WITHDRAWN

HARVARD LIBRARY

WITHDRAWN

Wanda Alberts

Integrative Religious Education in Europe

A Study-of-Religions Approach

Walter de Gruyter · Berlin · New York

BL
42.5
.E85
A43
2007

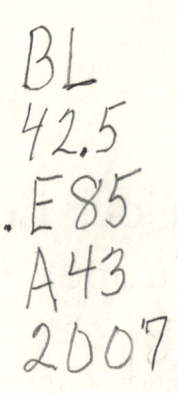

♾ Printed on acid-free paper which falls within
the guidelines of the ANSI to ensure permanence and durability.

ISSN 0080-0848
ISBN 978-3-11-019661-0

Library of Congress Cataloging-in-Publication Data

A CIP catalogue record for this book is available from the Library of Congress.

Bibliographic information published by the Deutsche Nationalbibliothek

The Deutsche Nationalbibliothek lists this publication in the Deutsche Nationalbibliografie;
detailed bibliographic data are available in the Internet at http://dnb.d-nb.de.

© Copyright 2007 by Walter de Gruyter GmbH & Co. KG, 10785 Berlin

All rights reserved, including those of translation into foreign languages. No part of this book
may be reproduced or transmitted in any form or by any means, electronic or mechanical, including
photocopy, recording or any information storage and retrieval system, without permission in
writing from the publisher.

Printed in Germany
Cover design: Christopher Schneider, Berlin
Printing: Hubert & Co. GmbH, Göttingen

Foreword

by Rosalind I. J. Hackett

In reading Wanda Alberts' lucid and engaging study of integrative religious education in Europe, one might be led to think that the notion of religious education is as contested a concept as that of religion itself. They are of course related, as Alberts demonstrates so admirably in this important work. Both are imbricated in cultural history, ideological battles, political debates, theological wranglings, and pressing social issues; their interpretation carries legal and policy implications for both individuals and communities.

Alberts chooses to focus her expertise as a religious studies scholar on the burgeoning, yet much debated, branch of religious education that she has termed "integrative religious education." This refers to the non-religious teaching about religion in schools with religiously mixed classrooms. Europe is her primary research area, with particular attention to the cases of England and Sweden, and additional examples from Norway, the Netherlands, and Germany. This lends both breadth and depth to her analysis, as Europe constitutes a varied and lively forum for debates over religious education, and England and Sweden have a long history of employing approaches that emphasize the teaching of various religions as an obligatory subject in schools. Yet their similarities and differences invite helpful comparison in assessing the merits of this particular model.

The integrative religious education approach in Europe has been shaped by a series of theoretical and methodological debates among a range of stakeholders, whether scholars, educators, religious and political leaders, or parents. Deploying to advantage her comparative and critical skills as scholar of religion, Alberts carefully unpacks the dynamics of each context and elucidates the various positions. The main difference between integrative and separative approaches with regard to teaching about religions in schools in Europe appears to derive from divergent conceptions of education and the task of the school in general. But, as Alberts revealingly demonstrates, when one examines more closely the arguments tendered by the various groups involved in these debates over the character of religious education then the question of power relations between religions and the state becomes more apparent. Alberts proffers some interesting reflections on which religion-state configurations are likely to be more conducive to favoring the integrative approach. It seems fair to say that religious education, especially non-confessional integrative religious education, appears to excel in bringing out the ideological and political dimensions of education, as well as religion ("church")-state entanglements.

These issues of secularity, plurality, religious heritage, and interculturalism will clearly resonate with American readers—whether specialists in the field of religious education or not. If they are involved with school education then they may be inspired by some of the courageous efforts of academics, teachers, religious leaders, and policy-makers in various European contexts to develop educational policy and content more in keeping with the times. There are initiatives in California,[1] Iowa,[2] and Massachusetts,[3] for example, to develop curricular materials from a non-confessional, comparative religious perspective. Some schools allow teaching about religion and religions within the context of other courses, such as history and social studies, and there are wider efforts to promote this as good education—especially post 9/11.[4] But these are still a drop in the ocean; university students arrive in our classes with virtually no knowledge of the world's religions, and little understanding of how religion operates in the lives of individuals, communities or nations. In contrast to fears in some European quarters about disestablishmentarianism or loss of religious privilege, in the U.S. context it is rather the specter of establishmentarianism that looms large. Furthermore, debates over whether and what to teach about

---

1 See, e.g., the Religion and Public Education Resource Center (RPERC) "http://www.csu-chico.edu/rs/rperc/" (accessed September 11, 2007) and Religious Studies in Secondary Schools http://www.rsiss.net/ (accessed September 11, 2007).

2 The University of Northern Iowa publishes the journal *Religion and Education* "http://www.uni.edu/coe/jrae/index.htm" (accessed September 11, 2007).

3 Program in Religion and Secondary Education at Harvard Divinity School http://www.hds.harvard.edu/prse/hstars (accessed September 11, 2007).

4 See Council on Islamic Education/First Amendment Center (2000) *Teaching About Religion in National and State Social Standards* "http://www.freedomforum.org/templates/document.asp?documentID=3976" (accessed September 11, 2007).

religion in U.S. schools tend to get sidelined by law suits over school prayer, vouchers, student religious groups, and creationism.[5]

Little wonder that Kwame Anthony Appiah in his recent book on *The Ethics of Identity* claims that:

> The greatest controversies about education in democracies, as we know, tend to occur when people feel that their own children are being taught things that are inconsistent with claims that are crucial marks of their own collective identities.[6]

Throughout the present book, Alberts has been concerned to link her careful exposition of theory and methodology pertaining to the academic study of and teaching about religious diversity to discussions of relevant educational theory and philosophy. It is in the last part of the book that she really comes to the fore with not only her critique of misguided policy and approaches, but with her advocacy of what an educationally sound integrative religious education should look like. She sensitively addresses the ambivalences but also underscores the vital importance of moving forward with a more inclusive and less discriminatory model of religious education. Her ideal curriculum would include not just religious traditions but also worldviews and ideologies, in a discrete subject. As she rightly argues, these educational options have implications for questions of citizenship, minority rights, religious pluralism, and intercultural coexistence. She is in good company. The former UN Special Rapporteur on Freedom of Religion or Belief, Professor Abdelfattah Amor, placed considerable emphasis on school education because of its power to influence the protection of the precarious right to freedom of religion and belief and to promote tolerance and understanding.[7]

---

5   See the Pew Forum on Religion and Public Life, "Religion & Public Schools," 2007 "http://pewforum.org/religion-schools/" (accessed September 10, 2007).
    See also the People for the American Way, "Teaching Religion in Public Schools" "http://www.pfaw.org/pfaw/general/default.aspx?oid=2462" (accessed September 11, 2007) and Charles Haynes (First Amendment Center), "Religious Liberty in Public Schools" "http://www.firstamendmentcenter.org/rel_liberty/publicschools/topic_faqs.aspx?topic=teaching_about_religion" (accessed September 11, 2007). See also Thomas, R. Murray. 2006. *Religion in Schools: Controversies around the World*. Westport, CT: Praeger, pp. 135-150.
6   Appiah, Kwame A. 2005. *The Ethics of Identity*. Princeton, NJ: Princeton University Press, p. 208.
7   The Oslo Coalition project on School Education, Tolerance, and Freedom of Religion or Belief was formed in 2001 to this end "http://www.oslocoalition.org/html/project_school_education/index.html" (accessed September 10, 2007).

If one thought for a moment that the field of religious education was not rich terrain for a contemporary scholar of religion to investigate, Wanda Alberts' work proves otherwise. Similarly, if one imagined that religious education, particularly integrative religious education, could make headway without the insights that religion scholars have with regard to interpretation, authority, representation, and plurality, then Alberts' work again proves otherwise. Despite the author's expressed concerns about the resistance of conservative religious forces and the challenge of increasingly centralized and standardized education practices, she is not without optimism. She looks forward to increased momentum for integrative religious education at the European level and the possibility of reviving the more progressive, emancipatory dimension of religious education.[8]

---

8   See, in this regard, Robert Jackson's upbeat editorial for the *British Journal of Religious Education* 29,3 (2007): 213-215.

Table of Contents

Foreword by Rosalind I. J. Hackett v
Acknowledgements xv

Introduction 1
Integrative religious education 1
The academic study of religions and RE 2
Aims, contents and limitations of this study 5
A note on citations and translations 7

Chapter I
Theory and methodology in the
academic disciplines relevant to integrative RE 8

1 The Study of Religions 8
   1.1 The character of the subject 9
      1.1.1 The general character of the academic study of religions 9
      1.1.2 Implications from the history
            of the academic study of religions 14
      1.1.3 Recent developments in the study of religions 20
      1.1.4 Limitations of the study of religions 28
   1.2 The concept of religion 31
      1.2.1 The variety of concepts of religion 32
      1.2.2 The "subject matter" or "field" of the study of religions 37
   1.3 Methodology 41
      1.3.1 Methodological variety 43
      1.3.2 Methodological integration 46
      1.3.3 The representation of religions 51

2 Education 55

2.1 Critical educational theory 55
2.1.1 Two aspects of education: "Erziehung" and "Bildung" 55
2.1.2 Critical theory 58
2.1.3 Towards a critical theory of education 60
2.1.4 A critical and constructive theory of education 63

2.2 Didactics 66
2.2.1 The focus on education: critical constructive didactics 67
2.2.2 The focus on teaching:
the "Berlin" and "Hamburg" models 69
2.2.3 The focus on interaction:
critical communicative didactics 70
2.2.4 General didactics and individual school subjects 71

2.3 Intercultural education 74
2.3.1 What is intercultural education? 75
2.3.2 Areas of intercultural learning 80
2.3.3 Intercultural education and educational systems 83

Chapter II
Integrative Religious Education in England 86

1 History and organisation of integrative RE in England 86

1.1 History of integrative RE 86
1.1.1 Developments until the 1960s 87
1.1.2 Ninian Smart's phenomenological approach to RE 88
1.1.3 The Shap Working Party for
World Religions in Education 91

1.2 Organisation of integrative RE 94
1.2.1 Agreed syllabuses 94
1.2.2 The model syllabuses of the School
Curriculum and Assessment Authority 99
1.2.3 The legal situation 105
1.2.4 Teacher training 109

2 Current approaches to RE in England 111

2.1 The Westhill Project 112
2.1.1 Aims and contents of integrative RE 112
2.1.2 The concept of religion and
the representation of religions 114
2.1.3 The notion of education and teaching strategies 117
2.1.4 Comment 119

2.2 "A Gift to the Child":
The Religion in the Service of the Child Project 120
2.2.1 The representation of religions 122
2.2.2 The concept of religion 125
2.2.3 The notion of education 126
2.2.4 Comment 127

2.3 The Experiential Approach 130
2.3.1 Aims and contents of integrative RE 130
2.3.2 The concept of religion and
the representation of religions 133
2.3.3 The notion of education 135
2.3.4 Critical evaluation 137

2.4 The Interpretive Approach 142
2.4.1 Aims and contents of integrative RE 143
2.4.2 The concept of religion and
the representation of religions 143
2.4.3 The notion of education 159
2.4.4 Recent developments and projects in interpretive RE 160
2.4.5 Comment 161

2.5 The Critical Approach 162
2.5.1 The critique of the "liberal consensus"
about representing religions in RE 163
2.5.2 Reconstruction: The representation
of religions in a critical framework 165
2.5.3 The notion of education 169
2.5.4 Critical evaluation 171

2.6 The Constructivist Approach 173

2.7 The Narrative Approach 179

Approaches to teaching Christianity 187
2.8 The Chichester Project 187
    2.8.1 The general framework 188
    2.8.2 Aspects of teaching Christianity 189
    2.8.3 The notion of education and teaching strategies 193
    2.8.4 Comment 195
2.9 The Stapleford Project 196
    2.9.1 Influences on the Stapleford Project 197
    2.9.2 Concept cracking 198
    2.9.3 Diversity within Christianity 200
    2.9.4 RE: religious or educational? 202
    2.9.5 The notion of religion 205
    2.9.6 Critical evaluation 207

Chapter III
Integrative Religious Education in Sweden 211
1 Religions in Sweden and the Swedish school system 213
    1.1 Religions in Sweden 213
    1.2 The Swedish school system 215
    1.3 Democracy and basic values in Swedish schools 217
2 The history of integrative RE in Sweden 219
3 Aims and contents of integrative RE in Sweden 226
    3.1 Aims of integrative RE 226
    3.2 Contents of integrative RE 229
        3.2.1 Official documents 229
        3.2.2 Academic literature 230
        3.2.3 Teaching material 234
4 The concept of religion 236
    4.1 The concept of religion in official documents about RE ... 236
    4.2 The concept of religion in academic literature 237
    4.3 The concept of religion in textbooks 241

5 The representation of religions 245
5.1 Official requirements for the representation of religions in RE 245
5.2 Academic discourse about the representation of religions in RE 247
5.2.1 General observations 248
5.2.2 Examples of the representation of religions in academic literature about RE 251
5.2.3 Further issues in the representation of religions in academic literature about RE 268
5.3 The representation of religions in textbooks 273
5.3.1 General observations 273
5.3.2 Example: the representation of Islam in Swedish textbooks 278

6 The notion of education in Swedish RE 282

Chapter IV
Evaluation and Conclusions 290

1 English and Swedish concepts for integrative RE 290
1.1 General features of integrative RE in England and Sweden 290
1.2 Individual aspects of integrative RE in England and Sweden 293
1.2.1 Aims of integrative RE 294
1.2.2 The concept of religion 296
1.2.3 The representation of religions 298
1.2.4 Teaching methods and the concept of education 305

2 Integrative RE in the European context 312
2.1 Learning and teaching about different religions in Europe 312
2.1.1 European RE in transition 312
2.1.2 Accounts of the situation of RE in Europe 315

2.2 Examples of models and changes in
    individual European countries.. 324
    2.2.1 Integrative RE as an individual
          school subject – Norway.. 324
    2.2.2 A separative framework and
          exceptions to the rule – Germany 328
    2.2.3 Integrative RE as a "learning dimension"
          of other subjects – the Netherlands.............................. 343
2.3 Integrative or separative RE in state schools?............................ 347

3 A framework for integrative RE in Europe 353

3.1 The general character of integrative RE.................................. 355
    3.1.1 The profile of integrative RE... 355
    3.1.2 The notion of education.. 360
    3.1.3 Integrative RE in the context of
          wider cultural, social and political debates 366

3.2 Individual features of integrative RE...................................... 372
    3.2.1 The name of the school subject...................................... 372
    3.2.2 The concept of religion and
          the delineation of the subject matter............................. 373
    3.2.3 The representation of religions....................................... 376
    3.2.4 Organisation and transformation................................... 382

3.3 Academic and political desiderata 385

Epilogue: The potential of integrative RE 388
Bibliography... 391
Index 437

Acknowledgements

"There must be an alternative to separating children by confession when it comes to teaching and learning about religions in schools." These were my thoughts when I studied German accounts of school religious education in the face of increasing plurality and globalisation. In Germany, because of the dominant separative-confessional model, integrative RE is still somewhat of a taboo topic. Therefore, I sometimes have to think twice, even at social events, when people ask me about my work, before I start to talk about it, as there is always the risk of provoking a heated controversy. In England or Sweden, however, people find it difficult to believe that we really have this separative approach in Germany. It took a while before I was able to break away from my situatedness in the German context, in which one always has to excuse oneself for deviating from the dominant model, and dared to come forward with and stand by my own position about the appropriate educational response to recent challenges for religious education.

Without any doubt, my concept will not be without inconsistencies. However, in the young field of integrative religious education, where we are still debating very basic questions such as the general character of the subject, it is necessary for us to actually begin to develop concepts from a study-of-religions point of view. It may take some time until the basic issues concerning integrative RE, as seen from a study-of-religions perspective, are settled and generally accepted models are developed. However, I regard being part of this current liminal phase of RE politics as an exciting challenge and look forward to being involved in further developing models and methods for integrative RE, together with my colleagues from Northern Europe and elsewhere, whose work and friendship I appreciate very much.

I wish to thank the people who have supported me while I was writing this book: the supervisor of my thesis, Michael Pye, Professor of the Study of Religions in Marburg, supported me in various ways. Above all, by his example, my interest in international cooperation was raised. Furthermore, he was there (physically or virtually) to help whenever there was a problem. I am grateful for the many inspiring discussions we had. Elisabeth Rohr, Professor of Education in Marburg, also helped me to develop my ideas about the topic of this thesis from the very beginning. I would like to thank her for her unpretentious and sincere support.

During my stay in Oxford, Susan Hector and Peggy Morgan helped me to get access to the English landscape of religious education. I am also grateful for their general support, companionship and encouragement during that time. While I was in Sweden, my good friend Maria Andersson helped me in various ways and made her flat feel like a second home to me.

Alexander Rödel, Konstanze Runge, Peter Schalk, Monika Schrimpf and Katja Triplett have helped me with comments on the manuscript. I am particularly grateful to David Smith, who, under an enormous pressure of time, helped me with errors and infelicities in English before I submitted my thesis to the University of Marburg. I am also particularly grateful to Alexander Rödel, who did the time-consuming formatting of this book, including night shifts, despite his contempt for the word-processor I used.

Furthermore, I would like to thank Albrecht Döhnert and Winnifred Sullivan, who have helped to bring this book into the Religion and Reason series, and Rosalind Hackett for writing a foreword from a North-American perspective. My thanks extend also to Charlotte Fields, who proofread the final manuscript.

My research project was made possible by a scholarship from the German National Academic Foundation (*Studienstiftung des Deutschen Volkes*). I am particularly grateful to Thomas Ludwig, who took a close look at my case in the application procedure, when it emerged that I had embarked upon a rather controversial topic.

I am also grateful to Julia Bokowski, Andreas Grünschloß and Hans Wißmann, who, in my time at the University of Mainz, raised my interest in the academic Study of Religions. Furthermore, I would like to thank Bernd Päschke for our discussions and his uncompromisingly critical view of the social and political contexts in which we live. His ideas and outstanding example of partiality for less privileged people have encouraged me to articulate my own positions more clearly. I would also like to thank Gritt Klinkhammer, who has supported me in many ways since I started as a lecturer at the University of Bremen, so that I was actually able to complete this book.

Finally, I would like to express my gratitude to all my friends, including many of the above, who have accepted my life as migrating bird, and to my parents, Frauke and Peter Alberts, whose belief and interest in what I am doing have always been a wonderful support in my life and work.

Introduction

Integrative religious education

In this thesis the term "integrative religious education" is used as an analytical category referring to a particular form of school religious education in which the children of a class are not separated – as opposed to separative confessional approaches – but learn together about different religions. "Integrative" refers to two distinctive aspects of this kind of religious education (RE): (1) the non-separative educational framework, which takes religious plurality – in schools and society in general – as its starting point and which requires a concept for dealing with diversity in the classroom, in particular with respect to teaching about different religions, and (2) making various religions the subject matter without taking the perspective of any of these religions as an overall framework.[1] Thus, "integrative RE" means non-separative and non-confessional school education about different religions.

In different countries and languages various terms have been used to describe this kind of RE. In Germany, for example, "interreligiöser Religionsunterricht" (interreligious RE), "Religionsunterricht für alle" (RE for all), "allgemeiner Religionsunterricht" (general RE) and "Religionskunde" (knowledge about religion) have been suggested.[2] The latter is also used in Sweden, where this school subject is called "religionskunskap". Unlike "interreligious RE", which implies a religious encounter, "multifaith RE", which is widely used in English, encapsulates the character of the subject quite well. However, I prefer to use "integrative RE" in the above sense in order not to emphasise any as-

---

1 "Integrative" should not be misunderstood as describing an attempt to integrate the positions of the different religions into a coherent whole.
2 "Interreligiöser Religionsunterricht" and "Religionsunterricht für alle" have been used, for example, for the Hamburg model, cf. chapter IV, section 2.2.2. "Allgemeiner Religionsunterricht" was used for example by Gert Otto, who later preferred "Religionskunde", as it is less ambiguous than the former (see Otto 1992: Allgemeiner Religionsunterricht – Religionsunterricht für alle). "Religionskunde" is also used in the new school subject "Lebensgestaltung – Ethik – Religionskunde" (ways of life – ethics – knowledge about religion), which was introduced in the state of Brandenburg in the 1990s, see chapter IV, section 2.2.2.

pect of religion, for example faith, in the name of the subject.[3] Some European countries, particularly in northern Europe, have integrative RE as an individual school subject.[4] Sweden and England have had the longest traditions of integrative RE as an individual compulsory subject for all pupils from primary up to secondary levels.

The academic study of religions and RE

If integrative RE is to be educational and not religious in itself, the academic disciplines of the study of religions and education ought to be responsible for the design of programmes for this school subject. The reason for this is that – unlike theologies, which study one or more religions within a religious framework[5] – the academic discipline of the study of religions deals with religious diversity from a non-religious perspective and has, therefore, sought to develop a methodology for an impartial approach to different religions.

However, the field of didactics has been neglected in the academic study of religions in many countries for a long time. This is because, until recently, in most countries of the world school curricula did not normally include a study of different religions from an impartial point of view but particular religions were taught from a confessional point of view. In countries with separative confessional school RE, a need for the kind of knowledge that the study of religions can provide was first recognised when so-called alternative subjects, like "ethics", "philosophy of life" or "values and norms" were introduced for children who did not want to participate in confessional instruction. However, this has still not brought about the development of a coherent didactics of the study of religions. This may be demonstrated using the example of Germany. As most of German RE is confessional, RE in general is re-

---

3 I have found one article in German that uses the phrase "integrativer Religionsunterricht", see Knauth and Weiße 1996: Lernbereich Religion/Ethik und integrativer Religionsunterricht aus SchülerInnensicht. Like its English equivalent, this did not use to be a common term for this kind of RE. The formulation "integrative religious education", which I have used in conference papers since 2003 (cf., e.g., Alberts 2005: European models of integrative religious education), has been taken up by some other scholars, for example Pye and Franke (2004: The study of religions and its contribution to problem-solving in a plural world, 14), or Thomassen (2005: RE in a pluralistic society: experiences from Norway, 241).
4 For integrative RE in the European context see chapter IV.2.
5 It is often overlooked in the debates about integrative RE that this also holds for universal theologies. Unlike the study of religions, pluralist theologies of religions are still normative, seeking to make sense of religious diversity.

garded as a matter of individual religious traditions and theologies rather than of the study of religions. Recently, more and more theologians have started to reflect upon how learning about different religions may be included in confessional RE.[6] However, this kind of reflection must not be mistaken for a didactics of the study of religions, as these approaches still operate in a general theological – and not impartial – framework.[7] Apart from a few exceptions, for example, Peter Antes or Udo Tworuschka,[8] most German scholars of religions have shown little if any interest in school RE until very recently. This also involves a lack of research from a study-of-religions point of view about existent concepts for teaching different religions in RE.[9] The situation is better in countries with a longer and wider tradition in integrative RE. However, even in those countries the distinction between the different functions of the study of religions and various theologies with respect to RE is not always clearly made and responsibilities are sometimes confused.[10]

On an international level, RE is again mostly conceived of as separative confessional instruction in a particular religion. Therefore, only a few scholars of religions have taken an interest in RE, but this field has rather been regarded as an area of interest for theologians. The fact that integrative RE, which directly relates to the study of religions, may actually be an alternative or a complement to common practice of RE in many countries in order to enhance knowledge about different relig-

---

[6] See for example Lähnemann 1998: Evangelische Religionspädagogik in interreligiöser Perspektive, Meyer 1998: Zeugnisse fremder Religionen im Unterricht. "Weltreligionen" im deutschen und englischen Religionsunterricht.

[7] Confusion is, for example, caused in the section "Religionen-Didaktik" by Martin Jäggle in Johann Figl's *Handbuch Religionswissenschaft* (2003). Contrary to what one may expect from a compendium in the study of religions, Jäggle, a Catholic theologian, does not distinguish between teaching different religions in confessional and non-confessional frameworks. Therefore, theological approaches (e.g. by Johannes Lähnemann), designed for confessional RE and therefore frequently operating with a "we" vs. "the other" dichotomy, are presented along with the English *A Gift to the Child* approach, which was particularly designed for an integrative framework.

[8] See the diverse publications by Antes and Tworuschka, e.g. Antes 1995: Religionspädagogik und Religionswissenschaft, Tworuschka 1982: Methodische Zugänge zu den Weltreligionen. Along with several publications about the representation of different religions, Tworuschka has recently also published a CD-ROM for the exploration of different religions (2004: Religiopolis – Weltreligionen erleben).

[9] For accounts of the scarce coverage of questions of didactics in the study of religions in Germany see Körber 1988: Didaktik der Religionswissenschaft (in: Handbuch religionswissenschaftlicher Grundbegriffe, vol. 1) and Fauth 1998: Zur Didaktik der Religionswissenschaft. Cf. also Bauer 1996: Zwischen Religionenkunde und erfahrungsorientiertem Unterricht, 155ff.

[10] See my criticism of some English approaches, e.g. sections 2.3 and 2.9 in chapter II, or of the Norwegian approach (chapter IV, section 2.2.1).

ions, which is more and more acknowledged as an important element of education, has only recently attracted the interest of more scholars in the study of religions. Above all, scholars from countries which already have integrative approaches have been working for an internationalisation of the debate. Apart from the early ground-breaking work by Ninian Smart,[11] recently the work of the Danish scholar Tim Jensen, who has for years been engaged in promoting a study-of-religions approach to school RE on a European level,[12] or the contributions by the English scholar Robert Jackson, who has developed a consistent study-of-religions approach to teaching different religions in integrative RE and established an international network of scholars who use similar methods,[13] are particularly important in this respect, but there are also a number of other valuable contributions.[14] Furthermore, the participation of scholars of religions in the creation or revision of syllabuses for integrative RE, and exchange beyond national levels about these procedures, are important for the development of sound concepts for integrative RE.[15]

However, as the panel sessions on RE at the world congress of the *International Association for the History of Religions* (IAHR) in Tokyo in 2005 have shown, there is still anything but a consensus about a study-of-religions approach to integrative RE. While some papers clearly emphasised the possibilities and limits of a sound study-of-religions position, others did not as clearly distinguish between theological and study-of-religions positions, leaving confusion rather than clarification about the general role of the study of religions with respect to RE. However, the fact that questions about RE were discussed in several

---

11   For the work of Ninian Smart see chapter II, section 1.1.2 and cf., for example, Smart 1968: Secular Education and the Logic of Religion.
12   For the work of Jensen see chapter IV, section 2.1.2 and cf., e.g., Jensen 2002: RE in public schools – a must for a secular state. Jensen is also one of the few scholars of religions who take an interest in the increasingly international debate about models of RE in Europe.
13   For the work of Jackson see chapter II section 2.4. and chapter IV, section 2.2.1 and cf., for example, Jackson 1997: RE. An Interpretive Approach and 2004: Rethinking RE and Plurality.
14   See, for example, the work of Nils G. Holm, e.g. Holm (ed.) 2000: Islam and Christianity in School Religious Education or Holm (ed.) 1997: The Familiar and the Unfamiliar in the World Religions: Challenges for Religious Education Today. Cf. also the European research project on Islam in textbooks, see Falaturi and Tworuschka 1992: A guide to the presentation of Islam in school textbooks, and the recent study on Christianity, Islam and Judaism in European curricula by Kaul-Seidmann, Nielssen et al. (2003: European Identity and Cultural Pluralism).
15   Here I refer, for example, to the work of the Norwegian scholar Einar Thomassen in the committee that revised the syllabus for Norwegian integrative RE, cf. Thomassen 2005: Religious education in a pluralistic society: experiences from Norway.

panel sessions at all reflects the general trend that education, and school RE in particular, are increasingly claiming their place on the agendas of departments for the study of religions in many regions of the world.[16] Nevertheless, beyond the important work of a few individual scholars,[17] the development of a coherent school didactics of the study of religions, which includes recent considerations within this academic discipline as well as within education, is still in its infancy. For example, a comparative analysis and criticism of concepts for integrative RE in different countries from a study-of-religions perspective still remains a desideratum, as does the development of a clear study-of-religions position about the general character and individual features of integrative RE.

Aims, contents and limitations of this study

This study aims at contributing to the development of a school didactics of the study of religions. It provides an analysis of a number of existent academic concepts for integrative RE from a study-of-religions perspective. The main focus of my analysis will be on concepts for integrative RE in England and Sweden (chapters II, III, and IV.1), while the general situation of integrative RE in Europe will also be taken into account and further examples from other countries will be discussed (chapter IV.2). The criteria for my analysis build on my conclusions about the debates on theory and methodology in the academic disciplines which I regard as responsible for integrative RE. My approach to these debates in the study of religions and education as well as my conclusions about the character of these disciplines will be outlined in chapter I. These theoretical and methodological considerations, together with the results from the analyses of different approaches to integrative RE in Europe, form the basis for the framework for integrative RE which I suggest in the final part of this study (chapter IV.3).

Sweden and England have been selected for their long and extensive traditions in integrative RE. The situation of integrative RE in Norway is briefly discussed in chapter IV, section 2.2.1, as an example

---

16 The regional conference of the IAHR in Yogyakarta and Semarang on Java with the theme "Religious Harmony. Problems, Practice and Education" (cf. Pye, Franke et al., ed., 2006: Religious Harmony) also reflected this trend. At this conference a clear study-of-religions approach to RE was put forward in the panel on "RE in global perspective". The conference of the *European Association for the Study of Religions* (EASR) in Bremen in 2007 also had education as one of its conference themes.

17 Such as Ninian Smart, Robert Jackson or Tim Jensen, as mentioned above.

of recent developments in the European landscape of RE. Without any doubt, an in-depth study of other models of integrative RE, for example, in Denmark or Estonia,[18] would have contributed to the completion of the picture. However, there is a limit to what can be done in an individual study. Furthermore, the issues that have arisen in the study of integrative RE in Sweden, England and Norway, as well as of other models for teaching about different religions in Germany and the Netherlands (chapter IV, sections 2.2.2 and 2.2.3) are indicative of the kinds of debates about RE in other countries as well, for example with respect to policies towards religious plurality, responsibility for RE in state schools or the general character of integrative or separative RE.

The main focus of my analysis of current English and Swedish approaches to integrative RE is on academic concepts for this subject that have been published by scholars of RE. These concepts are analysed with respect to the following aspects: aims and contents of integrative RE, the underlying concept of religion, the representation of religions and the notion of education. The historical and social contexts in which these concepts have been developed, including, for example, changing legal requirements, national guidelines or institutional responsibilities, are also considered.

This is a theoretical study based on the study of different kinds of written sources, for example, official documents, academic literature, teachers' manuals and textbooks for RE, which I collected during my research in England and Sweden between 2002 and 2005, and not an empirical study of actual classroom practice of integrative RE, even though visits to schools and teacher training institutions have complemented my study of the textual sources.

The framework for integrative RE which I suggest in the final part of this study (chapter IV.3) has been designed for the European situation in particular, but may also be transferred to other regions, possibly with some modifications that other contexts make necessary, however without changing its general character.

---

18 For Denmark cf. the publications by Jensen, e.g. 2005: European and Danish RE, or Buchard 2004: RE in the school: approaches in school practice and research in Denmark. For Estonia cf. Schreiner 2005: RE in Europe and the information on Estonia on the website of the European Forum for Teachers in RE, see EFTRE 2005: Estonia.

A note on citations and translations

References to literature that is quoted or mentioned in the text are given in the footnotes, citing the last name of the author(s), the year of publication and a short title, which may correspond with the original title but may also be an abbreviated version, for example without subtitle or with "RE" as an abbreviation for religious education. Citations may vary slightly if the author is not a person but an institution. Italics in quotations are original, unless stated otherwise. Translations from the German and Swedish are my own.

Chapter I
Theory and methodology in the academic disciplines relevant to integrative RE

1 The Study of Religions

This chapter is an introduction to the academic study of religions as the discipline which is most closely related to integrative RE as a school subject. As many theoretical and methodological questions which have been discussed at length in the study of religions are also relevant for RE – and have frequently been discussed with respect to RE without reference to the corresponding debates in the study of religions – these issues will briefly be introduced in this chapter in order to provide a study-of-religions background for the development of theory and methodology for integrative RE. Needless to say, there is no one-to-one correspondence between method and theory in the academic and in the school subject. A careful evaluation of those aspects of the academic subject that can be transferred to the school subject, and of the question as to how this is possible is the delicate task for the development of a didactic framework for integrative RE, which is still in its infancy in many countries, including Germany. However, it is important to draw on insights in the study of religions in order not to blindly reproduce the debates on issues which have long been settled on other levels, but to initiate a cross-fertilisation of ideas with respect to similar questions.

This chapter starts by generally introducing the study of religions, with reference to implications from its history as well as to recent developments, and as distinct from other disciplines which are concerned with religion(s), above all theology and philosophy (1.1). It then goes on to look more closely at the subject matter of the study of religions. Different concepts of religion will be briefly assessed, followed by conclusions about the delineation of the subject matter (1.2). The third section of this chapter deals with questions of methodology, in particular with methodological variety and integration in the study of religions as well as with selected issues concerning the representation of religions from a study-of-religions point of view (1.3).

1.1 The character of the subject

In the context of this study, an outline of the general character of the study of religions is helpful, particularly since it is frequently confused with dialogical theologies and theologies or philosophies of religion. This section will discuss the distinctive features of the study of religions as the academic discipline which deals with the variety of religions explicitly not from a normative point of view. For this purpose, after an outline of the general character of the academic study of religions (1.1.1), insights and implications from its history will mapped out (1.1.2), before some recent developments within this discipline are mentioned (1.2.3). The section concludes with some considerations about the limitations of the academic study of religions, which result from its self-set secular and scientific framework (1.2.4).

1.1.1 The general character of the academic study of religions

The academic study of religions is a historical, empirical and comparative discipline which deals with the different religious traditions of the world. As distinct from any theology it is a secular discipline which does not make judgements about religious truth claims. Neither does it construe any meaning behind the variety of religions. As a branch of the social and cultural sciences, it is methodologically agnostic with respect to religious claims which are not empirically verifiable. Its interest is in the study, analysis and description of religions as anthropological phenomena, using a methodology which does not prefer any religion over another.[1]

The study of religions exists worldwide and there is a variety of national, regional and international organisations. There is no consensus about the name of the subject. The German term *Religionswissenschaft*, which is rather uncontroversial[2], has been designated in English in

---

[1] The following titles may serve as examples of outlines of the general character of the study of religions to which the characterisation in this section owes a great deal: Flasche 2000: Von der Selbstbeschränkung und Selbstbegründung der Religionenwissenschaft, Pye 1999: Methodological integration in the study of religions, Pye/Franke 2004: The Study of Religions and its contribution to problem-solving in a plural world, Stolz 1997: Grundzüge der Religionswissenschaft, Waardenburg 1986: Religionen und Religion. Systematische Einführung in die Religionswissenschaft.

[2] Apart from Rainer Flasche's suggestion to call the subject *Religionenwissenschaft* in order to include the plurality of religions in the name, cf. Flasche 2000: Von der Selbstbeschränkung und Selbstbegründung der Religionenwissenschaft. Another point, which has been discussed in a number of countries, is the question of whether

various ways. Clearly, *Theology* or *Divinity*, which are often still the names of faculties which also include *The Study of Religions* are misleading names for the subject as they explicitly point at a theological character of the enterprise. *Religious Studies*, frequently used in Great Britain, may also be misleading as it implies a religious character. *The Study of Religion* or the *Science of Religion* are acceptable names for the subject. They do, however, refer to religion in the singular and the latter might also imply proximity to the sciences as opposed to the humanities. Therefore, in my view, the best solution is to call the subject *The Study of Religions*,[3] because it does not confine it to any individual aspect, such as the comparative aspect in *Comparative Religion*, or the historical aspect in *History of Religions*, and includes the plurality of religions.[4]

Two complementary branches of the study of religions can be identified, a historical descriptive and a theoretical and comparative branch.[5] Traditionally, the historical-descriptive branch is concerned with the history, development and contemporary situation of individual religions or religious phenomena. For instance, the development and expansion of different Buddhist traditions from their origins up to the present day is a classical topic of this branch. The theoretical, comparative and systematic[6] branch develops theories on the basis of a comparative study of religions and religious phenomena from the whole range of religions. As it is de facto only possible to compare

---

the name of the subject should emphasise the historical aspect of the discipline. In Germany the names *Religionswissenschaft* (the study of religions) and *Religionsgeschichte* (the history of religions) are often used interchangeably. In order to overcome the emphasis on the historical aspect, the German Association for the History of Religions (*Deutsche Vereinigung für Religionsgeschichte*, DVRG) changed its name to German Association for the Study of Religions (*Deutsche Vereinigung für Religionswissenschaft*, DVRW) in 2005. Other national and international associations have kept the emphasis on history, for example, the *Danish Association for the History of Religions* (DAHR) or the *International Association for the History of Religions* (IAHR).

3   The plural in the title seems more felicitous in English than in German.
4   This is, for example, the solution of the European Association for the Study of Religions (EASR) or the British Association for the Study of Religions (BASR).
5   An early convincing description of the distinction between those two branches can be found in Wach 1924: Religionswissenschaft. Prolegomena zu ihrer wissenschaftstheoretischen Grundlegung, 21, where he uses the word "längsschnittmäßig" for the historical and the word "querschnittmäßig" for the systematic branch.
6   Note that systematic is used here in a way which is different from frequent use in English RE, where the distinction between systematic and thematic refers to different approaches to RE: in the former ("systematic" or "systems-" approach) religions are discussed individually, one after the other, and in the latter ("thematic" approach) phenomena that occur in different religions are discussed comparatively. I find this systematic - thematic distinction in English RE somewhat misleading as it is inconsistent with the common understanding of "systematic", especially in *the study of religions*.

some religions in some respects at a time,[7] general theories about religions, which claim validity also beyond the direct focus of a study have to be based on further empirical evidence and have to be modified if any contradictory evidence is found. Therefore, taking account of mistakes that have been made in the history of the subject, a certain amount of caution is advised when it comes to general theories or statements. The subject matter or "field" with all its phenomena worldwide is so diverse that general statements are almost impossible, since nobody could ever have enough knowledge to verify such a statement in every tradition. This becomes evident also in the difficulties that scholars of religions have in defining "religion" itself (see section 1.2). In order to preserve the scientific character of the subject it is important to clearly define the field for which a theory was developed. In fact, general theories do not really seem to be necessary in the study of religions. A consensus has emerged among many scholars of religions that an analysis and description of structural similarities or "family resemblances"[8] of aspects of religions is a more adequate methodology in the comparative study of religions. To dispense with general theories and formulate theories of limited range seems to be more academically sound in such a complex and disparate field.

Classical comparative studies – for example of rituals, special texts, postulated superhuman beings[9] – have also been criticised for their disregard of dynamics or the respective contexts or intentions behind phenomena that seem superficially similar (see section 1.1.2). These criticisms, which are in fact often justified, point at shortcomings in the way those comparisons were carried out. They do not, however, call comparative methodology as such into question, as a comparative study of dynamics, contexts and intentions is also possible.[10] Generally,

---

[7] Cf. Pye 1972: Comparative Religion: An Introduction through Source Materials, 22.
[8] "Family resemblances" is a term that Wittgenstein introduced. For a reception of this term in the study of religions cf., e.g., Kippenberg 1983: Diskursive Religionswissenschaft, 11; Pye 1994: Religion. Shape and shadow, Pye 2000: Westernism unmasked, Wiebe 2000: Problems with the family resemblance approach to conceptualizing religion.
[9] The frequently used phrase "culturally postulated superhuman agents" was coined by Milford E. Spiro, see Spiro 1966: Religion: problems of definition and explanation, 96.
[10] Cf., e.g., Michael Pye's ideas about a comparative study of religious innovation, see, e.g., Pye 1969: The transplantation of religions, 1991: Reflections on the treatment of tradition in comparative perspective, 109.

in comparative studies equal attention should be paid to similarities and differences.[11]

The study of religions analyses and describes religious phenomena from an academic meta-level, which is independent from the insider perspective, even though the latter is an important voice to be included in any study (see section 1.3 on methodology). This standpoint of independent reflection does not claim to be superior to any religious truth, but presents a scientific approach to religions, which – by definition – must not make any religious truth claim itself. One of the important tasks of the study of religions is the development of concepts that can be used for different religions without being caught in the mindset of one tradition (see section 1.3.3).

As the study of religions restricts itself to the study of those aspects of religions which can be studied scientifically, it has to restrict its field to what can be studied using scientific methods. Religion is regarded as a human phenomenon. Therefore, the study of religions approaches its material with a limited set of specific questions. It is a study of religions "from the outside" as opposed to the theological endeavour of studying one or more religions "from the inside". The methodology has to be comprehensible ("nachvollziehbar")[12] for other scholars. It is grounded in empirical evidence, not in philosophical or theological speculations. The study of religions is a discipline, i.e. a methodically ordered approach to the study of a field. It cannot be integrated into any other discipline.[13]

The most common misunderstanding of the study of religions is mistaking it for a kind of universal theology which includes theological reflection about religious diversity. This may be due to the dominance of theologians in public discourse on religions which can in many countries be regarded as a result of the residual power of institutional-

---

[11] Thus, we could speak of the "comparative and contrastive" study of religions, cf. Pye 1972: 24; cf. also Segal 2001: In defence of the comparative method; Martin 2000: Comparison; Paden 2004: Comparison in the study of religion.

[12] This German concept, which means something like "comprehensible", in this context particularly to people who have access to the same kind of material or on material which was collected and made available by other scholars, seems to be particularly helpful in describing the requirements of the research process, see also Pye 2000: Westernism unmasked, 218.

[13] Cf. Pye 1999: Methodological integration in the study of religions,189, where he shows that the study of religions can neither be integrated in history, as the methods of historians do not normally involve field-work, nor in sociology, as there is more to religions than just their social aspects. See also Pye 1982: The Study of Religion as an autonomous discipline.

ised religion.[14] It seems to be difficult to communicate the basic distinctions between religious (universalist theologies), secular (the study of religions) and secularist (comprehensive secular explanations of religions) approaches to religions beyond – and even within – academia. This is one of the reasons why the role of the study of religions as the academic partner for integrative RE has not yet been fully acknowledged.

Michael Pye draws attention to some other important factors that contribute to misunderstandings about the general character of the study of religions: first, the interdisciplinary character of the subject creates a situation in which people who come from other disciplines, for example, anthropology, often do not "go to the trouble of acquiring a methodological orientation in the discipline of the study of religions".[15] Second, different emphases in the study of religions – such as phenomenology of religion, anthropology of religion or psychology of religion – have resulted in some kind of compartmentalisation which is detrimental, because "if the field is regarded as coherent, then a greater degree of methodological coordination, or even integration, is intellectually desirable and ought therefore to be sought".[16] Finally, there is serious methodological divergence and sometimes methodological fashions are for a short period of time regarded as *the* appropriate method, while other important methods are neglected.[17] What I am trying to outline as a contemporary consensus about the general character of the subject – despite its, in many respects, contested nature – is the preliminary result of an ongoing process of continuous reflection and modification of theory and methodology in the worldwide study of religions. In the next section, important aspects of the history of the subject and their implications for its present state will be considered.

---

14 Cf., e.g., McCutcheon 2000: Critics not caretakers: the scholar of religion as public intellectual, 170.
15 Pye 1999: Methodological integration in the study of religions, 193.
16 Ibid., 192.
17 Cf. ibid., 193. Pye refers to cognitive science as a fashion in the study of religions, which leads many scholars to neglect the need for fieldwork, textual studies and comparison.

1.1.2 Implications from the history of the academic study of religions

A useful distinction between four major phases in the history of the academic study of religions is made by the Danish scholar Armin W. Geertz.[18] He regards the second half of the 19th century as the formative or "classical" period (phase 1) in which the differences between the study of religions and theology were formulated. The first 60 years of the 20th century may be called the adolescent or "modern" period (phase 2), in which the differences between the study of religions and basically everything else were formulated and an attempt was made to provide the study of religions with a positivist, empiricist and historicist foundation. Geertz calls the years between 1970 and 1990 the rebellious early adult period (phase 3) which, according to him, represents the critical turn in the study of religions and in which everything was subjected to doubt except the premises of the doubters. In the current phase (phase 4), which Geertz calls "the-approaching-the-maturity-of-harried-parents phase", hard decisions at the cost of ideals have to be made in order to get on with one's life. Geertz's somewhat humorous account of the history of the subject in analogy to developmental stages of human beings does in fact address the important phases and turning points which are all still relevant for the present state of the study of religions. I am going to demonstrate this with a spotlight discussion of selected issues from those phases and their implications for today.[19]

In the first phase (second half of the 19th century) the work of F. Max Müller is one important starting point for the emergence of the study of religions as an independent discipline. Many of the issues that became central questions in the study of religions later were already addressed by Müller. The editor of the *Sacred Books of the East*, who saw close resemblances between religions and languages, regarded a study of different religions as a necessary prerequisite for an approach to the phenomenon "religion" in general. He coined the famous phrase about religions, which has been cited numerously in the history of the study of religions since then: "He who knows one knows none."[20] Müller distinguished between a historical study of religions, which deals with the historical phenomena of religion and a theoretical one, which stud-

---

18 Cf. Geertz: 2004: Definition, categorization and indecision: or, how to get on with the Study of Religion, 109f.
19 For a detailed account of phases 1 and 2 cf. also Sharpe: Comparative Religion. A History.
20 Müller 1876: Einleitung in die vergleichende Religionswissenschaft, 14.

ies the conditions that make religion possible.[21] His attachment to traditions that were fashionable at the time when he wrote – for example his belief that all of humankind unconsciously progresses towards Christianity, which has a special position among the religions of the world[22] – does not belittle his merit for the academic study of religions as a discipline independent from theology.

Another development with important impulses for the emerging identity of the subject took place in the late 19th century Netherlands, where the history of religions was introduced very early as an academic discipline. In the work of Cornelius Petrus Tiele, who was Professor of the History and Philosophy of Religion in Leiden, we can again find a number of ideas about the character of the subject, that were to be discussed intensively later. In his *Inleiding tot de godsdienstwetenschap* (1898), for example, he distinguishes between the general history of religions and the study of religions which builds on the results of the general history of religions in that it answers the question of what the nature of religion is, which reveals itself in all the different phenomena.[23] His methodology is an early version of "the phenomenological method", which was used widely in the next phase of the history of the study of religions: "We study these phenomena [religious ideas and actions] in order to deduce what is concealed behind the phenomena."[24] The discrepancy between the proclaimed methodological presuppositions for the study of religions as a discipline and the methodology actually used in one's own work is also similar in the work of Tiele and the later phenomenologists. On the one hand, Tiele writes that "[t]he subject matter of our discipline is not the superhuman itself, but religion which is based on the belief in the superhuman. And to study this religion as a historical-psychological and at the same time social, i.e. purely human phenomenon, is definitely a task of science."[25] On the other hand, Tiele presupposes a unity within the diversity of religions and thereby leaves the methodological framework which he himself introduced, as he structures his study from a particular metaphysical/theological perspective.[26]

---

21 Cf. ibid., 19. Müller uses the terms "historische Theologie" and "theoretische Theologie".
22 Cf. Müller 1979: Essays, XVIIf.
23 Cf. Tiele 1899: Einleitung in die Religionswissenschaft (German edition of the Dutch original from 1898), 11.
24 Ibid., 35.
25 Ibid., 4.
26 Cf. for example ibid., 257.

Two characteristic trends in the second phase (the first 60 years of the 20th century) are substantialist and functionalist definitions of religions and their implications for an understanding of the character of the study of religions. The phenomenologists of religion had a substantialist understanding of religion as a response to revelation. They did not differentiate between a religious and a secular study of religions. Most of them were Christian theologians[27] and understood the study of religions as a kind of universal theology[28] which includes reflection about the variety of religions. They coined, however, terms and concepts which have played an important role in the study of religions until today.

Söderblom regarded people as religious if something is holy to them.[29] Similarly, Otto regarded the "numinous"[30], which is accessible through experience, as the common aspect of all religion. His conclusion for the study of religions was that without any own experience of the numinous it is impossible to understand religious people and, therefore, to be a scholar of religion. Otto's conception of the holy as consisting in the *mysterium tremendum* and the *mysterium fascinans* can also be found in Gerardus van der Leeuw's *Religion in Essence and Manifestation* (1938). "Power" is the important concept in van der Leeuw's understanding of religion. He interprets the phenomenology of religion as a study of the ways that human beings respond to this divine power, i.e. mainly with fear and fascination.[31] Friedrich Heiler also demands that the scholar of religions approaches religion like a sanctuary with "the original religious emotions of reverent shyness and admiration".[32] For him, the study of religions is concerned with "religion as such".[33] The phenomenal world originates from the divine. The phenomena are interesting only insofar as they are approaches to the

---

27 Nathan Söderblom, for example, was Bishop in the Church of Sweden, Rudolf Otto was Professor of Systematic Theology in the Faculty of Theology at the University of Marburg, Friedrich Heiler was also for some time professor in this faculty.
28 Söderblom wanted to prove the existence of God from the history of religions, Otto intended to create a covenant of religious people (*religiöser Menschheitsbund*) and Heiler extended his efforts for a reunification of the major Christian churches (cf. his ideas about "protestant Catholicism" [*evangelische Katholizität*] and his participation as a Catholic in the Protestant Lord's Supper together with Söderblom) to include an attempt to unify the variety of religions with the help of the study of religions.
29 Cf. Söderblom 1913: Holiness, 731.
30 A word he invented to denote the holy minus its moral and rational aspects. Cf. Otto 1969: The Idea of the Holy [German original 1917], 6.
31 v.d. Leeuw 1956: Phänomenologie der Religion [1933], 33.
32 Heiler 1920: Das Gebet [1918]: VIII, similarly in 1959: Die Religionen der Menschheit in Vergangenheit und Gegenwart: 48.
33 Heiler 1920: Das Gebet [1918]: 17.

divine. The scholar of religions has to become immersed in the atmosphere of the holy in order to approach the heart of religious experience.[34] Heiler does not really see a difference between theology and the study of religions, because in his view the latter is likewise concerned with an experience of transcendent realities.[35]

From the point of view of the phenomenologists, religion is a phenomenon *sui generis*, which is given *a priori*. This is also evident in the work of Mirca Eliade, whose approach is somewhat different from the others, despite similar presuppositions and results. In contrast to the other mentioned phenomenologists, Eliade was not a theologian. His ideas are more independent from a Christian interpretation of the variety of religions. His work in the study of religions as well as in his fiction[36] is concerned with hierophanies, which he regards as the subject matter of the study of religions. At the heart of his philosophical construction is the assumption of an essential unity of religion and the holy, which can be studied in these various hierophanies, i.e. manifestations of the holy in space and time. Eliade describes the holy as qualitatively different from the profane, an eternal substance and ultimate reality opposed to the illusion of historical existence.[37]

In the course of the 20th century it became evident that this "classical" version of phenomenology of religion is religious in itself. It presupposed a unity of religion(s) as a starting point for comparisons. The assumption that it is possible to access the essence of religion by a study of the variety of phenomena is a philosophical construct which cannot be a premise of the study of religions if the latter is regarded as a discipline of the empirical social and cultural sciences and not of normative or speculative theology or philosophy. The phenomenologists of religion formulated a number of helpful methodological presuppositions for the study of religions, which helped to shape the character of the subject and to lay its academic foundations. Interestingly though, their own work was often inconsistent with those premises. The most illustrative example is perhaps the concept of intellectual

---

34 See Heiler 1961: Erscheinungsformen und Wesen der Religion, 14-17, where Heiler describes his understanding of scientific and religious prerequisites a scholar needs in the study of religions.

35 Heiler's famous phrase about the relationsthip between the study of religions and theology is: "Alle Religionswissenschaft ist letztlich *Theologie*, insofern sie es nicht nur mit psychologischen und geschichtlichen Erscheinungen, sondern mit dem Erlebnis jenseitiger Realitäten zu tun hat." (1961: Erscheinungsformen und Wesen der Religion, 17).

36 Eliade also produced a remarkable literary work.

37 Cf. Eliade 1954: Die Religionen und das Heilige: e.g. 12f, 56, 519; see also 1957: Das Heilige und das Profane.

suspense (*epoché*) or "bracketing", which can be regarded as an important part of "the phenomenological method". The idea was that in the study of religions one's own religious evaluations and convictions ought to be bracketed in order to approach the different religions without prejudice and partiality.[38] It is, however, easy to find examples to the contrary in the works of all the phenomenologists mentioned above.[39] In my view, the concept of "bracketing" is still helpful in order to demonstrate the attempted methodological agnosticism in the methodology of the study of religions, even though it is necessary to complement it with a clear reflection of one's own situatedness in a certain historical and social context. Influences and ideological presuppositions cannot be ignored or denied, but have to be made explicit if a study is to be academically sound.[40] This is, for example, an important point of postcolonial or feminist criticism of the study of religions, which will be discussed in the next section. Nevertheless, the attempt not to distort the representation of any religion unduly remains an inalienable and extremely important task in the study of religions.

As opposed to phenomenology, functional approaches to religion have often reflected the special interests of individual disciplines which deal with religion among a number of other phenomena or as a part of their actual object of study. Religion has been interpreted as compensation by psychologists like Freud and Jung, as a function of social integration by sociologists like Durkheim and Weber or as a means of catharsis by anthropologists like Malinowski, van Gennep and Turner. These analyses are helpful for an understanding of certain aspects of religions. They are, however, unacceptable as comprehensive explanations of the phenomenon "religion". There is no denying the fact that fear plays a certain role in many religions, that religions frequently constitute communities and structure contingency. These are, however, only certain aspects of religion(s) and none of them can serve as a com-

---

38 See for example the epilegomena of van der Leeuw 1938: Religion in Essence and Manifestation.
39 A number of such examples can be found in the above paragraph.
40 This also includes, for example, a distinction between one's own religious beliefs and the methodological agnosticism in the methodology of the study of religions. To avoid any misunderstanding let me give an example of what kind of reflection of one's own situatedness I mean. If for example the belief that there is no truth outside a certain religious group is taken as a starting point for a study of other religions, an impartial approach will not be possible. This presupposition is incompatible with the required methodological agnosticism. If, however, for example the influence of a certain religious and other ideologies on the culture in which one lives, e.g. organisational and economic structures that are taken for granted and recurrent processes of "othering" in societal life, are acknowledged, this may help to make explicit the context in which a certain study is conducted.

prehensively explanatory feature. The different perspectives on the multifaceted and disparate field "religions" have to be integrated into the discipline of the study of religions. The historical, sociological, psychological etc. perspectives are individually insufficient for an adequate study and representation of religions. Despite all interdisciplinarity, methodological integration under the premise of the study of religions is necessary in order to do justice to the breadth of the field and not to allow any individual aspect to be an explanatory feature for the whole phenomenon. This insight is an important result of phase 2. The differences in the understanding of the subject were an important issue at the 10th congress of the International Association for the History of Religions (IAHR) in 1960 in Marburg, where the gap, particularly between a universalist theological and an anthropological understanding of the subject, became evident. This gap can be regarded as the reason for the dispute on methods ("Methodenstreit") which was to follow in the next phase.

Even though Geertz emphasises the general scepticism in phase 3 (1970 to 1990), with an IAHR congress on methodology in Turku in 1973, which resulted in theoretical and methodological confusion, he acknowledges important decisions which were taken in this phase. In Turku, a growing dissatisfaction with Western science was expressed by intellectuals from former colonies. The relevance of research to society was discussed and in the debate about theory "[m]ost of the participants were aware of the fact that there was no meta-theory in the study of religion."[41] The meeting in Marburg in 1988[42] as well as the Warsaw statement in 1989[43] can be regarded as points of no return. In Warsaw, agreement was achieved on "conceptualizing religion as a historical phenomenon, engaging in empirically-based research, but perhaps more significantly, envisioning the study of religion in terms of the larger (theoretical) project of studying human society and culture."[44] The two quotations above illustrate that – despite all disagreement and difficulties – the two important issues which were discussed with respect to phase 2 (comprehensive functional explanations and the problems of the classical phenomenology of religion) were taken up and dealt with constructively at an international level in phase 3. The study of religions as an independent discipline – which consists of more than a collection of data from other disciplines – took its place among the social and cultural sciences. Important outcomes of the dis-

---

41 Geertz and McCutcheon 2000: The role of method and theory in the IAHR, 18.
42 Cf. Pye (ed.) 1989: Marburg Revisited.
43 See Tyloch 1990: Studies on Religions in the Context of Social Sciences, 8.
44 Geertz and McCutcheon 2000: The role of method and theory in the IAHR, 23f.

pute on methods was that the demand for an adequate, non-reductionist approach, which does justice to the delicate phenomenon "religion(s)" and takes seriously the perspective of believers, was supplemented by the paradigm of intersubjective verifiability on the one hand and by refraining from comprehensive explanations or definitions on the other.[45] Further issues and implications from the history of the study of religions which are relevant for phase 4 (from 1990 up to the present) will be taken up in the next chapter on recent developments.

1.1.3 Recent developments in the study of religions

Recent developments in the world-wide study of religions are certainly manifold and cannot be discussed at length here. My focus will be on a few trends that can be observed in a number of countries in Europe as well as in international organisations. Without any doubt, others would mention different developments here.[46] In recent years, increased attention has been paid to phenomena outside institutionalised religion, often as a direct or indirect response to the secularisation theory, which is questionable in many respects. Concepts like invisible religion (Luckmann)[47], civil religion (Bellah)[48] and implicit religion (Bailey)[49] point at influential aspects of religion beyond institutional organisation. In their study on "Theoretical correlations between worldview, civil religion, institutional religion and informal spiritualities" Helena Helve and Michael Pye present a set of concepts for the study of contemporary religion and conclude that "the trend is for institutional religion to weaken, while at the same time civil religion and informal spiritualities are not weakening. Rather, they are strengthening."[50] The inclusion of a study of worldviews and an increasing scepticism towards the holy-

---

45 Cf. Berner 1983: Gegenstand und Aufgabe der Religionswissenschaft, 98.
46 A similar perspective is taken by Armin W. Geertz (2000: Global perspectives on methodology in the study of religions), who regards the following issues as "postmodern challenges" to the study of religions: orientalism, the construction of the exotic, the representation and misrepresentation of other cultures, the politics of science and feminist criticism.
47 Luckmann 1991: Die unsichtbare Religion.
48 See Bellah 1970: Beyond Belief, especially pp. 168-189 and Bellah and Hammond 1980: Varieties of Civil Religion.
49 See Bailey 1997: Implicit Religion in Contemporary Society; cf. also the journal "Implicit Religion".
50 Helve and Pye 2001/2002: Theoretical correlations between world-view, civil religion, institutional religion and informal spiritualities, 101.

profane dichotomy can be observed in several countries, particularly in Scandinavia.[51]

Many of the recent developments are interconnected and influence each other. Internationalisation (especially growing participation of scholars from various countries in international conferences) is directly linked to postcolonial reflection and an awareness of orientalism and occidentalism. In the attempt to avoid discrimination by misrepresentation or negligence the criticism of colonialism and orientalism goes hand in hand with a criticism of androcentrism, which has until recently been another unquestioned paradigm in the study of religions. The change of perspective from a study of ancient texts to a study of contemporary religion(s) involved a change to empirical social research as well as an increasing awareness of the potential social and political relevance of the study of religions and an acknowledgement of the social responsibility of the scholar of religions, for example with respect to criticism of ideologies. In the following, postcolonial reflection, feminist criticism and the debate about social responsibility may serve as an illustration of the type of discussions which are going on in the study of religions at the moment.

Postcolonial reflection

Edward Said's seminal work Orientalism (1978) was a milestone in raising public awareness of the assumed cultural supremacy of the West in its study of other cultures. It disclosed convincingly the distortions in European constructions of other cultures. The relevance of Said's criticism for the study of religions cannot be overrated. Many of Said's points can be regarded as a direct criticism of the study of religions. One famous example of the kind of distortions of Eastern religions in the representations of Western scholars is Western constructions of Hinduism. It can easily be demonstrated that early Western understandings of Hinduism were to a considerable extent constructions based on Western models. A selected set of phenomena, which were assumed to be the important aspects of any religion – for example an-

---

51 Cf. for example the importance of the concepts worldview or view of life in the Nordic study of religions, e.g. Helve 1993: The World View of Young People: A Longitudinal Study of Finnish Youth Living in a Suburb of Metropolitan Helsinki or Helve 2000: The formation of gendered world views and gender ideology; see also Jensen 2002: From the History of Religions to the Study of Religions. Trends and tendencies in Denmark. A similar approach can be found in Berner 1983: Gegenstand und Aufgabe der Religionswissenschaft, which will be further discussed in chapter 1.2.2.

cient sacred texts in a learned language and a clergy – was taken to be representative of the entire tradition. Thus, the Brahmanic, scriptural and traditional aspects of Hinduism were mistaken for the religion Hinduism as a whole. Recently, there have been a number of attempts – in India itself and in the West[52] – to rewrite the history of Hindu traditions, with a particular emphasis on the inclusion of formerly marginalised groups, including above all women and lower-class people, in order to produce a more balanced and realistic account of the complex and multifaceted phenomena which together make up what is called "Hinduism". Apart from the special emphasis on the former exclusion and misrepresentation of women, the inclusion of popular, folk, non-Sanskritic and regional trends is inalienable in the attempt to appreciate Hinduism in its full diversity. The blatant distortions of the past – including questionable constructions of periphery (e.g. "the East", women) and centre (e.g. "the West", men) – are no longer admissible.

In 2001, Morny Joy complained that the implications of postcolonial reflection – in particular reflection on power relations, the discrimination of coloured or indigenous people, women and marginal groups, which has taken place in anthropology, history, literature and some contemporary philosophy – have not yet been adequately considered in the study of religions.[53] She shows repercussions for the study of religions if the charges are taken seriously and hopes that in the study of religions, postcolonial reflection, which is still peripheral, will in the future help to alter the subject considerably in order to free it from its 19th century mindset. Even though the full impact of these criticisms, which without any doubt involves a serious reconsideration of theory and methodology in the study of religions, are perhaps still to be expected, awareness about these matters is continuously increasing. An example of an important contribution to the debate is the book *Religion im Spiegelkabinett* (2003), in which different nuances of orientalism, as well as its equivalent "occidentalism" are discussed.[54]

---

52 For a survey of contributions from India cf. Joy 2001: Postcolonial Reflections. See also King 1999: Orientalism and the modern myth of "Hinduism".

53 Joy 2001: Postcolonial Reflections: 177. For a similar argument see Nye 2000. Cf. also Geertz 2000: Global perspectives on methodology in the study of religions.

54 See Schalk (ed.) 2003: Religion im Spiegelkabinett.

The gender debate

Feminist criticism – or perhaps more generally: the academic debate about gender – has become increasingly influential in the study of religions, even though, as always when residual privileges are at stake, it is still a long way until the relevant issues obtain due consideration not only by a committed minority. Feminist criticism is directed at both the study of religions as an academic institution in which men are overrepresented in many respects[55] and theory, methodology and representation of religions, which are often androcentric in that they exclude, marginalise or misrepresent women. Gender has become an issue to be considered in the study of religions somewhat later than in theology. At the congresses of the International Association for the History of Religions (IAHR) there have been panels on gender from 1980 (Winnipeg) onwards, the British Association for the Study of Religions (BASR) made "Religion and Gender" the theme of its annual conference in 1989. Ursula King recommends two ways of looking at women and religion: (1) the contribution of women to religion, how they influence and shape religion, and (2) the different and complex ways in which women are influenced and shaped, oppressed and liberated by religion. In a gender-reflected approach to religions a study of the role of women is particularly important, as it has been neglected for such a long time. However, "the topic has to be an integral one, concerned with both women and men, and a study to be undertaken by both sexes jointly."[56] An important contribution to the debate is the book Women and Religion, which Ursula King edited in 1995. An update of the developments and the progress that was made can be found in King and Beattie (2004) and the new edition of the Encyclopedia of Religion (2005).[57]

Donate Pahnke regards "substantial feminism" as particularly relevant to the study of religion. It deals with the clichés about male and female, rejects the dominant gender stereotypes and questions the categories male and female insofar as it assumes non-existence of innate gender differences until there is evidence to the contrary. Pahnke observes that, in the study of religions and its tradition of androcentric

---

55 For example, in *The Encyclopedia of Religion* (Eliade 1987) only 175 out of 1357 contributors are women and among the 142 significant "scholars of religion" there are only four women, two American and two British. Cf. King 1990: 284.
56 King 1990: Religion and gender, 285.
57 For the reception of the gender debate in the study of religions see also Mikaelsson 2004: Gendering the history of religions; Clark 2004: Engendering the study of religion.

research about patriarchal major religions, women appear mostly in their relationships to men or as deviation from the male norm.[58] The task for the study of religions is a comprehensive one:

> "Mit der einfachen Lösung, ab jetzt in jedes religionswissenschaftliche Buch ein Kapitel über ‚die Frau' einzufügen, wo vorher keines war, wird es auch nicht getan sein. Gender-Studies gehören nicht in ein separates Kapitel oder eine sonstige Enklave, sondern müssen in die ganze Breite des Forschungsspektrums als eine anthropologische Neubestimmung des homo religiosus eingehen, welche die ‚femina religiosa' und ihre Religiosität sowohl in den Entdeckungszusammenhang als auch in den Begründungszusammenhang der Forschung einbezieht."[59]

Edith Franke notes that taking up results from gender studies makes possible more precise academic work in the study of religions as it corrects the notion of the field and enables a critical perspective towards society, religions and ideologies. She calls for a cross-fertilisation of the study of religions and feminist criticism with respect to the following points: (1) experience of women and men as a field for empirical research (e.g. interviews), (2) partiality and reflexivity: the necessity to reflect one's own position, (3) contextuality and particularity: clear definition of the context for which a statement is valid, and (4) reconsideration of the subject-object dichotomy in the tradition of critical social empirical research. As in other academic and societal fields, the androcentric position must not be mistaken as impartial any longer.[60]

Randi R. Warne formulates it succinctly when she writes: "Androcentrism is a prescriptive ideological stance which is untenable on logical grounds."[61] She regards the gender-critical turn in the study of religions as essential "not only for the intellectual integrity of our project, but for our plausibility and usefulness as intellectuals."[62] The importance of a reflection of gender differences from the point of view of the study of religions is a recurrent issue in this work, particularly with respect to the representation of religions (chapter I, section 1.3.3) and as an aspect of the framework I suggest for integrative religious education (chapter IV, section 3).

---

58 This is obviously not a problem of the study of religions alone, but is part of a societal context in which women are marginalised. Analogous observations can be made e.g. for women in politics (e.g. the famous "first ladies") or in sports (e.g. that women's sports are often labelled explicitly "women....", for example, in the "Women's Championship" in football while men's sport is regarded as the norm which is given far more attention).

59 Pahnke 1993: Feministische Aspekte einer religionswissenschaftlichen Anthropologie, 22f.

60 See Franke 1997: Feministische Kritik and Wissenschaft und Religionen, 107-119.

61 Warne 2000: Making the gender-critical turn, 257.

62 Ibid., 258.

Social responsibility

The third recent development in the study of religions which I would like to outline briefly is the increasing acknowledgement of the social responsibility of the study of religions as an institution. Especially since it has become obvious also to the general public that religion is not a relic from the past which is gradually going to disappear, but which is very much present in societal and political life in various regions of the world, scholars of religions have become aware of their possible and actual contribution to public discourse about religion. In fact, in many countries the voice of scholars of religions with their impartial perspective on the variety of religions is virtually absent in public discourse, contrary to the voice of representatives of the different religious groups, who are frequently consulted, when it comes to statements about religious matters.[63] The manifold reasons for that cannot be discussed here.[64] What is, however, important is that more and more scholars – quite rightly – regard this as a problem and present ideas on how to change this unsatisfactory situation.

Kurt Rudolph, whose important paper "Die ideologiekritische Funktion der Religionswissenschaft" was published in *Numen* in 1978, regards a criticism of ideologies as an important aspect of the social responsibility of the scholar of religion. In a more recent article, he draws attention to the values of tolerance and humanity, which he describes as an inheritance of the Enlightenment. They can be a starting point for the study of religions:

> "For scholars of religions, human rights are not part of a creed that one merely recites without conviction. Furthermore, despite the value-neutrality of work in the field human rights should not be left at the door when one is required to take stances on public issues. ... Here belongs the impetus to ideological criticism that I have described, as well as its various effects, whose potential contribution to public life must be emphasized more strongly than ever."[65]

As an example of the kind of contributions to public life that he has in mind, he cites the charter of Remid, the Religionswissenschaftlicher

---

[63] This situation is described, for example, by Rudolph (2000: Some reflections on approaches and methodologies in the study of religions, 241) or Baumann (1995: "Merkwürdige Bundesgenossen" und "naive Sympathisanten". Die Ausgrenzung der Religionswissenschaft aus der bundesdeutschen Kontroverse um neue Religionen) with respect to Germany and by McCutcheon (2000: Critics not caretakers: the scholar of religion as public intellectual) with respect to the United States of America.

[64] The texts mentioned in the above note provide some points of this discussion.

[65] Rudolph 2000: 242.

Medien- und Informationsdienst (Religious Studies Media and Information Service) in Germany.[66] This registered society, which was founded by young scholars of religion in 1989, communicates knowledge about different religions (with an emphasis on contemporary religion and new religious movements) "in order to foster a peaceful and tolerant coexistence of people and of the various religions and to facilitate mutual understanding and respect."[67] Rudolph emphasises that for the scholar of religions today it is very important to foster a climate of tolerance toward "the other" in academic and public life.

Similarly to Rudolph, who sees a close link between the criticism of ideologies and the criticism of religions in this respect, Edith Franke demands that the results of the study of religions should be used in public debates about religious and social conflicts in order to help objectify and clarify the problems. She writes: "Meines Erachtens sollte Religionswissenschaft die Religionskritik nicht nur als einen ihrer Untersuchungsgegenstände betrachten, sondern ihre Forschungsergebnisse zu kritischen Stellungnahmen heranziehen."[68] The study of religions as an academic discipline cannot itself provide any criteria for a critical assessment of religions. However, criteria can be developed out of political positions (Franke also mentions respect for human rights) and the study of religions can analyse carefully if and in how far religions and the creation of religious symbols stabilise and legitimise social inequalities. What Franke means is not a substantial evaluation of beliefs, but a close look at the consequences of particular religious beliefs for social life.[69]

Russell T. McCutcheon sparked off a debate about the scholar of religions as public intellectual. He also is concerned with the critical potential of the study of religions with respect to statements about religions and ideologies. McCutcheon regards scholars of religions as culture critics who ought to challenge the ideological mechanisms and alignments "whereby description becomes prescription and the local is represented as universal."[70] His criticism of the current – virtually ab-

---

66 See www.remid.de.
67 Remid: Satzung §2 as cited by Rudolph 2000: Some reflections on approaches and methodologies in the study of religions, 242 (translation: Gregory Alles), the German original can be found in: www.remid.de/remid_verein_satzung.htm.
68 Franke 1997: Feministische Kritik and Wissenschaft und Religionen, 118.
69 Cf. ibid., 119. Franke mentions these tasks for the study of religions in the context of the relationship between a feminist study of religions and the criticism of religions. Her ideas about the possible contribution of the study of religions to public debates are, however, relevant not only with respect to gender issues.
70 McCutcheon 2000: Critics not caretakers: the scholar of religion as public intellectual, 177.

sent – role of scholars of religions in public discourse in North America points primarily at the concept of religion which the current study of religion has inherited from phenomenology and hermeneutics and which is still widely used: "religion is comprised of *sui generis*, non-falsifiable meaning derived from a private experience of mystery, awe, power, or the sacred ...".[71] What is required is a fundamental reconsideration of the concept of religion which acknowledges the political and social aspects of religion:

> "[S]o-called religious systems are perhaps the pre-eminent site for creating social continuity amidst the discontinuities of historical existence. If this was our understanding of religion, we would see all the more clearly just what is at stake when our colleagues obscure matters by uncritically teaching and writing on insider claims concerning certain behaviours and institutions being socially and politically autonomous systems of faith or salvation."[72]

The debate about what the social responsibility of the study of religions exactly comprises and what its limits are, is certainly not uncontroversial.[73] On the contrary, it could hardly be any more diverse.[74] Nevertheless, that there is a social responsibility of the scholar of religions can hardly be questioned. In a political climate in which stereotypes predominate, an important function of the study of religion is to provide reliable analyses of religious systems. Apart from making its knowledge public, the study of religions can, moreover, have important functions as a provider of mediation for dialogue, as the academic discipline responsible for the development of curricula for integrative RE, and as social mediator in conflicts with a religious dimension, in particular in helping to overcome false or misleading images of other cultures which may be current in the media and public life.[75]

In contributions to public debates about religion, it is important not to simply reproduce the rhetoric of the innate relatedness between religions and conflict. As Michael Pye has pointed out, the potential for harmony ought to be studied just as the potential for conflict. To regard

---

71 Ibid., 168.
72 Ibid., 177.
73 Cf. for example Donald Wiebe's response to McCutcheon's ideas about the scholar of religion as public intellectual at the IAHR world congress in March 2005 in Tokyo.
74 Cf. for example the very different papers which were presented in the panel "Angewandte Religionswissenschaft" (applied study of religions) at the conference of the German Association for the History of Religions in Erfurt in September/October 2003, see DVRG 2003: Thematisches Raster (http://www.uni-erfurt.de/religion_im_konflikt/beitraege.htm).
75 For this paragraph cf. Franke/Pye 2004: The study of religions and its contribution to problem-solving in a plural world.

religious diversity as a problem is a normative position, untenable on scientific grounds. Currently the link between violence, conflict and religion is all too present in the consciousness of many people, whereas the facts that religions also actually contribute to peace, and that there are various interesting models of religious pluralism in different parts of the world, are easily overlooked. Analyses of models of religious pluralism are as important as analyses of religious conflicts in order not to allow the so-called "clash of civilisations" to become a self-fulfilling prophecy, but instead to actively contribute to a peaceful coexistence of different religions.[76]

What I have described here are but spotlights on and opinions about recent developments in the study of religions, which are in many ways interrelated. The concept of religion and the delineation of the subject matter, as well as questions of methodology and the representation of religions, continue to be contested issues, particularly in the context of a growing internationalisation of the discipline. As these issues are important for an understanding of the study of religions as an academic discipline and, moreover, have implications for theory and methodology of integrative RE as the corresponding school subject, they will be discussed in more detail in the following chapters.

1.1.4 Limitations of the study of religions

As will be demonstrated in the next chapter, in the academic study of religions, the "field" or subject matter has to be delineated in such a way that it can be studied with the various methods of historical, social and cultural research. The fact that, in the study of religions, the approach to the variety of religions is not religious or normative in itself results in an exclusion of a certain type of questions which cannot be answered (and sometimes not even asked) from a secular point of view. Questions about, for example, the origin of "religion", the meaning behind the variety of religions, the truth of religious claims etc. lie beyond the responsibilities or rather possibilities of the study of religions. The search for religious truth is no more appropriate a task of the study of religions than the evaluation of religious theory and practice or the attempt to identify the "essence" of any religion or even of "religion" as such. As aspects of its own theory and methodology, metaphysical speculations are beyond the reach of the study of religions, even

---

[76] See, for example, Franke and Pye (ed.) 2006: Religionen nebeneinander. Modelle religiöser Vielfalt in Ost- und Südostasien, and Wasim, Mas'ud et al. (2005) Religious Harmony: Problems Practice and Education.

though they are an important part of the field which is studied. Likewise, any integral understanding of the phenomenon "religion" or religion as such cannot be achieved with the methods of the study of religions. Moreover, an attempt to do justice to the self-understanding of the believers requires an anti-reductionism of the following kind: (1) no comprehensive explanation of "religion" as such may be given and (2) religion must not be understood merely as a function of something else.

Scholars of religions approach religions with a limited set of questions when they undertake a delineation of the field which is not already religious itself. Some aspects of religions, which may be important and constitutive for an understanding of religion(s) from an insider's point of view are therefore not directly accessible to the researcher, except from a study of testimonies of believers. The conflict between the role of the scholar of religions as representative of the discipline of the study of religions and his or her private interests in finding (religious) truth have often led scholars of religions to go beyond what is acceptable within the study of religions. A clear distinction is necessary between what can be said within the limits of the discipline of the study of religions and private insights or beliefs which are acquired through the study of religions. The descriptions of Michael Pye and Ulrich Berner with respect to questions which lie outside the strictly defined academic study of religions are helpful for an understanding of the limitations of the subject. Pye (1972) regards the following considerations as being beyond the reach of the study of religions:

> "We may wish to examine the inner consistency of a belief system from a critical point of view, or to assess its consistency with our own manner of understanding the world, or its consistency or manner of conflict with the views of some philosopher or with the generality of scientific thinking in the world. We may wish to consider what kind of criteria might be appropriate for testing or evaluating the statements made by religious persons. Or we may wish to embark on the systematic formulation of value judgements."[77]

He emphasises the difference between the rationality of a scientific theory of religions on the one hand and philosophy on the other, which has various tasks, including the study of religions. A rational scientific theory of religions has to be independent from the rationality or irrationality of any religious system. Questions within religious or metaphysical circles are "questions to be set aside" by the scholar of religions.[78] Berner mentions the following ways in which the border of a

---

77 Pye 1972: Comparative Religion: An Introduction through Source Materials, 31.
78 Cf. Pye 2000: Westernism unmasked, 226f.

strictly defined study of religions may be crossed: (1) criticism of ideologies, e.g. from the point of view of normative positions which have to be made explicit; (2) art, e.g. fiction;[79] (3) ethics, for example if principles like reverence for life, human dignity or tolerance are used in order to measure the extent to which religious teachings and practices are in harmony with or in opposition to those principles; (4) theology. Berner draws attention to the fact that there is always the danger of crossing the boundaries of the study of religions unconsciously or without making it explicit. It is important to clearly distinguish between theory formation in the study of religions and those ways of crossing the borders of the subject.[80]

It may be helpful to distinguish between the study of religions as a *discipline* and as an *institution*. While the study of religions as a discipline (i.e. the study of religions in a narrow sense) has to be methodologically agnostic with respect to values as well, the study of religions as an institution (i.e. the study of religions in a broader sense) can look at the same field from a subjectively justified point of view which has to be made explicit. This may be a political agenda (such as human rights, international law), an ethical or religious stance (such as reverence for life) or a pedagogical programme (e.g. emancipation). Then, criteria which are not produced by the study of religions itself serve as reference points for statements about different religions. Whatever those criteria are, it is important to make them explicit and to clearly indicate at which point the study of religions in a narrow sense is departed from.[81] To distinguish between the study of religions as a discipline and the study of religions as an institution helps to preserve the character of the subject on the one hand (in particular in its delimitation to theologies or philosophies) and on the other hand fosters an ability to contribute to social and political questions.

---

79 Berner refers to Mircea Eliade's novels and quite rightly notes that the formal distinction between scientific literature and fiction seems to point to the border between what is within the limits of the study of religions and what is not, while the proclamatory impetus can in fact be found in both Eliade's literary and scientific work. Cf. Berner 1983: Gegenstand und Aufgabe der Religionswissenschaft, 114.
80 Cf. ibid., 113-116.
81 For the distinction between the study of religions as a discipline and as an institution cf., e.g., Pahnke 1993. Feministische Aspekte einer religionswissenschaftlichen Anthropologie, 28.

1.2 The concept of religion

The discussion about the concept of religion that can be used in the study of religions has been an important concern since the early origins of the subject. That the debate is still relevant today can be seen in the great number of recent publications which deal with the topic. After all, concepts of religions delineate the subject matter for the discipline of the study of religions. They are constituents of the discipline as they imply preliminary decisions about what is considered a part of the study of religions and what is not. To some extent, concepts of religion precede the other steps taken in the study of religions. They have implications for the selection of sources, for the choice of methods and the process of theory formation. One example of the topicality of the task to reflect upon what can be regarded as the subject matter of the study of religions was the conference of the British Association for the Study of Religions (BASR) in Oxford in 2004, which had the title "Mapping the Field".

As Armin W. Geertz points out, the most appropriate answer to the question "What is religion?" is: "Who wants to know?".[82] What will be discussed here is the attempt to find a concept of religion for the academic discipline of the study of religions. This is not to say that this generally is the only acceptable or possible concept of religion. For other purposes and contexts, other concepts of religion may be acceptable. Furthermore, religious concepts of religion (e.g. those of classical phenomenology) or functional comprehensively explanatory concepts of religion are important areas of research for the study of religions, despite the fact that they are unacceptable as a basis for our subject, as both these groups are reductionist in their own ways. Likewise unacceptable as a concept of religion for the study of religions is an understanding of religion that is highly influenced by what is commonly regarded as "religion" in that particular part of the world. Michael Pye has demonstrated that it is necessary to differentiate between those memes which are pre-scientific cultural assumptions that are deeply entrenched in the consciousness of people on the one hand, and scientific concepts with designatory, analytical and explanatory functions on the other.[83]

---

[82] Cf. Geertz 2004: Definition, categorization and indecision: or, how to get on with the Study of Religion, 113.
[83] See Pye 2002: Memes and models in the Study of Religions. For his analysis of different memes about "religion" or "new religions" in various parts of the world see also the section about the representation of religions, 1.3.3.

The attempt to define the subject matter of the study of religions and to provide an adequate concept of religion involves reflection about what the common denominator of the phenomena that are called "religious" is. As religion does not exist in a vacuum, a consideration of interrelations between religion and e.g. culture, social and political contexts, worldview or ideology are indispensable. Furthermore, as recent anthropology has shown, the interrelations between definition and power, which are often subtle but pervasive, have to be taken into account in order to fully acknowledge the circumstances in which the research process takes place.[84]

In the following, I am going to present some examples of the variety of concepts of religion within the study of religions (1.2.1). This confusing variety may, however, be overcome with a broad delineation of the subject matter (1.2.2), which is as necessary for integrative RE as it is for the academic study of religions.

1.2.1 The variety of concepts of religion

The variety of definitions, concepts and theories of religions could hardly be greater. In 2000, Kurt Rudolph mentions Marxist analysis, psychoanalytic theories (Sigmund Freud and Carl Gustav Jung), the "communicative theory" (Émile Durkheim and his school), the "purposive" theory (Max Weber) and its adaptations (e.g. Peter Berger) and functionalism (e.g. Bronisław Malinowski) as older profane theories or religion. Among the more recent ones he mentions the following approaches: cultural anthropological (Ralph Linton, Edward E. Evans-Pritchard), structural (Claude Lévi-Strauss), semasiological (Clifford Geertz), ethological (Konrad Lorenz, Walter Burkert), systems-theoretical (Niklas Luhmann), cultural-critical (Hans G. Kippenberg) and his own ideological-critical approach.[85] This survey of a selection of well-known concepts of religion can give a first impression of the diversity of approaches to religion from several academic disciplines which are concerned with religion. One important finding of Per Bilde, who conducted a study of a number of definitions of religion which he

---

[84] For spotlights from the debate in anthropology, see the works of Clifford Geertz, James Clifford and Vincent Crapanzano in the bibliography. One obvious example of the interrelations between definition and power is when the legal status of a community is decided upon: Can it be registered as a "religion" or not? For the procedure in Denmark see A.W. Geertz 2004: Definition, categorization and indecision: or, how to get on with the Study of Religion, 116ff.

[85] See Rudolph 2000: Some reflections on approaches and methodologies in the study of religions, 233.

organised into 18 types,[86] was that the definitions clearly reflect the disciplines from which the respective scholars come.[87] Thus, the fact that religion is approached from different disciplines is one important reason for the multiplicity of definitions of religion. Before I move on to the question of what characteristics a study-of-religions concept or definition of religion should have, I would like to demonstrate the variety within the existent approaches to religion with a selection of four well-known and widely discussed examples from the range of definitions, namely the ones by Émile Durkheim, Mircea Eliade, Clifford Geertz and Jonathan Z. Smith.[88]

Durkheim, from his sociological perspective, defines religion in 1899 as

> "a unified system of beliefs and practices relative to sacred things, that is to say, things set apart and forbidden – beliefs and practices which unite into one single moral community called a Church, all those who adhere to them."[89]

For Eliade, along with other phenomenologists of religion, religion refers to the experience of the sacred, which manifests itself in various forms. Eliade regards religion as an important aspect of being or becoming truly human.[90] Clifford Geertz regards religion as a cultural system and defines it as

> "(1) a system of symbols which acts to (2) establish powerful, pervasive, and long-lasting moods and motivations in men by (3) formulating conceptions of a general order of existence and (4) clothing these conceptions with such an aura of factuality that (5) the moods and motivations seem uniquely realistic."[91]

---

86 The types that Per Bilde identified are: religion as the fulfilment of human destiny, the feeling of absolute dependence, a flight of fancy or the need for consolation, belief in supernatural powers and concomitant behaviour, an expression of society and social solidarity, communication with the sacred, aspiring to the ultimate, anxious piety and conscientious devotion, communication with the world, the means to overcome the gap between humans and their world, giving meaning, order and completeness in an otherwise chaotic existence, ensuring the reality of the world, a part (almost biologically) of being human, what basically motivates humans, an explanation of the world, the aspiration of values, ideology and concomitant behaviour, consisting of five (or six) dimensions; cf. Bilde 1991: 9, quoted in: Geertz 2004: Definition, categorization and indecision, 114.
87 Cf. Geertz 2004: Definition, categorization and indecision, 113f.
88 Here I follow A.W. Geertz (ibid., 113f).
89 Durkheim 1995: The Elementary Forms of Religious Life, 4, quoted in Geertz 2004: Definition, categorization and indecision, 113.
90 Cf., e.g., Eliade 1969: The Quest, preface.
91 Geertz 1966: Religion as a cultural system, 4.

In contrast to Eliade, he shows much more attention to the differences between insider- and outsider-perspectives. Jonathan Z. Smith emphasises the outsider perspective even more decisively when he writes that religion

> "is a term created by scholars for their intellectual purposes ... It is a second-order, generic concept that plays the same role in establishing a disciplinary horizon that a concept such as 'language' plays in linguistics or 'culture' plays in anthropology."[92]

What can the consequences for the study of religions be in view of the diversity of approaches to "religion", of which the above examples are just spotlights? Some basic considerations can provide a starting point here: an adequate study-of-religions concept of religion should not be religious in itself and needs to do justice to the plurality of religions and cultures.[93] Taking account of the fact that scholars of religions often found in the empirical material what they had previously defined and constructed, it is important to emphasise that concepts and definitions should be preliminary in character and always open to improvement and modification by the empirical data. They should not be regarded as an end point but as a programme, their failure providing a new starting point.[94]

Jacques Waardenburg suggests "orientation" as a preliminary concept of religion as a starting point for further research. In this concept the different religions are regarded as different systems which provide some kind of orientation. Taking up ideas by Niklas Luhmann, Waardenburg writes that "a system of orientation enables human beings to find their ways in life and the world by referring to a framework which provides meaning."[95] However, the question of what is specifically religious in a religious system of orientation as opposed to a non-religious system of orientation remains. Waardenburg suggests specific elements, for example the idea that there are spiritual beings to whom one can relate, norms and values which are regarded as ultimate, or "bestimmte jenseitige, unbedingt, ja absolut geltende Bezugspunkte, die sinngebend wirken."[96] He modifies the distinction between religious and non-religious systems of orientation when he says that there are also non-religious systems of orientation which have a reli-

---

92 Smith 1998: Religion, religions, religious, 281f.
93 A good selection of articles about secular theories of religion can be found in Jensen and Rothstein (ed.) 2000: Secular Theories of Religion. Current Perspectives.
94 Cf., e.g., Michaels 1997: Einleitung, 13.
95 Waardenburg 1986: Religionen und Religion, 34.
96 Ibid., 35 (i.e. "particular transcendent, absolute or ultimate points of reference which have a meaning-creating effect").

gious character or effect, if ideologies or ways of life have an "absolute" quality for the people who relate to them and if they contain elements with a powerful symbolism.[97]

Similarly, Rainer Flasche regards religions as "Welterklärungs- und Lebensbewältigungssysteme in einer Gerichtetheit auf eine wie auch immer geartete Unverfügbarkeit."[98] They are at the same time open and closed systems, partial systems in relation to the whole system and to other parts of it, for example, the language system, the system of thought, the gestural system, the cultic system etc. Flasche regards the dichotomy of *heil* and *unheil* ("healed" and "not healed") as the fundamental structure of religions.[99] Waardenburg's distinction between religious and non-religious systems of orientation and Flasche's reference to "Unverfügbarkeit" point at an important question about concepts of religion: Is reference to transcendence in any form a necessary criterion for "religion"? Many definitions take up this criterion, often referring back to Spiro's famous definition of religion as "an institution consisting of culturally patterned interaction with culturally postulated superhuman beings".[100] Spiro himself claimed that "religion can be differentiated from other culturally constituted institutions by virtue only of its reference to superhuman beings."[101] Similarly, Tylor already suggested the belief in spiritual beings as a minimum definition of religion in the late 19th century.[102] In fact, reference to some kind of transcendence, be it in the form of spiritual beings or any other form, continues to be an influential criterion in the concepts of religion of many scholars, particularly in the sociology of religion.[103] Other scholars define religion without any reference to transcendence. For example, Ninian Smart, who understands religions as worldviews, as systems of belief "which, through symbols and actions, mobilize the feelings and wills of human beings."[104] Then, so-called ideologies or non-religious worldviews also come into perspective.

---

97 Ibid., 35.
98 Flasche 2000: Von der Selbstbeschränkung und Selbstbegründung der Religionenwissenschaft, 164; for the following see 168.
99 Cf. ibid., 172ff.
100 Spiro 1966: Religion: problems of definition and explanation, 96.
101 Ibid., 98.
102 Tylor 1873: Primitive Culture, 424.
103 See e.g. Pollak 1995: Was ist Religion? Probleme der Definition.
104 Smart 1983: Worldviews: Cross-Cultural Explorations of Human Beliefs, 2f., quoted in Smith 1998: Religion, religions, religious, 281.

In order to deal with phenomena which are actually relevant to society, Russell T. McCutcheon claims that we need a critical theory of religion as an all too human institution, because:

> "Whatever else religion may or may not be, then, it is at least a potent manner by which humans construct maps by which they negotiate not simply their way around the unpredictable natural world but also through which they defend and contest issues of social power and privilege in the here and now."[105]

His concept of religion refers to a number of phenomena of which no single one may be universalised:

> "religions are systems of social signification, encoded within narratives of the epic past and the anticipated future, coordinated within behavioral and institutional systems of cognitive and social control, all of which characterizes human responses to the various incongruities and disruptions that come with historical existence."[106]

The task to "scrutinize the ideological sleight of hand that leads to a seemingly perfect fit between the model constructed and sanctioned by the group in question, on the one hand, and reality, on the other"[107] shows once again the ideology-critical impact, which was already addressed by Kurt Rudolph in the 1970s,[108] which makes the study of religions extremely relevant in a vast number of topical discourses about the nature of reality, be it in relation to power and privilege, ethical questions, ideologies behind different economic models, notions of progress, to name just a few examples.

Before I present a few recent suggestions for a delineation of the subject matter, which may help to overcome the bewildering variety of definitions or concepts of religion – most of which have been normative or otherwise flawed – I would like to consider the term "religion" itself. The metalinguistic category "religion" is Eurocentric in origin but now used world-wide as a notion which refers to the phenomena outlined above. Despite the usual dangers of using the term uncritically, "religion" is, as Kurt Rudolph suggested, as good an umbrella term as would-be alternatives like "worldview" or "culture". It remains, however, *in fieri*, as Ugo Bianchi pointed out.[109]

---

105 McCutcheon 2000: Critics not caretakers, 173.
106 Ibid.,
107 Ibid., 175.
108 Rudolph 1978: Die ideologiekritische Funktion der Religionswissenschaft, cf. also the section on social responsibility in 1.1.3.
109 Cf. Rudolph 2000: Some reflections on approaches and methodologies in the study of religions, 240f.; Bianchi, Bleeker and Bausani 1972: Problems and Methods of the History of Religions, 33.

1.2.2 The "subject matter" or "field" of the study of religions

Despite differences in recent delineations of the field of the study of religions, there seems to be some broad consensus about the subject matter, even with respect to phenomena whose position in or outside the field is contested.[110] In the study of religions, religion is studied as a human phenomenon, i.e. religion as it is lived, expressed and described by human beings.[111] Broadly speaking, the subject matter of the study or religions are the concrete, empirical religions in their diversity, characterised by multiplicity and multifacetedness. The singular "religion" can only be used operationally in an academic context, as "religion" is always a construct.[112]

Ninian Smart's delineation of the field as structured by six dimensions, namely the doctrinal, mythological, ethical and the ritual, experiential and social levels of religion has been a widely accepted model for some time.[113] Michael Pye distinguishes between four basic aspects of religions, religious concepts, groups, states of mind and actions.[114] This distinction is also the basis of his "adumbration" of the field:

> "The term religion may be used to refer to patterns of (i) various inter-related behaviours including, for example, ritual practices and the design and use of special sites and buildings, (ii) more or less normative beliefs, symbols, images and other representations, (iii) a variety of social forms such as mass movements, local gatherings, churches, special interest groups and the specialised roles of individuals, and (iv) a subjective focusing in an awareness of power, otherness, holiness, depth, security, healing, release, and so on."[115]

Pye notes that the order of the individual aspects is immaterial and no single aspect determines the others exclusively. The relations between them are as significant as the aspects viewed severally. His examples show that with this adumbration the field is broad enough to include phenomena like civil, invisible and implicit religion and common re-

---

110 For example, recurrence of a certain set of topics on conferences may be regarded as an indication of that.
111 See e.g. Waardenburg 1986: Religionen und Religion. Systematische Einführung in die Religionswissenschaft, who therefore talks about "human religion" (17).
112 Cf., e.g., Flasche 2000: Von der Selbstbeschränkung und Selbstbegründung der Religionenwissenschaft, 164f. Flasche specifies the subject matter further by taking up the interrelations between religions and their contexts: "die konkreten Religionen in ihrer gemeinschaftsbildenden, denk- und sprachstrukturell bedingten, umweltbezogenen und gesamtstrukturellen Eingebundenheit" (ibid., 164).
113 Cf. Smart 1975: What is religion? Smart amended his model by a 7th dimension later, see Smart 1996: Dimensions of the Sacred.
114 Pye 1972: Comparative Religion: An Introduction through Source Materials, 12.
115 Pye 2000: Westernism unmasked, 212.

ligiosity. Furthermore, he shows that a heuristic, open-ended, family-resemblance- operational definition of religion is best not described as "functional", since this commonly implies a functional*ist* explanation which goes beyond the heuristic. It is also preferable to normative definitions, for example that of Paul Tillich, which regards "ultimate concern" as the characteristic feature of religion. Noting that "there is much religion which is not really about 'ultimate concern'", Pye makes an important point and shows that Tillich's notion of religion seems to be generally formulated but "in fact implies a normative, participant's view as to what should count as valid or significant religion."[116] Too narrow conceptions of the field can be avoided if care is taken not to regard a prevalent characteristic of one religion as the specific characteristic of all religions.[117]

Another interesting way of mapping the field has been presented by Ulrich Berner. He attempts to isolate those features from the broad general field of the social and cultural sciences which the study of religions is supposed to deal with. For this reason, he exemplarily analyses three texts, which are commonly regarded as "religious": The Buddha's Sermon at Benares, the Bhagavadgita and the Sermon on the Mount in the New Testament. What they have in common is that they establish a link between universal interpretation and normative implication. In Buddha's Sermon at Benares the eightfold path with its methodical steps which have to be practiced is offered as a way of overcoming suffering, which is regarded as characteristic of all existence. In the Bhagavadgita the idea of an unchangeable core of human personality is used as a justification for the permission to kill under certain circumstances (which is directly opposed to the observance of *ahimsa*, not harming other beings), as the bodies exist independently from the transcendent *atman*. In the Sermon on the Mount, the norm of loving one's neighbour is implied by reference to the law and the prospect of Judgement Day as anticipated, for example, in the Beatitudes. Berner concludes that religions are "Daseinshaltungen" (views of existence), which are grounded in universal interpretation and provide a normative framework for one's actions. He shows that his delineation of the field is broad enough to include e.g. texts like *The Myth of Sisyphus* by

---

116 For both quotations see ibid., 213, cf. also Pye 1972: Comparative Religion: An Introduction through Source Materials, 10ff.

117 Cf. Pye 1972: Comparative Religion: An Introduction through Source Materials, 9f, where he gives "belief in spiritual beings", "belief in a supreme being or god", "symbolic reference to supernatural values or beings", "experience of the holy", "sacred things in the sense that they are apart and forbidden" and "the expression of a dependence" as examples of characteristics which have been mistaken for being universal.

Albert Camus. Thus, not even the creation of meaning is taken as a necessary condition for religion, as *The Myth of Sisyphus* can be regarded as an interpretation of existence void of any meaning.[118]

What is important is a reflection about what kind of phenomena come into focus with a certain delineation of the field, and what is excluded. Quite clearly, "God", "the divine", "the numinous" or "the holy" cannot be part of the field which is studied by a scholar of religion. Kurt Rudolph formulates it somewhat radically when he says that "for the scholar of religions there is, strictly speaking, nothing 'holy' or 'sacred' that would occasion him or her to abandon the rational methods of the study of religions".[119] His point is, however, definitely correct: the field of the study of religions is a field which is accessible with empirical and rational methods. Therefore, *belief* in God, *belief* in the divine, *belief* in the numinous or holy are within the field, as they are part of the manifold evidence and multiple data for human belief and action, which can be accessed with the rational and empirical methods of the cultural and social sciences. Similarly, Waardenburg emphasises that the field for the study of religions is always "human religion", i.e. religion as it is expressed and described, thought and lived, believed and pursued by human beings.[120] Therefore, the study of religions does not deal with a metaphysical idea or substance of "religion", but with concrete religious aspects of a society or culture, such as religiously interpreted realities, religiously interpreted experiences and religiously interpreted norms. As further characteristics of religion Waardenburg mentions (1) reference to something which is not empirically accessible, e.g. reference to something holy beyond what is given empirically, (2) a tension between the world and "the other", an interpretation of the world in the light of "the other", (3) a dichotomy of the earthly "religious reality" vs. the reality of religion and (4) the creation of meaning and the reality of religion as the ultimate reason of human meaning, orientation and order.[121]

With respect to such assertions about the contents of religious claims, it is important not to universalise a certain concept which is important in one or more traditions and claim that it is a necessary

---

118 For Berner's approach to the delineation of the field see Berner 1983: Gegenstand und Aufgabe der Religionswissenschaft, 100-107. Contrary to this approach Waardenburg regards the creation of meaning as a feature of religion (1986: Religionen und Religion, 24).
119 Rudolph 2000: Some reflections on approaches and methodologies in the study of religions, 234, referring to an earlier formulation by himself.
120 See Waardenburg 1986: Religionen und Religion, 17.
121 Cf. ibid., 23f.

feature for any religion. Care has to be taken to avoid gross generalisations, which have often led to a premature, contextually motivated, exclusion of phenomena which do not have that specific content, which is, furthermore, determined by linguistic categories which may not be easily transferable to other cultural and religious contexts.

Perhaps it has become evident in this section that the delineation of the subject matter or adumbration of the field of the study of religions is not as easy as it may seem at first glance. A popular argument against renouncing criteria for the contents of beliefs as necessary aspects of a delineation of the field is that the notion of the field then becomes so vague that almost everything could then be included, for example, football, television etc. However, I think that this challenge has to be dealt with constructively. Turning a blind eye to the religious aspects of these phenomena is no solution and will only exclude the voice of scholars of religion from social discourse. On the contrary, a reassessment of the field is necessary if the study of religions does not want to be concerned with constructs which seem often rather like relics of the past than presently culturally relevant phenomena. The attempts to delineate the field which I described in this section point in the right direction and avoid a number of mistakes that were made earlier.

In order to find a viable solution for the delineation of the subject matter or adumbration of the field and a concept or definition of religion in the study of religions, a few points that have been mentioned above ought to be recalled: the need for a secular approach, the call for multiperspectivity – including, for example, insider perspectives as well as further explanations – and the warning not to universalise features of any one religion. Furthermore, it has become evident that operational and preliminary definitions of religion are preferable to closed and comprehensive ones, as the former acknowledge the empirical base of the subject in contrast to prescriptive or normative definitions of religion. In the study of religions, a definition of religion has to be open to adjustment and modification if required by the material, as it presupposes knowledge about the whole range of religions, which is, strictly speaking, hardly comprehensively achievable. Attention to the ambivalence of religion is necessary. Religions may be harmful as well as beneficial. It is important to attempt to fully acknowledge the facts and not to distort the perspective from the very beginning by overemphasising any individual feature of religion and thereby losing sight of the variety of the phenomena.

Careful reflection about what comes into focus and what is left out is required with respect to any delineation of the field. This is an important issue, for example, in the above-mentioned question, if reference to any kind of transcendence is regarded as a minimal criterion for religion. In my view, to put it somewhat radically, to claim that reference to transcendence is a necessary criterion for religion, is already a religious statement in itself which does, in fact, universalise one aspect of religions. I think, a dynamic polycentrism of a number of criteria which have been mentioned as important aspects of religion, such as *Welterklärung und Lebensbewältigung* (Flasche), orientation (Waardenburg) and *Kontingenzbewältigung* (Luhmann), worldview (Smart) or *Daseinshaltung* (Berner) may serve to demonstrate the range of phenomena relevant to the scholar of religions. It is more academically sound to include borderline cases and discuss why they have been chosen or what kind of arguments may be presented for excluding them, than to exclude them from the very beginning.[122]

1.3 Methodology

This chapter will address some basic issues concerning the methodology of the study of religions. Starting from the "dispute on methods" in the 1970s and the agreements achieved by the end of the 20th century, it will show interrelations between methods and theory, subject matter and sources. In the section on methodological variety, general features of the methodology used in the study of religions will be outlined before some important methods from the range of methodological plurality are introduced (1.3.1). After that, possible ways of methodological integration will be shown, while particular attention will be given to the role of the perspective of insiders of a religion and of the researcher (1.3.2), before conclusions for a study-of-religions representation of religions are drawn (1.3.3).

The "dispute on methods" was basically about the different approaches of the phenomenology of religion with its implicitly religious presuppositions, interpreting religion as a response to revelation, on the one hand, and the social and cultural sciences on the other, which are committed to preserving the scientific character of the subject and keeping a critical distance to religious points of view and which thereby neglect a particular concern of the phenomenology of religion. On an international level, the discussion culminated in a debate about the appropriateness of Mircea Eliade's methodological programme. The

---

[122] This is definitely also important for integrative RE in order to introduce the pupils to the relevant questions.

conflict between the phenomenological and the social and cultural sciences approaches cannot be fully resolved and to some extent it still continues to this very day, particularly in North America, where Eliade has had many followers. However, in order to preserve the secular and scientific character of the study of religions as opposed to various theologies, many scholars, and in particular those who are engaged in the international associations, have agreed on a set of methodological presuppositions which make it possible to do justice to the subject matter (an important concern of the phenomenology of religion) while at the same time maintaining scientific standards such as intersubjective verifiability.[123] An important outcome of the debate is that neither one's own religious experience nor an antireligious attitude are prerequisites for the study of religions, but that it is important not to let one's own religious or antireligious presuppositions distort one's representation of religions.[124]

The study of religions does not have any one single method which is unique to itself. Rather, it requires "a particular *clustering* of methods in order to do justice to its subject matter."[125] This clustering of methods arises partly out of the nature of the sources, which may be written, oral or material and therefore require different methods, for example, linguistic analysis or fieldwork. Therefore, it is evident that no individual method – such as the "historical" or "historical-philological" method – is sufficient by itself. The methods are to be selected according to their appropriateness to the material which is studied and to be used complementarily. For example, texts require philological research, possibly including translation and critical hermeneutics, while contemporary religious practice requires empirical methods such as interviews and observations.[126]

---

[123] For the dispute on methods see e.g. Berner 1983: Gegenstand und Aufgabe der Religionswissenschaft, and Geertz and McCutcheon 2000: The role of method and theory in the IAHR, 6ff.

[124] See e.g. Franke and Pye 2004: The Study of Religions and its contribution to problem-solving in a plural world, section 4.

[125] Pye 2000: Westernism unmasked, 214.

[126] Cf. Pye 1999: Methodological integration in the study of religions, 202, for a more detailed account of the interrelationships between method and subject matter, sources and theory formation see ibid., 197-203. See also Franke and Pye 2004: The Study of Religions and its contribution to problem-solving in a plural world, section 2.

1.3.1 Methodological variety

The preliminary cessation of the dispute on methods does not mean that the approaches in the study of religions are not methodologically diverse any more. On the contrary, the realignment of methods following a re-examination of the traditional historical-philological, comparative and textual approaches resulted in even greater diversity. However, there are some characteristics which can help to delineate a broad framework within which the variety of methods ought to be situated. As Michael Pye has emphasised, methods used in the study of religions should be rational, empirical, explanatory and testable ("nachvollziehbar").[127] Furthermore, an unbiased, value-free attitude should be attempted in the tradition of "methodological agnosticism".[128]

General developments in the study of religions also have an effect on the selection of methods. Traditional methodology has been supplemented with methods from the social and cultural sciences, for example, linguistics, discourse analysis, narratology, semiotics etc. Furthermore, several criticisms, for example, of orientalism and the construction of the exotic, the misrepresentation of other cultures, the politics of science and power, as well as feminist criticism, have also led to a modification of methods.[129] Basically, the integration of qualitative and quantitative empirical research in the context of the move towards the study of contemporary religion has led to a new set of questions and problems which have to be dealt with.[130] This is not to say that older methods are less valid, as long as they are compatible with the above-mentioned framework, which means, for example, that they may not be grounded in claims that cannot be verified empirically.

Widely used methods in the study of religions are understanding (hermeneutics), description, (non-comprehensive) explanation, comparison, contextualisation and classification. Each of these methods is the subject of controversial discussion and different scholars interpret them differently. A few points from the debates may help to understand the issues at stake. Berner emphasises that understanding religions as possible views of existence (*Daseinshaltungen*) is something dif-

---

127 See Pye 2000: Westernism unmasked.
128 See Franke and Pye 2004: The Study of Religions and its contribution to problem-solving in a plural world, section 4.5 and 5.3.
129 Cf. Jensen 2002: From the History of Religions to the Study of Religions.
130 For qualitative and quantitative empirical research methods in the study of religions see e.g. Baumann 1998: Qualitative Methoden in der Religionswissenschaft, Greschat 1994: Mündliche Religionsforschung, Hase 2000: Quantitative Methoden in der Religionswissenschaft, Knoblauch 2003: Qualitative Religionsforschung.

ferent from intuitive empathy, which presupposes truth. The respective *Daseinshaltungen* should be understood as possibilities of existence, including one's own. There are no special subjective prerequisites for understanding, the research process should be "nachvollziehbar" and open to criticism at all stages. Poetic interpretations of the field should be included.[131]

Description of the variety of religious phenomena has been regarded as one of the most important tasks of the study of religions. The *epoché* with which these phenomena were to be approached has, however, been criticised recently. Russell T. McCutcheon, for example, demands that scholars of religion should not linger in mere description, repetition and appreciation of the insider's point of view, but instead proceed to critical analysis and explanation. He sees the task of the study of religions in comparing and contextualising competing representations, a juxtaposition of different models of the world, as well as a contextualisation and redescription of normative, dehistoricised discourses as human constructs.[132] Other scholars emphasise the importance of *epoché* or "bracketing" at the recognitional[133] stages of the research process – i.e. elucidation and characterisation – while the other methods are preserved for further steps.[134] As indicated earlier, at the explanatory level a distinction between preliminary or partial and comprehensive or conclusive explanations is required. While the latter are incompatible with the principle of *epoché*, the former do not endanger the operational framework.[135]

Comparisons may be made both in the recognitional and the explanatory phases in the study of religions. When phenomena are compared, it is wrong to presuppose essential unity or difference from the very beginning. In the study of religions it is, in fact, only possible to compare some religions in some aspects. A consideration of developments and dynamics has often been neglected in comparative analyses. Therefore, a comparative and contrastive study of religious dynamics is a particular desideratum for research.[136] Contextualisation is also one of the important tasks in the study of religions. It is particularly relevant

---

131 Cf. Berner 1983: Gegenstand und Aufgabe der Religionswissenschaft, 110.
132 See McCutcheon 2000: Critics not caretakers, e.g. 175ff.
133 "The term 'recognitional' means that the researcher gives full recognition to the complex of experience covered by all four main aspects of religion for those who are involved in it" (Pye 1999: Methodological integration in the study of religions,199), cf. also ibid., 198f.
134 See Pye 1999: Methodological integration in the study of religions, 198.
135 Cf. Pye 1972: Comparative Religion: An Introduction through Source Materials, 17ff.
136 Cf. ibid., 24f.

in order to overcome common prejudice or generalisations about religions – such as claims like "Buddhism is peaceful" – and to deconstruct decontextualised "wholes". Contextualisation means considering one or more of the aspects of a given case of religion in the setting of its historical, socio-cultural or even biological context.[137] As McCutcheon puts it,

> "our scholarship is not constrained by whether or not devotees recognize its value for it is not intended to appreciate, celebrate or enhance normative, dehistoricized discourses but, rather, to contextualize and redescribe them as human constructs."[138]

In comparisons contextualisation is necessary as it helps to avoid superficiality. An important criticism of classical phenomenological approaches is its lack of attention to the intentions behind the visible phenomena.[139] A careful appreciation of the individual contexts – be they intentional, historical, social etc. – of the phenomena which one intends to compare is an important step towards preventing premature conclusions about similarity.

Classification refers to the process of grouping phenomena due to structural similarities. The creation of adequate categories which are applicable to the range of phenomena without forcing the conceptual framework of one tradition upon others is a difficult task in this process.[140] Types may not be misunderstood as ideal types of which the individual religions are expressions or materialisations. On the contrary, the types refer to family resemblances which can be found among the different phenomena. Their function is to make the range of phenomena more accessible, draw attention to similarities and to provide some structure from an academic point of view.[141] Taking up insights from "grounded theory",[142] initial questions ought to be modified in the research process if this is implicated by the material. Often a direct confrontation with the material raises new questions which were not considered central from the beginning. Stolz calls this to-ing and fro-ing an attempt to reach a synthesis between the theoretical horizon of the questions and the horizon of the material. This synthesis can, how-

---

137 Pye 1999: Methodological integration in the study of religions, 203.
138 McCutcheon 2000: Critics not caretakers, 178.
139 See e.g. Waardenburg 1986: Religionen und Religion, 241ff.
140 Cf. Pye's distinction between memes and models (Pye 2002: Memes and models in the Study of Religions), to which I referred earlier.
141 For issues about classification see also Flasche 2000: Von der Selbstbeschränkung und Selbstbegründung der Religionenwissenschaft, e.g. 168.
142 See e.g. Glaser and Strauss 1979: The Discovery of Grounded Theory: Strategies for Qualitative Research.

ever, only be understood in terms of approximation, as some aspects of the field are not accessible to the researcher. For different questions, different models should be tried. When taken to the field, these questions and models may be revised, reformulated and completed. Thus, a pattern of questions, hypotheses and models emerges which enables a description and analysis of religious phenomena.[143]

1.3.2 Methodological integration

Considering the variety of methods used in the study of religions, the question emerges of what is or what ought to be common to all these approaches. In their account of the role of method and theory in the IAHR, Armin W. Geertz and Russell T. McCutcheon conclude that integrating the various theoretical and methodological approaches is the future task for the discipline of the study of religions:

> "[U]niting the diversity and creativity of contemporary theoretical perspectives ... into a coherent institutional framework conducive for theorizing about, defining, and studying religion as a sub-category of human culture will be the challenge of the future. The question that the twenty-first century study of religion must pose is: What do all these diverse methodologies and theoretical perspectives have in common? In the postmodern age, will they share anything at all? In the postmodern university, will it have a place? Once we have completely shaken off earlier theological and dialogical models, what will unite us?"[144]

In the following, I would like to take up two issues in methodology – attention to the insiders' perspective and the background of the researcher – in order to highlight in an exemplary fashion what may be regarded as common ground despite methodological variety. Thereafter, I am going to conclude with a few basic points about methodological integration.

Attention to the insider's perspective

In rejection of earlier – often theological – accounts of "other" religions, in which the researcher's own point of view frequently led to distortions in the representation of the insiders' point of view of adherents to a religion, W. Brede Kristensen and Wilfred Cantwell Smith developed their somewhat radical partiality for the perspective of insiders. Two

---

143 Cf. Stolz 1997: Grundzüge der Religionswissenschaft, 42.
144 Geertz and McCutcheon 2000: The role of method and theory in the IAHR, 35.

characteristic quotations from their work have been very influential in the history of the study of religions, numerously cited – often disapprovingly – in various works of scholars of religions to this very day:

> "For the historian only one evaluation is possible: 'the believers were completely right.'"[145] (W. Brede Kristensen)

> "[N]o statement about a religion is valid unless it can be acknowledged by that religion's believers."[146] (W. Cantwell Smith)

Even though these quotations are, of course, only highlights from a more sophisticated argument by Kristensen and Smith and therefore merely present a simplified keyword-account of their positions,[147] they nevertheless represent one important strand in the range of positions about the role of the believer's view. Recently, scholars of religion have developed a more subtly differentiated perspective on this issue. Without any doubt, attention to the believers is an indispensable first element in the process of studying a religion. The believers' perspectives present necessary data for an account of a religion. The attempt must be made to take the subject matter as seriously as possible. As Michael Pye points out,

> "[T]he poly-aspectual subject-matter should be studied, in the first instance, in terms of its integral meaning for the believers or participants in question. That is to say, it should be studied without reference to the value orientation or possible explanatory hypotheses of the researcher."[148]

This first phase in the process of studying a religion can be called the recognitional phase, i.e. the phase in which the complex of experience covered by the different aspects of religion for those who are involved in it are fully recognised. During the recognitional stages of elucidation and characterisation, the internal coherence of any one of the systems which are studied should be respected.[149] However, in later phases of the process of studying a religion, tension with believers or participants may arise. For example, a structure may appear which is not or only

---

145 Kristensen 1960: The Meaning of Religion: Lectures in the Phenomenology of Religion, 14. Cf. also p. 13: "If the historian tries to understand the religious data from a different viewpoint than that of the believers, he negates the religious reality. For there is no religious reality other than the faith of the believers."
146 Smith 1959: Comparative religion: wither and why?, 42.
147 Smith, for example, admits himself that there are difficulties with this position.
148 Pye 1999: Methodological integration in the study of religions,197.
149 See ibid., 198, also Pye 2000: Westernism unmasked, 216. In this context, Pye takes up the problem of the impossibility of a completely objective account. He emphasises that "there remains a difference between achieving a good elucidation and characterisation of the religion of a specified group of people, or getting it all wrong because one's own beliefs and values continually get in the way." (1999: Methodological integration in the study of religions, 199).

partially apparent to the believers or participants. Hence, the believer is not always completely right.[150] Furthermore, the theoretical perspective resulting from comparative knowledge may not be visible to the believers or they may not agree with e.g. sociological or historical explanations. Therefore, the tension-with-believers (TWB) factor rises when one proceeds from the recognitional to the explanatory phase.[151]

It can be regarded as a consensus that "a religion's self-interpretation provides only a necessary aid to understanding, [but] never a normative approach".[152] Religious people's own self-awareness is not a criterion for truth or falsehood in the study of religions, despite its value as a source of data. Frequently, representations by scholars of religions and by members of a religion do not correspond. Therefore, a study-of-religions account of a religion is normally not acceptable as a personal account to an adherent to this religion. Nevertheless, the fact that agreement of believers to a study-of-religions analysis may rather be the exception than the rule[153] does not mean that it is not desirable that believers find themselves correctly represented in a study-of-religions account of their own position. In this context, Pye's distinction between the recognitional and the explanatory phases and his considerations about the different degrees of the TWB-factor are helpful in order to draw attention to the different levels and characteristics of the research process and thus to overcome the simplistic alternative if the believer is or is not always right.

Attention to the researcher's background

The perspective of the study of religions has often been described as an "objective" or "impartial" point of view on the different religions. On closer consideration, however, the concepts of objectivity or impartial-

---

150 Pye 1999: Methodological integration in the study of religions, 199. For this paragraph, cf. ibid 199f.
151 See ibid. and Pye 2002: Memes and models in the Study of Religions, 250.
152 Rudolph 2000: Some reflections on approaches and methodologies in the study of religions, 240. For the following cf. Stolz 1997: Grundzüge der Religionswissenschaft, 42f.
153 This is illustrated convincingly by Donate Pahnke when she asks if an Ayatollah or a Bishop would agree with a study-of-religions analysis of Christian or Muslim patriarchalism, cf. Pahnke 1993: Feministische Aspekte einer religionswissenschaftlichen Anthropologie, 26. For this issue see also Gladigow: 1988: Religionsgeschichte des Gegenstandes - Gegenstände der Religionsgeschichte, 21; Stolz 1997: Grundzüge der Religionswissenschaft, 42f and Flasche 2000: Von der Selbstbeschränkung und Selbstbegründung der Religionenwissenschaft, 167.

ity become problematic, as no individual can claim to have an objective point of view. The question emerges to what extent impartiality and objectivity are possible and desirable. As complete objectivity is an illusion, careful consideration of one's own situatedness and its various implications is preferable to naive claims to objectivity. The important insight in the recent study of religions is that it is more academically sound and therefore preferable to make aware and explicit the historical, social, intellectual and also personal contexts in which a study is carried out than to simply adhere to the claim of objectivity.[154]

Pye addresses an important point when he claims that neo-confessionalism, cold-war-ism, oil wealth, intercultural exotism and Westernism serve as widely unrecognised contextualisers in the present study of religions, whereas the influences of e.g. the Enlightenment, Romanticism, colonialism, the missionary movement, evolutionism, historicism and orientalism on the study of religions in its different phases and their functions in shaping the intellectual framework are more comprehensively acknowledged.[155] Morny Joy's claim that, "by and large, the status of the investigator and his/her preconceptions have, until recently, not been subjected to serious scrutiny",[156] is however also convincing, particularly when the kind of reflection that is going on in other disciplines – for example, anthropology – is considered. In the light of postcolonial and feminist criticism, Joy observes that "we are always already implicated in the definitions/traditions we inherit and by whatever attempts we instigate to extricate ourselves. It is this more nuanced appreciation of deconstruction that is coming to prevail."[157] Taking up ideas by Indian women scholars on the representation of cultures, Joy draws attention to the fact that everybody

> "needs to take vigilant account of their own varying allegiances and boundaries, recognizing a contingent rather than absolute subjectivity where their ideas are constantly being revised and recast, reflecting the mobile conditions of their own society and culture."[158]

She concludes that if this state of fluctuation is admitted the static patterns of the old subject-object dichotomy are no longer adequate as the basis of analysis. Full recognition of one's own situatedness is necessary:

> "It is time that we admitted that all too often the presumed God's-eye-view, that governed and still governs much of our deliberations, was one

---

154 Cf. for example Stolz 1997: Grundzüge der Religionswissenschaft, 39.
155 See Pye 2000: Westernism unmasked, 220f.
156 Joy 2001: Postcolonial reflections: challenges for Religious Studies, 179.
157 Ibid., 188.
158 Ibid., 189.

that is myopic, or simply a self-authenticating narcissistic gaze. It is time to accord 'the other' – be it a person or a religion – the integrity that is their due in an age when it is becoming increasingly difficult to do so."[159]

Joy's account of the background of the researcher takes a global perspective, which considers economic and political factors as part of the multiple, contingent and frequently contradictory affiliations of every thinker.[160] Like other disciplines, the study of religions is "caught up in a complex capitalistic system of competing discourses where both academic and developmental enterprises continue to mouth platitudes regarding the redeployment of resources and vistas of streamlined productivity".[161] Joy points out that scholars of religions are not operating in a neutral, let alone a benign, universe. The study of religions has never been immune to the political and economic agendas which provide the backdrop and sustenance of research work. Therefore, she takes the view that

"it is only honest to admit that we are always already compromised. That the best we can do is to recognize the constant realignment of powers and principalities that continue to influence both our self-perceptions and to circumscribe the parameters of our actions. This is not postmodernism in its relativist posturing, but an acknowledgement of the specific and contemporaneous confluence/dissonance of forces that ceaselessly impinge on all our activities."[162]

The failure to address or admit to one's own presuppositions and the factors that influence one's research, which Morny Joy criticises convincingly, is also one of the main points of feminist criticisms of methodology in the study of religions. With respect to the lack of reflection of the anthropological situation of the typical scholar of religions – being white, mature, educated, successful, healthy, heterosexual, male[163] – or the general failure to acknowledge male gender embeddedness, which easily results in the construction of maleness or androcentrism as norms, feminist critics agree that scholars of religion have to acknowledge their own identities, prerequisites, contexts and interests instead of clinging to this alleged objectivity which has already been successfully unmasked as an illusion.[164]

---

159 Ibid., 192.
160 Here she refers to a formulation by Rajeswari Sunder Rajan (1993: Real and Imagined Women: Gender, Culture and Postcolonialization, 8).
161 Joy 2001: Postcolonial reflections: challenges for Religious Studies, 190/191.
162 Ibid., 191.
163 Cf. Pahnke 1993: Feministische Aspekte einer religionswissenschaftlichen Anthropologie, 23.
164 See, for example, Warne 2000: Making the gender-critical turn, Franke 1997: Feministische Kritik and Wissenschaft und Religionen, King 1995: Religion and Gender.

Returning to our initial question about methodological integration, I agree with Michael Pye that this can be achieved with relative simplicity, despite the variety of methods and despite the far-reaching consequences of the recent developments I have mentioned. Issues like reflexivity, feminist criticism etc. are not problems of the study of religions alone, an interdisciplinary cross-fertilisation of ideas is without any doubt necessary here. Even though Morny Joy is right to emphasise that a lot of work still needs to be done in this respect and that taking the criticisms seriously will possibly change the subject considerably, a particular coordination and clustering of the various methods used in the social and cultural sciences in correspondence with the sources which are available for scrutiny and within the general epistemological framework of the study of religions (see above, e.g. methodological agnosticism, refraining from comprehensive explanations or theological interpretations, a non-prescriptive approach which studies from a particular point of view what religions are like and not what they ought to be like) can be regarded as a common agenda in the study of religions.[165] Nevertheless, defining and contesting this common agenda, most importantly, perhaps, in delimitation to universal theologies, remains a very important task for the study of religions, in particular on an international or global level.[166]

1.3.3 The representation of religions

In this section the interdependencies of the different aspects of theory and methodology in the study of religions will become apparent once again. Many features which are relevant to a study-of-religions representation of religions depend on decisions to be made at earlier stages of the research process. Without any doubt, the representation of religions is again a wide field whose complexity can hardly be grasped in a few paragraphs. However, it is – as in the earlier sections in this chapter – my intention here to make complex issues comprehensible in order to facilitate the process of transferring basic insights of the academic study of religions to other fields, in particular to theory and methodology development for integrative RE. I am fully aware that this involves omissions and simplifications which would be inexcusable in other contexts.

---

165 Cf. Pye 1999: Methodological integration in the study of religions, 203f.
166 At the 19th world congress of the IAHR in Tokyo, for example, it became obvious that the distinction between the study of religions and universal theologies is by no means universally accepted.

Representation is a delicate field which is inextricably intertwined with various levels of political and social hegemonic discourses, as it is part of the continuous process of constructing "the other" and thereby also constructing oneself in relation to this other. What has been discussed with respect to the representation of cultures in recent anthropology[167] is to a great extent also relevant to the representation of religions. In any representation of religions, the power relations between the scholar and the represented should be reflected, as well as the artificiality of constructed "wholes" in contrast to the diversity and dynamics of cultural and religious life, which are so hard to grasp and describe in academic accounts. Tensions between academic representations and self-representations have to be made explicit. They are not a problem, but reflect the variedness of the aims and approaches of the different agents involved.

In the following, I shall illustrate some basic points which need considering in a study-of-religions representation of religions. One important concern is that a representation reflects the breadth of the field, i.e. that a religion or religious phenomenon is appreciated in its full diversity. This is, unfortunately, to this date often overlooked in accounts of religion. Frequently, a small selection from the range of phenomena is claimed to be representative of the whole tradition, whereby many groups and individuals are overlooked, be it by unconscious or intentional exclusion. Important factors concerning an acknowledgement of the breadth of the field are gender, age, ethnicity, class (social status), education, urban/rural, majority/minority, past/present etc. The constructions of centres and peripheries have to be challenged. All too often they are mere reflections of power structures whose blind reproduction ought to be avoided in academically sound scholarship. In a balanced account of a religion, the whole range of phenomena, in particular with respect to the above mentioned factors, has to be considered. This does not at all mean that it is impossible or undesirable to describe just a small selection of a complex field. On the contrary, it has to be acknowledged that any account is necessarily a selection and that it is very important to clearly state for which group a particular account is valid. This means, for example, that a description

---

[167] See, for example, Geertz 1973: The Interpretation of Cultures, 1983: Local Knowledge: Further Essays in Interpretive Anthropology, 1988: Works and Lives: The Anthropologist as Author; Said 1978: Orientalism, 1989: Representing the colonized: anthropology's interlocutors, 1993: Culture and Imperialism; Clifford 1988: The Predicament of Culture: Twentieth-Century Ethnography, Literature and Art; Clifford and Marcus 1985: The making of ethnographic texts. A preliminary report, 1986: Writing Culture: The Poetics and Politics of Ethnography; Crapanzano 1986: Hermes' dilemma: the masking of subversion in ethnographic descriptions.

of a ritual for a Brahmanic Hindu boy in India as was performed many years ago is by no means representative of "Hindu rituals". It is but one aspect of it, neither more nor less interesting than other rituals such as the one performed for a lower caste Hindu girl in Britain today.

In addition to a consideration of the above-mentioned factors, which are relevant to the representation of cultures and religions alike, the particular structure of the "field" or "subject matter" of the study of religions requires a balance of the different aspects of religions. Therefore, the breadth of the field refers also to concepts, experiences, practices and social structures for the various groups and individuals, be they institutionalised in a traditional sense or not. If all these aspects are considered, a classification of the individual phenomena becomes more transparent. Using this model, the place of, for example, the worldview of old educated Buddhist convert women in Swedish cities today can be located within a framework which considers them among related phenomena and thereby a premature classification based on any single aspect can be avoided. Without any doubt the model is complex, but so are the phenomena themselves. An acknowledgement of this complexity is in any case preferable to gross distortions due to simplification.

Other distortions may occur if the data are arranged according to some preconceived idea about an "essence" or "meaning" of the phenomena, which is in fact a theological presupposition and therefore counterproductive to the task of the study of religions. An example of this is if one starts from the idea of an essence of a phenomenon, which one then "finds" in all the different traditions. In contrast, a study-of-religions account ought to employ operational neutrality and consider the different dimensions of religions in relation to their social, psychological and political contexts. In comparative analyses or representations, a contextualisation of the phenomena is essential and careful attention should be paid to the different surroundings and environments in order to achieve a reliable account of similarities as well as differences, rather than premature conclusions about alleged similarity. In this context, Rainer Flasche emphasises that, in comparisons, the focus ought to be on relations and relationships rather than on contents, forms or even terms. The researcher has to take care not to be misled by superficial similarities, which may lead to an equation of structurally and relationally different phenomena. Comparisons should concentrate on the material rather than the formal dimension.[168]

---

168 See Flasche 2000: Von der Selbstbeschränkung und Selbstbegründung der Religionenwissenschaft, 170.

One important task in the representation of religions is to use an adequate meta-language which is in fact applicable to the variety of traditions. The universalisation of terms or concepts from one individual tradition has led to many misunderstandings. Instead, it is the task of the study of religions to develop a general terminology which can be used for the various phenomena without imposing the frame of reference of one tradition onto another, even though the underlying concepts may be very different. As the study of religions has not invented a completely new language or terminology, every term which is taken from a certain religious or academic context has to be tested in terms of its applicability to its intended use. For example, if the term "soul" is used to refer to the Christian concept of a "soul" as well as to concepts in Shamanism or the religion of Ancient Egypt, the different connotations and concepts behind the term have to be considered.[169] Terms may be drawn from various cultural contexts, but have to remain independent of particular religious or ideological assumptions or claims.[170] Michael Pye's distinction between memes and models is helpful in establishing an adequate terminology for the representation of religions. While the presence and influence of memes in common discourse needs to be recognised and taken into account, the academic study of religions has to produce scientific models which are to some extent independent from the different memetic assumptions in various cultural contexts.[171]

---

[169] Cf. Stolz 1997: Grundzüge der Religionswissenschaft, 41.
[170] Cf. Franke and Pye (2004: The Study of Religions and its contribution to problem-solving in a plural world, section 3), who emphasise with respect to mistakes that have been made in the past that those terms should, in particular, not be euro- or christocentric.
[171] See above (section 1.2 on the concept of religion), cf. Pye 2002: Memes and models in the Study of Religions.

2 Education

The intention of this chapter is to provide the educational background for an analysis and development of concepts for integrative RE. For this purpose, main aspects of critical educational theory will be outlined (2.1), before a selection of relevant didactic models is presented (2.2). The third section (2.3) deals with approaches to intercultural education, which are particularly relevant for integrative RE for several reasons. The chapter is based on the German discussion on critical educational theory – referring back to the critical social theory of the *Frankfurt School* – but takes an international perspective.

2.1 Critical educational theory

In the first section, different aspects of education are introduced with the help of the German concepts *Erziehung* and *Bildung* (2.1.1). Then, some main points of the critical theory of the *Frankfurt School* will be outlined (2.1.2) as a background for the presentation of attempts to develop a critical theory of education (2.1.3). The first section concludes with an outline of Wolfgang Klafki's critical and constructive theory of education, which successfully introduced the critical dimension to general educational theory (2.1.4).

2.1.1 Two aspects of education: "Erziehung" and "Bildung"

It is not easy to define what exactly education is.[172] The German distinction between "Erziehung" and "Bildung" points to two important aspects which are incorporated in the concept "education". However, the German terms mentioned are often not clearly defined either, but their meaning remains contested to this date. Furthermore, in academic as well as in common discourse, they are often used interchangeably, as if they were synonyms. There are, however, important differences in their respective connotations. In the following, I shall attempt to shed light

---

172 Bernhard (1997: Bildung, 62f.) gives an impression of the range of interpretations when he starts his article about *Bildung* with the following list of different understandings: an accumulation of knowledge; mastering social conventions perfectly; passing through educational institutions or leaving those institutions with a "high" qualification; an application of knowledge like a technique or a power which enables the individual to oppose social requirements.

on different facets of the terms *Erziehung* and *Bildung* in order to approach the more general concept of education from these angles.[173]

Erziehung and *Bildung* refer to different dimensions of human individualisation. They are both processes which serve to reproduce society. Whereas *Erziehung* means the adaptation of the young generation to particular social contexts, *Bildung* is more than that: it is related to the formation of consciousness. *Erziehung* aims at teaching social standards in order to provide patterns of behaviour and strategies of survival. It is often rather about conditioning by means of examples or models than about rational communication, but also involves experiences in one's social surroundings. *Bildung*, on the other hand, has to do with developing consciousness of the world and of one's own situation in the world. It transcends the immediate surroundings of daily life. In contrast to *Erziehung*, which aims at the formation of basic components of one's personality, *Bildung* aims at a mental reconstruction of the world. It provides an opportunity to develop from a pre-rational to a reflective phase of dealing with reality. *Erziehung* can be understood as the manipulative equipment of a person to fit a given social environment, but *Bildung* may result in the independence of a person from social norms and conventions. It incorporates a rational approach to the world and at the same time a conscious reconstruction and development of one's own personality, an active mental relationship to the social environment and one's own place within it, as opposed to an unconscious adaptation to social constraints. *Erziehung* is concerned with personality, while *Bildung* includes the acquisition of cultural knowledge as a basis for a further development of one's own personality. The philosopher of education H.-J. Heydorn calls *Erziehung* a "windowless aisle"[174] which is indispensable for human development, but can only provide a basis for personality-building. By itself, it cannot produce emancipatory tendencies. *Bildung*, however, enables the liberation of a person with the help of consciousness.[175] The given framework of daily routine is confronted with the culture and knowledge of humanity and thus with a wide range of alternative options.

Despite the differences which I have tried to illustrate above, the distinction between *Erziehung* and *Bildung* remains somewhat artificial, particularly if critical concepts of *Erziehung*, which emphasise its emancipatory along with its adaptational character, are considered. Critical concepts of education respect the autonomy of the individual and do

---

173 For the following paragraph on the differences between *Erziehung* and *Bildung* cf. Bernhard 1997: Bildung, 65f.
174 Heydorn 1995: Über den Widerspruch von Bildung und Herrschaft, 4.
175 Cf. Heydorn 1995: Bildungstheoretische und pädagogische Schriften 1967-1970, 201.

not regard conventions or moral values as a set of timeless norms, but as reflexive categories which are permanently contested, particularly in educational contexts.[176] Therefore, the two aspects, which are separated in the German terms, are meaningfully integrated in the English concept "education".

In the following, I shall outline the contours of a critical theory of education, which was developed in the context of the philosophical and sociological framework of the "critical theory"[177] of the *Frankfurt School*. Critical educational theory was developed in direct delimitation to other paradigms of educational theory which were influential in 20th century Germany, particularly the educational theory of the humanities (*geisteswissenschaftliche Pädagogik*)[178] and empirical educational theory (*empirische Erziehungswissenschaft*).[179] As distinct from these approaches,

---

[176] For a discussion of a critical concept of *Erziehung*, see, for example, Kunert 1997: Erziehung. Kunert defines *Erziehung* as "symbolic interaction" (58) with the ambiguous function of making the individual fit for social interaction – the adaptational, functional, manipulative aspect on the one hand – while at the same time empowering the individual to make critical use of his or her reason – striving to enlighten people and enable emancipation on the other. These functions, which conflict to some extent, constitute the contradictory reality of *Erziehung* (cf. 61).

[177] "Critical theory", as opposed to "traditional theory", not only tries to map society, but distinguishes between reality in bourgeois society and the idea of a future society as a community of free human beings. Therefore, unlike traditional theory, critical theory criticises the reproduction of social injustice and thus a social order that is content with its current state, despite the pervasive mechanisms of oppression, exploitation and domination, be they obvious or subtle. Critical theory may be regarded as an ideological basis for social reform. It combines the interest in overcoming dominion and violence with an interest in the emancipation and development of human beings. See Horkheimer 1970 [1937]: Traditionelle und kritische Theorie. For a summary of Horkheimer's ideas about traditional and critical theory see Wulf 2003: Educational Science, 97ff.

[178] The educational theory of the humanities was the important paradigm in German pedagogy up to the late 1960s. The origins of this tradition, which is by no means a homogenous phenomenon, go back to the late 19th century and works of philosophers like F.D.E. Schleiermacher and W. Dilthey. Important theorists in the 20th century, who built on these philosophies are e.g. H. Nohl, E. Spranger, T. Litt and E. Weniger. Many of its points, for example, the historicity of education and educational theory, the significance of hermeneutics and the pedagogic relationship, have influenced educational theory considerably up to the present day. Cf. Wulf 1995: Paradigms of educational theory, 36.

[179] A prominent example of empirical educational theory is Wolfgang Brezinka's model (1972: Von der Pädagogik zur Erziehungswissenschaft), which is oriented towards Karl Popper's critical rationalism. Important points are e.g. the distinction between metascientific normative decisions which pertain to basic values and the demand for ideological neutrality in the object sphere of the scientific system of statements, as well as the need for intersubjective falsification as a methodological requirement. Brezinka shows the limited range of empirical educational theory and supplements

critical educational theorists provide a critique of bourgeois society and its scientific industry and emphasise the social and historical character of education in the general context of the proximity of educational theory to a critical theory of society, science and the individual.

2.1.2 Critical theory

The works of Horkheimer, Adorno, Marcuse and Habermas provide the philosophical groundwork for critical educational theory, but can already be regarded as critical educational theory, even though others who built on their ideas may have emphasised the relevance of those ideas for direct educational contexts more clearly or have "translated" the complex ideas of the Frankfurt School into a language that is actually also comprehensible to people who are not initiated into the sophisticated register of these philosophical circles.

In their seminal work *Dialektik der Aufklärung* (1947, Dialectic of Enlightenment) Horkheimer and Adorno seek to undermine the Enlightenment belief in progress. Despite the unquestioned power of reason to enlighten and liberate, they argue, there are dark side effects of the Enlightenment, which threaten to turn it into its opposite: reason has been "eclipsed" by technical interests, and, when allied with capitalism, it became identified with domination and mastery rather than with freedom and justice. Nevertheless, Horkheimer and Adorno remained committed to many of the central concerns of Enlightenment thought – such as reason, freedom and truth – and attempted to transform and rehabilitate these concepts in order to contribute to a more just and democratic society.[180] In his article *Theorie der Halbbildung* (1959, Theory of Semi-Education) Adorno is directly concerned with the role of education in the social context which he and Horkheimer had previously analysed. Semi-education[181] is a product of a societal decline, which is caused by the conditions which determine socialisation and life in general in industrial capitalist societies. The idea of education serving the upbringing of politically mature and responsible

---

it with a philosophy of educational theory and practical educational thought. Cf. Wulf 1995: Paradigms of educational theory, 37f.
180 Cf. Kohli 1996: Critical Theory, 116; Wulf 1995: Paradigms of educational theory, 40.
181 The concept Halbbildung (semi-education) was not invented by Adorno, but was already used in pedagogical reform movements of the late 19th and early 20th centuries, cf. Bernhard 1997: Bildung, 70f.

individuals[182] is corrupted by the social context in advanced industrial societies, where education is dominated by economic interests and daily life is permeated by the constant stream of products of the cultural industry.[183] In this context, education (*Bildung*) is articulated as being superficially and briefly informed without any critical consciousness. This declined form of education is based on an arbitrary acquisition of arbitrary elements of education. Semi-educated consciousness is therefore inconsistent, discontinuous, unstable and generally susceptible to manipulation. Various elements of education may still enter consciousness, but they are not integrated into its continuity. Therefore, they cannot become reflective elements of human experience and thus they can hardly contribute to further building up one's identity. The lack of integration of individual pieces of information into a continuous reflective consciousness is the distinctive feature of semi-education.[184]

Herbert Marcuse also focused on the pervasiveness of the technical apparatus of production in advanced industrial societies. The relations of domination, which incorporate social life as a whole, make any kind of criticism impossible, as criticism appears irrational in a framework in which the irrationality of a society based on domination and technological control is taken for granted as a model of rationality. Technological control, which appears as the incarnation of neutrality and reason itself, engenders a one-dimensional life, which in turn produces a one-dimensional mind, immunised not only against transcendence, but also against criticism. Thus, the one-dimensionality of human beings in modern industrial societies is caused by the relations of domination, in which any revolutionary potential is paralysed. Furthermore, Marcuse argues, in heavily administrated societies, it is difficult to attain the kind of freedom which is necessary in order to make truly rational choices about one's real needs as opposed to needs that were manufactured to uphold the philosophy and economic processes of consumption. He also draws attention to the part language plays in this context, particularly to its manipulative functions in the mass media. Marcuse regarded intellectual and emotional refusal to participate in and cooperate with the system of technological control, even if many people consider this a sign of neurosis and powerlessness, as the only way of

---

[182] Adorno uses the concept *mündig*, a German word which incorporates maturity, responsibility and participation, cf. also Adorno 1970: Erziehung zur Mündigkeit.
[183] See also Horkheimer and Adorno 1998 [1947]: Kulturindustrie, Aufkärung als Massenbetrug in: Dialektik der Aufklärung, 128-176.
[184] See Adorno 1972: Theorie der Halbbildung, esp. 112ff.

opposing this system of irrationality which appears disguised as rationality.[185]

Jürgen Habermas shares Marcuse's concern about the vulnerability of language to ideological distortion, but holds out hope for the realisation of ideal non-hierarchical speech situations in which all participants act autonomously. These self-reflective dialogues could help people to distinguish between "distorted" and "nondistorted" forms of communication. In his discourse ethics, Habermas argues for the "necessary linkage between rational consensus through dialogue and democratic participation in society."[186] Habermas, more decidedly than his predecessors in the *Frankfurt School*, attempts to relate critical theory to practice and emphasises the practical relevance of theory in that it anticipates and guides action. His ideas about the interrelations between practical, instrumental and critical reason are directly transferable to educational contexts. What is more, his identification of human interests – in *technology* in order to make objects accessible, in *practice* in order to approach central questions of life and in *emancipation* in order to eliminate domination – and his theory of knowledge imply a concept of education which he suggests may be applied in practice, since it not only provides critical theorems and explanations but also ideas about appropriate strategies, the resolution of tactical questions, and agendas for political struggle.[187]

2.1.3 Towards a critical theory of education

As mentioned above, the critical theory of the Frankfurt School was, to some extent, itself already a critical theory of education, even though the Frankfurt School dealt with education as but one part of a critical theory of society in general. Moreover, the ideas put forward by the authors mentioned above influenced educational theory in many ways. The relevance of critical theory for general educational theory has been widely acknowledged, as critical theory carefully analyses the contexts in which the educational enterprise takes place and provides a philosophical framework that enables a formulation of aims and purposes of

---

185 Marcuse 1979 [1937]: Philosophie und kritische Theorie; 1967: Der eindimensionale Mensch; English summaries of Marcuse's arguments are given in Wulf 2003: Educational Science, 102ff and Kohli 1996: Critical Theory, 117.
186 Kohli 1996: Critical Theory, 118.
187 See Habermas 1974: Theorie und Praxis, for an English summary of main points of his work that are relevant to education see Kohli 1996: Critical Theory, 117f and Wulf 2003: Educational Science, 105ff.

education. Among the educationalists who introduced concepts of critical theory into educational theory are Herwig Blankertz, Klaus Mollenhauer, Gernot Koneffke, Hans-Jochen Gamm, Heinz-Joachim Heydorn and Wolfgang Klafki, just to give some prominent examples.

Blankertz and Mollenhauer both tried to develop a critical theory of education distinct from former traditional humanist or strictly empirical approaches. They regarded education as a social phenomenon and emphasised the importance of autonomy and emancipation, for which a criticism of ideologies is a prerequisite. Heydorn, Koneffke and Gamm consider the relationship between education and development. Koneffke emphasises the subversive possibilities of development which make possible a resistance against the integration in existing power systems which attempt to reproduce themselves. Gamm criticises the lack of political engagement in educational science and undertakes a criticism of capitalism, out of which he develops the educational principle of taking the side of the exploited classes. He also draws attention to the difference between affiliating with the young or with the established generation.[188]

Critical educational theory is by no means a homogeneous phenomenon – despite certain characteristic similarities – but functions as a cover term for a variety of approaches within the contested field of education. In the following, I shall portray some key features of critical concepts of education, highlight the particular contribution of Heydorn, before I introduce Klafki's critical and constructive concept of education, which builds on different educational traditions including critical theory and which has become highly influential in various educational contexts.

Apart from the common interest in the emancipatory function of education, the following issues are main concerns of most critical concepts of education:

(1) *a critical evaluation of the historical and social character of education*, including a critical analysis of the interdependence of the educational system and the structure of society, which results in a realisation that the given social conditions produce inequality and therefore unsatisfactory educational situations. Along with a study of

---

[188] Cf. Wulf 2003: Educational Science, 131ff. This distinction is also relevant in the Scandinavian debate about RE, where the view can be found that integrative RE tends more towards the interest of the young generation in broad information, whereas confessional RE tends more towards the interests of the established generation (or: the parents), who prefer an introduction of the young generation to their own particular worldview. For this issue see Almén 2000: RE in Sweden, 63 and Olin 2000: RE in Finland, 114.

the mechanisms that impede the developments of self-confident individuals, a critical theory of education also studies how emancipatory energy can be set free. Nowadays, it is widely acknowledged that critical theory alone cannot overcome this dependence on the social context, but may help to reduce it by elucidating basic facts. This is directly linked to

(2) *a criticism of ideologies*, particularly of the dominant capitalist ideology and its consequences – above all the reproduction and legitimation of social inequality and injustice – as a concern of an educational theory which attempts not to become part of an educational system at the mercy of the interests of power. The interdependencies between power and education are a major concern of critical educational theory. Referring to the basic principles of enlightenment, emancipation and self-determination, social facts such as domination, oppression, reification and self-alienation are targeted. Furthermore,

(3) *the need for both theory and practice* has become apparent. Sound theory is a prerequisite for the development of methods. Therefore, a constructive theory for practice – as opposed to mere criticism or negativity – is needed, in which complex theoretical issues are translated into practice and furthermore into a language that can be understood by the people who are meant to apply theory in practice.[189]

Heinz-Joachim Heydorn can be regarded as a main exponent of a critical theory of education and development. His approach is based on a criticism of power structures which institutionalise the domination of people. He highlights the unresolved contradiction between education and power and develops a concept which aims at reducing power and progressively improving society by assisting people in the emancipatory educational process. However, he acknowledges the actual situation of education in a society which is based on social injustice: social investments in education are not driven by an interest in politically mature and responsible citizens, but by an interest in maintaining economic wealth and stability. In this context, education is alienated from its emancipatory impetus and reduced to schooling, qualification and training. Nevertheless, education still remains peculiarly antagonistic. If the contradiction between rhetoric (human rights, equality, justice etc.) and reality (domination, inequality, privilege etc.) is perceived, the violation of one's own humanity in the face of this schizophrenic real-

---

[189] For a more detailed account of features of critical educational theory see Wulf 2003: Educational Science, 128-146.

ity, in which one voluntarily or involuntarily participates, may be felt and this can be a source of revolutionary potential.[190]

Therefore, despite restrictive social environments, the emancipatory power of education cannot be fully suppressed. Critical education must resist the attempts to integrate the young generation into the institutional power system without helping them to find a critical perspective on it. Education and development ought to be regarded as a continuous path towards liberation. An important aspect of this process is to become conscious of the circumstances and peculiarities of one's own socialisation.[191] Perhaps Heydorn was still so close to the register of the Frankfurt School that it was difficult for him to introduce his concept of education to educational institutions, despite his merits in establishing a critical theory of education.[192] Wolfgang Klafki's critical and constructive theory of education, however, enjoys great popularity, not least because of the didactic programme which he presented to be used as a direct application of his theoretical ideas to practice.

2.1.4 A critical and constructive theory of education

Wolfgang Klafki, born in 1928, who started his academic career in the context of the educational theory of the humanities (geisteswissenschaftliche Pädagogik),[193] critically reflects upon educational theories of different traditions and builds his own critical and constructive theory of education on his criticism of former approaches. He locates his model, on which he has worked and published for more than 20 years now but which he regards as an unfinished project in the making, within the context of German and recent international approaches to a critical theory of education.[194] Perhaps it is the constructive character of Klafki's approach that has made it so well known. Like other critical theorists, he clearly criticises the social mechanisms and economic structures that produce inequality, but his approach emphasises the constructive side and presents strategies for educational institutions – and school in particular – to respond to these problems. He calls for taking small steps while keeping the broad perspective in mind.

---

190 Cf. Heydorn 1995: Bildungstheoretische und pädagogische Schriften 1967-1970, 144ff.; also: Über den Widerspruch von Bildung und Herrschaft, 284.
191 Cf. Heydorn 1995: Über den Widerspruch von Bildung und Herrschaft, 323.
192 Cf. Wulf 2003: Educational Science, 133.
193 See section 2.2.1 of this chapter. Klafki studied with E. Weniger and T. Litt.
194 See for example Klafki 1998: Grundzüge kritisch-konstruktiver Erziehungswissenschaft, which was also published in Japanese.

Klafki attempts to develop a concept of general education (*Allgemeinbildung*) which acknowledges the relations between the ability to look after one's basic personal rights, the idea of a fundamentally democratic society and a consistently liberal and social democracy. In order to help the young generation to engage actively and constructively in the future development of society – and not to accept the given social situation as an unchangeable fact – education must be understood as a process which fosters three basic abilities: (1) *individual self-determination* of life and meaning in social, vocational, ethical and religious matters, (2) *participation* in decision-making about cultural, economic, social and political issues and (3) *solidarity* in order also to grant the right to self-determination and participation to everybody else. Education has to be education for everybody, which deals – in a global perspective – with the tasks, problems and dangers of humankind considering history, the contemporary situation and future outlooks. In order to take seriously the right to a free development of one's own personality, education has to embrace all areas of human abilities and interests, including cognitive, social, technical, aesthetic and physical dimensions, as well the ability to take ethical, religious and political decisions. With regard to the organisation and content of education, the idea of providing "education for everybody" implies the gradual removal of selective and separating elements in school structures, learning areas and methodology in order to increase common learning as far as this is possible.[195]

Klafki's suggestion for an adequate contemporary concept of education is to concentrate on the key problems that mark our epoch in the cultural, social, political and individual dimensions and to respond to this situation by promoting key qualifications which may help to tackle these problems. He identifies the following issues as key problems of our epoch:[196] (1) questions of war and peace in the face of the destructive potential of modern weapons; (2) the problems surrounding questions of nationality, internationality, cultural identity and interculturality as well as the quest for a common ethos in our global world; (3) the environmental crisis; (4) the rapid growth of the world population; (5) the very topical problem of socially produced inequality within and among societies, for example with respect to class, gender, health and

---

[195] It may be noted here that the introduction of integrative RE is an important step in this direction.
[196] For Klafki's own summary of his main points see Klafki 2001: Zur Frage eines zeitgemäßen Bildungsbegriffs, 25f.; for a more detailed version see Klafki 2001: Grundlinien eines gegenwarts- und zukunftsorientierten Bildungsbegriffs und didaktische Konsequenzen, 31-38.

employment; (6) the dangers and possibilities of the new media of control, information and communication; (7) personal relationships, hetero- or homosexual love and sexuality in the context of conflicts between an individual pursuit of happiness, interpersonal responsibility and a respect for difference; (8) religious and ethical pluralism in modern secular societies, which requires a reconsideration of different processes such as identity formation, the development of an ability to deal with questions about meaning, religious or ethical orientation and the assumption of responsibility for personal decisions.[197] Addressing those key problems in educational contexts involves not only dealing with examples which may result in respective problem-specific and structural knowledge, but also an acquisition of attitudes and skills which are relevant beyond the immediate contexts of the specific problems. These competences may be called "key skills" (*Schlüsselqualifikationen*), which involve the ability as well as readiness to participate in debates, to criticise oneself and others constructively, empathy, to cooperate creatively and consider various interdependencies.

The implications of the concept put forward by Klafki for teaching methodology will be discussed in the next session. To conclude this section on educational theory, I would like to draw attention to the fact that such a concept of education implies a radical reassessment of the concept of achievement, too. Klafki suggests that concepts of achievement which are oriented towards measurable skills and knowledge and traditionally focus on individual and competitive achievement must be partly replaced and partly complemented by a dynamic notion of achievement which takes cooperation into account. Assessment should be understood above all as feedback and support in the learning process, not only as a "final account".[198]

---

[197] In this context, Klafki emphasises that this last problem cannot be dealt with satisfactorily within traditional confessional religious education – as taught in most German states – any longer. He mentions the new school subject "Life-Ethics-Religion" (LER, *Lebensgestaltung-Ethik-Religionskunde*) that was introduced in Brandenburg as a compulsory subject as an example of a broader framework in which these questions about religion and ethics can be addressed, see Klafki 2001: Grundlinien eines gegenwarts- und zukunftsorientierten Bildungsbegriffs und didaktische Konsequenzen, 37; also 1999: Braucht eine "gute Schule" einen neuen Unterrichtsbereich LER?

[198] Cf. Klafki 2001: Zur Frage eines zeitgemäßen Bildungsbegriffs, 26f, 2001: Grundlinien eines gegenwarts- und zukunftsorientierten Bildungsbegriffs, 43f.

2.2 Didactics

Didactics, the science of teaching, is one part of the wide field of educational theory. Until the 1960s, the educational theory of the humanities was the dominant paradigm for didactics. Two articles in the late 1950s and early 1960s, Klafki's "Didaktische Analayse als Kern der Unterrichtsvorbereitung" (Didactic analysis as the heart of lesson planning, 1959) and Paul Heimann's "Didaktik als Theorie und Lehre" (Didactics as theory and teaching, 1962) anticipated further developments and provided first outlines of models that were to become highly influential later.[199] This was the beginning of an intensive debate about a diversity of different approaches, which, however, practically ended in the mid 1980s and left an unproductive silence, because none of the models managed to integrate the various aspects (the social context, aims, contents, structures and processes, teaching and learning, communication and interaction, *Erziehung* and *Bildung*) into a comprehensive approach which could then be applied in practice.[200] In 1993, Friedrich W. Kron provided an overview of recent didactic theories and models. He identified 30 different approaches, which he classified into three groups with respect to their main foci: (1) education (*Bildung*), (2) learning and (3) interaction.[201] This distinction, which was later taken up by other scholars of education,[202] provides helpful categories for structuring the various approaches to didactics. In the following, I shall present one prominent example of a didactic theory from each of the three categories in order to give an introduction to the main issues at stake. For present educational and didactic theory, it is important to acknowledge the range of models and foci in order to approach the interdependencies of "the whole" of the didactic field with its complex and composite nature. Only then can the particularisation of ideas be overcome in a model which considers and integrates the different aspects.[203]

Criteria for my selection of examples include the potential relevance for integrative RE, since this introduction to didactic theories is given in order find appropriate models for this particular school sub-

---

[199] See Klafki 1969 [19591]: Didaktische Analyse als Kern der Unterrichtsvorbereitung; Heimann 1962: Didaktik als Theorie und Lehre.
[200] Cf. Stadtfeld/Diekmann 2005: Einleitung, 7f, Lersch 2005: Modellierungen der didaktischen Fragestellung, 70.
[201] See Kron 1993: Grundwissen Didaktik, 117f.
[202] Cf., e.g., Stadtfeld/Diekmann 2005: Einleitung, 8, and Lersch 2005: Modellierungen der didaktischen Fragestellung, 69f.
[203] Cf. Lersch (2005: Modellierungen der didaktischen Fragestellung, 91f.), who tries to elucidate "the whole" of didactics in its school-theoretical context.

ject. Therefore, some popular and frequently cited models – for example Felix von Cube's cybernetic model or Christine Möller's model, which is oriented towards learning outcomes – will not be discussed as they cannot really be meaningfully applied to integrative RE.[204] Among the models which focus on education, I have selected Klafki's critical-constructive model (2.2.1), which is a direct application of his educational theory as introduced above. The teaching theory developed by Schulz ("Hamburg Model"), which builds on earlier ideas put forward by Heimann, Otto and himself in the "Berlin Model", serves as an example of the approaches which concentrate on learning (2.2.2). Several concepts focus on the interactive processes in teaching and learning contexts. The models by Schäfer/Schaller and Winkler will be briefly outlined as examples of this group (2.2.3). The section concludes with a reflection about the relationship between general didactics and the development of teaching strategies for individual subjects (2.2.4).

2.2.1 The focus on education: critical constructive didactics

Klafki's critical and constructive didactic model builds on his theory of education and is primarily concerned with the aims and contents of school education. Klafki understands didactics as the theory of the tasks, contents and categories of education, which considers their relevance, the criteria for their selection, as well as their structure and stratification.[205] Every didactic decision depends on the concept of education which serves as the general framework. Didactic considerations, again, precede methodology, which can only be one further step once didactic decisions have been taken. Klafki's didactic concept is "critical" in so far as it is directed towards the pupils' progressive self-determination, participation and solidarity and "constructive" in that it is directly related to practice and pedagogical strategies.

---

204 Within a critical concept of education, the models of v. Cube and Möller are problematic anyway, as they do not include a reflection of the actual contents of education, but provide rather technological didactic methods, which reduce pupils to mere objects in the learning process and neglect emancipatory and participatory elements, cf. Kremer 1997: Didaktik, 80. In contrast to those models which regard learning as a kind of technical process, models which actually consider the development of critical consciousness integral to the learning process ought to be preferred.
205 Klafki 1963: Das Problem der Didaktik, 21. As this is only a brief outline of Klafki's main points, several interesting aspects, for example the way Klafki's model changed over the years (see Plöger 1999: Allgemeine Didaktik und Fachdidaktik, 168ff.), cannot be dealt with here.

Teaching needs to be oriented towards the key problems which are characteristic of our epoch and enable an acquisition of key skills which are required for this task.[206] The interplay between teaching and learning has to be conceived of as a process of interaction in which the learners – with the help of the teachers but also with an increasing independence – acquire knowledge and skills which enable a critical perspective towards historically and socially constituted realities. This process has to be organised as democratic social education with the pupils' participation as an integral element, for example through planning or feedback. In this context, teaching means "helping to learn" and enabling social and political maturity.[207]

Klafki identifies four main tasks for didactics: (1) to uncover the historicity of didactic decisions on which curricula are based in critical analyses; (2) to orient the curriculum towards the perspective of an educated layperson, an enlightened contemporary and politically responsible citizen and to include scientific perspectives if they contribute to a better understanding or to the development of strategies for action in the present or future; (3) to describe the educational relevance of a subject with respect to aesthetic, theoretic, pragmatic, ethical or religious meaning in order to justify its place in the canon of school subjects and (4) to analyse the general educational content of a specific element of education, be it with respect to elementary, exemplary or fundamental aspects of education.[208] Klafki uses the concept "categorial education" (*kategoriale Bildung*) in order to refer to the complexity of the educational process in which the material and the formal aspects are integrated into a coherent whole, whereby categories are acquired and an awareness for the elementary, exemplary or fundamental is raised.[209] Didactic analysis, which has to precede methodological preparation, is an indispensable aspect of actual lesson planning. It is important for the teacher to identify the educational value (*Bildungsgehalt*) of every individual educational element (*Bildungsinhalt*). If teachers become aware

---

206 For a further specification of these problems and skills see the section on Klafki's educational theory above (2.1.4).
207 Cf. Klafki 1985: Neue Studien zur Bildungstheorie und Didaktik, 199f.
208 Cf. Klafki 1963: Das Problem der Didaktik, 41ff.
209 *Kategoriale Bildung* is realised in a process of a two-sided elucidation: "Diese doppelseitige Erschließung geschieht als Sichtbarwerden von allgemeinen, kategorial erhellenden Inhalten auf der objektiven Seite und als Aufgehen allgemeiner Einsichten, Erlebnisse, Erfahrungen auf der Seite des Subjekts. Anders formuliert: Das Sichtbarwerden von ‚allgemeinen Inhalten', von kategorialen Prinzipien in paradigmatischem ‚Stoff', also auf der Seite der ‚Wirklichkeit', ist nichts anderes als das Gewinnen von ‚Kategorien' auf der Seite des Subjekts." (Klafki 1974: 43; quoted in Kron 1993: 123) See also Plöger 1999: Allgemeine Didaktik und Fachdidaktik, 269.

of covert decisions behind the curricula, a decentralisation of educational decisions is possible. What is taught in schools needs to be legitimised on the basis of the social and political context and not on the basis of the structure of the related academic subject.[210]

2.2.2 The focus on teaching: the "Berlin" and "Hamburg" models

This didactic model which focuses primarily on teaching was originally proposed by Heimann, Otto and Schulz (1965) of the "Berlin School" and further developed above all by Schulz as the "Hamburg Model". The Berlin Model was – unlike Klafki's model discussed above – less concerned with the question of what should be taught, but rather with the questions of how teaching should be organised and what kind of methodologies are necessary for good teaching practice. Schulz' Hamburg Model however, resembles Klafki's concept in that he conceives of education as a dialogue of different individuals as agents, not as the subjugation of an object of teaching and education to the intentions of a teacher and educator, and relates its partiality for the pupils to the intentions of promoting their competence, autonomy and solidarity.[211] At the centre of the Berlin Model lies a structural analysis of the teaching process in which anthropogenic and social, situational and cultural circumstances have to be considered – which means e.g. a study of related research about social and developmental psychology – when decisions about intentions, topics (contents, objects), methods and media (means of communication) are taken. Schulz emphasises that the educational value of a lesson is determined exclusively by its effect on the progress of the learners. Therefore, individual and social effects of the teaching and learning processes have to be studied in order to evaluate the success of the enterprise. His concept is based on four didactic questions: (1) aims: what do we want pupils to learn? (2) prior experiences, knowledge, attitudes and intentions: who learns from whom? (3) decisions about the structure of the project/lesson: what are the variables of the teaching process (methodological steps, forms of interaction, media etc.)? and (4) assessment and evaluation: how successful was the lesson? Among the factors that influence the teaching

---

210 Cf. Klafki 1958: Didaktische Analyse als Kern der Unterrichtsvorbereitung, see also Plöger 1999: Allgemeine Didaktik und Fachdidaktik, 269; Lersch 2005: Modellierungen der didaktischen Fragestellung, 71.
211 See Schulz 1995: Die lehrtheoretische Didaktik, 31; Schulz 1981: Unterrichtsplanung, 39ff.; see also Kremer 1997: Didaktik, 78, Kron 1993: Grundwissen Didaktik, 143; Plöger 1999: Allgemeine Didaktik und Fachdidaktik, 274.

and learning processes are institutional conditions, for example, curricula, the school context, locations, available material and the composition of the group as well as social conditions like the terms of production and power or the worldview of the participants.[212]

These conditions have to be considered in lesson planning, which Schulz divides into four levels: (1) perspectives, which include the broad, long-term perspective as well as the structure of an individual sequence; (2) outlines of individual sessions on the basis of the long-term perspective; (3) processes, in which the outline is translated into a concrete lesson plan and (4) correction or refinement during a lesson as a reaction to unexpected events. Due to its practical orientation, this model has been widely used in the second phase of teacher training.[213] In the more recent version (*Hamburg Model*), Schulz complements the suggestions for teaching strategies with general curriculum- and school theory and emphasises the participatory character of interactive teaching- and learning processes in which the role of the teacher is that of an advisor and not of a "know-all". The task of school as an institution is twofold: to enable children to participate in social life, but at the same to enhance their independence so that they can actively and responsibly take part in shaping and transforming social life.[214]

2.2.3 The focus on interaction: critical communicative didactics

Critical communicative didactics is among the approaches which Kron mentions in the group of didactic models in which the interactive process that characterises education is the main concern. "Critical" refers to the attempt to permanently improve teaching and learning processes and "communicative" points at its focus on the communicative or interactive character of these processes.

Karl-Hermann Schäfer and Klaus Schaller refer to the theories of the *Frankfurt School* (Horkheimer, Adorno and Habermas in particular), Paul Watzlawick's theory of communication and later also to "symbolic interactionism" following George Herbert Mead, for their analyses of structures of communication and interaction in teaching and learning processes, which they undertake in order to suggest a model in which power differences are reduced in the interest of contributing to emancipation and the development of the identities of all participants, in-

---

212 Schulz 1995: Die lehrtheoretische Didaktik, 32ff.
213 Cf. Kremer 1997: Didaktik, 78f.
214 Cf. Schulz 1981: Unterrichtsplanung, 11.

cluding the teacher. Like any other form of communication, teaching- and learning processes consist of a content- as well as a relational aspect. The relationship between teachers and pupils may be progressive-complementary (dominating the interactive process) or regressive-complementary (reducing this dominance). Emancipation can only take place in an interactive process approximating symmetrical structures which constitute a form of communication in which the participants in principle have equal rights.[215] Winkel (1995) is particularly concerned with disruptions of the interactive process, for example lack of discipline, provocation, or refusal to learn. He analyses interpersonal relationships as well as reasons for and effects of disruptions and draws attention to the fact that, in the presentation of topics, the manner of interaction is just as important as the contents.[216] The critical communicative model may be regarded as a complement to the other two models as it highlights another important aspect of educational processes.

2.2.4 General didactics and individual school subjects

Didactics, the theory of teaching, is concerned with what is common to all teaching processes. It ought to be regarded as a corrective, preventing the domination of teaching processes by single-minded political or academic interests. The didactics of an individual subject or the theory of teaching a subject has to be conceived of as part of a comprehensive general educational process. Skills and knowledge to be acquired in an individual subject have to be related to the educational aims of the school in general. The didactics of an individual subject is a relatively independent mediator between general didactics and academic subjects. General didactic theory and didactic theory for the individual subjects should engage in permanent critical dialogue in order to enable a cross-fertilisation of ideas.[217]

In the course of the educational orientation towards science from the late 1960s onwards, the contents of many school subjects were justified and determined solely by the structures and developments of the respective academic subjects. The abstract emancipatory constructs of critical theory, which educational theory produced at the time, were not able to avert this "colonisation of general didactics by the individ-

---

215 Cf. Schäfer/Schaller 1971: Kritische Erziehungswissenschaft und kommunikative Didaktik; for my summary cf. Lersch 2005: Modellierungen der didaktischen Fragestellung, 74f.
216 Cf. Winkel 1995: Die kritisch-kommunikative Didaktik.
217 Cf. Lersch 2005: Modellierungen der didaktischen Fragestellung, 92f.

ual academic subjects".[218] I suggest that this dialogue between general didactics and the didactics of individual subjects, which practically ended in the 1970s,[219] should be taken up again and general didactic theory should be related to the subject matter of individual subjects in order to develop educationally justified didactic concepts for each school subject. As Kremer notes, this involves research about the effects of different didactic models in general, as well as their application to individual school subjects. Aims, contents and methodology of individual school subjects have to be justified on educational grounds within general educational and didactic theory, as general didactic decisions – consciously or unconsciously – inevitably precede any subject-specific curriculum.

If we consider the general didactic models presented above, what can be regarded as their contribution to theory, analysis, planning and methodology in the didactics of individual subjects? Wilfried Plöger undertakes this translation for the models by Klafki and by the *"Berlin"* and *"Hamburg" Schools*. Klafki's model emphasises the primacy of didactics over methodology and implies that the theory of tasks, contents and categories for the didactics of any subject has to be set in a context of educational theory. On the basis of Klafki's model, Plöger identifies five main issues to be considered for the didactics of each subject: (1) the contribution of the subject to general aims of education, with an orientation towards the perspective of an educated layperson; (2) the educational dimension to which the subject contributes, e.g. aesthetic, theoretical, pragmatic, ethical, religious; (3) the relationship between the school subject and the academic discipline; legitimation of the content of the school subject based on its relevance for the presence and future, not on the structure of the academic discipline; renunciation of an exclusively academic approach; (4) a critical consideration of the history of the school subject: which interests have shaped it?; (5) an evaluation of the adequacy of the contents of the subject in the light of the general task of education and decisions about their refinement or replacement; formulation of a curriculum in which the different levels of abstraction (fundamental, elementary, exemplary) within the general concept are stated.[220] Plöger acknowledges that in Klafki's later work the political dimension of the didactic process is even more explicit. For

---

218 Kremer 1997: Didaktik, 82. In the 1970s, didactic sections were established by several academic associations. These gained influence with regard to the contents of the respective school subjects (cf. ibid.). Note that in Germany this did not happen within the study of religions as no related school subject existed at the time.
219 Cf. ibid.
220 Cf. Plöger 1999: Allgemeine Didaktik und Fachdidaktik, 270.

the didactics of a subject, this means that one ought to start from a broad societal perspective and translate it into specific contexts and tasks. The teaching process and the selection of contents ought to be conceived of as elements of an enterprise in which the socio-political intentions of self-determination, participation and solidarity are communicated.[221]

The model of the *Berlin School*, focusing more on methodology than on general educational theory, provides helpful suggestions for actual lesson planning. It reminds the educator to consider "the whole" of the teaching process, including anthropogenic and socio-cultural presuppositions. Careful decisions have to be taken about intentions, topics, methods and media. The central question is what kind of aids the teacher can provide for the pupils to acquire the intended patterns of thinking and acting and reflect upon and evaluate them.[222] As mentioned above, Schulz' *Hamburg Model* complements these methodological considerations with an educational theory that builds on emancipation and participation and thereby provides a philosophical background for the development of adequate teaching methods. Critical communicative models draw attention to hidden agendas behind different modes of discourse and call for a responsible choice of interactive strategies in teaching and learning processes. The decision about the roles of all participants and the mode of communication ought to be grounded in the principle of democratic participation, which seeks to counter hierarchies.

Finally, it is important not to fall victim to compartmentalisation and consider the whole complex of didactics, including educational theory, teaching theory and methodology, as well as the character of the interactive processes in which teaching and learning take place. The different didactic models which I introduced should not be regarded as alternatives, but as complementary aspects of a comprehensive didactic theory which is relevant for the didactics of any subject.

What is "critical" in critical didactics is the continuous reflection upon variables which seem to be given and a decision about whether one is really willing to accept these as "given" or whether one wishes to contribute to changing them towards more democratic and equitable models. The emancipatory aspect, which always allows for a consideration of alternatives or alternative perspectives and which means preferring to introduce children to the complexity of the world rather than to simplified bite-sized positions, enables the pupils to form their own

---

221 Cf. ibid., 271.
222 Cf. ibid., 273.

opinion and take responsible decisions on the basis of the multi-perspectival knowledge they have acquired. Critical scrutiny of the variables of the educational process may also include a criticism of the canon of school subjects. Kremer, for example, criticises the notion that the existence of some school subjects is justified merely by the existence of corresponding academic disciplines. If Klafki's concept of key problems and qualifications is taken seriously, traditional subject borders and curricula mirroring this reductionist model in which school subjects are regarded as "copies" of academic disciplines, have to be reconsidered.[223]

2.3 Intercultural education

For the following reasons, approaches to intercultural education are particularly relevant to the theory and method of integrative RE:

(1) the proximity of the concepts "culture" and "religion", which bring about similar issues concerning the relationship between academic subjects (anthropology, the study of religions) and school contexts, particularly as both academic disciplines do not have directly related school subjects in many countries;
(2) the similarity of educational justifications of intercultural education and integrative RE, such as social and historical contexts like multicultural societies, globalisation etc.

In international perspective, intercultural education is far more developed and debated than integrative RE (apart from the few countries that actually have integrative RE), but religious traditions are sometimes included as contents of intercultural education, when religion is regarded as a sub-category of culture. Therefore, the discussion about intercultural education is a valuable resource for the development of theory and method of integrative RE. It is, however, necessary to evaluate, in any individual case, if aspects of concepts of intercultural education are transferable to integrative RE. In this section, the main concerns of intercultural education will be introduced (2.3.1), before some important areas of intercultural learning are outlined (2.3.2) and a few issues concerning the relations between intercultural education and educational systems will be addressed (2.3.3).

---

223 Cf. Kremer 1997: Didaktik, 83.

2.3.1 What is intercultural education?

"Intercultural education" and "multicultural education" are often used synonymously. In the German context, intercultural education is used more frequently, while in the English speaking world multicultural education is a popular concept, sometimes as an object of criticism from an antiracist perspective,[224] which draws attention to the importance of a consideration of the political aspects of the way the term "culture" is construed. Some authors relate the connotations of the prefix "inter-" to interaction, exchange, openness, mutuality, acceptance of difference or even the creation of something new "between" other positions, and give these associations as reasons for choosing the term intercultural education, as they underline dynamics and interaction.[225] I also choose to use the terms intercultural education and intercultural learning as comprehensive concepts which include multicultural education along with antiracist criticism and acknowledge that intercultural education and learning always necessarily also have a political dimension.[226]

Multicultural societies are the starting points for concepts of intercultural education, however on different levels. Renate Nestvogel distinguishes between three different kinds of concepts of intercultural education, which respond to the situation in one's own country, the European unification or the world system respectively.[227] These three foci can also be regarded as reference points in the history of intercultural education, as they mark decisive turning points in the develop-

---

224 Cf. Hormel and Scherr 2004: Bildung für die Einwanderungsgesellschaft, 33.
225 Cf., e.g., Secco 1993: Interkulturelle Pädagogik, 27; See also Auernheimer 2003: Einführung in die interkulturelle Pädagogik, 25.
226 For a similar argument, see Auernheimer 1997: Interkulturelle Pädagogik, 345, 2003: Einführung in die interkulturelle Pädagogik, 2. For the German context Auernheimer (2000: Ziele und Bedingungen interkultureller Bildung, 16) suggests using the term "interkulturelle Bildung" rather than "interkulturelle Erziehung", as the latter is associated with pedagogic insistence and dominance. This problem does, however, not arise with the English concept *education*.
227 In the concepts Nestvogel refers to in the first category, the "own" country is Germany, see 2002: Zum Verhältnis von 'interkulturellem Lernen', 'globalem Lernen' und 'Bildung für eine nachhaltige Entwicklung', 32; for her description of the three models see 32f. For a similar analysis of concepts of intercultural education for individual subjects, see Roth 2000: Allgemeine Didaktik, 46. It has to be noted that the German debate about the multicultural character of society is somewhat odd if compared to the debate in other countries, for example, the United Kingdom or Sweden. It seems to be difficult for conservative German politicians to accept at all that Germany is a multicultural country. As Auernheimer notes, in this debate "multicultural" is often misinterpreted as "multiethnic" (1997: Interkulturelle Pädagogik, 347). For a discussion of different normative academic concepts of a multicultural society see ibid., 58ff.

ment of the discipline in which a global perspective considering worldwide interrelations and dependencies is inevitable for the present. Nestvogel regards *intercultural learning* as

> "Lernen von ‚fremden' Kulturen bei gleichzeitiger kritischer Auseinandersetzung mit der ‚eigenen' Kultur und Gesellschaft (kulturelle Selbstreflexion). Diese Auseinandersetzung reicht vom Makrosystem historisch gewachsener weltsystemischer Verflechtungen (incl. der darin wirksamen Herrschafts- und Interessenstrukturen) bis in den Mikrobereich der psychischen Strukturen des Subjekts (incl. der eigenen Person). Interkulturelles Lernen umfasst damit kognitive, affektive und konative (handlungsorientierte) Dimensionen und erfordert die Fähigkeit zu vernetzter Wahrnehmung und einer Reflexions- und Handlungskompetenz in komplexen Zusammenhängen."[228]

Nestvogel links the macro- and microsystemic relations with different aspects of intercultural learning, such as global learning on the macrosystemic and social or antiracist learning on the microsystemic level, while learning for democracy, human rights or peace education fall within both categories.

In the analyses of the contexts of intercultural education, the global economic and political systems and their effects on the lives of individuals and groups receive due attention. Auernheimer, for example, refers to the global markets for capital and labour, economic dependencies, the decrease of national regulation, the global cultural industry, the negation of distance by modern means of communication and worldwide migration as the setting in which nationalism and religious fundamentalism arise and in which there is no alternative to intercultural dialogue if the common global tasks are faced.[229] He emphasises that in any dialogue, the contexts, which often include hegemony, dependencies and privileges, have to be taken into account. Otherwise, dialogue is feigned from the very beginning.[230] Nestvogel elucidates the continuity between the historical processes of colonialism, development and globalisation and shows that racist violence is only the tip of an iceberg whose invisible part is located at the centre of our society. She quotes Zimmer, who regards intercultural education as education

---

228 Nestvogel 2002: Zum Verhältnis von 'interkulturellem Lernen', 'globalem Lernen' und 'Bildung für eine nachhaltige Entwicklung', 35f.
229 As examples of common global tasks he names the preservation of the eco-system and the provision of food for the growing world population; see Auernheimer 1997: Interkulturelle Pädagogik, 344.
230 Ibid., 344. For a similar argument about interreligious dialogue see Auffarth 1999: Dialog der Religionen: Vom Dialog vor dem Dialog.

for international cooperation on one's own doorstep, where the conflicts are in fact located.[231]

Intercultural education builds on the concepts of critical educational theory, which include equality, participation and coexistence with equal rights, respect for different cultural identities and universal principles – like human rights – which can be justified from different cultural traditions.[232] Alexander Thomas' definition of intercultural learning includes the initial open attitude required for successful intercultural learning, the performative aspect, as well as the integration of other cultural elements in one's own system of orientation:

> "Interkulturelles Lernen findet statt, wenn eine Person bestrebt ist, im Umgang mit Menschen einer anderen Kultur deren spezifisches Orientierungssystem der Wahrnehmung, des Denkens, Wertens und Handelns zu verstehen, in das eigenkulturelle Orientierungssystem zu integrieren und auf ihr Denken und Handeln im fremdkulturellen Handlungsfeld anzuwenden."[233]

Intercultural education needs to use research results from various disciplines depending on the different foci or aspects in question. Particularly relevant are comparative pedagogy and anthropology.[234] The latter can contribute to an understanding of the complex relationships within and between cultural systems and help to avoid mistakes in the interpretation of cultures. It is important to realise that one cannot simply use one's own patterns of description and interpretation for a study and valuation of another culture. An attempt to understand another culture in its own terms has to be the first step of any analysis.[235] There are many definitions of culture, and the difficulty of defining culture at all is generally acknowledged.[236] Auernheimer notes that most theories refer to the symbolic aspect and the orienting function of culture. However, in any account of culture, cultural hegemony, which is present not only in the selection and presentation of topics, traditions etc., but also in the very process of interpretation itself, has to be considered. A the-

---

231 Nestvogel 2002: Zum Verhältnis von 'interkulturellem Lernen', 'globalem Lernen' und 'Bildung für eine nachhaltige Entwicklung', 36ff.
232 Cf. Auernheimer 2000: Ziele und Bedingungen interkultureller Bildung, 11, 1997: Interkulturelle Pädagogik, 348f.
233 Thomas 1988: Psychologisch-pädagogische Aspekte interkulturellen Lernens im Schüleraustausch, 83.
234 For an adaptation of anthropological methods in intercultural education see Fillitz 2003: Methodische Reflexion, 341ff.
235 Cf. Secco 1993: Interkulturelle Pädagogik, 25f.
236 See. e.g. Nestvogel 2002: Zum Verhältnis von 'interkulturellem Lernen', 'globalem Lernen' und 'Bildung für eine nachhaltige Entwicklung', 39, Auernheimer 1997: Interkulturelle Pädagogik, 349.

ory of culture has to acknowledge its dynamic nature and consider the difference between constructed wholes and individuals in order not to make the latter prisoners of their alleged culture.[237]

Marianne Krüger-Potratz's analysis of the motivations behind different interpretations of culture and cultural difference shows that the rhetoric of cultural difference can be highly problematic when it serves – be it consciously or unconsciously – to cover for real differences of privilege and power.[238] Krüger-Potratz suggests regarding cultural difference as but one aspect of the dynamics of the social debates in which individuals and groups fight about resources. "Cultural difference" provides a seemingly legitimate opportunity to dispute other people's rights to resources by defining one's rivals as "other". She points out that cultural difference is neither new nor special, nor something that is related to migration, being foreign etc., but that it refers to the simple fact that we are different in different ways. At all times, there have been attempts to instrumentalise particular – collective – differences in order to attain or legitimate hegemony. Therefore, the relevant issues are not the existence or the ways of dealing with cultural difference, but a correct definition of the problems, which is independent from the old patterns of attempting to achieve homogeneity.[239] The aims stated for intercultural education by the different authors can be divided into three groups:

(1) knowledge and understanding of different cultural traditions in their social and political contexts
(2) recognition of the subtle and pervasive mechanisms which are at work in the construction of cultures and "otherness"
(3) intercultural competence on different levels, including cognitive, affective, emotional and behavioural levels.

With respect to the first category of aims, Auernheimer emphasises that understanding involves a reconstruction of meaning. Communication is codification. Understanding requires a deconstruction and reconstruction of codes. Intercultural education has to contribute to deeper – "second order" – understanding which incorporates knowledge about value systems, living conditions and historical experiences of others.[240]

---

237 Cf. Auernheimer 2003: Einführung in die interkulturelle Pädagogik, 73ff.; 1997: Interkulturelle Pädagogik, 349; 1995: Einführung in die interkulturelle Erziehung, 167.
238 Krüger-Potratz 2002: Kulturelle Differenz, 59ff.
239 Cf. ibid., 61f.
240 Cf. Auernheimer 2000: Ziele und Bedingungen interkultureller Bildung, 11; 1997: Interkulturelle Pädagogik, 350f.

An orientation towards the individual and his or her immediate contexts helps to avoid premature conclusions about cultural traditions as wholes.[241] The second category of aims involves a recognition of inequality and racist discrimination in school and society, a critical reconsideration of concepts of "otherness", reflection upon cultural self-evidence, and learning to change perspectives and consider a variety of approaches towards a phenomenon. A development of trans-cultural perspectives helps to decentralise one's own point of view, a prerequisite for understanding other points of view.[242]

Bearing the problems of the various constructions of cultural difference in mind, Krüger-Potratz demands that our constructs of what we define as our own history be analysed with respect to patterns by which we construct normality and define what is "generally so". Furthermore, we have to take account of the plurality within this history we call our "own" in order to do justice to the actual pluralism in school and education. Cultural difference must not only be regarded as a distinctive feature of foreigners and locals but also of sex/gender, class, religion etc. It is important to understand that, frequently, the rhetoric about cultural difference is in fact about claims to positions and privileges.[243]

The third category of aims involves intercultural understanding on the cognitive level, education for openness, empathy, interest, tolerance and the acceptance of difference on the affective level, and commitment to equality as well as competence for encounters, dialogue and constructive conflict-management on the behavioural level.[244] What is actually meant by these rather vague keywords will become clearer in the next section, which discusses the different aspects of intercultural education. At any rate, intercultural competence involves constructively dealing with crises, which are inescapable in intercultural learning processes. In self-reflexive dialogues it means

> "mit eigenen wie fremden, individuellen wie kulturellen Schwächen, mit regressiven wie aggressiven Impulsen umgehen zu können, Ohnmachtsgefühle, Versagensängste, Insuffizienzgefühle bei sich und anderen auszuhalten und die erlebte Krise produktiv und kreativ zu wenden."[245]

---

241 Roth 2000: Allgemeine Didaktik, 48.
242 Cf. Auernheimer 2000: Ziele und Bedingungen interkultureller Bildung, 11; Roth 2000: Allgemeine Didaktik, 47.
243 Cf. Krüger-Potratz 2002: Kulturelle Differenz, 61.
244 Cf. Auernheimer 2000: Ziele und Bedingungen interkultureller Bildung, 11; 1995: Einführung in die interkulturelle Erziehung, 168.
245 Rohr 2003: Interkulturelle Kompetenz, 517.

Elisabeth Rohr shows convincingly that intercultural competence must not be regarded as expert knowledge only, but is a skill which is highly relevant at different (including grass-roots) social levels in our globalising world. It involves reciprocal learning processes in which tolerance towards different and often ambiguous feelings of closeness and distance to others can be practised. What is most important is to learn to continue conversation, even if mutual understanding seems impossible at the time.[246]

2.3.2 Areas of intercultural learning

Intercultural education is a composite field which comprises a variety of aspects or sub-fields, such as political-, antiracist-, feminist-, (third- or) one-world-, international-, peace-, development-, human rights-, diversity- and environment education, social and global learning, education for Europe and education for the preservation of our world cultural heritage.[247] At the heart of all these aspects lies the question of how intercultural education can contribute to a fair, sustainable and future-oriented development.[248]

If the global world is considered the context for learning processes, intercultural education as part of a general education concentrating on key problems that are common to humankind necessarily has a political dimension and includes a critical analysis of imperialism and our global economic system. Furthermore, it may contribute to building up a political consciousness which includes a reflection of international relations and of the social structures within one's own country and awakening people's sensibility for structural violence and discrimination. If the political dimension of intercultural education is taken seriously, then important demands of antiracist criticism of multiculturalism have to be taken up. Intercultural or multicultural education has often focused on similarities, enjoyable and pleasant aspects of other cultures, such as food and folklore, and systematically excluded differences from consideration or even treated differences and conflicts as

---

246 Cf. Rohr 2003: Interkulturelle Kompetenz.
247 For lists of aspects of intercultural education see Hormel and Scherr 2004: Bildung für die Einwanderungsgesellschaft, 285, Nestvogel 2002: Zum Verhältnis von 'interkulturellem Lernen', 'globalem Lernen' und 'Bildung für eine nachhaltige Entwicklung', 31, Roth 2000: Allgemeine Didaktik, 46, Auernheimer 1997: Interkulturelle Pädagogik, 345, Fritzsche 1997: Multiperspektivität, 201.
248 Cf. Nestvogel 2002: Zum Verhältnis von 'interkulturellem Lernen', 'globalem Lernen' und 'Bildung für eine nachhaltige Entwicklung', 31.

taboo topics. Reflecting upon how to deal with collective concepts of otherness, stereotypes and prejudices, unconscious expectations and fears have to be an integral part of intercultural education in order to address structural as well as everyday racism. Here, it can help to equip people for responsibly dealing with this uneasiness caused by difference, on which everyday racism builds. Political and antiracist education strives for the ideal of non-hierarchical communication, even though this can only be realised partially in practice.[249]

Social learning includes learning to empathise and sympathise, to be respectful towards other ways of thinking and living, to co-operate, deal constructively with conflicts and to learn solidarity, which is a prerequisite for overcoming ethnocentrism and rivalry. In a long-term perspective, considering the respective developmental stages of the pupils, this involves a change of attitudes and learning to deal with the discrepancy between cognitive insights and spontaneous emotional responses, in which unconscious fears may be at work, fears which one thought to have already overcome. Children should be introduced to normative flexibility – as opposed to normative rigidity. In school, strategies should be learnt for practicing solidarity and sensitivity for people in outsider-situations. The close link between discrimination and poverty should be addressed, but awareness of the fact that sympathy may be or may become discrimination in disguise is also necessary.[250] Nestvogel draws attention to the fact that psychological factors also play an important role in intercultural processes and that both the social-interactive and the personal-interactive levels have to be considered. She highlights the importance of a global perspective in education but is sceptical about the continual introduction of new concepts (such as *global learning*) which partly overlap with other concepts and frequently remain rather vague. At any rate, what is meant by global learning, namely practising to look at phenomena from a global perspective, is an integral part of intercultural education, even though establishing a dualistic opposition of traditional vs. global learning is questionable and counterproductive.[251]

Educators have to become clear about their own *attitude towards cultural diversity*. Both idealisation and negation of differences are detrimental as they distort the real issues. An important step in intercultural

---

[249] Cf. Auernheimer 1997: Interkulturelle Pädagogik, 345, 351f.; 1995: Einführung in die interkulturelle Erziehung, 194ff.
[250] Auernheimer 1995: Einführung in die interkulturelle Erziehung, 171ff., Schmitt 1979: Kinder und Ausländer, 273f.
[251] Nestvogel 2002: Zum Verhältnis von 'interkulturellem Lernen', 'globalem Lernen' und 'Bildung für eine nachhaltige Entwicklung', 38f.

learning is the realisation that one's own position or way of life is but one among many. This decentralisation and relativisation of ethnocentric positions helps to understand the motivations of other people to act as they do. Auernheimer would like to free the term "syncretism" from its condescending connotations and regards it as a positive result of mutual acculturation. When different horizons merge, former coordinate systems are put into perspective and a new broader perspective and meta-communication are possible.[252]

Hormel and Scherr describe *diversity-perspectives* as a logically consistent continuation of a reflective intercultural education, which enable a critical distance to ethnicist or culturalist assumptions and static concepts of culture.[253] Diversity education starts from the breadth of distinctive categories, including social class and status, sex/gender, sexual orientation, ethnicity/nationality, race, age, language, religion, mental and physical health, handicap and regionality, which serve as reference points for identity constructs and possible causes of conflict and discrimination. It includes an acknowledgement of the difference between individuals and groups and of the ambiguous character of social identities with complex and situative variation. A self-reflective approach to identity constructs and a consideration of social and cultural environments and their interrelations with hegemonic structures helps to overcome simplistic notions of society, culture, social group, individuality and cultural identity.[254]

In intercultural education, *identity* is regarded as the product of increasingly self-reflective active processes, constructs and integrations. It is a life-long task to work on the idea of what one is and/or would like to be. This developmental process of life-long self-definition takes place in the context of interdependent relationships between individuals and their environments. Most concepts follow a middle path between psychoanalytic determination of the self and interactionistic dynamisation of identity.[255] Hormel and Scherr write that individuals are not identical with themselves. It is important to include heterogenic and dynamic elements in identity-constructs. The rhetoric of "cultural conditioning" is sometimes detrimental as it helps to keep up stereotypes and prejudice without leaving room for individual variation.[256] On the other hand, the concept of "cultural identity" is often used in self-interpretations. In modern societies, identity is not created by the

---

252 Cf. Auernheimer 1995: Einführung in die interkulturelle Erziehung, 181.
253 Hormel and Scherr 2004: Bildung für die Einwanderungsgesellschaft, 208, 205f.
254 Cf. ibid., 205-207.
255 Cf. Mertens 1999: Identität/Identitätsfindung, 269f.
256 Hormel and Scherr 2004: Bildung für die Einwanderungsgesellschaft, 205ff.

community, so every individual has to construct it. Identity constructs can be regarded as narratives, as modes of representation with a political aspect. Education has to support reflection upon and criticism of social constructions and borders and help in the process of building up one's own identity.[257] Personal identity is to be conceived of as an active and dynamic principle of individual personality. It is at the same time the starting point and product of a synthesis, an intersection between the individual and reality.[258]

It has become evident that *multiperspectivity* is an important aspect in different fields of intercultural learning. In order to overcome monocultural orientations, multiperspectivity, which strives for a consideration of the variety of positions, worldviews and arguments, needs to be established as a dimension of the curricula of various subjects. Auernheimer indicates the shortcomings of existent curricula in this respect and outlines how mulitperspectivity can be integrated into curricula for literature, language and religion. He mentions the potential of concepts for "interreligious" religious education from Great Britain and the Netherlands.[259] Fritzsche lists three areas in which multiperspectivity ought to be established: lesson planning, teaching material and the competences of the pupils. Unlike many other theorists of intercultural education, he does not seem to favour cultural "syncretism" (e.g. Auernheimer, see above) as a possible effect of intercultural encounters, because he explicitly rejects "multicultural patchworks".[260]

2.3.3 Intercultural education and educational systems

Comparative studies show, that intercultural education is embedded in the educational systems of different countries to very different extents. Several authors come to the conclusion that the German educational system is not as advanced as other countries like Great Britain, the USA or Canada when it comes to the realisation of intercultural learning as a dimension of school education. An integration of the different aspects of intercultural education in the German educational system is still

---

257 Cf. Auernheimer 1997: Interkulturelle Pädagogik, 249f.
258 Secco 1993: Interkulturelle Pädagogik, 28.
259 See Auernheimer 1995: Einführung in die interkulturelle Erziehung, 192-194.
260 Fritzsche 1997: Multiperspektivität, 201. Fritzsche also presents some considerations about a multiperspectval representation of Islam (198-200) in order to show how mutual fear can be reduced and modes of showing mutual respect can be established.

rather an "exotic playground"[261] than daily routine. In Germany, curricula are still widely monocultural or eurocentric, many teaching books are not multi-perspectival and minority languages scarcely receive any attention. The situation of religious education is unsatisfactory, as it privileges the two major Christian churches and produces segregated learning groups.

Auernheimer detects several structural problems which impede the implementation of intercultural learning in German schools: competitiveness, selection mechanisms and early decisions about careers, which already create pressure to do well in primary school, impede learning co-operation, conflict-management and a constructive approach to diversity. Homogenous learning groups are commonly regarded as a prerequisite for successful teaching and learning processes. Therefore, dealing with heterogeneity is often neither taught nor learnt.[262] The fact that our social system often contradicts its own stated principles is reflected in the educational system. As in the wider social context, in the educational system there is a discrepancy between the rhetoric of democratic self-understanding and the reality of politics and economics, which is often ignorant about inequality. Furthermore, different lobbies continue to promote competing tasks for the educational system, which range from an education for the labour market to critical theories of education as described above.[263] Education needs to provide room for reflection about these issues. Furthermore, intercultural education requires an adequate institutional framework, otherwise it is corrupted from the very beginning and cannot be much more than lip service to idealised principles without any basis in reality.

Hormel and Scherr suggest a particular strategy for the implementation of intercultural education on the following levels: (1) legal and political frameworks, (2) schools as organisations and institutions, (3) professional development and teacher training as well as (4) pedagogical concepts and curricula.[264] Schools need to have a transparent educational philosophy. So far, this philosophy often remains unarticulated and reflects the interests of dominant groups. There has to be an explicit basic consensus, which needs to be discussed and reconsidered from time to time. Furthermore, the educational philosophy has to be consistent with pedagogical programmes and the school structure. This

---

261 Roth 2000: Allgemeine Didaktik, 48. Cf. also Hormel and Scherr 2004: 284f., Auernheimer 2000: Ziele und Bedingungen interkultureller Bildung, 12f.
262 Auernheimer 2000: Ziele und Bedingungen interkultureller Bildung, 12f.
263 Cf. Hormel and Scherr 2004: Bildung für die Einwanderungsgesellschaft, 34, 283. Auernheimer 2000: Ziele und Bedingungen interkultureller Bildung, 12f.
264 Hormel and Scherr 2004: Bildung für die Einwanderungsgesellschaft, 285.

means, for example, an adequate representation of minorities among teachers and heads and self-reflexivity among the pedagogical personnel. Multiculturalism ought to be visible in school. Impacts of the social climate of the school are further starting points for critical assessment of present structures. Pressure for achievement, competition and asymmetric teacher-student-relationships may act as a counterproductive hidden curriculum which corrupts the principles stated in the formal curricula. A good social climate can be established by symmetric and trustful teacher-student relationships, a culture of open doors, transparent decisions and participation of the pupils. This may help to prevent the hidden curricula of discrimination and segregation from taking effect. Extra-curricular activities like workshops, clubs, theatre groups etc., in which co-operation and living together can be learnt in a relaxed atmosphere, can also help to improve the social climate. These activities may also include learning at different places – also outside school – and cooperation with various groups of the community.[265]

An integration of intercultural learning requires reflection about the role of multiculturalism for every individual school. "Monitoring" is a helpful means of avoiding institutional discrimination, for example with respect to recommendations for secondary or special schools or decisions about moving a pupil up to the next year. Furthermore, mediation and supervision are effective ways of methodical democratic conflict resolution which ought to be integrated into school life. If teachers are to provide models of intercultural competence and enable meta-communication, teacher training also needs to be reformed so that teacher trainees actually get a chance to acquire these skills themselves and to build up a wide repertoire of methods.[266]

Intercultural education, which can be regarded as a touchstone for the quality of educational institutions,[267] is not a distinct pedagogical discipline but should be part of all educational processes. It is a basic educational perspective, a principle of all didactic planning and reflection. A diversity perspective ought to be a cross-section perspective for different themes and topics for schools, universities, further and adult education, altogether a continuous element of education as such.[268]

---

[265] Cf., e.g., Auernheimer 2000: Ziele und Bedingungen interkultureller Bildung, 13f., Hormel and Scherr 2004: Bildung für die Einwanderungsgesellschaft, 185.
[266] Cf. Auernheimer 2000: Ziele und Bedingungen interkultureller Bildung, 15.
[267] Auernheimer 1997: Interkulturelle Pädagogik, 353.
[268] Cf., e.g., Binder and Daryabegi 2003: Interkulturelles Lernen, 34ff, Reich 2000: 47, Hormel and Scherr 2004: Bildung für die Einwanderungsgesellschaft, 36, 232, Auernheimer 1997: Interkulturelle Pädagogik, 346.

Chapter II
Integrative Religious Education in England

Introduction

This chapter is mainly about recent academic concepts for RE in English state schools in the context of the history and organisation of English integrative RE. Therefore, it is by no means a comprehensive survey of integrative RE in England, but restricts itself to a certain set of questions concerning academic concepts for RE. Other important aspects of RE, for example, details of teacher training at different universities or colleges, a close analysis of a wide range of teaching material or empirical research in classrooms have not been part of my study, even though visits to teacher training institutions, observations in classrooms, interviews with lecturers, teachers and teacher trainees have complemented my study of academic literature on the subject.

As my interest in this study is particularly in concepts for integrative RE as defined in the introduction, other topics, for example, *collective worship*, which is a very interesting aspect of English school life, are also deliberately excluded here. The topics described in the section on history and organisation of integrative RE in England (II.1) were selected for their relevance to current academic approaches to RE (II.2).

1 History and organisation of integrative RE in England

1.1 History of integrative RE

This section will give an overview of important stages in the history of integrative RE in England. After an outline of the developments until the 1960s, the preconditions for the establishment of integrative RE (1.1.1), special attention will be given to Ninian Smart's approach to RE, which has considerably influenced integrative RE, particularly in its early years but to some extent up to the present (1.1.2). Furthermore, the role of the *Shap Working Party for World Religions in Education* for the development of integrative RE will be discussed (1.1.3).

1.1.1 Developments until the 1960s

Until the mid-1960s, RE in England was about Christianity only. The educational system in England and Wales has its roots in church activities. From the beginning of the 19th century, churches founded schools, trained teachers and organised the school curriculum. Since 1833, the state contributed to the expenses of church schools and took over some of the responsibility for the schools. The first state schools were founded in the 1870s when the increase in population made it impossible for the churches to deal with the need for education on their own. In the following years, church and state schools existed in an integrated system which was administered by local education authorities.[1]

In the 1870 Education Act, RE is defined as Christian RE, however, not as denominational instruction. The so-called Cowper-Temple Clause states that "no religious catechism or religious formulary which is distinctive of any particular denomination shall be taught in the school."[2] Parents are allowed to withdraw their child from RE. The 1944 Education Act transfers the responsibility for RE from the churches to the state, which means, for example, that RE teachers do not need approval from the church any longer. The 1944 Act requires RE to be based on a syllabus which is agreed upon by different parties in the following way: the Local Education Authority (LEA) convenes an agreed syllabus conference, which consists of four committees with representatives of (1) the Church of England, (2) other denominations, (3) the LEA and (4) teacher's organisations.[3] This conference has to agree upon a syllabus – hence the term *agreed syllabus* – for *Religious Instruction*, as the subject was called at the time. This agreed syllabus is obligatory for all schools for which the LEA is responsible. First versions of agreed syllabuses have existed since the early 1920s.[4]

In the 1960s, several scholars questioned the way religious instruction was practiced in schools at the time, with a clear focus on the study of biblical texts. The ideas of Harold Loukes and Ronald Goldman were particularly influential. Loukes, who studied religious questions and attitudes among youths, intended to make RE more relevant to the interests of the pupils by dealing with problems with which human be-

---

1 Cf. Barnes and Kay 1999: Developments in Religious Education, 23f.
2 Jackson 2000: Law, politics and RE, 87.
3 In Wales there were only three committees, as the Church in Wales did not form a committee of its own but was represented in the committee made up of religious denominations, cf. ibid.
4 Cf. Jackson 2000: Law, politics and RE, 87.

ings are inevitably confronted, such as questions of responsibility or the meaning of suffering and death. In his book *Teenage Religion* (1961), Loukes describes his "life-centred" or "problem-centred" approach to RE.

Goldman transferred Jean Piaget's theory about different stages of psychological development of children to RE and observed that the progress of the pupils in acquiring conceptual knowledge is dependent on the stages of their development. In his book *Religious Thinking from Childhood to Adolescence* (1964), Goldman follows Piaget's ideas and identifies three main stages of cognitive development among pupils between the ages of 6 and 17: *intuitive thinking, concrete operational thinking* and *formal operational thinking*. Before children have reached the stage of *formal operational thinking*, Goldman finds, they misunderstand biblical texts, for example by concentrating on minor aspects of a story, which inhibits their understanding of the main idea. Therefore, he concludes, dealing with biblical texts makes sense only from a certain age onwards. Goldman elaborates on this theory in his book *Readiness for Religion* (1965) in which he compares readiness for learning about religion with readiness for learning to read, write or count, which seems to emerge among most children in a certain phase of their development. Young pupils ought to explore "life themes", for example, "shepherds", "water" and "light". Goldman regards this as a basis for a later understanding of the figurative meaning of these words in biblical texts. Attention to the lives of the pupils, which scholars like Loukes and Goldman propagated, gained great popularity and resulted in a reconsideration of the contents of RE. However, a much more important change in RE, the transformation of Christian religious instruction to education about world religions, also began in the 1960s.

1.1.2 Ninian Smart's phenomenological approach to RE

The establishment of the study of religions at British universities brought about a reassessment of school RE from a different angle. Ninian Smart, professor of the then young subject "Religious Studies" at the University of Lancaster and chair of the *Schools Council Project on RE in Secondary Schools*, criticises confessional RE in a society which is to a great extent secular and plural. He calls for an objective RE about the world's religions – analogous to the academic study of religions. Smart emphasises the unity of the educational system, in which it is unnecessary "to draw a line between the logic of religious studies at one level of age as opposed to another."[5] Smart's phenomenological approach to RE, which he regards as an alternative to confessional RE, is outlined in his *Secular Education and the Logic of Religion* (1968) and in the *Working Paper 36* (1971) of the Schools Council.

Smart understands phenomenological RE as an initiation of the children into understanding religion and engaging them in questions about the truth and value of religion.[6] This may be attained by a combination of an explicit and an implicit approach. On the one hand, children may deal with the explicit phenomena of religions – including a consideration of the intentions behind the visible phenomena –, on the other hand, they may acquire a consciousness of implicitly religious ultimate questions. RE ought to be determined by the nature of the subject matter. Smart regards religions as consisting of six mutually dependent dimensions: the doctrinal, mythological, ethical, ritual, experiential and social dimensions.[7] This model of religions can be the basis for a compilation of relevant facts about religions, which may be looked at from a historical-descriptive perspective. "Parahistorical" questions, which pertain to the truth and value of religions, can however also be addressed in RE.

Smart distinguishes between the terms *religion* and *religious*. He regards the six dimensions which were mentioned above as formal characteristics of any religion. This model of religions is open in the sense that it includes secular worldviews such as Maoism or Marxism. Religious questions, for example, "Why do men suffer?", "Why does anything exist at all?" or "What lies beyond death?", have to do with the meaning and purpose of human existence. They can be distinguished from non-religious questions by their degree of depth, dealing with ultimate meaning and values.[8] What follows for RE is that it is concerned with religions and values, in a plural, non-dogmatic way. Non-dogmatic teaching can be understood as "teaching how" as opposed to "teaching that", which happens in religious instruction. The teacher is above all a teacher and not a representative of a religious institution. He or she is committed to education and to being an empathic educator. This does not mean that he or she may not express his/her own re-

---

5   Smart 1968: Secular Education and the Logic of Religion, 96.
6   Ibid., 105.
7   Ibid., 15ff; See also Smart 1975: What is religion?, 14-16.
8   Smart 1975: What is religion?, 16ff. Smart refers to Paul Tillich's concept of "ultimate concern", but rejects Tillich's idea that ultimacy is absolute and rather regards ultimacy as a matter of degree of depth (ibid., 18f).

ligious view. However, this must not result in distortions of or a lack of openness for other positions.[9]

Education in general, not only RE – here Smart addresses similarities between the school subjects RE and history – ought to transcend the informative. For RE this means a school-appropriate introduction to the study of religions, "to give people the capacity to understand religious phenomena, to discuss sensitively religious claims, to see interrelations between religions and society and so forth."[10] RE ought to include a careful evaluation of various positions. Before pupils can form their own opinions about different religions, they have to understand the ideas of these religions. For this purpose, narrow theological concepts of RE are as inadequate as intellectualist devaluations of religion. Religions and cultures cannot be approached merely from the outside. The insider perspective has to be taken into account, one has to enter into dialogue with different positions, as in discussions about philosophical questions.[11]

Teaching material should not be religious itself. In the selection of religions to be presented in RE, the cultural and religious environment of the pupils ought to be considered. If this means that dealing with Christianity continues to be a dominant aspect of RE in Britain, care has to be taken that the general character of RE is acceptable to Christians and non-Christians, religious and non-religious people alike. The examples which Smart gives for possible topics in RE show that he has, above all, the so-called "world religions" and secular ideologies in mind. They may be studied *thematically* (comparing themes from different traditions) or *systematically* (dealing with the individual religions separately).[12] Moral education, which was traditionally understood as a task of RE, is not a responsibility of RE alone, but a task for the school in general. RE is not committed to the values of any particular tradition. It can, however, contribute to moral education by dealing with the relationships between moral ideas or problems and religious belief.[13]

Smart uses the word "phenomenological" in a particular way. He avoids many of the weaknesses of the classical phenomenology of religion. He uses the ideas of empathy and of preliminarily bracketing one's own presuppositions about truth and value from "the phenomenologi-

---

9   Cf. Smart 1968: Secular Education and the Logic of Religion, 95f.
10 Ibid., 96.
11 See ibid., 104 and 93f. Smart clarifies what he means with reference to Plato's philosophy and how this could be discussed in school.
12 Cf., e.g., Schools Council 1971: Working Paper No. 36, 83f.
13 Cf. ibid., 67-70.

cal method". He does not, however, presuppose universal essences which may be inferred from a study or experience of the concrete phenomena. Smart talks about the "nature" of religion in general but, unlike many phenomenologists, he does not define this nature from an insider-perspective but with his formal multidimensional model. A fair evaluation of his approach requires a consideration of the context in which he wrote. At a time in which the study of religions was emancipating itself from the classical phenomenology of religion, Smart uses particularly those aspects of phenomenology for his concept of integrative RE, which were still acceptable later.

The very name "phenomenological RE" exposed Smart's approach to various kinds of criticism, even though these can often not be applied to his approach directly. Comprehensive and generally justified criticism of the phenomenology of religion, for example, referring to the "phenomenological understanding of the nature of religion, its implicit confessionalism, and its 'non-reductionist' account of religious truth and authenticity"[14], can only partially – if at all – be applied to Smart's model of phenomenological RE. Furthermore, other approaches, which lacked Smart's sensibility for the subject matter and applied stereotypically simplified versions of his six dimensional model of religion, were also labelled "phenomenological" and gave rise to justified criticism. Again, these criticisms are only partially – if at all – applicable to Smart's original model.[15] Another point of confusion emerged from the polarisation of *confessional RE* vs. *phenomenological RE*. This polarisation resulted in criticism of phenomenological approaches to RE being interpreted as a general criticism of non-confessional RE, as if these two models were the only alternatives for RE in schools.

1.1.3 The Shap Working Party for World Religions in Education

In 1969, when religions other than Christianity were hardly taught in RE in England, the Department of Adult Education of the University of Newcastle organised a conference in a hotel near the village of Shap in the Lake District, where the *Shap Working Party for World Religions in*

---

14 Barnes 2000: Ninian Smart and the phenomenological approach to RE, 325.
15 Cf. ibid., 316, see also Jackson 1997: Religious Education. An Interpretive Approach, 10ff.

Education (Shap) [16] was founded in order to bring together people who have expertise in both religious studies and RE and to encourage the study and teaching of world religions on the different levels of the educational system. This aim was achieved mainly by the gradual transformation of RE in England and Wales into integrative RE. Another important commitment of Shap, the provision of accurate information for people who are professionally involved with RE, Religious Studies or work with different religious communities, continues to be important today. Members of Shap have different religious backgrounds and come from different levels of the educational system. Shap is a forum in which experts from Religious Studies and RE meet. Their main concern is to understand religious beliefs and practices, and their meaning for the life of believers in particular.[17]

Shap issues the annual journal *World Religions in Education*, which elucidates – from different perspectives – topics relevant to integrative RE, e.g. "Time" (2000/1), "Can I teach your religion?" (1999/2000), "Faith, values and religious education" (1998/9), "Who am I?" (1997/8), "Exploring conflict and reconciliation: issues for religious education" (1996/7), "From syllabuses to schemes – planning and teaching in religious education" (1995/6), "Exploring loss, grief and change" (1994/5), "Exploring journeys" (1993/4), "Religion and truth" (1992/3), "Religious education and the creative arts" (1991/2). The journal also contains reviews of recent publications which are relevant to teaching world religions and recently a supplement for primary school teachers of RE was added. Very popular is the *Calendar of Religious Festivals*, also published by Shap. In 1986, Shap published the book *Festivals in World Religions*[18] in order to provide more information about religious festivals than can be included in the annual calendar.

Another well-known publication by Shap is the teacher's manual *Teaching World Religions* (1993),[19] which deals with world religions in the curriculum, the points of view of faith traditions – including small traditions like Rastafarianism or New Age spirituality – and how they can be included in school RE. The *Shap Handbook on World Religions in*

---

16 Thus, Shap is not an acronym, but refers to the place where the working party was founded. In the following, the name *Shap Working Party for World Religions in Education* will be referred to by the common abbreviation *Shap*.
17 See Shap's mission statement, published in every volume of the journal *World Religions in Education*, e.g. 1999/2000: vi, or on its website (http://www.shap.org).
18 Woodward 1986: Festivals in World Religions, revised edition by RMEP 1998.
19 Erricker et al. 1993: Teaching World Religions.

Education (1987)[20] comprises articles about RE methodology, a list of resources for different religions (among them Baha'ism, Humanism, Jainism and Primal/"Tribal" religions) as well as short chapters on new religious movements and ideas and examples for classroom-situations. The book *Religions and Education. Shap Working Party 1969-1989* (1989)[21] is helpful when it comes to forming an impression of the work and aims of Shap. Again, it contains contributions to individual religions and teaching methods, further articles on multifaith themes, for example, "Worldview analysis: a way of looking at our field" by Ninian Smart or "Women and religion" by Ursula King.[22]

An important Shap initiative, the *Chichester Project* (cf. chapter II.2.8), is concerned with the representation of Christianity within integrative RE. When RE in England and Wales gradually became education about world religions, a new perspective on teaching Christianity within this changed framework was required. The publications by the *Chichester Project* provided models for the representation of Christianity in agreed syllabuses.

Shap regularly holds conferences and members meet annually. Although these meetings have also been attended by experts from Scotland, a distinct Scottish branch of Shap, *The Scottish Working Party on Religions of the World in Education*, was founded, as the Scottish RE system was found to be too different from the English and Welsh one. Recently, a European branch of Shap was also founded. The *European Association for World Religions in Education* (EAWRE) publishes a calendar of religious festivals – based on the Shap model – in English, French and German.[23]

Even though Shap has undoubtedly achieved many of its aims already, two of the tasks that still remain are to continually provide reliable information and to encourage the production of teaching material about world religions. Looking back on 30 years of Shap history, John Rankin describes the spirit in which this work has been and ought to be done: "Shap ... has always had a propaganda function, and needs to go on convincing the doubters about the positive value of understanding

---

20 Brown 1987: The Shap Handbook on World Religions in Education.
21 Wood 1989: Religions and Education. Shap Working Party 1969-89.
22 Smart 1989: Worldview analysis: a way of looking at our field, King 1989: Women and world Religions.
23 See e.g. EAWRE 2006: *Kalender der Feste der Religionen* for the German version of the calendar for 2006.

religion and teaching young people to have respect and insight into the religious beliefs of others."[24]

Apart from the aspects described in this chapter, changing syllabuses also contributed to the transformation of RE in England into an integrative approach. Before the publication of national model syllabuses in 1994, locally agreed syllabuses considerably shaped the character of RE in the different areas of England and Wales. Therefore, the next section pays particular attention to the influence of agreed syllabuses (1.2.1) before discussing the standardising effects of the national model syllabuses (1.2.2). The section also provides an outline of the legal situation (1.2.3) and basic information about teacher training (1.2.4).

1.2 Organisation of integrative RE

1.2.1 Agreed syllabuses

RE in England and Wales is organised locally. The *Local Education Authority* (LEA) convenes a conference, the *Standing Advisory Council for Religious Education* (SACRE), which is responsible for the RE syllabus for the area under the authority of the LEA. In England, this committee consists of representatives of four groups: the Church of England, other religions and denominations, teachers and the LEA. In Wales there are only three groups, one for all religions together, one for teachers and one for the LEA. In meetings that are open to the public, the representatives of these groups draw up a syllabus which has to be approved by each of the groups. This "agreed syllabus" is obligatory for all schools under the responsibility of the LEA.[25]

The first "multifaith" syllabus was created in Birmingham in 1975.[26] Other than in traditional Christian RE, this syllabus propagates a descriptive and existential approach to world religions. Furthermore, it includes non-religious worldviews, for example, Humanism or Communism. After Birmingham, more multifaith agreed syllabuses followed and when the Swann Report *Education for All*, which claimed

---

24 Rankin 1999: 30 Years On..., 16.
25 For the procedure of drawing up agreed syllabuses cf., e.g., Hull 2002: Der Segen der Säkularität, 170f.; Jackson 2000: Law, politics and religious education in England and Wales, 87; Lankshear 2000: Religious Education in England and Wales, 56.
26 See Hull 1994: Geschichte und Entwicklung des Lehrplans für den Religionsunterricht in Birmingham, Copley 1997: Teaching Religion. Fifty Years of Religious Education in England and Wales, 197f.

that multireligious[27] RE is the adequate kind of RE for a multicultural society, was published in 1985, many LEAs already had multifaith syllabuses, not only in urban areas with multicultural schools like e.g. Bradford (1983), but also in more rural areas like e.g. Hampshire (1978) and Berkshire (1982).

Thus, in a movement from the bottom to the top, by means of changed agreed syllabuses, the transformation from Christian to integrative RE took place in an increasing number of LEAs, before it was formally legalised in the 1988 *Education Reform Act* (ERA). This act, which was preceded by a great deal of debate, comprised the explicit inclusion of different religions in the second group and the claim that any new syllabus "shall reflect the fact that the religious traditions in Great Britain are in the main Christian, whilst taking account of the teaching and practices of the other principal religions represented in Great Britain".[28] With another Education Act in 1993, all LEAs which had not yet produced a new agreed syllabus after the 1988 ERA were asked to do so. Furthermore, the 1993 Act requires SACRE meetings to be open to the public, agreed syllabuses to be revised every five years and the agreed syllabus conference to reflect the local religious landscape.[29]

Agreed syllabuses often have the following structure: the members of the SACRE are listed at the beginning or the end. The second group with the representatives of "other religions and denominations" is normally the biggest group. Often it also includes smaller religious groups like e.g. the Baha'i and representatives of secular worldviews like Humanism among the "world religions". The introduction normally provides information about the character of the subject, above all about the secular nature of RE as a subject in which pupils may learn about and from different religions and are encouraged to form and critically reflect upon their own opinions. The Oxfordshire Agreed Syllabus (1999), for example, states:

> "There is a clear distinction between the role of the faith communities in nurturing pupils in a religion and the role of the school in teaching pupils to reflect on religion in its many forms in the world. Religious Education

---

27 In fact, the report uses the term "phenomenological RE". For the temporary identification of integrative or (to use the common English term) multifaith RE with phenomenological RE cf. also section 1.1.2.
28 ERA 1988, section 8.3, quoted in Hull 1989: The Act Unpacked, 9.
29 Cf. Jackson 2000: Law, politics and religious education in England and Wales, 91f.

seeks to develop an awareness of the variety of human responses to life's key experiences."[30]

Frequently, the educational character of the subject is emphasised, for example, in the Kirklees Agreed Syllabus (1995):

> "If Religious Education is to have a proper place and status within the school curriculum it must be justified on educational rather than on religious grounds ... Religious Education is the education of young people about religion. We need to help them to learn how the lives of believers are affected by religion, faith and spiritual experience ..."[31]

Thereafter, an outline of the legal framework for RE often follows, which reflects in particular the relevant sections of the 1988 ERA. The aims of RE are also stated in the introduction. After the model syllabuses by the *School Curriculum and Assessment Authority* (SCAA) were published in 1994, the two aims *(learning about religions* and *learning from religion)*[32] which are given in the model syllabuses are often mentioned as general aims in the agreed syllabuses and then further specified. Frequently, the explicit and implicit dimensions of RE are linked to the aims, for example, in the list of aims stated by the following agreed syllabuses:

Bradford 1992:
- understanding and evaluating values, commitments and questions of meaning
- knowledge, understanding and evaluation of religious belief and practice

Devon 1992:
- reflection on meaning
- knowledge and understanding of religion[33]

---

30 Oxfordshire 1999: 1.
31 Kirklees 1995: 1.
32 The use of the singular or plural for "religion(s)" in statements of the attainment targets (AT) vary in different syllabuses. While the model syllabuses of 1994 use the plural for AT1 ("learning about religions"), the QCA non-statutory national framework of 2004 uses the singular ("learning about religion"). Often the question of whether the singular or plural should be used is related to the discussion of whether religions should be studied "thematically" (i.e. comparatively) or "systematically" (i.e. one after another). For this discussion, see Wright 1997: Mishmash, religionism and theological literacy, 143ff.
33 The aims of RE in the Devon and Bradford syllabuses are quoted in Copley 1997: 170f.

Oxfordshire 1999:
- to be aware of and respond to life experiences and the questions they raise
- knowledge and understanding of religious beliefs and practices
- evaluation of the significance of religious concepts, beliefs and practices by being able to express personal opinions based on the use of appropriate evidence and argument.[34]

Among the main aims, like knowledge and understanding of different religions and reflection on questions of life, meaning and value, many syllabuses mention the spiritual, moral, cultural and social development of the pupils[35] as well as further aims, like developing a positive awareness of one's own worth[36] or "a positive attitude towards other people and their right to hold beliefs different from their own, and to living in a religiously diverse society."[37]

Some SACREs explicitly state what RE is not about, for example, personal statements the pupils prefer to keep to themselves or evaluations of the beliefs and values of the pupils as "right" or "wrong",[38] and emphasise that RE neither propagates nor undermines any religious tradition.[39] After a statement of the aims of RE, some syllabuses list the skills that pupils are expected to acquire in RE. These are often quoted from the model syllabuses. Many syllabuses give recommendations about which religions to deal with at which key stage. Following the legal requirements, every key stage[40] includes a study of Christianity as well as two other "major religions" represented in Great Britain. Dealing with more religions or worldviews is recommended, particularly for thematic approaches.[41]

The main part of the syllabuses normally comprises keyword lists with aspects of the individual religions which are recommended to be studied at the respective key stages. The syllabuses are structured

---

34 Oxfordshire 1999: 5f.
35 E.g. Hertfordshire 1995: 5, Kirklees 1995: 2.
36 Kirklees 1995: 2, cf. also The London Borough of Redbridge 1995: 12.
37 Kirklees 1995: 2, cf. also e.g. Birmingham 1995: 3, Warwickshire 1996: 1 and Hertfordshire 1995: 5.
38 Birmingham 1999: 10.
39 The London Borough of Redbridge 1995: 12.
40 The different key stages (KS) are: KS 1 (year 1 and 2, age 5-7), KS 2 (year 3-6, age 7-11), KS 3 (year 7-9, age 11-14), KS 4 (year 10 and 11, age 14-16). Year 12 and 13 are informally called KS 5 or "post 16" education (former upper sixth form); cf. Copley 1997: Teaching Religion. Fifty Years of Religious Education in England and Wales, xiii; Jackson 1997: Religious Education. An Interpretive Approach, 119.
41 See e.g. Oxfordshire 1999: 15.

around a set of topics, which are different in the individual syllabuses. The main part of the Birmingham syllabus (1995), for example, has the following structure: (1) making sense of the world, (2) living together, (3) following guidance, (4) expressing meaning, belief and value, (5) marking special times, places and events. These topics are related to the attainment targets learning about religions – "knowing and understanding" – and learning from religions – "questioning, evaluating, applying".[42] The Kirklees syllabus deals with the topics (1) belief, (2) people, (3) practice and (4) influences. For each key stage (with an increasing level of abstractness) some aspects of the religions are listed in relation to these topics. This structure is also used for the last key stage, in which the religions are meant to be studied comparatively.[43] The Warwickshire syllabus (1996) identifies three areas of learning which should be covered in any teaching unit:

(1) "The development of awareness of the spiritual and moral dimensions of life experiences and the identification of questions and issues they raise."[44] This aspect comprises a study of experiences of the natural world and experiences in human relationships.
(2) "The development of knowledge and understanding of belief and practice in religious traditions and other value systems,"[45] including devotion and meditation, celebration, lifestyle, authority and expression of belief.
(3) "Exploring, reflecting and responding",[46] including a reflection about the topics of the aspects (1 and 2), which may serve as starting point for further reflection.

The Redbridge syllabus (1995) is called "Exploration & Response". It identifies these two processes in relation to religion and human experiences as the dynamic of RE, which is meant to enable the pupils to develop four capacities: to gain knowledge and understanding of religions and human experiences from which fundamental questions of belief and value arise (exploring); to raise questions about belief and value, to evaluate issues of belief and value, and to relate knowledge and understanding to their own outlook and experience (responding).[47] This teaching programme is then allocated to six learning areas at each

---

42 Birmingham 1995.
43 Kirklees 1995.
44 Warwickshire 1996: structure 2.
45 Ibid., 3.
46 Ibid., 5.
47 The London Borough of Redbridge 1995: 13.

KS: (1) special times, places and events, (2) lifestyle and community, (3) nature and the world, (4) awareness of self and others, (5) expressing meaning, belief and value, (6) sources of authority. Most syllabuses are structured like the above examples for key stages 1-4. Key stage 5 (post-16 RE) syllabuses often consist of thematic modules, e.g. religion and science, sexuality and religion, death, evil and suffering, religion and art or forms of religious experience.[48]

Some syllabuses include a chapter on resources for RE, e.g. addresses of religious communities, places that can be visited, religious items, books or internet resources.[49] Frequently, a glossary, which explains important concepts of the individual religions as well as terms for the description of religious phenomena, is provided at the end of a syllabus.

1.2.2 The model syllabuses of the School Curriculum and Assessment Authority

In 1994, the *School Curriculum and Assessment Authority* (SCAA) published model syllabuses and required agreed syllabus conferences and teacher trainees to have knowledge of these. *Model 1: Living Faiths Today* is structured around knowledge and understanding of what it means to belong to a religious community and *Model 2: Questions and Teachings* is structured around knowledge and understanding of the teachings of religions and their relation to shared human experience. These two models are for key stages 1-4, another publication is concerned with post 16 RE. *The Faith Communities' Working Group Reports* is a brochure about six religions, based on the work of members of religious communities and experts for the respective religious communities.

Model 1 and 2 have a common introduction which outlines the legal framework for RE, including the non-conversion clause of the 1944 Education Act (section 26.2) and the relevant sections of ERA 1988. After this, aims for RE, regarded as reflecting a "broad consensus about the subject's educational rationale and purpose"[50] are stated. The aims may be summarised under three main points:

(1) knowledge and understanding of religions

---

48 Cf. for example Oxfordshire 1999.
49 The Warwickshire syllabus, for example, has 11 pages on resources.
50 SCAA 1994: Model 1, 4.

(2) respect for other beliefs; a positive attitude towards other people and life in a pluralistic society
(3) promotion of the spiritual, ethical, cultural and social development of the pupils

In fact, these three aims recur in the debate about integrative RE in England. However, they reflect individual aims of concepts for RE, which sometimes cannot – as Judith Everington shows – be easily integrated into one single coherent approach.[51] In an RE which aims at promoting knowledge and understanding of religions, the representation of religions may be different from an RE which seeks to promote intercultural respect and harmony. The latter may be liable to give a "purified" or domesticated account of religions, avoiding controversial issues.[52] In a concept focusing on the spiritual, ethical, cultural and social development of the pupils (like the "a gift to the child" approach), the representation of religions is dependent on this aim and therefore different again. Everington claims that each of these aims can only be followed at the cost of the others. Therefore, a decision should be taken about which of the aims is regarded as most important.[53] As can be seen, the question about the aims of RE is far from being settled and influences many current debates about what RE ought to be like.

The model syllabuses recommend including the following two main attainment targets in any agreed syllabus:[54]

(1) learning about religions
(2) learning from religion

These attainment targets reflect the two main strands of English RE, descriptive and existential approaches. Attainment target 1 is mainly about understanding religions, attainment target 2 is about reflecting upon religious questions. These attainment targets are related to the following skills and abilities to be fostered in RE: investigation, interpretation, reflection, empathy, evaluation, analysis, synthesis,[55] applica-

---

51 Everington 2000: Mission Impossible? Religious Education in the 1990s.
52 Cf. Wright's criticism of the "liberal consensus" in English RE (see chapter II.2.5 and particularly Wright 1993: RE in Secondary Schools, chapter 4), cf. also Everington 2000: Mission Impossible? Religious Education in the 1990s, 188f.
53 Everington 2000: Mission Impossible? Religious Education in the 1990s, 193.
54 SCAA 1994: Model 1, 7.
55 While the other skills are perfectly acceptable in secular integrative RE, "synthesis", further specified as "linking significant features of religions together in a coherent pattern" and "connecting different aspects of life into a meaningful whole" (SCAA

tion and expression. Among the attitudes to be promoted, respect, care and concern are mentioned, which ought to be at the heart of all school activities, furthermore commitment, fairness, self-understanding and enquiry.[56]

After this introduction, the model syllabuses are structured according to the individual key stages (1-4) with short suggestions about how to learn about and from religions at any particular stage. Intended learning outcomes related to the attainment targets are also given for each key stage. At any of the key stages, dealing with Christianity and one other world religion is suggested. Model 1 gives keywords for dealing with the individual religions at any key stage with respect to

- **knowledge and understanding**, e.g. for Buddhism at KS 1:[57] the life of the Buddha (being human, not divine; a prince who gave up his wealth for the search for truth; how he reached perfection), the moral teaching of the Buddha (kindness and compassion, generosity, truthfulness and patience; not hurting any living thing, no stealing or telling lies), the Buddhist community (lives out the teachings of the Buddha; made up of ordained monks, nuns, priests and lay people; all members support each other).

- **possible learning experiences for the pupils related to attainment target 1**, e.g. for Buddhism at KS 1: e.g. listening to or reading stories about the life of Siddhartha Gautama; hearing what the Buddha taught about the way people should treat one another; watching a film about Buddhist monks in Great Britain or other parts of the world.

- **possible learning experiences for the pupils related to attainment target 2**, e.g. for Buddhism at KS 1: e.g. talking about one's own ideas of the perfect person; talking about how people show kindness to one another; thinking about instances when we hurt people or animals, steal and tell lies, and about why people believe these things are wrong; identifying people in our society who have different roles.

1994: Model 1, 5), seems to imply a religious character of RE. For further considerations on this issue see chapter IV, section 1.2.1.

56 Cf. SCAA 1994: Model 1, 7f.
57 See ibid., 15 for the list of keywords, from which the following points (also for learning experiences) are selected.

Model 2 relates – in similar tabular and keyword style – knowledge and understanding of religions to shared human experience. For Buddhism at KS 1, for example, reflection on the following topics relating to the Buddha, Buddhist teaching and the Buddhist community is suggested:[58]

- **Buddha – wise teacher**: wise people in the pupils' lives or in the stories they read; what a good teacher does; the signs of a good person.

- **Buddhist teaching – values**: the need for rules in everyday life; how we show kindness to each other; how people hurt each other, and how that feels; why stealing and lying are wrong; other things which are wrong.

- **The Buddhist community – following the example of the Buddha**: different communities to which the pupils belong; how they look after each other in school and at home; people who wear different clothes to show that they do a special task.

Note that these examples of the representation of Buddhism in the SCAA model syllabuses are for KS 1, i.e. for five to seven year-old children. The complexity of the tasks for the pupils rises with the key stages. [59]

---

58 See SCAA 1994: Model 2, 18, which also quotes the "knowledge and understanding of Buddhism (1)" section of Model 1.
59 Thus, the suggested topics for KS 4 (14 years and older) require a far more detailed study of Buddhism and Buddhist teachings (model 1), including for example the "diversity of different images which reflect the variety of Buddhist schools of thought"; Buddhist teachings, e.g. texts like the Dhammapada, Metta Sutta or the Lotus Sutra, or "the three signs of being/ marks of existence" (anicca, dukkha, anatta); Buddhist attitudes to contemporary issues, e.g. the environment, peace and conflict; and Buddhism in the 20th century, e.g. the sangha in different countries, adaptation to Western society, new movements in the East and West, practical works such as, for example, peace movements, prison chaplains, hospitals and hospices. The "key ideas and questions arising from human experience" in relation to Buddhism (model 2) which pupils are encouraged to think about at KS 4 include, for example, the value of concentration, the power of art to convey beauty and uplift us; the purpose of life, human destiny, "what happens at death?", the possibility of immortality, the nature of truth; issues involved in practising a minority religion, community – shared values, why people who belong to the same religion have different beliefs and traditions. See SCAA 1994: Model 1, 62 and Model 2, 54.

The key achievement of the model syllabuses was an establishment of a co-operation with different religious communities at a national level. However, these two model syllabuses have had a serious impact on recent agreed syllabuses and contributed to the disappearance of other approaches. Furthermore, being very similar to each other, they have manifested the idea of dealing with the religions separately rather than comparatively, and the way religious traditions are represented in these models tends to the essentialist.[60] Many RE professionals have taken a critical view of these developments and one group even published an alternative model syllabus which identifies supporting pupils in their search for meaning and purpose in life as the main aim of RE, which they claim cannot be attained with a curriculum that centres on the religions.[61]

In 1995, the SCAA published *Religious Education 16-19*, which is intended as a guideline for SACREs and agreed syllabus conferences with respect to RE for 16-19 year olds. This booklet contains general considerations about RE for students at that age, including intended learning outcomes related to the attainment targets *learning about religions* and *learning from religion*. It provides an overview of the categories of topics which are currently offered in RE courses and emphasises that coverage of the topics "should reflect the mainly Christian heritage of this country, as well as drawing on other principal religions. The balance between these will also take account of the local area and the pupil population."[62] The topics comprise "Principal religions of the world, including Christianity"; "Traditional and contemporary Christian Theologies" (Eastern Orthodox, Catholic, Protestant); "Philosophy of Religion"; "Sacred Texts"; "Aspects of religious life" (nature of religious discipleship and experience, prayer in world religions, mysticism in world religions, monastic life and other forms of asceticism); "Religion and Ethics"; "Religion and Science"; "Other aspects of religion" (psychology, politics, the arts, religion as a driving force for division or healing). The booklet then gives examples of how key issues in RE may support knowledge and understanding in other subjects. The appendix gives examples of RE courses ("investigating religious experience", "creation and evolution", "film and faith") and of the use of study visits in a course. *Religious Education 16-19* is not a model syllabus, but rather a list

---

60 For this issue cf., e.g., Jackson 2000: Law, politics and religious education in England and Wales, 92.
61 Baumfield, Bowness et al. 1994: A Third Perspective; and Baumfield, Bowness et al. 1994: Model syllabuses: a contribution.
62 SCAA 1995: Religious Education 16-19: 9.

of possible study areas which may be covered in post 16 RE with some suggestions for activities. Rather than providing a stringent concept, it collects different examples of common practice as a first guideline about what to include. The focus is more comparative than in the model syllabuses which are, as we have seen, structured around the individual religions. The special emphasis on Christianity is manifest not only in the selection of topics, but also in the vocabulary used for comparative study, which basically consists of Christian concepts or questions that have emerged particularly in Christian theology.

The *Faith Communities' Working Group Reports*,[63] which were created in order to find out what representatives of individual religions regard as important for an understanding of their own religions and the resulting suggestions for topics in RE, are also written in tabular and keyword style. This report is intended as a suggestion for agreed syllabus conferences about which topics to include for the individual religions. Covering five pages per religion, following a brief introduction, keywords about aspects of the religion in question are listed under headings which were also chosen by the representatives of that religion, structured according to the key stages. This procedure of identifying "essential knowledge" about religions for RE has been heavily criticised, particularly because this brochure, having been created by a small group of informants from each religion in question and by no means constituting a representative sample of the adherents, has often been mistaken for an account of what adherents of these religions in general would like to have taught in RE about their religion.[64] The introductory note that "the Working Group Reports are not designed to be used as teaching programmes"[65] is important when it comes to finding an appropriate place for them in the landscape of RE in England, where they provide one source among many others that may be considered as suggestions for the selection of contents for RE.

---

63 SCAA 1994: Faith Communities' Working Group Reports.
64 For a critical view of this report see e.g. Everington 1996: The relationship between educators and practitioners, 69f., 76; Jackson 1997: RE. An Interpretive Approach, 135.
65 SCAA 1994: Working Group Reports, 4.

1.2.3 The legal situation

The Education Reform Act of 1988 (ERA 1988) brought about a substantial reform of the educational system in England and Wales. A *national curriculum* was created for all state schools with obligatory syllabuses for 10 subjects in England and 11 subjects in Wales. With this, the LEAs lost much of their influence and the state school system moved towards central organisation. RE, however, was the only subject which was not included in the national curriculum. Thus, its local organisation was retained. The *national curriculum* and RE together form the *basic curriculum* to which every pupil in England and Wales is entitled. The ERA 1988 interprets the task of the school in general as contributing to the "spiritual, moral, cultural, mental and physical development of the pupils".[66] The name of RE was changed from *Religious Instruction* to *Religious Education* in order to emphasise the educational character of the subject. In this context, the reinterpretation of the Cowper-Temple clause, which prohibits that a syllabus be based on the teachings of a particular religious denomination, is interesting. With respect to this clause, the 1988 ERA states that "this provision is not to be taken as prohibiting provision in such a syllabus for *the study* of such catechisms or formularies".[67] This leads John Hull to conclude that the concept of studying different religious traditions is anchored in the new legislation.[68]

The 1988 ERA also deals with the procedure used to draw up agreed syllabuses. For the first time, it recognises officially the variety of different religious traditions by making the second group in agreed syllabus conferences include other religions and denominations (than the Church of England, which still has its own group of representatives). The ERA 1988 is, furthermore, the first act concerned with the content of RE syllabuses. The formulation in section 8.3, that every new agreed syllabus shall "reflect the fact that the religious traditions in Great Britain are in the main Christian, whilst taking account of the teaching and practices of the other principal religions represented in Great Britain"[69] refers to the multireligious landscape in Great Britain but particularly mentions Christianity as the biggest religion in that landscape. This gave rise to numerous discussions about the contents of

---

66 ERA 1988, section 1.2, quoted in Hull 1989: The Act Unpacked, 3.
67 ERA 1988, quoted in Hull 1989: The Act Unpacked, 4, emphasis in original.
68 Hull 1989: The Act Unpacked, 4.
69 ERA 1988, section 8.3, quoted in Hull 1989: The Act Unpacked, 9.

RE. The opinions of scholars of RE about this passage vary. The special emphasis given to Christianity is generally regarded as counterproductive to the multireligious character of RE.

The range of positions towards the formulations about RE in the ERA 1988 may be illustrated by the different opinions of John Hull and Michael Grimmitt: John Hull welcomes the legal recognition of the multireligious character of RE in England and Wales and states that, on these grounds, the multireligious syllabuses can be kept while other syllabuses have to be changed.[70] Michael Grimmitt, however, regards the formulations of the 1988 ERA as going back 30 years in time and as a set-back for RE, from which it will not recover before the passage in section 8.3, which specifically mentions Christianity, is changed so that no individual religion is particularly emphasised any longer.[71] With the debate about the new regulations concerning the national and basic curriculum in mind, Grimmitt criticises the idea of quantitatively measurable knowledge, which is implied in the new regulations, as well as the idea of pre-determined levels of attainment, which the pupils are required to reach at certain ages. He regards this as a misconception of education resulting from an attempt to regard schools as part of the *enterprise culture*, which are expected to compete with each other in *marketing* their *product* and attracting *consumers*, with headteachers *managing* their schools by models of efficient business management.[72] This market-dominated, output and assessment-orientated centralised educational system with a national curriculum which deliberately leaves out curriculum theory and employs a technicist understanding of teaching and learning, puts RE under an enormous pressure to accept this ideology of standardisation and assessment. Many LEAs give in to this pressure despite the fact that RE is not part of the national curriculum and therefore does not have to define itself in terms of *attainment targets, programmes of study* and *levels of attainment*.[73]

Irrespective of the different interpretations, the relevant clauses of the ERA 1988 legalise a posteriori the procedure by which multireligious agreed syllabuses have been formulated for years – in cooperation with representatives of different religions. However, they also gave rise to a number of arguments and debates. For example, referring to the phrase "that the religious traditions in Great Britain are in the main

---

70 See e.g. Hull 1989: The Act Unpacked, 1994: Geschichte und Entwicklung des Lehrplans für den Religionsunterricht in Birmingham.
71 Grimmitt 2000: Introduction, 12.
72 See ibid., 9.
73 See ibid., 7ff.

Christian", there were objections to the multireligious agreed syllabuses of the London boroughs of Ealing and Newham on the grounds that they were not "mainly Christian". The responsible barrister, who was consulted by the Secretary of State on this issue, however, rejected the argument and decided that the syllabuses were acceptable as they contained information on all major religions in Great Britain.[74] In contrast to this wide interpretation of the ERA 1988, a circular of the Department for Education from 1994 employs a very different interpretation of the legal framework for RE:

> "The legislation governing religious education ... is designed ... to ensure that pupils gain both a thorough knowledge of Christianity reflecting *the Christian heritage of this country*, and knowledge of the other principal religions represented in Great Britain".
>
> "Religious Education in schools should seek: to develop pupils' knowledge, understanding and awareness of Christianity as the *predominant* religion in Great Britain, and the other principal religions represented in the country; to encourage respect for those holding different beliefs; and to promote pupils' spiritual, moral, cultural and mental development."
>
> "As a whole *and at each key stage*, the relative content devoted to Christianity in the syllabus should *predominate*. The syllabus as a whole must also include all of the principal religions represented in this country."[75]

Many RE professionals regard the latter statements as problematic and recommend avoiding ambiguous formulations like *predominant* or *predominate*, which imply a hierarchy of religious traditions.[76]

In 2004, the Qualifications and Curriculum Authority (QCA) published *The non-statutory national framework for Religious Education* on behalf of the Secretary of State for Education and Skills, supported by a steering group consisting of members of various faith and belief communities and professional organisations. The booklet in which it is published, to be used by LEAs, Agreed Syllabus Conferences and SACREs as well as by other people involved with RE, is intended as a contribution to raising standards in the learning and teaching of RE.

The introductory section emphasises the importance of RE for intercultural understanding in a plural world. The pictures underline this harmonising understanding of the character of RE, showing symbols of different religions, a jigsaw puzzle in which these symbols are put to-

---

74 Cf. Jackson 2000: Law, politics and religious education in England and Wales, 90f.
75 DfE circular 1/94, quoted in Jackson 2000: Law, politics and religious education in England and Wales, 93, emphases by Jackson.
76 See e.g. Grimmitt 2000: Introduction, 13f, Jackson 2000: Law, politics and religious education in England and Wales, 93.

gether, children of different ethnic origins playing together and the word "peace" formed by human beings lying on the ground. The introductory section is followed by a general outline about the place of RE in the curriculum, including sections on attitudes in RE (encouragement of positive attitudes to learning and to the beliefs and values of others, such as self-awareness, respect for all, open-mindedness, appreciation and wonder), the contribution of RE to learning across the curriculum (e.g. promoting spiritual, moral, social and cultural development; promoting citizenship, personal, social and health education and key skills) and RE and general teaching requirements like inclusion, the use of language and the use of information and communication technology.

The non-statutory national framework for RE follows the format of other subjects in the national curriculum. It has a section on the foundation stage (ages 3-5) during which "children may begin to explore the world of religions in terms of special people, books, times, places and objects...".[77] It outlines the contribution RE can make to the early learning goals, particularly to personal, social and emotional development; communication, language and literacy; knowledge and understanding of the world and creative development. For key stages one to three it outlines programmes of study which list the knowledge, skills and understanding with respect to *learning about religion*[78] and *learning from religion* that the pupils are expected to acquire at any particular stage. A *breadth of study* section suggests areas of study *related to religions and beliefs* (including Christianity, "other principal religions", religious communities with a significant local presence "where appropriate" and a secular worldview "where appropriate"[79]), *themes* and *experiences and opportunities* for every key stage. Depth of knowledge is supposed to increase at any key stage. Notes in the margins give intertextual references concerning opportunities to develop certain attitudes, links to other subjects or ICT opportunities. The framework also includes a short section on knowledge, skills and understanding at the ages 14-19.

As with the national curriculum subjects, the section on attainment targets gives eight-level descriptions of increasing difficulty,[80] which

---

77 QCA 2004: The Non-Statutory National Framework, 21.
78 Note that, unlike the formulations in the 1994 model syllabuses, the singular is used in "learning about religion".
79 One might ask in which contexts the study of a secular worldview may not be considered appropriate.
80 Plus the description of one additional level of "exceptional performance" above level eight.

summarise the types and range of performance that the pupils working on the respective levels should characteristically demonstrate. These level descriptions relate to the two attainment targets *learning about religion* and *learning from religion*. Compared to other official documents for RE, the *Non-Statutory National Framework for Religious Education* does not say anything fundamentally new about RE. It does, however, bring the organisation of RE more closely in line with the national curriculum subjects and the national standards (including programmes of study and expected levels of attainment) rather than local responsibility, which has been characteristic of the organisation of integrative RE in England since its beginnings.

1.2.4 Teacher training

Teachers in secondary schools often have a first degree in the study of religions or theology, but candidates with degrees in other subjects such as history or anthropology may also be accepted for teacher training for RE. Following this first degree, there are one-year courses which prepare teacher trainees directly for teaching RE.[81] These courses comprise study phases and school practice in cooperation with local schools. In the study phases, teacher trainees acquire knowledge about world religions and about ways of teaching about these in RE. This theoretical knowledge can be applied directly in the school practice phases in which the candidates have the opportunity to acquire teaching experience.

Teacher training for primary schools comprises RE as one component. Furthermore, students who want to become primary school teachers may specialise in RE. Alternatively, they may specialise in RE in their Bachelor of Education course, which qualifies them to become an RE co-ordinator in a primary school later. Primary RE teachers may also have been trained at church colleges of higher education. These colleges also offer teacher training for RE, which is independent from anyone's own religious beliefs. In general, teachers of RE are selected by their academic and didactic qualifications alone; the religious background of a teacher is immaterial. The teachers' task is to help their pupils to reflect about religions, norms and values, but not to impose their

---

81   These courses are called Post Graduate Certificate in Education (PGCE) programmes.

own particular religious beliefs on the pupils.[82] The secularity of the profession of the RE teacher can be regarded – as John Hull suggests – as a cornerstone of the justification of the existence of RE in state schools in a multicultural democracy.[83]

A big problem is the lack of qualified RE teachers. In many schools there are fewer qualified RE teachers than needed. In some schools, only the RE co-ordinator is an academically qualified RE teacher, while teachers of other subjects also teach RE after having participated in special training courses. However, the breadth of knowledge which is necessary for teaching this subject can hardly be communicated in a few extra training courses. Furthermore, teachers who have not had academic training for RE sometimes have problems in understanding the secular character of the subject.

---

82 For a comparative account of the different understandings of the role of the teacher in a number of English approaches to RE, see Copley 2004: Is UK RE failing to address its own culture context?

83 Hull 2002: Der Segen der Säkularität, 169, for teacher training see 168f., cf. also Lankshear 2000: Religious Education in England and Wales, 58, Jackson 1999: The training of RE teachers in England and Wales. Some observations about power relations.

2 Current approaches to RE in England

Introduction

This chapter analyses recent English academic approaches to integrative RE with respect to the following: aims and contents ascribed to integrative RE, the underlying concept of religion, the way religions are represented, and the notion of education on which the approach is based. As many of these points as possible have been analysed, depending on the information available. However, it has not always been feasible to cover all of them. This analysis is based on the criteria developed in the chapter on theory and methodology in the study of religions and in education.[84] Each section on individual approaches concludes with a general comment or critical evaluation of the respective approach. More detailed criticism is included in the sections on the points mentioned above.

The length of the sections varies because of the diverse characters of the approaches. These differences are due to the material that is available. Some approaches have existed for more than twenty years and include a range of publications, for example, monographs, journal articles, handbooks for teachers and teaching material. Others have been developed very recently and not much literature is yet available. I have identified nine different influential academic concepts for RE, which are currently used for teacher training, curriculum development or as teaching strategies. Frequently, they have been developed by a project team over many years. Despite their considerably different conceptions of RE, religion(s), the representation of religions, education and teaching strategies, all of these are widely used together in current RE in England. My intention is to evaluate these concepts with respect to their contribution to an integrative RE which is based on basic insights from the discussions about method and theory in the study of religions and education.

---

84 See chapter I.

2.1 The Westhill Project

The Westhill Project is a curriculum development project for RE in primary and secondary schools. In the context of the changes RE was undergoing in the 1960s and 1970s in England, the RE centre at Westhill College in Birmingham was established in 1973. Its first director, Michael Grimmitt, together with Geoff Robson, compiled resources and established a programme for training teachers of RE. After 1980, a new team[85] produced further materials with a focus on curriculum development and pedagogy for teachers of RE. The project builds on the work of scholars with backgrounds in different disciplines relevant to RE: insights by Robert Goldman and Harold Loukes (see also section 1.1.1), especially their intentions to make RE relevant to the lives of the pupils; educational theories of Jean Piaget and Jerome Bruner, particularly in relation to the conceptual development of children; the philosophy of religion of Wilfred Cantwell Smith and John Hick and the phenomenology of religion as understood by Ninian Smart.[86]

2.1.1 Aims and contents of integrative RE

In the Westhill Project, religions are regarded as instrumental in the process of the development of a child. The aim of RE is defined as "to help children mature in relation to their own patterns of belief and behaviour through exploring religious beliefs and practices and related human experiences."[87] In a dynamic process, by getting to know traditional belief systems and talking about shared human experience, individual patterns of beliefs are the focus of reflection. The teachers' manual *How do I teach RE?* states principles for RE, among them the children's need to develop their own beliefs and values and a consistent pattern of behaviour, and the contribution of RE to the spiritual, moral and social development of the children, helping them to develop a positive and understanding attitude towards diversity in a pluralistic society.[88] Desired learning outcomes comprise the acquisition of knowledge and understanding of religions, personal development

---

85   With Garth Read (a curriculum specialist), John Rudge, Roger Howard (teachers) and Geoff Teece.
86   Cf. Rudge 2000: The Westhill Project, 88f.
87   Ibid., 92; Read et al. 1992: How Do I Teach RE?, 2.
88   For the principles of RE see Read et al. 1992: How Do I Teach RE?, 2f.

through involvement with issues fundamental to one's life, the development of an awareness about experiences of life and the issues they raise, an awareness of and a sensitivity to the religious dimension of life through a personal encounter with experiences such as awe and wonder, belonging and commitment, caring and compassion, as well as the capacity to reflect on, respond to and express one's own beliefs and values in relation to the knowledge, understanding and awareness one has developed.[89]

The Westhill Project provides a model of the field of enquiry from which the content of RE can be drawn. In this model, the focus is on the interaction between the three following areas: *traditional belief systems*, *shared human experience* and *individual patterns of belief*. "Traditional belief systems" is used as a generic term for the major religions of the world. With respect to shared human experience, the focus is on those experiences which raise profound issues and questions about the human condition, such as, for example, the awareness of human limitations and the finite nature of life; questions which concern the purpose of life, its meaning and value, people's sense of identity and issues about personal and cosmic origins and destiny. These questions may be summarised as "what does it mean to be human?".[90] Individual patterns of belief are seen as a part both of the content and of the process of RE.

The RE Process
Learning about

Traditional belief systems ←→ Shared human experience

Learning from   Individual patterns of belief   Learning from

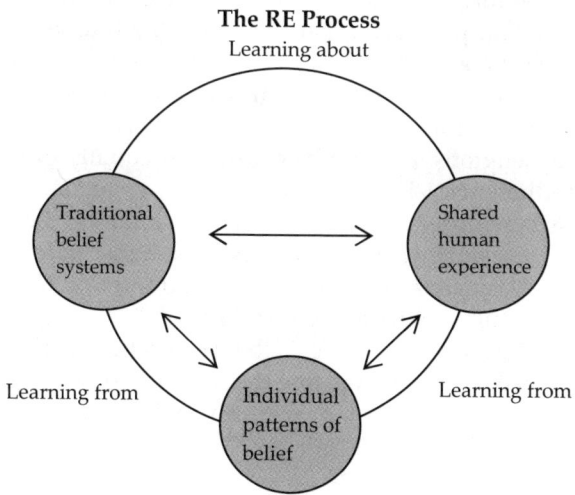

Figure 2.1 - The RE Process (Rudge 2000: The Westhill Project, 103)

---

89 Cf. Rudge 2000: The Westhill Project, 92, 102.
90 Ibid., 96.

2.1.2 The concept of religion and the representation of religions

The concept of religion is carefully reflected in this approach. First of all, the difficulty of defining religion is acknowledged. This is, however, not seen as a major problem for RE, as the focus on the field of study is selected on the basis of the experiences children have in their daily lives:

> "In RE we are concerned with the more practical question of how children are to make sense of the many ways in which they will encounter religious (and non-religious) belief and practice in their daily lives – in the media, in their local communities or among their friends."[91]

Therefore, the focus is more on living and contemporary religion than on historical study. The dynamic character of religions is emphasised when they are regarded as "akin to living and moving organisms, changing and developing, responding to situations, manifested in many colours, varieties and forms."[92] Despite problems surrounding any concept of religion, the generic term "traditional belief systems" is suggested for referring to the major religions of the world. The choice of this term is explained in detail: "system" refers to the common bond that, despite varieties of interpretation, outlook and behaviour, holds together a tradition and provides a distinctive worldview with which certain people identify; "traditional" refers to the fact that those systems are durable and pervasive, that they have (had) an influence and are part of the heritage of ideas and inspiration of cultures; "belief" refers to interpretation of life and the world as one important aspect of religions. The authors emphasise, however, that this does not mean that other aspects of religions may not be considered equally or even more important by adherents.[93] The expression "belief systems" is preferred over "religions" in order to make explicit that other views of life "which do not necessarily include a theistic or transcendent perspective",[94] such as Theravada Buddhism, some strands of Hinduism or secular humanist philosophies are also included.

In the Westhill Project, John Hick's theory of religion is regarded as relevant for RE insofar as it claims that the most important aspect religions have in common is that they provide an analysis of human insuffi-

---

[91] Read et al. 1992: How Do I Teach RE?, 4.
[92] Ibid., 9.
[93] For explanations of the term "traditional belief systems", see ibid.: 9f. and Rudge 2000: The Westhill Project, 94.
[94] Read et al. 1992: How Do I Teach RE?, 10.

ciency and thus a theory of human nature. Hick's claim that they also provide a path to transcend this imperfect state and thus help people to become more truly human is considered a good starting point for a concept of religion in RE, which does not corrupt religious beliefs.[95]

For the representation of religions in RE, a combination of the "systems approach" and the "life themes approach" is suggested. In the *systems approach*, material from one tradition only is presented in order to shed light on the question of what it means to be a follower of that particular religious tradition and to "build up a conceptual awareness of the key beliefs, values and world-views found within that tradition."[96] In the *life themes approach*, a particular issue or question about life, an aspect of shared human experience, is explored in order to develop an awareness of ultimate questions. These issues are, however, meant to be contextualised with reference to the teachings and practices of at least two different religions. The systems may thereby serve to illuminate the life theme and – mutatis mutandis – knowledge about one tradition may be contextualised with reference to a life theme. Thus the same material may be used in either approach, but the approach determines how the material is used. If the representation of religions is limited to these two approaches, other ways of representing religions are explicitly excluded. Teaching religions, for example through themes

> "which purport to transcend traditions, such as festivals, founders and holy books, is representative of neither the life themes nor the systems approach ... This kind of thematic planning and teaching tends to distort any possible understanding of what it means to be a believer in any one tradition, and it does nothing to illustrate how the theme may be related to issues about life and ultimate questions."[97]

Teachers are advised to identify suitable topics, present different perspectives in an objective way, including considerations about "the essential" and "the cultural", the majority and the minority, the local and the global, the popular and the intellectual and the traditional and the radical.[98]

Spirituality is regarded as an important concept in RE, as spiritual development is seen as a major aspect of RE.[99] The project uses a broad understanding of spirituality, which is regarded as something unique to human beings. The following features are mentioned in order to out-

---

95 Teece 1997: Why John Hick's theory of religions is important for RE, 3-5.
96 Rudge 2000: The Westhill Project, 101.
97 Rudge 2000: The Westhill Project, 102.
98 Read et al. 1992: How Do I Teach RE?, 16f.
99 See Rudge 1993: RE and Spiritual Development.

line the way the concept of spirituality is used: transcending the immediate and the mundane; developing particular temperaments and dispositions; developing particular sets of character traits and values; the awareness of being an enduring entity which persists over time and retains a continuity of self-consciousness and personal identity; detecting and responding to some of the wonder, mystery and awesomeness of the natural world, social living and personal experience; recognising, remembering and reliving a select number of significant experiences.[100] An understanding of religious beliefs, values and experiences is regarded as a prerequisite for spiritual development. Rudge emphasises that in this process, which is grounded in understanding and encounter, it is important to draw on the spiritual heritage of the whole of humankind, not just of the locality or of religious people only.[101] Hence, spirituality is interpreted as a broad concept that comprises both religious and non-religious features.

Interrelations within the field of enquiry

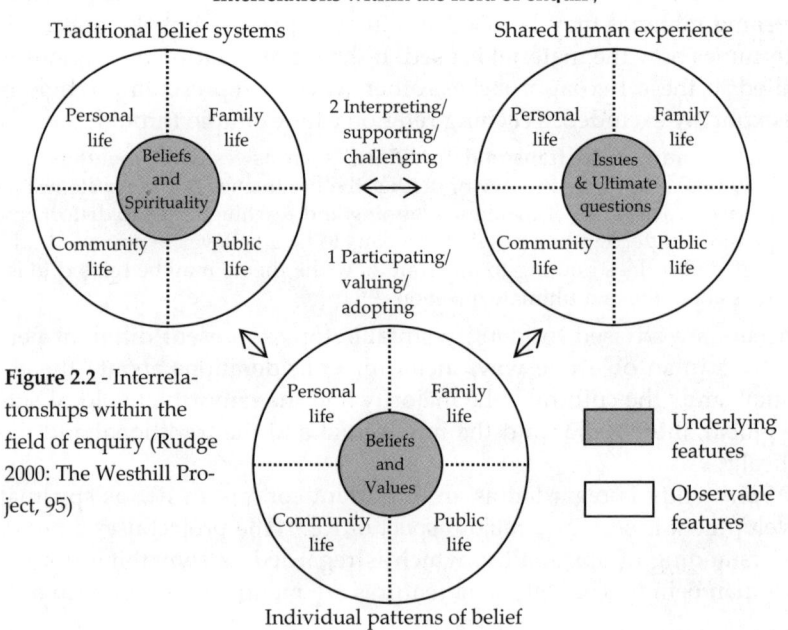

Figure 2.2 - Interrelationships within the field of enquiry (Rudge 2000: The Westhill Project, 95)

---

100 Further explanations about these features are given in Read et al. 1992: How Do I Teach RE?, 13f.
101 Rudge 1993: RE and Spiritual Development, 17.

In all the three areas of content of RE (traditional belief systems, shared human experience and individual patterns of belief) the observable features are identified as personal life, family life, community life and public life. Beliefs and spirituality are mentioned as the underlying features of traditional belief systems, whereas issues and ultimate questions are mentioned as features of shared human experience, and beliefs and values as features of individual patterns of belief.

The dynamic relationship between the three areas of content of RE is itself regarded as an important part of the field of enquiry. A careful consideration of this relationship may help to avoid over-simplifications. Rudge states, for example, that religious beliefs should not simply be regarded as answers of particular communities to ultimate questions, as they also have the function of raising questions about life.[102] The content of RE should be selected according to its expected educational value for the pupils. In this process, the study of observable features may serve to illustrate the underlying features. They can be regarded as a means of exploring beliefs, values, spirituality, issues and ultimate questions.[103] Generally, priority is given to the pupils' personal development. Knowledge and understanding of the subject matter is not regarded as "an end in itself, but as a means to an end. The content of [the] field of enquiry is *instrumental* in the process of personal development."[104]

2.1.3 The notion of education and teaching strategies

The educational strategy of the project is based on the assumption that every human being has to respond to experiences, situations and events and is thus inevitably involved in the process of the formation of beliefs and values. RE can make a contribution to developing beliefs and values of pupils in their formative years. Pupils are meant to learn in relation to their ages, abilities and stages of development[105] in order to acquire an autonomy that is based on the ability to reflect upon one's

---

[102] Rudge 2000: The Westhill Project, 97. Cf. the discussion about the *livsfråga*-concept in Swedish RE, chapter III, section 5.2.1.
[103] Rudge 2000: The Westhill Project, 99f.
[104] Ibid., 93.
[105] Rudge refers to the work of Jean Piaget, but notes that the categories Piaget invented have often been taken at face value by people who interpreted them and, therefore, an impression of overly neat and tidy developmental stages has sometimes been created. See Rudge 2000: The Westhill Project, 100.

own beliefs and values in relation to those of others. Responsibility for one's own beliefs and actions is regarded as an important aspect of maturity.[106] Education is understood as the widening of one's horizon, deepening the perception of the world around oneself and reflecting one's own perspective in the light of the study of other outlooks. This is regarded as an open process in which the will to ask questions is more important than necessarily arriving at conclusive answers. In this process, the role of the teacher is that of an educator. Teachers should encourage and promote an open, critical and sympathetic approach to the subject. In this context, the general ethos of the school with its hidden or informal curriculum is also considered important. Teachers have their contribution to make with respect to the values promoted in the school surroundings. Beliefs such as the value of human life in all its diversity should be supported by encouraging attitudes of sensitivity, respect, open-mindedness and empathy in children.[107]

One strategy that is recommended for discussions in RE in order to discriminate clearly between facts and beliefs is particularly remarkable: "owning and grounding" is regarded as a task for teachers and pupils alike in order to retain an impartial perspective and to avoid entering the realm of theological argument. *Owning* implies marking a particular statement as one's own belief, using terms such as "I believe...", "It seems to me that...", "I feel...", "I think...", "In my experience..." etc. *Grounding* means attaching a particular belief to some groups of people who hold it, for example "Muslims believe...", "It says in the Qur'an...", "Many people think..." etc.[108] If one owns or grounds a statement, one does not presume that its truth or authority holds for others. This may, on the one hand, often be a useful means to make clear that in RE no particular beliefs or values are being forced upon the pupils. On the other hand, practising owning and grounding in the classroom can help the pupils to see the difference between facts and beliefs more clearly, an ability that is certainly useful also beyond the immediate context of RE.

---

106 Rudge 2000: The Westhill Project, 93f, Read et al. 1992: How Do I Teach RE?, 2.
107 Read et al. 1992: How Do I Teach RE?, 3.
108 For *owning* and *grounding* see ibid., 67f.

2.1.4 Comment

The Westhill Project presents an interesting and workable approach to integrative RE. The different aspects of the field of enquiry and the suggested process in which the interrelations between those aspects can be explored show a good way of combining the existential and descriptive dimensions of the subject. A broad concept of religion ensures the coverage of a wide range of phenomena from different contexts, always contextualised with respect to the life world of the pupils. The underlying concept of education focuses on the process of maturing and learning to take responsibility for one's beliefs and actions. Education is also understood in a broad sense, combining intellectual, emotional and affective learning with the aim of acquiring not only knowledge but also skills that are necessary for responsible social interaction. The emphasis on spirituality and spiritual development raises general questions about the character of RE and its role in the curriculum. In how far is it possible to promote "spiritual development" in a non-religious school environment? This, however, is by no means a dilemma of the Westhill approach alone, but generally an ambivalent issue in RE in England. It will be taken up again in the evaluations and conclusions of English and Swedish concepts for integrative RE (chapter IV.1).

However, there are a few points concerning the notion of religion and the representation of religions in RE which may have to be reconsidered if the non-religious integrative framework is taken seriously. Whereas the authors emphasise that any theological or philosophical perspective is not of much use as a framework in which to describe religions in RE, Rudge nonetheless follows a theological line of argument when he supports Hull's claim that holiness is discovered through encounter.[109] Furthermore, the adoption of Hick's philosophy of religions[110] can also be regarded as problematic, as it represents a particular interpretation of religious diversity, contradicting the self-understanding of many religious people. It superimposes a universalistic interpretation of religions, if it is taken as a starting point for RE. Rather than using it as a general framework, Hick's philosophy of religion – as well as other interpretations of religious diversity – have to be discussed critically in integrative RE, so that the pupils are not introduced into a particular unquestioned paradigm but have a chance to

---

[109] See Rudge 1993: RE and spiritual development, 13, referring to Hull 1991: Mishmash, 38.
[110] Teece 1997: Why John Hick's theory of religions is important for RE.

encounter different accounts of religious diversity and get a chance to make up their own minds about it. The presuppositions of any framework for the representation of religions need to be considered, including the notion of religion behind the suggested distinction between "the essential" and "the cultural", which presupposes that it is possible to distinguish between "essential" and "cultural" aspects of religions.

The considerations around the term *traditional belief systems* are sophisticated and helpful. It may be necessary to use such an expression in order to avoid the limited scope commonly associated with "religion", which is frequently defined in relation to one or more gods or transcendence in general. These ideas remind one of Smart's suggestion to call our subject *worldview analysis* rather than the *study of religions*.[111] One could, however, argue that worldview is but one aspect of religion and does not cover the whole range of phenomena that the term religion covers. Another suggestion would therefore be to promote a broad concept of religion that includes worldviews which do not refer to any gods or transcendent spheres. The Westhill team acknowledges the importance of handling controversial issues responsibly. They claim that not to deal with controversial questions is to rob the subject of its relevance. Children have to understand that issues of belief are often controversial and represent different outlooks and interpretations of human experience. Therefore, differences must not be played down. In order to do justice to the variety of, and differences between, religious positions, the authors correctly emphasise that it is important not to create false impressions about the variety of religions, such as the idea that "all religions amount to the same thing".[112]

2.2 "A Gift to the Child"
The Religion in the Service of the Child Project

The other famous developmental approach to RE has also been developed by a team of scholars from the city of Birmingham. The *Religion in the Service of the Child Project*, which was launched in the mid 1980s, builds on earlier work by Michael Grimmitt and John Hull. After preparation work by Grimmitt and Hull, in the first phase, which started in 1987 under the title *Religious Education in the Early Years*, an outline of the new approach was created. This approach employs a par-

---

111 Cf. Smart 1989: Worldview analysis: a way of looking at our field.
112 Read et al. 1992: How Do I Teach RE?, 6, see also ibid., 3-6.

ticular method to contribute to the development of children. In the second phase, which started in 1989, the name was changed to *Religion in the Service of the Child Project* and the method was tested and evaluated. The project materials, which consist of a teachers' book, pupil books and an audio cassette, were published in 1991 under the title *A Gift to the Child: Religious Education in Primary School*.[113] The project material was developed through classroom research. As the title suggests, the approach focuses on teaching RE to young children in nursery, infant and junior classes.

The project is about teaching methodology, not curriculum development. Therefore, it is not concerned with the syllabus or curriculum for RE (i.e. the question of what should be taught) but with the question of how to teach effectively. It illustrates a teaching strategy. The authors emphasise, however, that the method or strategy they suggest is but one among many.[114] The basic idea underlying the teaching strategy is that each religion contains gifts which are valuable not only to adherents of that religion but also to other people. Those gifts can be obtained in an encounter with objects from the different religions. Most of those gifts are of educational nature and therefore fall within the responsibility of secular RE. Some of the gifts are, however, of a religious nature and are regarded as relevant only for children who belong to the one particular tradition the items are taken from. Even though religious gifts go beyond the proper scope of RE in state schools, the authors emphasise that there is no need to deny that they exist even within RE.[115]

The overall aim of the "gift" approach is a contribution to the spiritual, moral, cultural, mental and emotional development of the children rather than an understanding of religions, even though the latter is certainly regarded as a welcome side effect. As in the Westhill project, knowledge and understanding of religions are regarded as means to an end. As the project title suggests, religions are instrumentalised to serve the development of the child.

---

113 Grimmitt et al. 1991: A Gift to the Child.
114 See for example Hull 2000: Religion in the Service of the Child Project, 125.
115 Grimmitt et al. 1991: A Gift to the Child, 13.

2.2.1 The representation of religions

For an encounter with the religious items the authors suggest the following pattern, in which the order of the stages may vary slightly:

The *engagement stage* should be a stimulus to the perception of the children in order to raise their curiosity and interest. A first relationship between the pupil and the material is created, often by means of controlled disclosure. *Entering devices* mark the transition into the realm of the religious item. They may comprise, for example, the use of a story ring, lighting a candle, sitting on a circular rug or listening to the sound of a bell. In the *discovery phase* children may explore the material for themselves, for example by becoming involved in play, fantasy or drama.

After the discovery phase, a boundary between the children and the religious item is created with the help of *distancing devices*, for example a physical space which the pupils may not cross, or the introduction (e.g. through photographs) of a child of the religion for whom the item has a particular significance. The religious material can thus be discussed in the third person. In the *contextualisation phase*, the material is placed in its wider social and religious context, and its status within the religious tradition from which it is taken is

ENGAGEMENT
Introducing pupils to the religious item and inviting them, through sensory perception, to become familiar with it

⇩

ENTERING DEVICE
Candle, story ring, story mat, bell, incense

⇩

DISCOVERY
Allowing pupils to explore the religious item for themselves through story, play and fantasy

⇩

CONTEXTUALISATION
Enabling pupils to see the religious item in a wider social and religious context

⇩

REFLECTION
Encouraging pupils to reflect on their own lives from a new perspective, in the light of their experience of the religious item

Figure 2.3 – The Teaching Strategy (Grimmit et al. 1991: A Gift to the Child, 12)

appreciated. The last phase – *reflection* – provides an opportunity for the pupils to look at their own lives in the light of their encounters with the material. Questions raised through the encounters with the religious object may be reflected upon and the gifts can be articulated.

In the project material, this teaching strategy is exemplified by reference to a set of "items" from different religions, including e.g. "Ganesha", "The Call to Prayer", "Angels", and "Jonah".[116] These aspects of individual religions were selected by the project team for the potential lively response that a confrontation with them may provoke on the part of the pupils, as this material may make a strong appeal to the senses of the pupils and because of its specific, explicit and concrete character. For each of the "items" the project team has collected material which may be used in the classroom in order to teach about these aspects of religions. A closer look at the example of "Ganesha" may help the reader to acquire an impression of how this strategy can be applied with respect to a single item. The authors present the following sketch of the strategy for teaching about the Hindu god Ganesha.

In the *engagement stage*, the children are asked to imagine a boy with an elephant head and to say the name Ganesha. Then the teacher

THE TEACHING STRATEGY

ENGAGEMENT
Introduction to Ganesha through the child's imagination

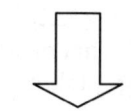

⇩

ENTERING DEVICE
Candle

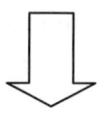

⇩

DISCOVERY
Story of Ganesha's birth, unveiling the figure of Ganesha, story of the broken tusk

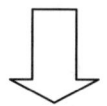

⇩

CONTEXTUALISATION
Kedar worships Ganesha

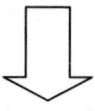

⇩

REFLECTION
Where do you belong and to whom? What or who do you worship?

Figure 2.4 – The Teaching Strategy: Teaching about Ganesha (Grimmit et al. 1991: A Gift to the Child, 33)

---

116 These "items" either represent aspects of individual religions, such as the Hindu god Ganesha or the Muslim Call to Prayer, or they relate to figures which are relevant in several religions, such as angels or the Prophet Jonah in Jewish, Christian and Muslim traditions.

lights a candle (entering device). In the *discovery stage*, the teacher tells stories about Ganesha and unveils a figure of Ganesha. The authors suggest several activities of how to work with stories in that phase. As a *distancing device*, a boy called Kedar is introduced in a special book. What has been learnt about Ganesha so far is *contextualised* by means of a story about the Hindu boy Kedar, who worships Ganesha in a *puja*. In the context of Kedar's activities, additional information is given about *pujas*. In the *reflection stage*, general questions are considered, e.g. the question of what or whom the children worship or where and to whom they belong – taking up the idea that Kedar feels he belongs to Ganesha.[117]

In a "grid of gifts"[118] the authors present possible gifts (learning outcomes) that may be obtained in an encounter with religious items. Those gifts comprise the following skills:[119]

- *communicating* – especially learning to express one's own deep thoughts and learning important words from the religion studied.
- *questioning* – with an emphasis on questions stimulated by the material,
- *imagining* – Children can often link images intuitively. The imagery they use should be affirmed, extended and sometimes challenged to promote development.
- *empathising* – In an encounter with the religious material, children may explore their own life and feelings and those of others. The bounds of sympathy can thereby be widened.
- *identifying* – The different stories from the religions offer a variety of opportunities for identification. General questions about identity may also be raised.
- *valuing* – Widening one's treasury of values can be regarded as RE's contribution to moral education. In this process, the emphasis is, however, not on rules, obligations and laws that can be found in religions, but rather on experiences, situations and feelings that may be valued.
- *believing* – The authors claim that "all religious material worth including in the maintained school curriculum should make some offering of worthy belief to all children."[120] Other special

---

117 See Grimmitt et al. 1991: A Gift to the Child, 33ff.
118 Grimmitt et al. 1991: A Gift to the Child, 13ff, 124f.
119 Cf. ibid., 14f.
120 Grimmitt et al. 1991: A Gift to the Child, 15. Unfortunately, the authors do not specify any further what they mean by "worthy belief" in this context.

aspects of belief are regarded as appropriate only for children that come from the religion that is represented in the material. The authors emphasise, however, that even the gift of belief does not necessarily have to be religious.[121]

With respect to the Ganesha example, the possible gifts are specified as follows: *understanding* of the concepts shrine, God and worship; *asking questions* like "Who or what is God?", "What makes me angry?" (referring to the story of Ganesha's broken tusk); *imagining* which animal one would like to be, imagining that God may have many forms; *empathising* with children caught in conflict and with those who lose someone they love; *identifying* by considering to whom one belongs oneself and what one worships; valuing worship, anger, humour and the positive aspects of conflict; *believing* (for everybody) that painful losses may be healed and that there may be more to God than can ever be known, and (for the believing child) believing in Ganesha.

2.2.2 The concept of religion

In the presentation of their strategy, the authors do not provide an overall concept of religion, as they deal only with certain aspects of religions. There are, however, some statements in their publications that hint at some aspects of the concept of religion that lies at the heart of this approach to RE. Following Rudolf Otto's idea of the holy, religious objects are interpreted as *numina*, i.e. religious elements "charged with the sacred beauty of faith and thus offering to the child something of the numinous."[122] The authors of the teachers' manual speak of the "dynamism of the religious materials".[123] The basic idea is that religions contain a range of gifts that can be obtained by followers of a particular tradition and other people alike and that there are other gifts which are accessible only to the people belonging to that tradition. This is why a distinction is made between the gift of believing for all children in the classroom, regardless of their religion, and for the child that belongs to the tradition in question. John Hull phrases this idea as follows: "There

---

121 Grimmitt et al. 1991: A Gift to the Child, 14f.
122 Hull 2000: Religion in the Service of the Child Project, 115.
123 Grimmitt et al. 1991: A Gift to the Child, 6.

is a holiness about religion which everyone can experience, but there is a deeper holiness which only the faithful know."[124]

The framework for the representation of religions in this approach is based on an interpretation of the religious items as beautiful and holy objects.[125] A survey of the publications of the *Religion in the Service of the Child Project* reveals that this approach takes over more ideas from the early phenomenology of religion as promoted, for example, by Rudolf Otto, than just the idea of the holy and the classification of certain objects as numina. Certain formulations imply – though subtly – a common essence behind the variety of religious phenomena. Suggested attainment targets, for example, that children should "be familiar with a range of various images of the divine" and "appreciate that devotion to the divine takes many forms",[126] imply a unity of "the divine" (as an entity) in the variety of religious phenomena. It has been pointed out that this approach to the variety of religions is based on theological assumptions and can therefore not provide a framework for RE that tries to avoid taking a theological perspective on religions.[127]

2.2.3 The notion of education

As in the Westhill Project, in the *Religion in the Service of the Child Project* education is also seen as the process of widening one's horizon. The process of teaching and learning consists in an interaction between the teacher and the pupils and is therefore not predictable. Teachers of RE need sufficient background knowledge, but their own religious beliefs are irrelevant to their qualification as a teacher as long as they are open to the "beauty and pain" of the material they teach.[128] The suggested teaching strategy consists in a direct confrontation with the material and a fixed pattern for this encounter with the religious items. In this

---

124 Hull 2000: Religion in the Service of the Child Project, 121.
125 I found only one passage which might be interpreted as not presupposing the holiness of the objects. In Grimmitt et al. 1991: A Gift to the Child, 12, the authors write: "The beauty and holiness of religious material are not of an automatic or magical kind. All human meaning emerges in human contexts, and the teaching is a partly controlled activity that enables certain aspects of meaning to emerge from the material and from the children."
126 Both quotations are taken from Grimmitt et al. 1991: A Gift to the Child, 130.
127 See for example Jackson 1997: RE. An Interpretive Approach, chapter 1, where Jackson refers for example to Jacques Waardenburg's criticism of the classical phenomenology of religion.
128 Grimmitt et al. 1991: A Gift to the Child, 15.

intensive and in-depth study of selected religious objects, the abilities to communicate and empathise are regarded as central.

The authors emphasise that parents should be informed about the character and contents of RE. Thereby, RE could also contribute to better community relations.[129] The *Religion in the Service of the Child Project* acknowledges the multireligious classroom with children of different religious or non-religious backgrounds. One characteristic acknowledgement of the difference in religious orientation of the children is the distinction the authors make with respect to the gift of belief:

> "The numen might give a child a gift of *belief*. Faith itself or the strengthening of faith might be the gift. At this point, and only at this point the grid of gifts distinguishes between the gift of belief or faith offered to the believing child, and that offered to the unbelieving child."[130]

2.2.4 Comment

Taking up what Hull said in the quotation above, I am not sure if the idea of the gift of belief can be upheld in secular integrative RE. The very classification of belief as a gift seems indebted to a particular belief system and therefore problematic in this context. Is belief really an educational learning outcome, i.e. can you really say that belief is a desirable aim of RE? Or is an identification of aims in the category belief not necessarily a theological statement promoting particular beliefs? If we look at the examples of possible gifts in the category *believing*[131] (for all children, not just the believing child) we find, on the one hand, empirically verifiable statements such as "that life can be lived with hope and purpose", "that painful losses may be healed", "that the direction of one's life can unexpectedly be changed". On the other hand, we find specific beliefs, such as "that life is a mystery", "that everybody is called in some way", "that there is more than this world", which express a worldview that may not be shared by the pupils and which I think cannot really be desired learning outcomes of integrative RE. On what grounds can one claim that it is better to believe that there is more than this world than not to believe it? And if a child does not agree with the belief "that there is always hope"[132], is that less desirable than

---

129 Ibid., 15.
130 Hull 2000: Religion in the Service of the Child Project, 118.
131 In the grid of gifts in Grimmitt et al. 1991: A Gift to the Child, 124. The following quotations are taken from there.
132 Grimmitt et al. 1991: A Gift to the Child, 125.

the contrary, i.e. is the former belief a gift and the latter not? To categorise beliefs as gifts (and in this approach as desired learning outcomes) is a theological statement that ought to be avoided in integrative RE.

My view of the gift of believing for the believing child is also critical. At this point, the general aim of integrative RE is at stake again: In integrative RE, is it a desired learning outcome for e.g. a Christian child to believe "in angels" or "that God is worthy of praise", "that one's life should be full of praise" and "that God is known through emotions"?[133] Regardless of whether one agrees with the selection of theological assumptions that underlie those beliefs – which are, of course, by no means representative for the whole range of Christian theological ideas and beliefs – I am not convinced that particular beliefs like these fall within the realm of desirable learning outcomes of integrative RE at all, even if they are only meant for the children that belong to that particular religion. The authors ask: "Why should not Muslim children become better Muslims through an encounter with the Call to Prayer at school?"[134] I again regard this sentence as problematic. In the ideological framework of integrative RE there should be no room for an unquestioned concept like "better Muslim" (which of course implies that there are also "worse Muslims"). Theological concepts of this nature may be discussed in class, but cannot be accepted as given.[135]

I suggest replacing the category "believing" with the category "understanding", even though the authors do not see understanding as a primary aim of RE, but rather as secondary to the goal of the strategy.[136] However, I think it is important that the children understand claims such as "that there is always hope", "that God is worthy of praise" or "that one's life should be full of praise" (see above), independently from the question of whether this corresponds to their own beliefs or not. This is, in my view, the only way to preserve the secular character of the subject, while due attention is still given to the development of the children. Understanding may be an understanding of religious and non-religious beliefs, but also an understanding of the difference between beliefs and verifiable facts. In contrast to promoting beliefs, promoting an understanding of beliefs is an appropriate aim of an integrative RE that is not indebted to any theological point of view. Pro-

---

133 All quotations are taken from the "grid of gifts" in ibid., 125.
134 Ibid., 13.
135 And again, would Muslim parents agree with the idea that their children may become "better Muslims" through an encounter with the Call to Prayer in school RE?
136 See Grimmitt et al. 1991: A Gift to the Child, 124f.

moting beliefs cannot be an aim of integrative RE, as this would always be the promotion of particular beliefs at the cost of others.

In a primary RE context, the "gift"-concept is creative, original and helpful in many respects. The methods which are based on this idea provide valuable tools for representing ideas, wisdom, inspirations and insights from different religions. However, at the same time, the very concept "gift" obscures the learning outcomes in this approach. This is because the learning outcomes are not clearly defined themselves but somehow mystified and surrounded with an aura of spirituality when they are referred to as gifts. It is not entirely clear which skills are regarded as essential and desirable for RE and which as possible side effects, especially with respect to belief. The teaching strategy, with its entering and distancing devices, seems to create an atmosphere in which children may be introduced to – in Rudolf Otto's terms – the mystery of "the holy" or encounter "holy" objects. Even though these devices may be helpful for creating respect on the part of the pupils, the interpretation of the religious items as numina takes this idea too far, as it seems to try to elicit a religious appreciation of the items, because the holiness of the items is presupposed as the general framework in which the encounters take place. Furthermore, the lack of reference to the ambivalence of religions, which are not always just "nice", presents holiness and religion as inherently valuable. Thus, the impression is created that religious worldviews (and related "items") have a particular quality that non-religious worldviews, which are not related to the holy in Otto's sense, lack. Thereby, religious worldviews are privileged over non-religious worldviews and the secular character of integrative RE is at stake.

In the teaching sequence, the contextualisation phase is crucial for the acceptability of this approach. The contextualisation of an item, which is deliberately left out in the beginning in order to enable a direct and uninhibited encounter, is not called off completely but presented a little later. Thus, the religious material is not corrupted, but only temporarily instrumentalised and taken out of its context. This is a helpful concept for enabling an initial direct encounter between the pupils and the religious item. Background information, which is necessary in order to understand the role of the religious item in its original contexts, is provided immediately after the first impressions of the pupils. The project team presents well reflected distancing devices which make this sequence possible. Thus, the teaching strategy succeeds in serving two different purposes: an immediate encounter with religious items as well as an understanding of the role of religious items in their original contexts.

2.3 The Experiential Approach

The experiential approach to RE emerged from the work of the *Religious Experience and Education Project* (REEP), which was established in the second part of the 1980s at the University of Nottingham. It refers to the theories of the biologist Alister Hardy, who regarded religious experience as a characteristic of every human being and as a criterion in the process of natural selection. David Hay, the main exponent of the experiential approach, links his own findings about spirituality in Great Britain to Hardy's theories, assuming that the majority of people interpret at least a part of their experience spiritually or religiously. Hay regards this as a fundamental contradiction to the dominant secularity in modern Britain, which he believes has an indoctrinatory function leading to the suppression of religious experience and a climate in which not many people dare to talk about religious experience for fear of being called stupid or mad. In this context, Hay and his colleges regard the questioning of, and acting against, this concealed secular indoctrination as one important task of RE in order to make the religious worldview plausible again. For this reason they developed a handbook for teachers, which outlines exercises for extending the pupils' awareness.[137] They regard these exercises as a necessary complement to the existing syllabuses for religious education.

2.3.1 Aims and contents of integrative RE

In the experiential approach, the main task of RE is regarded as *deindoctrination* in order to show that there is more than one – the perceived dominant secularist – perspective on reality. The idea is to help the pupils to extend their awareness and to promote their respect for the various responses to reality. Additionally, teachers are supposed to attempt to show the pupils that the different ways of being human actually present personal possibilities for themselves. It is the purpose of RE to provide assistance for the pupils to open their consciousness to those aspects of ordinary human experience which religious people take particularly seriously. This is called *relational consciousness*, an increased awareness or perceptiveness. Hay regards nurturing relational consciousness in the classroom as a "first step in creating the conditions for

---

137 Hammond, Hay et al. 1990: New Methods in Teaching RE.

an insight into the roots of religion".[138] The stimulation of relational consciousness is described as a kind of preparation for one's own religious experience. In RE, pupils are meant to be encouraged to develop their own individual response to the spiritual dimension in order to deepen their personal consciousness of the spiritual. Consciousness of one's own spiritual experience is regarded as a prerequisite for empathy with other religious experiences. Looking at one's own experience of the sacred enables a better understanding of the religious experience of others, because understanding believers is only possible on the basis of an acknowledgement of the fact that all visible phenomena of religions have emerged as a response to the experience of a sacred dimension of reality.[139]

The project team illustrates this position with the help of a story in which religions are compared to maps which show a beautiful land, the sphere of the sacred. It is the aim of RE to get to know this sphere itself. It is, therefore, not enough just to study the maps (i.e. the religions), but it is necessary to visit the lands they describe in order to really understand what the maps want to express. On this journey, one is supposed to rely on one's own experience and use the maps for orientation.[140] To concentrate on external phenomena of religions, for example, doctrines, ethical questions, pilgrimage or rituals "is to ignore the most central issue in religion – its spirituality".[141] This is the project team's main criticism of a descriptive approach. A descriptive approach also makes conversation about experience possible, but it regards active involvement as inappropriate in RE. Therefore, the project team claims, it cannot offer methods for accessing the experience of believers. An RE based on the methods of the world-religions school runs the risk of being clinical and sterile, as it cannot convey the fascination of a faith: "The affective dimension is wholly ignored as the passion of belief is dispassionately presented"[142]. Thus, the descriptive approach cannot communicate anything of the actuality of the experience that lies at the heart of faith. Brian Netto concludes that, without the aims, activities

---

138 Hay 2000: The Religious Experience and Education Project, 83.
139 See for example Hammond, Hay et al. 1990: New Methods in Teaching RE, 12.
140 The story *The Limits of Maps* can be found on p. 19 in Hammond, Hay et al. 1990: New Methods in Teaching RE. As no source is given, I suppose that this story was written by the project team for this particular purpose. The project team's own interpretation of the story, which is described in this paragraph, follows on p. 20ff.
141 Hammond, Hay et al. 1990: New Methods in Teaching RE, 13.
142 Ibid., 21. The terms "descriptive approach" and "world religions school" are used interchangeably.

and methods of the *Religious Experience and Education Project*, integrative RE is reduced to a dry "naming of parts".[143]

The project team regards their approach as a bridge between the study of religion and the experience of religion.[144] RE ought to provide, they claim, both the diversity and openness of the descriptive approach and at the same time a "real sense" of the spiritual experience which "lies behind the wide spectrum of belief and practice".[145] In the conceptual framework of the *Religious Experience and Education Project*, the inner experience of the pupils is an important aspect of RE, as becoming aware of and trying to understand one's own inwardness is regarded as a prerequisite for understanding the subjectivity of other people. The process of understanding is rooted in the pupils' own experience. It is determined by their experience of faith and not by a mere study of its underlying concepts.[146]

The project team developed a set of exercises by which teachers may guide the pupils towards an experience. These exercises are regarded as ways for the pupils to approach their spirituality by raising their awareness for the world of the spiritual. The exercises are also regarded as a means of communicating the spiritual insights of the religious traditions of the world.[147] The exercises follow a fixed structure:

- *Getting started*: creation of a climate in which the pupils can share their views comfortably and safely.
- *Raising awareness*: the attention of the one's consciousness should be directed at the here-and-now. This phase comprises exercises in stilling and listening for the pupils "so that they gain insight into the dimensions of ordinary human awareness attended to by religious believers in the practices of prayer and meditation."[148]
- *Embodying awareness*: being mindful of one's own body and body language; exploring the uniqueness of personal identity;

---

[143] Netto 1990: Multi-faith RE and experiential learning, 198.
[144] Cf. also Potter 1990: The Durham Pilot Project, 184.
[145] Hammond, Hay et al. 1990: New Methods in Teaching RE, 21. Here, they also claim that recent documents (which they unfortunately do not specify any further) imply that "it is this sense of experience which is essential if the real nature of religion is to be grasped."
[146] Cf. Netto 1990: Multi-faith RE and experiential learning, 198. See also Hammond, Hay et al. 1990: New Methods in Teaching RE, 17.
[147] Cf., e.g., Hammond, Hay et al. 1990: New Methods in Teaching RE, 21, 28; Hay and Hammond 1992: When you pray, go to your private room, 149 and Netto: Multi-faith RE and experiential learning, 198.
[148] Hay 2000: The Religious Experience and Education Project, 79.

recognising the embodied nature of one's own human consciousness and empathising with the self-perceptions of others.
- *Framing awareness*: looking at metaphors and symbols which frame our awareness; as religious metaphors are vehicles used for articulating religious experience, pupils should investigate how metaphors affect their own and others' perceptions of reality.
- *Extending awareness*: investigation of the imaginative use of symbols; use of story and guided fantasy.
- *Endings*: time for the pupils to reorientate themselves.[149]

2.3.2 The concept of religion and the representation of religions

The attempt to find a middle way between the study of religions and theology leads the *Religious Experience and Education Project* to form a notion of religion which, in many respects, resembles the concepts of religion of phenomenologists of religion like Rudolf Otto, Friedrich Heiler or Mircea Eliade[150]: The historical religions are interpreted as the outer expressions of inner experiences of the sacred. For Hammond, Hay et al. the experience of the sacred is the unquestioned criterion for telling if something is religious or not:

> "The historical religions, endlessly colourful, creative, tangled up with politics and every other dimension of life, are in all cases the public expression of an inner experience of the sacred. And if the rituals and activities of religion, however vivid, politically significant or aesthetically moving are not an expression of, or response to, the human experience of the sacred, then they are not religious. At best, they are well-meaning make-believe, at worst, corrupt."[151]

The sacred is regarded as a reality to which the different religions refer. In order to understand the religions one has to get to know the sacred itself. The project team uses the map analogy to clarify their view: religions refer to the sphere of the sacred, however imperfectly, like maps which do not provide a perfect image of a land either. Religions can be

---

[149] For a description of the activities see e.g. Hay 2000: The Religious Experience and Education Project, 78-82. The main part of Hammond, Hay et al. 1990: New Methods in Teaching RE (p. 31-176) also follows this structure and suggests activities for the individual aspects.

[150] See, for example, Otto 1979: Das Heilige, Heiler 1920: Das Gebet, and 1961: Erscheinungsformen und Wesen der Religion, Eliade 1957: Das Heilige und das Profane.

[151] Hammond, Hay et al. 1990: New Methods in Teaching RE, 10.

regarded as a means to explore the reality that lies behind them. They may, however, also be obstacles, if one is content with studying only the religions themselves and does not set off to explore the path to the land of the sacred for oneself, which may, for example, happen in an RE which does not refer to the spiritual realities behind the religions.[152]

This notion of religion is based on a liberal Christian philosophy of religion which is concerned with an enquiry into the source and essence of religion.[153] Religions are regarded as responses to the experience of the sacred, they represent different paths to experiencing the sacred. Experience is identified as the central aspect of religiosity and personal experience is regarded as a prerequisite for understanding the experience of others. This approach is very similar to Rudolf Otto's view in *Das Heilige*, where he writes on one of the first pages that those who have not yet experienced the sacred for themselves should not read any further, as they would not be able to understand what follows.[154] This approach to understanding religions is based on the assumption that there is a common source for the different religions, which is rooted in experience. Religious experience as well as religion are interpreted as something that transcends the actual phenomena and religions. The essential unity of religious experience, with no considerable differences in the individual religions, is claimed. This theory is the presupposition for the methods described in the activities for experiential RE, by which understanding is sought. These methods can be regarded as one way of applying Heiler's idea that it is necessary to "immerse oneself in the atmosphere of the sacred" in order to get a feeling for religion(s) at all.[155] A limitation of RE to a study of religions – to use the words of the map analogy: map reading – means that the sphere of the sacred cannot be accessed at all.[156]

Meditation, prayer and profound contemplation are seen as the heart of religion for committed believers. These activities enable them to immerse themselves in the deepest way in the reality of their religion. A causal relationship is established between experience and action. Experience may result in action, for example if the experience of God's love in prayer gives rise to the motivation to take action in social or po-

---

152 Cf. ibid., 19ff.
153 This is made explicit in, e.g., Netto 1990: The changing nature of religious education, 198.
154 Cf. Otto 1979: Das Heilige, 8.
155 The original phrase is "[E]intauchen in die Atmosphäre des Heiligen", see Heiler 1961: Erscheinungsformen und Wesen der Religion, 16.
156 Cf. Hammond, Hay et al. 1990: New Methods in Teaching RE, 19f.

litical matters. In line with Mircea Eliade's philosophy of religion, rituals are interpreted as actions in which believers re-experience important moments of the history of their religion. These moments are interpreted as particularly powerful manifestations of the sacred.[157]

The experiential approach is based on the thesis that, in order to really understand the diversity of religious experiences represented in Great Britain, one has to learn to empathise with that realm of human experience. In order to gain some insight into the realm of the spiritual, one has to be introduced to the "knowledge" out of which religion grows. This knowledge is different from knowledge about religion. The former kind of knowledge, which resembles sensory and affective consciousness, though it cannot be separated from cognition, is logically prior to it.[158] A basic assumption of the approach is that the different traditions use different languages and metaphors to refer to the world of the sacred.[159] This implies that it is one single world of the sacred which can be accessed by the different traditions. On this condition, the conclusion that an understanding of one's own experience enables a better understanding of others is consistent, because then what is experienced is actually the same. Against this background the extension of one's own awareness, which is the aim of the activities suggested by the project team, can be described as pointing directly at the sources of religious motivation for the believer.[160]

2.3.3 The notion of education

The notion of education in the experiential approach rests on the proposition that the potential for religious experience is inherent in every human being. From their recent research, David Hay and Rebecca Nye conclude that every child has a spirituality and is able to talk about it. Uncovering and developing the pupils' relational consciousness, which they see as necessary for survival, is regarded as the central task of education.[161]

---

[157] Cf. ibid., 12, Hay 1985: Suspicion of the Spiritual: 143, cf. also Eliade, e.g. 1953: Der Mythos der ewigen Wiederkehr or 1957: Das Heilige und das Profane.
[158] Cf. Hay 1998: The naturalness of relational consciousness, 144f.
[159] Cf., e.g., Hammond, Hay et al. 1990: New Methods in Teaching RE, 16.
[160] Cf. ibid: 11.
[161] Cf. Hay 2000: The Religious Experience and Education Project: 83, see also Hay and Nye 1996: Investigating children's spirituality and 1998: The Spirit of the Child. Their findings about the spirituality of children are based on children's reactions to photos. Children were asked to comment on photos which showed children of about

The very essence of education is a widening of perspectives. The project team claims that in a country like the United Kingdom, which is secular to a large extent, this widening of perspectives involves helping the pupils to overcome the constricting influence of the culture of which they are a part. They need to become open for alternative worldviews. Teachers and pupils should cooperate in the process of extending their own personal freedom and understanding of others. Education must not be understood as meaning that somebody who knows instructs somebody who does not know. The project team refers to ideas of Plato about education when they write that a teacher assists the pupils in the process of discerning what they already potentially know. Thus, it is the task of an RE teacher "to identify what ... pupils already 'potentially know' about religion."[162] In order to achieve that, the teacher has to help the students to overcome any barriers which prevent them from bringing to light what they already know.

An appreciation of, and respect for, the experience of others requires becoming aware of ones own subjective experience first. As participant observers, pupils ought to try to enter as far as possible into the metaphors and experiences of believers. The idea is to get an impression "from the inside". In the words of the map-story, this means that one has to visit the places oneself in order to really learn something about them.[163] RE teachers have to know the territory of religious experience themselves. On this basis they are able to identify a starting point from which their pupils may explore it. The teacher functions as a facilitator rather than somebody who transmits information, as a teacher-controlled transmission of knowledge is not regarded as beneficial to the pupils' understanding and appreciation of inner experience. The project team of the experiential approach acknowledges the limitations of human reason and logical thought – a position they find in all major religious traditions. Therefore, they concentrate on the necessity of action, of doing and being, rather than on cognitive understanding.[164]

---

the same age in situations in which it can be expected that spiritual ideas may arise, e.g. a girl looking out of a window, a boy standing at the window of his bedroom looking at the stars, or a girl which cries because her hamster has died.

162 Hammond, Hay et al. 1990: New Methods in Teaching RE, 7. For this paragraph, cf. ibid., 7, 18; see also Hay 2000: The Religious Experience and Research Project, 74.

163 Cf. Hay 1985: Suspicion of the Spiritual, 147; for the interpretation of the map-story with respect to education see Hammond, Hay et al. 1990: New Methods in Teaching RE, 19f.

164 Cf. Hammond, Hay et al. 1990: New Methods in Teaching RE, 21, 24; see also Potter 1990: The Durham Pilot Project,184.

Ordinary, not specifically religious aspects of human experience, which tend to become stunted in secular culture, need to be formally introduced "if the pupil is to have any grasp at all of the ways in which religious people view life".[165] Pupils have to be encouraged to open their consciousness to the here and now of experience. This *point mode* of consciousness is the common experiential basis of children and religious people. It is also the basis for exploring different ways of seeing. Pupils should take seriously the role of metaphors in the process of interpreting and focussing on their own experience of life. Thereby, they may become aware of the power of language and intentions in the process of structuring experience.[166]

2.3.4 Critical evaluation

A discussion of the problematic aspects of this approach is difficult because of the interrelations between different levels of argument. Some criticism is only possible if one temporarily takes for granted the authors' acceptance of some problematic assumptions in order to pursue their line of argument, because otherwise certain aspects could not be addressed at all. A generally critical perspective on those assumptions is, however, also necessary. The main focus of my criticism of this approach is on its concept of religion and the representation of religions. The concluding general evaluation, which includes a criticism of the concept of education at work in this approach, shows that the experiential approach may have its place within a particular framework which is based on theological assumptions, but cannot be applied in an integrative RE which acknowledges basic principles of the academic study of religions.

In the authors' analysis of contemporary society, Great Britain is on the one hand regarded as a highly secular society, on the other hand the pupils' multireligious environment is acknowledged. The task of helping pupils to develop a genuine understanding of other faiths than their own is regarded as difficult "in a multi-faith environment where differences of culture involve wide differences in the language and

---

[165] Hammond, Hay et al. 1990: New Methods in Teaching RE, 17.
[166] This point mode of consciousness is contrasted with the ordinary *line mode*, see Hay 2000: The Religious Experience and Research Project, 76. To illustrate what he means by exploring different ways of seeing Hay uses the example of the Necker cube, see ibid., 75f., Hay and Nye 1998: The Spirit of the Child, 165ff, cf. also Hammond and Hay 1990: New Methods in Teaching RE, 13f.

metaphors used to refer to the world of the sacred."[167] Apart from the fact that the theory of religions underlying this claim is problematic, I am not sure if this view of religious plurality is helpful in this context. The variety of language and metaphors is regarded as a problem rather than a natural expression of difference which could also be seen as an interesting starting point for learning something about human beings and thereby widening one's horizon. It seems to me that, in contemporary educational contexts, it would be wiser to see variety as an opportunity rather than a problem, if children are to learn to deal with the actual situation rather than a distorting construct suggesting a (lost?) unity which does not necessarily correspond to the children's actual experience. And – taking account of the multireligious context – it may on the contrary be argued that in an environment in which children encounter different religions and worldviews every day it may be much easier to establish mutual understanding than in a context in which there is no actual contact with the other positions.

The concept of religion

The concept of religion underlying this approach is a theological construct that interprets the variety of religions as different expressions of the experience of the holy and all phenomena that are not human responses to the experience of the holy as not religious. In the story "The Limits of Maps"[168] the theological character of the approach is made explicit. The individual religions cannot fully reveal the true nature of the realm of the sacred. This claim conflicts fundamentally with the understanding many religious people have of their own religious traditions and can therefore not form the framework for the representation of religions in integrative RE. In his criticism of this approach, Kevin Mott-Thornton asks, for example, what Muslims would think about the claim that their religion provides an inadequate path to Allah or that it is an insuperable obstacle for the spiritual journey. He also criticises that "[t]he notion that the religious tradition is 'made' by earlier religious pioneers and is therefore intrinsically faulty runs directly against the Islamic view that the central elements of the tradition are directly from Allah."[169] In my view, Mott-Thornton is absolutely correct when

---

167 Hammond, Hay et al. 1990: New Methods in Teaching RE, 16.
168 Ibid., 19, see description above.
169 Mott-Thornton 1996: Language, dualism and experiential RE, 162.

he criticises that this approach to the different religions as exemplified in the map-story suggests that many adherents misunderstand their own tradition. He regards this as "evidence of an emerging and uncritical neo-confessionalism, which embodies fashionable and questionable theological assumptions."[170] The theological presuppositions at heart of the approach make it unacceptable for integrative RE.

Andrew Wright identifies the Christian theological roots of the concept of religion used in this approach. Schleiermacher's interpretation of religion as an expression of human experience, the experience of ultimate dependence (*schlechthinnige Abhängigkeit*) in particular, and the following traditions of liberal Protestantism (as promoted, for example, by Ritschl, Harnack and Bultmann) was transformed into a universal theology that embraced all religious traditions, for example by Wilfred Cantwell Smith and John Hick. This model of religions is, however, only one among many and Wright asks on what grounds it could be justified as a framework for modern RE given "its geographical and temporal limitations as a product of occidental modernism, and ... its primarily apologetic origins"[171]. Wright also uses Islam as an example to show the tensions between this model and the understanding adherents have of their religions. He regards the idea that religious experience lies at the core of Islam as patronising and as one which forces Islam into a liberal Western mould.[172]

The representation of religions

Integrative RE is one area of children's lives in which they can actually learn about and from the different religions. Attempting to analyse the representation of the different religions in the experiential approach is not an easy task, as the empirical religions themselves are not really being dealt with at all in this approach. In the handbook for teachers we do not find religious people's descriptions of their own experiences, which could have been presented as a starting point for empathy. My criteria for analysing the representation of religions cannot be applied to this approach, because a representation of the different empirical religions is virtually absent. In this approach, one aspect of religion –

---

170 Ibid.
171 Wright 1996: Language and Experience in the Hermeneutics of Religious Understanding 170, for the argument see p. 169f.
172 See ibid., 173. Cf. also section 2.5 in this chapter on Wright's critical approach to RE and his critique of the "liberal consensus".

experience – is decontextualised to such an extent that its character as an empirical phenomenon within different traditions cannot be made plausible any more.

The theological view of the plurality of religions, which is used as a framework for experiential RE, makes a study of the individual religions unnecessary. The religions themselves are just seen as maps on the way to the experience of the holy, which is what "religion" is really about. Within this philosophical construct the individual ways in which human beings may approach the holy are not even studied (contrary to the methods of most scholars who used "the phenomenological method"), but another path – the different exercises for raising awareness – is created in order to accompany the children on their way to a state of mind in which they may experience the holy for themselves. Ironically then, in this approach to a subject that is supposed to be about the different religions, there is hardly any room for those at all. A study of the individual religions is made superfluous by an overall theological framework which claims an essential unity of religions. The combination of this theology of religions with an emphasis on experience results in a purported study of religious experience "as such", independent from the study of individual religions.

General evaluation

Notwithstanding its possible applicability in contexts in which the theological presuppositions mentioned are accepted, the experiential approach is highly problematic within a framework which takes seriously the premises of an integrative RE based on insights from the academic study of religions.[173] This is not only a criticism of minor points that may be modified, but the very concept of this approach rests on assumptions that are unacceptable in an integrative RE environment. Several problems of this approach have been addressed before[174] but have not led to convincing modifications in more recent publications of the project team. This is perhaps not possible as the criticism addresses the premises, general framework and methodology of the approach as such.

---

173 For example, taking seriously the individual religious traditions, not using one particular theological construct as an overall framework, trying to be acceptable to the variety of religious traditions etc.
174 See, for example, Wright 1996: Language and experience in the hermeneutics of religious understanding.

The approach is theological and therefore indebted to one particular religious tradition; the subject is instrumentalised for a particular theological interest. The concept of religion is part of the liberal Christian tradition, extended to include other religions within this framework. It fundamentally contradicts the view many people, for example Muslims or Buddhists, have of their own religions. Furthermore, the main "field" of integrative RE, the different religious traditions, hardly finds a place at all in this approach. The notion of education is also problematic because of its over-emphasis on experience, which makes the learning outcomes dependent on religious experience. If we apply the message of the map-story about education to other subjects, it would mean, for example, that it would be necessary to visit the different countries of the world in geography lessons[175] and make journeys through time in history lessons, etc. in order not to just "learn about" the issues at stake.

In the publications of the *Religious Experience and Education Project* there is a lack of clarity with respect to basic concepts. Ideas are sometimes introduced by means of brainstorming, thought-experiments or images and the reader is left with the vagueness of these ideas which are not followed by a clear definition of concepts. This is most obvious in the way the difference between spirituality and religion is explained.[176] This vagueness obscures the basic presuppositions of the approach. Furthermore, different levels of understanding are confused. The authors are absolutely correct in their call for an acknowledgement of the intentions and the implicit aspects of religion in order to understand religious traditions. But they erroneously identify this acknowledgement with the claim that one's own religious experience is necessary in order to understand religious people. What they mean is a kind of religious understanding which is possible only in a generally religious framework, presupposing their assumptions about the unity of religious experience. That is something completely different from the kind of understanding that can be sought in a secular educational subject.

---

[175] The important difference is, however, that there is at least general agreement that these countries actually exist, contrary to the sphere of the sacred.
[176] See Hammond and Hay 1990: New Methods in Teaching RE, 6ff.

2.4 The Interpretive Approach

The interpretive approach to RE was developed by a team around Robert Jackson, the director of the *Warwick Religions and Education Research Unit* (WRERU) in the Institute of Education at the University of Warwick. Other members of the team are, for example, Eleanor Nesbitt, Judith Everington and Julia Ipgrave. In this approach a methodological rationale for the subject is combined with ethnographic theory and fieldwork among children in Great Britain as a basis for curriculum development. The representation of religions is one of the main concerns in this approach, which can be described as a middle way between a reification of cultures and religions as discrete entities and complete deconstruction. Textbooks like those of the series *Bridges to Religions* or *Interpreting Religions* build on the methodology and field work of the *Warwick RE Project* (WREP). The project team cooperates with scholars from different countries. Therefore, projects based on its methodology have also been developed in other countries. The interpretive approach is outlined comprehensively in the works of Jackson, for example *Religious Education. An Interpretive Approach* (1997). Other publications of the project team focus on individual aspects of the project, for example, the role of ethnographic research, fieldwork, the representation of individual religions or further methodological questions like the integration of interpretive methodology in agreed syllabuses.[177] Recent developments and a contextualisation within other approaches to RE are given in Jackson's *Rethinking Religious Education and Plurality. Issues in Diversity and Pedagogy* (2004).

In the following characterisation of the interpretive approach, after an outline of the project's general perspective on the aims and contents of integrative RE in multicultural societies, emphasis will be placed on the way the different religions are represented and the concept of religion on which this representation is based. This will be illustrated with examples from the representation of Hinduism and the methodological considerations around it. Then, the project's approach to education will be outlined, also taking account of the way the individual is interpreted in this context. After an overview of recent developments and projects which employ the theoretical framework and methodologies developed in the interpretive approach, its general contribution to an integrative RE which is based on principles of the academic study of religions is evaluated.

---

[177] See for example Nesbitt 2001: Ethnographic research at Warwick: some methodological issues, 2001: What young Hindus believe, 2002: Ethnography and religious education, Everington 1998: Evolution not revolution, Ipgrave 1999: Issues in the delivery of RE to Muslim pupils.

2.4.1 Aims and contents of integrative RE

Integrative RE in multicultural societies ought to be secular, but not secularist. In a conversational framework which respects the existence of different truth claims without taking one of them as given – but also not excluding the possibility that one of them may be correct – the aim of the subject is described by Robert Jackson as follows:

- to develop an understanding of the grammar – the language and wider symbolic patterns – of religions and
- to foster communication across different religious and cultural positions.[178]

Thus, the aims of integrative RE are twofold: in addition to the basic aim of developing an understanding of the religious worldviews of others, their religious language and symbols, feelings and attitudes, it is hoped "that good relationships between those from different religious and cultural backgrounds will be promoted".[179] The first of the aims also requires a development of interpretive skills which are necessary for the kind of understanding attempted. Children should be helped to reflect their studies of ways of life which differ in many respects from their own. In the terminology of Richard Rorty, the project team calls the deepening of one's self-understanding by studying other worldviews *edification*, a new perspective on the familiar as a result of a study of the unfamiliar. The effects of edification, which in some points resembles M. Grimmitt's idea of *learning from* religion, cannot, however, be precisely predicted.

2.4.2 The concept of religion and the representation of religions

In the Warwick RE project, a concept of religion which is carefully elaborated and which draws on insights from the academic study of religions as well as anthropology forms the basis for the development of methods for representing religions in RE. The close relationship between religions and cultures allows a combination of methods building on theories from the different disciplines, which often overlap. Jackson is critical of the concept *world religion* which has often been used in British RE since the rise of "Religious Studies" at British universities in the

---

[178] Jackson 1997: RE. An Interpretive Approach, 76 and 92.
[179] Ibid., 112.

mid 1960s. There are different interpretations of what *the world religions* are about, including, for example, "(living) religions of the world", or the distinction between *world religions* and other religions – as e.g. primal religions – according to criteria like a universal message or mission. The liberal Christian influence on the development of the idea of a world religion and the general problem of the power relations inherent in the process of definition led Jackson to conclude that, if one continues to use the term *world religions*, one should do so critically.[180] The concept of religion on which the representation of religions in the interpretive approach is based builds on a critical evaluation of the methods of the phenomenology of religion, interpretive anthropology as carried out by Clifford Geertz, Wilfred Cantwell Smith's concept of religion and considerations concerning the relationship between religion and culture.[181]

The phenomenology of religion

As has been shown in section 1 of this chapter, phenomenology has been highly influential in the emergence and development of integrative RE in England. In the late 1960s and early 1970s, the phenomenological or "undogmatic" approach was regarded as the secular counterpart to confessional RE. Phenomenological approaches to RE following the ideas of Ninian Smart and his curriculum development project have become important aspects of RE in England. However, the different versions of phenomenological RE have also provoked severe criticism focusing on five main characteristics of the approach:

(1) Phenomenology's apparent sole concern with the external actions of religious practitioners and the observable phenomena of religion and its consequent lack of concern with the motivations of religious believers.
(2) Its over-wide coverage of religions, leading to a superficial treatment or trivialization of faiths.
(3) Its juxtapositions of material on common themes from different religions, leading to confusion.

---

180 Cf. Jackson 1997: RE. An Interpretive Approach, 53ff.
181 See chapters 1 to 3 of Jackson's RE. An Interpretive Approach (1997). Chapter 1 deals with the phenomenology and RE, chapter 2 with anthropology and interpretation, and chapter 3 with the representation of religions.

(4) The remoteness of its subject matter from the experience and concerns of most school children.
(5) Its lack of concern with issues of truth, and its consequent implicit relativism.[182]

Jackson reminds the reader that these criticisms are not applicable to phenomenology *per se*, but that they are applicable only "to some poorly designed materials described by their authors as phenomenological".[183] Much of the criticised material does, in fact, not correspond to the intentions of the phenomenologists. Therefore, the existence of poor thematic materials "should not obscure the possibilities of juxtaposing material from different traditions in illuminating ways that do not compromise the coherence of each one".[184] Furthermore, there is no reason why phenomenological methods may not be combined with others which are more likely to arouse the pupils' interest.

Jackson shows that the work of most early phenomenologists of religion (though not necessarily Smart's) is based on an essentialism related to philosophical phenomenology and theology. The early phenomenologists were almost all Christians trying to make sense of other religions in relation to their own.[185] Jackson considers phenomenology's weaknesses and strengths in order to evaluate which aspects of phenomenological methodology may be saved for RE today. His criticism of phenomenology comprises the following points: knowledge is derived subjectively, with no reference to historical or cultural contexts; the concepts *religions* and *religion* are accepted uncritically, despite the problems surrounding these recently constructed notions; the terminology for describing the different phenomena is taken from a Western and Christian background; the *epoché* principal is not obeyed; the notion of empathy is rather vague; religious data are taken out of their original contexts in place, time society and culture; phenomena are regarded as expressions of universal essences. With reference to the latter point Jackson notes that

> "any cross-cultural search for religious 'essences' is philosophically dubious and lacks a grasp of historical influences on the building of concepts. Rudolph [sic] Otto's contention, for example, that the 'numinous' is a

---

[182] Jackson 1997: RE. An Interpretive Approach, 10.
[183] Ibid., 11.
[184] Ibid., 12.
[185] He mentions, for example, Chantepie de la Saussaye, Brede Kristensen, Heiler, Frick, Söderblom, Widengren and Eliade as emphasising the classificatory aspect, while van der Leeuw's *ideal types* closely correspond to Husserl's *eideia* and make his approach more akin to philosophical phenomenology. Cf. ibid., 13ff.

'unique ... category of value' and a mental state 'perfectly sui generis and irreducible to any other', cannot be regarded as an axiom."[186]

There are, however, also considerable strengths of phenomenology, which make it possible to save some of its methodology while avoiding or laying aside the problematic aspects. The insight that the process of interpretation has to start at the point of the interpreter, for example, is very valuable. The reconstruction of meaning can start from there. Nevertheless, the intention to lay aside one's presuppositions (*bracketing* them out) is methodologically important as a step towards impartiality. The notions of empathy and sensitivity are helpful, but they have to be preceded by the process of grasping the grammar of somebody else's discourse. An acknowledgement of the importance of the insider's testimony is another important aspect, even though one cannot go as far as W. Brede Kristensen who said that "we must refer exclusively to the believer's testimony".[187]

Jackson regards the "new-style" phenomenology of J. Waardenburg as one example of how helpful ideas from the phenomenological tradition may be preserved in an approach which takes on board most of the criticisms.[188] This new-style phenomenology focuses on intentionality in order to reconstruct meanings with particular reference to intentions. Rather than concentrating on secondary textual accounts like the classical phenomenology, it undertakes a contemporary study of living religions. The concept of *epoché* is extended to a suspension of one's own presuppositions about the nature of religion itself. The study of religions is set in the context of a study of other factors, for example social, cultural, political or economic life. Systematic reflection includes checking one's own hypotheses by further empirical research. New-style phenomenology is also concerned with linguistic issues concerning translation and a critical use of scholarly concepts rooted in a Western cultural and religious tradition. Moreover, despite its scholarly character, new-style phenomenology may also be regarded as an art. According to Waardenburg, the researcher's role in the reconstruction of a religious universe resembles that of an actor playing a part, in

---

186 Ibid., 24, referring Rudolf Otto's *The Idea of the Holy*.
187 The original phrase in Norwegian is "Vil vi lære virkelig religion å kjenne, er vi utelukkende henvist til de troendes vitnesbyrd" (Kristensen 1954: Religionshistorisk Studium, 27).
188 It may be added here that the revision of the "phenomenological approach" to religions was by no means undertaken by Jacques Waardenburg alone, but this work of Waardenburg is part of a general trend in the reflection about method and theory in the academic study of religions from about the 1970s onwards. For this debate in the discipline of the study of religions, see chapter I, section 1.1.2.

which an "imaginative faculty" is required. While Husserl referred to *eideia* and van der Leeuw to *ideal types*, Waardenburg tries to identify "structures of intentionality" and discards any quest for a universal, abstract classificatory scheme.[189]

Jackson concludes that standard criticisms of phenomenological approaches to RE are often misplaced, "being applicable only to poorly designed materials which misapply principles from phenomenology".[190] Classical phenomenology does have a number of methodological and philosophical weaknesses and some questionable theological assumptions. Nevertheless, core elements may be preserved in a different approach which includes a consideration of the criticisms of the classical approaches. This may be called a first pillar of the concept of religion and a framework for the representation of religions in interpretive RE. Phenomenology in its new-style version, as suggested by Waardenburg, begins to resemble hermeneutical approaches from interpretive anthropology. One example of that is Waardenburg's interpretation of *epoché* as being aware of the factors that influence one's presuppositions, rather than trying to "bracket them out".

Anthropology and interpretation

Recent interpretive anthropology is the second pillar on which the interpretive approach rests. It provides techniques which the classical phenomenology of religion lacks. A critical examination of the colonialist history of anthropology, which enabled white, Western, male anthropologists to study the exotic "other", raised the issue of reflexivity and provoked a search for less prescriptive and more self-critical methodologies. Jackson refers to the works of Clifford Geertz and his account of the interpretive process. In the reconstruction of the complex interaction between "parts and wholes", field notes, for example, are interpreted as *inscribed actions* or *textualisations*, and not as raw discourse. The complexity of the field, with its different levels of relationships between parts and wholes, should be preserved through the accumulation of detailed field notes in a "thick description". Ethnography is an interpretive activity and may be compared to literary criti-

---

[189] See Waardenburg 1978: Reflections on the Study of Religion, e.g. 102, 110f; cf. Jackson 1997: RE. An Interpretive Approach: 25ff.
[190] Jackson 1997: RE. An Interpretive Approach, 27.

cism: "what we call our data are really our own constructions of other people's constructions of what they and their compatriots are up to".[191]

Ethnography ought to create a balance between *experience-near concepts* (ones easily used by informants themselves) and *experience-distant concepts* (specialist accounts aimed at forwarding scientific, philosophical, or practical aims). This balance is necessary in order "to produce an interpretation of the way a people lives which is neither imprisoned within their mental horizons ... nor systematically deaf to the distinctive tonalities of their existence".[192] The distinction between experience-near and experience-distant concepts is sometimes a matter of degree. However, there is overlap but not identity between concepts used by the insider and the outsider. The benefits of empathy are evaluated critically, as empathy inadvertently comprises a projection of one's own concepts and ways of using them onto different concepts which are structured by a different grammar. Geertz sometimes describes the interpretive process as "translation", which should not be misunderstood as a technical process.[193]

Jackson identifies similarities between Waardenburg's new-style phenomenology and Geertz's ethnographic approach: both describe the hermeneutic exercise as an art and use the oscillation between individual experience and the wider signification system as a means to interpretation.[194] Before Jackson goes on to describe the implications of his survey of the phenomenology of religion and the ethnographic approach for interpretive RE, he takes up criticisms of the works of Geertz by deconstructivist ethnographers like Vincent Crapanzano and James Clifford, who are concerned with issues of authority established in the eyes of the readers of ethnographic works and hierarchies (for example, the hierarchy of ethnographers, readers and the Balinese in Geertz' description of a Balinese cockfight) created in ethnographic descriptions. In his analysis of Geertz' description of a Balinese cockfight, Crapanzano claims that it comprises no understanding of the native from the native's point of view, but only a constructed understanding of a constructed native's point of view. When Geertz constructs constructions of constructions, Crapanzano concludes, this appears to be little more than a projection of his conceptions onto Balinese practice. Another criticism is the absence of dialogical situational aspects, which are re-

---

191 Geertz 1973: The Interpretation of Cultures, 9.
192 Geertz 1983: Local Knowledge, 57.
193 Cf. Jackson 1997: RE. An Interpretive Approach, 37.
194 Cf. ibid., 37f.

garded as important elements of the ethnographic process, in the final representative text. Clifford regards this as a suppression of the dialogical dimension in Geertz's works.[195] In defence of Geertz, Jackson notes that Geertz "is only too aware that ethnographic accounts inevitably obscure the various levels of construction to be found in thickly described field data" and concludes that "Clifford and Crapanzano do not offer anything more convincing than Geertz's hermeneutical method for establishing the relationship between 'parts' and a more general picture of a cultural scene".[196] Jackson's own criticism of Geertz is that some of his work lacks in its form and style the sensitivity that he himself claims should be present in ethnographic work. Furthermore, Geertz fails to relate experience-near and experience-distant concepts in the meticulous way which he himself advocates.[197]

The potential weaknesses of interpretive anthropology ought to be kept in mind when it is applied to the representation of religions in RE. These weaknesses may comprise, for example, the possibility of the interpreter's abuse of authority, the projection of one's own subjective experience on those studied, the tendency to suppress individual voices of insiders and the possibility to construct artificial 'wholes' from the experience of individuals. Having those in mind, the Warwick RE Project suggests methods for the study of religion in the field, the selection of material for the content of RE and the developments of methods for representing the material in the classroom. Interpretive methodology raises several issues of reflexivity, among them (1) the importance of the students' self awareness, the attempt to be aware of the impact of some of one's own presuppositions which are shaped e.g. by gender, academic background, religious views, nationality, ethnicity, class and age; (2) the problems around empathising, such as that one may easily convince oneself of having empathised while this has not actually been the case. Therefore, in order to elucidate other ways of life, it is necessary to compare and contrast elements of one's own language and experience with that of insiders and examine the interplay of the individual insider's experience and behaviour with the wider symbolic context of language, imagery and practice; and (3) edification as a possible personal response of the student to the interpreted material. Generally, a combination of a good technique and sensitivity, including methodo-

---

[195] Cf. ibid., 42; Jackson refers to Crapanzano 1986: Hermes' dilemma: the masking of subversion in ethnographic descriptions, e.g. 71ff. and Clifford 1988: The Predicament of Culture, e.g. 40.
[196] Both quotations are taken from Jackson 1997: RE. An Interpretive Approach, 44.
[197] See ibid., 45.

logical self criticism – a continual self-examination of methodology and practice, is required in order to represent religions and cultures in a vibrant, flexible and organic way.[198]

Religion and religions, culture and cultures

The third pillar on which the methodology of the interpretive approach rests – along with a revised phenomenology of religion and interpretive anthropology – is a consideration of different concepts of religion and religions in relation to what has been developed above, in order to work out criteria for the representation of religions in RE. Jackson follows Wilfred Cantwell Smith's analysis of the emergence and development of the concept *religion* as denoting the totality of all belief systems, a prerequisite for the idea of the phenomenologists that "religion" itself has an essence.[199] Jackson draws attention to the Western and Christian influence on the dominant concept of religion. Generally, power relations are crucial in the process of defining religions and cultures. This has been addressed, for example, by Edward Said in his work *Orientalism* (1978), in which he reveals the tendency of Western writers to superimpose ideas on "other cultures" dichotomising, for example, *the Orient* (them) and *the Occident* (us). Jackson exemplifies Said's ideas with respect to Hinduism.[200] The mistake of constructing static images instead of historical or personal narratives in presenting another culture can be avoided by a criticism of inherited conventions and traditions and an integration of self-criticism as an inherent feature of academic methodologies. Jackson follows the emergence of the terms *Christianity, Judaism, Islam* and *Hinduism* to show their fairly recent make-up and construction. Nevertheless, they have influenced RE in Great Britain to a considerable extent.[201]

Searching for alternative ways of presenting religious data by taking account of their organic, personal and changing nature, Jackson regards Smith's distinction between *faith* (inner religious experience or involvement of a particular person) and cumulative *tradition* (data of

---

198 As opposed to the representation of *religions* as discrete belief systems and *cultures* as separate, bounded entities. Cf. ibid., 45ff.
199 Smith 1978: The Meaning and End of Religion, cf. Jackson 1997: RE. An Interpretive Approach, 51f.
200 Cf. Jackson 1997: RE. An Interpretive Approach, 56f.
201 Cf. ibid., 55ff.

the past religious life of the community) as helpful.[202] Even though Smith's concepts have to be examined critically and may need to be modified with respect to social and political awareness or other issues,[203] the interplay between cumulative tradition as a *whole* and the faith of the individual as a *part* are useful concepts for describing complexities and interdependencies within the framework of the hermeneutic circle. Jackson modifies Smith's *faith and tradition* matrix in order also to take account of significant membership groups of which individuals are parts. For studying and representing religions, he suggests an examination of the relationship between (a) *individuals*, (b) *membership groups*, i.e. relevant groups to which the individual belongs and (c) *the wider religious tradition*. This three-layer matrix serves as a structure for research projects of the Warwick team and is also used in the school books. The distinction between those three levels can help the pupils to appreciate the complexity of religious life and religious traditions by assembling a multi-dimensional picture of the meaning and significance of beliefs and practices.[204]

That the notions religion and culture are regarded as closely related in the interpretive approach has already become obvious from the above, where the implications of recent anthropology for RE were considered. Jackson dedicates one chapter in his *RE. An Interpretive approach* to cultural issues,[205] in which he discusses different notions of culture and their impact on RE in multicultural societies. He takes up anti-racist criticism of multicultural education – e.g. a lack of attention to hierarchies or to the dynamics of and interactions within and between cultures – in order to find more flexible ways of representing and interpreting cultural material. Unlike in a closed view of cultures, the dynamics and the processes of permanent development have to be taken into account, including a study of the peripheries as well as the centres (and the interaction between the two). Jackson refers to the debate about cultural heritage and the role of Christianity in Britain and notes that

---

[202] Jackson does not go as far as Smith, who suggests abandoning the word *religion* completely, cf. Smith 1978: The Meaning and End of Religion: 50. For Jackson's discussion of Smith's ideas see 1997: RE. An Interpretive Approach, 60-69.
[203] For example, Jackson suggests referring to "individual" rather than "personal faith" and draws attention to the fact that there is often disagreement about the borders of a religious tradition. See Jackson 1997: RE. An Interpretive Approach, 62.
[204] See also Everington 1998: Evolution not Revolution, 150.
[205] Chapter 4, "Cultural Issues" in Jackson 1997: RE. An Interpretive Approach.

"Christianity should have an important place in religious education, but not on the grounds that there exists a fixed and unchanging culture or 'British way of life' that requires a study of an equally static Christianity for its preservation. ... Christianity and the other faiths need to be seen as living and internally varied traditions, relating, responding and reacting to one another and to the secularism they all encounter. The Christian tradition also needs to be presented as theologically and ethnically pluralistic."[206]

The notions of culture, ethnicity and nationality have to be examined critically, taking account of the fuzzy boundaries, internal variety and the ongoing process of re-formation. Furthermore, social and personal interaction in schools is itself an important part of the process of cultural and religious re-formation.

This approach – developed on the basis of new-style phenomenology, recent anthropology, Smith's categories of faith and tradition and a consideration of cultural issues – may be used as a tool for organising ethnographic data on living religions, avoiding the imposition of a general schema. It provides a sound methodology for the representation of religions in an integrative framework, on the basis of ethnographic research data. The approach is self-critical with respect to assumptions about "the nature of religion", the numinous etc. and reconsiders the character of "religions" against the above background. It avoids positing universal essences or entrapping insiders within schematic formulations of key beliefs or concepts, either by identifying them simplistically with outsider constructions, or with insider institutional views. Instead, it includes more personal accounts and thereby pays more attention to internal diversity of religious traditions and to phenomena which do not fit neatly into taxonomies based on six world religions.[207] It has to be made explicit that the constructed "wholes" are abstractions. Voices of and co-operation with insiders are included as integral elements of the research process as well as of representation. Religions and cultures are recognised as dynamic and changing, their content and scope as being negotiated if not contested. They may be delineated differently by insiders and outsiders. The threefold model *individual*, *membership group* and *wider religious* tradition is regarded as a means to give a looser, more personal and organic picture of religious traditions.

---

206 Jackson 1997: RE. An Interpretive Approach, 79. Here Jackson also refers to the work of Nesbitt, cf. Jackson and Nesbitt 1992: The diversity of experience in the religious upbringing of children from Christian families in Britain, Nesbitt 1993: Drawing on the ethnic diversity of Christian tradition in Britain.
207 Talking about six world religions (i.e. Buddhism, Christianity, Hinduism, Islam, Judaism and Sikhism) is quite common in Great Britain, cf. section 1 of this chapter.

The attempt to achieve authentic interpretation requires a permanent reconsideration of methodology and praxis. One permanent concern is the projection of assumptions from one religious tradition onto others. This ought to be avoided both in its obvious forms, in which a concept from one tradition is used for the description of another tradition, but also in its less obvious forms, for example, in generalisations about "religion".[208]

To ground the representation of religions in ethnographic research also means an inherent inclusion of insider voices, which has to be built on a special cooperation between educators and practitioners. The way the relationship between these groups is interpreted in the Warwick RE Project is very different from other approaches – for example, that of the SCAA model syllabuses – which employ other criteria for the selection of representatives focusing on theological authority rather than on the views of children. The opportunities and challenges of the collaboration of educators and practitioners in the context of the Warwick RE Project are described in detail by Judith Everington.[209]

The textbooks

In the textbooks which were developed by members of the project team, the interpretive methods are put into practice. They are based on ethnographic studies in Britain, considering individual children in their religious membership groups and with reference to wider religious traditions. The textbooks introduce children of about the same age as the target audience. The relationship between their individual situations and narratives, groups to which they belong, as well as aspects of the religious traditions they relate to, is to be studied with the help of interpretive methods. Jackson explains the different steps of the interpretive process, which also serve as a structure for the study of the topics presented in the textbooks, as follows:

- *making it clear*: ensure that students have familiarized themselves with some of the basic facts and ideas featured in the unit before proceeding to interpretive tasks.
- *working it out*: encourage students to begin the process of interpretation by relating material drawn from one of the three 'levels' – individual, membership group, tradition – to material

---

208 Cf. Jackson 1997: RE. An Interpretive Approach, 69, 108ff.
209 Everington 1996: A question of authenticity.

drawn from another 'level'. The aim here is to bring two pieces of material together so that each sheds light upon the other.
– *building bridges*: draw on ... own experiences or on familiar ideas in order to interpret material featured in the unit. The aim here is to encourage the student to focus upon personal knowledge and experience which can be related analogically to material from the religious tradition. The familiar is used to make sense of or to gain insights into the unfamiliar.
– *thinking it through*: encourage students to use material from a religious tradition as a stimulus to reflecting upon matters of personal significance or concern ... encourage students to examine or re-examine aspects of their own understanding in the light of questions, issues or experiences which are encountered in particular religious traditions, but which also have universal significance.[210]

The last of the activities – *thinking it through* – refers to what Jackson means by edification, which cannot, of course, be guaranteed through the activities provided in curriculum materials. The books can, however, serve as a stimulus for activities which may – also with the support of teachers – result in edification. Different books are designed for the individual key stages, taking account of the developments of the children.

One other important concern of the Warwick RE Project is *bridging*, a concept which is used to describe two different processes. In the first sense, it refers to building bridges between the world of the pupils – their personal knowledge, experiences and feelings – and the world of the individuals, groups and traditions they encounter in RE. Pupils are encouraged to explore similarities and differences, a process in which the familiar can be used to shed light on the unfamiliar and remote. For example, in the context of exploring Christian understandings of prayer, the children are asked to recall recent experiences of sadness, joy or worry. Thereafter, they may read a poetic description of prayer from a Greek Orthodox book of prayers and reflect on similarities and differences between their own experiences and those described in the poem.[211] The second understanding of *bridging* concerns the gap be-

---
210 Jackson 1997: RE. An Interpretive Approach, 115f., Cf. also Everington 1998: Evolution not revolution, 151f.
211 Cf. Everington 1998: Evolution not revolution, 151f., where she refers to an activity from a textbook by Robson (1995: Christians, 22). See also Jackson 1997: RE. An Interpretive Approach, 111.

tween young people's experiences of their religious traditions at home and the way these traditions are represented in RE. Nesbitt argues that this gap may be bridged with the help of ethnographic research, which provides a source of data and contains interactive processes as integral elements.[212]

Example: the representation of Hinduism

One example for the ethnographic research conducted in the context of the Warwick RE Project and its implications for the representation of religions in RE is Eleanor Nesbitt's study of the beliefs of young Hindus in Britain. Nesbitt argues that it is necessary to look critically at categories like belief and religion which are easily reified in RE and elsewhere. Her research in the Coventry area reveals that young British Hindus are faced with permanent choices between alternative value systems and behaviours. She found a diversity of interpretations of different aspects of Hindu beliefs. When talking about God, for example, most interviewees slid from singular to plural with no sense of contradiction. God's singularity or plurality is not a problem, contrary to many outsider perspectives on Hinduism. The following quotations illustrate some of the views:

> "In the words of one female Gujarati employee: 'If an English person said to me, "I believe in God, do you believe?" ... I would go [ie say], "I believe in every god,"' and in the words of a female Punjabi employee: 'In my house every god's obviously welcome ... God's God, there's one God out there, so that's what I believe in as well.'"[213]

Even though only a few of the interviewees used the term *karma* unprompted, there was a general feeling or belief that good deeds are rewarded and bad deeds punished. Most young Hindus emphasised that repercussions are more likely to be expected in this life than in a future existence. Some scepticism about reincarnation (in the words of one female Gujarati undergraduate because there is 'no real evidence') was voiced, but some people appeared to accept that punishment or reward for actions in a previous life may result in rebirth as a creature of a different species. One male Gujarati undergraduate said, for example, "I believe if you do nice things and help a lot of people well you can come

---

[212] See Nesbitt 1998: Bridging the gap between young people's experience of their religious traditions at home and school, see also Ipgrave 1999: Issues in the delivery of RE to Muslim pupils, 155.
[213] Nesbitt 2001: What young Hindus believe, 151.

back as a nice person or a nice animal ... I think that if you do good things then you can come back as a nice say plant," while a Punjabi female university student dismissed the notion of "coming back as a dog" as "silly".[214]

Nesbitt also asked the young Hindus about *dharma* and responsibility, science and creation, Christianity, atheism (which was, in contrast to Christianity, totally rejected), and areas of interaction, like home and family, the media, *sampradayas* ("sectarian movements") and ritual action. A study of those different areas of a religion is intended to illuminate the interactions between *individual, membership groups* and the *wider religious tradition*. Two quotations by young Hindus may give an impression of the issues that come up in the dynamics of cultural change and encounters between different cultural or religious positions. With respect to science and religion, one male Gujarati undergraduate pointed out that:

> "the Hindu timescale is completely different from the timescale of scientists in the order of how things happened, when people appeared on earth and things like that ... the *yuga*'s huge and Ram was born a whole *yuga* before Krishna, so that was several hundreds of thousands of years before, and scientists say that by that time you know civilisation weren't there and people weren't around, but that doesn't stop me from believing."[215]

The other quotation is a response by a female Punjabi sixth former to a televised version of the Ramayana. She said:

> "The kala tika idea, I saw it in the Ramayan[a] when Sita was getting married they put a kala tika on her, and then I asked my mum, 'that's what we believe in as well?' She said, 'Yes'. So you can see that's what the gods all used to believe in as well."[216]

These examples from Nesbitt's research give an impression of the complexity of the field and the diversity of interpretations of elements from Hindu traditions such as the belief in God or gods, *karma*, cosmic time or ritual practice. Nesbitt concludes that this research indicates that young British Hindus are comfortable with a variety of dissimilar worldviews ranging from encompassment, mutual endorsement to compartmentalisation. Further research is necessary, however, to identify whether what she has observed is characteristically Hindu and to

---

214 Ibid., 152.
215 Ibid., 153. The term *yuga* denotes four recurrent periods of time in which the *dharma* decays. The current *yuga*, the *Kali yuga*. is the worst of the four.
216 Ibid., 155. *Kala tika* is the term for a black mark applied to the face in order to avert harmfully envious glances, cf. ibid.

further examine Hinduism's adaptability and comfort with post-modernity.[217]

The variety of interpretations of and ways of life within Hindu traditions is also represented in the books for teaching Hinduism written by members of the Warwick RE Project team. The book *Hindus* (1996) of the *Interpreting Religions* series for key stage 3 introduces four British Hindu children, who accompany the reader through the book, which focuses on a variety of topics from Hindu traditions.[218] The *teachers' notes* explain the methodology of the approach and the concept of religion. The introduction explains the purpose of the book to the pupils, including an outline of the methodology and pictures of four young Hindus, Tina, Bhavesh, Tejal and Amit. After that, two pages are devoted to each of the children. The descriptions comprise direct statements by the children and information about their cultural and family backgrounds as well as about their daily lives in Britain. Statements by the children (always with name and picture) are also given in each of the following chapters on aspects of the Hindu traditions.[219] In the chapter *Karma and the law of karma*, for example, after a short explanation of the concept karma,[220] the following statements are given by the children:

(1) Amit: "If I do something good, I hope for a good life next time. If you do good it will be better next time, I hope!"
(2) Bhavesh: "If all of this life's actions are going to affect the next life, I hope it is for the better each time."

Additionally, the following responses to the question of what counts as good or bad action are quoted:

---

217 Cf. ibid., 160.
218 Wayne, Everington et al. 1996: Hindus.
219 After an introduction of the four children, the book is structured around the following topics: Worship and prayer: ways of worshipping; Worship and prayer: picturing God; Arti and prashad; The mandir – the temple; The atman and the cycle of life, death and rebirth; Karma and the law of karma; Food and fasting; Marriage and the family; Learning about Hindu traditions; Learning from stories; The Bhagavad Gita; The Ramayana; Holi and Janmashtami; Keeping in touch – Raksha Bandhan; Navaratri; Divali; Family celebrations – life names; Mother Ganga – a sacred river of India; Respect for the natural world; Respect for life; Visiting gurus; Jalaram Bapa – a saint from Gujarat; Mahatma Gandhi; Belonging to a community of communities; Who am I?
220 "Karma means 'action'. According to the law of karma, the life that we lead now is the result of the good and the bad things that we have done in a previous life. Similarly, the good and bad things we do now will affect the kind of life we will live after death." (Wayne, Everington et al. 1996: Hindus, 24).

(3) Bhavesh: "The animals and plants are serving their duty in giving us food. Being vegetarian is quite important to me. Animals are another form of life. I don't eat meat or fish. I do eat dairy products as you're not killing anything."

(4) Tejal: "It's important that you are honest. I don't like people who cheat or are evil."

Along with the statements by the children, the Bhagavad Gita (3:8) is cited:

(5) Do the work that is prescribed [for you] for to work is better than to do no work at all, for without working you will not succeed even in keeping your body in good repair.[221]

The chapter also provides pictures from banners put up at a Hindu outdoor event as examples of which actions are regarded as good and which as bad. The banners say "Share your daily bread with others so that your other brothers may also have a thrill of life" and "Do not treat others as you would not like to be treated". In the *making it clear* section, the students are asked to think about what Amit and Bhavesh hope for when they think about the far-off future and to use the information of the quotations 3-5 to write down some of the good actions that might help the boys to get what they hope for. In the *building bridges* section, the pupils are asked to write down good and bad things they have done in their own lives and think about the consequences that resulted from those. After that, they are encouraged to write down what many Hindus believe about actions and their consequences. In the *thinking it through* section, the pupils are asked to design a game – similar to the "Snakes and Ladders" game which is given as an example – in which good actions bring good consequences and bad actions bring bad consequences. In designing this game, they are supposed to consider the good and bad actions given in the quotations 3-5.[222] This example of the representation of karma as one important aspect of Hinduism clearly demonstrates how different voices are included in the representation of a religious tradition, with a special emphasis on children in Britain today. The suggested activities may serve as an example of how the teaching methodology can be put into practice.

---

221 All quotations in Wayne, Everington et al. 1996: Hindus, 24.
222 Cf. ibid., 24f.

2.4.3 The notion of education

In the interpretive approach to RE, individuals are seen in relation to religions and cultures, which are characterised as ever changing and intermingling with each other without any clear borders between them. Individuals are capable of combining different cultural resources and thus becoming *skilled cultural navigators* with *multiple cultural competence*.[223] Education ought to promote conversation. Reference points for the study of different religious traditions are children in Great Britain today. Children learning from their peers is seen as one important aspect of understanding each other in a multicultural society. The study of religious and cultural traditions which are different from one's own may – in addition to the educational aim of promoting knowledge and understanding – bring about *edification*, a different view on the familiar, having been challenged by the unfamiliar. Other people's "peculiarities" can serve as a mirror of one's own (Edmund Leach) and by "unpacking" another worldview, we can become a new person (Richard Rorty).[224] Studying other ways of life and reflecting about what has been studied cannot be separated from each other. Reflexivity is an integral part of the interpretive process. In addition to these general findings, further research is necessary into which means (teaching methods, teaching material) serve the aims that have been identified for RE.[225]

Teachers of RE may come from any religious or non-religious background. They ought to be impartial, not neutral. The professional requirement is a commitment to an open and dialogical or *conversational* RE. In the framework of a conversational approach some aspects of knowledge can be regarded as socially constructed, but this does not mean that the notion of ultimate truth has no meaning at all. The different positions – also about the nature of truth – ought to become part of the discourse in RE without any of those positions being accepted as given in the first place, not even the relativistic one.[226]

---

[223] Jackson 1997: RE. An Interpretive Approach, 83, 90.
[224] Cf. ibid., 130.
[225] See Everington 1998: Evolution not revolution, 153.
[226] Cf. Jackson 1997: RE. An Interpretive Approach, 135f.

2.4.4 Recent developments and projects in interpretive RE

Recent publications by the project team deal with the role of ethnography and ethnographic research in RE, examples of ethnographic research which is relevant to RE, the integration of the approach into the general framework for RE (for example, presented in the SCAA model syllabuses), possibilities of introducing a historical dimension and examples of other projects which use the methodology developed by the Warwick team.

Eleanor Nesbitt describes the methodology of the ethnographic research carried out in the Warwick RE project among children from different religions. She emphasises the project's advantages, which may serve to modify the essentialising tendencies of the syllabuses.[227] Similarly, J. Everington shows how interpretive methods can be used in order to overcome the stereotypical representation of religious traditions as clearly defined "sets" of beliefs and practices in the SCAA *Working Party Reports* and *Model Syllabuses* (1994) and the resulting "discrepancy between the simplified, normative picture presented by the syllabus ... and the 'messy', complex picture presented by real people."[228] These methods can be applied using a combination of different commercially and self-produced resources together with first hand experiences of visits and visitors.

Jackson takes up suggestions by the Dutch philosopher of education, Wilna Meijer, about how a historical dimension may be introduced into the interpretive approach to RE. Meijer refers to Hans-Georg Gadamer's *Truth and Method* (1975), in which he argues that preconceptions are in our eyes, not in front of our eyes, and Paul Ricoeur's *Time and Narrative* (1988), in which the concepts of temporality (an awareness characterised by anticipation of the future) and historicality (recovery of the past through reflection) are established in order to show how reflection enables new interpretations of the past and may reveal new potentialities for the future. Meijer argues that in order to make full use of the notion of *tradition* in the three-level model suggested in the interpretive approach (see above), a discussion of pupils themselves as parts of traditions in relation to their own pasts and futures may be added.[229]

---

[227] See Nesbitt 2001: Ethnographic research at Warwick, 2002: Ethnography and RE.
[228] Everington 1998: Evolution not Revolution, 150.
[229] See Meijer 2004: Tradition and reflexivity in RE, quoted in Jackson 2004: Rethinking RE and Plurality, 92ff.

Recent projects which build on integrative methodologies comprise, for example, an approach to teaching African Religion in post-Apartheid South Africa, an RE project in a special school in London and an attempt to involve pupils in planning RE and school-based research on values in Swedish schools. These examples show that the interpretive approach is not confined to the use of ethnographic methods or school books, but can be developed in other directions and adapted creatively to different classroom situations. Furthermore, they demonstrate the importance of the pupils' own experiences, reflections and interactions as an integral part of the subject matter.[230] A list of recent projects and publications can be found on the WRERU homepage.[231]

2.4.5 Comment

The interpretive approach is very reflexive about the issues around the representation of different religions in RE. Its theory and methodology reflects recent developments in the study of religions. The approach builds on a critical evaluation of past approaches to cultures and religions in the study of religions and anthropology and transfers more recent approaches from these disciplines to RE. This process proves useful for a responsible representation of the diversity of religions and religious phenomena in integrative RE. The methodology in which the approach is grounded is very sophisticated. Perhaps it is justified to use the concept "bridging" in a third sense, as the approach successfully builds a bridge between the academic study of religions and school RE. Curriculum development is grounded in well reflected ethnographic research and considerations about an adequate representation of religions, which includes an account of cultural and religious dynamics and change. Furthermore, the international orientation of the project team and the variety of follow-up projects building on the interpretive methodology suggested, for example, by Jackson and Nesbitt, are exceptional and very promising for the further development of the subject.

The recently suggested integration of a historical dimension into the interpretive is definitely useful. Another point which deserves further consideration is gender differences. They are not covered specifi-

---

230 Cf. Jackson 2001: Creative pedagogy in RE, 2004: Rethinking RE and Plurality, 94-108.
231 See WRERU 2006: Current WRERU Research Projects
(http://www2.warwick.ac.uk/fac/soc/wie/wreru/aboutus/research_projects/current/).

cally in the Warwick RE Project, as Jackson notes self-critically.[232] Including a reflection of gender-related issues may complement the interpretive approach in all its dimensions, on a theoretical level, in the ethnographic research as well as in the representation of religions in the teaching material with respect to individual, membership group and wider religious tradition. It has to be added, however, that a convincing inclusion of the gender dimension is not presented in any of the other English approaches to RE either. Taking this up, the introduction of a gender dimension to interpretive RE may help to further improve a generally convincing and very important approach to RE which owes its quality not least to its strict methodological self-criticism.

2.5 The Critical Approach

Andrew Wright's critical approach to RE builds on his critique of what he calls the contemporary liberal consensus of RE. The *Spiritual Education Project*, which is closely related to the critical approach to RE, was based at King's College of the University of London. It consisted of three phases between the years 1996 and 2002: a survey, critique and reconstruction of the conceptualisation of spiritual education, an application of the theoretical aspects to the practical teaching context and an attempt to apply the findings of the other phases beyond the boundaries of RE, for example with respect to cross-curricular issues or school policies. This project is part of a broader attempt to develop a critical rationale for RE, a critical theory based on a deconstruction of the mind-set of contemporary RE in England. Above all, Wright talks about spirituality, spiritual education and spiritual literacy. To some extent the words "spiritual" and "religious" seem to be interchangeable in his approach. Spiritual education, however, comprises more than RE, but RE is regarded as an important part of it. Most of Wright's considerations are relevant to RE, as they concern the framework for the representation of religions in school and a critique of common practice in RE.

Wright's concept for critical RE, which promotes the religious or spiritual literacy of children, will be analysed against the background of his critique of contemporary liberal RE, before his approach is evaluated with respect to its benefits for an integrative RE based on the principles of the academic study of religion. Special attention is given to his concepts of religion and education and their implications for the representation of different religions in RE.

---

232 Cf. Jackson 2001: Creative pedagogy in RE, 48.

2.5.1 The critique of the "liberal consensus" about representing religions in RE

Wright's criticism is directed towards the experiential-expressive model of religion which has become the dominant framework for the representation of religions in RE. In this model

> "religious language is concerned to express experience rather than describe the way things are in the world. As a result religious doctrines are important not as cognitive truth claims, but merely as expressions of religious piety. This is reflected in liberal classrooms, with religious teaching concerned more with the stimulation of the child's capacity for spiritual experience than with issues of religious truth."[233]

Wright shows convincingly how the liberal consensus led to a specific universal theology, as the diverse religious expressions are regarded as equally valid representations of a common – generic[234] – religious experience which must be approached with empathy and tolerance. In this framework, doctrinal differences are mere accidents of culture, without any inherent cognitive significance. As this framework for the representation of religions is itself rarely questioned, but superimposed on the pupils as an unchallenged interpretation of religious diversity, Wright talks of a "liberal indoctrination" of the pupils in RE:

> "The liberal indoctrination of children into this particular theology is supported by the liberal commitment to the twin principles of freedom of belief and tolerance, one effect of which is to locate religious dogma within the subjective sphere of private belief, effectively withdrawing it from public discourse. It is at this point that liberalism ceases to function as an interim ethic intended to facilitate dialogue between contrasting traditions, and takes on instead the form of a closed ideological world-view into which pupils are indoctrinated."[235]

RE, which has emancipated itself from Christian confessionalism, needs to recognise its compliance with the neo-confessionalist affirmation of the inherent universal value of religion and advocacy of generic human

---

[233] Wright 2000: The Spiritual Education Project, 171f, see also Wright 1996: Language and Experience and the Hermeneutics of Religious Understanding, where he shows how a representation of religions based on the experiential model of religion in some cases fundamentally contradicts the view religious people have of their own religions. On page 173 he exemplifies this with reference to Islam.

[234] For Wright's understanding of the distinction between generic and nominalist interpretations of religion and its consequences for RE see 1997: Mishmash, religionism and theological literacy, 143ff.

[235] Wright 2000: The Spiritual Education Project 172, see also Wright 2000: Religious education, religious literacy and democratic citizenship.

religiosity. However, it has not yet developed a tradition of hermeneutical liberation, but has drawn uncritically on the positions of Romanticism and Post-Modernism. Therefore, the possibility of an authentic understanding of religions is constrained.[236]

The important didactic questions are: *why* should *what* be taught and *how* should the material be presented? The liberal approach to the latter issue is particularly problematic as it imposes premature solutions onto the children. In order to draw the unconscious presuppositions of the liberal approach into the conscious sphere, Wright deconstructs the liberal consensus. He shows that the understanding on which the liberal approach is built is, in fact, not valid across all cultures and traditions. What is more, it excludes all spiritual traditions apart from the liberal. Wright uses the examples of Trinitarian Christianity and Islam to support his argument that a range of religious traditions are "incompatible with the predominantly western, white, male, middle-class, academic liberal spirituality presently imposed on the majority of our children".[237] He argues that the spiritual resources of Trinitarian Christianity do not begin with inner subjectivity, but with the objective reality of God the Father, Son and Holy Spirit. The roots of this spirituality lie in divine revelation, not in human experience. The Trinitarian God reveals himself through creation, history, scripture and the teachings of the church. The possibility of an authentic relationship between God and human beings becomes reality in the public worship of the Christian community, in which sacramentally the divine realm breaks into the immanent realm of creation. Therefore, Trinitarian Christian spirituality has little to do with introspective experience, but with developing a relationship with an objective deity.[238] Wright uses similar arguments with respect to Islam. In Islam, he writes, the heart of religion is not to be found in inner experience, but in the revelation of Allah in the Qur'an. The words of the Qur'an are important, as is the truth they proclaim about the will of Allah for his creation:

> "The submission of a Muslim to these words entails an active obedience to that ultimate reality which creates the universe and reveals himself to humanity. An authentic Muslim attempts to live a life related to the actuality

---

236 Cf. Wright 1997: Hermeneutics and religious understanding. Part one: the hermeneutics of modern RE, 212f, and Wright 1998: Hermeneutics and religious understanding. Part two: towards a critical theory for RE, 59.
237 Wright 2000: The Spiritual Education Project, 175, for a more detailed elaboration of his argument about Trinitarian Christian Spirituality, see Wright 1998: Spiritual Pedagogy, chapter 5, 69-81.
238 Cf. ibid.

of Allah, not to her or his sinful experience. ... Indeed, the contemporary expectation that religious education take children beyond the externals of Islam and allow them to enter into its experiential heart appears on this reading rather close to the old orientalist's references to 'Muhammadenism' for liberal comfort."[239]

Wright concludes that a relativist classification of the language of the Qur'an as a second-order expression of human experience runs counter to Islamic self understanding. It implies the relativity of Islamic doctrine alongside other religions, because all religions are seen as expressions of a common religious experience. This view "may be attractive to Cantwell-Smith and liberal universalists, but it is not Islamic and indeed is offensive to Muslims."[240] These examples show that a critical awareness of the ideology which underlies the representation of religions is necessary in order to do justice to the religious traditions and not to distort them unduly from the very beginning.

2.5.2 Reconstruction: The representation of religions in a critical framework

In order to avoid gross distortions in the representation of religions, an alternative framework for the representation of religions in RE is necessary. A critical awareness of ideology demands a reassessment of the concept of religion underlying the liberal consensus and the experiential-expressive approach to RE. This is crucial, as the concept of religion or spirituality necessarily influences the way religions are represented in RE. The theological presuppositions of the experiential-expressive approach and the consequential discrepancy between the self-understanding of religious people and the way their religion is represented in RE have been explored above.

An alternative definition of religion and spirituality is required, which does not propose a common universal spirituality, but operates within a broad framework in which the different religious traditions can be placed without compromising their distinctive identities. Wright defines spirituality as "the developing relationship of the individual

---

[239] Wright 1996: Language and Experience in the Hermeneutics of Religious Understanding, 173. Despite the somewhat infelicitous phrase "an authentic Muslim" (are there inauthentic Muslims?) the point Wright makes here is important, as it shows clearly how imposition of a particular liberal theology onto other traditions distorts their representations.

[240] Ibid.

within community and tradition, to that which is – or is perceived to be – of ultimate concern, ultimate value and ultimate truth."[241] Spirituality is an ambiguous realm of human knowledge and understanding. There is a diversity of contrasting and competing traditions of spirituality. In order to take account of this fact, a choice between a post modern-relativist and a universalist position is not an option for a framework of RE:

> "Rather a critical spiritual education will give children access to the diversity of spiritual options available, together with the skills and insights through which they can enter into contemporary debate and learn how to differentiate and make informed judgements between a variety of possibilities."[242]

Children need to be equipped to explore these conflicting worldviews rather than to be introduced to a single unquestioned paradigm, which does not correspond to reality. Wright refers to the critical realism of Hans-Georg Gadamer and Jürgen Habermas in order to establish a hermeneutics on which a critical approach to RE may build. Both reject romantic and post-modern hermeneutics and appreciate the diversity and cognitive potential embodied in language. Furthermore, they recognise the two horizons of interpreter and text and affirm the possibility of a transformative reading of a text. A critical hermeneutics for RE ought to be grounded in the notion of linguistic competence. Building on Habermas' theories of communicative action, it can be said that mutual understanding may be established through the quality of shared discourse rather than through a premature agreement about a false consensus or any imposition of the views of one group upon another. In this view of communicative processes,

> "ongoing conversation between horizons replaces the idealised hope of their fusion. If the long-term hope is for the establishment of common agreement, the short-term goal, given the limitations and contingency of human knowledge, is that of a mutual understanding that recognises areas of fundamental agreement and disagreement."[243]

A genuinely transformative hermeneutics can be opened up if the children are not expected to rely merely on their own experiences, preferences and inclinations, but are encouraged to also consider other options. In this process, encounters with other religious and non-religious worldviews can serve to broaden, deepen and challenge their own ini-

---

241 Wright 2000: The Spiritual Education Project, 175, also 1998: Spiritual Pedagogy, 88.
242 Wright 1998: Spiritual Pedagogy, 96.
243 Wright 1998: Towards a critical theory for RE, 66f., for whole paragraph cf. ibid., 64ff.

tial perspectives. The study of religious traditions has to "transcend the limits of neutral phenomenological description"[244] and acknowledge the specific truth claims embodied in the different linguistic traditions. With respect to the general framework, children have to access both nominalist and generic concepts of religion in order to critically assess the nature of the dispute. Academic disciplines and theories, such as anthropology, literary criticism, philosophy, psychology, phenomenology, sociology, feminist theory and theology can provide tools for a secondary interpretation of the primary religious narratives.[245]

Wright identifies five pedagogical principles in which his critical approach to RE is grounded:[246]

(1) justice to the horizon of religion

(2) justice to the horizon of the pupil

(3) appropriate responses to power structures

(4) dialogue between the horizons

(5) religious literacy rooted in attentiveness, intelligence, reasonableness and responsibility

(1.) Doing justice to the horizon of religion requires a *qualitative* pluralism – as opposed to a *quantitative* pluralism of, for example, six major world religions, which implies that they are generically related and supposes their general compatibility. Qualitative pluralism "reflects the genuine diversity of religious and secular perspectives on religion, and accepts the ambiguous, controversial, and conflicting nature of theological truth claims"[247]. Tensions within specific religious traditions have to be taken into account. They may provide a starting point for RE. Attention must also be given to the variety of attempts to understand the interrelationship between religious traditions – ranging from exclusivism to an all-embracing universal theology. Pupils ought to be encouraged to engage with an adequate range of contrasting and conflicting positions, including non-religious worldviews.

(2.) Doing justice to the horizon of the pupils implies that it must be possible for the children to recognise and articulate their emergent beliefs and attitudes without constraint or manipulation. Other than in the liberal idealised and abstract view of the horizon of the pupils,

---

244 Ibid., 68.
245 Cf. Wright 1998: Towards a critical theory for RE, 67f.
246 Cf. Wright 2000: The Spiritual Education Project, 177ff.
247 Ibid.

which assumes that the pupils are implicitly religious and possess the innate potential for religious and spiritual sensibility – a view in which the horizon of the pupils is seen in terms of future potential rather than present reality – the actual horizons of the pupils have to become a conscious and integral part of the learning process.

(3.) RE has to aim at equipping the pupils to recognise and respond appropriately to power structures inherent in religious and educational discourse. There is no such privileged perspective as a neutral vantage point from which religions can be explored without prejudice. Ideological bias should, therefore, not be denied, but rather drawn to the surface and acknowledged openly. Teachers as well as pupils have to learn to recognise and admit their underlying presuppositions. The two extremes of a traditionalist subject-based pedagogy and a progressive child-centred pedagogy without any rule guidance or restraint have to be avoided. Pupils ought to be provided "with the skills, knowledge and wisdom through which they can identify and explore both their own ideology and the various ideologies presented by religious and secular traditions".[248]

(4.) In the attempt to enable a critical dialogue between the horizon of the child and the horizon of religion, attention must be paid to two possible dangers: the colonisation of the child's horizon by any one particular religious horizon as well as the colonisation of the horizon of religion by the unchecked horizon of the child. In an intelligent conversation between the two horizons, the child encounters a variety of religious perspectives. This encounter can be regarded as a means of further clarifying, enriching and developing the child's religious beliefs.

(5.) The aim of critical religious education, the religious literacy of the pupils, ought to be rooted in attentiveness, intelligence, reasonableness and responsibility. Convergence and dissonance in the dialogue between different horizons stimulate further reflection, conversation and study. Critical reflection is vital. For the educator, what the children believe is not so important, but the way they come to acquire their beliefs is of great interest. The outcome of the discussion in RE is necessarily open:

> "The reality is that religion simply is an ambiguous entity within contemporary society, and any education that does not accept this, and does not actively seek to allow pupils a critical grasp of the situation for themselves, will inevitably collapse into ideology. A communicative openness is thus

---

248 Wright 2000: The Spiritual Education Project, 179.

simply a better option than a prematurely conceptualised and pre-packaged solution to contentious religious issues."[249]

The pedagogical principles suggested by Wright for a critical approach to RE do not demand any specific pedagogy. He suggests, however, one model as an example, following the idea of spiral learning, i.e. continually circling around a series of topics, which enables the exploration of a topic with ever increasing depth. The pedagogical strategies he proposes comprise three phases, dealing with the horizons of the pupils, the horizons of religion and the engagement of the horizons, respectively.[250] The first phase consists of a basic introduction to the topic, an open exploration of the topic and an articulation of initial beliefs. In the second phase, a spectrum of conflicting religious and secular perspectives are presented before the pupils' positions are located within this spectrum. The third phase is designed to serve the development of critical thinking skills, a conversation across and between horizons and a re-articulation of the pupils' initial positions. Authentic religious literacy can only emerge when pupils learn to engage in informed conversation about their beliefs and the beliefs of others.

Wright describes the questions that should be addressed in a series of lessons about the existence of God. He says that it is neither sufficient to simply affirm the children's particular beliefs, nor to introduce them to a range of beliefs with theistic, atheistic and agnostic contours. Rather, children need to engage with the question of which particular account of 'God' is true. The rational and moral arguments of secular atheism will need to be set alongside post-modern agnosticism, rational philosophical arguments for the existence of God, and arguments for belief in God rooted in religious authority and faith commitment.[251]

2.5.3 The notion of education

Wright's response to the debate about RE and nurture is the claim that nurture is inevitably an integral part of RE. Therefore, the question of whether RE ought to nurture or not is invalid and the task is to ensure that the spiritual tradition in which the children are nurtured is appropriate and that the process of nurture is effective. Effective nurture in

---

249 Wright 1998: Towards a critical theory for RE, 68.
250 For an outline of the pedagogical strategies and the individual phases, see Wright 2000: The Spiritual Education Project, 180-183.
251 Ibid. 183.

RE needs to be founded in a clearly articulated and implemented ethos statement which takes "account of national concerns regarding basic values as well as specific local concerns of the school's foundational spiritual tradition."[252] Spiritual literacy, an important aim of RE, may be enhanced if teaching acknowledges the various traditions in which human spiritual understanding is embodied, focuses on the question of spiritual truth, "embodying not merely human concerns about the ultimate meaning and purpose of life, but also of the ultimate nature of reality"[253] and promotes a critical wisdom which transcends the modernist polarity of rationalistic sense and emotive sensibility.

After a presentation of the main contours of the debate about traditional vs. progressive education, Wright discusses three concepts of education which attempt to establish pupil autonomy within a broadly progressive educational framework: *negative education, deconstructive education* and *compensatory education*.[254] All three concepts recognise the dangers inherent in regarding education as nurture and attempt to protect and enhance the freedom of the child. Wright concludes, however, that in all three approaches, the search for freedom has resulted in the imposition of an alternative ideological framework on the pupils, in *negative education* by imposing the view on the pupils that their natural untutored instincts are always right – which actually denies them access to positive development of their critical faculties, in *deconstructive education* by imposing the ideology that there is no ultimate meaning or purpose in life other than that which pupils create for themselves and in *compensatory education* by simply inducting children into an ideological worldview which is supposed to be preferable to the status quo, for example in David Hay's programme of compensating for the marginalisation of spiritual experience with a programme of re-sensitising children's capacity for spiritual awareness.[255]

Wright claims that all these approaches to education present no more than a benign form of educational paternalism. They are inextricably bound up with a variety of ideological commitments. Despite the rhetoric of freedom and emancipation, contemporary education has failed to develop a genuinely critical stance. In order to take account of the legitimate point which advocates of progressive concepts of education wish to make, and in order to truly respect the children's auton-

---

252 Wright 2000: Spirituality and Education, 124. Cf. also Wright 1998: Spiritual Pedagogy, 93ff.
253 Wright 2000: Spirituality and Education, 112, for the whole paragraph cf. ibid.
254 Cf. ibid. 125ff.
255 Cf. Wright 2000: Spirituality and Education, 130f.

omy and freedom, Wright suggests supplementing the notion of education as nurture with an interpretation of the process of education as critical emancipation.[256] He refers to Paolo Freire's notion of conscientisation (the cultivation of a critical awareness) and his concept of education to support his argument for a critical education grounding in the cultivation of skills of critical reflection in the context of cultural pluralism. Freire, starting from a concern for the poor and dispossessed, claims that education must enable children to break through to an awareness of the ideological structures permeating their schooling, cultural and economic backgrounds, peer groups and society at large, through appropriate skill formation.[257] Ideological structures are at work in any educational process. This has to be made explicit and become a matter of debate. For spiritual education this means that spirituality must always be taught as a controversial issue, which demands the cultivation of appropriate levels of spiritual literacy.[258]

2.5.4 Critical evaluation

Wright's criticism of the liberal consensus in contemporary English RE is extremely helpful, as it addresses – with unusual clarity – the theological assumption behind many common practices in RE, which are supposed to be independent from particular religious beliefs, but are, in fact, not. Wright provides the kind of criticism which British integrative RE lacked for a long time. He demonstrates in a number of examples that the experiential-expressive approach to RE is misleading and compromises the self-understanding of many religious people. In contrast to the experiential-expressive model, Wright's own definition of religion, which is broad enough to include secular worldviews, strongly emphasises truth claims.[259] Conversation about these compet-

---

256 A critical understanding of education, Wright argues, might help to create a better political debate in order to overcome the current ideology that 'might is right' with respect to controversial areas of the curriculum, allowing the political victor to impose the value system they believe to be appropriate on the children's curriculum. Cf. ibid., 131.
257 Cf. ibid., 132, for Freire's position, see e.g. Freire 1997: Erziehung und Hoffnung.
258 Ibid. 137. If I understand Wright correctly, the words "spiritual" and "spirituality" in the last sentence could also be replaced with the words "religious" and "religion", which would mean that his ideas may be transferred to the general framework of integrative religious education.
259 His reference to "ultimate concern, ultimate value and ultimate truth" (2000: 175) as a criterion for spirituality or religion may be questioned from a study of religions

ing truth claims, which entails a reconsideration of one's own initial perspectives, is regarded as one of the main tasks of RE. This is definitely an important element of integrative RE. Care should be taken, however, not to over-emphasise the conceptual aspect of religion at the expense of other aspects.

His approach to education has a clear critical and emancipatory impetus. His position that pupils should be introduced to the complexity and ambiguity of phenomena rather than to simplified models which do not correspond to what children encounter in their daily lives, is very relevant for integrative RE. His reinterpretation of the concept of nurture acknowledges that any concept of education must include ideological and political stances. Denying them only obscures the real character of education. Therefore, political and ideological decisions have to be made explicit in any concept of education or of RE.
Wright's model for the path to religious literacy, taking due account of the horizon of the religions, the horizon of the pupils and the interaction between these two, is well-reflected, convincing and shows a way to overcome the dichotomy of "pupil-centred" and "subject-centred" approaches. His argument about attention to power structures in religious and educational discourse, takes up important points from recent debates about the representation of religions as well as from critical educational theory. His point that it is necessary to acknowledge the ambiguous character of religion(s) and equip the pupils with methods of dealing with this ambiguity is an important corrective for RE which only deals with the pleasant and uncontroversial aspects of religions.

With some of Wright's formulations about the contents of RE it remains unclear to me how these ideas can be translated into practice. In his example of a series of lessons about "the existence of God", he is definitely right to emphasise that the pupils must be introduced to the full range of positions about the question of the existence of God.[260] However, how exactly the pupils may – as Wright wishes – engage with the question of which particular account of 'God' is true, remains unspecified. A study of the different truth claims and the arguments in which they are grounded is unquestionably an important part of the study of different theistic, atheistic or agnostic concepts. The different

---

point of view. Cf. Pye's criticism of (Kishimoto's, Eliade's and Tillich's) reference to the "ultimate" as a criterion for Religion (Pye 1972: 10f).

260 Even though asking this very question ("Does God exist?") in the context of dealing with the topic God/gods shows a particular interest which has been much stronger, for example, in Christian than in Hindu traditions and means approaching the topic with the tools of a particular Western tradition.

arguments about which of the accounts of 'God' may be true can also be studied and discussed. However, the matter can, of course, not be decided in integrative RE.

Similarly, it remains unclear as to why and how the "limits of neutral phenomenological description" ought to be "transcended". What exactly does Wright mean by "phenomenological" here? Why should an acknowledgement of different truth claims require going beyond neutral description? What is necessary is an effort of the imagination to understand why a particular statement or "account" of God, which has the implication of a "truth claim", is important for those who advance it. The meaning of this truth claim, for them, has to be elucidated. Even though I am not entirely sure if the latter conclusions correspond to Wright's intentions, this is what is possible and desirable with respect to truth claims in integrative RE.

2.6 The Constructivist Approach

The constructivist approach to RE has recently been suggested by Michael Grimmitt, who has been involved in the development of concepts for integrative RE from the very beginning.[261] He outlines this new approach for the first time in a chapter in his book *Pedagogies of RE* (2000)[262]. His basic idea in this approach is that constructivist theories of learning, in which knowledge is regarded as a human construct rather than a reflection of an objective ontological reality, can form the pedagogical basis for RE. As a framework for this approach, Grimmitt outlines four constructivist theories of learning:

(1) *Piagetian constructivism* claims that the objective world is only accessible through experience. The acquisition of knowledge is regarded as an active process of "assimilation" in which new information is integrated into existing cognitive structures. In *The Psychology of Intelligence* (1950), Piaget identifies four distinct stages in the process of conceptual development, the sensori-motor stage, the pre-operational stage, the concrete operations stage and the formal operations stage. These stages mark an ascent towards more com-

---

[261] Note his contributions to the two developmental approaches as well (sections 2.1 on the *Westhill Project* and 2.2 on the *Religion in Service of the Child Project* in this chapter). See also for example Grimmitt 1973: What Can I Do in RE? and 1987: Religious Education and Human Development.
[262] Grimmitt 2000: Constructivist Pedagogies of RE Project, 207-227.

plex and 'objective' thinking. Progress from a situated egocentric interpretation to a decontextualised 'objective' or rational point of view is, according to Piaget, the end and purpose of cognitive development.

(2) *Social constructivism* as outlined by Vygotsky regards knowledge as a product of social interaction. In Vygotsky's theory the emphasis is on the dialectical relationship between individuals and their social contexts. The particular relevance of the teacher's intervention is recognised in the discrepancy between actual and potential development, the "zone of proximal development". Given the relevance of collaborative work between dyads (a child and a more mature person) for success, the teacher needs to know the pupils' conceptual structures in order to build upon, challenge and extend those constructions. The process of building up knowledge through this kind of interaction is interpreted as appropriation (Leont'ev) rather than assimilation (Piaget).[263]

(3) *Emancipatory constructivism*[264] emphasises the influence of the sociocultural context as a striking factor in the construction of reality. If pupils are expected to learn how to build up a critical point of view, existing knowledge, as well as social and cultural structures that reflect the relationships of power and privilege in societies – such as ethnicity, class and gender – have to be questioned and problematised.

(4) *Radical constructivism*, mainly associated with the work of von Glaserfeld, regards knowledge not as a reflection of an objective ontological reality, but as an order and organisation of a world constituted by our experience. In this approach, the relationship between knowledge and reality can at best be described as 'viable', i.e. as possibly helpful for accomplishing a task that one has set oneself. Von Glaserfeld emphasises the role of language and the process in which every individual has to reconstruct the meaning of words solely on the basis of their own subjective experience. Teachers

---

[263] See Vygotsky 1962: Thought and Language and 1978: Mind in Society; Leont'ev 1981: Problems of the Development of Mind (quoted in Grimmitt 2000: Constructivist Pedagogies of RE Project, 208f).

[264] The term "emancipatory constructivism" was first used in O'Loughlin 1992: Engaging teachers in emancipatory knowledge construction, see Grimmitt 2000: Constructivist Pedagogies of RE Project, 227, note 6.

need an understanding of the conceptual networks of their pupils in order to 'orient' their efforts at construction.[265]

Drawing on these approaches, Grimmitt develops several principles for applying constructivist theory to RE, which involves a major re-orientation and re-thinking of current theory and practice. Main points are a critical reflection of one's own knowledge, beliefs and value assumptions and contrasting these with alternative perspectives in order to arrive at true interaction, challenge and collaborative and co-operative problem-solving. The constructivist process consists in linking one's own experiences and thoughts with the content that is being studied. Thereby, one's own meanings are created and there is an individually consistent path for arriving at conclusions. In this process, a critical examination of the role of language is essential, because of its function of conveying meanings and interpretations which represent interests and values of certain groups. In order to acknowledge or express interests and values of alternative groups, these meanings and interpretations may be de- and reconstructed.

On the basis of these principles, Grimmitt suggests a three stage pedagogical strategy, in which an attempt is made to establish a dynamic relationship between the subject content and the critical and reflective thought of the pupils as situated and contextualised individuals. The sequence of learning in this strategy always starts with an encouragement of the pupils' own interpretations of experience and continues with the provision of alternative contextualised interpretations to evaluative judgements about interests that are expressed and served in any interpretation:

(1) *Preparatory pedagogical constructivism*: exploration and reflection of the pupils' own experience as a conceptual and linguistic preparation for the encounter with an item of religious content.

(2) *Direct pedagogical constructivism*: direct confrontation with the item of religious content without explanation or instruction in order to present to the pupils a stimulus to construct their own understanding of the item in relation to their prior experience and ideas.

(3) *Supplementary pedagogical constructivism*: provision of additional or supplementary information to enable the pupils' constructions to

---

[265] Cf. von Glaserfeld, E. 1995: Constructivism: A Way of Knowing and Learning, London: Falmer Press; Watzlawick, Paul (ed.) 1984: The Invented Reality: How do we know what we believe we know?, New York: Norton; Larochelle, Bednarz et al. (eds.) 1998: Constructivism and Education, Cambridge, UK: CUP; all quoted in Grimmitt 2000: Constructivist Pedagogies of RE Project, 210.

become more complex and make possible a consideration of alternative perspectives. In this constructivist interpretive process, pupils are meant to consider new information critically. It is important, however, that their own earlier constructions are not abandoned or replaced by the newly acquired "objective" knowledge, but that they integrate the latter into their prior understanding.[266]

In order to illustrate this teaching and learning process, Grimmitt uses the example of teaching and learning about Shiva as *Nataraja*, king or lord of the dance, as an item of religious knowledge in RE. He identifies the background knowledge that is necessary in order to learn about Shiva *Nataraja* (p. 211-214) and outlines how this may be taught in an instructional approach (p. 215). In contrast to this, Grimmitt exemplifies the above mentioned stages of the constructivist process with respect to Shiva as *Nataraja* as follows: In stage 1, *preparatory pedagogical* constructivism, questions about life and death, the meaning of life, the idea of reincarnation, creating and destroying, reasons for being happy or sad are addressed by the teacher and explored by the pupils. In stage 2, *direct pedagogical constructivism*, the teacher shows a photograph of Shiva as *Nataraja* and the pupils are encouraged to ask questions. In the emerging conversation, the teacher gives some information about the item (for example that it is from Hinduism, that Shiva is a god, that he dances on the demon of ignorance) and asks questions that aim at an interpretation of the statue, e.g. about the circle of life, reincarnation and its end, the truth about human life. In stage 3, *supplementary pedagogical constructivism*, links between aspects of the discussions in the earlier stages and Hindu concepts like *karma*, *samsara*, *maya* and *moksha* are established. This is again done in a dialogue between the teacher and the pupils.[267]

Even though Grimmitt acknowledges that there is some room for an instructional approach in RE, he emphasises the importance of constructivist theories in order to promote more complex and sophisticated forms of learning, such as inter- and intra-subjective understanding through imagination, empathy, connections between one's own feelings, acts and experiences and the content studied. The merit of the constructivist approach is that pupils are encouraged to explore ideas and issues for themselves and arrive at their own conclusions. Inevita-

---

[266] See Grimmitt 2000: Constructivist Pedagogies of RE Project, 216f.
[267] Grimmitt quotes examples from the discussions he had with pupils in class about Shiva as Nataraja in the different stages of the constructivist process when he used this strategy, see ibid.: 217-222.

bly, learning is a matter of interpreting and constructing meaning. In RE, "pupils do this through considering the inescapable, ultimate questions that arise from reflecting upon the human condition."[268] In a constructivist environment, the influence of the socio-cultural context of individuals upon this interpretational process is considered and deliberately taken up in the strategic questions of the teacher.

Grimmitt emphasises the challenge which emancipatory constructivism in particular presents for other methods in RE that draw on ethnography or phenomenology, especially as it enables a problematisation of religious knowledge and understanding and a deconstruction of language and meanings related to power and privilege. Thereby, emancipatory constructivism makes possible an evaluation of the positive as well as the negative aspects of religion, including "its intrinsic sexism and racism"[269], since all items of religious content are placed within a critical framework. The content of RE thus consists of a deconstruction and reconstruction of traditional religious interpretations and meanings in light of the pupils' own experience and alternative perspectives.[270] Grimmitt clearly addresses the social and political relevance of the emancipatory potential of this approach to RE which would

> "prevent RE from furthering the hegemony of cultural and social reproduction involving the perpetuation of injustice, inequality and oppression and would challenge concepts and practices which have become reified by tradition and which may no longer be worthy of support or toleration. It would also represent a significant advance in ensuring that RE has a direct effect on sensitising pupils to matters of social and political concern in a pluralistic democracy."[271]

This is a clear statement about the general character of the subject, which is interpreted as an emancipatory process in which the pupils are encouraged to interact with and critically respond to the subject content. This constructivist teaching model has important implications for the role of the teacher and thus also for teacher training. Grimmitt emphasises that the way teachers themselves have acquired their knowledge about religions cannot provide a model for teaching RE.

---

268 Ibid., 224.
269 Ibid., 224.
270 Examples of relevant questions in this context are: "How does this religious text, belief, practice or value present the possibilities of being female and male? From where or from whom does it derive and for whom is it intended? To whom does it give power and privilege? To whom does it deny power and privilege? etc." (ibid., 225).
271 Ibid., 225.

Teacher trainees need to transform their own knowledge within a wider pedagogical focus and subject it to the same process of deconstruction and reconstruction they intend to take the pupils through.[272] The concept of teaching as simply transmitting knowledge has to be questioned, as a consideration of RE in the light of constructivist learning theories implies, that the concept of knowledge must also be reconsidered by taking up the realisation of the learner's integral part in the construction of meaning.

Comment

In his article, Grimmitt mainly outlines how constructivist ideas can be transferred to RE. He writes about his understanding of education in general and exemplifies this with respect to RE and the teaching of one religious item in particular. The main focus in this approach is on a new understanding of education as an emancipatory process and on an outline of how this notion can be put into practice. As this approach is seen as compatible with other approaches, in particular with those drawing on phenomenology and ethnography, Grimmitt does not provide a new outline of his understanding of the notion of religion or what he regards as suitable contents for RE. By transferring constructivist ideas to RE, he provides a new framework for aims of RE within a general pedagogical concept of learning and teaching.

The constructivist approach, in my view, is a challenge for most common practices of current RE. The constructivist interpretation of "knowledge" and "reality" sheds a different light on contents and learning outcomes of RE, if compared, for example, to the national guidelines for RE in England and Wales.[273] If reality is always seen as somebody's reality, the simple distinction between facts and beliefs cannot be upheld easily. The representation of facts also has to be considered critically and no construction of reality can be accepted as ultimately correct. Furthermore, the approach takes seriously the environment and developmental stages of the children and empowers them to play an active role in the process of learning by acknowledging their own constructions as important parts of the inevitable process of constructing, deconstructing and reconstructing.

---

272 See ibid., 225f.
273 See, for example, the national model syllabuses (SCAA 1994).

Grimmitt's example for presenting Shiva as *Nataraja* in RE can provide a model for the representation of other aspects of religions, following the three constructivist stages. It is a helpful example for dealing with the different constructions that influence the RE process. The constructivist approach is another contribution to teaching about individual religious items, however, leaving behind the problematic notion of religion in the "A Gift to the Child" approach of the *Religion in the Service of the Child Project* and acknowledging the ambivalence of religion.[274]

2.7 The Narrative Approach

The narrative approach to religious education has been developed mainly by Clive and Jane Erricker in cooperation with Danny Sullivan, Cathy Ota and Mandy Fletcher in the period from the mid-1990s up to the present. It is based on a combination of a pedagogical concept, the *education of the whole child* and empirical research about the worldviews of children, including qualitative interviews, within the general framework of grounded theory.[275] The approach is structured around the idea that the narrative dimension ought to be used in the classroom within a general framework of a narrative pedagogy, in which the small narratives of the pupils are given preference over the grand narratives of the world religions. The approach has a clear primary school focus.[276]

The narrative approach starts from a radical reassessment of traditional concepts of education, knowledge and learning. Empowerment, discernment and sensitivity are identified as aims of education. The authors take a critical view on the common understanding of education as the transmission of knowledge and of the idea of delivering a curriculum. Their aim is therefore to deconstruct curriculum constraints. The current curricula overemphasise subject knowledge at the cost of

---

274 Cf. section 2.2 in this chapter.
275 See Erricker et al. 1997: The Education of the Whole Child, C. Erricker and D. Sullivan 1994: The development of children's worldviews, Erricker 1998: Journeys through the heart, C. and J. Erricker 2000: Children's Spirituality and the Transformation of Education and C. and J. Erricker 2000: Reconstructing, Religious Spiritual and Moral Education, C. and J. Erricker 2000: The Children and Worldviews Project, C. Erricker 2001: From Silence to Narration. See also CWVP 2006: *The Children and Worldviews Project* (http://www.cwvp.com).
276 In the *Children and Worldviews Project* children between the ages of 5 and 10 were interviewed, cf. Erricker 2001: From Silence to Narration, 160.

the experience of learning and the development of the "whole child". The curriculum ought to be less content centred. The Errickers go as far as to state that the idea of "subject matter is wrong in itself".[277] Learning, particularly in RE, is regarded as unfolding one's identity, constructing a worldview by means of communication and developing emotional literacy. Therefore, education inevitably has to be child-centred and child-led.[278]

Curriculum content and pedagogical practice are regarded as two incommensurable paradigms. If subjectivity and relationships are to be considered, there is no choice but to concentrate on the children's narratives at the cost of the "grand narratives" of religious or ideological traditions, as only one of these can be at the centre of the educational process. The authors draw on the ideas of the French philosopher Jean-François Lyotard about postmodern knowledge.[279] Lyotard identifies a crisis of narratives (*crise de récits*) in the postmodern world and demands a critical view of the discourse about knowledge. In this meta-discourse, the grand narratives (*grand récits*) of, for example, the Enlightenment or the philosophy of history have to be deconstructed and their legitimation through power (alone) has to be acknowledged.

Referring back to Lyotard's call for a discourse about the rules of science, C. Erricker calls for a reconsideration of what is regarded as education. On what grounds should the grand narratives be handed down from generation to generation and knowledge be assessed with respect to the extent to which those grand narratives can be reproduced? Would that not be a reinforcement of power structures which ought to be assessed critically? If unfolding one's identity is taken seriously as an aim of education, this has to be regarded as an open and dynamic process. There is no discontinuity between children and adults in the sense that there are adult skills resulting from a maturity that children lack. Children have to learn for themselves, however, with the help of peers and adults. This concept of learning is fundamentally opposed to the syllabus approach in which children have to learn what is being taught. A critical view is also taken of the creed of rationalism that knowledge can be objective and value-free. In this construction, the affective and emotional dimensions of knowledge and development are neglected completely. The conceptual and the affec-

---

277 C. and J. Erricker 2000: The Children and Worldviews Project 195.
278 C. Erricker actually prefers the term "person-centred", cf. 2000: True stories and other dreams, 3. For these issues see also C. and J. Erricker 2000: Narrative constructions towards community, 126 and 2000: The Children and Worldviews Project, 202.
279 See Lyotard 1979: La condition postmoderne.

tive dimensions are, however, inseparable. Therefore, the curriculum can be a part, but not the dominating feature, of the process of identifying the aims of education.[280]

This involves a radical reassessment not only of how to teach, but also of what ought to be taught and how teaching and learning may take place. Listening and responding to the children ought to be the heart of education. The Errickers refer to what F. Newman and L. Holzman call "the performance of conversation"[281] in order to illustrate what this process may comprise, for example, attending to the question a child asks, trying to identify the experience from which it derived and talking about the issues underlying it. Verbalising experiences and feelings is part of the process of understanding oneself, as emotions may become clearer to oneself and sharing them, as well as respecting other people's feelings, may contribute to empathy and mutual understanding.[282]

The scepticism of the narrative approach to a clearly defined subject matter in general has serious consequences for the delineation of aims and contents of RE. If the traditional concept of knowledge is challenged and a kind of knowledge that takes account of subjectivity and emotions is desired, Lyotard's ideas become relevant again, as an attempt should be made not to silence the *small narratives* of the pupils by means of reproducing and reinforcing *grand narratives* and an orthodox view. Knowledge can be perceived as narrative knowledge. Conventional subject knowledge may be replaced by a process, a narrative process, in which the children acquire certain skills that may in turn form a basis for RE. Clive Erricker identifies the following 12 skills which may result in the recognition of the complexity of social discourse as well as of one's own role and responsibility within this process:

(1) reflection of one's own emotions;
(2) self knowledge (understanding why one does something);
(3) understanding of consequences;
(4) self criticism (according to one's own recognised principles);
(5) self control;

---

[280] Cf. C. Erricker 1998: Journeys through the heart, 117, C. and J. Erricker 2000: The Children and Worldviews Project 196, 203, and Erricker 2000: True stories and other dreams 1ff.
[281] Newman and Holzman 1997: The End of Knowing: A New Developmental Way of Learning.
[282] Cf. C. and J. Erricker 2000: The Children and Worldviews Project 190, 198f.

(6) reflection on the emotions of others;
(7) empathy;
(8) criticism of others (according to one's own recognised principles);
(9) understanding why others do things
(10) recognition of relationship;
(11) recognition of difference;
(12) recognition of the complexity of social discourse[283]

The small narratives of the children themselves should form the centre of RE. The world religions – in contrast – are regarded as grand narratives. They are "constructs with political purposes, in the context of which they make truth claims".[284] Even though teachings of religious traditions are often reflections of experience, theologies are nevertheless meta-narratives which systematise those teachings and construct knowledge.

Unless it is justified through theological truth claims or empirical research, "religion does not consist of a body of knowledge in the scientific or social scientific sense". Religion deals with "faith in that which is beyond such forms of assertion and enquiry"[285] and this is existentially significant for the pupils. It is the task of RE to provide an opportunity

> "for the expression of different 'spiritual voices' i.e. the inclusion of different faith and non-faith positions within the process of addressing spiritual development; but we cannot allow any position to construct the foundations of such a development."[286]

A relativist position is regarded as the only possible starting point for integrative RE, as beliefs and values are regarded as utterly subjective with no object of reference outside the relationships between subjects. Truth is created by means of consensus. There is nothing like objective truth, as agreement does not constitute epistemological knowledge in itself. Therefore, the pursuit of consensus is regarded as an acknowledgement of relativism, both epistemologically and socially. Clive Erricker uses this line of argument to shed light on "why the theological position can never act as the foundation of curriculum innovation in

---

283 Ibid., 200.
284 Ibid., 194.
285 This and the above quotation are taken from Erricker 2000: True stories and other dreams, 4 and 5.
286 Erricker 1998: Spiritual confusion, 61.

spiritual development in a plural society".[287] If the children are at the centre of RE, listening to their stories as a prerequisite for understanding their spiritualities is one essential element of RE. Children are encouraged to pursue narrative reflection, for which existential questions may be a starting point. If the small narratives of the pupils replace traditional knowledge, narratives from different religious traditions can nevertheless be valuable for the pupils who may choose to establish links between the different types of narratives.[288] Faith, which has become a concept exclusively appropriated by religion, has to be approached also and perhaps primarily beyond its institutionalised forms and contexts: "It is by releasing the grip religion has on faith that the subject can achieve its pedagogical potential."[289]

Generally, the authors wish to transform the subject into something broader than traditional RE, but suggest a provisional integration of the basic ideas of their approach into the current structures of RE. With respect to the representation of religions this includes introducing pupils "to the struggles and joys of faith, the difficulties and successes of constructing values and community without recourse to simply presenting them with the sanitising ideological platitudes of religious tradition," because they clearly sense the difference between "the authenticity of the individual voice and the rhetoric of ideological pronouncements."[290]

In the context of a narrative approach to RE, trust, respect and a willingness to listen are important professional qualities of teachers. Establishing a relationship that encourages trust also includes a deconstruction of the traditional power relationship between teacher and pupils. Referring back to ideas of McGuinness about counselling, C. Erricker identifies four dimensions of the relationship needed between teacher and pupils: empathy, unconditional positive regard, genuineness and immediacy. Teachers have to develop these skills in order to communicate them to the pupils and encourage the pupils to also develop them. They should be able to analyse the conceptual relevance as well as the affective significance of the pupils' responses. If students are given the chance to associate freely, unexpected reflection is often a result. In acknowledgement of the importance of peer to peer communication pupils may be challenged by other pupils prior to any inter-

---

[287] Ibid., 60.
[288] Cf. C. and J. Erricker 2000: The Children and Worldviews Project, 203.
[289] Ibid., 203.
[290] Both quotations in C. and J. Erricker 2000: The Children and Worldviews Project, 204.

vention by the teacher. Children may be allowed to know as much as or even more than the teacher.[291] To prevent what is being taught having hardly anything to do with those who are expected to learn, teachers in their role as nurturers have to show sensitivity to the needs of the children, to the way they express their experiences and values and to the basis on which these are formed. The whole RE process can be regarded as a process of creating a community through trust and respect.[292]

Critical evaluation

The Errickers suggest the transformation of the subject into something broader than RE in order to overcome exclusivist claims, the dichotomy religious vs. secular and the assumption that all children are implicitly religious. However, it remains unclear to me what exactly this transformed subject would look like.

The Erricker's criticism not only applies to RE, but to the whole school curriculum, which is to some extent suited to the reproduction of grand narratives. A conscious evaluation of the extents to which grand or small narratives ought to be dealt with in school can be regarded as a helpful corrective to current educational practice. This is, however, not a matter for RE alone but for many school subjects. Therefore, I see no reason why RE should be transformed into something broader while other school subjects (for example, history) remain as they are. Despite the legitimate criticism of the reproduction of grand narratives, the different religions of the world in their variety – not only a selection of "world religions" – including the disparate views of various insiders, do, in fact, constitute a legitimate and worthwhile subject for study. The subject integrative RE is needed for this. This does not mean, however, that there is no room for the small narratives of the children. RE ought to be one, but not the only, forum in which these small narratives may be articulated.

A criticism of grand narratives has to become an integral part of RE. Clive Erricker is right when he emphasises, with respect to phenomenological and interpretive approaches, that

"[w]e are still working within a conceptual model that is determined by tradition. What we study is what has survived and been legitimated. This

---

291 See ibid., 196-201.
292 See Erricker 1998: Spiritual confusion, 62.

is the case even if we regard tradition as dynamic and cumulative. What we study is what the gatekeepers or authority figures in traditions, communities and groups wish to be acknowledged as the representation of themselves."[293]

Furthermore, he claims:

"This model presumes that what is to be studied is what tradition presents, or at least what we interpret tradition as presenting, even when conveyed through the plurality of its membership groups. What has been edited out is what tradition has discarded as heresy rather than orthodoxy, or has been reinterpreted to conform to its orthodoxy."[294]

His point that the metanarrative itself is never contested is important, but why should it be impossible to include a reflection about the metanarratives and the processes by which they are created in RE? Unquestionably, metanarratives have a great influence. Therefore, it is an important aspect of education that the children learn about them. If this happens within a general critical framework which acknowledges their character as constructions emphasising certain aspects and excluding others, RE unfolds its ideology-critical potential, which makes this subject a very relevant part of the school curriculum. Despite Erricker's legitimate and thought-provoking criticism, I think that interpretive RE, as put forward by Robert Jackson and his team, provides a good methodology for this purpose, especially as it pays attention to small narratives, e.g. through ethnographic research among children and including children's voices in the textbooks. However, Erricker's criticism of the notion of tradition ought to be taken into account. Jackson's three-layer matrix (individual – membership groups – wider religious tradition) is helpful for a representation of diversity within "traditions". However, phenomena outside these "traditions" must not be left out. This is a serious challenge for contemporary RE in England.

Even though I agree with Erricker in many points of his criticism of current RE practice, I do not see why it should not be possible to integrate many of the changes he suggests in integrative RE. He addresses important issues when he writes that there is

"a bias to representation in favour of the idea that the truth claims of 'orthodoxies' occupy a central position in any attempt to understand religion – a sort of fixed (ahistorical) point from which there is only (temporal) de-

---

293 Erricker 2000: A critical review of RE, 30.
294 Ibid.

viation. This model is underpinned by a judgement that, despite their shortcomings, ... religious systems are intrinsically valuable."[295]

He criticises the implicit assumption that orthodoxies ought to be trusted and supported as vehicles for human progress towards wisdom and that, "however much we may advocate internal criticism as part of the dynamic of their maintenance, we do not regard it as suitable, in relation to our educational purposes, to undermine their truth claims".[296] For RE, he concludes that

> "the assumption behind this sort of study is an implicitly religious one: defence of our subject as it represents itself to us, and defence of its claims to knowledge, or at least the right to those claims, however much we may observe conflicting expressions of such claims."[297]

The narrative approach provides an excellent critical corrective for the selection of the phenomena to be represented and discussed in RE. It shows that a permanent reconsideration of the subject matter – even though the authors reject the notion of a subject matter – is a very delicate and important task. Clive Erricker addresses an important point when he writes that the common map of the subject matter

> "is precisely the one that orthodoxies wish to impose as a representation of religion in order to gain hegemony over both deviance (heterodoxy) and secularity. This map acts in the self-interest of orthodoxies and their truth claims".[298]

To overcome this unsatisfactory situation, he suggests studying what purposes the concepts "tradition" and "orthodoxy" serve from a meta-level. This is exactly the kind of criticism that has come up in the recent study of religions, for example with respect to the reification of constructions of centres and peripheries.[299] In my view, this ideology-critical dimension, also with respect to the choice of narratives which are regarded as parts of the subject matter, can and has to be a part of integrative RE.

---

[295] Ibid. 31, referring to Bowker (1987: Licensed Insanities), who addresses the unacceptable face of religion and regards the destructive character of religious ideologies as a reason for why they should be studied (cf. Erricker 2000: A critical review of RE, 29).
[296] Ibid.
[297] Ibid.
[298] Ibid. 32.
[299] See chapter I, section 1.1.3, particularly Joy 2001: Postcolonial reflections: challenges for Religious Studies.

Approaches to teaching Christianity: The Chichester and Stapleford Projects

The question of how to teach Christianity as part of an integrative approach to RE is of particular relevance because of the long tradition of teaching Christianity within a monoreligious framework before the transformation of the subject. Obviously, the change of the character of the subject following the 1960s also required reconsiderations about teaching Christianity. There are two projects that deal particularly with teaching Christianity within an integrative approach to RE, the Chichester and the Stapleford projects.

2.8 The Chichester Project

The Chichester Project is based on ideas of the *Shap Working Party of World Religions in Education (Shap)*.[300] The necessity of a new approach to teaching Christianity in a non-confessional framework to pupils of diverse religious and non-religious backgrounds, is the starting point for the attempt to teach Christianity from a new perspective in the context of other "world religions", as one religion among many. The project is mainly concerned with RE in secondary schools. The project team, which included John Rankin, David Naylor, Alan Brown and Mary Hayward, first met in 1977 in order to consider issues like problems of objectivity, methodologies and the religious commitment of teachers. There was general agreement about the following aims of the project:

(1) to extend knowledge of the beliefs, practices and values to be encountered within Christianity;
(2) to encourage appreciation of the importance and influence of these beliefs, values and practices in the lives of Christians;
(3) to develop an awareness of the wide diversity of interpretation contained within the Christian tradition;
(4) to encourage serious reflection on the evidence upon which Christian claims are based;
(5) to develop an understanding of the language of Christian discourses and Christian worship.[301]

---

300 For *Shap* see also chapter II, section 1.1.3.
301 Brown 2000: The Chichester Project: teaching Christianity: a world religions approach, 55f.

The development of a curriculum or learning unit was not intended, but the team produced a range of materials for pupils and teachers for learning and teaching about Christianity in secondary schools.[302] The teacher's manual *Teaching Christianity. A World Religions Approach* (1987), for example, comprises contributions concerning the approach in general, individual aspects of Christianity (Jesus, the Bible, worship, festivals, communities and ethics) and a section on teaching practice. Articles mainly from this publication will be used to illustrate the issues considered relevant for teaching Christianity within integrative RE.

In my description of the Chichester approach to teaching Christianity, I will focus on the following characteristics: its attempt to achieve a balance between understanding and reflection in the learning process; its attendance to the internal diversity of religions and its broad recognition of diverse religious phenomena, including, for example, the political dimension of religions and phenomena like implicit and civil religion; considerations about the commitment of teachers and suggested strategies for teaching RE.

2.8.1 The general framework

Understanding is seen as the main aim of RE. Special emphasis is given to understanding Christianity in Great Britain. The project attempts to balance informing the pupils about Christianity with involving them in active learning strategies aimed at developing their own understandings and perspectives:

> "Successful learning and understanding follows when students can be encouraged to 'engage with' not just 'learn about' Christian experience and belief and when they can 'appreciate' why Christians (or members of any other religion) choose to believe or belong, not just 'know the facts' about what Christians do and what they believe."[303]

The approach to religions in RE in which the Chichester Project locates itself is committed to nurturing knowledge, understanding and freedom. An understanding of what their religion means to believers is an important aspect of this.[304] No religion is preferred over another:

---

302 See ibid., 69 for a list of publications by the Chichester Project.
303 Brown 2000: The Chichester Project, 67.
304 Cf. Smart 1995: Foreword, VIII; Rankin 1995: Christianity as a world religion; Doble 1995: Commitment and an open approach to teaching Christianity, 15, 22f; Erricker 1995: Christianity in its cultural contexts, 35.

"The teacher might help the pupil explore the question of truth by diverting questions away from the desire to know which religion is correct towards a more specific exploration of what each religion says and how each religion expresses itself."[305]

The project seeks to encourage teachers and pupils to approach Christianity with the same methodology they use for other religions and thereby ensure that the teaching of Christianity is placed firmly within an integrative framework. Different aspects of Christianity are suggested for investigation, for example, topics like communities, foundation documents, Christianity in literature, art and music, what Christians believe, individuals, spirituality, festivals, Christianity in non-western cultures and ethics.[306] Along with the acquisition of factual knowledge about these topics, the pupils are encouraged to empathise with the feelings and experiences of the people involved. An important aspect in the study of any religion is the notion of "taking seriously": taking seriously, for example, an offering of flowers to the Buddha, the pilgrimage to Mecca, a bath in the holy Ganges, the Eucharist etc.[307]

The Project acknowledges the difficulty of defining "religion", but pursues a pragmatic approach to this issue, which neither tries to solve the problems around definitions of religion nor to define the boundaries of Christianity: "... given this important caveat we can proceed without attempting to resolve it because we will, generally, be dealing with 'mainstream' religious traditions."[308] Christianity is regarded as a world religion among other world religions. It has to be approached in the same way as other religions. Teaching Christianity is a test case for the successful implantation of an integrative framework into RE.[309]

2.8.2 Aspects of teaching Christianity

It is important not to present any religion as superior to others, even though the time allocated to the different religions in the timetable may vary considerably. In the representation of religions the "diversity within diversity" has to be considered, i.e. the diversity *of* different religions as well as the diversity *within* religions. Consideration for the internal diversity of religions means, for example, that one cannot say

---

305 Brown 1995: Christianity and other religions, 13.
306 Cf. Brown 2000: The Chichester Project, 57.
307 Rankin 1995: Christianity as a world religion, 6.
308 Brown 1995: Christianity and other religions, 10.
309 Cf. Erricker 1995: Introduction, IX.

that all Lutherans believe that there is no truth in any religion except Christianity. This position is possibly held by some Lutherans, while others disagree with it.[310] Doble suggests the following model as an account of internal diversity within Christianity:

- A family of traditions: Orthodox, Catholic, Protestant, non-white, indigenous and fringe;
- Communities in process: developing liturgies, interpreting scripture, encountering new cultures, growing through mission;
- A cluster of faith systems: doctrinal formulations interacting with ever-changing world views and reinterpreting their primal vision;
- Faith encounters with the world: Christian moral and political responses to the primal vision, diverse, sometimes contradictory, yet with degrees of unity.[311]

This model takes up diversity with respect to organisation, practice, concepts and their interpretation, and ethics.

Minton emphasises the relevance of the political dimension of religions. A tension between a homoeostatic or conservative function and a radical, reformative, or even revolutionary function seems to be characteristic of almost any religion. Both these functions ought to be dealt with in RE. The political dimension of Christianity consists of two aspects, an historical immanentism – including, for example, the covenant between God and Moses and the prophetic tradition in the Old Testament, the Sermon on the Mount and the Parables of the Kingdom in the New Testament – and a sapiential pragmatism found, for example, in the Wisdom tradition of the Old Testament. These traditions are confronted with the political situation in the modern world which is dominated by the capitalist bloc, "which is the strongest explicit link to Christianity, declaring a great emphasis on freedom and human rights, but operating an economic system which is not easily sustained from early Christian principles referring to the distribution of wealth".[312] The communist bloc is declaredly atheistic, but proclaims "economic and social aims which comply with both the teaching of Jesus about responsibility for other people and the 'primitive communism' of the earliest Church" and the Third World, "emerging from colonisation and exploi-

---

310 Cf. Brown 1995: Christianity and other religions, 10.
311 Doble 1995: Commitment and an open approach to teaching Christianity, 19.
312 Minton 1995: The political dimension of Christianity, 27.

tation by Christian countries, but in a large measure exhibiting an economic status vis-à-vis the first two worlds which some Christians would consider is materially the most comparable of the three with Jesus's teaching about suffering and service." [313]

On the basis of this account of the encounter of Christian political traditions with the political situation in the modern world, Minton draws several conclusions for the representation of Christianity in RE. The role of Christianity in political changes and conflicts in the past and present has to be studied. This should be done in comparison with the political character of other religions. Attention has to be paid to the perspective from which the topic is presented. The relations between Christianity and politics should be presented as a "cluster of concerns" rather than as an "agenda for action". The ambiguity of and tension between those concerns are at the centre of Christian inspiration. The whole range of dimensions of the relationship between Christianity and politics ought to be considered, including the global level as well as the national, local and individual levels. Minton suggests three questions for the study of the political dimension of any religion: "What is the ideal political state of affairs envisaged by the religion?", "What have been and are the actual effects of the religion on politics?" and "What kind of politics exists within the religion's own organisation of itself – in its hierarchies, councils and decision making?".[314]

Christianity should also be studied in its different cultural contexts. Christianity as taught in the classroom may differ completely from what the pupils know as Christianity. Incongruities, paradoxes and contradictions are inherent in the nature of religions. Presenting examples from implicit and civil religion in the United States, Clive Erricker shows the complexity of the relationship between religions and social and political life. One important learning outcome is that the pupils understand that what they perceive as a largely or wholly secular

---

[313] Ibid., 28 (both quotations are taken from there). Despite recent changes in the global political landscape, especially transformations in Russia and Europe, which also brought about some changes in the language used for describing the different ideologies, Minton's analysis and conclusions are basically still applicable, as they demonstrate the tensions between political reality and important ideas from the Christian tradition.

[314] Minton 1995: The political dimension of Christianity, 28. Minton says that ideally the answers to those questions should be the same, which would mean that religions are successful in "practicing what they preach" (ibid., 29). But perhaps it is a task for the adherents rather than for teachers of religion to decide what an ideal answer might be, as this includes a decision about what religions should be like rather than a study of what they are like.

world around them is, in fact, permeated with religion.[315] In support of this claim, Erricker quotes, for example, a newspaper article about what Miss America (1984) said after her enthronement: "When the new Miss America met the Press, she said that God should never have been expelled from the classroom, that she followed the flag with her whole body and that she tried to live her Christian values seven days a week."[316] Even more compelling – and sadly very topical – is his argument about the following quotation from an American general: "Our patriotism must be intelligent patriotism. ... If we maintain our faith in God, our love of freedom and superior global air power, I think we can look to the future with confidence."[317] Erricker shows how firmly held religious convictions, such as, for example, the idea of waging a just war, can form the basis for political decisions. He provides the following analysis of the quotation above:

> "The speaker feels no incongruity when suggesting that faith in God, love of freedom and superior global air power go together and it is significant that he believes faith in God to be as important to the American way of life as the other two. If we believe such faith to be threatened by the evil of atheism, which is coupled with a disregard for freedom, as he clearly does, we arrive at a rationale for superior air power starting from a religious point of view."[318]

Erricker argues that the representation of a religion has to include mainstream traditions and dissent. With respect to Christianity, this should include the general influence of Christianity in societies (for example, the architecture of the Oxford and Cambridge colleges in Britain),[319] responses of the churches to political issues, such as poverty and economic growth, and the religious aspects of nationalism as exemplified in morally healthy Americanism.

---

315 Cf. Erricker 1995: Christianity in its cultural contexts, 34.
316 Observer, 5 November 1984, quoted in Erricker 1995: Christianity in its cultural contexts, 31.
317 General Lemay (in: Agee 1975: CIA Diary, 14; quoted in Erricker 1995: Christianity in its cultural contexts, 32).
318 Erricker 1995: Christianity in its cultural contexts, 31.
319 Until the 19th century, these college buildings were constructed with a chapel and a dining hall with a layout that "reflects the hierarchical structure of a society supported by a mainstream Anglican tradition whose own organisation was of the same kind. Implicit in this are certain national beliefs in the way things ought to be ordered which are reflected in the denomination's teachings." (Erricker 1995: Christianity in its cultural contexts, 31).

2.8.3 The notion of education and teaching strategies

In a thematic approach to religions in RE, attention should be paid to the fact that similar concepts often have different meanings in different religions. Every religion has its own structure. This has to be acknowledged in order to avoid simplifying comparisons. A common mistake is the transference of concepts that were developed in the study of one religion to other religions. The distortion which results from this procedure is often not intended, but originates from lacking reflection on the complex issues at stake. In the context of this question, Brown asks: "How many syllabuses and textbooks take a 'Christian' model by looking at a 'founder', building, scriptures, worship etc. without really thinking out whether such a structure is acceptable to other religions?".[320] One element of getting to know religions is encounters with people who belong to the religion studied in RE. It is the teachers' task to prepare those meetings carefully and to discuss what happened at such a meeting afterwards with the pupils. Doble suggests establishing long-lasting contacts. He also regards this as an establishment of dialogue.[321]

In the Chichester Project, education is interpreted as "the helping of pupils to move towards personal maturity, that is, towards becoming the most complete, stable, self-fulfilled persons possible for them".[322] Minton emphasises that education also has a political dimension: in a closed society, its intention is to educate its citizens to believe in and serve the ideology of the state, whereas in an open society, it is about bringing up citizens to exercise their democratic rights on the basis of a maximum of information and integrity.[323] The reaction of the pupils is an integral part of the educational process. Brown sees the main task of the teacher in the awakening and educating of a religious sensibility, which he regards as "an essential dimension of human development" and "however diverse its manifestations ... an inherent human capacity".[324] Doble addresses possible tensions between different commit-

---

[320] Brown 1995: Christianity and other religions, 12. For the whole paragraph cf. ibid., 10ff.
[321] Doble 1995: Commitment and an open approach to teaching Christianity, 22.
[322] Ibid., 17.
[323] Cf. Minton 1995: The political dimension of Christianity, 23. Perhaps a more differentiated account of the different political systems, which acknowledges the difference between rhetoric about democratic societies and actual practice, may be helpful in this respect.
[324] Brown 2000: The Chichester Project, 62.

ments of teachers, including religious and professional ones. As long as teachers are religiously open,[325] this tension is not a major problem. There is, however, a problem with single-minded teachers, whose commitment does not allow other positions than their own:

> "How can they properly serve the county schools of a pluralist Britain whose educational aims differ significantly from those of the teacher's own group? While integrity demands that they find a subject other than RE to teach, realism recognises that such teachers develop different responses: some continue to teach as they have always taught; others swallow their scruples and try the form and content of open teaching, though their heart is not in it and their conscience is bruised."[326]

Open teaching, however, may also comprise commitment and does not reduce RE to an "objective" study of "facts". An attempt to actively engage the pupils in reflection which enhances their understanding of religious phenomena can be seen, for example, in two of the project's publications by Clive Erricker, *Christian Experience* (1982) and *Christian Ethics* (1984), in which the pupils are, for example, encouraged to express what a passage they have read says about themselves and about the relationship between human beings and the world or god. Another task for the pupils is to rank characters according to their moral acceptability and give reasons for this ranking, or to consider which of the characters acted in a Christian way. In the project, "a balance has been sought between a didactic approach to informing students about Christianity and involving them in active learning strategies intended to develop their own understanding and perspective."[327]

---

[325] Apparently, he thinks of this group as being "pluralists", cf. Doble 1995: Commitment and an open approach to teaching Christianity, 20.

[326] Doble 1995: Commitment and an open approach to teaching Christianity, 20. Doble uses the (fictional?) example of the teacher John in order to show some possible ways of dealing with competing commitments. Unfortunately, it is not always clear if certain positions are held by John alone or if Doble also supports them or even thinks they are generally correct. If the latter was the case the following statements could be criticised as being based on theological presuppositions and therefore being religious themselves and inappropriate in an integrative framework: "While he does not share their beliefs and practices, his Christian experience has prepared him to recognise 'the holy' in the experiences of others. ... His own religious experience has helped him to enter more surely into this dialogue and so into a way of teaching that can do nothing but good for the pupils, his commitment allows him to recognise and value the commitment of another." (ibid., 22). When Doble says that it is this very insight which may be seen as John's resource for his way of teaching Christianity, he seems to support the theological premises underlying those views. In any case, he does not criticise them at all.

[327] Brown 2000: The Chichester Project, 66.

One strategy in the presentation of Christianity may be to start with an experience, a phenomenon or an action which can be observed, and ask questions which lead to the ideas behind them.[328] Pupils are encouraged to engage with the material, "and not simply be taught about it."[329] If a pupil is moved by an account of the experience of somebody else, they may understand something which they cannot understand on an intellectual level alone. A concrete starting point for the interpretive activity of the pupils may be a phenomenon of the civilisation we live in – for example what different buildings say about certain forms of Christianity – or a study of Christianity in the context of world affairs such as, for example, an understanding of the US equation of civilised life, freedom, belief in God and confidence in military power as a prerequisite for understanding US strategies and activities, for example in Nicaragua or El Salvador.[330] "This face of Christianity is also an important one to understand in order to make sense of international affairs, in the context of World Studies as well as Religious Education".[331]

The Chichester approach to teaching Christianity is clearly designed for a multireligious classroom. It presents strategies for teaching children of any religion or none and therefore does not assume a pupil's prior commitment to or participation in the religion studied. A consideration of the different commitments and other experiences of, as well as influences on, the pupils remains a continuous task for any integrative RE.[332]

2.8.4 Comment

The Chichester project is dedicated to the important task of placing the teaching of Christianity within an integrative approach to education and suggests teaching strategies for this purpose. Apart from a few minor exceptions,[333] it is successful in clearly distinguishing between a confessional and an integrative framework. The contributions discussed above show different ways in which the internal diversity of Christianity – in relation to local and global social and political contexts

---

328 Cf. Rankin 1995: Christianity as a world religion, 6f., Brown 2000: The Chichester Project, 62ff.
329 Brown 2000: The Chichester Project, 69.
330 Afghanistan and Iraq could be given as further recent examples.
331 Erricker 1995: Christianity in its cultural contexts, 36. See also ibid., 35.
332 Cf. Doble 1995: Commitment and an open approach to teaching Christianity, 15ff.
333 Cf. my notes in the text above.

– may be presented in the classroom. The attempt to approach Christianity with the same tools as other religions involves overcoming merely text-based approaches, for example, interpretations of the Bible or other documents from church history, and taking account of the various aspects of this religion. Furthermore, the authors provide helpful approaches to the political dimension of Christianity. These – as well as other considerations about the representation of religions which they exemplify for Christianity – can also be transferred to the representation of other religions within an integrative approach to RE. The concept of education on which the Chichester approach is based includes the main points of critical educational theory, particularly with respect to the aims of education (and RE) as well as the role of education in its socio-political contexts.[334] Doble's idea that RE teachers need to be able to take a pluralist view of religions is a particularly relevant point in the discussion about prerequisites for this profession.

2.9 The Stapleford Project

The Stapleford Project is another project providing a concept for teaching Christianity within integrative RE. It was launched in 1986 by the *Association of Christian Teachers in England* in order to produce material for teaching Christianity in RE on the basis of a distinctive theoretical rationale. Its main idea and method, *concept cracking*, was developed mainly by Trevor and Margaret Cooling of the *Stapleford House Education Centre*, the conference and study centre of the *Association of Christian Teachers*. In addition to the printed publications about the project, which comprise academic articles, a handbook for teachers, a termly magazine for primary schools, *Cracking RE*, and teaching material, there is also a project website on which much of the material can be accessed.[335]

As the Stapleford Project is only a concept for teaching Christianity – and Christian concepts in particular – but not other religions in RE, it is concerned with the more general questions about integrative RE only in relation to this part of it. Therefore, it does not provide a general outline or framework for aims and contents of RE or the representation of different religions within RE, but concentrates on one particular

---

334 Cf. chapter I.2.1.
335 The address of the project website is www.stapleford-centre.org. The handbook for teachers (Cooling 1994: Concept Cracking) can be downloaded from the website as pdf-files and there is also an online edition of the magazine *Cracking RE*.

method of representing aspects of Christianity, which may perhaps be transferred to the representation of other religions.[336] For this reason, some general questions about integrative RE, which have been analysed in the other concepts, cannot be dealt with in the same detail in this section. The characterisation of Cooling's approach will start with an outline of the influences on the project, and proceed from a description of its methodology to wider issues about teaching Christianity and other religions in RE. Individual aspects of the concept are criticised when they arise in the text, a general evaluation of the project and further reflections on some of its basic assumptions and the questions of transferability to the representation of other religions in integrative RE will be given in the concluding section.

2.9.1 Influences on the Stapleford Project

The background of the project is a criticism of Ronald J. Goldman's thesis that only older children (in their teens) are able to understand abstract religious ideas. According to Cooling Goldman's idea, which builds on the works of Piaget on the development of children, leads to a negligence of conceptual knowledge in RE. The work of Jerome Bruner and its criticism of Goldman's idea of readiness is an important source of inspiration for the Stapleford approach.[337] Bruner argues that it is possible at any stage of children's development to translate concepts into terms that make sense to them. These terms may be *enactive* (making mental models through action), *iconic* (making mental models through visual and sensory organisation) or *symbolic* (representation in words and language). Concepts may also be learnt intuitively and this intuitive learning is regarded as a prerequisite for later formal understanding. In contrast to Goldman, Bruner maintains that, when young children are introduced to abstract concepts at the early stages of their development, it is not necessarily true that they are unable to grasp these concepts just because they see the world in more concrete terms at that age. He suggests overcoming the problem of "disembedded

---

336 This possible transference of the method is not specified any further, but suggested as a task for specialists in other religions. Cf. Cooling 2000: The Stapleford Project, 166 and Cooling 1994: Concept Cracking, 6.

337 This idea of readiness builds on the assumption that learning of abstract concepts can only take place once the level of formal operational thinking is achieved. Cf. Goldman 1964: Religious Thinking from Childhood to Adolescence and Goldman 1965: Readiness for Religion. Cf. also chapter II, section 1.1.1.

thinking" – confrontation with abstract concepts outside a frame of reference which is meaningful to the children – by translating concepts into terms which the children can make sense of at their respective stages of development.[338] On the basis of Bruner's ideas, the Stapleford Project suggests attention to the development of the pupils in a new light, acknowledging the pupils' ability of understanding concepts and ideas at all stages of their development as long as these are translated into their world of experience, but at the same time taking account of their increasing capacity to understand more and more complex issues. Cooling's basic concern is an adequate representation of Christian concepts – as expressed in narratives in particular – in RE, in contrast to a distortion engendered by an over-emphasis of the educational character of the subject, which he fears might include a representation of Christian narratives that does not pay due attention to Christian interpretations of those narratives. He is particularly concerned with the framework of the Christian "meta-narrative" as an expression of a world-view in which the individual elements make sense.[339]

2.9.2 Concept cracking

In order to contribute to a better practice of teaching Christian concepts in RE by means of translating abstract ideas into forms appropriate to the developmental stages of the pupils, the *concept cracking* method was developed. Concept cracking involves identifying a focus within one topic and unpacking related themes and concepts. One or a few of those ideas or concepts should be chosen for further attention within a unit of work. Then, the concept has to be translated into a form that makes sense to the pupils. Therefore, a relation to the world of the pupils has to be established. In order to make sense to the pupils, beliefs which may seem strange to them have to be related to their own beliefs. A bridge has to be built between the world of Christian beliefs and the world of the experience of the pupils. This process means reformulating a concept in a way that helps the pupils in their own personal development and their understanding of the world. In short, concept cracking comprises four steps:[340]

---

338   Cf. Bruner 1977: The Process of Education and Bruner 1966: A Theory of Instruction; quoted in Cooling 1987: Christian Doctrine in RE, 154.
339   See Cooling 1996: Education is the point of RE – not religion?, especially p. 170.
340   See Cooling 1994: Concept Cracking, 11.

(1) Unpacking the cluster of ideas
(2) Selecting one idea to explore
(3) Relating it to the pupils' world of experience and reflecting on that experience
(4) Introducing the explicitly religious idea and making it relevant to the modern world

Cooling exemplifies this method with a selection of topics, such as the story of Ruth, the covenant between God and Israel, Easter and adult baptism. He gives keywords for the individual steps required for cracking the concepts behind those topics. With respect to Easter, for example, he mentions sin, love, sacrifice, forgiveness and reconciliation, and new life for step 1, forgiveness and reconciliation for step 2, falling out with someone and then restoring the relationship with forgiveness for step 3 and Joseph and his brothers, Jesus' attitude to his persecutors, Coventry Cathedral reconciliation service and the Corrymeela community for step 4.

According to the respective stages of the pupils' development, the way the concepts are presented may proceed from a fairly simple to a rather sophisticated one. The same topic (for example, Christmas) may be dealt with at different stages emphasising different aspects with an increasing level of complexity. Cooling explains possible ways for this progression to greater complexity by the "onion-" and the "jigsaw-method".[341] Like peeling away the layers of an onion, an ever deepening exploration of the same material can be achieved, proceeding e.g. from (1.) an outline of the story of Jesus' birth to (2.) explaining why the birth of Jesus is important to Christians, (3.) investigating the differences between the accounts in Luke and Matthew and (4.) exploring the theological significance of the gifts from the wise men. The jigsaw method depends on the identification of a cluster of beliefs which underpin a main belief or practice like sin, forgiveness, atonement, rescue and a new start as aspects of the concept of salvation. "These can be likened to the parts of a jigsaw, which when joined together give a reasonably comprehensive picture of the Christian belief in salvation."[342] Easier ideas like "new start" can be introduced earlier than difficult ones like atonement. Generally, the status of development of the pupils has to be considered for the selection of concepts.

---

[341] Cf. ibid., 12f.
[342] Ibid., 13.

Cooling provides a table with suggestions for individual concepts and ideas around the topics God, Jesus, church, the Bible and ways of life for key stages one to four.[343] For example, incarnation and redemption are identified as key concepts around Jesus. The suggested distribution of topics over the key stages is as follows: Jesus – a special person for Christians, Jesus changed/changes people's lives (KS 1); Jesus' birth and life reflecting God's presence in the world; new beginnings as a result of Jesus' death and resurrection (KS 2); the two natures of Christ – human and divine, the purpose for which Jesus came (KS 3); the messianic kingdom – the heralding of a new age in history, and eternal life – a new dimension experienced in relationship with Christ (KS 4). In the section "ways of life" the human condition and discipleship are identified as key concepts and the following topics are suggested: the worth of people, following a leader (KS 1); humans as created, rebellious but redeemed, personal and corporate commitment through following Jesus (KS 2); the perfect relationship between God and humanity and its loss; (again) personal and corporate commitment through following Jesus (KS 3); purpose in life defined in relation to obedience to God, witness and mission – spreading the good news (KS 4).

2.9.3 Diversity within Christianity

Cooling reflects on the internal diversity of Christianity and concedes that there is, in fact, a pluralism of "Christianities". In his reflection about a perceived common essence of faith, he distinguishes between the postulate of "a set of timeless truths which all Christians are expected to believe"[344] and the attempt to specify characteristics of the family resemblances which the various Christianities share. The second approach to the plurality of Christian beliefs makes it possible to identify commonalities and bonds between different traditions without "implying that every Christian has to hold to all of these identified characteristics".[345] This distinction is very important for the representation of religions in integrative RE, as it marks the difference between a normative and a descriptive approach.

The keywords for the representation of Jesus and "ways of life" above, however, do not show an acknowledgement of this variety, but

---

343 Ibid., 14.
344 Cooling 1996: Education is the point of RE – not religion?, 174.
345 Ibid., 175.

seem to present a particular theological interpretation of the issues. Perhaps this impression is caused by the keyword-style of presentation, while proper attention to the variety of Christian views on Jesus or "ways of life" might become apparent in more elaborate outlines of possible topics to be discussed. Despite his consideration of internal diversity, however, Cooling states that it is the first responsibility of RE to teach the pupils to understand "creedal orthodoxy" and "mainstream Christianity as believed by the majority of Christians" and that helping them to understand "variations on that" is only a secondary responsibility.[346] The question is, however, who defines what "creedal orthodoxy" and "mainstream Christianity" are. Does "mainstream Christianity" refer to lay members of different Christian denominations (whose views often differ considerably from "creedal orthodoxy", as, for example, the popularity of the concept of rebirth among Christians shows) or to theologians and the clergy? Cooling sees one example for his argument in that it is possible "to identify a core of beliefs which the vast majority of Christians would recognise and identify with"[347] in the *Faith Communities' Working Group Reports* of the model syllabuses of the SCAA, which "led to an agreed statement among Christians from many different denominations as to what Christians believe and think should be taught in schools".[348] There are, however, also very critical views on this report.[349] Again, a close look at who agreed on what in this report is necessary. What criteria were used to select the representatives? Was breadth attempted only with respect to denominations or also with respect to other factors like gender, class, education etc.?[350] The importance of an adequate attention to the variety of interpretations within a religion and its implications for the selection of topics and the manner of representing different aspects of religions can hardly be overrated.

---

346 Cooling 1997: Theology goes to school, 52f.
347 Cooling 2000: The Stapleford Project, 159.
348 Ibid., 160.
349 Cf. the section on this report in chapter II, section 1.2.2.
350 How (the results of) this report may be used in RE is another issue. It is a source which was created by selected "representatives" of faith communities in order to give an account of what Christians want to have taught about their religion in integrative RE. It is unquestionably a very interesting source worth considering in RE. However, pedagogical guidance for dealing with it is required, taking up the issues addressed above. If this was transferred to other subjects, what would, for example, have to be considered when dealing with a report of selected French people about what they want schoolchildren to learn about France? Would that be the same as what pedagogues want children to learn about France?

2.9.4 RE: religious or educational?

In the context of debates about the religious or educational character of RE, the Stapleford method of representing Christian beliefs in RE defends itself against reproaches of indoctrination or nurture, which are seen as tasks for religious communities and not the secular school. Cooling argues against a polarisation of or tug-of-war between educational and religious approaches to RE.[351] He is right when he notes that it is incorrect to assume "that the concern for the transmission of an accurate understanding of the religious content is a religious use of the same order as nurture."[352] The attempt to understand religions in their own terms is unquestionably an important task for integrative RE, irrespective of the way the existential dimension of the subject is interpreted. Cooling regards the "religious" (in the sense of "about the religions") and educational aspects of the subject as complementary: "RE should not simply be religious in the sense of conveying an understanding of the faith as understood by believers. It should also be educational in the sense of promoting reflection and self-understanding by the student."[353]

There is confusion, however, owing to different ways in which Cooling interprets the word *religious*. In the above sense, which Cooling also describes as "transmitting an accurate understanding of the religions to the children",[354] a "religious" dimension of secular RE is perfectly acceptable. This use does not, however, correspond to the common use of *religious*, neither in academia nor in daily life. Cooling himself also uses *religious* in a different sense as "entailing the promotion or development of faith",[355] which would be problematic in an integrative framework. As both these understandings of religion are used in the context of the question of whether RE ought to be religious or educa-

---

[351] His article *Education is the point of RE – not religion?* (1996) is a response to the educational approach to RE presented by the Birmingham team. He concedes that there can be (using the vocabulary of the *Religion in Service of the Child Project*, cf. chapter II, section 2.2) non-religious gifts from religions to people that do not belong to that religion. He sees, however, a problem in separating aspects of religions from the interpretations that exist within the religions themselves and thereby neglecting the meaning those aspects have in their original surroundings. The latter is seen rather as an impediment to than a means of understanding religions in their own terms.

[352] Cooling 1996: Education is the point of RE – not religion?, 179.

[353] Cooling 1997: Theology goes to school, 55.

[354] Cooling 1996: Education is the point of RE – not religion?, 165

[355] Ibid., 180. In fact, he talks about *non-religious* as "in the sense of not entailing the promotion or development of faith".

tional (or rather in the context of an argument to overcome the polarisation of religious and educational) the different uses of the term "religious" are misleading and inhibit a clear argument about the character of RE. It is, after all, not clear, if "religious" in this context refers to doing justice to the individual religions by representing them accordingly or if it also entails the promotion or development of faith. The suspicion that the latter notion is also included in Cooling's understanding of "religious" is reinforced by a look at what he mentions as possible benefits of understanding Christianity in its own terms within an RE framework: He mentions (1.) conversion to Christianity, (2.) partial acceptance of Christian teachings and (3.) rejection of Christian interpretations of Christian narratives.[356] These possible outcomes or "benefits" of teaching Christianity in the way suggested by Cooling indicate an understanding of "religious" in the second sense. All three reactions are confessional reactions, located among different confessional positions. "Religious" in the first sense would imply an understanding of what those narratives mean for Christian people of different denominations and perhaps also for non-Christian people who relate to those narratives. Perhaps the words "descriptive" (rather than "religious") vs. "educational" are more appropriate to describe the two basic dimensions of RE, as confusion about the interpretation of how RE may be religious itself can thereby be avoided.[357]

Even though this approach focuses very much on concepts, as its aim is the communication of Christian concepts and their meaning to believers, the interrelatedness of different aspects of religions is also considered. The meaning of narratives to believers is often set within an existential framework and cannot be properly understood without that. An interaction between the horizon of the pupils and the horizon of the aspect of the religion in question is regarded as necessary in order to enable the pupil's understanding. Cooling takes up hermeneutical considerations about studying texts, which suggest that, unless

---

[356] See ibid., 177f.
[357] Another problem is, however, the term *Religious Education* itself as – if we start from what has been said above – it also implies that the subject itself is religious and not secular, contrary to the general character of integrative RE. Cf., e.g., Hull 2002: Der Segen der Säkularität. The same problem exists with the term *Religious Studies*, which is often the official name of departments for the study of religions. Perhaps the name of the subject is still a relic from its confessional past. As the word "instruction" was replaced with "education" in the respective clause of the 1988 ERA, a consideration of an alternative for the word *religious* or a general reformulation of the name of the subject might be a sensible next step in order to facilitate a general understanding of the character of the subject.

there is some collision between text and reader, misunderstandings are very likely: "If, as reader, we do not allow our own horizon to be challenged by the horizon of the text, we will simply read what we expect to find and reinforce our own prejudices, whilst being under the illusion that we have read and understood the text."[358] The pupils should be encouraged to reflect upon their own understandings of the world in light of the material they study. Cooling emphasises the importance of children learning both abstract ideas and concrete examples. The latter can foster a proper understanding of the former. Children of any age are able to understand fairly complex ideas, if these are presented in a way that makes sense in the children's world of experience. Thereby, the communication gap between the children and religious concepts can be bridged from the very beginning. For this purpose, the concepts and ideas have to be translated into a form that makes sense to the children at each stage of their development.[359]

Knowledge has intuitive, emotional and tacit dimensions. Pupils may understand a concept better than they are able to express it. Understanding a concept means more than a cognitive process, but also involves emotion. In explorative conversation, children may expand their own religious ideas and vocabulary. The polarisation of content-centred and pupil-centred approaches to RE is misleading. The form of teaching ought to be chosen according to the intended aims: "The Project has sought to achieve a balance between content-centred and child centred poles of the methods debate by being *content-structured, but child related.*"[360]

Even though the project locates itself rather in the *learning about religion* dimension of RE, Cooling is also concerned with the question of how concept cracking serves the spiritual development of the children, which he calls "the heart of what learning from religion means".[361] He suggests four points, namely (1.) standing in another's shoes: empathy and pursuing one's understanding of what beliefs mean for the believer; (2.) reflection on the way beliefs shape attitudes and behaviour, followed, for example, by a reflection on what one regards as holy oneself. With respect to Christianity, this may mean learning something

---

358 Cooling 1996: Education is the point of RE – not religion?, 171. Cf. also: Cooling 1997: Theology goes to school, 54, Cooling 2000: The Stapleford Project, 161.
359 Cf., e.g., Cooling 1994: Concept Cracking, 17.
360 Cooling 1997: Theology goes to school, 57.
361 Cooling 1994: Concept Cracking, 21. For the following, see pages 22-24.

from Christianity without having to be Christian;[362] (3.) change by knowledge[363] and (4.) the promotion of conversation, by which he understands a facilitation of the process of theological exploration through language. With regard to the latter point, it may be asked if theological exploration is not a step beyond what is possible in secular RE. Does not theological exploration already imply a religious view on religions? One has to be clear about the perspective on religions. Cooling's claim that "we need to develop a style of question and response which encourages children to explore language about God"[364] may be justified with respect to an understanding of Christian concepts. However, his examples of questions which are intended to enable children to unpack and explore their own imagery – like "Why does God need sharp elbows?" or "Can't it rain without God?"[365] – seem to imply an exploration within a Christian-theological way of thinking and thereby engaging children in a kind of conversation that has its place in church rather than in a secular school. In any case, careful attention to the use of language (and perhaps especially for theologians who teach or write about teaching their own religion) is vital in order not to corrupt the integrative character of the subject.

2.9.5 The notion of religion

The notion of religion behind the Stapleford Project identifies concepts as the keys to religions. With respect to Christianity, Cooling emphasises that "doctrine defines the nature of Christianity and should therefore provide the fundamental framework within which to set the teaching of Christian texts and practices".[366] Regardless of whether one agrees with this emphasis on concepts or regards this as an overemphasis of one single dimension of religions, the concept of religion underlying the Stapleford Project is too rooted in a Christian-theological framework and cannot serve as a general concept of religion

---

362 In the words of the Religion in Service of the Child Project, he calls this "religion making a non-religious gift to the child" (Cooling 1994: Concept Cracking, 23).
363 As an example, Cooling describes how he was changed through his encounter with philosophy at university in contrast to his knowledge about physics, which was just a means to the end of passing his A-level, cf. Cooling 1994: Concept Cracking, 23.
364 Cooling 1994: Concept Cracking, 24.
365 Ibid.
366 Cooling 2000: The Stapleford Project, 159, see also Cooling 1997: Theology goes to school, 52.

on which a representation of religion in integrative RE may be based. In contrast to a particular variation of a functional definition of religion, which Cooling locates within a pupil-centred approach (religion as "constituting the human activities of seeking to understand oneself and of trying to lead a more fully human existence") the Stapleford Project is built upon the view of religion "as the means by which humans seek to discover the truth about God and to reflect on the implications this has for their own lives",[367] which is seen as the common position of content-centred approaches. This is a particular Christian-theological view of religion, which cannot be transferred to the variety of religious traditions and is therefore not applicable to integrative RE. Positions like this one ought to be taken up and discussed in RE, because they are widely spread in theological and common use of the word "religion". They cannot, however, provide the general framework for the representation of religions in integrative RE.

In connection with Cooling's ideas on the representation of Christianity, some general questions emerge about the representation of religions in integrative RE. The project is not meant as a complete package for teaching religion, but as a contribution to a greater enterprise. Its particular concern is the effective teaching of theological concepts with Christianity as a case study. The teaching method needs, however, to be balanced with other approaches. Cooling supposes that the method can be transferred to the teaching of other religions, but he wants to leave that to specialists in those religions. He sees the Stapleford project as a contribution to the systematic approach to teaching religions in RE, which has its legitimacy along with the thematic approach.[368] The thematic and systematic approaches should not be polarised as alternatives, but the approach ought to be chosen according to the purpose one pursues. Forced links which distort the representation of religions are a possible danger of the thematic approach. In contrast, "the theological conceptual approach has something to offer to a thematic approach by encouraging the formation of legitimate themes and links between religions that are theological in nature."[369] This may help to avoid a compilation of aspects of religions which seem similar, but have, in fact, different meanings in the different religions.[370]

---

367 Both quotations in Cooling 2000: The Stapleford Project, 163.
368 Cf. Cooling 1997: Theology goes to school, 58f, Cooling 2000: The Stapleford Project, 164ff, Cooling 1994: Concept Cracking, 6.
369 Cooling 1997: Theology goes to school, 58.
370 Cooling's examples (cf. Cooling 1994: Concept Cracking, 15f) of those distortions within a badly planned thematic approach are, however, not very convincing. The

Parallels are also drawn to other approaches, for example, the ideas of "bridging" and "edification" in the interpretive approach or the "gift"-idea in the *Religion in Service of the Child Project*. Additionally, methodological insights – like "owning and grounding" (*Westhill-Project*) or the use of "distancing devices" (*Religion in Service of the Child Project*) – from other approaches are acknowledged.[371]

2.9.6 Critical evaluation

Cooling's basic idea and method, concept cracking, is a helpful approach for the representation of religions in RE. To make it applicable for representing concepts from different religions in integrative RE, some modifications have to be made in order to move away from a framework that is often so deeply rooted in Christian theological thinking that it inhibits its transference to a non-confessional approach. First, as has been shown above, the notion of religion on which the concept builds is too narrow to comprise the actual variety of religions. Second, it does not really become clear if this concept is really intended for a secular RE and is not implicitly theological or confessional. Suspicions of implicit confessionalism arise out of a.) Cooling's vague use of the terms "theological" and "religious" to describe aspects of the character of RE,[372] b.) his description of possible learning outcomes,[373] and c.) individual formulations which make it hard to imagine that Cooling

---

first example he mentions is treating the Bible, the Qur'an and the Guru Granth Sahib "as having exactly the same significance in the religions Christianity, Islam and Sikhism respectively" (ibid.) within a thematic study of sacred texts. His second example is a representation of Jesus, Muhammad and the Buddha as having the same status for their respective followers. Those two examples are – in my view – an oversimplified characterisation of the thematic approach. Sacred texts or role models (the topic he names as the framework for dealing with Jesus, Muhammad and the Buddha) are completely legitimate topics in RE and it goes without saying that comparison does not imply saying that the items compared are basically the same. It is a strength of the thematic approach to draw attention to similarities as well as differences between aspects of different religions. An oversimplification as described by Cooling has to be regarded as a result of poor training in the study of religions and teaching RE. Cooling is, however, right in emphasising the importance of the meaning behind the phenomena, a point that has also often been made about early phenomenologies of religion (cf. chapter I, section 1.1.2).

371 Cf. Cooling 1997: Theology goes to school 51, 53. A detailed discussion of the presuppositions of the SCAA model syllabuses and the *Religion in Service of the Child* approach can be found in Cooling 1996: Education is the point of RE – not religion?
372 See above.
373 See also above and below.

would agree to a transference of these ideas to the representation of other religions. For example, if we take another look at Cooling's ideas about possible benefits for non-Christian pupils from studying Christianity and transfer those to the representation of *Islam*. Would he agree with the following statements?

> First, pupils may find the *Islamic* world-view articulated through *Islamic* narrative so compelling that they decide to accept it as providing a more satisfactory identity than that provided by their current view. This is conversion and represents a very radical form of learning from *Islam*, one that state school teachers in England cannot actively seek. On the other hand neither should they resist it if it is the chosen outcome of a pupil's studies.[374]

This version of "learning from religion" may actually happen in integrative RE and Cooling is right in saying that teachers should not resist it. His classification of this outcome as a benefit and the formulation "cannot actively seek" imply, however, that this outcome – at least with respect to Christianity – is in fact favoured by Cooling. This impression is reinforced by the description of the two other possible benefits (see above), a transmission of which to other religions may seem similarly awkward, as they also include a – positive or negative – confessional response to the tradition in question.[375] This is particularly obvious in Cooling's description of a rejection of the traditional Christian interpretation of a narrative. His example for this seems somewhat hypothetical and unlikely: a student interprets the Genesis account of the Fall as the ultimate liberation of human beings from the rule of a tyrant God. The construal of such an example – which is, on close inspection, a confessional statement within a religious framework that accepts that there is a God and that there has been a Fall as described in Genesis – makes it hard to believe that the author really takes criticism of the Christian tradition seriously.

Another issue arises from his statement that "this is an acceptable educational outcome so long as the student clearly understands the traditional Christian interpretation and appreciates that they are reinterpreting the narrative in a way that contradicts its purpose in its 'home' tradition".[376] What if there are different views of different

---

[374] This is the transference of a quotation from Cooling 1996: *Education is the point of RE – not religion?*, 177, from what he said about Christianity to Islam. The quotation is unchanged except that "Christianity" was changed to "Islam" and "Christian" to "Islamic" (see italics).
[375] Cf. Cooling 1996: Education is the point of RE – not religion?, 177f.
[376] Ibid., 178.

"home traditions" on the same event, for example, Jewish, Christian, Muslim or even Buddhist views on Jesus? This issue shows that a meta-level which is independent of any particular religious view is required in order to acknowledge the different positions on phenomena in their own terms, without necessarily having to take over one of those positions, which means, after all, entering the sphere of religious discourse.

Andrew Wright's comment on Cooling's approach also shows the need for a framework that critically reflects the presuppositions of any approach. In the context of the debate about a nominalist or generic interpretation of religion,[377] Wright shows that Cooling's concern for comprehension has to take up questions about legitimacy, coherence and authority if the charges of neo-confessionalism and implicit nurture are to be invalidated. The debates about Christian nominalism and generic liberalism have to become part of RE, either position has to be evaluated critically, but neither of them can serve as an ideological framework for integrative RE. Any attempt "to resolve theological disputes ... before teaching begins inevitably descends into educational paternalism".[378] In one case, in fact, Cooling argues against integrative RE in primary school. He does so in the context of a response to the question why *Christian* doctrine in particular ought to be taught. He argues that in Britain, in most cases, Christian concepts abound in the

---

[377] The nominalist view of religion, which "rejects the notion that there is such a thing as religion, only specific and incompatible 'religious' systems" (Wright 1997: Mishmash, Religionism and Theological Literacy, 143) is often related to a systematic approach to religions in RE while the generic view of religion, which is built on the idea "that the religious history of humanity is indivisible, that no religion has evolved in isolation from other religions" (Hull 1994: Editorial: 'model syllabuses', 4) is often related to a thematic approach to religions.

[378] Wright 1997: Mishmash, Religionism and Theological Literacy, 154. See also 153. Cooling takes up Wright's criticism. In 1997: Theology goes to school, 59 he regards Wright's suggestions as a task for the subject to address, in 2000: The Stapleford Project, 165, he gives Brown et al. 1997: *God Talk: Science talk – a Teacher's Guide to Science and Belief*, as an example for a critical encounter with Christianity and emphasises that comprehension, which is one of the main aims of the Stapleford Project, is a prerequisite for criticism. The question of representation, as addressed by Wright, however, still remains. Cooling's response seems to suggest that his concept is intended for comprehension which has to precede criticism. Understanding is, however, a complex process which also includes a critical dimension. It is not a legitimate procedure in RE to give an uncritical account from a particular Christian perspective (i.e. one that does not include the questions of legitimacy, coherence and authority) first and address the issues mentioned by Wright later. This might result in a theological introduction to Christianity followed by a presentation of criticisms of it. In contrast to that integrative RE requires a generally impartial and to some extent critical perspective from the very beginning.

experience of children.[379] Even though the approach may just as well be applied to teaching other faiths, Cooling doubts that this is sensible at primary level. He writes:

> "The question is, however, whether children in the primary school have reached a sufficient stage of maturity to be able to take on board such plurality without distorting their understanding of the religions studied. The overall aim of the pupil being able to appreciate diversity is one the primary school teacher should have clearly in mind. The experience of diversity, however, may have to wait until the secondary school if this aim is to be achieved."[380]

It has to be considered, however, that the latter statement is taken from a publication of an early phase of the project, before the official acknowledgement of the integrative character of RE in the ERA 1988.[381] In a modified version, which takes up the above criticism, the method of concept cracking can be used in integrative RE. The consideration of the meaning of phenomena and its integration into RE is definitely a major contribution to good teaching practice in RE. However, at each stage of the elucidation of religious phenomena, attention should be paid to the general secular framework of the subject.

---

[379] For a minority of children, Cooling concedes, for whom Islam and other faiths will be a part of their everyday environment, the approach can be applied with respect to their religions. Cf. Cooling 1987: Christian Doctrine in RE, 156.
[380] Cooling 1987: Christian Doctrine in RE, 157.
[381] This is not the place for a discussion of arguments for or against integrative RE from the very beginning. For this issue cf. chapter IV, section 2.3.

Chapter III
Integrative Religious Education in Sweden

Introduction

This chapter will discuss different aspects of integrative religious education in Sweden. After a brief outline of the religious landscape in Sweden and an overview of the Swedish school system (1.), the history of integrative religious education in Sweden will be outlined, taking account of important developments from its origins in the 1960s until the present (2.). These sections provide background information necessary for understanding the different aspects of the main part of this chapter, the situation of integrative RE in Sweden today. In this part, the main focuses of interest are the concept of religion (4.) and the representation of religions (5.) in contemporary Swedish RE, while the debates about aims and contents of the subject (3.), as well as the notion of education (6.), are also considered.

In the context of my study of different concepts for integrative RE, a close examination of Swedish models is of special relevance as a counterpart to the study of English concepts, which are generally far better known in other countries. My particular interest in Swedish RE (as also in English RE) lies, above all, in the concept of religion which is used as a general framework for this subject and the way the individual religions are represented within this framework. These aspects can, however, only be properly understood if broader contexts are considered, the intended aims of the subject in particular, but also the further societal and educational environments in contemporary and historical perspectives.

My study is based primarily on written sources, which can be grouped in the following way: official documents issued by the government, in particular the National Agency of Education (*Skolverket*), academic literature of different kinds, and teaching material. Official documents issued by the government included in this study comprise the *skollagen* (the school law), *läroplaner* (curricula), giving a general outline of the subject, *kursplaner* (syllabi), specifying the aims and contents of the respective subjects in more detail, and *timplaner* (timetables), allocating a certain number of hours to every subject that is taught in school. Academic literature in integrative RE comprises different kinds of publications, including monographs, edited books and journal articles (in print and online). Particularly relevant are handbooks for teachers and studies of individual aspects of the representation of religions in RE. The publications by the RE teachers' association (*föreningen lärare i religionskunskap, FLR*), the *årsbok FLR* and the journal *Religion och Livsfrågor* (RoL) were excellent sources for my particular interests in Swedish RE. Even though this is not a detailed study of Swedish teaching material for RE, textbooks were also consulted in order to examine how the governmental requirements and academic concepts are translated into actual teaching environments. My consideration of teaching material is by no means a comprehensive survey, but also helps to shed light on the relevant issues from a different angle. Certainly, this can only be a first glance at a field of study which deserves to be dealt with in far more detail.

Another area which would be an interesting field for further research, the actual practice of integrative RE in the classrooms, i.e. the application of the academic ideas in practice, is not included here at all. The present study is an examination of the different levels of published *concepts for RE* (in official documents, academic literature and teaching material) only, without empirical research into classroom practice. Nevertheless, the substantial documentation available makes it possible to discern and analyse the leading trends quite satisfactorily.

Within the framework of this study of recently published concepts for RE in Sweden, my particular interest concerns the underlying notions of religion as well as the ideas in academic discourse about how to present the different religions and religious phenomena in integrative RE.

1 Religions in Sweden and the Swedish school system

1.1 Religions in Sweden

Given the existence of a state church until the year 2000, there has been a long tradition of Lutheran-Protestant Christianity in Sweden. While the policy on other religions was rather strict after the reformation in the 16th century – it was, for example, decided at the Church Synod in Uppsala 1593 that all Roman Catholic priests and teachers must leave the country and that Catholic places of worship should be closed – there was a change towards religious freedom in the 19th century when several religious groups were granted the right to practice their faiths. The "dissenter laws" (*dissenterlagar*) of 1860 and 1873 allowed citizens to withdraw from the Church of Sweden, if they joined one of the other denominations that were approved by the state. The most significant changes for centuries, however, took place in the second half of the 20th century, when secularisation and pluralism became important characteristics of Swedish religious life. In 1951, full freedom of religions was implemented, i.e. the right to belong to any religious body or none. Immigration, mainly of workers to start with (1950s – 1970s) and later mainly refugees (up to the present), has brought about the culturally and religiously plural situation of today.[1]

The fact that more than 80% of the total population[2] belong to the Church of Sweden – despite e.g. the high degree of secularisation and low church attendance[3] – is partly due to the fact that the policy on religious freedom has not been entirely consistent. For example, until 1996, children were automatically registered as members of the Church of Sweden when one parent was a member. Similarly, Lutheran-Protestant immigrants were automatically registered as members and many members of free churches simultaneously belong to the Church

---

[1] The immigrant population in Sweden rose from about 0.7% to about 20% between 1900 and 2000. The fastest increase took place from the 1960s onwards, in 1950 there were still only 2.9% immigrants in Sweden. See Anderson and Sander 2005: Det mångreligiösa Sverige, 9.

[2] Sweden has a population of about 9 million (cf. The Swedish Institute 2006: SWE-DEN.SE).

[3] Obviously, the question of how to measure religiosity or secularisation is a very difficult one. Traditional sociological studies (which in Western contexts normally deal almost exclusively with Christianity) in which church attendance or belief in God are used as criteria – are often simplistic and of limited value for a sound study-of-religions analysis. Nevertheless, in this context these questions about religious belief and practice help to demonstrate that official numbers about membership do not necessarily say much about the actual beliefs and practices of the people in question.

of Sweden. Since 1996, baptism has become the basis for membership and about 70% of all children are baptised in the Church of Sweden, while 87.5% of all burials are conducted by a pastor of the Church of Sweden. In the year 2000, church and state were officially separated. The Church of Sweden relinquished its role as State Church and became one of many religious communities in Sweden – though by far the largest.[4]

It is, of course, highly problematic and controversial to illustrate the religious landscape of a country in terms of membership numbers. Some of the problems were demonstrated in the last paragraph. Nevertheless, despite the problems involved in any numerical account of religious affiliation, numbers of adherents of the different religions may serve as a first orientation about religious diversity in a plural society if the difficulties are kept in mind. Andersson and Sander (2005), for example, refer to religions in an "ethnic" sense, i.e. they count individuals with a background in a culture in which a particular religion predominates culturally and socially. Additionally, for some traditions they include converts with a Swedish background.[5] In the past 50 years, the number of adherents of different religious traditions has increased considerably. Among Christian churches, the largest growth was in Orthodox and Oriental churches, which now have about 100,000 members altogether. There are about 170,000 Roman Catholics in Sweden today, of whom about 80% have an immigrant background. Judaism has existed in Sweden for a long time, the first congregation having been established in 1776. Many Jews fled to Sweden during the World War II. Most Jews who arrived in the Cold-War period came from the former Soviet Union or the Eastern bloc. Today, more than approximately 11,000 Jews belong to one of Sweden's three congregations. Andersson and Sander count approximately 22,000 Jews in Sweden. The number of Muslims in Sweden has increased steadily since the 1980s, from approximately 30,000 in the early 1980s to about 200,000 in the mid-1990s. It is difficult to give an exact number for the present. Including the so-called second-generation immigrants the number today is probably about 350,000, referring to an internally diverse group of different Muslim traditions. In 2000, the large central mosque in Stockholm was opened.

There are approximately 6,000 Hindus, who come mainly from Sri Lanka, India and Uganda. Among the approximately 15,000 Buddhists

---

4 Cf. the fact sheet on Sweden "Religions and religious change in Sweden" (2003), see also: Karlsson and Svannberg 1997: Religionsfrihet i Sverige, 7, 17f.
5 Andersson and Sander 2005: Det mångreligiösa Sverige.

in Sweden, most are immigrants, but there are also many Western converts, especially in Tibetan and Zen groups and among the Soka Gakkai. There has also been an increase in membership in new religious movements, including, for example, the Baha'i, New-Age-oriented religions, ISKCON, the Church of Scientology, Mormons (8,500, with a temple near Stockholm since 1985), Jehovah's Witnesses (23,000, mainly immigrants) and neo-pagan groups. Andersson and Sander estimate that people with "other" religious traditions than "traditional Swedish religiosity" nowadays represent perhaps roughly about 7% of the population in total.[6]

1.2 The Swedish school system

The current structure of the Swedish school system has its roots in the school reforms in the 1960s, when different types of schools (*folkskola, fortsättningsskola, högre folksskola, kommunala mellanskola* and *realskola*) were brought together and one compulsory school (*grundskola*), which all pupils are required to attend for 9 years, was created.[7] In the late 1960s, the vocational school (*yrkesskola*) and the technical college (*fackskola*) were integrated into one upper secondary school (*gymnasieskola*), which is not compulsory.[8]

The Swedish Parliament (*riksdag*) and government have the general responsibility for education in Sweden. They provide the municipalities with guidelines, a national curriculum and objectives, which are enforced by the local bodies and the schools themselves. The principle of equal opportunities for all children is generally considered an integral element of the Swedish educational system. According to the Education Act (*skollagen*) all children and youths, regardless of gender, geographical, social or economic background, are to have equal access to education. Education provided by the state is generally free of charge in Sweden. Most schools in Sweden are state schools. There is, however, a small percentage (ca. 4%) of independent schools, which may belong to a particular religious denomination or follow a special educational approach, for example Waldorf or Montessori. Independent schools also receive state funding. They are required to provide the children

---

6   Andersson and Sander 2005: Det mångreligiösa Sverige, 31.
7   For general information on the Swedish school system, see the information sheets provided by Svenska Institutet, e.g. *Compulsory schooling in Sweden* (2001); Skolverket, e.g. *Det svenska skolsystemet, Grundskola, Gymnasieskola, Demokratie och värdegrund* (English translations are available as well); Werler 2002: Schweden; Rudvall and Stimpel 1998: Bildungspolitik.
8   Werler 2002: Schweden, 456.

with an education equivalent to that of state schools. Independent schools have to be approved by the National Agency of Education (*Skolverket*). The standards of the schools are supposed to be the same for the whole country. The responsibility of the individual is regarded as an important presupposition about the human condition and it is one main task of the school to provide children and youths with an environment in which this responsibility can be developed. In the Education Act, the aim of education is defined as to "provide the pupils with knowledge and, in co-operation with the homes, promote their harmonious development into responsible human beings and members of the community."[9]

All children in Sweden have to attend the *grundskola* for nine years from the age of seven onwards, with the exception of Sami childen who may attend Sami school (*sameskolan*), or children with special needs or learning disabilities, who may attend special schools (*specialskola* or *särskola*). The idea is, however, that as many pupils as possible attend the *grundskola* together. There are special programmes within the *grundskola*, e.g. Swedish as a Second Language, to foster the integration of immigrants. The recent national curriculum (*läroplan*) for the compulsory school (Lpo 94) is from 1994 and was amended in 1998. It comprises a statement of the fundamental values on which each school is to be based, as well as basic objectives and guidelines. Complementary to the curriculum, there are also national syllabi (*kursplaner*) which state the aims and contents for each subject and a timetable (*timplan*) that states the number of hours the students are entitled to be taught in each subject. Every municipality should also have a local school plan (*skolplan*) in which the organisation and development of the schools in that municipality is outlined.

Generally, there are no final examinations in the Swedish educational system. Grades are regarded as personal feedback for the pupils or students. There are no grades until year eight of the compulsory school, when a distinction is made between pass (*godkänd*, G), pass with distinction (*väl godkänd*, VG) and pass with special distinction (*mycket väl godkänd*, MVG). The current curriculum for the *gymnasieskola* (Lpf 94) also came into effect in 1994. The *gymnasieskola* is not compulsory, but it is attended by almost all youths (96%-98%). This is due to the fact that there are 17 different national programmes[10] with different vocational or academic specialisations. All programmes are three-year programmes and can be attended by every student who has received a

---

9   The Education Act, quoted in Skolverket 2005: The Swedish School System.
10 For a list of the programmes see Skolverket 2005: Gymnasieskolan.

pass in Swedish, English and Maths in the compulsory school. For students who do not have these qualifications, there are special individual one-year programmes that qualify them to attend the upper secondary school. There are eight core subjects that are included in each of the national programmes: English, the Arts, Physical Education and Health, Maths, General Science, Social Studies, Swedish (or Swedish as a Second Language) and Religion (*religionskunskap*). The core subjects account for about 1/3 of the credits, while the programme-specific subjects form the other 2/3. Most programmes include 15 weeks of workplace-training; only in the Arts-, Natural Science-, Social Science- and Technology-programmes is this not compulsory. There are also special upper secondary schools (*gymnasiesärskolor*) with four year programmes for youths who cannot attend the regular upper secondary schools due to e.g. severe learning disabilities.

The school reforms from the 1960s onwards with the intention to provide a broad education for as many children and youths as possible, brought about an educational generation gap, because many more young people than before had access to broad education. With the intention of bridging that gap, the concept of lifelong learning (*det livslånga lärandet*) became the motto of the whole educational system and adult education (*komvux* and *särvux*) was given special emphasis with programmes equivalent to *grundskola*- and *gymnasieskola*-education, which are also free of charge. Teacher training for the compulsory school takes between 3.5 (teachers for years 1-7) and 4.5 (teachers for years 4-9) years depending on the chosen track. Teacher training consists of a combination of pedagogic and subject-related studies. Teachers in secondary schools normally do one year of pedagogic training after studying their own particular subjects.[11]

1.3 Democracy and basic values in Swedish schools

Generally, the *värdegrund*, the fundamental value system, is regarded as the foundation of the Swedish school system. According to the National Agency of Education (*Skolverket*), the *värdegrund* should permeate school life on three different levels: (1) The pupils are to gain knowledge about democracy and fundamental values. This can to a large extent be done in conventional teaching. (2) The schools themselves are to operate democratically, i.e. in a framework in which pupils and staff are empowered to actively influence school life. This participation can be formally organised – e.g. by way of unions – or realised informally, e.g. in giving

---

11   See Werler 2002: Schweden, 466.

the pupils an opportunity to discuss and influence the content and methods of the lessons. (3) The third level concerns the responsibility of the school to educate democratic members of society. This involves working with the *värdegrund*, i.e. democratic values such as solidarity, equality of all human beings and equal opportunities. Thus, the development of social competence is a – if not *the* – key element in the Swedish school system. The *värdegrund* should lie at the heart of all school activities to strengthen democracy in school and society in general and to counteract all forms of abusive treatment, discrimination and expression of lack of respect for the equality of people. The importance of the school in the enterprise of educating responsible members of a democratic society can hardly be overestimated. Therefore, a holistic approach to teaching and the development of young people is required. The National Agency of Education has published a list with factors which can help to measure whether the *värdegrund* has actually become the ethical foundation of school life.[12] Other official documents also emphasise the importance of shared fundamental values. According to the Education Act, "school activity shall be structured in accordance with fundamental democratic values ... Persons active in the school system shall in particular promote equality between the genders and actively counteract all types of insulting treatment such as bullying and racist behaviour."[13]

The curricula for the *grundskola* as well as for the *gymnasieskola* emphasise the importance of a democratic framework as a prerequisite for preparing pupils for taking personal responsibility. Basic values have to be visible in daily life. It is the task of the school to shape and communicate them. They comprise inalienable human rights, freedom and integrity of the individual, the equal value of all human beings, equality between the genders and solidarity with the weak and deprived.[14] Although the *värdegrund* is mostly defined as a general foundation of values, in some documents it is linked to specific worldview systems that have had a strong influence on Swedish society. The curricula include the phrase "In accordance with the ethics borne by Christian tradition and Western Humanism...".[15] Formulations like these were heavily debated before the final drafts of the curricula.[16]

---

12 Skolverket 2005: Demokratie och värdegrund.
13 The Education Act, quoted in Skolverket 2005: Democracy and Fundamental Values, 2f. One example of ways of attaining these aims is the requirement that textbooks be approved by an "ombudswomen" who checks them for an adequate representation of women.
14 See Utbildningsdepartment 1994: Lpo 94, Lpf 94, and Lärarförbundet 1998: Lpfö 98.
15 For example Utbildningsdepartment 1994: Curriculum for the Non-Compulsory School System Lpf 94, 5.
16 See for example Borevi 1997: Religion i skolan, 42; Hartmann 2000: Hur religionsämnet formades, 223f. See also section 5.2.3 of this chapter.

2 The history of integrative RE in Sweden

The history of religious education in Sweden is closely related to developments in the Swedish school system in general.[17] As in England, the Swedish state school system emerged out of a school system provided by the church. The tradition of the *gymnasia* in cities with a cathedral dates back to the 17th century, the public *grundskola* (basic school) under the authority of the vicar was introduced in 1840. Along with preparation for confirmation, writing, maths, history and sports became school subjects. In 1870, it became obligatory for every child to attend school. The influence of the church, however, remained very strong, particularly in the curriculum. The Bible and Luther's catechism were regarded as central elements of the curriculum.

One important turning point was the reforms that led to the new syllabus of 1919. Different groups – for example the temperance movement, the free churches and the labour movement – had questioned the confessional character of school RE and the close relation between the schools and the Church of Sweden. The question now was what was regarded as more important: the confessional character of the school and religious education (with the obvious risk that other religious or political groups would open their own schools based on their own creeds) or the unity of the school system and perhaps even of society in general. Sweden opted for the latter. In order to preserve the unity of the school system, confessionalism was abandoned. This was a decisive turning point in religious education, making integrative RE possible later, the introduction of which in the 1960s was a development in accordance with the basic decisions taken in 1919.

With regard to religious education in Sweden, the right of children to access broad information, is regarded as more important than the right of the parents to have their children instructed in the belief they choose.[18] This idea was first formulated in 1919 with respect to Christian denominations, but paved the way for further developments with

---

17 For information about the history of RE in Sweden, see e.g. Almén 2000: RE in Sweden, Hartmann 1996: Uniformity and pluralism in Swedish school curriculum development, Hartmann 2000: Hur religionsämnet formades, Härenstam 2000: Kan du höra vindhästen?, 145ff., Larsson 1992: Introduktion till religionspedagogiken, Larsson 1996: A Reformed School and RE in Sweden, Larsson 1997: Pluralität als Herausforderung, B. und S. Rodhe 1996: Tradition, identity, authority in Swedish religious education, Selander 1993: Undervisa i religionskunskap, 12ff; Selander 1994: Livstolkning. Om religion, livsåskådning och etik i skolan i ett didaktiskt perspektiv.
18 See for example Almén 2000: RE in Sweden, 63 and 72; Borevi 1997: Religion i skolan, 38 and 57f.

respect to different religions and worldviews later. This particular emphasis on and interpretation of the rights of children is a characteristic feature of the Swedish state school system – in contrast to many other European countries.[19]

With the decision in 1919, religious education became "broadly Christian", explicitly non-denominational in character. The curriculum content was now selected by state, not church, bodies. Luther's catechism disappeared from the schools and in religious education, the emphasis was now on what was regarded as the common ground of all Christian denominations: the New Testament (the Sermon on the Mount in particular), ethics and the history of Christianity, while denominational peculiarities were avoided.[20] The name of the subject was changed from *Biblisk historia, bibelläsning & katekes* (biblical history, bible study and catechesis) to *Kristendom* (Christianity). Generally, the different names that were given to the subject in the 20th century also mark significant changes in the approaches to the subject. The underlying idea of communicating an ethic which is independent from individual denominations, provides the ideological basis for later developments in the subject where this claim is broadened to include other religions and worldviews as well. The other idea which has continuously permeated the concept of the subject is its instrumentalisation for the attainment of social and educational aims, particularly with respect to ethical responsibility.

After World War II, growing secularisation and religious plurality raised the issue of the character of religious education again. With the Act on Religious Freedom in 1951, Christian education in state schools seemed to have lost its legal basis. Again, the decisions concerning RE have to be seen in the context of other school reforms. In 1946, the school commission published a report which focused on the general aims of education. The questions about the character of the school were located within a wider social context. "What kind of society do we want?" was identified as the important question and within this framework the school has a special role to play. It was regarded as a key factor in the project of creating a better society based on a shared pluralism.[21] After the Second World War, the main groups who criti-

---

19 For this issue see e.g. Olin 2000: Religious Education in Finland.
20 Cf. Hartmann 2000: Hur religionsämnet formades, 216f; Catholics and Jews were given the opportunity to attend religious instruction in their religious community instead of school RE. This remained a possibility even after integrative RE was introduced, but hardly anybody made use of this right (cf. Almén 2000: RE in Sweden, 63f).
21 Cf. Almén 2000: RE in Sweden, 64.

cised RE were no longer different Christian denominations, but people from various other political, religious, or ideological backgrounds. The groundwork for the significant changes in the 1960s was laid in the decade before. In 1950, the resolution *In principle* called for an objective RE which is not exclusively about Christianity but also about other religions and outlooks on life.[22] The reforms in the 1960s were regarded as the beginning of a "rolling curriculum reform", i.e. a continuous revision of the curriculum. In 1962, the first curriculum for the *grundskola* was introduced. One of the main intentions of the curriculum reform was the intellectualisation of the school, objectivity and neutrality being key concepts of the project.

This had serious implications for RE. The most significant changes were the claim for objectivity and the broadening of the scope of the subject to include different religions and outlooks on life. It can be said that the 1962 curriculum marks the beginning of the history of integrative religious education in Sweden, because RE became a compulsory subject in the new *grundskola*, in which different religions and worldviews were presented and discussed. At this stage the focus was, however, still very much on Christianity. The name was changed from *Kristendom* (Christianity) to *Kristendomskunskap* (knowledge about Christianity). With the requirement of objectivity and neutrality in mind, providing the pupils with reliable and unbiased information about religions was regarded as one of the main aims of the subject:

"Undervisningen skall vara objektiv i den meningen, att den meddelar sakliga kunskaper om olika trosåskådningars innebörd och innehåll utan att auktoritativt söka påverka eleverna att omfatta en viss åskådning. Den skall vara präglad av vidsynhet och tolerans."[23]

The emphasis was on historico-critical studies with religious phenomena as starting points. The underlying pedagogical idea was that the topics studied stimulate the pupils to reflect about questions of life, not least because it was assumed that religions have to do with recurrent existential questions, which retain their relevance in different historical contexts. The general approach was, however, still content centred

---

22 B. and S. Rodhe 1996: Tradition, identity, authority in Swedish religious education, 41. The term *livsåskådning* is sometimes translated as outlook on life, sometimes as view of life. Even though the focus is more on human life than on the world and thus emphasises a special aspect of worldview, it corresponds roughly with what is commonly understood by worldview.

23 "Teaching is meant to be objective in the sense that it communicates factual knowledge about the meaning and contents of different kinds of faith, without trying to influence the pupils towards a particular one. Teaching ought to be characterised by an open perspective and tolerance." (Utbildningsdepartement 1962: Lgr 62, 217, quoted in Hartmann 2000: Hur religionsämnet formades, 219).

rather than pupil centred, the communication of subject knowledge and critical thinking being the central pedagogical task for the teacher. The areas of content comprised the Bible, Christian beliefs and ethics, important aspects of the history of Christianity and other religions and outlooks on life.[24] It has been pointed out that RE in schools was at that stage very similar to theology as taught at university.[25]

The approach to RE in the 1962 curriculum has been criticised for its lack of a basic pedagogical concept. Apparently, stimulating the pupils' interest with a cognitive approach based on objectivity and neutrality was a very difficult task. Teachers found it hard to live up to those requirements and were unsure about their teaching styles.[26] The next steps of the rolling curriculum reform were the curriculum for the *gymnasieskola* 1965 and the new curriculum for the *grundskola* 1969. The name of the subject was now changed from *kristendomskunskap* (knowledge about Christianity) to *religionskunskap* (knowledge about religion). Impartiality towards the different religions became an important presupposition of the subject. The representation of religions changed from a focus on dogmas and history, to a focus on different interpretations of life and existential questions. The concept *livsfråga* became an important feature in the process of structuring the subject matter. The main areas of content in RE were now fundamental questions of life, attitudes towards life, ethics, values, religious and non-religious worldviews. In the discussion about the curriculum reforms at the end of the 1960s, the phrase *"med engagemang och saklighet"* (with commitment and objectivity), was employed to modify the objectivity claim which had dominated the discussions in the early 1960s. Thus, the importance of the personalities and views of the teachers and pupils were acknowledged and teachers were given more freedom in organising and presenting the material. These early transformations of the subject were partly influenced by the discussions about RE in England. Particularly the works of Ronald Goldman and Harold Loukes became well known in Sweden.[27] The general trend to integrate single subjects into bigger units, however, had a harmful effect on RE. Still being un-

---

24 Hartmann 2000: Hur religionsämnet formades, 219.
25 Hartmann 1996: Uniformity and pluralism in Swedish school curriculum development, 125. This is an obvious similarity to early integrative RE in England, as developed by Ninian Smart. Smart explicitly emphasised the unity of the educational institutions and did not see a clear-cut border between RE in schools and Religious Studies in universities (cf. Smart 1968: Secular Education and the Logic of Religion, 97ff).
26 Hartmann 2000: Hur religionsämnet formades, 219.
27 Cf. Larsson 1992: Introduktion till religionspedagogiken, 35f, for Goldman and Loukes see also chapter II, section 1.1.1.

sure about the scope and the teaching methods of the subject, teachers often avoided the subject, which therefore faced the risk of being "integrated away".[28]

The new curriculum for the *grundskola* of 1980 is one of the rare examples of a political decision taken as a result of pedagogical research.[29] The reform was marked by a pedagogical paradigm shift from a content centred to a pupil centred approach, i.e. from an approach which takes a description of different religious phenomena as its starting point to an approach that starts with the pupils' situations and questions. The name of the subject was changed from *religionskunskap* (knowledge about religion) to *människans frågor inför livet och tillvaron; religionskunskap* (human questions in the face of life and existence; knowledge about religion). This rather long-winded title can be regarded as the new agenda of the subject. The focus is now on the present, on the pupils' situation, their questions and problems, as well as on current events and phenomena. The content of the subject is identified as

> "vital issues, faith and ethics; how different ethical views govern our actions and our attitudes towards different vital questions, for example of right and wrong, good and evil, our view of mankind and existence. The significance of religious belief when in various ways throughout life one is deciding about vital issues...".[30]

The approach to religions becomes a functional one in the sense that the potential meaning for the individual pupil is regarded as one of the most important issues.[31] The aim of the subject is now a reflection of *livsfrågor* (questions of life), beliefs and ethics: "how ethical views influence our actions and our points of view on different questions of life, for example about right and wrong, good and evil, view on the human being and existence".[32]

---

28 Cf. Hartmann 2000: Hur religionsämnet formades, 248.
29 Several studies (e.g. Ronnås et al. 1969: Tonåringen och livsfrågorna) had shown that the pupils were not particularly interested in studying the different religions but had a great interest for *livsfrågor* and existential questions. Cf. Hartmann 1992: Barns livsfrågor, 31ff. The comparatively large number of publications about the attitudes of pupils and teachers to RE and the reforms resulting from it is a Swedish particularity and shows another level of the democratic organisation of Swedish schools.
30 Utbildningsdepartement 1980: Lgr80, quoted in Hartmann 1996: Uniformity and pluralism in Swedish school curriculum development, 127.
31 See Hartmann 2000: Hur religionsämnet formades, 221: "Lgr 80 markerar en övergång från de tidigare läroplanerna, som beskrivit religion och livsåskådning som sociala och kulturella *fenomen* i historien och omvärlden, till en ämnesbeskrivning som i stället betonar religionernas och livsåskådningens *funktion* för den enskilde."
32 Lgr 80: 127, quoted in Hartmann 2000: Hur religionsämnet formades, 221.

The approach to RE as outlined in the 1980 curriculum can be regarded as an attempt to integrate the descriptive (religions and *livsåskådningar*[33]) and the existential (the pupils' situation and *livsfrågor*) dimensions of RE. However, the main focus was now on the existential dimension and that raised certain problems: for example, the relation to the subject content remained unspecified. For many teachers it wasn't clear any more what the subject was actually about. Having started with the pupils' *livsfrågor*, what were they going to do next? How to bridge the gap between the dimensions mentioned? It was often felt that the subject lacked an underlying pedagogical concept that was based on subject theory and teaching methodology.[34]

The 1990s again witnessed characteristic school reforms. An important aspect of these is the project of *kommunalisering*, an attempt to redistribute some of the responsibility from central to local bodies. The idea is to have a few documents which state the aims for the schools and the individual subjects for the whole country and leave further responsibility to the local bodies. In the preparations for the new curriculum, which was introduced in 1994, several documents are worth mentioning. In the report *Skola för bildning* (1992, school for education) the general desire to find a common code of values is expressed in the passages on the *värdegrund* of the school. In the formulations on the *värdegrund*, the Christian tradition made a comeback: "Det är värden som bland annat genom kristen etik och västerlandsk humanism har djup förankring i vårt land."[35] In the debates about these controversial formulations, critics from many different backgrounds pointed out that it was infelicitous to tie the common code of values of the state school to one particular religious tradition.[36] In contrast to the 1980 curriculum, the syllabus proposal that came with *Skola för bildning* was again characterised by a cognitivist, knowledge-based concept of education. There was a shift back from the pupil centred approach to a more scientific approach to the subject content once more. Faith and *livstolkning* (interpretation of life) became the central concepts for RE around which teaching should be structured. The aim of the subject was now defined as "att stimulera och främja elevernas livstolkningsprocess och därvid

---

33 Views of life.
34 Cf., e.g., Almén 2000: RE in Sweden, 73, Hartmann 2000: Hur religionsämnet formades, 222.
35 Läroplanskommittén 1992: Skola för bildning, 147, quoted in Hartmann 2000: Hur religionsämnet formades, 223.
36 Hartmann 2000: Hur religionsämnet formades, 224.

låta dem få möta de viktigaste livsåskådningstraditionerna."[37] A revised syllabus proposal for RE (SOU 1993) emphasised the communication of knowledge as a prerequisite for reflection. In the representation of religions, an approach was called for that studies religions and worldviews as phenomena rather than trying to find their potential function for the pupils. This is a similarity to the 1962 curriculum.[38]

The reform in 1994 was based on the ideas of the earlier reports. The importance of the *värdegrund* as well as the influence of Christian ethics and Western humanism on that *värdegrund* were emphasised in the curricula for the *grundskola* and the *gymnasieskola*. The name of RE was now changed back to *religionskunskap* (knowledge about religion). It became a compulsory subject without any possibility of opting out and was regarded as an important part of the curriculum within the social sciences unit. The focus of the subject content changed to current issues (for example internationalisation, tolerance, solidarity, respect for others, peace and war, national vs. global interests) in relation to religions, *livstolkning* and ethics. The educational idea behind the new approach is that knowledge acquired through objective and multifaceted teaching is a prerequisite for developing one's own view of life, point of view on existential questions and ethical issues in order to take responsible decisions, which is regarded as an important aim of the subject. This approach is characterised by a complementary balance of the descriptive and existential dimensions of the subject. The interplay between these dimensions – described, for example, in the syllabuses from 2000 onwards – will be an important element of the following analysis of integrative RE in Sweden today.

---

37 "To stimulate and support the process of interpreting life among the pupils and in this process let them encounter the most important traditions of interpreting life." (Läroplanskommittén 1992: Skola för bildning, p.237f, quoted in Hartmann 2000: Hur religionsämnet formades, 225).

38 Cf. Hartmann 2000: Hur religionsämnet formades, 225.

3 Aims and contents of integrative RE in Sweden

The next sections deal with aims and contents of integrative RE in Sweden (3.), the concept of religion (4.), the representation of religions (5.), and the notion of education (6.). These aspects are analysed in academic literature,[39] documents issued by the National Agency of Education (*Skolverket*) and teaching material.

Even though RE in Sweden has been integrative since 1962 and has always been attended by almost all pupils (with only a few exceptions), it was not until the school reform of 1994 that it became an obligatory subject without any possibility of withdrawing from it and attending an RE provided by the religious communities instead. *Religionskunskap*, allocated to the social sciences unit, is now an obligatory subject in both the *grundskola* and the *gymnasieskola*. In the latter, where *religionskunskap* has the status of a core subject (*kärnämne*) the course *religionskunskap A* is compulsory for all national programmes, while *religionskunskap B* is part of the social sciences programme.

An interplay between a descriptive and an existential dimension can be observed with respect to aims and contents of integrative RE in Sweden.[40] While on the descriptive level the focus is on an encounter with and an understanding of religions and other views of life, the existential level has to do with the development of the pupils' own identities and individually reflected views of life.

3.1 Aims of integrative RE

In general, the aims of integrative RE in Sweden are laid out quite clearly and they secular in nature. Basically, the aim is to develop one's own view of life through the study of different religious and non-religious traditions in order to act responsibly as a member of a democratic society. The descriptive and existential dimensions are regarded as interconnected and an attempt is made to keep a balance between the two.

The aims on the descriptive level of RE are mainly characterised as knowledge and understanding of different religions. In addition to

---

39 Academic literature about RE is by far the biggest part of the sources used in this study. It comprises articles and monographs by Swedish scholars of religion and/or education as well as further literature on RE as found in handbooks for teachers and teacher training. Important sources are also the publications of the *föreningen lärare i religionskunskap* (FLR), especially its *årsbok* and its journal *Religion och Livsfrågor*.

40 This issue is also the main characteristic of integrative RE in England.

intellectual understanding, the importance of empathic understanding is acknowledged.[41] Reflection about methodology is sometimes also mentioned as an integral part of studying religions in school RE. Almén, for example, emphasises the importance of an awareness of the possibilities and limits of different tools of analysis which make insights into different kinds of knowledge possible.[42]

In the Skolverket documents, the focus concerning the aims of the descriptive dimension of RE in the *grundskola* is on knowledge and understanding of the following: tradition and cultures, religions and other outlooks on life in our time and in history, the problems surrounding fundamental values (for example, the value of each human being, the equal value of people and support for the weak), the relationship between society and religion over different periods and in different places, Swedish society and the influence of Christian and other religious traditions on it, the interplay between society and religion today and in historical perspective, similarities and differences between established religions, other outlooks on life and new religious movements and phenomena, attitudes towards religious and ethical questions, aesthetic expressions such as art, music and dance in different religious contexts. For the *gymnasieskola*, familiarity with the languages, concepts, stories and pictures that express views of life within religious and secular traditions (such as Existentialism, Marxism etc.) is additionally mentioned. Generally, the aims for the *grundskola* and the *gymnasieskola* are very similar, though in the latter a deeper understanding is attempted.[43]

The teaching material emphasises the importance of learning about religions in order to understand the influence of beliefs in ethical discussions and on how people think and act. Högberg and Sunqvist (1999) state, for example, that this is not only relevant with respect to the great questions about life and death, but for all situations in life. They regard the study of religions as helpful for understanding why human beings are different from each other.[44] Understanding beliefs, ethics and views of life and their interplay and interdependence with

---

41 Furenhed 2000: Undervisning och förståelse, 131f.
42 Almén 2000: Vad studerar vi som "religion", 208.
43 For the aims of RE in the Skolverket documents see e.g. the syllabuses 2000ff for the *grundskola* (Compulsory School. Syllabuses), 70 and the programme manual for the *gymnasieskola* (Programme Manual), 123.
44 Högberg and Sunqvist 1999: Religionsboken, 9.

society is emphasised in many textbooks as the main aim of the descriptive dimension of RE.[45]

Aims concerning the existential level of RE mainly have to do with a reflection of one's own situation and general existential and ethical questions such as man's situation in the universe, questions about good and evil, life and death and values.[46] While the development of one's own identity is regarded as an important task of the school in general, the development of one's own view of life as a part of that is regarded as a central task of RE.[47]

In the *Skolverket* documents, the aims for the existential level of RE also have an affective dimension. Among reflections about oneself, one's life and surroundings, the development of a sense of tolerance and being prepared to act with responsibility are mentioned as important aims of RE. Generally, the aims on the existential level are seen in close relation to the aims on the descriptive level, and the main focus is on the interplay between these two. The subject is regarded as a forum which enables a meeting between the personal experience of the pupils of what it means to be a human being and the subject material.[48] In the *skollagen*, the interdependence of the communication of skills and knowledge and the fostering of a harmonic development of the pupils towards becoming responsible human beings and members of society is emphasised. An exemplification of this task for RE is made by Almén, who sees the potential of the subject in showing how other people deal with occasions of joy or problems in their lives in order to offer the pupils the possibility of taking up different elements of mankind's collected wisdom.[49] His interpretation of the interplay between the different levels is that it is the aim of RE that the pupils understand and apply concepts in order to use them as tools in the development of their own knowledge and personal orientation in the world.[50] The importance of a careful examination of the methods used to achieve different aims is also acknowledged by Almén. Since there are many different perspectives on the phenomena, informed decisions are necessary about which method or concept proves most appropriate for which aim. Furthermore, the different concepts, perspectives, learning

---

45 See e.g. Rodhe and Nylund 1995: Nya Studietexter i religionskunskap, Förord; or Thulin and Elm 1995: Religion: 2.
46 See e.g. Ohlsson 2002: Att förnya och vidga religionskunskapsämnet, Hallberg 2000: Reflektioner kring kursplan 2000, 14f.
47 Almén 2000: Vad studerar vi som "religion", 205.
48 See for example Ohlesson 2002: Att förnya och vidga religionskunskapsämnet.
49 Almén 2000: Vad studerar vi som "religion", 204f.
50 Ibid.

strategies and aims to be achieved in RE are mutually dependent. An understanding of this issue itself is also considered an aim of RE:

> "Religionskunskapsundervisningen borde kunna ge eleverna en inblick i detta samband, kunskap om olika analysverktygs möjligheter och begränsningar och därmed en insikt om vilket slags kunskap de kan ge."[51]

Thus, methodological reflections about the general approach are an integral part of RE. Understanding the problems, difficulties and possibilities of different perspectives on religious diversity is, in a certain respect, a meta-level aim of the subject.

3.2 Contents of integrative RE

The contents of Swedish RE correspond to the aims. Existential and ethical issues are regarded as contents of RE. These are to be dealt with on the basis of the study of different religious and secular traditions of interpreting life and the world.

3.2.1 Official documents

Skolverket suggests three main areas of content for the compulsory school:

(1) *Livsfrågor och livstolkning* (issues concerning life and its interpretation): "The subject takes as its starting point Man's questions concerning life and existence, irrespective of whether these are expressed in religious terms or not. Consciously and methodically working through life issues is the core of the subject."[52]

(2) *Etik* (ethics): At this point the relevance of ethical questions for every human being is acknowledged. Everyday ethical issues are regarded as another starting point for reflection and discussion in RE. General reflection on ethical behaviour and the study of different views on ethics are regarded as complementary: "Discussion on ethical issues may be deepened through

---

51 "It should be possible in the subject *religionskunskap* to give the pupils some insight into these relationships, [i.e.] knowledge about the possibilities and limits of different tools of analysis with respect to the question of what kind of knowledge they can produce." (Almén 2000: Vad studerar vi som "religion", 208).
52 Skolverket 2001: Compulsory School. Syllabuses, 71.

familiarity with ethical principles, thinking and systems from different religions and outlooks on life."[53]

(3) *Tro och tradition* (belief and tradition), involving the study of different religious and secular traditions.

Similarly, in *Religionskunskap A*, which is compulsory for all students in the *gymnasieskola*, the emphasis is supposed to be on ethical and moral issues, different interpretations of life and religions and *livsåskådning* as parts of societal life. *Religionskunskap B*, which can be found in both the cultural and social science branches of the Social Science Programme (*samhällsvetenskapsprogrammet*), is meant to contribute to deepening and broadening the content of course A: "Based on the chosen study orientation and their own needs, pupils receive opportunities to further develop their knowledge and skills in the areas of belief and outlooks on life."[54]

3.2.2 Academic literature

In the academic literature, a combination of issues concerning ethics and the interpretation of life with the study of religious and non-religious traditions is regarded as the content of RE, while knowledge about methodology is also indispensable.[55] Two very important sources, which can be regarded as an overview of what is being discussed in academic literature about RE, are the journal *Religion & Livsfrågor* and the yearbook (*årsbok*) published by the *Föreningen lärare i religionskunskap* (union of RE teachers). Examining the topics dealt with in the Årsbok in the past 14 years we can get an impression of the range of issues covered. Årsbok 1990/91, *Östeuropa*, comprises articles about RE in Eastern Europe and the Baltic countries. Årsbok 1992, *Norden*, is about RE in Denmark, Finland, Norway and Sweden. *Miljö* (the environment, 1993) is about *livstolkning*, *livsåskådning*, ethics and ecology and how these issues can be dealt with in RE. In the section about world religions and ecological issues there are chapters on Christianity, Judaism, Islam, Hinduism and Buddhism. The importance of dealing with these questions in RE is upheld in order to avoid a situation in

---

53 Ibid., 72.
54 Skolverket 2001: Programme Manual. Programme goal and structures, core subjects, subject index for upper secondary school, 125.
55 See for example Myrgård 2000: Ny kurs... *för religionskunskapen!*, 11; Almén 2000: Vad studerar vi som "religion".

which pupils are simply educated into a scientific-technical view of these issues, but to also make them familiar with alternative views. *Kristendom och etik* (Christianity and ethics, 1994) acknowledges the difficulty of teaching Christianity in integrative RE and that new ways of teaching Christianity are necessary. *Religionernas pedagogik* (the pedagogies of the religions, 1995) has articles on pedagogical traditions in individual religions including also, for example, the Quakers.

Afrika – en glömt kontinent (Africa – a forgotten continent, 1996) contains articles about, for example, the Yoruba, men and women, religion and magic in Zimbabwe, the African Association for the Study of Religions, Algeria and Islamism and the role of the church in the new South Africa. *Etiska perspektiver* (ethical perspectives, 1997) deals with teaching ethics and issues like human dignity, freedom and responsibility, animal testing, genetic conditioning, sexuality, universalism vs. particularism and human rights from a comparative perspective. In the preface (*"till läsaren"*) Nils-Åke Tidmann sees a consensus of the authors in the book about good ethics: "En framåtsyftande etik är en blanding av känsla och rationalitet, varmt hjärta och kallt huvud."[56] *New Age – den nya folktron* (New Age – the new folk belief, 1998) deals with different aspects of what is summarised under the heading New Age, including, for example, popular beliefs in Sweden and New Age as a synthesis of pre-modern, modern and post-modern elements, mystic and knowledge in New Age. In the 1999 yearbook, *Into the third millennium*, most of the articles, which are papers presented at an international RE conference in Copenhagen in 1998, deal with the situation of RE in different European countries, including e.g. Denmark, Finland, Germany and England.

Heliga skrifter (holy texts, 2000) comprises articles on texts from different religions also including New Age, and, interestingly, an article on legend and life in the works of the Swedish authors Selma Lagerlöf and Astrid Lindgren. In the preface, Olof Frank explains what is meant by "holy texts". "Holy" may be understood in this context as religious or sanctioned by religion. With respect to the works of Lagerlöf and Lindgren, Frank explains that they also refer to the essence and meaning of life and show bridges between reality and possibility, the concrete and the incomprehensible, between what is and what could be. Thus, "holy" is interpreted as appealing to the essence and meaning of life. *Kvinnligt, manligt, barnsligt* (female, male, childlike, 2001) has only two articles that deal explicitly with individual religions (Islam and

---

[56] "A progressive ethic is a blending of emotion and rationality, of a warm heart and a level head." (Tidman 1997: Till läsaren in: Årsbok FLR, 6).

Christianity) in relation to society. The other articles deal with biological and social differences between men and women, parenthood (including interviews with mothers and fathers), homosexuality, and pedagogical perspectives on gender issues focusing on ethical, philosophical and spiritual aspects. Human rights of individuals are interpreted with respect to the inescapability of social relations and everybody's responsibility within these interdependencies. The three articles on homosexuality deal, for example, with the difficulties of defining homosexuality, historical and contemporary perspectives on homosexuality and the rights of homosexuals, and the view of homosexuality that has prevailed in certain conservative circles. In the preface to this volume, Olof Franck summarises the common framework on which the different articles are based, by quoting the philosopher Ingemar Hedenius: "Att alla människor har samma värde är detsamma som att alla människor har samma mänskliga rättigheter och samma rätt att få dem respekterade och att ingen i detta avseende är förmer än någon annan."[57]

Most articles in *Att tro, att tvivla – och att veta* (To believe, to doubt – and to know, 2002) deal with reflections about Christian beliefs with respect to criticisms, today and in history. The only article on another religion is one on the relationship between revelation and reason in Islam.[58] Some other articles in this volume deal with more general issues in this context, for example, the question of whether contemporary physics has a religious dimension[59]. *Liksom värden, typ. Moral och mening med fokus på skolan* (Values, ethics and meaning with a focus on school, 2003) is again less comparative with respect to the individual religions, but covers important issues relating to ethics and values in contemporary society. In the context of the *värdegrundsdebatten*, the authors of the book reflect on the possibilities of contributing to the promotion of central values – such as democracy, freedom and integrity of the individual, equality between men and women – and their implementation in daily social relations and in school. The articles deal, for example, with the notion of the individual and the ideal of a citizen in a democracy and the limits of an individual within a democratic framework.

---

[57] "That all human beings are of equal value means that all human beings have the same human rights and the same right to have these respected, and that in this respect nobody is above anybody else." (Ingmar Hedenius, quoted without reference in Franck 2001: Förord to the FLR Årsbok, 7).

[58] See Roald 2002: Den muslimska traditionen. This very dichotomy of revelation and reason is, however, again an issue with particular relevance in the Christian tradition, as exemplified for example by Paul Tillich in his Systematic Theology.

[59] Cf. Nordén: 2002: Har nytida fysik religiös betydelse?

Gender issues are covered, for example, in articles on dealing constructively with homophobia or on how the images of men and women in society may be changed, particularly with respect to parent-child relations. Jan Hjärpe shows the differences between a theological and an anthropological approach within the study of religions. The different perspectives on religions[60] can be studied in texts as well as in field studies. There has been a development from the former to the latter in the past years, but a lot more anthropological/empirical work is necessary. The contributions in *Om stora barn och små* (About big and small children, 2004) deal with the roles, rights, problems and representations of children in different contexts. Most articles deal with aspects of the United Nations' *Convention on the Rights of the Child*. Special attention is paid to the relationships between adults and children. Other issues in this context are multicultural identities, ethnic segregation, gender, respect for children (and the pedagogical ideas of Janusz Korczak), vocational ethics, spiritual development and the *värdegrund*.

This browsing in the yearbooks of the FLR can give an impression of the breadth and variety of topics which are being discussed around RE in Sweden. Definitely remarkable is the breadth of perspectives and the acknowledgement of developments in other countries, be it Eastern Europe (1990/1991), Scandinavia (1992) or Europe in general (1999). Equally remarkable is the range of religions covered, including, for example, indigenous religions (Africa, 1996) and new religious movements, not a set of so-called "world-religions" only. The ethical focus and relation to current issues in a number of volumes makes a contemporary perspective necessary. What is more, starting from a *livstolkning/livsåskådning* approach to the study of religions, methods from other social subjects are used as impulses, demonstrating a firm location of the subject in the social sciences unit. The implementation of an integrative framework since the 1960s required a reconsideration of the representation of all religions, and of Christianity in particular. In the comparative volumes, the issues in question are studied in several religions, the majority of articles, however, are about Christianity. Thematic volumes show an even greater attention to issues concerning Christianity, and sometimes a general, broadly Christian frame of reference seems to have survived from earlier times. This is very obvious in the volume about belief (2002), in which the preface gives a short overview of different interpretations of belief in the history of Christianity and most articles also focus on aspects of Christian beliefs. The bridge that is built

---

60 Hjärpe mentions the following perspectives: "psykologi-individen, sociologi-gruppen, politologi-sammhällen", Hjärpe 2003: Att studera religioner och normsystem, 53.

between the demands and normative implications of the *värdegrund* and the promotion of democratic values around it and the attempted impartiality towards different religions and worldviews is of particular interest in illuminating the general character of and discourse about the subject. This is, however, not so much perceived as a tension, but the *värdegrund* – despite all discussions about it – is often interpreted as a kind of meta-ethic and scale or standard by which different phenomena can be measured. To what extent a certain ethic – and thereby necessarily also a particular worldview – can be promoted in integrative RE and what this means for the representation of religions, which ought to be as undistorted as possible, remains, however, a matter of debate.

3.2.3 Teaching material

Most teaching material contains sections on *livsfrågor, livsåskådning* and various religious and secular traditions, but there are also books that focus on one of the different aspects of the subject. A typical structure of a textbook can be found, for example, in Thulin and Elm's book for the *gymnasieskola*[61] with chapters on different traditions (*naturfolkens religioner*,[62] Hinduism, Buddhism, Judaism, Christianity, Islam, new religious movements, *livstro utan Gud*[63]), as well as on ethics and on *livsfrågor* and society. Westerberg and Linnér's *Tio frågor*,[64] also a book for the *gymnasieskola*, deals exclusively with *livsfrågor*. It contains chapters on "the future", "freedom and responsibility", "what is a human being?", "whom can we rely on", "nature and the environment", "*livets gränsstationer*" (existential situations),[65] "good and evil", "the others", "the meaning-seeking person", and "presentation and competition".

The results of my survey of what textbooks reveal about their underlying understanding of what the contents of RE should be will be included in the section on the representation of religions in textbooks (see section 5.3) and will therefore not be discussed at length here. At this point, I would only like to add what advertisements for textbooks in the teacher's journal *Religion och Livsfrågor* emphasise about the contents of textbooks. About Ola Björlin's *Människan och tron* [advertised in Rol 1, 2004] we learn that human beings, their beliefs and doubts are at

---

61 Thulin and Elm 1995: Religion.
62 I.e. religions of people living in traditional ethnic situations.
63 I.e. non-theistic beliefs concerning life.
64 Westerberg and Linnér 1997: Tio frågor till livet.
65 This chapter is about rites of passage which frequently accompany important situations in life.

the centre of what is studied: What does it mean to be a human being? What gives meaning to my life? Can you live life without any belief? What is good and evil? What is moral action? The book is about *livsfrågor*, ethics, the secular view of life, the variety of beliefs and their historical backgrounds, near-death experiences, PSI phenomena and more. The book provides encounters with people who give their points of view about life. It shows different ways of working with one's own view of life, getting to know more about the ideas of other people and how to take ethical decisions.

Leif Berg's *Religion och liv* is advertised in *Religion och Livsfrågor* 2004/1 as starting from the world of the pupils and stimulating them to compare, analyse, discuss and comment on ethical and religious beliefs. The principle of the equal value of all people is central, as well as the ambition to present the world from different perspectives, e.g. male and female, historical and contemporary. The provision of background knowledge is also mentioned: "Naturligtvis ger läromedlet också rejäla baskunskaper. Allmänbildning är viktig även i religionskunskap."[66] *Religionskunskap A. Om livsfrågor, religion och etik* by Carl Olivestam et al. also contains a CD with three Swedish people talking about their views about religion.[67] This shows the inclusion of qualitative social research data in the teaching material. *Relief A Plus* is advertised as making comparisons between religions easier, for example with respect to sacred places, images of god, or life after death. "Ge en påtålig bild av det abstrakta" is the heading of the advertisement which continues: "Religion har två sidor. En abstrakt och en konkret. Alltför sällan sätts de ihop till den helhet som förståelsen kräver."[68] Apart from including information about the contents of the textbooks, these advertisements also hint at their underlying ideas of religion and frameworks for representing religions. The questions of what kind of concepts of religion are used in RE and how the different religious traditions are represented will be discussed in the next sections.

---

66 "Of course the textbook also provides reliable background information. General knowledge is important also in *religionskunskap*." (Advertisement in Religion och Livsfrågor 2004.37, 1).
67 Advertisement in Religion och Livsfrågor 2004.27, 1.
68 "Religion has two sides. One is abstract, one is concrete. Only too rarely do these complement each other to the totality that reason would require." (Advertisement in Religion och Livsfrågor 2003.36, 3).

4 The concept of religion

In Swedish RE, the hermeneutical key to the different religions is the concept *livsåskådning*. The wide scope of phenomena covered by this concept shows that, in Swedish RE, the difference between religious as opposed to non-religious is not much of an issue.[69] This is evident in the whole range of sources studied, despite the different levels of differentiation in the descriptions and uses of the concept of religion. The secular and broad concept of religion that has been employed since the beginnings of integrative RE in Sweden is widely accepted in academic literature on RE and also mirrored in the *Skolverket* documents as well as in the textbooks. There are, however, different nuances in the use of this concept and those will be highlighted in the following discussion, in which the straightforward legal documents are taken as a starting point from which more complex issues from academic literature are unfolded and which concludes with an overview of how this matter is presented in teaching material.

The amount of information that can be found in the different sources about the concept of religion varies considerably. As the *Skolverket*-documents have only short passages on RE, the first of the following sections is naturally shorter than the ones on academic literature and teaching material.

4.1 The concept of religion in official documents about RE

In the syllabuses (*kursplaner*) for RE, the general understanding of religion on which the subject ought to be based is made explicit:

> "Religion should be understood in a broad sense. In many cultures, religion is an all-embracing system, which determines how Man views the whole of his existence. From a historical perspective, it is clear how religion has shaped the way in which individuals and their cultures express themselves."[70]

The efforts of human beings to find coherence and interpret and clarify their existence are seen as the main driving force for religious activities

---

69 Several studies in the 1960s and early 1970s about the interests of pupils had shown a great interest in existential and ethical questions on the part of the pupils, but far less interest in "religious" questions. This was one influence leading to the broadening of the concept of religion and the introduction of the concepts *livsfrågor* and *livsåskådning* as hermeneutical keys to the study of religions within RE. See Almén 2000: RE in Sweden, 67f.

70 Skolverket 2001: Compulsory School. Syllabuses, 71.

which are "expressed in traditions, rites, narratives and myths"[71]. Belief is regarded as a fundamental concept in religious traditions, of which texts, cult, symbols, art and ethical positions are seen as expressions. Furthermore, the concept of religion is quite closely related to the concept of culture. Religion seems to be regarded as a sub-category of culture, for example when the students' traditions from different *cultures* are mentioned in the context of the study of beliefs.[72] The structure *Skolverket* suggests for RE can be regarded as another hint at the concept of religion underlying the subject. In order to understand religions, a reflection on the following elements is considered important: *livsfrågor* and *livstolkning*,[73] ethics, belief and tradition.

Interpretation of life and the construction of meaning are important topics. The need for interpretation and the construction of meaning and purpose are considered universally human features across different cultures:

> "Fundamental to the study of religions and other outlooks on life are questions concerning belief and the interpretation of life, that is issues about reality and the world, Man and values. In all cultures and at different times, people have expressed their needs to interpret and clarify life in order to give it meaning."[74]

Generally, in the *Skolverket*-documents, the different religions and secular worldviews represent different interpretations of life. In addition to the aspects mentioned above, those interpretations of life also find their expression in social structures, architecture and town-planning, music and literature, traditions and stories.[75]

4.2 The concept of religion in academic literature

In the academic literature about RE in Sweden, there is broad agreement that, as a general framework for RE, functional definitions of religion are preferable to substantial ones, despite a general caution with respect to defining "religion" at all. Björn Skogar, for example, acknowledges that by starting from a substantial definition a variety of

---

71 Ibid.
72 Ibid., 72.
73 This concept is somewhat similar to Ninian Smart's idea that what a scholar of religion does is "worldview-analysis". See Smart, e.g. 1989: Worldview analysis, cf. also Morgan 2001: Ninian Smart, 347.
74 Skolverket 2001: Programme Manual. Programme goal and structures, core subjects, subject index for upper secondary school, 124.
75 Ibid.

phenomena as well as the majority of teachers and pupils would be excluded from the very beginning and the subject would mainly deal with "other" people (who are religious according to that definition) without any existential appeal to the pupils. From a functional point of view, however, Skogar regards religion as something that is common to all human beings, who are involved in the process of trying to find meaning, interpreting and valuing:

> "Utifrån det vidare, funktionella perspektivet kan däremot den som studerar, fostrar eller underivsar aldrig själv ställa sig helt utanför. Eftersom det handlar om livstolkningar handlar det om alla."[76]

In this version of a functional definition of religion, *livstolkning* is again the central concept. *Livstolkning* is regarded as a task and a process that cannot really be avoided by anybody. Therefore, this definition of religion makes the subject relevant to all pupils and teachers and includes all kinds of views of life irrespective of whether they are commonly regarded as religious or non-religious.

In a similar vein, Ragnar Furenhed claims that religions deal with *livsfrågor* of human beings and thus also with the pupils' *livsfrågor*. He writes: "Även om religioner inte i första hand är ideologier innehåller de ändå en livsåskådningsdimension."[77] He describes the difficulty of differentiating between what is religious and what is not and recommends not to emphasise the difference between religious and non-religious worldviews too much. Furenhed discusses the relation he observes between the existential needs of human beings and religions. Religions serve the needs of a pattern/order (*mönster*), aims (*mål*), community (*samhörighet*), mysticism (*mystik*) and confidence (*tillit*) as follows: religions form patterns and structure reality. They have an integrating and a segregating function. Religions cater for the need of aims in different ways, with inner aims, such as living as close as possible to an ideal and outer aims, such as pilgrimage. Furthermore, religions contribute to the formation of groups and make room for social occasions, for example, festivals. Furenhed sees the need for mysticism as a counter-movement to secularisation. He writes: "Kanske har vi nått en punkt då sekulariseringen vänder mot en ökad andlighet. Världens

---

76 "From the broader, functional perspective, however, the one who studies, educates or teaches can never take the perspective of a complete outsider. As the topic [of the subject] is interpretations of life, it is about everybody" (Skogar 2000: I stormens öga, 109).

77 "Even if religions are not in the first place ideologies they have nevertheless a dimension of interpretation of life" (Furenhed 2000: Undervisning och förståelse, 121).

avförtrollning vänds i återförtrollning."[78] Many new religious phenomena and movements show this move towards a reenchantment of nature, being, life or the world. As in the *Skolverket*-documents, in academic literature belief is regarded as a major aspect of religion of which confidence is an important part.

A very sophisticated discussion of a possible concept of religion for RE is presented by Edgar Almén in his article *Vad studerar vi som "religion" – hur och varför studerar vi just det?*.[79] Almén points to the interplay between different concepts (of religion, education, learning, the individual) and different aims of RE. With respect to delineating religion, he regards the following concepts (*begreppsapparater*) as helpful: culture, individual, tradition and confession.[80] When religions are described as areas of culture, which influence the people growing up in these surroundings, a reflection about which notion of culture is appropriate in this context is important. He introduces the notion of culture as propounded by Jan Hjärpe in "Islam – kultur- och kommunikationssystem",[81] which takes account of the internal pluralism of religions – i.e. pluralism within religious traditions, for example, within Islam – Peter Berger's ideas on "the socially constructed world"[82] and the following deliberations of Clifford Geertz about religion:

> "Whatever else religion may be, it is in part an attempt (of an implicit and directly felt rather than explicit and consciously thought-about sort) to conserve the fund of general meanings in terms of which each individual interprets his experience and organizes his conduct."[83]

These concepts are regarded as helpful, above all in assisting the pupils to understand people from other backgrounds. Almén also points to the interrelations between the concepts of the individual and of religion. Religion can also be described as the inner conviction, experiences and spiritual life of a person. Despite the influences of the cultural and social surroundings, religious ideas can be maintained and lived against one's environment. In contrast to this individual approach, the notion of tradition can be emphasised, as religions and *livsåskådningar* are also collective phenomena with a history. If one uses a part of a

---

78 "Perhaps we have reached a point at which secularisation turns towards increased spirituality. The disenchantment of the world turns into reenchantment." (Furenhed 2000: Undervisning och förståelse, 127).
79 Almén 2000: Vad studerar vi som "religion", 192-211.
80 In Swedish: *kultur, individ, tradition* and *bekännelse*, ibid., 198-204.
81 Hjärpe 1980: Islam – kultur och kommunikationssystem, in Liberal debatt, quoted in Almén 2000: Vad studerar vi som "religion", 198.
82 See Berger 1973: The Social Reality of Religion.
83 Geertz 1975: The Interpretation of Cultures, 126f., quoted in Almén 2000: Vad studerar vi som "religion", 199.

tradition as a building block for another tradition, there is always a relation to how this part has been used before. And, obviously, by using elements from a tradition, one also contributes to the way this tradition is continued. Almén transfers Michael Pye's ideas of "comparative hermeneutics"[84] as a means of dealing with innovation in religion in RE. With respect to immigrant children in Sweden and the issues of tradition and innovation he suggests the following:

"Måste vi inte försöka skapa begreppsapparater som t.ex. gör det möjligt för ett barn till turkiska invandrare att skilja mellan islam och turkisk kultur och att bearbeta både islam och turkisk kultur som traditioner, som man kan vara trogen på olika sätt? Därmed skulle kanske barnets islam och 'turkiska kultur' kunna bli ganska olik islam och turkisk kultur i föräldranas barndomsmiljö, men barnet skulle (om det vill) kunna se sig självt både som muslim och som arvtagare till turkisk kultur utan att tvingas leva avskilt från svensk kultur."[85]

The notion of religion as confession (*bekännelse*) is introduced by Almén as a complement to the other three ways of approaching religion (culture, individual and tradition). He regards it as helpful for taking seriously insiders' conceptions of their religions in order to understand what is important to them, what kinds of solutions they see for certain problems and what tasks they have to fulfil. Almén understands the notion of confession in a broad sense. He says, for example, that we can "bekänna oss som uppvuxna i den västerländska kultursfären".[86] It is important also to study the notion of confession (or the equivalent, should there be any) of the people one tries to understand. Similarly, the notions of religion which exist within the different religions (and again as above: or the equivalents, should there be any) ought to be discussed in RE. Almén discusses different notions of religion and what their implications are for RE. About a concept of religion which emphasises tradition and innovation as elements of religions, Almén

---

84 Almén refers to Pye's articles "Comparative hermeneutics in religion" (1973), "Syncretism and ambiguity" (1971) and his book *Skilful Means. A Concept in Mahayana Buddhism* (1978[1]), of which a second edition was published in 2003; see Almén 2000: Vad studerar vi som "religion", 202, 211.
85 "Do we not have to try to establish terms and concepts that e.g. make it possible for a child of Turkish immigrants to differentiate between Islam and Turkish culture, and to study both Islam and Turkish culture as traditions to which one can be faithful in different ways? The children's Islam and Turkish culture can thereby perhaps become a completely different Islam and Turkish culture from the ones their parents experienced in their childhood. However, the child (if it wants to) ought to be able to regard itself both as Muslim and as an heir to Turkish culture without being forcibly cut off from Swedish culture." (Almén 2000: Vad studerar vi som "religion", 202f).
86 "We can bear witness to our upbringing in the Western cultural sphere" (Almén 2000: Vad studerar vi som "religion", 203).

writes: "Sådana begrepp blir användbara, när man ser på eleven som en individ som står i traditioner som binder honom/henne i lojaliteter till föräldrar och släkt, till kamratgrupper och kanske både till Sverige och till ett annat land."[87]

Even though the dominant concept of religion as *livsåskådning* does not necessarily correspond with the understanding people from different religions have of their own religions, it has had an influence on the self-understandings of many religious people in Sweden. The terminology has influenced the way many people talk about their own beliefs, their religion or non-religious worldview, and the Church of Sweden has even chosen this very approach for teaching material used in their preparation classes for the confirmation.[88]

4.3 The concept of religion in textbooks

The *livsåskådnings*-approach is also the most influential concept of religion in the teaching material used in Swedish RE. Religions are often regarded as answers to questions about important issues in life, such as life and death or the meaning of life.[89] The academic debates about what religion is or what religions are have been taken up in some textbooks, but sometimes theories of religion that cannot actually be maintained in the study of religions today are still taken as starting points. When this is the case, it often has to do with over-generalisations that cannot really be made on scientific grounds or with the transference of concepts that emerged in a Western (and often Christian) context to other cultures or religions without a careful consideration of the implications of this process.

In their book for the later years of the *grundskola*, Högberg and Sunqvist start from the question of the meaning of one's own life, which they regard as common to most human beings, as a motivation to turn to religions. They conclude the following about the character of religion(s): "Religion has in all times dealt with the questions that people held to be the most important ones in their lives".[90] The questions

---

87 "Such concepts can be used if the pupil is regarded as an individual who is part of [different] traditions that require loyalty to parents, relatives and friends and perhaps both to Sweden and another country." (Almén 2000: Vad studerar vi som "religion", 202).
88 See Almén 2000: RE in Sweden, 69f.
89 See, for example, Thulin and Elm 1995: Religion; Högberg and Sunqvist 1999: Religionsboken.
90 "Religion har i alla tider handlat om de frågor som människor tyckt vara viktigaste här i livet." Högberg and Sunqvist 1999: Religionsboken, 6.

they mention are: "Is there a god or some power which influences my life?", "Who am I and what is the meaning of my life?" and "Is there a life after death?". Their conclusions about religions are clearly influenced by notions of religion that emerged in a Christian context; they write, for example, that the conviction that there is a kind of power or god can be found with every human being who has a religion or that the word religion means "reverence for the holy"[91]. They are a little more careful when they say that it is difficult to tell what is common to all religions. They list elements which they say can be found in "almost all" religions (existence of one or several gods; division of the world into a material and a spiritual one which one wants to belong to and to which contact can be established through holy action and ceremonies; that things in the world happen according to God's [*now in the singular*] law and that "to obey God's laws is the meaning of life"[92] and that there is a life after death).

These features of religion, however, are too deeply rooted in and indebted to Christian worldviews, so that they cannot really be generalised as criteria for the identification of religions in general. Furthermore, they exclude a variety of *livsåskådningar* that do not include belief in god(s), spiritual beings and life after death. Interestingly, there are chapters on e.g. Buddhism or Humanism in the book – despite the fact that they do not necessarily meet the criteria above. The impression that the features mentioned are actually presented as universal to all religions is reinforced in the task for the pupils, where the question is asked, "Vilken övertygelse – tro – finns hos alla religiösa människor?",[93] and where the pupils are encouraged to memorise what they have read in the text. Thus, what is communicated to the pupils is that there are actually universal features which can be found in every religion – despite the fact that these features were introduced not as universals but as ideas which can be found in most religions. Furthermore, the inclusion of traditions which do not fit into this pattern shows, that these generalisations are somewhat premature and contradict the actual empirical data used for the representation of religions in this book.

Some textbooks, especially those for the *gymnasieskola*, take up theoretical and methodological considerations from the academic study

---

91 "Ordet religion betyder just 'vördnad för det heliga'." Högberg and Sunqvist 1999: Religionsboken, 6.
92 "Att följa Guds lagar är livets mening." Högberg and Sunqvist 1999: Religionsboken, 8.
93 Högberg and Sunqvist 1999: Religionsboken, 9 ("Which conviction – beliefs – can be found among all religious people?").

of religion. Rodhe and Nylund[94] briefly discuss issues from the history of the study of religions in the West. Different religions have often been described from a European or Northern American perspective. The very concept of "religion" is regarded as problematic, since it was formed in a particular Western context and its denotations are not necessarily transferable to other contexts, for example India or East Asia. Rodhe and Nylund mention Rudolf Otto's and Nathan Söderblom's ideas about the holy as a criterion for religion and acknowledge that their theories avoid including belief in god(s) in a definition of religion.[95] In the chapter on *världsreligionerna* (world religions) they draw attention to the difficulty of saying what "religion" is. They refer to different ideas about religion, that some people say religion is a private matter and others that it is something that permeates one's whole life, also including, for example, politics and economics. Pragmatically, they say that there is something that is called religion – despite all debates around it –, which can be found in many forms in our world and that world religions are a selection of those forms that have influenced and have been influenced by the parts of the world in which they have prevailed.

In most textbooks, religion is discussed as a human phenomenon which is often seen in relation to questions about life. In the textbook by Arlebrand, Arvidsson et al.,[96] the heading of the first chapter "Religion – ett mänskligt uttryck" (religion – a human expression) can be regarded as a key to the author's concept of religion, which the students are encouraged to discuss in the task section at the end of the chapter. This whole introductory chapter is written in a descriptive mode presenting different theories on religion and religions from the history of the academic study of religions. The authors do not present one authoritative definition of religion, but discuss the implications of different theories on the scope and the methods of the subject. For example, they present a theory of religion which defines religion as a human reaction to a perceived power that religious people believe to have ultimate control over one's fate. The authors go on to show that this definition of religion excludes "den sydliga buddhismen" (Southern Buddhism) which would, however, commonly be regarded as a religion.

94　Rodhe and Nylund 1998[5]: *Religionskunskap*, (textbook for the *gymnasieskola*) 23ff.
95　From a contemporary study-of-religions point of view, Otto's and Söderblom's theories are, however, problematic. Their attempts to find a broad concept of religion are too rooted in their own religious tradition and are not generally applicable to the diversity of religious traditions. For this issue cf. chapter I, section 1.1.2.
96　Arlebrand, Arvidsson et al. 1998: Relief. This is a textbook for the different forms of the gymnasieskola including *komvux* (communal adult education).

They give popular examples from the history of the academic study of religions to describe key topics relevant to the question "what is religion?". Among them are Nathan Söderblom's, Rudolf Otto's and Mircea Eliade's conceptions of "the holy", attempts to find the origin of religion, and concepts of god(s) (*gudsföreställningar*). The authors comment on the contexts and the benefits of the different ideas from the history of the subject[97] and draw their own conclusions about an acceptable concept of religion for the subject:

> "Basic to all religions is that they intend to put the life of a human being in a broader context than the reality which we can see and perceive with our five senses. Religions express people's striving for eternity. The perspective of eternity puts the life of a single individual in a meaningful context. The person is not any longer left to herself but can for some time forget herself and be taken up with something greater."[98]

Despite the definitions of religion that sometimes exclude certain phenomena or generalise a concept of religion that is indebted to one particular religious tradition (which is almost exclusively Protestant Christianity) the concept of religion as interpretation of life (*livsåskådning*) is the most common one in Swedish textbooks, which can also be seen in the fact that phenomena which would be excluded by a certain definition are nevertheless treated. Therefore, it seems consistent to conclude that there is some agreement on a broad concept of religion, including also a variety of worldviews which are not always classified as religious.

The way the concept *livsåskådning* is used in most sources (official documents, academic literature and teaching material) reveals that it means much more than just interpretation of life. Analogous to the complexity of the concept "religion", it comprises many more levels than just the conceptual one. The actual usage of *livsåskådning* implies that *livsåskådningar* are also perceived as complex systems with ethical and practical implications and consequences.

---

97 For example: "The attempts to explain religions are interesting as an expression of the optimistic belief in science as being capable to answer all questions, which is characteristic of the time in which they lived. Today no scholar of religion claims to be able to give a full explanation for why people have developed religions." (Arlebrand, Arvidsson et al. 1998: Relief, 4).

98 Arlebrand, Arvidsson et al. 1998: Relief, 3f.

5 The representation of religions

This chapter deals with the different ideas about the representation of religions in the three types of sources which are considered particularly relevant for Swedish RE. After a brief look at *Skolverket*-requirements concerning the representation of religions in RE (5.1), special attention is given to academic discourse about representing religions in RE (5.2). This section makes up most of this chapter, as academic concepts for integrative RE are the particular concern of this study. The chapter concludes with a survey of the representation of religions in teaching material (5.3).

5.1 Official requirements for the representation of religions in RE

In the syllabuses (*kursplaner*)[99] published by the National Agency of Education (*Skolverket*) there is only a very general outline of how the different religions should be represented in RE, almost without reference to the representation of individual religions.[100] There is some general information about aspects of religions which should be studied, but those are only exemplified for Christianity.

In the syllabus for the *grundskola*, the following aspects of Christianity receive particular mention: its influence on Western culture and the development of society, including values; its influence on Swedish society, for example on the value-system, legislation and the legal system, culture and traditions (e.g. the role of the Bible and the ecclesiastical year); expressions of beliefs, such as psalms, hymns and songs, ethical principles and customs. At this point, other religions are only mentioned by way of analogy: "På liknande sätt har andra religioner och livsåskådningar sådana uttrycksformer".[101] Similarities, which can create a community between religions, as well as differences, which can create antagonisms that sometimes result in conflicts between religions, are considered in the subject. This is supposed to occur within a framework which attributes equal value to every human being: "En grundsten i ett mångkulturellt och demokratiskt samhälle är att män-

---

99 The syllabuses (*kursplaner*) for the year 2005/2006 were introduced in 2000.
100 Unlike in England, where the model syllabuses by the School Curriculum and Assessment Authority (SCAA) give rather detailed information about the areas of the religions that are to be studied in RE, cf. SCAA 1994: Model Syllabuses for RE.
101 Skolverket 2000: Kursplan religionskunskap grundskola: "Other religions and views of life have similar forms of expression."

niskor är lika värda trots sina olikheter."[102] The common origins of Judaism, Christianity and Islam are emphasised. These three religions are recommended to be studied in depth. Established religions, new religions and phenomena are regarded as the scope of the subject. In the syllabuses for the *gymnasieskola*, these are identified as well known traditions, modern phenomena such as youth culture and workplace culture (*arbetsplatskultur*), which are not immediately perceived as being related to religious belief, and other outlooks on life.[103]

In the study of religions in schools, one focus ought to be on interpersonal relations and gender issues from religious and *livsåskådnings*-perspectives together with consequences for decisions in life (*livsbeslut*) and relationships between people. The experiential dimension of religions should also be studied, for example through an interpretation of aesthetic expressions and symbols (e.g. music, art, rites and ceremonies), which can be regarded as a complement to more theoretical knowledge: "Upplevelse- och känslodimensionerna i ämnet ger möjligheter till fördjupade insikter och personligt engagement."[104]

In the syllabuses for the *gymnasieskola*, the different aspects of religions that ought to be studied in RE are broadly outlined. They comprise the following dimensions: (a) historical: focus on the historical background of the phenomena studied, (b) institutional: focus on institutions which have determined, and continue to determine, developments today in churches, communities, religions and other outlooks on life, (c) cultural: what Christianity and other religions and *livsåskådninar* have meant for cultural development, (d) belief: beliefs and ideas of religions and other *livsåskådningar*, (e) ethical: how different attitudes towards questions of belief and life determine views on ethical issues, and (f) gender: the role of religions and other *livsåskådningar* in shaping attitudes about values and tasks of men and women. The ethical dimension and its potential relevance for social life is regarded as particularly important:

"In Sweden the traditions upheld by Christianity and Western humanism have shaped the interpretation of fundamental values for a long time. In an increasingly multicultural society, the same awareness of the importance of

---

102 Ibid.: "A cornerstone of a multicultural and democratic society is the equal value of people despite their differences."
103 Skolverket 2000: Kursplan religionskunskap gymnasieskola.
104 Skolverket 2000: Kursplan religionskunskap grundskola. At this point what is meant by *personligt engagement* remains rather vague and could be interpreted as both academic or religious engagement. In my view, the latter would lie beyond the scope of a secular subject. "Experiental and emotional dimensions of the subject make possible deeper insights and personal engagement".

common fundamental values can also be created through other religions and views of life."[105]

These formulations refer to specific traditions which have influenced Swedish society to a great extent, but at the same time take account of change and an increasingly multicultural and multireligious society, which requires new foundations for the values on which contemporary society may build.

For the representation of religions, the development of concepts (*begreppsbildning*) is generally seen as a central task, be it with respect to concepts deriving from the dimensions of religions and *livsåskådningar* or concepts relating to existential issues.[106]

The official documents, both for the *grundskola* and the *gymnasieskola*, emphasise that in RE, a wide range of phenomena from different religions and worldviews should be studied, keeping in mind the question of a common value base for society, in Sweden and internationally. With respect to the selection of religions, the breadth of the field is acknowledged, including non-religious worldviews and contemporary phenomena which show some resemblance to what is traditionally regarded as religious. In this context, the interpretation of religion as *livstolkning* is again decisive. Considering the increasingly multireligious situation and growing awareness of the plurality of religions worldwide, the special roles of Christianity and Western Humanism in having shaped the Swedish tradition are emphasised, notwithstanding the impartial treatment of the variety of religions. Interestingly, the suggestions for the representation of religions in RE do not differ significantly for the *grundskola* and the *gymnasieskola*.

5.2 Academic discourse about the representation of religions in RE

Academic literature about the representation of religions in RE is concerned with a range of issues, all of which cannot be covered in my survey. The following section on general observations (5.2.1) deals with the general perspective from which religions are presented, the selection of religions or religious phenomena dealt with, the aspects of religions that are presented, as well as the methods of presentation. Attention is also given to the way the descriptive and existential dimensions are bridged. After a general outline of these issues, individual examples of suggestions for the representation of religions (Buddhism, "tribal

---

105 Skolverket 2000: Upper Secondary School.
106 Skolverket 2000: Kursplan religionskunskap gymnasieskola.

religions" and "Euro-Islam") in Swedish RE will be discussed (5.2.2). The section concludes with a brief consideration of further issues in the representation of religions, which have emerged from the study of academic literature (5.2.3).

5.2.1 General observations

The general perspective from which the religions are presented is an important concern. Its relevance is generally acknowledged and since RE is regarded as informative rather than instructional (i.e. no training into any religious way of life) the approach is basically descriptive. Rodhe describes the perspective on the different religions as intellectual information about something that is basically not intellectual.[107] The perspective should be the same on all religions, an impartial view on the different traditions. Notwithstanding the attempt to understand the individual traditions, the importance of a critical eye is also emphasised. An identification of intellectual inconsistencies, for example the lack of logic or paradoxes and ambiguities, can be important in many respects: it can contribute to an understanding of ideological tensions and arguments within and between religions. Furthermore, it can help to overcome the view that religious people have coherent and unproblematic answers to every possible question and it can be a means for students to formulate their own scepticisms about or criticisms of religions.[108]

The concepts *livsfråga* and *livsåskådning* serve to bridge the gap between the existential and descriptive dimensions of the subject. There has been a shift from the *livsfråga*-approach, in which religious concepts are regarded as answers to existential questions,[109] to the *livsåskådnings*-approach, in which religious concepts are regarded as dealing with questions concerning the interpretation of life and the world. This shift has taken place due to some inconsistencies in the *livsfråga*-approach: presenting religions merely as answers to a certain type of question is an oversimplification and, additionally, is not always convincing, especially as religious concepts sometimes raise questions which they do not necessarily answer. A distinction can be made between questions which may be answered and the mysteries of life which remain con-

---

107 Cf., e.g., Rodhe 1996: Tradition, identity, authority in Swedish religious education.
108 See Furenhed 2000: Undervisning och förståelse, 121.
109 This approach owes much to the theology of the Protestant theologian Paul Tillich and his idea of a correspondence between existential questions and theological answers.

stant causes for struggles.[110] The very idea that the questions of the pupils are excellent starting points for studying different religious traditions was confronted with some problems. First, the questions of the pupils did not necessarily correspond to the issues at stake within the religions. Second, approaching religions from a set of supposedly universal existential questions means transferring a single concept from a particular context (and concept of religion) as a key to complex phenomena. This allows only one reading, or at least influences the representation of the religion in question considerably from the very beginning, and thereby possibly distorts it unduly. Another problem with the *livsfråga*-approach to religions is that the tendency to concentrate on thoughts and opinions may distort the relevance of different aspects of religions in favour of the conceptual level.[111]

Nevertheless, the *livsfråga*-approach to religions has the advantage that it starts from something which is common to all human beings, for example the fact that they have to die, and the questions that emerge from these universal facts. The different answers to these questions of life can be compared and discussed. The "community or fellowship" of all human beings is thereby emphasised to a greater extent than if one used "the concept 'religion' as a similar tool, when the non-religious are left outside and the subject tends to stress what is common to the religions as against those who are not religious".[112] These considerations show a truly integrative approach, which is integrative not only with respect to religions, but also with respect to non-religious worldviews.

The relationship between the *livsfrågor* or *elevfrågor* (questions of the pupils) and the religious traditions has never been outlined convincingly. The lack of criteria for structuring the subject content lead to a general uncertainty on the part of the teachers.[113] Almén concludes that the *livsfråga*-perspective is helpful in the long run only if attention is paid to the pluralism of perspectives and material (including e.g. fiction, newspaper articles, utterances of "normal" people in their daily lives) and if those perspectives are used as methods for deepening one's understanding: "What does a certain religion or 'livsåskådning' look like, if you use this kind of material and this way of understanding 'livsfrågor'? In which respect seems a certain perspective to be fertile, and in which respect can another perspective be more helpful?"[114] If teaching methodology shows such a high level of reflection (also of its

---

110 Almén: RE in Sweden, 83.
111 Cf. ibid., 70.
112 Ibid.
113 Larsson 1992: Introduktion till religionspedagogiken, 37.
114 Almén 2000: RE in Sweden, 89.

own presuppositions) RE can be an important contribution to "the common cultural consciousness and to real knowledge about how meaning is created and sustained in that society of which their school is a part".[115] Thus, the idea of the relevance of *livsfrågor* within the subject *religionskunskap* still survives, but the over-simplified view of the relationship between *livsfrågor* and the religions has been overcome. The concept is still important, but somehow absorbed within the idea of *livsåskådning* as a key to religions, avoiding the simple question – answer scheme.

A variety of methods are suggested for the representation of religions. Work with classical texts from the religions, for example, ought to be supplemented with encounters with real people in order to give an impression of the internal variety of a tradition and thereby avoid presenting religions as something from the past with no relation to the present lives of people. Many authors emphasise the importance of approaching religions from different angles. A variety of sources may be studied, including literature, drama, art and music, but also people and places in different parts of the world. Thereby, historico-critical work can be combined with empathy in order neither to refrain from rational judgement nor to make understanding impossible due to perhaps rationalistic presuppositions. Generally, the question whose religion is to be presented is worth considering, keeping in mind the range of possible sources from official statements to statements by individuals without any representative function. Comparison is also an important aspect of the representation of religions. The different dimensions of religions provide starting points for comparisons, for example the informative, existential or conceptual dimensions.[116]

In his book *Undervisa i religionskunskap*, Selander presents different possible approaches to the religions in RE, including the historico-critical method, *livsfrågepedagogik*, analysis and phenomenology. A phenomenological analysis and comparison of religions starts from central concepts or dimensions. Ninian Smart's model of six dimensions of religions (cf. chapter II, section 1.1.2) was also very influential in Sweden. A phenomenological comparison of religions based on this model acted as a complement to a historical description of religions.[117] The selection of the phenomena that should be compared is not easy. In order to combine the phenomenological approach with the existential

---

115 Ibid.
116 See, for example: Skogar 2000: I stormens öga, Furenhed 2000: Undervisning och förståelse, Selander 1994: Livstolkning. Om religion, livsåskådning och etik i skolan i ett didaktiskt perspektiv.
117 Selander 1993: Undervisa i religionskunskap, 20f.

task of RE, different interpretations of this existential-phenomenological approach can be found.[118]

Two different perspectives on the representation of Hinduism are the subject of dispute in the so-called Geels-Johannesson debate. Geels claims that a study of the Upanishads does not help to understand the religion of an ordinary Hindu. For that purpose, a study of funeral rites in Indian villages, for example, would be considerably more beneficial. Johannesson replied that the latter would not challenge pupils in the same way as studying Upanishad texts.[119] From this debate it becomes obvious that the issue is not just what aspects of religions may be presented, but also what purposes this is meant to serve. Should religions be represented in their cultural settings or as something to choose from? The representation of religions is heavily influenced by the general framework of the subject. As *livsåskådning* is the pivotal concept in Swedish RE and since it is one of the important aims of the subject to communicate methods and possible contents to the students so that they may responsibly form their own *livsåskådning*, the issue of an instrumentalisation of religions emerges. Is an instrumentalisation of religions for pedagogical purposes (for example, forming one's own *livsåskådning*) justified? This question will be reconsidered after a discussion of examples for the representation of religions in academic literature.

5.2.2 Examples of the representation of religions in academic literature about RE

Buddhism

One example of the representation of Buddhism in Swedish RE was developed by Ragnar Furenhed and presented in an article in a well-known book for teachers.[120] Furenhed's article starts with a Buddhist description of an unenlightened person as a mad monkey who runs around in the forest in order to find the best banana, which is not possible, since better bananas can always be found. He asks whether people in the West, under the stress of searching for "the best" while missing the meaning of life, are not exactly like mad monkeys. Furenhed

---

[118] Including e.g. existential-philosophic phenomenology, humanist psychology and Jungian phenomenology, cf. Selander 1993: Undervisa i religionskunskap, 21f.
[119] See Geels 1988: Buddhism som "folkreligion" and Johannesson 1988: Skev bild, quoted in: Almén 2000: RE in Sweden, 80
[120] Furenhed 2000: Den buddhistiska vägen, 161-175.

sets a description of the Buddha taken from Hermann Hesse's Siddharta[121] against that in order to illustrate the different ways of life. The following is an attempt to describe "the Buddhist way" in a series of lessons concentrating on points of contact between teenagers' ideas about life and Buddhist psychology, for example breaking with authorities or searching for one's own way of life. Issues from the Buddhist tradition – mainly taken from texts of the Pali canon – are juxtaposed with universally human experiences and questions. The series of lessons is structured around several "dilemmas" experienced by Buddha's father Shuddodana or by the Buddha himself. It starts with the question if Shuddodana, after he was told that his son would become a great worldly or spiritual ruler, ought to support his son Siddharta Gautama so that he may become a king or a monk later in his life. The students are encouraged to think about the following issues: the respective influence and power of worldly and spiritual rulers in history; what would the alternative king – monk be in our time? Do parents still have expectations about what their children "should become"? And are they right to have those? Since Shuddodana decides to try to bring up his son to become a worldly leader, his next dilemma is how this can be done. The students are asked to discuss several questions concerning this dilemma, for example the responsibilities of parents or the wish to have wealth and power.

Important Buddhist teachings, such as the legend of the four encounters of the Buddha, the four noble truths and the eightfold path are introduced, starting from dilemmas of the Buddha himself. With respect to his encounters with illness, age, death and an ascetic on these journeys out of the protected and beautiful palace area, the students are asked to think about issues like: do we only begin to take questions about the meaning of life seriously once we have problems or a crisis? Why do people choose to do something else, something unusual or difficult rather than enjoying a comfortable and quiet life? Was Siddharta right to leave his wife and child? A gender perspective is also introduced by the question of whether a departure to a new life is typically male behaviour. Furenhed mentions the work of Carol Gilligan[122] about differences between male and female development to draw attention to questions about gender which can be raised with reference to the story of Buddha's life: do more women seek the meaning of life and

---

[121] His statement that he does not know a more beautiful description of the Buddhist ideal personality (ibid., 161) is perhaps slightly infelicitous in this context as it implies that the most beautiful description of the Buddhist ideal personality cannot be found in Buddhist literature, but in a description by a Western author.

[122] Gilligan (1982): In a Different Voice, cf. Furenhed 2000: den buddhistiska vägen, 166.

their identity in interpersonal relations, while departing and moving away from others is more common among males? Prophets and founders of religions, almost all men, set off to new shores and this departure makes them break with existing relationships and their bonds of responsibility and compromise. Regardless of the question of whether these frequent differences between men and women are genetically determined or brought about by social environments, they may lead to different attitudes of men and women towards ethical conflicts.

Furenhed draws attention to the importance of the Buddhist notion of suffering (Swed. *lidande*) as a characteristic of human life. He explains the Pali concept *dukkha* and chooses to use this Pali word rather than a translation in order to stay as close as possible to the original context of the concept and to avoid connotations of the word *lidande* in Swedish which are alien to the Pali concept. Furenhed quotes Pali and Zen sources to explain the concept of *nirvana*.[123] The questions to be discussed at this stage are, for example: Is the Buddha right when he says that all life is suffering? Is it correct that affluence and deprivation create dependencies? Think about what "the golden middle way" may look like in your life; what is *lagom*[124] between affluence and deprivation? Is it possible not to expect too much of life without becoming a pessimist? Is "the golden mean" more suitable for older people than for younger ones? Could the way of moderation also be an ideal for society?

After a consideration of the four noble truths, the eightfold path (*den ädla åttafaldiga vägen*)[125] from dukkha to nirvana is discussed with the pupils, relating the single aspects to general questions about values and to the pupils' own behaviour. The elements of the eightfold path (*fullkomligt insikt, beslut, tal, liv, yrkesval, strävan, medvetande* and *meditation*) are explained with reference to original texts before the Buddha's last dilemma concerning the question of whether he should attain nirvana or continue to help others on their paths is succinctly phrased in the question: "Bör livet levas i avskild lugn eller i aktiv medmänsklighet?"[126] Starting from this question, a few issues of inner-Buddhist discourse and some differences between Theravada- and

---

123 Furenhed uses the Sanskrit term *nirvana* rather than Pali *nibbana*, possibly due to common use outside academia.
124 The Swedish word *lagom* means something like "just right" between possible extremes.
125 Furenhed 2000: Den buddhistiska vägen, 171. Here Furenhed also mentions a different translation by Gunnar Gällmo, who says "åttafiliga vägen" in order to emphasise that the different ideals have to be followed simultaneously.
126 Furenhed 2000: Den buddhistiska vägen, 174. "Should life be lived in silent seclusion or in active humanity?".

Mahayana-Buddhism are introduced. The students are asked to discuss their views on the relationship between the two ideals of harmony and humanity.

Furenhed shows convincingly how basic Buddhist teachings and concepts can be communicated to the pupils in a way that relates the contents of what is being taught to broader issues and contexts and thereby also to questions that are particularly relevant to the pupils. His approach is mainly text-based and he quotes famous Buddhist sources, carefully considering the translation of Pali concepts in order not to distort them unduly or to impose Western interpretations on them from the very beginning. After a consideration of the original texts, however, the pupils are asked to reflect on the issues which have arisen, independently from the immediate contexts in which they arose. A connection between the pupils and some important teachings in the Buddhist tradition is thereby established. The pupils have learnt something about Buddhism and are encouraged to consider the relevance of what they have studied even beyond Buddhist contexts. However, in RE this approach to Buddhist scripture ought to be complemented with other ways of representing Buddhism, which include, for example, contemporary Buddhism and Buddhist practice.

Varieties of contemporary Buddhism are considered in Kjell Härenstam's book about the representation of Buddhism – and Tibetan Buddhism in particular – in RE, *Kan du höra vindhästen? Religionsdidaktik – om konsten att välja kunskap*.[127] Härenstam has a background in teaching as well as in the academic study of religions and teacher training.[128] He has analysed the way Tibetan Buddhism is presented in textbooks for RE. Tibetan Buddhism is mentioned only in textbooks for the later years (*högstadiet*) of the *grundskola* and for the *gymnasieskola*. Härenstam found that these representations of Tibetan Buddhism were often permeated by ethnocentric, colonialist and even racist ideas.[129] His intention is to find a better way of teaching about Tibetan Buddhism based on the assumption that the academic subject of the study of religions and its theories cannot be separated from the way it is taught in schools. Härenstam's book starts with two diametrically opposed views on Tibetan Buddhism: in 1909 Sven Hedin, a Swedish explorer, described religious people in Tibet as parasites. In his view, Lamas hold their people in captivity and are themselves slaves of narrow-hearted

---

127 Härenstam 2000: Kan du höra vindhästen?
128 He is based at the University of Karlstad.
129 See his preface, Härenstam 2000: Kan du höra vindhästen?, 5-6.

(*trångbröstade*) dogmas.[130] In 1994, on the other hand, Lama Anagarika Govinda, a Western convert to Buddhism, claims that "Tibet has become the symbol of all that present-day humanity is longing for ...".[131] These two different conceptions of Buddhism show the range of perspectives one is likely to come across in different types of literature about Tibetan Buddhism.[132]

In the next chapter, Härenstam introduces the Buddhist monk and teacher Pema Dorjee from Tibet, who used to be head of a teacher training college in Dharamsala in India and who is now the head of a big study-centre in which Buddhist philosophy is taught to both laypeople and monks. As part of a university exchange programme in 1998, Pema Dorjee came to Sweden to give lectures at universities and schools.[133] One incident during his stay illustrates the issue at stake with respect to different representations of a religion. Pema Dorjee was portrayed in *Värmlands Folkblad*.[134] Most of the article consisted of an interview with him, but the journalist also added a little information window with "facts on Buddhism".[135] When these "facts" were translated for Pema Dorjee, he was very surprised and asked: "Who says that life is suffering?" To the answer "Buddha" he responded: "Nej, nej, man kan inte uttrycka det på det sättet! Nirvana kan inte översättas med utslocknande! Om detta skulle vara vad den tibetanska buddhismen står för skulle ja inte vilja vara buddhist och ingen annan tänkande människa heller."[136] This discrepancy between the views on what Bud-

---

130 See Sven Hedin 1909: Transhimalaya Del I, 546f., Stockholm, quoted in Härenstam 2000: Kan du höra vindhästen?, 7.
131 Lama Anagarika Govinda 1994: The Way of the White Clouds, xi, New Delhi, quoted in Härenstam 2000: Kan du höra vindhästen?, 7.
132 Cf. Härenstam 2000: Kan du höra vindhästen?, 7-8.
133 Groups of students from Sweden have also visited Dharamsala. This exchange on the academic level is one way of bringing about a modification of the general and stereotypical constructions of Buddhism that can be found for example in textbooks (see below).
134 Värmlands Folkblad, 16.5.1998, 34. See Härenstam 2000: Kan du höra vindhästen?, 9ff.
135 "Fakta om buddhismen / Religion grundad cirka 500 f.Kr. av Buddha (den upplyste) med huvudtesen att livet är ett lidande som upprepas genom ständig återfödelse. Men genom att utplåna tankar, känslor, begär och släcka livstörsten kan man få slut på lidandet och uppnå nirvana (utslocknandet). / Buddhism har sedan dess förgrenats och flera riktningar har lånat inslag från andra religioner, till exempel gudsbegreppet. / Den tibetanska formen av buddhismen, lamaismen är en utpräglad präst- och munkreligion. I det tibetanska kungariket utvecklades ett mäktigt klosterväsande av feodalt slag. Förnämste präst och politiskt överhuvud var Dalai lama i Lhasa." (Härenstam 2000: Kan du höra vindhästen?, 11).
136 "No, no, one cannot say that in this way. Nirvana cannot be translated as fading away! If that was what Tibetan Buddhism stands for, I would not want to be a Bud-

dhism is shows impressively how complex the issue of representing a religion (in whichever context) is. A famous Buddhist monk and teacher questions even the basic "facts" on which most European constructions of Buddhism are based. To understand the view that life is suffering was also one of the central points of Furenhed's suggested representation of Buddhism in school RE, which was discussed above. Furenhed's construction of Buddhism was based on a selection of texts from the Pali canon, in which this idea is in fact very important. The response by Pema Dorjee, however, shows that – even though the texts he quotes have been very influential on many forms of Buddhism – they are not representative of all Buddhists. Even though Pema Dorjee's reaction to the "facts" in the article seems to reflect an inner-Buddhist dissent, it also raises the issue of translation and shows how delicate a matter it is to "transplant" concepts from one cultural background to another and what kind of problems generalisations can bring about.

The third chapter of Härenstam's book deals with Western images of Buddhism and discusses issues concerning representations and misrepresentations of Buddhism. In Swedish textbooks, Theravada Buddhism is often described as a religion that suits modern Western individuals who are critical of metaphysical speculations. Mahayana Buddhism, on the other hand, is described as much more similar to what is traditionally understood (by Westerners) by "religion": the Buddha as a kind of cosmic god, the ideal of a *bodhisattva* who loves all living beings – rather than that of an *arhat* in Theravada traditions, concepts of heavens and hells and many traditional ideas about gods and spirits. Tibetan Buddhism is frequently introduced as the most degenerated form of Buddhism. The textbooks refer to Shamanistic influences of older religious traditions and do not go much beyond a description of ritual practice such as the use of prayer wheels.[137]

To describe the difference between those stereotypical representations of Buddhism and the self-representation of many Buddhists or Buddhism as a living religion, Härenstam refers to two publications by specialists in Buddhism, Damien Keown's *Buddhism. A Very Short Introduction* (1996) and Richard Gombrich's *Precept and Practice. Traditional Buddhism in the Rural Highlands of Ceylon* (1971). Keown shows that, in many studies on Buddhism, only a very small part of the Buddhist tradition is studied and what is found there is assumed to be characteristic or representative of the whole tradition. In fact, however, Bud-

---

dhist and no other thinking human being either" (Härenstam 2000: Kan du höra vindhästen?, 11).

137 Cf. ibid., 12.

dhism is very complex and versatile so that it is impossible to infer the whole from a study of only a part. Many constructions of Buddhism by Western scholars mirror their own expectations about what Buddhism ought to be rather than the complex and multifaceted phenomena behind the concept "Buddhism". Keown emphasises that, with respect to the study of Buddhism, "we must be alert to the risk of 'culture-blindness' and misunderstandings which can arise from the assumption that Western categories and concepts apply to other cultures and civilisations."[138] This is certainly relevant not only for the study of Buddhism. The search for adequate terms and concepts is a recurrent issue in the study of religions. Outsider constructions always run the risk of culture-blindness or a superimposition of concepts which are, in fact, alien to the religion or culture in question. Keown refers to some reductionist conceptions of Buddhism such as Buddhism as the religion of peace, or as a philosophy rather than a religion or even as a purely ethical system. None of these captures the complexity of Buddhism, but "they suffer from being incomplete, and typically represent a reaction of some kind to the perceived deficiencies of religion in the West."[139]

In the West, Buddhism has become popular as a kind of rational philosophy which is – contrary to traditional religion – compatible with science. This interpretation of Buddhism, however, is very different from the forms Buddhism has actually taken in Asia. Since its very beginnings, belief, for example, in the power of mantras, in other spheres that are populated with gods, in spirits and the merciless law of *karma* has been a characteristic of many forms of Buddhism. Keown shows that in the West, people have often selected only those aspects of Buddhism which correspond to their own religious, philosophical and ideological interests and neglect other aspects that do not match their expectations about Buddhism. Buddhist teachings, for example, were used as a framework for a critique of Western materialism. Buddhism seemed to be an answer for people who were looking for a rational religion. This interpretation of Buddhism, however, overlooks many characteristics of Buddhism in the past and present. It is, in fact, a Western ideal-Buddhism.[140]

Richard Gombrich, to whose book *Precept and Practice. Traditional Buddhism in the Rural Highlands of Ceylon* (1971) Härenstam refers next, arrives at a similar conclusion. "Pure" rational Buddhism is a philosophical abstraction independent from Buddhism as it is actually prac-

---

138 Keown 1996: Buddhism, 3.
139 Keown 1996: Buddhism, 14.
140 Cf. Härenstam 2000: Kan du höra vindhästen?, 15f.

ticed. The idea of a rational Buddhism has to do with the way Buddhism and European culture met:

> "The missionaries decided with some justice, given their own frame of reference, that Buddhism was an 'atheist creed', since they were told that the Buddha was not a god. This information was seized on by western rationalists, atheists and agnostics, who were delighted to hear of a religion which was atheistic, and even claimed to be rational; Buddhism as they understood it seemed an ideal ally in the fight against Christianity."[141]

Gombrich differentiates between two types of Buddhism, the "traditional" and the "modern" one. Modern Buddhism corresponds to Western expectations of what true Buddhism should be like. Traditional Buddhism includes many more elements of what is normally seen in relation to folk religion or Hinduism. Gombrich emphasises that the Buddha grew up in a Hindu society and accepted many Hindu beliefs, such as the universe being populated with many living beings which are hierarchically structured in several layers. Human beings are in a middle position with different classes of gods and spirits above them and other spirits and demons below them. Every living being, including the gods, is subject to the circle of rebirth (*samsara*) and composed of five components (*skandha*). One important idea in traditional Buddhist philosophy is the concept of non-self (Sanskrit *anatman*, Pali *anatta*). Gombrich sees this idea as frequently being in conflict with a common affective belief in the reincarnation of one's personality or the more cognitive concept of merely karmic survival.[142] He draws attention to another issue about which he detects a frequent misunderstanding in Western constructions of Buddhism. According to the tradition, the Buddha was against caste distinctions between monks, but in Sri Lankan Buddhism as actually lived, the caste system has played a considerable role. The monastic community consists of different groups (*nikayas*) which are defined merely by cast borders. Gombrich says that the view that Buddha was against the caste system is a misunderstanding for which mainly Western authors are responsible.[143] He uses another example to illustrate the difference between Buddhist texts and practice: it is commonly assumed that monks strive for *nirvana*, whereas laypeople try to accumulate good karma for their next life. This is correct if one looks at the texts only, but it is incorrect for Buddhism as it is practiced. Monks – exactly as laypeople – also try to accumulate good karma for their next life.

---

141 Gombrich 1971: precept and practice, 51, quoted in Härenstam 2000: Kan du höra vindhästen?, 17.
142 Cf. ibid., 73, quoted in Härenstam 2000: Kan du höra vindhästen?, 17.
143 Cf. ibid., 295, quoted in Härenstam 2000: Kan du höra vindhästen?, 18.

Considering the ideas of Keown and Grombrich, Härenstam concludes that many representations of Buddhism in the West (including the teaching material he analysed) concentrated on India, early Buddhism and a few prominent texts. These representations were transformed into an "idealised Western export-Buddhism", which ignored several aspects that have always been parts of actually existent Buddhism in its many forms. With this background, it became possible to label Tibetan Buddhism as degenerated and regard it as particularly distant from original Buddhism. Interestingly, however, Gombrich demonstrates that many of the aspects that have been ignored are not even unfamiliar to Theravada Buddhism, which is often seen as closest to 'original Buddhism' as described in the ancient Pali texts, as the Sri Lankan example shows. Härenstam concludes:

> "Kanske är detta, som vi kallar ursprunglig form, inte något annat än ett bestämt sätt att se på och välja kunskap från det mångfacetterade och svårgripbara fenomen som termen buddhism används för att beteckna."[144]

This process of selection of what is characteristic of a complex phenomenon is an important issue in the representation of *any* religion. Therefore, it is important to be conscious of the fact that one inevitably selects certain aspects from reality and to be aware of one's motives for the particular selection one undertakes. Every selection includes a decision about what is considered essential or at least important or worth mentioning. The existing representations of Buddhism go back to the selection of different scholars and other informants. It is necessary to consider their respective backgrounds, interests and ideologies. The *varför-fråga* – the question of why which aspects are chosen in a particular context – is crucial in any representation of religion. It has to be considered for which purpose a particular representation of religion is constructed. The selection an author of a textbook undertakes can be a result of values and ideological convictions which may be completely different from what lies behind the sources written by scholars or travellers. At any rate, Härenstam concludes, "när det gäller kunskap om andra kulturer, kan man aldrig bortse från frågan varför denna kunskap har valts ut och presenterats."[145] Referring back to the findings of Keown and Grombich, Härenstam claims that what they label as Western export-Buddhism is in fact not a misrepresentation of Buddhism, but a representation that was made from a certain perspective

---

144 "Perhaps what we call original is nothing but a certain way of looking at and choosing knowledge about the manifold and not easily comprehensible phenomenon that the term Buddhism seeks to describe." (Härenstam 2000: Kan du höra vindhästen?, 20).
145 Ibid., 20.

and with certain aims. The study of Buddhism ought to take place within a framework which considers the environment of the process of representation. In Härenstam's words: "När man studerar buddhismen, så torde det alltså vara mycket väsentligt att fundera över ideologiska och sociala förhållanden i det västerland som söker kunskap om andra kulturer."[146]

In the following chapters of the book, Härenstam compares different representations of Tibetan Buddhism, including reports from Tibet before and after the flight of the 14th Dalai Lama to India in 1959, and teaching material from the 1970s, 1980s and 1990s. The representation of Tibetan Buddhism in the textbooks changed considerably during this period. The older books focused mainly on practice, which was often described in terms like *magi* (magic) or *besvärjelser* (incantation). The prayer wheel is regarded as a symbol of mechanistic religion. The Dalai Lama is labelled *gudakungen* (god-king) and the processes of finding a new Dalai Lama are described in detail while the importance of divination is emphasised. According to Härenstam, those descriptions probably communicate to the pupils an impression of Tibetan Buddhism as something primitive and exotic, and definitely not as something which can contribute to their own spiritual development. Among the more recent books, Härenstam observes a different trend. The focus is much less on religious practice. The prayer wheel is no longer mentioned. Instead, symbolical meanings are emphasised. The 14th Dalai Lama is seen as a warrior of peace. The ideological contents of the tradition are dealt with. Now there is much more for the pupils to pick for their own spiritual development. This example of the representation of Tibetan Buddhism in Swedish textbooks is Härenstam's starting point for more general reflections: "I all sin korthet aktualiserar också beskrivningarna av den tibetanska buddhismen problem som har att göra med alla tolkningar av så svåravgränsade och diffusa fenomen som världens olika religioner."[147]

These more general issues concerning the representation of religions are considered in the last two chapters of the book. Härenstam refers to Tibetan writers to explain the problem inherent in the "transplantation" of concepts. Dawa Norbu problematises this for the use of serfdom, feudalism and theocracy in the Tibetan context.[148] These con-

---

146 Ibid., 20.
147 "In all their brevity these descriptions of Tibetan Buddhism raise issues related to any interpretation of phenomena which are as difficult to define and as varied as the world's different religions." (ibid., 108); for the representation of Tibetan Buddhism in textbooks see chapter 5, summary on page 108.
148 Norbu 1987: Red Star, 190, quoted in Härenstam 2000: Kan du höra vindhästen?, 117.

The representation of religions 261

cepts with roots in societies that are very different from Tibetan society are often applied completely uncritically for Tibet. For want of better solutions, one often has to use terms and concepts which emerged in certain circumstances and cannot have exactly the same meaning in others. Problems arise, however, if those terms and concepts are transferred unconsciously or without any comment. This also applies to the concept *religion* itself. Pema Dorjee finds it difficult to translate this concept into the Tibetan tradition. It has emerged from Western European history and its meanings have been shaped by European religious traditions. A Buddhist concept like *dharma* does not have the same connotations at all.[149]

Against this background, Härenstam takes up questions concerning the attempt to pay respect to and understand religious beliefs. To take religious beliefs and practice seriously makes a reductionist perspective that tries to explain religion solely by means of external influences impossible. He also detects a limit to what can be "explained" about other religions: "Det kändes plötsligt futtigt att försöka 'förklara' bönevimplarna, de olika religiösa ceremonierna. Hur ska man förklara eller begreppsliggöra ljudet av galopperande vindhästar ut över Himalayas berg?".[150] Respect for the people to whom the traditions have a meaning and respect for the descriptions the people give about these is important.

One of Härenstam's conclusions is that ethnocentrism and reductionism are a matter of degree. Ethnocentrism becomes a big problem if one's whole terminology is formed from a cultural background that is different from what is described. And to some extent explanations are necessary in the study of religions. Therefore, even though neither ethnocentrism nor reductionism can be avoided completely, being aware of them and continually reviewing one's own work with respect to them are indispensable for the study and representation of religions in different contexts, including the academic study of religions and RE.[151] For any representation of religions, there is no choice but to select – a perspective and contents. It is important to be conscious of this process of selection and to consider carefully the criteria which shape this process. In any case, it is better to make explicit those criteria than to pretend – perhaps even to oneself – not to have any at all. Härenstam suggests that the *värdegrund* as a means for

---

149 This is what Perma Dorjee told Härenstam when the latter talked about "Tibetan religion", cf. ibid., 117.
150 Ibid., 118.
151 Cf. ibid., 118f.

gests that the *värdegrund* as a means for selection is worth considering.[152]

The approaches to teaching Buddhism in school by Furenhed and Härenstam were designed for different purposes and can hardly be compared. Furenhed has presented an article with one model for presenting Buddhist teachings in RE, while Härenstam wrote a monograph that discusses in detail various issues concerning the representation of Buddhism in RE. Furenhed's model can be regarded as a design for a series of lessons, in which descriptive (information about Buddhist texts and teachings including the life of the Buddha) and existential (reflection about one's own life and worldview in relation to the issues raised in Buddhist texts, stimulated e.g. by questions about the omnipresence of suffering, or about dependencies caused by affluence or deprivation) elements are combined in order to show the relevance of Buddhist teachings for the life of the pupils. He outlines how in school RE pupils may engage with Buddhist texts in a more existential way than is possible in the academic study of religions, without, however, taking a religious perspective. This is a very good example of how the gap between the study of religions at universities and RE in schools may be bridged. Furthermore, it demonstrates that non-confessional RE does not at all need to be a cold, dry and detached study of visible phenomena of religions without any deeper understanding.[153] It is evident, though, that Furenhed's model is by no means a comprehensive framework for teaching Buddhism in schools, but has to be complemented with other approaches, which deal e.g. with contemporary Buddhism, Buddhism and migration, and Buddhist practice. To further Furenhed's intention to build bridges between Buddhism and questions and problems of the pupils, it may be particularly interesting to include voices of and information about Buddhist children in teaching material.[154]

Härenstam transfers general considerations about the representation of religions in the study of religions to the representation of Buddhism in school RE. His study highlights dramatic changes in the representation of Tibetan Buddhism in the 20th century. Furthermore, it reveals the

---

152 Cf. ibid., 120f. Härenstam's further ideas about didactics are taken up in section 6 on education.

153 The latter is a reproach which is frequently used as an argument against non-confessional RE. See e.g. Hammond, Hay et al.1990: 21, Netto 1990: Multi-faith RE and experiential learning.

154 This kind of teaching material may be similar to the material presented in the interpretive approach in English RE (see chapter II.2.4), i.e. material about Buddhist children in one's own country, but material about Buddhist children in different parts of the world may also be helpful.

limits of stereotypical representations of Theravada, Mahayana and Tibetan traditions, as well as the discrepancy between frequent Western images of Buddhism and Buddhism as a living religion today. Referring to academic literature about Buddhism, Härenstam shows a way of avoiding common errors and frequent misunderstandings about Buddhism. His own approach to teaching Buddhism includes a plurality of voices in written material as well as encounters with Buddhists, not least through an exchange programme with Indian universities and contacts with Tibetans in Dharamsala. Härenstam contextualises his ideas about the representation of Buddhism within a broader framework for the representation of different religions in integrative RE. Therefore, this example of the representation of a particular religion may also serve as a guideline for considerations about the representation of other religions.

"Tribal religions"

In academic literature about RE in Sweden, some consideration is given to the representation of "tribal religions".[155] In this section, I briefly illustrate some issues that have emerged in two approaches to teaching "tribal religion" in RE, again by Furenhed and Härenstam. The book *Livstolkning och Värdegrund*[156] includes an article about the representation of "tribal religions" (*naturfolkens religion*) by Furenhed. According to Furenhed, tribal religions are often misrepresented in teaching material where people are described as being busy mainly with performing religious rites. The agenda is often exotistic, thus widening the gap between the pupils and the religions in question even further. Furenhed's outline of a series of lessons he suggests for the representation of tribal religions in RE starts with an article in *Dagens Nyheter* in the early 1980s, which describes the clash of interests of a Western European company that wants to build a factory in Liberia and the locals worrying about their ancestors who live in the trees which have to be cut down if the factory is built. He takes this story as an illustration of the fact that Western "rationality" in the long run often turns out to be

---

[155] I translate the Swedish terms *naturfolkens religion* and *naturreligion* as "tribal religions". The concepts *naturfolkens religion* and *naturreligion* are certainly not unproblematic, as they imply that these religions are somehow closer to "nature" than most other religions, which is not necessarily correct.

[156] Almén et al. 2000: Livstolkning och värdegrund.

unwise and that African "irrationality" may be useful in a longer perspective.[157]

Furenhed regards the following as the main aim of teaching about tribal religions: "att visa på de positiva värden som finns i naturmänniskans levnadsform och livssyn."[158] When teaching about *"naturreligion"*, four aspects should be considered: (1) the physical environment, (2) the interdependence of living conditions and ideas, beliefs and ideals about living together, (3) the interdependence of ideas, ideals and aims, and (4) universally human attitudes and reactions expressed in myths, beliefs and rites. Furenhed emphasises the importance of empathy. With the help of slides, poems and stories, he wants to convey a feeling of familiarity in order to create respect for tribal religions and thereby moves away from exotising and distancing tendencies. One aim is to communicate the universality of the human condition and different ways of interpreting it. Ideas from tribal religions are also seen as a means of criticising Western culture. Incomprehensible or unacceptable behaviour in tribal religions is not to be ignored, but should be discussed in class, even though in general there should be an emphasis on positive aspects in order to create an understanding for other cultures: "... om en av våra viktigaste läraruppgifter är att skapa förståelse för främmande kulturer, är det ändå nödvändigt att fokussera de positiva värdera i dessa."[159] It may be questioned if these latter considerations are consistent. Perhaps emphasising positive aspects too much can also create a distorted idealised impression, which certainly does not contribute to a better understanding either. Would not a balanced account, which tries not to distort the representation in either direction, be more appropriate? Furenhed has a point, however, if his intention is not to make empathy or understanding too difficult from the very beginning by starting with aspects that are incomprehensible at first sight.

One other point in Furenhed's account of the representation of tribal religions in RE seems, however, more problematic. What I mean is his focus on "irrationality" as a feature of tribal religions, despite his questioning of the dichotomy between "Western rationality" and "Afri-

---

157 "... att den västerländska 'rationaliteten' på längre sikt ofta är oklok, och det är tankeväckande att den afrikanska 'irrationaliteten' i ett längre perspektiv kan vara ändamålsenlig." (Furenhed 2000: Naturfolkens religion, 144).
158 "to show the positive values that can be found in tribal forms of living and views of life" (Furenhed 2000: Naturfolkens religion, 144).
159 "... if one of our most important tasks is to create an understanding for different cultures, it is important to focus on their positive values" (Furenhed 2000: Naturfolkens religion, 146).

can irrationality". Is not this very focus on "irrationality" in the representation of tribal religions a hidden agenda of a superiority of the bigger religions? Or would a representation of Christianity also focus on its "irrational" features, for example, Christ's presence in the Eucharist? Perhaps Furenhed is only referring to common prejudice about tribal religions and attempting to show its inadequacy. Failing to name the conditions in which this prejudice has emerged and survived is, however, to contribute – though unintentionally – to an agenda that is not completely independent from racist ideas, which have frequently prevailed in the representation of tribal religions.

Kjell Härenstam also reflects on the representation of tribal religions in RE. His main point is that a representation is always a representation *by somebody* and that knowledge is always *somebody's* knowledge.[160] He also found many representations of tribal religions exotistic, ethnocentric or racist. The terminology used to describe these religions is part of this problem. Words like magic (*magi*),[161] belief in spirits (*andetro*), taboo (*tabu*) or ancestor worship (*förfädersrdyrkan*) occur frequently in the description of tribal religions. As the pupils are not at all familiar with these terms, which possibly sound strange and different to them, they may conclude that "det måste alltså handla om *mycket konstiga och avvikande människor.*"[162] Thereby – whether consciously or unconsciously – the difference between "us" and "tribal religions" is marked clearly. The issues concerning the creation and use of terms is interesting. Härenstam mentions several approaches to tribal religions from the late 19th century and shows that the categories which were developed then often still dominate in descriptions of other cultures today.[163] An uncritical adoption of the old approaches also means an adoption of problematical theories which were fashionable at the time, for example, evolutionism or original monotheism. Most of these theories were *skrivbordsprodukter* ("armchair theories") or at least *utifrånskonstruktioner* (constructions from the outside), as Evans-Pritchard already observed.[164] As much as a scholar might try to give an objective account of a phenomenon, they are always bound by concepts which imply certain value presuppositions already. A nice example of the

---

160 Härenstam 2000: Kan du höra vindhästen?, 123ff.
161 For an account of the problematic oppostion religion vs. magic, see e.g. Kippenberg and von Stuckrad (2003): Einführung in die Religionswissenschaft, 155f.
162 Härenstam 2000: Kan du höra vindhästen?, 124 ("therefore, these people must be *very strange and different*", emphasis in original).
163 He refers to, for example, James George Frazer's *The Golden Bough* and the works of Robert Ranulph Marret, Henri Levy-Bruhl and Wilhelm Schmidt. Cf. ibid., 124f.
164 Cf. Evans-Pritchard 1965: *Theories of Primitive Religions*.

implications of the concepts used in the representation of a religion can be found in Ulf Drobin's *Afrikanska religioner i västerländska belysningar*.[165] He says that, briefly, one can say that there are two different "African religions", one as described by scholars with a Protestant background and one as described by scholars with a Catholic background. The different conceptual structures result in different accounts of the same phenomena. One example of this hermeneutic circle is John S. M'Biti's account of African religions, in which he claims that African religions are in all important aspects basically like Christianity. M'Biti, an Anglican bishop, uses Western-Christian terms and concepts and "finds" many structures which are similar to Christianity in what he calls "African religion".[166]

Härenstam draws attention to critical views of these deeply ideologically shaped representations of different religions. The writer and scholar Okot p'Bitek, for example, in his book *African Religions in Western Scholarship* criticised the "hellenisation" of African traditions, when, for example, the word *jok* is translated as *god*. The African word *jok* has many connotations that hardly match the concept of god in a Western-Christian context. According to p'Bitek, any such translation is an "ideological import" already and therefore alien to the phenomenon in question, undermining a fair account of it.[167]

These few points from contributions to the discussion about the representation of *naturfolkens religion* in RE once again show the importance of a critical awareness of the limits of one's own perspective and the complex processes by which representations of religions are shaped. The issues that have been raised, by Härenstam in particular, demonstrate that the development of responsible didactics of tribal religions, including appropriate terminology, in integrative RE is yet a desideratum.

"Euro-Islam"

An interesting example of the representation of Islam in the Swedish *gymnasieskola* is the Euro-Islam course at Rudbeck's school in Sollentuna, 15 km north of Stockholm.[168] In Sollentuna, there are large immigrant groups from e.g. Turkey, Iraq, Iran, Syria, Bangladesh, Pakistan,

---

165 Drobin 1979: Afrikanska religioner i västerländska belysningar.
166 Cf. M'Biti: *African Religions and Philosophy* (1969), quoted in Härenstam 2000: Kan du höra vindhästen?, 126.
167 p'Bitek 1970: African Religions in Western Scholarship, quoted in Härenstam 2000: Kan du höra vindhästen?, 126f.
168 For an outline of the Euro-Islam course, see Wiberg 2000: Religious education in a Swedish upper secondary school perspective.

Somalia and ex-Yugoslavia. Many of the immigrants have a Muslim background. The Euro-Islam course was developed by two Swedish teachers, Anna Wilberg and Kristina Rosberg, not as part of the compulsory RE course,[169] but as one of several optional courses from which students with an interest in different religions may choose.

This 80-hour course, which includes several study trips in Sweden (e.g. to the Uppsala mosque, Sollentuna church and a Muslim school in Kista) and even one trip to a mosque in London, is about the meeting of Islam and Western culture. The aim of the course is to attain an increased understanding of how Islam has integrated into Europe. This is to be achieved through practical and theoretical studies, observations and experiences, as well as personal encounters and reflections. The students are meant to acquire knowledge about the following: how and when Christianity and Islam met in Europe; how Islam has influenced art, music, literature and architecture; how Islam and Muslims are portrayed in films and popular literature, central doctrines of Islam and Christianity, the significance of holy places, Islam in Europe and particularly in Sweden, the situation of Muslim women, the meeting or confrontation of Islam and secular society. Follow-up assignments can be about further issues, for example, different Muslim groups in Sweden or other European countries, mosques in Stockholm, Muslim dietary regulations etc.

Every student has to make his or her own survey by interviewing parents and grandparents about their religious backgrounds. Dialogue is an important aspect of the project and ideally about half of the students have a traditionally Swedish and the other half an immigrant background. On the trip to London, the students visited Regent's Park mosque and the Muslim students participated in the Friday prayers. They also visited a Muslim school, talked to the pupils there and met a Pakistani writer, who told them about his experience as a Muslim and immigrant in London.

This project – though so far only an optional course – is an excellent example of the variety of themes and activities which are possible in integrative RE. Focusing on one particular aspect of Islam – its acculturation in Europe – it presents a range of activities through which children from different backgrounds are enabled to explore the dynamic character of a religion in its contemporary shape.

---

169 Therefore, it is not really integrative RE according to my definition (see introduction). As it is, however, designed for a mixed group of students (of any religion or none) and is not indebted to a religious point of view, I include it in this study, because it is an interesting suggestion for the representation of Islam, which could also be used in integrative RE in a stricter sense.

5.2.3 Further issues in the representation of religions in academic literature about RE

Negative aspects of religions

In the new edition of *Om undran inför livet*, Bo Dahlin added a chapter "Vad är religiös tro – efter 'den 11:e september'?". He notes that in the debates around this event on September 11, 2001 in New York, people often talk about "Muslim terrorists", while in debates about terrorist attacks by Christians, for example bombings on clinics in North America that perform abortions, the attackers are not labelled "Christian terrorists". This can be seen as one example of an implicit (or sometimes explicit) islamophobia which established a close connection between Islam and terrorism.

The suicide bombings in the event referred to above lead Dahlin to reflect about the question of what religious belief is exactly. He says: "Ett första svar kunde vara att människor tror på något för att ge livet en *mening*. Det är vårt existentialla behov av mening som gör att vi anammar en viss trosuppfattning."[170] Dahlin regards two extremes as dangerous and possibly leading to death (suicide), extreme meaninglessness – totalised doubt resulting in depression – and extreme meaningfulness – totalised belief resulting in fanatic enthusiasm. Between those extremes there is room for a middle way with a combination of belief and doubt. Dahlin distinguishes between cognitive belief, which comprises a set of ideas about, for example, god, good and evil or the meaning of life and emotional belief such as confidence or trust in a god or higher power: "Tro i denna mening är en tillit till att livet, tillvaron, världen, universum eller Gud i någon grundläggande mening *bär mig*, eller oss, oavsett vad som händer."[171] It seems that Dahlin regards this general confidence which may be supplemented with rational considerations as a kind of healthy belief preferable to the extremes described above.[172]

The question of what is possible within the limits of the principles of the academic study of religions or in integrative RE may again be asked in this context. Is it possible to promote a particular kind of belief – in this case a moderate general confidence – in RE? On what grounds can that be done? Or would that mean giving up impartiality towards the variety of religious beliefs? In any case, the process which results in

---

[170] Dahlin 2004: Om undran inför livet, 66.
[171] Ibid., 68f.
[172] He clarifies what he means by that with the Muslim saying "Lita på Gud men bind fast kamelen", ibid., 69.

evaluations of different beliefs has to be made explicit. There is nothing wrong with showing in what kind of actions particular beliefs may result. And, perhaps, if these actions can be classified as "bad" on the grounds of the *värdegrund* or international conventions on human rights, which were drawn up in democratic processes, certain beliefs may be criticised in this procedure. The general attempt to use broad and balanced information is, however, particularly important in this procedure. There is always the risk of being biased because of propagandistic information. It is, after all, very difficult to decide which beliefs may result in e.g. violent behaviour and which may not. The framework Dahlin suggests, building on certain ethical principles, common sense and to some extent rationality, may perhaps be one difference between the representation of religions in academia and in state schools. Whereas in the academic study of religions an attempt is made to refrain from judgements about different beliefs, explicit adherence to certain ethical principles may be more appropriate in schools, which have, after all, also a fostering task. One has to be aware of the fact, however, that these principles have been developed and interpreted on the grounds of particular beliefs, even if they may rather be aspects of civil religion than of an individual religious tradition in the classical sense.

Methods of studying religions in RE

Considerations about the effects of certain representations of religions are necessary. For example, what is the effect of emphasising the ritual aspect of Tibetan Buddhism? In the textbooks, Tibetan Buddhist rituals are often interpreted as mechanistic practice. Härenstam compares those rituals to rituals in the Church of Sweden and shows convincingly that the latter are no less mechanistic than the former. Nevertheless, the stereotype prevails. The example of a Tibetan Buddhist headmaster of a school, who rarely has time for the rites, but for whom the most important element of his religion is sympathy for all beings, serves to illustrate that "normal" Tibetan Buddhists are rarely portrayed in textbooks. Are they less representative of their religion than the stereotypical old man with his prayer wheel, who often appears as a kind of cliché of a Tibetan Buddhist? Perhaps it is worth also considering the inclusion of pictures that do not imply that this religion does not have anything to do with the modern world, but is a kind of relic from a feudal middle age, a representation which is very close to the official Chinese view of Tibetan culture.[173]

Härenstam's analysis of the representation of Tibetan Buddhism in Swedish RE pays attention to two dimensions of RE, which can – using the words of the English debate[174] – be called *learning about* (descriptive dimension) and *learning from* (existential dimension) religions or, in the Swedish context, studying religions and building one's own *livsåskådning*. After these considerations about criteria for selecting information *about* Tibetan Buddhism in RE, the question remains what children may learn *from* it. A study of Tibetan Buddhism and its environment can in itself be a stimulus to reflect about one's own view of life and ethics. The non-violence tradition can be inspiring and the role of culture in the conflict with the Chinese occupational power may provoke various considerations and discussions. Härenstam concludes: "*Studium av den tibetanska buddhismen skulle med andra ord kunna förstärka de allmänna och grundläggande värden som läroplanerna fastslår.*"[175] It is also possible, of course, that the pupils' own *livsåskådning* will be influenced by their encounter with Tibetan Buddhism. This is again what is meant by *learning from* religions, which is possible for all the pupils, since "[e]ndast om man har en mycket monolitisk uppfattning om religionerna, kan man tro att eleverna därför måste beteckna sig som buddhister."[176]

Härenstam does not argue for not mentioning negative aspects of religions, but for a careful consideration and reflection of the ambivalent character of religions. If religions are interpreted as humankind's common cultural heritage, there are obviously many negative and suppressive aspects of it, but there are also other aspects, which can contribute to spiritual development and liberation or emancipation. In RE, these positive aspects can be communicated to the pupils:

---

173 Cf. Härenstam 2000: Kan du höra vindhästen?, 162.
174 Some influential concepts for RE in England also serve as a stimulation for the representation of Religions in Swedish RE. Härenstam, for example, refers to the works of Ninian Smart, Michael Grimmitt and Robert Jackson and their ideas about what integrative RE should be like, cf. Härenstam 2000: Kan du höra vindhästen?, 146ff.
175 "In other words, the study of Tibetan Buddhism is meant to contribute to strengthening the general and basic values laid down in the curricula." (Härenstam 2000: Kan du höra vindhästen?, 163).
176 "Only if one has a very monolithical understanding of religions can one think that pupils have to call themselves Buddhists for this reason." (Härenstam 2000: Kan du höra vindhästen?, 163).

"En icke-konfessionell religionsundervisning borde göra det möjligt för eleverna att vaska fram de äkta pärlorna i detta arv, utan att för den skull behöva släpa på allt detta andra."[177]

Even if this instrumentalisation of the different religions in order to create one's own *livsåskådning* may be a step beyond what is possible within the framework of the academic study of religions, a consideration and reflection of the different perspectives and an inclusion of those within one's own frame of reference is definitely within the limits of what is possible in integrative RE. These issues, however, make recurrent methodological considerations necessary. Critical reflection of one's own presuppositions about the study of religions in RE has to be an integral part of the subject. Härenstam formulates this with respect to teaching material:

"Det skulle vara spännande med läroböcker som eggade fantasin och väckte nyfikenheten, gärna genom att inspirera till ifrågasättande av läromedlens *egen* presentation. Läromedlet ses då inte som en slutpunkt, utan som en startpunkt för en *sökprocess* med både kognitiva, emotionella, estetiska och etiska aspekter."[178]

This claim about teaching material can be transferred to the other levels of integrative RE. In order to avoid a dogmatic point of view (be it a universal-theological or a rationalistic one) the whole framework for integrative RE always has to be open to criticism. Within the limits of some basic insights from the academic study of religions and intercultural education, a pluralist approach to the different phenomena seems to be an effective means of avoiding gross distortions.

Härenstam concludes that it is better to consciously choose a starting point for one's representation of religions (for example, the *värdegrund*) than unconsciously selecting according to a colonialist or racist agenda.[179] What is being written always says something about the writer as well. Can *allsidighet, saklighet* and *objektivitet*, demanded in the

---

177 "Non-confessional RE ought to enable the pupils to gather the real pearls of this heritage without their having to also to bear the weight of the rest." (Härenstam 2000: Kan du höra vindhästen?, 163). To support this claim, Härenstamm quotes Ninian Smart's call for "a worldview for the world, which does not however make all religions the same, but stresses their complementary values in helping to build a truly global civilization, ... a kind of spiritual democracy ... [in order to] eliminate inter-religious and inter-ideological violence." Smart 1999: Foreword, in Peter Conolly, ed.: Approaches to the Study of Religion, xiii.

178 "It would be exciting to have textbooks that stimulate the pupils' curiosity and imagination by inspiring them to question the position of the textbook itself as well. Then, a textbook may be regarded, not as a way of rounding-off, but rather as the starting point, for an exploration of cognitive, as well as emotional, aesthetical and ethical aspects." (Härenstam 2000: Kan du höra vindhästen?, 164).

179 Ibid., 133.

syllabuses, be achieved? "En intellektuell hederligare hållning torde väl vara att hävda, att informationen ska ta upp *så många sidor som möjligt* och *att man inte medvetet ska ljuga.*"[180]

RE, the "värdegrund" and "cultural heritage"

As we have seen, state schools in general and RE in particular ought to be non-confessional. The *värdegrund* is, however, seen as a kind a metasystem of values, independent from the specific traditions. It is regarded as a general minimum consensus and a kind of prerequisite for a functioning democratic society. Despite the fact that ethical principles are also something highly individual, educators regard fostering and maintaining these values as a collective responsibility.[181] For Almén, RE has always been an ideological instrument. Nowadays, however, it is no longer an instrument of churches and religions, but rather of the school system and the "Swedish model". In this context, high expectations were held for this subject.[182]

The controversy about reference to "den etik som förvaltats av kristen tradition och västerlandsk humanism"[183] as part of the *värdegrund* has been mentioned before.[184] This special reference only to the Christian tradition and Western Humanism but no other religion or worldview is frequently – in politics or the media – accounted for by the particular cultural heritage of Sweden and Europe, despite the dissent expressed by people who deal with RE professionally. In his reflection on "cultural heritage", Härenstam refers to Martin Bernal's *Svart Athena* (1997), in which Bernal articulates his reservations about the phrase "Western cultural heritage". In the context of this phrase, Rome, Jerusalem and Athens are often mentioned as influences, but the considerable influences of Egypt and the Middle East on ancient Greek culture are generally neglected. Why do we not refer to "our oriental cultural heritage", "our African cultural heritage" or maybe even to "humankind's cultural heritage"?[185] There are different cultural heritages, which the school selects and leaves out. Powerful groups are more likely to emphasise their heritage. Knowledge consists of a process both of selection and omission. The concept of knowledge is closely related to the ques-

---

180 Härenstam 2000: Kan du höra vindhästen?, 134.
181 Cf. Borevi 1997: Religion i skolan, 41f.
182 Cf. Almén 2000: RE in Sweden, 66.
183 Utbildningsdepartement 1994: Lpo 94, 5.
184 Cf. the section on the *värdegrund* (1.3) in this chapter.
185 Härenstam 2000: Kan du höra vindhäseten?, 129.

tion of power.[186] Härenstam suggests referring – like Edward Said – to human cultural heritage[187] and allowing the whole rich human cultural heritage to contribute to the spiritual and moral development of children. After all, RE is no longer about indoctrination into a certain interpretation of life and the world, in contrast to the time when RE was still confessional. Why should children not be influenced by the variety of traditions in this world?[188]

5.3 The representation of religions in textbooks

5.3.1 General observations

Most Swedish textbooks for RE present different religions and non-religious worldviews.[189] The concepts of *livsfrågor* and *livsåskådning*, which – as we have seen – play a key role in academic concepts for RE, are also influential in the textbooks. The overview of different religions (*jämförande religionsöversikt*) in a textbook by Thulin and Elm shows impressively how non-religious worldviews are integrated into the subject *religionskunskap*.[190] This overview shows religions Hinduism, Buddhism, Judaism, Christianity and Islam, and the scientist, socialist and existentialist worldviews in one table. For all these traditions, Thulin and Elm give keywords for the following aspects: founder, holy text, area of origin, creation, meaning of life and "after death". The respective keywords for the scientist and existentialist worldviews are, for example:[191]

---

186 Here Härenstam refers to the work of Gunilla Svingby (see Svingby 1987: Sätt kunskapen i centrum!, 16 ff).
187 Härenstam 2000: Kan du höra vindhästen? 155f.
188 Cf. Härenstam 2000: Kan du höra vindhästen?, 155f.
189 There are, however, a few textbooks which focus almost exclusively on Christianity or pay a disproportionate amount of attention to Christianity. An example of the first category is Eggehorn et al. 1996: Religion, in which 5/6 are dedicated to Christianity under different headlines, such as "kärlek, krig och kloka kunger" and other religions are mentioned only in the chapter "religion and culture", of which most space is, however, again dedicated to Christianity. Arlebrand et al. 1998: Relief A+B can be regarded as an example of the latter, in which there are three chapters about Christianity (one structured similarly to the chapters about other big religions, one about the history of Christianity and one about the Catholic Church) and only one at most about each of the other religions.
190 Thulin/Elm 1995: Religion, 132-133.
191 This is my translation of the respective part of the overview mentioned above.

Livs- åskådningar	Founder	Holy text	Area of origin	Creation	Meaning of life	After death
Scientist	Darwin 1809- 1882	On the Origin of Species...	Western Europe	Physical and biological development; Atheism	To make the best out of this only life that we live	To continue one's species
Existential- ism	Jean- Paul Sartre 1905- 1980	Existentialism is a Human-ism	Western Europe	Physical and biological development; Atheism	To make the best out of this only life that we live	Whatever you want to believe yourself

Figure 5.1 – The representation of the scientist and existentialist worldviews in Thulin and Elm 1995: Religion, 132-133.

This overview of the religions – as simplifying as it may be – demonstrates how religions and *livsåskådningar* are both represented by means of the same categories, even though a distinction is made between *religioner* and *livsåskådningar*. Texts like *On the Origin of Species*, *The Communist Manifesto* or *Existentialism is a Humanism*, are regarded as "holy texts" for their respective traditions. *Livsåskådningar* as well as religions are characterised by providing explanations or theories about issues such as the origin of the world or of life, the meaning of life and what happens after death. Interestingly, in this overview, the *livsåskådningar* are the only traditions with their origins in Western Europe, whereas the religions mentioned originate from India (Hinduism, Buddhism) or the Middle East (Judaism, Christianity and Islam).

In recent textbooks, authors often try to take a global perspective and to focus on contemporary religion. *Livets Kurs*,[192] for example, a textbook for the *gymnasieskola*, concentrates on *livsåskådningar* today. Human beings with their beliefs are at the centre of what is studied. Björlin wants to emphasise similarities between religions and values that are shared across different religions. He presents different types of texts and introduces different aspects of the religions, for example *livs-*

---

192 Björlin 1996: Livets Kurs.

frågor, ethical questions and descriptions of the variety of beliefs and traditions in Sweden, today and in historical perspective. Some representations of religions include statements of people belonging to these religions in Sweden today. At the end of the book, there is an anthology with texts from the different religious traditions.

Often textbooks also contain interviews with people from Sweden who belong to a religion. One example of this is the opening passage of the chapter "Buddhismen" in Högberg's and Sunqvist's *Religionsboken*.[193] They present an interview with Elin Lagerkvist, who has been an active Buddhist since 1978. The short interview is about why she is a Buddhist, what she thinks is most important about her religion, how her life is influenced by her religion, if she has problems practicing her religion and what her message for Swedish youth is.[194]

In Thulin and Elm's *Religion*[195] in the chapters on tribal religions, Hinduism, Buddhism, Judaism, Christianity and Islam, information is given about history, sacred texts, the concepts of god (or "Is there a god?" in the Buddhism chapter), beliefs, religion today, different denominations within the religion, the religion in different countries and important or famous people. Every chapter also has specific points concerning particular characteristics of the religion in question. There is also a chapter on new religious movements (e.g. Jehovah's Witnesses, Mormons, and Bahai) and one about *livstro utan Gud* (non-theistic beliefs about life), which includes Darwin and evolutionary theory, socialism, existentialism, naturalism and ecosophy. The chapter *Etik* (ethics) contains texts about ethical choices, patterns, moral problems (including life and death, abortion), euthanasia (including suicide), violence (including mobbing, maltreatment, racism) and non-violence, security and community (including family, friends), drugs, sex and living together (including homosexuality), work, justice among countries and the environment. The last chapter on *livsfrågor* and society deals with ideas about existence, religions and society, god, life, death and the

---

193 Högberg and Sunqvist 1999: Religionsboken: 376f.
194 Ibid., 377. Her message is somewhat pedagogic. She says: "Jag vil uppmana dem att leva uppmärksamt, att tycka om sig själva och sätta värde på att de just är födda till människor, som har så stora möjligheter jämfört med andra varelser. Förstör inte heller din dyrbara kopp med alkohol eller droger. Stanna upp och försök lyssna till ditt inre. Försök att nå en uppriktig kontakt med ditt inre. Var självständig! Följ inte flocken eller gänget. Då kan du ge mer till andra." (ibid.) Perhaps this representation of Buddhism was also chosen for its pedagogical content. Probably some fundamentalist's message for young Swedish people would not have been included in a textbook.
195 Thulin and Elm 1995: Religion.

message of love (*kärleksbudskapet*) in different traditions, including also the United Nations' *Universal Declaration of Human Rights*.

Relief A+B[196] for the *gymnasieskola* has chapters on Judaism, Christianity, Islam, Hinduism and Buddhism, and two more chapters on Christianity. The representation of the individual religions follows a fixed structure: rites and life (visible aspects of the religions), beliefs and ethics (stories, oral tradition, sacred texts, intellectual commentaries, moral claims) and culture and society (societal aspects of religion). There are, however, extra topics in some chapters, like e.g. "The Jewish People" in the Judaism chapter, "Islam in Europe" in the Islam chapter, "One continent – many cultures" in the Hinduism chapter and "Religion in China" and "Religion in Japan" in the Buddhism chapter. The fixed structure for the different chapters was chosen in order to make it easier for students to compare the different religions. Informal spiritualities are characterised in the chapter "New Age", in which the historical background, main characteristics, criteria for success and criticisms of New Age are presented. The chapter on belief in Sweden comprises influences on the current situation, churches in Sweden and immigrant religions, new religions and New Age. There is also a chapter on "blended religions" (*blandreligioner*) with examples from Africa, Japan and Brazil.[197] The chapters about "sacred space" and "death and mourning" are written from a comparative perspective. The composition of this textbook shows how different approaches to a number of religions and religious phenomena in integrative RE, including comparative studies, may be supported with adequate teaching material.

Compared to standards in the academic study of religions, the information communicated in textbooks for schools certainly does have to be somewhat simplified. To find acceptable ways of simplifying which distort the representation of religions as little as possible, is definitely a difficult task. Special caution, however, is necessary whenever concepts from one tradition are transferred to others or when statements about all religions (or religion in general) are made. In the introductory chapter "Vad är religion?" of one textbook, for example, we can read the following about prayer and rites: "Bön är en rit som förekommer i alla religioner och som uttrycker människans beroende av en högre makt. I riten möts människa och gud, syligt och

---

[196] Arlebrand et al. 1998: Relief A+B.
[197] It may be added that the term "blended religions" is not entirely unproblematic. As no religion has emerged from a vacuum, and all religions draw on a variety of sources and traditions, it may be asked which religion, in fact, is not a blended religion at all.

osynligt."[198] This concept of prayer, for example, is very close to Friedrich Heiler's, which has often been criticised.[199] Especially its claim to universality and the transfer of the Christian concept of prayer to other religions, which forms the basis of this claim, should be carefully examined. As we have seen in Härenstam's findings about representation, the choice of concepts continues to be one of the central issues in RE. In this respect, the unreflected use of the word *världsreligionerna* (world religions) is also a problem. As will be discussed later, this very concept of a world religion may be problematic in itself if it does not solely refer to all the religions in the world.[200]

Most problematic aspects of representations of religions in textbooks do, in fact, relate to such an unreflected use of concepts (which are often Christian or Western) or theories which cannot necessarily be verified. One section I found in a textbook can perhaps serve as an illustration for both these problems. In the last chapter (*apokalyps – världens slut*) of Högberg's and Sunqvist's *Religionsboken*, there is a section on world religions, comprising Judaism, Islam, Christianity and a few sentences on "repeated ends of the world" mentioning the Aztecs, Greeks and Hinduism. Then there is a section on cults and sects (*kulter och sekter*) which comprises cargo cults in the Pacific, the Anabaptists, the Korpela movement,[201] Aum Shinrikyo (*"mördande teknosekt"*, Engl. "murderous technosect") and UFO. First, apart from the fact that the concepts *sekt* (sect) and *kult* (cult) are at least as problematic as the concept "world religion", the criteria for the differentiation between "world religions" and "cults and sects" are not really clear,[202] and second, the task at the end of the chapter – "Vad är det för människor som söker sig till den här typen av sekter?"[203] implies that there is some-

---

198 "Prayer is a rite that exists in all religions. It expresses man's dependency on a higher power. Man and god, visible and invisible meet in rites" (Arlebrand et al. 1998: Relief A+B, 5).
199 See Heiler 1917: Das Gebet; for a criticism of Heiler, see Waardenburg 1992: Friedrich Heiler und die Religionsphänomenologie.
200 In this case, it would be superfluous anyway, as all religions we know are religions in this world. For an investigation of the problems of the term *world religion*, see e.g. Jackson 1997: Religious Education. An Interpretive Approach, 53f.
201 The Korpela movement, which took its name from its leader, Toivo Korpela, was a Swedish apocalyptic movement which expected the end of the world in the 1930s.
202 Why, for example, is the Aztec religion a world religion and cargo cults not? There is no convincing reason to distinguish between religion, *kult* and *sekt*, particularly since the Swedish terms *kult* and *sekt* have negative connotations due to polemic use by established religions.
203 Högberg and Sunqvist 1999: Religionsboken, 455, "What kind of people join these types of sects?".

thing like a cult personality, i.e. a personality that makes you liable to join "cults", a theory that cannot be empirically verified.

5.3.2 Example: the representation of Islam in Swedish textbooks

A good discussion of the representation of Islam in Swedish textbooks was presented by Härenstam. In 1993, he published a study *Skolboksislam. Analys av bilden av islam i läroböcker i religionskunskap*,[204] which was part of the European research project "Islam in Textbooks".[205] Against the background of the Swedish school subject *religionskunskap*, the market for teaching material[206] and images of Islam, Härenstam analyses representations of Islam in Swedish teaching material for RE. He compares these to Islamic self-understanding and the goals of the Swedish school curriculum. The "Western image of Islam" (*Västerlandes bild av islam*) and the "mass media image of Islam" (*Massmediabilden av islam*) are contrasted with Islamic self-understanding defined as "the writings of some Muslim authors in some books".[207]

In the textbooks that were published prior to 1962, at a time when RE was still Christian and not integrative, there was only very brief information about Islam. Islam was often represented as fanatical and fatalistic, with Allah as a dictator. After 1962, when the concept of objectivity was introduced, emotive words were removed from the texts. Now the books gave some short historical information about the life of Muhammad and the five pillars of Islam, but no information at all about present-day Islam. In the books published between the 1969 and 1980 curricula, there is an emphasis on internationalisation and gender equality. All textbooks now mention the "low status of women in 'Islam'", which was not an issue in the earlier textbooks.[208]

---

204 Härenstam 1993: Skolboks-islam.
205 This research project, in which 22 countries participated, was initiated by the Islamic Scientific Academy (*Islamische Wissenschaftsakademie*) in Cologne. It was aimed at improving the representation of Islam in textbooks for schools on the basis of an analysis of existing representations of Islam in those textbooks. Härenstam's study is the Swedish contribution to this project.
206 Monopolistic tendencies are identified as a problem of the Swedish textbook market: "a very small number of books play a very dominant role." (282) For example, *Religion and liv* has about 80% of the market of textbooks for the upper level of RE in the grundskola. Cf. part I chapter 2 "Läroboken och läromedelsmarknaden" in Härenstam 1993: Skolboks-islam.
207 Härenstam 1993: Skolboks-islam, 283.
208 For the analysis of textbooks published before the 1980 curriculum, see part II (Swedish summary on p. 261f, English summary on p. 284) of Härenstam 1993: Skolboks-islam.

In the textbooks published after the 1980 curriculum for the *grundskola* and the 1970 curriculum for the *gymnasieskola*, Härenstam analyses the representations of God, *jihad*, and "women/family" and also presents results from an analysis of the representations of the Qur'an, Muhammad, and Islam in the world of today.[209] The characterisations of Allah are more negative in the upper level books. This may partly be a result of the fact that, at lower levels, the "little world of Islam" (home, family, traditions etc.) is presented, whereas the textbooks for the upper level of the *grundskola* and for the *gymnasieskola* present the "big world of Islam" (current affairs, politics etc.).[210] *Religion och liv, högstadiet*,[211] which has the most aggressive image of Allah, is most widespread in Swedish schools. Other books, such as *Vad är religion?* (What is religion?), which was written by specialists in each religion, focus more on Islamic self-understanding.

Women and family[212] are central themes in Swedish textbooks. Härenstam finds that the textbooks convey "[t]he overall impression... that Islam in some way supports the suppression of women".[213] Often the situation of women in a few countries is presented as representing Islam as a whole. An improvement of the position of women in Islam is often linked with secularisation. Most textbooks do not distinguish between Islam in the Qur'anic sense and the way Muslims have lived or live their lives today. Härenstam quotes one example of an extremely negative and stereotyped view of the situation of women in Islam: in a study book, the model answer to the task of giving examples of how Islam influences the life of women is: "There is female circumcision; in many countries women should be veiled; women are often required to stay at home."[214] In the books for the upper secondary

---

209 In chapter 2.5 of part IV, Härenstam presents a summary of his analysis of the representation of Islam in textbooks also for the school subject history. The complete analyses thereof as well as of the representations of the Qur'an, Muhammad and Islam in the world of today, can be found in a supplement.
210 Härenstam 1993: Skolboks-islam, 285.
211 *Högstadiet* is the highest of the three levels of the Swedish *grundskola*: 1. *lågstadiet* (junior level): years 1-3, ages 7-9; 2. *mellanstadiet* (intermediate level): years 4-6, ages 10-12; 3. *högstadiet* (upper level): years 7-9, ages 13-15. Cf. Härenstam 1993: Skolboks-islam, 281.
212 Note that this juxtaposition of women and family already contains an agenda which maps a particular field in which the role of women is described. Characteristically, the representation of women (and not men) in relation to family matters is described, which establishes a closer link between women and family than between men and family.
213 Ibid., 286.
214 Ibid., 287, unfortunately in the English summary from which I quote, Härenstam does not give the source of the quote.

school, one can also find many examples of Islam as supporting the oppression of women. For example, in *Liv, Människa, Mening* (life, human beings, meaning), one can read that, according to the Qur'an, women are required to wear a veil. This is, however, an interpretation that has been heavily criticised by Swedish Muslims. On the junior and intermediate levels, parallels between the Qur'an and the Bible are often emphasised, but sometimes quotes from the Qur'an are used to illustrate problems of people – especially women – living in Muslim countries. Härenstam even found one teacher's manual in which all that was said about the Qur'an was that it sanctioned the suppression of women. With respect to the Qur'an, most books focus on problems, but in some books for the gymnasieskola there is some general presentation of the different contents of the Qur'an, which is not just used as an illustration of social problems.

At junior and intermediate levels, Islam in the world of today is often represented by children from a rural area in the Middle East. Härenstam comments that "[t]his, of course, gives present-day Islam an image of something 'outmoded'."[215] Two books for the intermediate level, however, chose to also present Muslim immigrants to Sweden. Here, Islam is not seen as a problem for modern lifestyles, but as an inspiration or source of life in present-day Sweden. In the textbooks for the upper level, there is a much more aggressive representation of Islam. In one book, the only Muslim who is given a name is Khomeini and in the complementary reader, the following examples for Islam in present-day politics are chosen: The murder of Sadat, executions in Iran and Draconian punishments in Pakistan. These features can also be found in textbooks for the *gymnasieskola*, even though there is more emphasis on different interpretations of Islam and the difference between "Islam as an ideal" and Islam as it is actually practiced. Generally, Härenstam concludes, the closer the authors of the textbooks are to current research, the more their view resembles Muslim scholars' accounts of Islam. The books that were written by scholars who also do research in the study of religions (for example, Jan Hjärpe) are best. There is, however, still a lot of work to be done, as books like these are still an exception rather than the rule.

The integration of the subject into the social subjects can be seen as one reason for the shift towards a social anthropological approach to the representation of Islam. Härenstam regards a dialectical approach to the representation of Islam – for example, the one by Akbar S. Ahmed – , which distinguishes between Islam as an ideal and the way

---

215 Ibid., 288.

people live in Muslim countries as a possible model for representing not only Islam, but also other religions in Swedish RE. In this approach, the "ideal" is used as an inspiration and a criticism of actual "realities".[216] This suggestion is, however, not entirely unproblematic. The construction of an ideal and a criticism of actual practice by means of this ideal can already be regarded as a theological enterprise. This "ideal" necessarily implies a selection from all the different sources that are available. A careful study of tensions between different positions can definitely be regarded as helpful for understanding a religion. The construction of an ideal, however, takes this idea perhaps a bit too far.

Härenstam's analysis of Islam in Swedish textbooks shows that debates in other social and cultural areas, such as public discourse, politics or the media, have been mirrored in the changing representations of Islam in school textbooks over the years. His analysis also reveals that a sound representation of Islam in textbooks, which goes beyond the reproduction of stereotypes, requires expertise in the study of religions as well as in education on the part of the writers of textbooks.

---

216 Cf. ibid., 291.

6 The notion of education in Swedish RE

Concepts for RE are influenced considerably by their underlying notion of education and related issues such as the question of what exactly constitutes knowledge and understanding. Compared to the academic study of religions, the educational (*fostrande*) task of the subject is more important in school RE. In Sweden, RE is considered a part of the programme to educate responsible and articulate citizens. In this enterprise, factors like the learning atmosphere, the forms of learning and the way the encounter between children and adults takes place (the teacher and student roles) play an important role.[217]

In the *Skolverket* documents, training in reflection and critical thinking is regarded as an important element of the subject. This should be practised particularly with respect to ethical issues, the surrounding world and survival, "the need for a universally accepted international system of values"[218], and the way religion and outlooks on life are related to culture and society. The new *kursplan* (2000ff) has to be understood and interpreted against the background of the *kunskapssamhället* (knowledge society) and it is rooted in the concept of knowledge which was formulated in *Skola för bildning*.[219] There has to be a mental, emotional and value- relation between the pupils and the material which is studied. In the educational process, the relationship between teachers and students is of utmost importance.

In academic literature, different metaphors are used to describe this relationship. Hallberg sees the teacher as a Rabbi or Guru, someone who teaches others how to think.[220] Skogar regards teachers as adult examples or role models. They have to educate pupils into democratic and humane (*medmenskliga*) values. It is also their duty to stimulate critical thinking, even if this should challenge their own points of view.[221] According to Furenhed, it is the task of the teacher to encourage discussion and reflection. In this process, the notion of respect is vital: teachers have to respect the pupils as human beings looking for meaning, the experiences and the degrees of maturity of the pupils, and the right of the pupils to communicate or to be silent. Teachers should

---

217 Cf. Skogar 2000: I stormens öga, 103f.
218 "behovet av en allmängiltig internationellt övergripande värdegrund" (Skolverket: Kursplan religionskunskap gymnasieskola), engl. Skolverket 2000ff: Programme Manual, 125.
219 Statens offentliga utredningar 1992: 94, quoted in Hallberg 2000: Reflektioner kring kursplan 2000, 14.
220 Hallberg 2000: Reflektioner kring kursplan 2000, 15.
221 Skogar 2000: I stormens öga, 104.

also offer challenges to the pupils. They ought to enable them to explore existential questions creatively. Here, however, the teacher does not have to wait until the students formulate such questions. Teachers have the difficult but not impossible task of awakening the students' interest in *livsfrågor* which are perhaps only latently present for them.[222]

Teacher training for *religionskunskap* was reformed several times in Sweden. It contains the study of religions as well as education. The recurrent question has been, however, how to organise the combination of these two aspects of teacher training. Traditionally, a teacher training course followed the academic study of religions and another academic subject. However, recent reforms have aimed at also including pedagogical reflection at earlier stages of teacher education. The different universities and colleges of higher education have different programmes for educating and training future teachers of RE. Following the National Teacher Education Reform (*Lärarutbildningskommitténs slutbetänkande*) in 1999, the School of Teacher Education at Malmö University developed a new programme for teacher training for RE, called *Religionsvetenskap och Lärande* (The Study of Religions and Learning). This programme includes thematically oriented courses which "combine more theoretical studies of the history of- and comparative- religions, ethics and sociology of religions, cultural studies and analysis, with didactic, methodological and pedagogical studies."[223] As the students regularly visit "partner schools", a didactic approach to the study of religions forms an integral part of the programme, which has a clear focus on ethics and existential questions as well as on a comparative approach to the religions of the world.[224]

Closely related to the question of what education is, should be the question of what exactly constitutes knowledge and what kind of knowledge is desirable. Härenstam, who visited Benares several times with groups of teacher trainees with the intention of widening their horizons, breaking with ethnocentric patterns of thinking and understanding more about another culture, made an interesting observation. Every visit to Aghori Ashram left him with a different impression, and new impressions/new knowledge resulted in new interpretations. This led him to conclude that one never really knows the whole "truth" about something.[225] Härenstam distinguishes between two different notions of knowledge (*kunskap*) and quotes several educationists who support this distinction. Basically, he emphasises the difference be-

---

222 Cf. Furenhed 2000: Undervisning och förståelse, 129 and 138ff.
223 Liljefors Persson 2004: Religious studies and learning – and beyond!, 216.
224 For this programme and recent reforms in teacher training, see ibid.
225 Cf. Härenstam 2000: Kan du höra vindhästen?, 134f.

tween (1) the reproduction of previously presented facts or ideas and (2) a reorganisation and transformation of one's understanding stimulated by open questions.[226] Similarly, Michael Grimmitt contrasts (1) "[k]nowledge as objectively existent, external to the knower, presented through certain 'disciplines', 'public traditions' or 'common culture' and there to be discovered, mastered and learnt" with (2) "knowledge as a social construct, socially related and socially relative."[227] The first conception of knowledge (1), which has been considerably influential on teaching traditions in schools, sees knowledge as something impersonal and permanent, something that exists relatively independently from the *kunskapsbäraren* (bearer of knowledge).

The second conception of knowledge (2), acknowledges that the construction of reality happens within a context: social and linguistic contexts frame our conceptions of reality. There is no vantage point from which reality can be regarded objectively. "Facts" are formed by social and linguistic circumstances. Terms and concepts form realities and not vice versa. The acquisition of knowledge is a dialectical process that develops through dialogue and contact with other horizons. In this process, the task of the teacher is not to pass on to the pupils his or her own concept of reality, but to create the preconditions for the pupils to perceive new horizons and to acquire new perspectives on reality. This is not a matter of addition, but of reinterpretation and reorganisation.[228] In the second conception of knowledge, the claim to objectivity becomes problematic: "Däremot kan man tala om att söka nya tolkningar och perspekiv och om att vidga sina horisonter."[229] Härenstam introduces the distinction by Lars Løvlie, a Norwegian pedagogue, between analytic/positivistic and hermeneutic/dialectic knowledge. Løvlie describes the peculiarity of concepts for the latter as follows: "Dialektiske begreper försøker ikke å klassifisere kjennetegn ved ting som sommerfugler, biler eller planeter. Heller en å tilsvare 'objekter' i verden, beskriver de forløp eller processer i livet. De foholder seg ikke fotografisk, men snarare filmatisk till verden."[230]

---

226 Here Härenstam (ibid., 136) follows the Göteborg pedagogue Ference Marton.
227 Grimmitt 1987: RE and Human Development, 18, quoted in Härenstam 2000: Kan du höra vindhästen?, 136.
228 Cf. ibid., 20ff, quoted in Härenstam 2000: Kan du höra vindhästen?, 136f.
229 Härenstam 2000: Kan du höra vindhästen?, 138.
230 "Dialectic concepts do not seek to classify knowledge as things like butterflies, cars or planets. They describe processes in life, rather than objects in the world. Their perspective on the world resembles a film rather than a photograph." Løvlie 1992: Pedagogisk filosofi, 26; quoted in Härenstam 2000: Kan du höra vindhästen?, 138.

It is important that *kunskapsteoretiska frågor* (questions concerning theories of knowledge) are taken up in teacher training. Erling Lars Dale draws attention to the fact that a simplified positivistic concept of knowledge leads to a distinction between knowledge as objective and values as subjective. Then, fostering based on values becomes irrational. However, knowledge also has to do with understanding (Swed. *förståelse*, Norw. *forståelse*). Dale concludes: "Forståelsen uttrycks i bruken av en skikk eller en norm. Det vil si, at forståelsen uttryckes i praksis. Praksis er regelfølgende atferd. Det sentrale er ikke 'å følge' selve regelen. Det sentrals er at regelen er i bruk. Det utgjør regelens liv."[231] Understanding builds on the ability to analyse the interplay between the relationship between parts and wholes.[232] Knowledge that comprises this kind of understanding cannot be separated from norms and values. Dale calls this kind of knowledge *kulturellt kodifierad intuition*.[233]

Bernt Gustavsson's considerations about knowledge take up, for example, Hans Georg Gadamer's insight that we cannot leave our contexts behind us but only understand the world from our contexts as a starting point. Learning is the interpretation of what is new from the point of view of the known and recognisable. With this preliminary understanding in mind, we meet something other and different and this encounter between what we do and what we do not know is the meaning of education. We are always prejudiced in the way we believe we know what things are like. It is difficult to learn something new and to be able to open oneself to the unknown and strange. To meet something new in this way is strenuous, because it forces us to partly give up our former interpretations of the world. Interpretation is like a game, it is a circular process taking place between parts and wholes. Knowledge is acquired in a dialogical process with language as a medium and is therefore discursive in character. The acquisition of knowledge can take place, for example, in encounters with texts that describe something. These encounters result in reinterpretations of reality. Interpretation and understanding are endless processes. Education is

---

[231] "Understanding is expressed in the use of a custom or norm. This is to say that understanding is expressed in practice. Practice is what follows after a rule. The main issue is not "to follow" the rule itself, but the fact that the rule is being used. This is the meaning of rules." Dale 1992: Kunskap, 52f; quoted in Härenstam 2000: Kan du höra vindhästen?, 138.

[232] Cf. the similar debate in England, especially Robert Jackson's critical adoption of theories and methods from modern anthropology (for example by Clifford Geertz and some of his critics), see the section on the interpretive approach in chapter II.2.4.

[233] "culturally codified intuition", Dale 1992: Kunskap, 52f; quoted in Härenstam 2000: Kan du höra vindhästen?, 139.

about widening horizons and perceiving other horizons. The horizon of a person is not fixed, but changes with new experiences. To extend one's knowledge means to extend one's horizon.[234] Similar ideas can be found in the philosophical hermeneutics of H.C. Wind. He compares the interpretation of reality to a game with a set of rules but endless possible variations. As in a game, interpretation has no *givet facit* (fixed outcome) but can continuously develop.[235]

After a consideration of these Scandinavian contributions to the debate about notions of education, knowledge and understanding, Härenstam draws the following conclusions for the representation of religions in RE: an analytic/positivistic notion of education (a) implies a distinction between facts as descriptions of reality and values as expressions of and attitudes towards these facts. In this framework it is possible to talk about objectivity with respect to higher or lower correspondence with reality, whereas in the hermeneutic/dialectic notion of education (b) there is no objective starting point for interpreting the world. There is always some prejudice about the phenomenon that one is going to study. An encounter with a phenomenon results in a reinterpretation and change of this prejudice and gives rise to new horizons. An encounter with other horizons is a dynamic process in which horizons merge, whereby new interpretations and perspectives on the phenomenon emerge: "Kunskapsutveckling innebär vidning av horisonter från de utgångspunkter man har."[236] The role of language in this process of structuring reality is crucial.

In concepts for a RE which is based on the first notion of education (a) the claim to present a more or less objective picture of religions is possible. Therefore, in teaching material, facts about religions ought to be presented as neutrally and objectively as possible. Questions like "What characterises Tibetan Buddhism?" and "What are the differences to other Buddhist traditions?" can guide the students through their study of Buddhist traditions. Concepts based on the second notion of education (b) include a consideration of ever changing perspectives. Widening one's horizon as far as possible is attempted, while the fact that understanding is a never-ending process is taken into account as well. Pupils already have ideas about the religion to be studied in RE. Their prejudice may be taken as a starting point. As religiously mixed

---

234 Cf. Gustavsson 1996: Bildning i vår tid, quoted in Härenstam 2000: Kan du höra vindhästen?, 139ff.
235 Cf. Wind 1987: Historie og forståelse, quoted in Härenstam 2000: Kan du höra vindhästen?, 141.
236 "The acquisition of knowledge consists in a widening of the horizon of one's starting point." (Härenstam 2000: Kan du höra vindhästen?, 142).

classes are normal in integrative RE, these starting points of the students may be very different from each other. Understanding more about a religion involves permanent processes of extending one's *förståelsehorisont* (horizon of understanding), which includes the consideration of as many perspectives as possible on a phenomenon. An understanding of a phenomenon which is as multifaceted as religion does not have a cognitive dimension only, but also an emotional one. Textbooks building on these insights may present more controversial material with opposed and different views, texts which make the reader curious for more texts and also include fiction and poetry.[237]

In his survey of recent concepts of education and knowledge, Härenstam has shown convincingly that the implications of the notions of education underlying any concept for integrative RE can hardly be underestimated. They have a considerable impact on the way religions are represented in RE. This has to be considered at all levels of concepts for RE, from the governmental documents to academic literature and textbooks up to individual lesson planning by teachers. The issue of implementing pedagogic concepts with a particular – if tacit or otherwise – understanding of education and knowledge in integrative RE is again related to the question about the aims of integrative RE, which has been discussed above.[238] Härenstam's view is succinctly expressed in a sentence which he often quotes: "Kunskap är någons kunskap",[239] which clearly locates his approach within the hermeneutic/dialectic notion of education.

What is remarkable in Swedish academic literature about RE is the amount of research about the attitudes of teachers and pupils. Studies about pupils' attitudes towards religions, *livsåskådningar* and *livsfrågor* have accompanied integrative RE in Sweden from its very beginnings. The study *Tonåringen och livsfrågorna* (1969)[240] revealed that the pupils had great interest in existential and ethical questions, but only little interest in religions. The study argues that religions provide answers to these very questions. *Barn och Livsfrågor* (1975)[241] is a study about young children and the way they deal with existential questions. Similar

---

237 Cf. Härenstam 2000: Kan du höra vindhästen?, 140ff.
238 See section 3.1 of this chapter.
239 "Knowledge is someone's knowledge", see e.g. Härenstam 2000: Kan du höra vindhästen?, 145.
240 Ronnås 1969: Tonåringen och livsfrågorna: elevattityder och undervisningen i livsåskådning och etik på grundskolans högstadium.
241 Projektet Barn och Livsfrågor 1975: Små barn och stora frågor: en probleminventering bland lärare om livsfrågor i förskolan, på lågstadiet och på fritidshem.

studies are *Gymnasieeleven och livsfrågorna* (1974)[242] and *Tonåringen och livet* (1980).[243] Another popular field of research are the students' and teachers' attitudes towards the subject itself. Florheden und Lifmark, for example, study teachers' views on how respect and understanding for other people may be fostered in RE.[244] Ove Larsson studies pupils' understandings of the phenomenon religion and the subject *religionskunskap* in year 9.[245] His findings are that most pupils have an inclusive understanding of "religion", but an exclusive understanding of "religious" as something for a special group with special characteristics. Most pupils distance themselves from traditional forms of Christianity, but have a feeling that "there has to be something there", while not knowing what that is. Some pupils see common traits in the world religions. The perspective on the different religions is vital in the process of the students' understanding. Larsson recommends a combination of the three perspectives suggested by Almén comprising perspectives on culture, tradition and the individual.[246] Another study about the attitudes of students is Gunilla Selander's *Gymnasisten och det heliga. Två eleverundersökningar och några religionsdidaktiska/metodiska undersökningar*,[247] which studies what students say is holy for them and what they think about belief in fate or god. On this basis, she identifies different topics which might be worth including in RE, such as environmental awareness, friendship, democracy and religion, belief in fate, astrology and different paranormal phenomena. Ulf Sjödin studies values among teachers and students of *religionskunskap* in the *gymnasieskola*. His study is about the students' view on RE, *livsfrågorna*, leisure, the future, the environment, ethics and society, and the teachers' view on teaching, *livsåskådningsfrågorna* and their view of the pupils' attitudes.[248]

The different perspectives on education and RE show once again that integrative RE is a dynamic field, which is dependent on a cross-fertilisation of ideas and knowledge from different groups: scholars of religions, scholars of education, politicians, teachers and pupils. With respect to concepts for RE, empirical studies, for example about RE in

---

242 Skolöverstyrelsen 1974: Gymnasieeleven och livsfrågorna: studiematerial för lärare i so-ämnen, i första hand religionskunskap, på gymnaseiskolan.
243 Hasselrot 1980: Tonåringen och livet: undersökning och diskussion kring tonåringen och livsfrågorna.
244 Florheden and Lifmark 1994: Hinder och vägar.
245 Larsson 1991: Religion i skolan.
246 Ibid., 39ff.
247 G. Selander 1997: Gymnasisten och det heliga.
248 Cf. Sjödin 1995: En skola – flera världer.

the classroom, attitudes of teachers and pupils towards the subject etc. have led to considerable changes in and modifications of the subject. This was already an important point in the chapter on the history of integrative RE in Sweden. It is to be hoped that this constructive model for adjusting a school subject to academic and educational insights – rather than to religious or economic interests – will be adopted by other countries as well, particularly by those who do not yet have integrative RE, thus transforming the subject.

Chapter IV
Evaluation and Conclusions

Introduction

This final chapter evaluates different models for teaching about religions in the European context by referring back to the debates about theory and methodology in the study of religions and education. Building on this evaluation, it suggests a framework for integrative RE in Europe. The first section of this chapter presents conclusions from the preceding analyses of English and Swedish models for integrative RE (1). The next section (2) provides an analysis of the general situation of teaching and learning about different religions in schools in Europe, including a discussion of further examples from Norway, Germany and the Netherlands, and evaluates these different approaches against each other. The chapter concludes with a section (3) that outlines a framework for integrative RE as the model which has been found to be most appropriate for teaching about different religions in schools in Europe.

1 English and Swedish concepts for integrative RE

In this section, after a comparison of general features of integrative RE in England and Sweden (1.1), features relating to individual points which have been the foci in the analysis of English and Swedish concepts for integrative RE will be dealt with (1.2). These concern the aims of integrative RE, the concept of religion, the representation of religions and teaching methods, as well as the notion of education.

1.1 General features of integrative RE in England and Sweden

First of all, the study of integrative RE in England and Sweden has shown that there are well-reflected, generally accepted – by educationists, teachers, parents, pupils, politicians and religious communities – models of integrative RE in Europe, which have been used in actual school contexts for many years.

In English, Welsh and Swedish state schools, integrative RE is a compulsory subject from the beginning of primary school until upper secondary levels, where older students can choose certain subjects and drop others. In England it is still possible for parents to withdraw their children from integrative RE. In Sweden this option, which contradicts the general character of a subject which is particularly designed for pupils from diverse religious and non-religious backgrounds, was abolished in 1994.

The history and development of integrative RE has been rather different in England and Sweden. In Sweden, considerations about the unity of the school system in the face of differences in religion or worldview were decisive in the transformation of RE from a monoreligious to an integrative approach in the 1960s. The various national school and curriculum reforms that followed included repeated transformations of the school subject RE, mirrored in the different names that were given to the subject (including *kristendomskunskap, religionskunskap* and *människors frågor inför livet och existens*). In England, however, initiated above all by the groundbreaking work of the scholar of religions Ninian Smart, the transformation took place from the bottom to the top, due to local responsibilities for RE. In the 1970s, the first "multifaith" agreed syllabuses were drawn up, but integrative RE was not officially introduced on a national level before the 1998 Education Reform Act, even though it had been practiced in many schools for years.

Furthermore, the educational surroundings have been different in England and Sweden. In Swedish school politics, priority has been given to the socially integrative function of the state school – with its 9 years compulsory *grundskola* and 3 years *gymnasieskola* which almost all pupils attend. Unlike in England, there has been only a small minority of private schools in Sweden until recently, and the character of RE has always been regarded as a national concern. In England, the education system comprises different types of schools, including a variety of private schools. Even though the potential of comprehensive schools for producing a more equitable society was recognised by a number of politicians, these ideas have never really challenged the existing plural system. As RE has been the responsibility of local education authorities in England and Wales, various syllabuses were drawn up by the different agreed syllabus committees in the country. Even in the 1988 reform, when a national curriculum was introduced for all other subjects, RE remained under local responsibility. However, following the general trend to introduce nationwide "standards" in education, which involves making students reproduce testable standard knowledge, non-statutory national model syllabuses were published in 1994, which include key-word style information about six religions (Christianity, Buddhism, Hinduism, Islam, Judaism and Sikhism) and an – again non-statutory – national framework for RE, similar to the frameworks of national curriculum subjects, was introduced in 2004.[1]

As can be seen from the above remarks about different developments of integrative RE in England and Sweden, the organisation of and responsibilities for RE differ considerably in the two countries. While Sweden, a highly secularised country, which abolished its state church in 2000, follows a strictly educational approach, with the state authorities deciding upon the character and broad content of RE in the whole of Sweden, the general framework for RE in England as well as local practice have been negotiated between different interest groups. On a national level, "representatives" of religions were invited to take part in the discussions that preceded the publication of national model syllabuses. On a local level, cooperation between representatives of religious communities and educationists has been institutionalised for many years in the composition of agreed syllabus committees. All four groups of an agreed syllabus committee have to agree upon a syllabus. However, the composition of agreed syllabus committees also shows the residual power of the Church of England, which forms a group of its own, while all other religions and denominations are integrated into another group. This approach gives equal responsibility of RE to religious (the Church of England, "other" religions and denominations) and professional (teachers, representatives of the local education authorities) interest groups, each of them having the power of veto.

Notwithstanding the positive effects of an institutionalised cooperation between RE professionals and religious communities, which is definitely to be encouraged, this situation shows the ambivalence of English RE as opposed to the Swedish model: if RE was truly educational (i.e. "secular" and not religious), no religious interest group, let alone any religious community in particular – like the Church of England in the English model – can be granted the right of veto in curriculum development. Generally, cooperation between RE professionals and "insiders" of different religions is more than welcome and definitely an important factor for the acceptance of integrative RE among religious communities. However, educators ultimately have to decide upon the contents of RE, drawing not exclusively on the opinions of certain "representatives". A dynamic model for such cooperation and ways of including the results of such cooperation in RE curricula has

---

1 See chapter II.1.2: Organisation of integrative RE in England and Wales.

been shown in the interpretive approach by the Warwick team around Robert Jackson. Their work also relates to the important issue of the subtleties of power relations in these consultation processes,[2] which have to be considered by RE professionals. Despite various cooperation and consultation dynamics, the responsibility for RE ultimately has to be with study-of-religions trained RE professionals who are not dependent on the benevolence of any religious interest group.

As in other countries, RE has been a political issue in England and Sweden. Its introduction and development was accompanied by heated debates about the roles of majorities and minorities in multicultural societies. Interestingly, opposition to integrative RE in England and Sweden came less from religious communities, but more from conservative politicians who tried to preserve their conservative understanding of education and RE for the modern school. This resulted in a number of compromises in English RE, one of them being the formulation in the 1988 Education Reform Act itself, which privileges Christianity over other religions.[3] In Sweden, it was possible to establish an educational approach to integrative RE with fewer concessions to political and religious lobbies. Nevertheless, in Sweden problematic formulations in the official documents about RE, privileging "Christian ethic and Western Humanism" as particularly valuable, have also prevailed.[4]

1.2 Individual aspects of integrative RE in England and Sweden

According to the aspects of integrative RE, which were analysed in chapters II and III, this section will draw conclusions with respect to the aims of integrative RE (1.2.1), the concept of religion (1.2.2), the representation of religions (1.2.3) as well as teaching methods and the notion of education (1.2.4).

---

2 For example, with respect to the role of religious and belief communities that participated in the creation of the SCAA national model syllabuses, cf. e.g. Everington 1996: The relationship between educators and practitioners, 69f., 76; Jackson 1997: RE. An Interpretive Approach, 135.
3 For the debates about the Education Reform Act 1988 see chapter II, section 1.2.3.
4 See, for example, the respective formulations in the syllabuses or statements about the *värdegrund*, cf. e.g. chapter III.1.3.

1.2.1 Aims of integrative RE

In both England and Sweden the integrative approach to RE – as opposed to confessional approaches – is regarded as an important element of education in a multicultural society. In Sweden, the aims of RE are firmly based on the general philosophy of the school and reflect the secular approach to religions: knowledge and understanding of various religions, worldviews and views of life are seen as a prerequisite for forming one's own worldview, be it religious or non-religious. As school education is regarded as a means of assisting children in becoming well-informed and responsible individuals that respect their own and others' rights as citizens in a plural democracy, the approach to RE is also consistently emancipatory within a generally plural and conversational framework in which different interpretations of life are studied, particularly with respect to fundamental ethical questions.

From the introduction of integrative RE up to the present, the aims of RE in England and Wales have been contested. Three major approaches can be identified: (1) knowledge and understanding of different religious traditions, (2) mutual respect and harmony in a multicultural society and (3) personal, moral and spiritual development of the pupils.[5] Different approaches to RE give different emphases to each of these aims. For example, the prioritisation of knowledge and understanding in the national model syllabuses has led to a great deal of criticism. A most obvious difference in comparison with the Swedish model is, however, the emphasis on "spiritual development" in many English approaches. Even though many interpretations of "spirituality" and "spiritual development" comprise a wide range of phenomena and ideas, the emphasis on "spiritual development" in some approaches seems to regard spirituality as something of inherent value that the secular world lacks. The question is, however, if religion and spirituality can be fully separated so that this approach to spirituality does not prioritise religious worldviews over secular ones.

Some examples of English approaches to integrative RE have shown that, unlike in Sweden, the secular character of the subject and its aims is not always asserted in England, despite a broad consensus that the approach to religions in integrative RE cannot be the approach of any particular religion. This is most visible in the experiential approach, which has been designed to help the pupils on their way towards the experience of the sacred. "Believing" as a possible learning outcome of the methodology suggested in the *A Gift to the Child Project*

---

5   Cf. Everington 2000: Mission impossible? RE in the 1990s.

also seems to be religious rather than secular. However, even the national model syllabuses suggest skills and processes which are beyond a secular approach to religions when they include "synthesis", which is explained as "linking significant features of religion together in a coherent pattern" and "connecting different aspects of life into a meaningful whole."[6] The former citation sounds very much like what phenomenologists – as theologians of religions – have tried to do with respect to their construal of "religion as such" and the latter reminds one of the classical work of theologians. What if a child cannot see this meaningful whole of life, e.g. because his/her mother has just died of cancer? Has he or she not attained the aims of RE? The fact that tasks like "synthesis" may take RE a little too far is indirectly recognised in the model syllabus for 16 to 19-year-old students, who are meant to realise "that life poses questions which cannot easily be answered."[7] However, the pictures in the brochure of the national framework reinforce the impression that, along with contributing to harmony in a multicultural society – photographs in which people form the word "peace" and children with different skin colours play happily together –, synthesis in the above sense may also be intended – a picture in which the different religions are parts of a jigsaw puzzle, fitting neatly into each other and together forming a circle.[8]

In most individual academic approaches to RE in England, more subtle reflection about the aims of RE is presented, as e.g. in the Westhill Project or the interpretive and critical approaches. In those concepts, the different aims are combined, while attention is paid to the generally secular character of the subject. A comparison of the English and Swedish approaches with respect to the aims of RE shows that, in Sweden, there is more emphasis on forming one's own opinions and drawing one's own conclusions, while the focus in England is more on learning to cope with the diversity of religions in the country and worldwide. This may partly be a result of the different social, cultural and religious contexts in England, which has large religious minorities e.g. from former colonies, and Sweden, where for many people institutionalised religion has lost its relevance.

Ninian Smart's conclusion from a survey of RE in Russia, Sweden and England constructively integrates the different levels of aims that have been mentioned above within a generally secular framework for the subject. He presents three aspects of "religious studies in school" – as he calls integrative RE – including (1) general knowledge about re-

---

6   SCAA 1994: Model 1. Living Faiths Today, 5.
7   SCAA 1994: RE 16-19: 6.
8   See QCA 2004: RE. The Non-Statutory National Framework.

ligions and, more generally, worldviews in terms of world history, (2) the exploration of worldviews to sensitise students to the understanding and evaluation of differing ideas and practices and (3) the exploration of living questions.[9]

1.2.2 The concept of religion

The notion of religion on which approaches to RE are based often determines the actual contents of RE and, in particular, the way the different religions are represented. In Sweden, "religion" in RE contexts clearly comprises different religions, worldviews and views of life. *Livsåskådning* (view of life) is the key concept and hermeneutic key to these phenomena. Therefore, the perspective is somewhat wider than in the traditional focus on "six major world religions" in much of English RE, particularly in the national model syllabuses. The limits of this "major world religions" approach are evident and have been criticised, for example by the Warwick team. In some English approaches the classical phenomenological notion of religion – as used, for example, by Rudolf Otto, Gerardus van der Leeuw, Friedrich Heiler and Mircea Eliade – that refers to religions as related to "the holy" has prevailed, despite compelling arguments which have shown that it is unacceptable in a non-confessional framework.[10] In the *A Gift to the Child* approach, for example, religious items which are presented in the classroom are regarded as "numina", directly referring to Otto's terminology. In integrative RE environments, however, essentialist understandings of religion, which affirm the ultimate value of "real" religion, conflict with the children's experience of the actual ambivalence of religion. Andrew Wright has demonstrated convincingly that what he calls the "liberal consensus" about experiential-expressive models for RE, referring to a "generic religious experience", is a patronising neo-confessional framework depriving children of opportunities for authentic understanding beyond that particular religious philosophy.[11] Nevertheless, the experiential model is still used among others in teacher training and as teaching methodology in England. Paradoxically, the experiential model seems to be so appealing to many RE professionals that they do not really want to do without it, despite its failure in a truly integrative framework.

---

9   Smart 2000: Reflections on RE in Russia, Sweden and England, 106.
10 For this discussion in an RE context, see e.g. Jackson's account of the phenomenology of religion in Jackson 1997: RE – An Interpretive Approach, chapter 1.
11 See chapter II.2.5: The critical approach.

In Sweden, the concept *livsåskådning* has made it easier to find broad agreement about a secular concept of religion. Even though sometimes a distinction is made between religions and *livsåskådningar* – as in a teaching book that in an overview presents Hinduism, Buddhism, Christianity and Islam as religions and the scientific worldview, Socialism and Existentialism as *livsåskådingar* – normally not much time, if any, is spent trying to define what the difference between these two is. Ultimately, it seems impossible to make out this difference without falling back into essentialist notions of religion. The concept *livsåskådning* widens the horizon so that traditions which are – outside the study of religions departments – not commonly regarded as religions are included. Contrary to the latter approach, in England more attention is paid to the difference between religious and non-religious worldviews, regardless of the problems this distinction presents for a secular framework. One of the national model syllabuses for RE even includes "learning to make distinctions between secular and religious interpretations of life in modern society"[12] among the aims of RE. Non-religious worldviews are sometimes included in English RE as well,[13] but the general focus is much more on what is traditionally called religion. Despite critical accounts of the "six-major-world-religions" typology, it is difficult for me to imagine, for example, the Warwick team producing a textbook *Socialists* along with the existent textbooks *Hindus*, *Christians* and *Muslims* in the *Interpreting Religions* series. This is, however, not really a criticism of the interpretive approach, but could equally be applied to study-of-religions programmes at university, which normally only very rarely deal with "secular" worldviews, even if this is inconsistent with the general understanding of religion of most European scholars of religions. The interpretive approach is built on a well-reflected notion of religion, which pays particular attention to the internal diversity of religions, drawing on insights from the study of religions and cultural anthropology.

The traditional understanding of religion is challenged in the narrative approach, which uses postmodern criticism for a radical reassessment of the "subject matter" of RE. The notion of "tradition" is criticised and the question is posed as to why RE ought to reproduce the *grand narratives* of religions, and thereby also reproduce existent power relations, and silence the *small narratives* of the children, which ought to be regarded as equally valuable. These criticisms are important points for methodological considerations about the representation of religions.

---

12 SCAA 1994: RE 16-19: 6.
13 For example, Humanism or Socialism are sometimes mentioned.

However, not dealing with the *grand narratives* of the religions at all would deprive the children of opportunities of learning about phenomena – be they narratives, constructions or whatever – that are actually highly influential in social, cultural and political life. The Westhill Project's concepts of religion and map of the field of RE were taken up as a general model in the "European RE-scene". At the EFTRE[14] conference in Edinburgh in 2001, a modified version of the Westhill concept of the field as consisting of *traditional belief systems, shared human experience* and *individual patterns of belief* has been used as the common understanding of the framework for RE in Europe, slightly rephrased as *living faith systems, shared human experience* and *ultimate questions*.[15] Even though the focus on the present, using "living" instead of "traditional", seems appropriate for RE, the formulation "ultimate questions" is reminiscent of particular Protestant traditions and the *livsfråga*-approach to RE, which has turned out to be not unproblematic in Sweden.

Edgar Almén's and Carl Axel Aurelius' observation that "new" non-confessional concepts of religion still resemble traditional ones is of interest here.[16] Even though it is evident that integrative RE cannot be built on a concept of religion that is applicable to one religion only – a problem that occurred, for example, in the Stapleford Project – a continual critical reconsideration even of currently acceptable concepts of religion on which integrative RE is based seems necessary, including their explicit or implicit presuppositions and consequences.

1.2.3 The representation of religions

The notion of religion, which underlies any concept for RE, has implications for the way religions are represented in this concept. In Sweden the *livsfrågor*- and *livsåskådnings*-approaches to religions have influenced the representation of religions in official documents and academic literature about RE, as well as in teaching material. The *livsfråga*-approach, which owes much to Protestant theological traditions, particularly the theology of Paul Tillich, caused several problems as an overall framework for the representation of religions in RE. Above all, it seemed difficult to bridge the actual questions and interests of the

---

14 The European Forum for Teachers of RE.
15 Schreiner 2002: Different approaches – common aims? Current developments in RE in Europe, 96f.
16 Almén and Aurelius 2000: Some second thoughts about RE in Great Britain, Russia, and Sweden, 134.

pupils with the material that was to be taught about the religious traditions. Nevertheless, the idea that questions about life and existence may present starting points in RE has survived, e.g. in the teaching book *Tio frågor til livet*,[17] which is structured completely around *livsfrågor*.

However, the concept *livsåskådning* has emerged as the more appropriate framework for the representation of religions. It provides a starting point for approaching different religions, worldviews and views of life from a non-religious point of view. Comparisons frequently emphasise the conceptual and the ethical dimensions of these traditions, with a particular focus on contemporary religion. The roots of the former can be seen in the focus on dogmas in the Lutheran tradition in Sweden, which is now reflected in the description of all religions, worldviews and views of life.[18] The latter – the focus on ethics – pertains to the particular relevance of RE in the context of the Swedish school system with respect to the common *värdegrund* in the face of diversity.

Academic literature about the representation of religions in Swedish RE provides sophisticated theoretical and methodological reflection that points a way to how study-of-religions expertise can be transferred to school contexts. This includes e.g. the use of primary sources, relating religious concepts to questions that transcend the immediate context, choosing a starting point which is interesting for all religions in comparisons, while leaving room for distinctive features of the individual religions. The Geels/Johanesson debate about the kind of selection of aspects of religions that may be most beneficial for the pupils (their argument relates to different ways of presenting Hinduism) is part of the general question of which aspects of religions should be selected and to what extent the representation of religions may be instrumentalised for pedagogical purposes. An answer to their immediate concern about whether a study of the Upanishads or of traditional Indian village spirituality is more appropriate in RE seems easy: both aspects of the Hindu traditions should have a place in RE, accompanied by reflection about these differences within "traditions". However, this debate addresses further questions concerning representation of religions within the framework of a particular philosophy of education.

Some scholars take up more general issues related to the representation of religions and cultures in plural environments. Kjell Härenstam's work about the representation of individual religions, for example Tibetan Buddhism, Islam and "tribal religions", is a particularly

---

17 Westerberg/Linnér 1997: Tio frågor till livet.
18 Cf. Almén and Aurelius 2000: Some second thoughts on RE in Great Britain, Russia and Sweden, 133.

valuable contribution to the debates about the representation of religions in RE as well as to broader questions about representation. In his analyses of the representations of these religions in academic literature and Swedish textbooks for RE, Härenstam shows what kind of misrepresentations and stereotypes of these religions have prevailed and offers creative strategies for avoiding them. His conclusions for adequate representations of religions in RE, including attention to the internal diversity of traditions, ethnocentrism, reductionism, and the discrepancy between different insider- and outsider-constructions of religions, are of substantial relevance to integrative RE as well as the academic study of religions in Sweden and beyond.

If in Sweden much consideration is given to concepts, in England the main focus of interest is more on religious practice and actual encounters with religious people, buildings, rites etc., possibly because RE is generally very much regarded as a means of promoting mutual understanding in multicultural Britain. The question of whether the different religions ought to be studied "thematically" (comparatively) or "systematically" (separately, one after another) is only the tip of the iceberg in an ideological battle about an appropriate concept of religion and religious plurality on which representations of religions in RE may be based. In the English debate, a generic concept of religions as essentially similar has been linked to the thematic approach, whereas a concept of different religions as discrete, incompatible entities has been linked to the systematic approach. In my opinion, close scrutiny of the different arguments reveals that these links are false. In fact, they are misleading and unnecessarily narrow perspectives for the representation of religions. By contrast, once an acceptable concept of religion and religious plurality beyond the simplifications mentioned above is found, the practical issue of whether religions ought to be presented thematically or systematically loses its ideological character and it will emerge that both approaches can be usefully combined in integrative RE. In the thematic approach, it is important to keep in mind that phenomena may look similar but have very different meanings. As a debate in the study of religions has shown, in order to avoid gross distortions, the intentions behind visible phenomena have to be given due consideration. This involves a careful selection of the concepts which are to be compared. It has been suggested by the Westhill team that concepts ought to be selected for their meaning rather than for their appearance. This means, for example, that a comparison of prophets, founders and holy texts may be less appropriate than a comparison of concepts of e.g. the human being, justice, community, or of life after death. A good combination of the thematic and systematic approaches, showing awareness of the futility of superficial comparisons, has been presented by the Westhill Project. The project team suggests starting either by presenting aspects of an individual religion in order to communicate conceptual knowledge about that religion or to start with "life-themes", aspects of common human experience, and contextualising these with reference to at least two religious traditions. These two ways of approaching religion in RE also reflect the distinction between explicit and implicit religion, which has been particularly influential in the British context.

To find a non-theological, secular framework for the representation of religions in integrative RE seems more difficult a task than may be expected. Andrew Wright's criticism of the "liberal consensus" about a particular – despite all claims to the contrary, in effect theological – concept of religion and the representation of religions it brings about, has revealed how deeply some representations of religions have been rooted in a particular theology of religions. It seems as if some groups do not really want to conceive of integrative RE as a secular subject and therefore just ignore criticisms like Wright's and promote their religious concepts nevertheless. This may be possible because not many people are experienced in clearly distinguishing between religious and secular concepts of religion. Pluralistic or universal theologies may seem to be appropriate solutions at first sight. However, as Wright has demonstrated, this approach creates insoluble problems, particularly with respect to the difference between this particular theology and the self-conceptions of adherents to different religions. In its most extreme form, the experiential approach concentrates solely on preparing pupils for this supposedly generic religious experience and dispenses completely with the representation of any lived religion, apart from its own universal theology. Contrary to this, a non-religious framework for the representation of religions needs to include voices of insiders about their religions, unfiltered by any universal philosophy or theology of religions. This opinion is shared by the majority of English academic concepts of religion which have been discussed in this study. Therefore, even though Wright definitely addressed an important problem and a blatant inconsistency in some concepts for RE, most recent approaches to RE avoid those mistakes and suggest useful strategies for representing religions in integrative RE.

The great variety of approaches to representing individual religions is mirrored in different kinds of teaching material. The *A Gift to the Child Project*, for example, has published teaching material that can be used to present individual items from different religions to very young pupils. The analysis of this approach has shown how important its "contextualisation stage" is, in which information is considered about the meaning that the items, previously introduced independently of their contexts, may have for believers from the tradition of which they are taken. Furthermore, the analysis revealed how difficult it can sometimes be to define the border between religious and secular activities in RE.[19] Very creative and well-reflected representations of religions, which include recent theory and methodology in the academic study of religions as well as cultural anthropology, are presented by the Warwick team. Starting from Robert Jackson's three-layer model of religions (individual, membership group, wider religious tradition) and the question of what is actually important for children to learn about different religions, it has produced teaching material which is partly based on ethnographic research among children of different religions in Britain. In these teaching books, young individuals are not only included, but provide the starting points for learning to interpret religions. Having been personally introduced in the beginning, they accompany the reader through the whole book, while different topics relating to the wider religious tradition to which they belong are explored. The methods of the Warwick project present various ways of bridging the world of the pupils and the religious individuals, groups and traditions which the pupils encounter in RE.[20]

In an integrative RE which has emerged from former monoreligious or confessional Christian models, intended to introduce children to this particular tradition, a new perspective on Christianity and new methodologies for teaching Christianity in a changed environment are necessary. In England and Sweden this issue has been given particular attention. In the Swedish context, Edgar Almén points out problems which may arise when Christianity is taught using an integrative approach.[21] In England, the Chichester and Stapleford projects both provide concepts for representing Christianity in integrative RE. Diversity and dynamics within Christianity, having frequently been neglected, are presented in the Chichester approach, in particular with respect to political dimensions, implicit and civil dimensions as well as the role of religion in world affairs. While the Chichester approach aims at firmly grounding teaching Christianity in an integrative framework and therefore employs a concept of religion that is not confined to Christianity, but is applicable to the variety of religions, the Stapleford approach with its "concept cracking" method is built on a concept of religion that focuses on Christianity only and cannot be transferred to other relig-

---

19   See chapter II.2.2.
20   See chapter II.2.4.
21   Almén 2000: Frestelser och vägmärken för undervisningen om kristendomen.

ions. Therefore, the latter approach is of limited value for integrative RE, failing to place teaching Christianity firmly in an integrative environment. Nevertheless, it is not impossible to transfer the method of "concept cracking" to teaching different religions in an integrative approach. However, in order to take it beyond its immediate applicability in a broadly Christian environment, where it was designed for teaching Christian concepts in particular, some aspects of the Stapleford project as it presents itself in its publications, would have to be modified.[22]

From the analysis of different approaches to representing the variety of religions in integrative RE, several points have emerged to which special attention ought to be given in teaching designs:

(1) The intended impartial treatment of the different traditions is at risk when the representation of religions is dominated by terms and concepts of one particular tradition without any reflection about this problem being included. This is, for example, the case in the English SCAA national model syllabus for 16 to 19 year old students, where only Christian concepts, including e.g. prayer, the existence of God, the problem of evil, miracles, discipleship and mysticism, are suggested as topics for a comparative study of religions. It would be interesting to try to design a similar comparative approach starting from e.g. Buddhist instead of Christian concepts. A comparison of these two approaches could show the limitations of either approach. Though this problem may not be so obvious in many other approaches, it is nevertheless often present. What is more, it may hardly be possible to avoid it completely. Therefore, it is even more important that this very problem itself is communicated to the students and that reflection about it accompanies comparative studies of religions. A related issue is the discrepancy between insider and outsider terminology with respect to the study of new or minority religions. This is obvious in clearly pejorative vocabulary, like "sekt" (sect) or "kult" (cult) in Swedish, but may be less apparent in other concepts.

(2) Another frequent problem is the unequal treatment of religions – despite all affirmations to the contrary – including a conscious or unconscious reproduction of various types of discourses of "othering". These forms of "traditional narrow-mindedness" may partly reflect "the colonial habit of describing the 'foreign' with help of parallels to the 'centre of the world'".[23] Generally, all rhetoric of, for

---

22 Cf. my critical evaluation of the Stapleford project in chapter II.2.9.
23 Almén and Aurelius 2000: Some second thoughts on RE in Great Britain, Russia, and Sweden, 133.

example, a "principal religion" that ought to "predominate" in RE as opposed to "other" religions[24] or the recurrent construction of a uniform and somehow Christian-Humanist "cultural heritage" of a country or a region, which – unlike "other" traditions – deserves special appreciation, is unacceptable in an integrative framework. National documents both in England and Sweden contain these problematic formulations and this issue remains contested among educationists, who want a truly impartial approach, and – mostly Christian-conservative – politicians who fear that their country or Europe may lose something when it really grants equal rights to all religions.

(3) A sole focus on only one of the different dimensions of religions has caused misunderstandings. For example, frequently religious concepts which are parts of canonical texts have been presented to the pupils while other dimensions were neglected. Therefore, an "ideal view" of a religion, often as described several hundred years ago, has been mistaken for the whole of this religion with its contemporary forms and internal diversity. This limited understanding of religions was challenged by the obvious discrepancy between these constructions and actual encounters with religious people, or the role of religions in social, cultural and political systems. Most approaches to RE have widened their perspectives about the variety of dimensions of religions in the context of a general focus shift from historical to contemporary aspects. However, care is still necessary to prevent over-emphasising any of the dimensions while leaving out others.

(4) Jane and Clive Erricker have drawn attention to an important question that ought to be kept in mind about the general framework in which religions are represented, as well as to the selection of individual phenomena presented in RE: to what extent does RE reproduce the *grand narratives* of major institutionalised religions, thereby strengthening their positions while excluding "heresies", minority voices and *small narratives* of individuals, including the children themselves? In my view, an appropriate reply to this problem cannot do completely without these *grand narratives*, as this would disregard the importance of knowing about their influence in the contemporary world. Attention to the subtleties of various

---

24 Sometimes even "other principal religions", which makes another dimension of the problem visible, as this phrase implies that there are even two types of "others": "other principal religions" than Christianity, referring probably to what is regarded as "other world religions", and "other other" religions which are not principal, referring probably to new, small, or indigenous religions.

power-relations and privileges makes it very important indeed for the children to learn to understand these processes while they are familiarised with *grand narratives*, so-called "heresies", minority voices and individual *small narratives*, as well as being given space for articulating their own ideas. Nevertheless, this point is a serious challenge for teaching methodology and demonstrates that avoiding a reification of concepts that are problematic in integrative RE may turn out to be more difficult than initially expected.

The analysis of concepts for representing religions in integrative RE shows that important decisions precede any such representation. These decisions have to be taken consciously on the basis of general theoretical and methodological considerations. Many of the problems that have arisen in individual approaches might have been avoided if such reflection had been included. Attention to the generally secular framework of RE, the selection of religions and phenomena to be represented, attention to dynamics, the ambivalence of religion as well as to internal diversity and various power relations, have turned out to be particularly delicate issues. Furthermore, my study of English and Swedish approaches clearly demonstrates that methodological considerations about the approach to the variety of religions, worldviews and views of life have to become an integral part of RE in order to avoid patronising the pupils by introducing them to unquestioned paradigms.

1.2.4 Teaching methods and the concept of education

Integrative approaches to RE involve a general shift from former religious approaches of instructing the children in one particular tradition to non-religious educational approaches which are intended to communicate to the children skills and knowledge that enable them to deal with the plurality of religions. The main task for teaching methodology is to find ways of engaging the pupils with the material they ought to study. In England and Sweden, a wide range of methods has been suggested, including, for example, visits, participant observation, direct encounters with believers, interviews, dialogue, text study, interpretive methods etc. Concepts for integrative RE offer a creative variety of approaches. For example, the *A Gift to the Child* approach introduces a particular strategy of presenting religious items in the classroom and contextualising them in the religious context from which they are taken. In a further development of this approach within a constructivist pedagogical framework, Grimmitt presents further teaching strategies, which start with an encouragement of the pupils' own interpretations and experiences and relate these to alternative contextualised interpretations, accompanied by a more general reflection about different interests in interpretation processes. A very interesting approach to learning about religions, concerned particularly with migrant religion, is the Euro-Islam course offered at Rudbeck's school in Sollentuna, north of Stockholm. It includes different kinds of activities in which the students themselves do empirical research, including observations, interviews and an analysis of the representation of religions in the media, all related to the pupils' own prior and possibly changing understanding of Islam in Europe.[25] The interpretive approach by the Warwick team offers activities which employ different interpretive methods (*making it clear, working it out, building bridges* and *thinking it through*) in order to promote conversation and bridge the worlds of the pupils and the material studied. As Jackson puts it, this learning process may result in "edification", a re-assessment of one's own way of life in the light of the study of other worldviews.[26] In a generally ideology-critical framework, the narrative approach rejects the notion of "subject matter" – the material pupils ought to study – and proposes a subject in which children are not presented "with the sanitising ideological platitudes of religious tradition",[27] but rather introduced to the complex processes in which meaning, values and community are constructed.

Some authors have paid particular attention to child development in their design of teaching methods. An early influential approach was that of Ronald Goldman, who applied the Piagetian framework of different levels of operational thinking to RE in order to find ways of teaching the Bible which are appropriate to the respective developmental stages of children. Most recent approaches include reflection about which methods may be appropriate for children of different ages. For example, the Westhill project includes reflection about educational aims that are particularly relevant for children of a certain age, while also paying attention to not distorting religions unduly when they are instrumentalised in the service of the development of the pupils. The *A Gift to the Child-* and Stapleford approaches are particularly concerned with methods for teaching selected religious items or complex concepts to younger children. However, other approaches also integrate reflection about child development, be it by letting children of the same age explain their views in textbooks (interpretive approach), starting with children's stories (narrative approach), paying respect to the "horizon of the pupils" (critical approach) or starting from the pupils' construc-

---

25   Cf. chapter III.3.3.2.2.
26   Jackson 1997: RE. An Interpretive Approach, 112.
27   C. and J. Erricker 2000: The Children and Worldviews Project, 204.

tions of the meaning of a religious object (constructivist approach). It goes without saying that, like in other school subjects, any development of teaching methods for integrative RE has to build on considerations about the target group for which these methods are designed. This includes age and development among other factors.

Experiences with teaching methods in integrative RE have shown that one of the major challenges is finding ways of bridging the two dimensions of the subject: the *descriptive* dimension, relating to phenomena of explicit religion, religions, worldviews and views of life, and the *existential* dimension, relating to implicit religion and the interests, interpretations, concerns and environments of the pupils with a particular emphasis on their development. The combination of these two aspects of integrative RE within a general non-normative framework is managed very well in most of the approaches from England and Sweden.[28] Among the creative strategies for practising ways of changing perspectives are *owning* (e.g. in phrases like "I think", "it seems to me that", etc.) and *grounding* (e.g. "some people say", "the Qur'an says that" etc.) of arguments in classroom conversation, suggested by the Westhill team.

Another important issue in the study of concepts for RE is the interplay between the educational task of the school subject and the representation of religions. This gives rise to the question in how far religions are instrumentalised to serve the development of the pupils. Furthermore, to what extent is this acceptable or even unavoidable? William Kay's account of the Swedish approach seems over-critical in this respect. He concludes from Almén's description of a particular trend in the history of Swedish RE, which argues that RE "should concentrate on those elements in the religious traditions that could be of special interest for Swedish adolescents today",[29] that in the Swedish model "[t]he religious tradition is in effect made in the image of the Swedish adolescent", not being allowed to speak for itself and therefore in danger of becoming "a domestic animal, tamed, losing its wild and rich contradictions and passions, something that makes it less radical, less able to form the foundation of a social critique and, therefore, perhaps less likely to allow religion to flourish within Swedish culture".[30] Even though Kay addresses an important challenge for any kind of integrative RE with respect to insider and outsider constructions of

---

28 There are, however, a few exceptions, in which the general approach to RE is still defined by a normative theological approach. This is the case in the English experiential and the Stapleford approaches.
29 Almén 2000: RE in Sweden, 80.
30 Kay 2000: British comment on the Swedish PPI, 119.

traditions, in my view his criticism of the Swedish model goes a little too far, particularly as these points have been integral parts of the Swedish academic debate about RE and strategies of how to deal with that challenge have been presented. Furthermore, this criticism may be equally addressed to some English models, as my own analyses and those of others have shown. However, these points have also been taken up in English approaches and it is to be hoped that they will continue to be considered in future approaches to RE.

Methodological self-criticism with respect to these questions and a continual reconsideration of the aims and methods of teaching RE may help to further improve models for integrative RE. The inclusion of different voices of insiders is another efficient means of raising awareness for the diversity of interpretations within traditions. A comparison and contrast of different interpretations may, furthermore, help to understand the dynamics between insider and outsider constructions, of which RE itself is a part. The study of different traditions as suggested in Swedish contexts, including a close scrutiny of concepts, actual practice and other dimensions, with respect to basic questions such as equality, human rights etc. within a generally critical framework, firmly places this model in an emancipatory educational approach.

As we have seen, the school subject integrative RE itself has a critical and emancipatory impetus, having emerged from a particular understanding of education in plural environments. A top-down approach, in which a curriculum is "delivered", is challenged by an approach that enables children to deal with various kinds of information. Beyond this background, the question of what exactly constitutes knowledge is considered a major concern in many approaches to integrative RE. This difficult and controversial issue involves the questions of what kind of knowledge is desirable in school contexts and how that knowledge can be communicated. Obviously, knowledge in integrative RE cannot mean unreflected acceptance of religious teachings, but includes knowledge about those teachings. Most approaches recognise that knowledge is socially constructed. This implies that they include in-class reflection about what kind of knowledge is acquired in RE. However, despite all constructivism, there are political and social facts, which often have to do with religion or worldview, that children need to learn about.[31] If Härenstam's claim that knowledge is always "somebody's knowledge"[32] is kept in mind, a conversational approach to religions, whose starting point is made explicit, is possible.

---

31 Smart 2000: Reflection about RE in Russia, Sweden and England, 104.
32 "någons kunskap", see Härenstam 2000: Kan du höra vindhästen?, 123ff.

In Sweden, knowledge and understanding of religions is regarded as a prerequisite for forming one's own view of life,[33] which again is an integral element of education towards emancipated and responsible citizenship in a country which is part of a globalising world. In England, the common understanding of the subject – outside academia – focuses more on the communication of respect for the traditions as such, as a prerequisite for harmony in a pluralist and multicultural society. While English concepts offer a variety of ideas about the existential dimension of RE, a dimension which not everybody clearly conceives of as non-religious – or at least not as non-spiritual, in Sweden, the existential dimension of RE is not tinted with an aura of spirituality. In fact, spirituality or even "spiritual education" is not much of an issue in Sweden at all. In England, however, "spiritual education" is regarded not only as an aim for RE, but also for school in general, which ought to promote the "spiritual, moral, cultural, mental and physical development of pupils".[34] Here, spirituality is regarded as a part of every human being. Therefore, spiritual education is regarded as an integral element of school life. As has been noted, however, interpretations of "spiritual" vary and range from very religious to (almost) secular concepts. Possibly this ambivalence is a compromise which again allows for a variety of interpretations, ranging from a religious to a secular understanding of the aims of the school. Clearly emancipatory approaches (e.g. by Jackson, Grimmitt or Erricker) conflict with conservative political trends which continue to regard education as a means of transmitting basically unquestioned values of particular traditions.

From my analysis of approaches to RE, the following general conclusions can be drawn about a concept of education on which integrative RE may be based:

(1) Wright's critical approach in particular has shown that, rather than imposing premature solutions on them, children have to be introduced to the relevant questions, encouraging a critical awareness of ideology, also with respect to the representation of religions. The quality of shared discourse enables understanding beyond premature agreement about a false consensus. Methodological considerations about different approaches to religious plurality – including integrative RE – have to be an integral part of the subject. Communicating these complex issues to pupils and students of different

---

33 The latter may be called the Swedish way of "learning from" religions, cf. Härenstam 2000: How to choose knowledge for Swedish schools and text-books in RE, 41.
34 UK Parliament 1998: Education Reform Act, section 1.2.

ages is by no means an easy task for teachers.[35] However, it is not impossible and several creative ways of doing this have been shown in the existent approaches.

(2) In England, new trends that have brought about a market-led, output and assessment orientated, centralised education system built on a technicist understanding of education in order to create common standards in terms of easily testable knowledge,[36] fundamentally contradict the emancipatory task of integrative RE. The idea of quantitative measurement in accordance with pre-determined levels of attainment is ignorant of the concept of the curriculum as a process. National attainment testing brings about the decrease of influence of teachers, educationists, academics and local authorities. Market-led, managerial, standards-driven and performativistic approaches to education are by no means a problem for integrative RE alone, but fundamentally challenge educational systems at all levels, not only in England, but in a number of European countries.

(3) Education always has an ideological and political dimension. As we have seen, even integrative RE that attempts to take an impartial perspective on the variety of religions is based on a number of ideological positions about education, democracy, human rights etc. In the face of this, it is very important to consciously choose this ideological framework and make explicit the presuppositions of an approach so that the kind of ideology children are being introduced to is clear. Despite the problems of individual formulations that privilege particular traditions and therefore ought to be revised, the *värdegrund* in the Swedish context is one example of how this may be done skilfully.

(4) Having said that, it has to be noted that there is a stark discrepancy between progressive concepts of education that attempt to communicate ideas about emancipation, democracy, equal rights, the dignity of human beings etc. and political realities, in which concepts like this have become dissolute, while mere rhetoric has survived. It may be difficult to inspire children with an enthusiasm for these values while many aspects of the ideology of the society they live in fundamentally contradict those values. On the other hand, this contradiction may make integrative RE a very relevant subject in the school curriculum, as it challenges different (overt or covert)

---

35 For a comparative account of the different understandings of the role of the teacher in a number of English approaches to RE, see Copley 2004: Is UK RE failing to address its own culture context?.

36 For these formulations cf. Grimmitt 2000: The captivity and liberation of RE and the meaning and significance of pedagogy, e.g. 13.

ideological positions and their consequences, including the dominant one, which may rarely be questioned elsewhere.

The continuing debates about different aspects of integrative RE have shown that an ideal model for integrative RE is unlikely to be found over night. However, an analysis of concepts for RE demonstrates that a number of excellent models already exist in countries in which integrative RE has been a school subject for some time. Furthermore, it demonstrates how important it is that educationists from different levels of the education system act responsibly in the interests of the educational task of the school in order to make sure that integrative RE is included as an integral element of school education.

2 Integrative RE in the European context

Learning and teaching about different religions in schools is organised differently in the individual European countries. The Anglo-Welsh and Swedish approaches are by no means representative of the situation of RE in Europe. On the contrary, integrative approaches to RE are still in the minority in Europe, despite a general acknowledgement of the challenges of religious plurality for traditional models of RE. This section starts with a description of the general situation of religious education in state schools in Europe, with a particular emphasis on the question about the general kind of frameworks (religious or non-religious) in which children are being taught about the variety of religions (2.1). After that, examples of the different approaches will be considered (2.2), and conclusions will be drawn about the different frameworks (2.3).

2.1 Learning and teaching about different religions in Europe

2.1.1 European RE in transition

RE and academic research about RE are both in a state of transition in Europe. A good outline of the social, political and religious contexts of these changes is provided by Nils G. Holm in his account of religious diversity in secular Europe,[37] in which he analyses the current religious situation in Europe as a background for the international research project *Understanding Christianity and Islam in Secular Europe*. I cannot refer to individual points of his analysis here, but what is important is his understanding of "secular" as something that is not influenced by religious institutions. Furthermore, his account of "secularisation" is helpful: he refers to Bryan Wilson's understanding of secularisation as a process "by which religious thinking, practices, and institutions lose their significance for the operation of the social system"[38] and gives examples of related phenomena, such as pluralisation, fragmentation and privatisation, but also draws attention to phenomena which contradict the secularisation thesis, such as the emergence of new religious movements or religious fundamentalism. The opposite of the so-called secularisation is even more clearly described by Tim Jensen, who talks

---

[37] Holm 2000: Introduction, 11ff.
[38] Wilson 1998: The secularization thesis. Criticisms and rebuttals, 49.

about a kind of de-secularization and re-vitalization of religion, which relates

> "a) to a tendency towards a relative increase in the degree that otherwise secularized individuals and larger groups of the otherwise secular society (politicians, decisionmakers, public opinion-makers), accept and use religious concepts and postulates to found, legitimize (or criticize) various opinions and aspects of life and society and to inform them when they want to make the "right" ethical and political choices, and
>
> b) to an increase in the efforts of certain more or less institutionalized religious (not always so-called fundamentalist) groups to regain lost domains in public and political life."[39]

These accounts of the ambivalence of the present religious situation of religions in Europe may suffice to set the scene of the debates about RE. Along with the general shift of RE research towards more attention to the plural religious landscape in Europe, increased international networking has characterised recent years of RE research, including, for example, organisations like the *European Forum for Teachers of Religious Education* (EFTRE), which supports cooperation of national and regional teachers' associations and other organisations and which has a very informative website with information on RE in individual European countries.[40] While many international RE organisations have special relations with particular religious communities,[41] the *European Association for World Religions in Education* (EAWRE) is an independent association of scholars and educators. It has a clear multi-religious orientation and intends to promote adequate teaching of world religions in European RE. Apart from other academic networks, such as the *European Network for Religious Education through Contextual Approaches* (ENRECA, set up in 1999), or the *European Network for Inter-religious and Inter-cultural Education* with scholars from North Europe and South Africa, there is also more informal international cooperation and exchange about research and teaching methods.

Cooperation among European scholars and educators about different approaches to RE in the face of religious diversity often takes place at international conferences with subsequent publications of the conference proceedings. This kind of cooperation is flourishing. Therefore, it is only possible to give examples of important and influential joint publications in recent years, which all deal with the situation and chal-

---

39 Jensen 1997: Familiar and unfamiliar challenges to the study and teaching of religions, 201f.
40 See EFTRE 2005: RE in Europe 2005 (http://re-xs.ucsm.ac.uk/eftre/reeurope.html)
41 E.g. the *Intereuropean Commission on Church and State* (ICCS) or the *International Association for Christian Education*.

lenges of RE in different European countries: Schreiner et al. 1997: *Identitätsbildung im pluralen Europa*, with articles on different responses of individual countries to recent challenges for RE; Tidmann 1999: *Into the Third Millenium – EFTRE conference August 1998 in Copenhagen*, which focuses particularly on approaches from Northern European countries; Chidester, Stonier and Tobler 1999: *Diversity as Ethos. Challenges for Interreligious and Intercultural Education*, which includes experiences from South Africa and Europe; Holm 2000: *Islam and Christianity in School Religious Education*, the result of a research project on the development of methods for "multi-cultural and multi-religious teaching, where the minorities are given a profile and can actually participate in the teaching process"[42] and a follow-up course for teachers from different European countries; Heimbrock 2001: *Towards Religious Competence. Diversity as a Challenge for Education in Europe*; Broadbent and Brown 2002: *Issues in Religious Education*; Jackson 2003: *International Perspectives on Citizenship, Education and Religious Diversity*; and Gustavsson and Larsson 2004: *Towards a European Perspective on Religious Education*, which focuses particularly on RE research. Furthermore, there are several journals that also provide a platform for the international debate, including *Panorama: International Journal of Comparative Religious Education and Values* or the *British Journal of Religious Education*. All these publications are treasure troves for RE research and practice in different European (and also some other) countries.

Two points, however, ought to be kept in mind about these international RE networks:

(1) Cooperation exists mainly between Northern European scholars. The networks of RE researchers do not yet involve many people from the Eastern and Southern parts of Europe or researchers representing traditions other than those of Western Europe.[43]

(2) Scholars and teachers from different countries often have very different ideas about what they mean by RE and what RE ought to be like. This is partly due to the different approaches in individual countries, and partly due to different ideological positions about the appropriate character of RE in state schools. Therefore, it is necessary to differentiate between some major approaches to teaching about different religions in school RE.

---

42 Holm 2000: Preface, 7.
43 Cf. Gustavsson/Larsson 2004: RE research for the future, 355f.

2.1.2 Accounts of the situation of RE in Europe

Several internationally engaged scholars have analysed the different approaches to RE in European countries from different points of view, among them Hans Spinder, Herbert Schultze, Hans-Mikael Holt, Peter Schreiner, Robert Jackson and Tim Jensen. Before I describe my own approach to this field, I would like to briefly introduce the analyses by Schreiner, Jensen and Jackson in order to highlight different foci of the debate. Almost comprehensive coverage of the general situation of RE in individual European countries has been provided in the publications by Schreiner, who works at the Comenius-Institut in Germany, a Protestant centre for research and development in education. In 1997 and 2002, he presented schematic overviews listing the following characteristics of the respective approaches to RE in almost all member states of the Council of Europe:[44]

- approach to RE, which divides the approaches in "confessional" (including the different religious groups who offer confessional RE) vs. "non-confessional"
- status of the subject: optional, compulsory or "optional-compulsory"
- substitute or alternative subjects
- responsibility for syllabuses
- remarks about individual points such as exceptions, majority and minority religions, faith-based schools or recent changes

These overviews are very valuable as first impressions of the general situation of RE in Europe. More detailed information is presented in a collected volume by Schreiner, *Religious Education in Europe* (2000), in which RE professionals from 24 different countries briefly describe the situation of RE in their own countries. They were asked to include the following information: the place of RE in the education system; names of the subject(s); the approach: "confessional – non-confessional, ecumenical and/or interreligious";[45] links with churches and other religious communities; status of the subject and any alternative subjects; responsibilities for curricula, syllabuses and teaching material; current problems, discussions and perspectives. This book is a rich source of information about the situation of RE in individual European countries. However, as the situation of RE has been changing rapidly in the past few years, the information may be somewhat dated by now. Recent

---

44 Cf. Schreiner 2002: Overview of RE in Europe, 91-93.
45 Schreiner 2000: RE in Europe, 7.

developments can be found on the homepage of the *European Forum for Teachers of Religious Education* (EFTRE).[46] In his article "Different approaches – common aims? Current developments in religious education in Europe" (2002) Schreiner identifies two main approaches to RE in Europe,

(1) *the religious studies approach* and
(2) *the denominational or confessional approach.*

He relates this difference to different RE "biographies" in European countries, with respect to the religious landscape of the country, the role and value of religion in society and the structure of the education system, its history and politics. These two distinct approaches involve different responsibilities with respect to the contents of RE, teacher training, curriculum development and teaching material. Schreiner also identifies an "overlapping area" where there is cooperation between the state and the religious communities. In this context, he mentions the Anglo-Welsh model with its agreed syllabus conferences as well as the shared responsibility of state and religious communities for the RE syllabuses in Germany. From his comparison of aims for RE, Schreiner concludes that in many European models there is convergence in practice, despite different theoretical approaches. He observes a general shift towards more educational (as opposed to religious) approaches. Starting from the aims of the subject, Schreiner (2002: RE in the European context, 2005: RE in Europe) also provides another distinction between the following main types of RE in Europe:

(1) *education into religion*: introducing pupils into one specific faith tradition;
(2) *education about religions*, referring to "religious knowledge"[47] and "religious studies"; and
(3) *education from religion*, which includes a consideration of different answers to major religious and moral issues as well as developing one's own views in a reflective way.[48]

However, Schreiner emphasises that this is an ideal-typical view of the different models. Often elements of all these models are integrated into one single approach. His view of "good RE" is that it should include elements from all these three perspectives.[49] With respect to the organi-

---

46 See EFTRE 2005: RE in Europe (http://re-xs.ucsm.ac.uk/eftre/reeurope.html).
47 Whatever that may be; for the time being I interpret it as "knowledge about religions".
48 See e.g. Schreiner 2005: RE in Europe, 3.
49 Schreiner 2002: RE in the European context, 87.

sation models for RE, Schreiner distinguishes between (1.) the complete absence of RE in public schools,[50] (2.) exclusive responsibility of the state, (3.) cooperative models where the state and religions share responsibilities and (4.) confessional or denominational approaches in which the religious communities alone are responsible for RE. Schreiner notes that denominational approaches are often considered as the realisation of state neutrality and individual freedom of religion,[51] and that in many countries, particularly in those where a state church has been dominant, there has been a development from a broadly confessional approach to a non-confessional one.[52] Schreiner describes his account of current problems of and obstacles – such as ambivalent terminology, language and culture barriers – to a "Europeanisation" of RE and identifies the following major challenges for RE in Europe: the tension between encouraging open-mindedness and transmitting values in RE; different concepts of education, particularly the tension between limited views pertaining, for example, to economic needs and professional views; and different accounts of the role of spirituality in RE. Regarding another important issue in the debate about RE in Europe, i.e. the question of the extent to which RE can be neutral with respect to different religious or ideological positions, he concludes that education in general cannot be neutral and always has to do with norms, values and different interests.[53]

The Danish scholar of religions, Tim Jensen, who is based at the University of Odense, takes a more evaluative view of the situation of RE in Europe. He regards confessional RE as biased solely in favour of the dominant majority religion. In his analyses, he identifies the following European ways of handling RE:[54]

(1) *no RE in public education at all*
(2) *state-guaranteed RE in public schools*
    a. *confessional*
    b. *non-confessional*

Jensen regards the first solution (1), *no public RE at all* (e.g. in France, with the exception of Alsace-Lorraine, and some post-communist states), in which RE is totally privatised, in the hands of parents and the respective religions only, as an expression of the view that RE can only

---

50 In most of France, Montenegro, Slovenia and Albania.
51 Schreiner 2002: RE in the European context, 88.
52 Schreiner 2005: RE in Europe, 3.
53 Ibid., 3.
54 See e.g. Jensen 1999: Religion and RE in a Europe of conflicting trends, 149ff., 2002: RE in public schools – a must for the secular state, 85.

be religious and confessional. However, he continues, this is untrue and, furthermore, runs contrary to essential interests of the secular state, preventing pupils from acquiring knowledge about important aspects of cultural and national history and neglecting the function that knowledge about different religions acquired in non-confessional secular RE may have for the promotion of peaceful interaction and communication in a multi-religious state and the world. What is more, this model, in which RE is solely confessional and almost exclusively assumes the form of instruction in the parents' and children's own religions at home or in religious institutions, is in total contrast to central ideas of the Enlightenment, and its educational concept disregards the importance of knowledge and critical faculty as a prerequisite for responsible citizenship. The second solution (2), *state-guaranteed RE in public schools* falls into two very distinct sub-categories, despite individual legal specifics: (2.a) *confessional RE*, "guaranteed and authorized by the state, but run and practiced by religious institutions – mainly the dominant Christian churches which also make up the syllabi – sometimes in cooperation with the state or the local authorities,"[55] for example in Finland, Austria, Belgium, Poland, and most federal states of Germany, (2.b) *non-confessional RE*, "guaranteed, authorized and run by the (secular) state which, via the Parliament and the Ministry of Education, draw up the (normative) executive order, syllabi and guidelines of the subject",[56] which can be found in England, Wales, Scotland, Denmark, Sweden and Norway. In contrast to the latter approaches, the confessional approach is also used in the Scholae Europaea of the European Union.

In countries with *confessional RE* (2.a) frequently alternative subjects, e.g. "ethics" or "philosophy" are offered to pupils who do not want to take part in confessional RE. In Jensen's analysis, the confessional approach is predominantly religious instruction, primarily in the majority religion (i.e. church) of the state. Teaching about religions may be included, particularly at secondary levels. However, Jensen's points that "the teaching about the other religions tends to be a teaching from the point of view of the dominant religious tradition" and that "teachers *may* be professional teachers, with or without a special and close relation to the church, but they may also be members of the clergy or teachers appointed by and educated by the church"[57] are crucial, particularly as this issue very often tends to be neglected in other accounts of the representation of different religions in confessional RE.

---

55 Jensen 2002: RE in public schools – a must for the secular state, 85.
56 Ibid.
57 Ibid.

In countries with *non-confessional RE* about different religions (2.b), teachers are educated via the departments of the study of religions at public universities, or teacher training seminars. National curricula may leave space for local variation, particularly at primary levels. Despite the common non-confessional approach, the models of the individual countries differ considerably, for example with respect to provision, the possibility to be exempted from RE or ways of cooperating with religious communities.

As we have seen, Jensen rejects solution (1), *no RE in public schools*, for a number of compelling reasons. However, he is equally critical of *state-guaranteed confessional RE* (2a) and argues that it is not in the interest of secular states to support one religion above others. Jensen convincingly refutes two common arguments against non-confessional RE, namely the positions that only people who know religion ("as such" or one religion) from the "inside" would be qualified to teach RE and that respect for other believers would be easier for a believer than a non-believer.[58] His position about arguments referring to the dangers of relativism, which is also often put forward in the confessional vs. non-confessional RE-debate, will be taken up later, when general issues that have emerged from the European debate will be discussed (section 3.1.3). Jensen supports his conclusion that "[t]his leaves us with something close to either the Scandinavian or the British (Scottish) ways of doing things"[59] with a statement made by teachers, mostly from countries without a state governed non-confessional or confessional RE, like France, Spain or some former communist countries, who attended a teachers' seminar at the Parliament of Europe in 1994. They argued in favour of a state-guaranteed, non-confessional RE about the diversity of faiths and diversity within faiths on the basis of a study-of-religions approach to the subject.[60] However, these recommendations have been ignored not only by the Council of Europe and many of its member states, but also by the various European RE associations.[61] Rather than

---

58 Jensen demonstrates that the former position would impede the development of knowledge and the transmission of knowledge, within both the natural and human sciences: "Veterinarians do not have to be cows to attain knowledge about cows. ... Likewise, psychoanalysts do not have to share the idiosyncrasies of their patients, gynaecologists do not have to be women, and political scientists do not have to be members of a party and supportive of the political ideology in question to analyze and understand a political party or ideology, nor politics in general." (2002: RE in public schools – a must for the secular state, 86). The latter position is even easier to refute, having a long and bloody history of empirical evidence against it (ibid.).
59 Jensen 1999: Religion and RE in a Europe of conflicting trends, 152.
60 Palmer 1995: "Studying Religions in Social Sciences at school". Report on the 65th European Teachers Seminar Donaueschingen, Germany, 24-29 October 1994.
61 Jensen 2002: RE in public schools – a must for the secular state, 86.

repeatedly trying to get hold of the differences between the respective backgrounds of European models of RE, Jensen argues, consideration ought to be given to what kind of RE is appropriate as an obligatory subject in secular European education systems today. His own ideas about this issue will be taken up later, when the general framework for integrative RE for European countries will be considered (section 3).

The third account of models of teaching different religions in RE to be discussed here is the one by Robert Jackson of the University of Warwick, England, whose own interpretive approach has already been discussed in chapter II.2.4. Unlike Schreiner or Jensen, Jackson is not directly concerned with the situation of RE in individual European countries, neither is he as keen on distinguishing precisely between confessional and non-confessional frameworks for teaching about religious diversity. In his recent publications, he analyses approaches to religion and RE in England and Wales, but also relates to projects and issues in other countries and international networks. His particular interest is in broader social, cultural and educational issues which lie behind different pedagogies of RE. In *Rethinking Religious Education and Plurality. Issues in Diversity and Pedagogy* (2004) he distinguishes between attempts to insulate young people from plurality and diversity and pedagogies acknowledging plurality. Among the former are e.g. approaches which (1.) regard Christianity as the religious heritage of British national culture, (2.) arguments against RE in state schools, as well as (3.) separating children by sending them to faith-based schools. While Jackson clearly states the inadequacy of (1.) and (2.) in plural societies, he only tentatively criticises faith-based schools (3.), taking a pragmatic conciliatory position in a country with a strong faith-based private school sector, which is unlikely to be integrated into the state school system in the near future.

Among the pedagogies which acknowledge plurality, Jackson discusses the *religious literacy* approach, as well as *postmodernist*, *interpretive* and *dialogical* approaches. He criticises the *postmodernist approach*, as put forward by Clive and Jane Erricker (cf. also chapter II.2.7), for its prerequisite of anti-realism and its total emphasis on the children's personal narratives, denying them opportunities to study wider issues, and the *religious literacy approach* by Andrew Wright for its tendency to reify religions and to pay little attention to emotional elements in religions. Despite these criticisms, he acknowledges the important contribution of these two approaches to the general debate about RE. In the postmodernist approach, he particularly appreciates that the pupils' concerns are made a key element of RE, the children are involved as agents, and educators are reminded not to lose sight of general education policy and its relation to socially instrumental goals. Furthermore, the inclusiveness of the religious literacy approach, which does not exclude any position (e.g. because it may be considered radical or conservative), is valued, as well as its acknowledgement of difference, attention to the power of language and insistence on the application of critical skills to data from religions.[62] The three *dialogical approaches* by Heid Leganger-Korgstad (Norway), Wolfram Weiße (Hamburg, Germany, cf. below: section 2.2.1) and Julia Ipgrave (England), which Jackson also discusses along with his interpretive approach, are appreciated in particular for their emphasis on pupils as agents, e.g. in the processes of selecting and reviewing topics and methods of study. The pupils are given opportunities to reflect critically on both contents and methods of study. Generally, the interpretive and dialogical approaches pay a great deal of attention to the development of skills and appropriate attitudes for the study of religions and issues concerning religion and values.[63] A very interesting example of how pupils may participate in planning and evaluating teaching and learning processes is the formation of a youth shadow Standing Advisory Council for Religious Education (SACRE) in the city of Bradford, whose suggestions for RE comprised an unbiased approach to RE which covers a range of religions, exploration of the full complexity of topics, and having specialist teachers.[64] In his conclusions, Jackson considers epistemological, political and ethical foundations for a pluralistic religious education and the contribution such an RE can make to multi- or intercultural education, citizenship education and values education in an international perspective. I shall return to this approach in section 3.1.3, where issues and questions related to integrative RE in the context of wider cultural, social and political issues are taken up.

The three accounts of teaching different religions in RE in Europe by Schreiner, Jensen and Jackson have different emphases, despite some similarities. Schreiner provides a descriptive and informative account of the situation of RE in almost all European countries. He does not evaluate the different approaches against each other, but seems to appreciate all the different ways of dealing with religious diversity in school RE. Unlike Schreiner, who claims that good RE ought to com-

---

62 For Jackson's account of the postmodernist and religious literacy approaches, see chapters 4 and 5 in Rethinking RE and Plurality. Issues in Diversity and Pedagogy (2004).
63 Cf. Jackson 2004: Rethinking RE and Plurality. Issues in Diversity and Pedagogy, 163.
64 See Miller 2003: "Faith and belonging in Bradford" in: RE Today, 20.3, 34, quoted in Jackson 2004: Rethinking RE and Plurality. Issues in Diversity and Pedagogy, 164.

prise all the three aspects that he identified: *education into religion, education about religion* and *education from religion*, I do not think that *education into religion* should be part of the curriculum of state schools in Europe. This seems to be something religious communities may wish to provide, but less so a task for secular schools. My account of the aims of RE in different European countries is also different from Schreiner's view that aims converge despite the difference between approaches. Confessional-separative and non-confessional integrative approaches are based on different notions of education and different accounts of the task of state schools. This can be demonstrated with the examples he uses from England, Finland and Germany. As in the Swedish model, the English example from the Manchester Agreed Syllabus of 1996 reflects the general aims of integrative approaches which have been called *learning about religion(s)* and *learning from religion(s)* in England. Christianity as the majority religion may be given special attention. However, the *approach* to Christianity is the same as the approach to other religions. This understanding is incompatible with the aims Schreiner quotes from Finnish and German examples for recommendations for confessional RE. The Finnish example states that the student should familiarise "him/herself *with his/her own denomination and religion* and its cultural inheritance in order to get stimuli to form a personal outlook on life", and study *"other religions and value and belief systems* with the aim of learning to respect people who carry different convictions...".[65] The confessional character of these aims cannot be overlooked: close study of and stimuli from one's "own" tradition (i.e. Lutheran Christianity for most Finnish students) and additional knowledge of "other" religions and value and belief systems in order to respect people with "other" religions and coexist with them in a multicultural society. The German example, a statement from an association of Protestant and Catholic RE teachers, is even more explicit about the confessional aims of the subject, which is intended to provide "orientation and advice" in questions of an ethically responsible life and "to pass on religious knowledge and religious experiences".[66] That "orientation and advice" in the latter example will be given from a particular religious point of view may be speculation. However, passing on religious knowledge and religious experience is obviously beyond what is possible in non-confessional integrative models.

---

65 Framework for the Senior Secondary School 1994: 87, quoted in Pyysiäinen 1999: 44 (italics WA).
66 Statement by the Association of Protestant and Catholic RE teachers in Württemberg (1997), quoted in Schreiner 2002: Different approaches – common aims?, 99.

Contrary to Schreiner, Jensen does not attempt to harmonise the differences between confessional-separative and non-confessional integrative approaches, but clearly addresses the fundamental differences between these approaches, above all with respect to the general responsibility for RE. He decisively rejects confessional RE in state schools on the grounds of his understanding of the task of education in secular and plural societies. His conclusion is that a non-confessional integrative approach, which is based on the methodology of the study of religions – similar to some British and Scandinavian models, is the only one acceptable for secular Europe. Jensen shows what is at stake in the debates about religions and RE in Europe: traditional power and privilege of established religions and worldviews vs. truly secular and educational approaches which relate to critical faculty and emancipation of young citizens.

Jackson's approach is, like Schreiner's, more conciliatory about different kinds of organising RE, including faith-based schools, as long as an open perspective is provided. However, he is severely critical of anti-plural positions. Furthermore, in his account of approaches to plurality, he uses academic expertise from different disciplines to show implicit and explicit racism inherent in some contributions to the debate about multicultural societies. His vision of pluralistic RE and its contribution to intercultural, multicultural, citizenship and values education in an international perspective, which comprises cooperation between educators and religious communities, is broad enough to meet with approval by different interest groups. Jackson's conciliatory approach may turn out to be an efficient means of making integrative RE – though not without compromise with respect to responsibilities – an element of different educational systems in the near future.

We have seen that RE is in a state of transition in most European countries. Apart from a small minority of countries which do not provide education about religions at all – although this is also changing, as the French example shows[67] – most models in some way or another respond to the challenge of including learning about religious diversity in the school curriculum. Focusing on the different general frameworks for teaching about religious diversity in state schools in Europe, I would like to suggest the following distinction between major approaches:

---

[67] In French education politics there have recently been initiatives to make learning about different religions an aspect of the school curriculum. Cf. Debray 2002: L'Enseignement du fait religieux dans l'école laïque.

(1) *integrative RE as an individual subject*
(2) *separative approaches: teaching about different religions in separative confessional or "alternative" subjects*
(3) *integrative RE as a "learning dimension": inclusion of aspects of integrative RE in other parts of the curriculum.*

In the following, individual examples of those approaches will be discussed (2.2), and conclusions about the different frameworks of teaching about religious diversity in Europe will be drawn (2.3).

2.2 Examples of models and changes in individual European countries

In this section, individual examples of the major approaches to teaching different religions in RE in European countries will be discussed. Particular emphasis will be given to recent changes. The examples are taken from Norway, which introduced the integrative approach in 1997 (2.2.1), Germany, where most RE is separative, i.e. children may chose between different forms of confessional RE or "alternative" subjects, although some integrative models exist in individual federal states (2.2.2), and the Netherlands, where integrative RE has been introduced as a "learning dimension" which may be realised in an individual subject or be integrated into other subjects or school activities (2.2.3).

2.2.1 Integrative RE as an individual school subject – Norway

Apart from England, Wales and Sweden, whose approaches have been discussed at length in chapters II and III, Scotland, Denmark and Norway also have integrative RE as an individual school subject. A brief look at the Norwegian example may help to highlight some of the issues that arise when formerly confessional approaches are transformed into integrative ones. Unlike England, Wales and Sweden, which can look back on decades of experience with integrative RE, Norway introduced this new subject, called *Kristendomskunnskap med religions- og livssynsorientering* (KRL, "Knowledge of Christianity with religion and life-philosophy orientation")[68] in 1997. In Norway, 88% of the population belong to the Church of Norway and the king as well the majority

---

68 The official English translation, "religious knowledge and ethical education" (see Børresen 2002: Interkulturelle und interreligiöse Bildung in Norwegen, 104), withholds information about the particular emphasis on Christianity in KRL.

of the government have to belong to the state church. About 7% of the 4.6 million inhabitants of Norway have an immigrant background.[69]

Before 1997, RE had been Lutheran confessional *kristendomskunnskap* (knowledge about Christianity) or, since 1971, alternatively *livssynskunnskap* ("philosophy of life"). Often, however, neither of these alternatives were an option for immigrant children, as these RE alternatives were taught at the same time as first-language education for those children whose mother tongue was not Norwegian.[70] In a plural society, where many people feel that the doctrines and values of the church have lost credibility, and other religions, most visibly Islam, have come to the country, a separative-confessional approach was no longer regarded adequate. As Breidlid and Nicolaisen put it: "Such deprivation of a common space for dialogue and exchange of existential views has been dissatisfactory for the teachers as well as for the students."[71] The idea was that, rather than being separated when it comes to religion, children ought to learn together about Christianity, the dominant religion in Norway, as well as about other religions and views of life. As in Sweden, the common *grundskolen*, a 10-year comprehensive school comprising primary and lower secondary levels, is regarded as a tool for creating social cohesion and national solidarity. Only a small minority of children visit private schools.[72]

The very name of the subject, which since 2001 has been called *Kristendoms- religions- og livssynskunnskap* (KRL, "Christianity and general religious and moral education"),[73] shows that it has been shaped by political compromises. Despite the fact that, in this subject, the different religions and views of life ought to be studied with the same impartial methodology, and despite the rhetoric of pluralism and dialogue, the subject still privileges Christianity. In 2001, the Ministry of Education appointed a group to revise the KRL syllabus on the basis of the first experiences with the subject. This group suggested, for example, abolishing the Christian bias inherent in the "Christianity and 'others'" structure of the parts into which the subject was divided for the lower grades: (1.) Bible knowledge, (2.) the history of Christianity, (3.) the Christian interpretation of life, (4.) other religions, and (5.) ethical and

---

69 Cf. Børresen 2002: Kulturelle und religiöse Vielfalt in Norwegen, 97f. see also Statistisk Centralbyrå 2003: Statistics Norway: Population.
70 Cf. Børresen 2002: Interkulturelle und interreligiöse Bildung in Norwegen, 103.
71 Breidlid and Nicolaisen 2004: Multi-faith RE in a religiously-mixed context: some Norwegian perspectives, 69.
72 Cf. Thomassen 2005: RE in a pluralistic society: experiences from Norway; Børresen 2002: Interkulturelle und interreligiöse Bildung in Norwegen, 101.
73 This is the official translation that Thomassen (2005) and Skeie (2004) use. The literal translation is "Knowledge of Christianity, Religions and Views of Life".

philosophical issues. The revision group presented an alternative, more thematic, structure with three parts: (1.) main narratives of the world religions, (2.) main festivals and worship, and (3.) ethical issues, while 55% of the classroom time should still be devoted to Christianity, a proportion prescribed by the Norwegian Parliament. However, this change was rejected after the Ministry of Education had collected reports from local school authorities and other interested bodies and organisations. The scholar of religions, Einar Thomassen, who was a member of the group, observes that "[t]hese reports showed that resistance to the new thematic structure as a rule coincided with vested Christian interests" and that reports "from educational institutions and local authorities which did not display this vested interest, however, were generally much more positive towards the proposal of a thematic approach, welcoming it as a stimulating pedagogical challenge".[74]

Thomassen concludes that this shows that the government, as well as a number of local authorities and educators, are still ambivalent about KRL. The rhetoric of pluralism, dialogue and equal worth is in stark contrast with a model of integrative RE which implies a hierarchy of religions with Christianity in a priority position over the "others". Furthermore, elements of Christian catechesis have remained, as it is still recommended to learn the ten commandments and certain Lutheran hymns by heart.[75] Therefore, it does not come as a surprise to learn that there is opposition to this kind of RE as a compulsory subject, from which complete withdrawal is not possible.[76] Reservations about KRL because of its Christian bias have been articulated by the Norwegian Humanist Association and organisations representing religious minorities. The Norwegian Humanist Association lost an appeal against KRL, which it regards as a means of Christian indoctrination, at the Supreme Court of Norway and has lodged an appeal with the European Court of Human Rights in Strasbourg. However, some Lutheran and neo-charismatic Christian groups also oppose KRL, as they suspect it teaches relativism and disregards the claim of religion to offer truth.[77]

The change of Norwegian RE from a separative-confessional to an integrative approach has brought about a new kind of RE research at the academic level, because new concepts are required, e.g. for teacher

---

74 Thomassen 2005: RE in a pluralistic society: experiences from Norway, 240.
75 Ibid., 239f.
76 Exemption is, however, possible from certain activities which may be regarded as taking part in religious practice, such as visits to places of worship, singing songs etc. Cf. ibid., 238.
77 Cf. ibid., 248f.

training and new textbooks on different religions and worldviews.[78] RE-related research, traditionally dominated by theologians, has recently included contributions from other subjects, such as the study of religions, educational studies, sociology and political science. Norwegian RE-related research has become part of the international landscape of research about RE. Approaches from other countries, above all from England, are taken up and transferred to the Norwegian context and Norwegian approaches to religion and RE in plural Europe are appreciated in other countries. An example of recent empirical research is Sissel Østberg's Warwick-RE-Project-inspired study about ethnicity, religion, nationhood and citizenship among Pakistani children in Oslo.[79] Another researcher, Geir Skeie, is particularly concerned with concepts for plurality and pluralism as challenges for RE and has studied Norwegian majority and minority discourse about nationalism, religiosity and citizenship.[80] Heid Leganger-Krogstad has developed a contextual dialogical approach from her experiences of the discrepancies between national syllabuses and textbooks, reflecting urban and Southern Norwegian concerns, and local Finnmark teaching environments with their own versions of ethnic and religious plurality. These consist of people with, for example, Norwegian, Sami and Kven backgrounds, as well as diverse forms of old shamanistic traditions and different variants of Christianity. Her approach involves ethnographic field studies, action research and experiments which she carried out together with her students. It aims at familiarising children with their local environment and relates local experiences to global issues and concerns.[81]

A most valuable contribution to the debate about representing religions in integrative RE is Halldis Breidlid's and Tove Nicolaisen's work about the representation of religious narratives.[82] They have studied the representation of religious narratives in textbooks with a particular focus on issues of ethnicity (e.g. in the Exodus story, which was frequently represented with a complete lack of empathy for the Egyptians who had to suffer for their Pharaoh's decisions) and gender (e.g. with respect to the role of Sita in the Ramayana, who was represented

---

78 For a recent account of RE research in Norway see Skeie 2004: An overview of RE research in Norway.
79 See e.g. Østberg 2003: Cultural diversity and common citizenship.
80 See e.g. Skeie 2002: The concept of plurality and its meaning for RE; 2003: Nationalism, religiosity and citizenship in Norwegian majority and minority discourse.
81 See e.g. Leganger-Krogstad 2001: RE in global perspective: a contextual approach; 2003: Dialogue among young citizens in a pluralistic RE.
82 See e.g. Breidlid and Nicolaisen 2004: Multi-faith RE in a religiously-mixed context.

either as an independent, active person in her own right, or as a subordinate faithful wife within the framework of traditional role models, or was invisible due to exclusive emphasis on her husband Rama). Breidlid and Nicolaisen advise teachers "to reflect upon the fact that some religious stories reveal negative and prejudicial attitudes towards other people and towards non-believers"[83] and suggest a further study of the challenges which gender roles in religious stories present for integrative RE. Their argument about how to deal with conflicting stories from different traditions, for example Christianity and Islam, is also constructive. Harmonising conflicting stories is not an option and trying to find out which one is the more original or historically probable story often does not help either (though this ought to be a topic for discussion at higher levels). However, if the children's backgrounds are to be taken seriously, conflicting stories have to be introduced side by side, as is also suggested in Robert Jackson's conversational (1997) or pluralistic (2004) approach.

Considering the discrepancy between this kind of advanced research and the political framework for KRL, Thomassen's conclusion about the present state of integrative RE in Norway seems to hit the nail on the head: "KRL is still best described as a halfway house between traditional Christian instruction on the one hand, and a multifaith study programme on the other."[84] However, despite unresolved tensions in its political and pedagogical ideology, KRL is well-received among teachers and pupils. Therefore, one may hope that politicians will follow academic insight rather than religious lobbying and take the necessary steps to transform this kind of integrative RE into a truly impartial approach, so that it can be accepted by pupils and parents from diverse religious backgrounds as a compulsory subject.

2.2.2 A separative framework and exceptions to the rule – Germany

German accounts of the situation of RE in this country typically begin with a description of the legal framework, particularly with article 7.3 of the national constitution, which says that in state schools RE is "an ordinary school subject" which is taught "in accordance with the principles of the religious communities" while the right to supervision is granted to the state.[85] This article is normally interpreted as the legal

---

83   Ibid., 76.
84   Thomassen 2005: RE in a pluralistic society: experiences from Norway, 239f.
85   The complete section in German says: "Der Religionsunterricht ist in den öffentlichen Schulen mit Ausnahme der bekenntnisfreien Schulen ordentliches Lehrfach.

basis for separative confessional RE. However, there is also a minority of other interpretations, which regard these formulations as a foundation for an integrative approach based on the cooperation of educators and religious communities, as we shall see below.

The federal structure of Germany necessitates that education is largely a responsibility of the federal states (Bundesländer). Therefore, the education systems in the individual states differ from each other, for example with respect to the years that children have to attend school before graduating from upper secondary school (Gymnasium) with their "Abitur". Unlike the "new Bundesländer" (former GDR), which emphasise state neutrality with respect to religion in education,[86] many of the "old Bundesländer" (former West Germany) have constitutions which prescribe the Christian character of school education in general. The constitution of Baden Württemberg, for example, states: "Young people are to be educated in reverence for God, in the spirit of Christian compassion, for the brotherhood of all human beings, and for the love of freedom, in love of their people and home [*"Heimat"*], for moral and political responsibility, for professional and social achievement, and to a liberal democratic way of thinking."[87] State schools in Baden-Württemberg ("Grund- und Hauptschulen") are regarded as Christian comprehensive schools: "In Christian comprehensive schools children are educated on the basis of Christian and occidental educa-

---

Unbeschadet des staatlichen Aufsichtsrechts wird der Religionsunterricht in Übereinstimmung mit den Grundsätzen der Religionsgemeinschaften erteilt. Kein Lehrer darf gegen seinen Willen verpflichtet werden, Religionsunterricht zu erteilen." (Grundgesetz der Bundesrepublik Deutschland, section 7.3).

86 See, for example, sections 15.4 and 15.5 of the school law of Mecklenburg Vorpommern: "Das Ziel der schulischen Erziehung ist die Entwicklung zur freien Persönlichkeit, die aus Ehrfurcht vor dem Leben und im Geiste der Toleranz bereit ist, Verantwortung für die Gemeinschaft mit anderen Menschen und Völkern sowie gegenüber künftiger Generationen zu tragen. Die Schulen achten die religiösen und weltanschaulichen Überzeugungen der Schüler, Eltern und Lehrer." (Land Mecklenburg-Vorpommern 2006: Schulgesetz). Similarly, § 4 of the school law of Brandenburg states: "Die Schule wahrt die Freiheit des Gewissens sowie Offenheit und Toleranz gegenüber unterschiedlichen kulturellen, religiösen, weltanschaulichen und politischen Wertvorstellungen, Empfindungen und Überzeugungen. Keine Schülerin und kein Schüler darf einseitig beeinflußt werden." (Land Brandenburg 2005). An exception among the "new Bundesländer" is the school law of the state of Saxonia, which particularly mentions the relevance of „the Christian tradition for the task of communicating values in school." See Freistaat Sachsen 2007: Schulgesetz, §1, section 2.

87 Land Baden-Württemberg 1953: Verfassung, section 12.1: "Die Jugend ist in der Ehrfurcht vor Gott, im Geiste der christlichen Nächstenliebe, zur Brüderlichkeit aller Menschen und zur Friedensliebe, in der Liebe zu Volk und Heimat, zu sittlicher und politischer Verantwortlichkeit, zu beruflicher und sozialer Bewährung und zu freiheitlicher demokratischer Gesinnung zu erziehen."

tional and cultural values. Children of a class attend all lessons together, with the exception of RE."[88]

The German policy towards religious pluralism is highly ambivalent at regional and national levels. It generally privileges Christianity and seeks to minoritise other religions, most explicitly Islam, as can be seen in the results of the so-called "Kopftuchdebatte", to give just one example, a public debate which emerged when a Muslim woman who wears a headscarf was refused a job as a teacher. The outcome of this debate – and a number of legal cases – was that in many federal states wearing headscarves was forbidden for teachers, while wearing Christian robes is still allowed. The argument is that teachers must not wear religious or other symbols which may endanger "the neutrality of the state towards pupils or parents" or "disturb the political, religious or worldview harmony." It is explicitly stated, however, that this does not apply to Christian and occidental traditions which serve the interest of the school as a whole.[89]

Normally, the approach to RE in Germany is separative: children may either take confessional RE provided by the Protestant or Catholic Church respectively, or attend an alternative subject, called e.g. "ethics", "practical philosophy" or "norms and values".[90] In the "old Bundesländer", before those subjects were introduced, children who did not want to attend confessional RE just had extra leisure time or first-language education for immigrant children with a foreign mother tongue, in most cases Turkish. Over the years, more and more "alternative" or "substitute" subjects, as they are called, were introduced. Very

---

88 Land Baden-Württemberg 1952: Verfassung, sections 15.1 and 16.1: "In christlichen Gemeinschaftsschulen werden die Kinder auf der Grundlage christlicher und abendländischer Bildungs- und Kulturwerte erzogen. Der Unterricht wird mit Ausnahme des Religionsunterrichts gemeinsam erteilt."
89 See, for example, the respective section in the legal framework for schools in Baden-Württemberg, which was changed in 2003: "Lehrkräfte an öffentlichen Schulen ... dürfen in der Schule keine politischen, religiösen, weltanschaulichen oder ähnliche, äußeren Bekundungen abgeben, die geeignet sind, die Neutralität des Landes gegenüber Schüler und Eltern oder den politischen, religiösen oder weltanschaulichen Schulfrieden zu gefährden oder zu stören. Insbesondere ist ein äußeres Verhalten unzulässig, welches bei Schülern oder Eltern den Eindruck hervorrufen kann, dass eine Lehrkraft gegen Menschenwürde, Gleichberechtigung der Menschen nach Art. 3 GG, Freiheitsgrundrechte oder die freiheitlich-demokratische Grundordnung auftritt. Die Darstellung christlicher und abendländischer Bildungs- und Kulturwerte oder Traditionen entspricht dem Bildungsauftrag der ... Landesverfassung und widerspricht nicht dem Verhaltensgebot nach Satz 1. Das religiöse Neutralitätsgebot des Satzes 1 gilt nicht im Religionsunterricht ..." (cf. Land Baden-Württemberg 2005: Schulgesetz für Baden-Württemberg).
90 After the German reunification, this Western German model was also introduced in most of the "new Bundesländer".

recently, confessional RE in religions other than Christianity has been introduced in individual places. Religious minorities, above all Islam, with about 3.3 million people the largest religious minority in Germany, claim their right to also offer confessional RE. However, organisation is difficult, particularly finding ways of offering teacher training, which for Christian RE is guaranteed in state-financed Protestant and Catholic theological faculties at universities. It seems unlikely that proportionally comparable means in terms of state-funding will be spent on teacher training for confessional RE in other religions.

As we have seen, confessional RE, mainly provided by the two major Christian churches, aims at supporting the children's development of a confessional identity in one particular tradition. Teachers may have been educated in teacher training programmes of confessional theological institutions, where this particular theology and its different aspects are studied. Teachers may also have been appointed by the churches. Frequently, Catholic priests and Protestant vicars also teach a few hours of RE in one of the schools in their parish. Generally, RE teachers need to be approved (they need, for example, a "vocatio" or "missio canonica") by the religious community they represent in RE. Theological teacher training programmes at university may include one or two classes in the non-confessional study of religions, provided that this discipline is taught at that particular university. However, a systematic study of religions other than Protestantism or Catholicism respectively, let alone the methodology of the study of religions, is not included in these programmes. Christian confessional RE deals mainly with Christianity. The study of other religions is often also included, particularly at secondary levels. However, it has to be kept in mind that these traditions are represented by teachers who studied one particular theology, not the study of religions. Therefore, these teachers are, in fact, not trained for teaching different religions and many teachers do not really know how to do so at all. Generally, in Christian confessional RE, different religions are represented as "other"[91] religions and are studied from a Christian perspective.

As attendance of confessional RE is not compulsory and since a growing number of pupils do not wish to participate in this subject, in more and more federal states alternative or substitute subjects have been developed. They are called e.g. *Ethik* (ethics) in Hessia and Bavaria, *Werte und Normen* (values and norms) in Lower Saxony, and *Praktische Philosophie* (practical philosophy) in North-Rhine Westphalia. The

---

91 Originally frequently called "Fremdreligionen" ("alien religions"), now "andere Religionen".

idea is that these subjects deal with the anthropological and ethical aspects of RE minus the religious dimension. Therefore, none of the substitute subjects has "religion" in its title. However, apart from philosophy and ethics, these alternative subjects also ought to include some study of religions, even though the emphasis is much more on the former. Teacher training for this school subject frequently lacks a sound pedagogical concept. Courses from different academic disciplines can be selected, often including, above all, theology [!], philosophy and some study of religions, however, far fewer than necessary of the latter to be actually qualified to teach about different religions. Moreover, many teacher trainees feel that they are left alone when it comes to combining these classes to form a coherent approach. Therefore, teachers of the "alternative" or "substitute" subjects – just as their colleagues who teach confessional RE – generally have not had sufficient training to be able to teach about different religions. To put it clearly: in most German schools, there is no room for children of different religious backgrounds to learn together about the different religions under the supervision of qualified teachers.

The dominant separative model has repeatedly been criticised for its educational inconsistencies and, furthermore, for the organisational difficulties it presents when more and more religious communities introduce their individual version of confessional RE. Alternative concepts and models have been developed in some federal states. I would briefly like to mention three examples in which educationists decided that an integrative model is more appropriate for state schools: The federal states of Hamburg, Bremen and Brandenburg have introduced non-separative integrative RE in which children of various religious backgrounds are expected to learn together about different religions.[92]

Integrative RE in Hamburg: "Religionsunterricht für alle"

RE in the City of Hamburg, which is an independent federal state of Germany, is integrative. After World War II, RE in Hamburg was provided by the Protestant church, to which more than 90% of the population belonged. Today, the percentage of the Protestant population has

---

92 Another step towards an integrative model is the very recently introduced compulsory subject "ethics" for the years 7 to 10 in Berlin. In Berlin, confessional (separative) religious or worldview education ("Religions- und Weltanschauungsunterricht") is a purely optional subject, which pupils may or may not attend in their leisure time. It is offered by several different religious communities. See the articles 12.6 and 13.1 of the school law of Berlin (Land Berlin 2006: Schulgesetz).

sunk below 40%, while increased immigration has also changed the religious landscape; above all more and more Catholics and Muslims have been coming to Hamburg. In the face of growing multiculturalisation, Horst Gloy, the director of the Pedagogical Theological Institute of the North-Elbean Protestant Church, began to promote an integrative rather than a separative approach to RE, interpreting the legal framework in a different way. In a religiously plural environment, Gloy said, RE can no longer be confessional instruction, but has to be an interreligious RE.[93] In order to meet the new challenges, a *Gesprächskreis interreligiöser Religionsunterricht* (round table for interreligious education) with representatives of different religions and educationists was initiated and a new concept for a *Religionsunterricht für alle* (religious education for all) was developed. This model also found the support of regional church representatives as well as the responsible education authorities. Academic support was e.g. provided in an interdisciplinary research project about "youth, religion and education in a multicultural society shaped by economic and social disparities."[94] Related research included theoretical and empirical studies on dialogue as well as on actual classroom practice.[95] The Hamburg dialogical approach to RE, which starts from the real-life environment of the pupils, is furthermore part of international research networks in which similarities and difference between approaches in different countries are being discussed.[96] In this approach to integrative RE, dialogue is an integral part of the methodology.[97] However, contrary to e.g. Hans Küng's concept of interreligious dialogue, the Hamburg approach focuses on dialogue at a grass-roots level and promotes a "dialogue from below". Children with different religious backgrounds are encouraged to talk about topics like the meaning of life and death, ethical questions about justice, peace or the integrity of the creation. Similarities and differences between religions can thereby be studied and children have opportunities to learn that differences do not have to alienate but can be integrated into everyday life.

---

93 Cf. Gloy 1997: Was für eine Schule schulden wir unseren Kindern und Jugendlichen in einer sich verändernden Welt?, and 1997: Dem interreligiösen Religionsunterricht gehört die Zukunft.
94 "Jugend-Religion-Unterricht in einer von ökonomischen und sozialen Disparitäten geprägten multikulturellen Gesellschaft", see e.g. Doedens and Weiße (ed.) 1997: Religionsunterricht für alle.
95 See e.g. Knauth 1996: Religionsunterricht und Dialog, or Asbrand 2000: Zusammen leben und lernen im Religionsunterricht.
96 Cf. e.g. Chidester, Tobler et al. 1997: Diversity as Ethos, Jackson 2003: International Perspectives on Citizenship, Education and Religious Diversity.
97 Cf. Weiße 1996: Vom Monolog zum Dialog.

The Hamburg model focuses particularly on Christianity and other "world religions", understood, however, as "neighbouring religions", referring to ordinary people in the neighbourhood rather than official representatives. The Hamburg model builds on different concepts from philosophy, pedagogy and theology. Wolfram Weiße, Professor of Education, RE, and Ecumenical Theology at the University of Hamburg, himself a key figure in the developments in Hamburg, sketches the main elements of the Hamburg dialogical approach as follows: "it is related to the experiences of the pupils and to stimulus material from religious traditions; it is contextual and intercultural; it is based on the approaches of ecumenical theology and inter-religious learning."[98] The social, religious, political and ecological environments of children, in Hamburg itself as well as in a global perspective, is given particular consideration and children are encouraged to respond responsibly to these environments. Therefore, integrative RE in Hamburg also includes citizenship education.

The organisation of the Hamburg model is shaped by compromises. Officially, RE in Hamburg is provided by the Protestant Church, despite its integrative vision. Therefore, there are some inconsistencies in the approach. For example, teacher trainees have to be a member of a Christian church in order to be allowed to take their examination. This means that only Christians can teach the subject. Furthermore, the different religious communities, although invited to participate in shaping the subject, do not have equal positions when it comes to drawing up syllabuses. In Hamburg, the academic study of religions is not regarded as the appropriate academic discipline for integrative RE, as the studies it produces are considered too remote from the actual horizons of the pupils. Rather, a model is favoured in which pedagogy and different theologies are brought together. A recent initiative in this direction is the plan for an establishment of an Academy of World Religions in which Christian, Jewish, Muslim and Buddhist scholars work closely together with educationists.

The integrative dialogical approach has been well accepted in Hamburg, even though there is some opposition from the conservative party (*Christlich Demokratische Union*, CDU). The Bishop of the Protestant Church in Hamburg, Maria Jepsen, also supports this model. However, national representatives of the Protestant Church in Germany (*Evangelische Kirsche in Deutschland*, EKD) oppose an introduction of a dialogical integrative approach on a national level. Compared to common RE in Germany, the Hamburg approach is among the few

---

98 Weisse 2003: Difference without discrimination, 193.

approaches to RE that really do take seriously the plural environments of today's pupils. However, it could definitely be improved in the direction of a more impartial approach, above all with respect to organisation and teacher training. For the time being and given the present political climate, it may be the best possible solution for Hamburg. However, future improvement would have to include theoretical and methodological reflections of the study of religions so that not one particular (though universalist) theological approach is made the starting point for integrative RE. A study-of religions-point of view may also help to achieve a more impartial approach to the different religions, with respect to subject content as well as to organisation. In my view, if a truly integrative approach is pursued, the planned Academy of World Religions would at least have to involve scholars of the study of religions, who together with educationists design the general approach, into which the insider information provided by the Muslim, Jewish, Buddhist, Christian and perhaps even other scholars can be integrated.

Integrative RE in Bremen:
"Biblischer Geschichtsunterricht auf allgemeinchristlicher Grundlage"

Bremen is also a federal state in its own right. It has the privilege to be exempted from the national law about RE. The so-called *Bremer Klausel* (Bremen clause) in article 141 of the national constitution says that all federal states that had different regulations about RE before 1949 may keep these regulations instead of the national ones. Until today, Bremen has kept its older regulation in article 32 of its constitution, which says that RE is "non-confessional education in biblical history on a general Christian basis."[99] The formulation "on a general Christian basis" is the result of a compromise in 1946 between state authorities and the churches who feared that this traditionally non-confessional subject could be interpreted as anti-Christian.[100] Despite its rather infelicitous name, RE in Bremen is a non-confessional integrative subject, open for all pupils with various religious or non-religious backgrounds. Officially, the federal state of Bremen, not the churches, has the responsibility for teacher training and the curriculum. However, since the Protes-

---

99 The whole sentence in German: "Die allgemeinbildenden öffentlichen Schulen sind Gemeinschaftsschulen mit bekenntnismäßig nicht gebundenem Unterricht in Biblischer Geschichte auf allgemein christlicher Grundlage." (Freie Hansestadt Bremen 1947: Verfassung, section 32)
100 Dommel 2002: RE in Bremen, 2. For the history of the Bremen model see also Lott 1998: Wie hast du's mit der Religion?, 83-91.

tant Church is the only religious community in Bremen which supports this subject and feels responsible for it, it is, in fact, the only religious community which is consulted by the state authorities for curriculum development.

The study of religions – not theology – is the academic discipline responsible for RE in Bremen. The teacher training programme, a course that includes the study of religions as well as RE, independent from theology,[101] but part of the Faculty of Cultural Studies ("Kulturwissenschaften"), is exceptional in Germany. It was developed after the University of Bremen was founded in 1971 and has been taught since 1977.[102] Bremen is a multicultural city with a religiously mixed population. In this context, the teacher training programme promotes an integrative educational approach to RE and refuses to split the subject up on the basis of different religions. Subject contents are European and non-European Christianity[103] as well as other established and new religions. Furthermore, students are acquainted with theological as well as study-of-religions methods of analysis.

Jürgen Lott, professor of RE and one of the founders of the RE programme at the University of Bremen, summarised the Bremen model for RE when he coined the phrase "identity by communication"[104] as a response to a memorandum by the Protestant Church in Germany called "identity and communication",[105] in which it argued for confessional RE as a basis for dialogue at a later stage. Lott's argument against a separative approach is that education is a part of life and not preparation for life. Identity is not static, but formed in various kinds of encounters. Lott emphasises the ideology-critical function of RE. Rather than being instructed in a particular religion, children ought to have a chance to critically study different religions and make up their own minds about ambivalences and tensions within and between different traditions.

---

101 There is no Faculty of Theology at the University of Bremen.
102 Cf. Otto: Das Ende des konfessionellen Religionsunterrichts. Auswege aus einer Sackgasse, 51.
103 This new approach to Christianity from a study-of-religions perspective is particularly valuable, as scholars in the study of religions have for a long time left the field of Christianity to theologians.
104 The German phrase is "Identität *durch* Verständigung", cf. e.g. Lott 1998: Wie hast du's mit der Religion?, 149f. It has to be added, however, that Lott used this formulation with particular reference to the debate about the new subject LER in Brandenburg, which he defends against church propaganda (see below). However, it is equally applicable to the Bremen model.
105 Evangelische Kirche in Deutschland 1994: Identität und Verständigung. Standort und Perspektiven des Religionsunterrichts.

Unlike the Hamburg model, in the Bremen approach, the study of religions is the academic discipline responsible training teachers for RE. The combination of the study of religions and RE works very well at the university level. An inconsistency of the Bremen model is, however, that once teacher trainees have graduated the influence of the study of religions abates and the Protestant Church reclaims its influence by providing resources and support. Like in the Hamburg model, the integrative vision of the subject is diluted by the actual influence of the Protestant Church, which is involved in all important decisions about RE. Therefore, it is not surprising that the way the subject is taught very much resembles traditional Protestant RE, as it is taught in other federal states of Germany.

Unlike other models for RE which have a strong church lobby to protect them, RE in Bremen, since it is officially independent from the churches, does not have a strong lobby and its position is, therefore, fairly weak. The education authorities do not allocate the full amount of hours to RE teaching and do not employ enough RE teachers. Furthermore, the integrative character was recently attacked by the churches and conservative politicians when they realised that Jewish or Muslim teachers may teach RE in Bremen. Opposition to the current approach also comes from the growing Muslim community in Bremen who, of course, cannot accept an integrative RE "on a general Christian basis" and from atheists for similar reasons. This kind of opposition is understandable, as the character of the subject is not consistently secular, despite its integrative vision and state responsibility.[106]

Integrative RE in Brandenburg: "Lebensgestaltung-Ethik-Religionskunde" (LER)

A recent bone of contention has been the question of whether the above mentioned *Bremen Clause* also applies to the "new Bundesländer", in which the churches have a far weaker position and which have tried to find their own models after the reunification in 1990. Unlike most other "new Bundesländer" to which the dominant Western German separative solution with Christian-confessional RE and alternative subjects was exported, Brandenburg went its own way. Soon after the German reunification, preparations were made to introduce an integrative subject in which children learn about different views of life, ethics and religion(s), taking up an older plan that existed already in the late GDR

---

106 Cf. Dommel 2002: RE in Bremen, 4.

to introduce a school subject "ethics".[107] After a test phase, the new obligatory subject *Lebensgestaltung-Ethik-Religionskunde* (LER: ways of life, ethics, knowledge about religions) was introduced in 1996. Different religious communities were invited to participate in the development of a concept for the new subject. The Protestant Church terminated its cooperation when it became clear that the final responsibility for the subject lay with state educationists and teachers and not with the religious communities.

What followed was massive propaganda against LER, above all by the churches, who advised their members to apply for exemption from LER, but severe criticism also came from the conservative party (CDU). The situation in Brandenburg was regarded as a threat to traditional confessional RE extending also beyond Brandenburg. I will not attempt to provide anything like a full account of the arguments that were advanced against LER in these (often public) debates and, furthermore, against non-confessional RE in general. A few points have to suffice for an impression of the character of the debate: there was general criticism that in such a subject the state had the presumption to convey values, which was rejected as dangerous with reference to German history. Moreover, it was claimed that religions cannot be represented by anybody other than themselves, which in fact implies that RE can only be confessional and that (academic/secular) knowledge about religions cannot be an element of education at all. Furthermore, a comparative study of religions could only be a superficial transmission of knowledge lacking attention to what religion "is really about". Impartiality, as implied in § 11, section 3 of the 1996 school law, which says that LER is taught in a "non-confessional" way, "neutral with respect to religions and ideologies"[108], was mistaken for arbitrariness and a complete lack of any point of view at all. An impartial treatment of religions, it was claimed, leads to indifference towards religion or to cynical, arrogant and distanced views of religions. On these grounds, alternatives to separative approaches were rendered impossible.[109] Law suits by the churches and the conservative party followed. One important issue was the question of whether the *Bremen Clause* does or does not apply to Brandenburg. A compromise was reached at the Supreme Court in 2002. The result of this was that LER can remain an ordinary subject in

---

107 For the origins of this idea, see Lott 1992: Wie hast du's mit der Religion?, 121ff.
108 The German formulation is: "bekenntnisfrei, religiös und weltanschaulich neutral".
109 For accounts of these and other arguments cf. e.g. Grötzinger, Gladigow and Zinser: Zur Einführung, Otto 1997: Das Ende des konfessionellen Religionsunterrichts, 50f., Lott 1998: Wie hast du's mit der Religion?, 10f.

Brandenburg, while the position of optional confessional RE is also strengthened. However, exemption from LER is possible.

Karl Ernst Grözinger, Burkhard Gladigow and Hartmut Zinser, three scholars of the study of religions, who edited a book about what the study of religions may contribute to subjects like LER,[110] explain the reaction of the churches as resulting from the fact that an impartial treatment of religions, where theologies themselves are the subject matter and not the overall framework of the subject, is perceived as an insult to the self-understanding of theologians. Of course, LER is not perfect and current practice could be improved, e.g. with respect to a didactic model that enables a consistent integration of the three aspects of the subject (ways of life, ethics and religions).[111] However, as the comparison with other countries has shown, a perfect integrative RE has never been introduced overnight. Integration of the different elements of the subject was for many years a major concern in Swedish RE, whose approach is – despite some differences – quite similar to the LER concept. LER in Brandenburg is the first consistently secular and educational approach to integrative RE in Germany, including an appropriate name for the subject as well as a correct distribution of responsibilities, which involves cooperation with, but not domination by, religious communities. An inconsistency of this approach is, however, like in England, that exemption is possible. But one may hope that, as in England, the actual practice of integrative RE will convince doubters and that almost all pupils will participate in it. A next step would be, as in Sweden, to abolish the right to exemption, so that all state-educated children may learn about different religions in an unbiased way.

Even though it was possible to keep LER in Brandenburg, the massive propaganda of the churches against integrative RE has had the effect that many people in Germany believe that integrative RE is just not possible. I experienced this personally at a seminar for PhD students funded by the *German National Academic Foundation* (*Studienstiftung des Deutschen Volkes*). After I had given a presentation about the ways in which integrative RE has been taught in England for many years, a student of theology got up and said: "It all sounds very good but it is just not possible." And he continued, "it just cannot be possible." This incident is indicative of the barriers in the minds of the people and the efficiency of the propaganda against integrative RE. In fact, RE in Germany is caught in a kind of vicious circle: RE is confessional, therefore university education and research about RE is done from a

---

110 Grözinger, Gladigow et al. 1999: Religion in der schulischen Bildung und Erziehung, see below.
111 Cf. e.g. Lott 1998: Wie hast du's mit der Religion?, 145.

theological confessional point of view. Only a small minority of scholars dares to suggest alternatives. And their positions (for example, the work by Gert Otto or Jürgen Lott) are normally effectively ignored or even stigmatised by most people who are concerned with RE. Highly relevant research by educationists from Germany and other European countries (in Germany e.g. by Wolfgang Klafki),[112] as well as international research by scholars of religions, which easily refutes the arguments against integrative RE, are simply ignored in the German debate. RE research in Germany is almost as a rule theological (i.e. religious) research. Politicians consult religious specialists, not specialists in religion. Therefore, apart from a few and very relevant exceptions, research about integrative RE in Germany has come to an intellectual standstill in a general climate in which conservative politicians have been trying for years to deny that Germany is a multicultural and plural society at all.

I have the impression that in Germany, questioning the separative approach as such is something like a taboo, which hardly anybody dares to break. Most politicians, who are themselves products of such an education, cannot imagine anything different from this. Models for the future which go beyond modified versions of current practice seem to be beyond reach. Politicians in the 1990s had no difficulty in changing the paragraph in the constitution which formerly granted asylum for those who needed it, by which they reduced the number of people who can apply for asylum at all to a minimum. However, making a law to guarantee that children learn from qualified teachers about different religions seems to be impossible. Politicians would be well advised to take a closer look at the intentions behind the different arguments for and against integrative approaches and to start differentiating between religious lobbying and academic educational expertise. I agree with the other scholars who favour integrative models,[113] when they say that in the present political climate in Germany, only a common European framework for RE seems to be a means of getting out of this educationally unacceptable situation, in which residual power of long established religions, effective lobbying and educational provincialism result in denying the majority of the future generations fundamental aspects of emancipatory education.

---

112 Cf. e.g. Klafki 1999: Braucht eine "gute Schule" einen neuen Unterrichtsbereich LER?
113 Cf. the positions put forward in favour of the Hamburg, Bremen and Brandenburg approaches above.

In the public and academic debates about RE, with very few exceptions,[114] the academic study of religions was conspicuous by its absence until very recently. Obviously, it was hardly concerned with confessional RE. Some scholars in the study of religions took the initiative for the establishment of alternative subjects to confessional RE in all federal states.[115] However, when more and more "substitute" or "alternative" subjects were developed, the study of religions found itself marginalised in the teacher training programmes for those subjects. Therefore, the *German Association for the History of Religions* (DVRG)[116] issued a statement about the necessity of making the study of religions an integral part of teacher training programmes for the so-called alternative subjects. This statement was sent to all federal ministries of education, the chancellors of the universities and other institutions.[117] Due to the federal responsibility for education, programmes for teacher training were developed at regional levels and often the study of religions has continuously had difficulties in being accepted as a major partner for this kind of teacher training. Only a few, if any, concepts have been developed that go beyond a broad outline of the traditional study-of-religions approach to religions, but systematically and educationally reflect teaching different religions in non-confessional school environments.

A first major contribution from the academic study of religions was *Religion in der schulischen Bildung und Erziehung. LER – Ethik – Werte und Normen in einer pluralistischen Gesellschaft* (1999), edited by Grözinger, Gladigow and Zinser. The editors state that the debate about LER made the academic study of religions known for the first time as a discipline related to a particular school subject. This challenge is taken up and different valuable contributions are presented by several scholars of the study of religions and education about individual aspects of represent-

---

114 These exceptions are e.g. Udo Tworuschka, who contributed on different levels to the inclusion of the expertise of the study of religions to RE in schools; for example, he studied the representation of religions in teaching material (see Falaturi and Tworuschka 1996: Der Islam im Unterricht) and developed teaching material, recently also ICT-based material (see Tworuschka 2004: Religiopolis - Weltreligionen erleben), and Peter Antes, who repeatedly argued for the study of religions as the responsible discipline for non-confessional RE, e.g. in the substitute or alternative subjects (e.g. Antes 1995: Religionspädagogik und Religionswissenschaft).
115 Cf. e.g. Zinser 1991: "Herausforderung Ethikunterricht". Ethik/ Werte und Normen als Ersatzfach in der Schule.
116 This association was renamed in 2005 and is now called DVRW (Deutsche Vereinigung für Religionswissenschaft), cf. chapter I, section 1.1.1.
117 Cf. Kippenberg 1996: Erklärung des Vorstands der Deutschen Vereinigung für Religionsgeschichte (DVRG): Beteiligung der Religionswissenschaft an der Ausbildung von Ethik-Lehrern.

ing religions in non-confessional RE, as well as about the necessity of this kind of education about religions. Very slowly, scholars in the study of religions in Germany are beginning to realise that unless they actively contribute to the debate about RE, their expertise, which is as relevant as ever in this changing educational landscape, will simply be ignored. Unlike church representatives, who have always been very active in contributing to public debates and curriculum development, scholars in the study of religions have so far frequently reacted to political decisions rather than played an active part in the debates that had led to these decisions. Taking initiative for integrative RE, not only within the small world of academia, but also in public debates, may be a way for the study of religions to make itself more heard, or perhaps, for the majority of the population, make known its existence at all, and show that statements about the relevance of the academic study of religions are more than mere lip service.

Conclusion

The current policy towards RE in Germany, which privileges the Christian churches over all other religions (e.g. by well organised state provision of theological teacher training), is confronted with serious educational and organisational difficulties since more and more religions have claimed their right to also offer confessional RE. Of course, within the dominant separative framework, it is only consistent that all religions may offer their particular version of confessional RE. However, this is generally a development in the wrong direction, leading to a further fragmentation of society, which is neither politically nor educationally desirable, and whose disastrous effects on national and international levels cannot be overlooked.

Nevertheless, a few integrative approaches to RE have been developed in Germany, although sometimes with considerable concessions to the churches. However, these approaches have been under permanent attack by national church representatives, who are – unlike educationists or scholars in the study of religions – very present in the media. These severe attacks by church representatives on any kind of integrative RE can be regarded as a symptom of the fact that church representatives also realise that models of integrative RE in fact deeply challenge the dominant confessional model, which has so far provided them with a privileged access to the young generation, but which they may not be able to retain in the long run, since arguments for educational (not religious) RE in secular state schools as a framework for teaching about different religions are simply more convincing. However, in the current political climate, a common European framework for integrative RE, which builds on the various experiences with integrative models in European countries, seems to be the only way out of this educationally unsatisfactory situation of RE in Germany.

2.2.3 Integrative RE as a "learning dimension" of other subjects – the Netherlands

In the Netherlands, out of the total population of about 15 million people, about 1.3 million have immigrant backgrounds. These include, for example, "guest workers" from Mediterranean states, people from former Dutch colonies (e.g. Indonesia, Surinam, and the Dutch West Indies), refugees from South America, South East Asia, Africa and the Middle East, Gypsies, Chinese from Hong Kong, the People's Republic of China and Taiwan. A distinctive feature of the education system in the Netherlands is its strong private school sector. About 75% of all schools are private schools (*bijzondere school*), leaving only a proportion of 25% for public state schools (*openbare school*). In the private schools, which also receive full state funding, education takes place within particular religious or educational frameworks. These schools are, for example, Roman Catholic, Protestant, Islamic, Jewish, Hindu, Monetessori, Jenaplan or Waldorf schools. Because of its particular focus on different private schools as opposed to, for example, the Scandinavian focus on comprehensive state schools, the Dutch system has been called a "pillarised" system of education.

About 65% of all schools in the Netherlands are – formally speaking – Christian schools. However, Bakker shows that there is a discrepancy between this formal affiliation and the actual identity of the school-population: "It is easy to see that the so easily presupposed homogeneity within a specific pillar as a whole does not exist at all. This is a typical Dutch educational myth."[118] This can be demonstrated by an example of the composition of the pupils of a Protestant primary school in Rotterdam in 1998-1999: only 11% of the parents were Christians, 48% Muslims and 17% Hindus. A further 24% indicated that they had no specific religious background. Of the 11% with a Christian background, a number belonged to a Chinese church, the majority were Roman Catholic, descendants of Cape Verde families. Therefore, Bakker concludes, names for schools which refer to a particular religious tradition

---

118 Bakker 2001: School as a place of diversity, 209.

imply a general character of the school which is different from the actual situation. Furthermore, they implicitly convey the idea of a homogenous and unambiguous interpretation of the particular religious profile of that tradition. This idea is, however, another myth.[119]

In the Netherlands, the primary school (*basisschool*) takes 8 years for children between the ages of 4 and 12. In public primary schools, religious communities, including Christian, Jewish and Muslim groups as well as the Humanist Association, are granted the right to offer (confessional) RE. The schools organise the timetables and offer alternative activities for children who do not want to participate in any of these lessons. In many schools, only Christian or Humanist RE is offered. Almost all free primary schools are confessional schools. They offer confessional RE as an obligatory subject. Christian schools with a high percentage of non-Christian children tend to develop a more open approach to traditional Christian confessional RE. The state has no control over the contents of confessional RE in private schools. A majority of the Protestant schools uses the material of the Dutch Sunday-School Association, which focuses more on practice, including praying, hymn or psalm singing and telling biblical stories rather than on providing information from an educational point of view. There are three types of secondary schools with 4, 5 or 6 years respectively. Public secondary schools have no RE at all, while confessional secondary schools offer confessional RE, mostly about Christianity with some attention to other religions.

Until 1985, this either-confessional-RE-or-no-RE solution meant that information about different religions was, if at all, provided from a particular confessional perspective or simply not provided at all. As this was regarded as unsatisfactory in a religiously plural society, the Education Act of 1985 (*Wet op het Basisonderwijs*) made *Geestelijke Stromingen* (GS, spiritual traditions) an obligatory learning area for all primary (*basis-*) schools. Based on insights from the academic study of religions, this learning area is meant to provide non-biased information about different religions, presented in an adequate vocabulary, and to communicate skills to explore in a respectful way the different religions and worldviews.[120] The education act states that the subject matter has to be taught in an "objective" way, clearly distinct from traditional "subjective" RE which provides an introduction to the particular religion to which the children belong. These formulations were used in order to make possible the introduction of GS as a compulsory subject or

---

119 Ibid.
120 Cf. Westerman 1996: 'Geestelijke Stromingen': a distinctive feature of RE in the Netherlands, 180.

learning area for all pupils in all schools. GS is meant to provide information about various religions and worldviews, encourage the discussion of various arguments and give insights into different norms and value systems in plural societies.

As we have seen, the Dutch school system gives great freedom to individual schools. Therefore, it was left for the schools themselves to decide if they wanted to offer GS as an individual subject or integrate that particular learning dimension into other subjects. Furthermore, schools may decide for themselves for which age groups GS is included in the syllabuses. The actual contents of the subject, e.g. which traditions in particular are being taught, only so called world religions or also non-religious worldviews, may also be decided upon by the individual schools. Since no overall general approach was developed for GS, actual teaching practice is often influenced considerably by the representations of religions given in textbooks.

Westerman shows what kind of problems may arise when GS is integrated into subjects such as history or geography. A survey of history and geography textbooks shows that while "history textbooks normally place world religions far away in time, most geography textbooks place them far away from home."[121] Geography textbooks often give little information about religious traditions in Europe and also very little about religions in North and South America, Africa or Australia. Thus, the impression is created that religions are only an Asian affair. Westerman conludes that "[m]ost geography and history textbooks give the impression that faiths and other world-views belong to 'there and then' and not to 'here and now'."[122] Furthermore, information is frequently presented in caricature (e.g. "the cows of Hindu India are sacred, they eat what they like, while millions of Indians starve of hunger"[123]) or exaggerations that sometimes remind one of stories of 19th century explorers. This means that the good intentions of GS may be reversed: "the exotic prevails while the plural situation round the street corner is ignored."[124] The information provided in these teaching books will reinforce colonialist points of view and stereotypes of religions rather than promoting better understanding of different religions. If teachers have no special knowledge in the study of religions, they may themselves be unable to criticise misrepresentations of religions in textbooks.

---

121 Ibid., 181.
122 Ibid., 182.
123 Quoted in Westerman 1996: 'Geestelijke Stromingen': a distinctive feature of RE in the Netherlands, 182, without any further reference.
124 Ibid.

In the Netherlands there has been a general tendency towards integrating subjects into wider learning areas. Without any doubt, teaching GS as part of such a wider learning area has advantages. However, apart from the problems addressed above, another issue is at stake here: religious private schools may also combine GS and confessional RE. One may wonder if the confessional or the impartial perspective will prevail in such a combination. In 1998, 13 years after GS was officially introduced, not all schools had yet included it in its curriculum. Where GS was taught, there were great differences with respect to contents, didactics and the time allocated to it. Nevertheless, as Griffioen and Bakker concluded in 2002, teachers have a positive view on the subject and 80% of the schools acknowledge its relevance.[125] However, that also means that 20% of the schools do not regard GS as a relevant learning area. Furthermore, as GS was only introduced for primary schools, learning about different religions from an impartial point of view is not yet included in the curriculum for secondary schools.

Introducing integrative RE as a "learning dimension" rather than as an explicitly individual subject gives rise to a number of conceptual and organisational problems such as, for example, teacher training, the development of a general concept, or of teaching material. Understanding integrative RE as a part of greater thematic units is definitely a valuable approach. However, this cannot be a substitute for integrative RE as an individual subject. The subject content is simply too wide to be fully integrated in other subjects. If individual religions have had their own school subjects for decades, how should a subject about the diversity of religions fare with less time allocated to it?

As the history of Swedish integrative RE, as well as the history of GS in the Netherlands has shown, if integrative RE is not introduced as an obligatory, distinct subject, it is in permanent danger of being integrated away. Schools may organise adequate integrative RE but they may as well not do so. Practice has shown that making IR a learning dimension is not sufficient to secure adequate teaching of the subject. Furthermore, when integrative RE is absorbed into other subjects, a question of responsibility arises: who trains these teachers, who develops curricula, who writes textbooks etc.? It is no surprise that scholars of history or geography are, as we have seen, not really capable of doing this. My conclusion from the Dutch experiences with GS is that the idea of integrative RE as a learning dimension is good, but practice has shown that it is not good enough. Unless integrative RE is introduced

---

125 Griffioen and Bakker 2002: Interkulturelles und interreligiöses Lernen in der niederländischen Bildungspolitik, 28.

as a distinct subject with an overall didactic concept, teacher training programmes and adequate teaching material, the way it is actually taught in schools will remain unsatisfactory.

2.3 Integrative or separative RE in state schools?

The comparison of different European approaches to teaching and learning about religions in state schools in Europe has shown that, despite a general acknowledgement of the importance of knowledge about different religions, the responses of the individual countries to these challenges are quite different from each other. While most North European countries have introduced integrative RE about different religions as an obligatory subject for all children, sometimes with possibilities of opting out, other countries have retained their old separative models and tried to communicate knowledge about different religions within these separative, often confessional frameworks with the exception of so-called "alternative subjects". Another model has been the integration of information about different religions into other parts of the curriculum, without an individual subject for integrative RE.

The main difference is between integrative and separative approaches to teaching about religions in schools in Europe. On the surface, this difference seems to be due to different conceptions of education and the task of the school in general. However, a closer look at the arguments used by the different groups that are involved in the debates about the character of RE shows that, at a deeper level, these differences have a lot to do with power relations between different religions and the state in the individual countries. Interestingly, the transformation of RE in the direction of an integrative approach seems to have been easier in countries like Sweden, Denmark, England or Norway, where state or "established" churches used to have a kind of monopoly on RE as unquestioned sole authorities, than in countries like Germany or Finland, where two or more denominations have insisted on their rights to their own versions of confessional RE. Perhaps it was easier for these former unquestioned authorities to make concessions with respect to RE than for the latter groups, which have always felt that they had to compete with another denomination, and recently also with other religions. The whole range of arguments for and against the transformation of separative (confessional) into integrative approaches, which have been put forward in the debates about RE in countries that still follow the separative approach, cannot be presented here.[126] I shall simply present a few major points with respect to the question of how the representation of religions differs in these two approaches and refer to the different notions of education behind these models.

It is important to mention that opposition to integrative approaches in countries with separative models comes almost exclusively from representatives of religious communites and conservative (Christian) politicians, but not from scholars of education. On the contrary, scholars of education emphasise with increasing urgency that some form of integrative RE is indispensable in contemporary schools.[127] Therefore, the arguments for separative RE are normally religious rather than educational, often building on concepts of education and development, which are questionable from a non-religious educational point of view. For example, in the German discussion the churches have claimed, against all educational insight, that identities have to be built up in one's "own" religious tradition first, before communication with "other" traditions is possible. This argument is understandable from a religious perspective and its interest in recruiting members for one's own religious community. However, this approach is completely unjustified on solely educational grounds, as Jürgen Lott has shown convincingly from an educational perspective.[128] Unfortunately, these different dimensions – religious vs. educational interests – have been effectively obscured in most of the public debates.

Similarly, matters are obscured when integrative RE is regarded as an inappropriate state authority on religion. In fact, a state guaranteed integrative RE about different religions by qualified teachers who have been educated in the study of religions is far more appropriate than the presumptuous claim that specialists in one tradition were also qualified to teach about different religions, which is still common practice in the confessional models in Germany. As experience with integrative models has shown, fears that children will get the religions mixed up if they learn about different religions from an early age onwards, have not proved well-founded. If children are already confronted with different religions and worldviews in nursery schools and have to develop their

---

126 For this issue cf. the publications by Jensen, e.g. 1999: Religion and RE in a Europe of conflicting trends, also Lott 1998: Wie hast du's mit der Religion?, Weiße, e.g. 1996: Religionsunterricht für alle.
127 Cf. e.g. Klafki 1999: Braucht eine "gute Schule" einen neuen Unterrichtsbereich LER? This is mirrored in the Norwegian situation where church representatives have opposed the revision of the curriculum for KRL towards a truly integrative approach, which had been suggested by the committee, cf. Thomassen 2005: Religious education in a pluralistic society: experiences from Norway, 240.
128 Cf. Lott 1998: Wie hast Du's mit der Religion?, 185ff.

own strategies of dealing with various kinds of inhomogeneity and plurality, why should a systematic study of these different traditions be delayed?

As the examples from Germany and Finland show, even apart from educational reservations, separative approaches are confronted with considerable organisational problems, if the current oligopoly of RE, which is in the hands of a few Christian denominations, is to be transformed into a model in which the different religions have equal opportunities. The schools do not have the means to organise separate RE for all religions and one may doubt that universities can afford to establish anything similar to the traditional theological faculties for all other religions so that there may be comparable teacher training courses for all religions. Furthermore, the Finnish and German approaches have shown that the confessional idea is not always consistent, as e.g. many non-Lutheran children participate in Lutheran RE. This makes the "one's own" vs. "the other" rhetoric even more problematic. Often different educational tasks have been mixed up in a separative approach. This was most obvious in cases where confessional RE, alternative subjects and first language education for immigrants were offered at the same time so that it was impossible to choose more than one of these options. The underlying assumption was that immigrant children need no education at all about religion, ethics or norms and values. The general idea behind the RE vs. "alternative-subjects" model, that some children ought to have confessional RE in "their own" tradition while others deal with norms, values and ethics in general, which again the former group does not, is somewhat inconsistent with respect to the justification of these separative subjects in the curriculum.

The real problems of the separative model are, however, not organisational but educational in nature. The very concept of separative RE in schools is highly questionable. Why can religions not provide confessional RE independently from state education if they wish to do so? In schools, a separation of pupils when it comes to religions and ethics is completely unjustified on educational grounds. Furthermore, as Breidlid and Nicolaisen have stated with respect to the Norwegian situation before the transformation of the subject in 1997, it deprives the children of essential elements of education:

> "The students were separated when religious and moral issues were dealt with. Such deprivation of a common space for dialogue and exchange of

existential views has been dissatisfactory for the teachers as well as for the students." [129]

How can children with different religions and worldviews learn to live together and understand each other if the hidden curriculum communicates that learning together is impossible and that these issues can only be discussed in a separative environment? In my view, a solely separative approach to RE and religious diversity in state schools is irresponsible in our contemporary world. If state education aims at laying the ground for common values and mutual understanding, as is frequently emphasised in the rhetoric about integration, it is educationally impossible to separate children when it comes to beliefs and values. The main challenge for contemporary education is to deal with these various particular religious positions educationally, rather than letting different interest groups choose their own policies as a general framework for reflection for a selection of pupils.

Furthermore, separative approaches to teaching about *different* religions often start from a misunderstanding of the subject matter. If knowledge about religions and worldviews as well as a methodology of dealing with the factual diversity is regarded as an element of education, it is important that this knowledge and these skills are communicated by qualified teachers. Only teachers who have actually studied the diversity of religions and reflected upon acceptable methodologies of presenting it, are in fact qualified for this task. Teachers who have been educated to teach confessional RE from an insider perspective in their own tradition normally have very little knowledge about other religions, let alone knowledge about an educationally acceptable non-religious methodology of dealing with the plurality of religions. For this and the above mentioned reasons, confessional RE alone is incapable of providing an educationally acceptable approach to different religions in state schools.[130]

---

[129] Breidlid and Nicolaisen 2004: Multi-faith RE in a religiously-mixed context: some Norwegian perspectives, 69.

[130] Another issue, which cannot be discussed at length here, but which is closely related to the questions about the integrative or separative character of RE, are faith-based schools. In some countries, private faith-based schools (e.g. Norway, Sweden) are only a small minority in the educational landscape, in other countries (e.g. England) they provide education for a considerable number of pupils. In the Netherlands, as we have seen, they even represent the great majority of schools, even though the religious affiliation of the school is not generally indicative of the actual composition of the pupils. Similarly to the debates about RE, it may be asked if faith-based schools strengthen or erode social cohesion. For an analysis of arguments for and against faith-based schools, see Jackson e.g. 2003: Citizenship, religious and cultural diversity and education, 16ff., and 2004: Rethinking RE and Plurality. Issues in Diversity and Pedagogy, 161f.

Another solution for including learning about different religions in school curricula was the introduction of integrative RE as a "learning dimension", e.g. in the Netherlands, but also in France, where information about religions was included in history, geography and literature syllabuses in a curriculum which formerly did not include any kind of RE at all.[131] The experiences with integrative RE as a "learning dimension" have shown that the idea is a step in the right direction, but does not go far enough. The breadth of the subject matter of integrative RE and the systematic reflection of theory and methodology cannot fully be covered as a part of another subject. The integration into other subjects resulted in poor provision. In busy school life, these "learning dimensions" tend to become marginalised and therefore, as the Dutch example shows, integrative RE has often effectively not taken place at all when it had not been introduced as an individual subject. Furthermore, teachers in other subjects do not have sufficient knowledge with respect to individual religions or to methodology to be able to teach about these complex matters.

To sum up, we can say that the *separative approach* (2.2.2) as well as *the inclusion of integrative RE-aspects in other parts of the curriculum without an individual subject* (2.2.3) are insufficient solutions for the task of providing all school children with unbiased knowledge about different religions, which is an indispensable element of education in a religiously plural world. *Integrative RE as an individual school subject* (2.2.1) is the only model in which all children are given a chance to learn from an impartial perspective about different religions. Therefore, unlike the Finnish and the majority of the German solutions, which cement the separation of the pupils, the recent introduction of integrative RE in Norway was a step in the right direction, even though the approach needs to be developed further into a truly impartial approach that does not privilege one religion over others. As the opposition to KRL in Norway has shown, this is the crucial point for the subject to find acceptance among all parents and children.

It is important that young European citizens do not leave school without having had an RE that has provided them with knowledge and understanding of different religions. Regardless of whether the pupils or their parents consider themselves religious or not, all pupils need to know about religions. Religions do not solely belong to their adherents, but they – as Tim Jensen puts it – "belong to the world, as part and parcel of past and present world history and European history, as part

---

131 With the exception of Alsace-Lorraine, which has confessional RE, for recent developments in France cf. Schreiner 2005: RE in Europe, 7f.

and parcel of the human cultures and societies. Religion is a human, historical, social and cultural fact."[132] Therefore, secular states and school authorities should have the obligation to provide children with a professional, secular integrative RE. I fully agree with Jensen's conclusion about RE, religions and secularity in Europe:

> "And if RE is to be compulsory, in line with the principles of the Human Rights articles on education and in line with the interests of a truly secular state, then the RE offered has to be informative, critical and pluralistic. It is, in my opinion, high time for the secular states to become truly secular, especially when it comes to religious education."[133]

My conclusion is that the only way to make sure that all state-educated children in Europe learn about religious diversity from an impartial perspective from qualified teachers is to introduce a common European framework for integrative RE as an individual obligatory school subject. Unlike separative-confessional approaches, this is in line with an appropriate concept of education in secular yet religiously plural democracies. In order to be acceptable to children, parents and teachers of diverse religious and non-religious backgrounds alike, this subject has to start from an approach to religions which is not religious in itself, i.e. an approach as has been developed in the academic study of religions.

---

132 Jensen 1999: Religion and religious education in a Europe of conflicting trends, 153.
133 Ibid., 159.

3 A framework for integrative RE in Europe

In this final part of my study of integrative RE in Europe, I shall outline a European framework for integrative RE, based on the academic study of religions and education. This framework for integrative RE grounds in a non-religious concept of education, as distinct from a number of *religious* – i.e. frequently Christian theological – concepts for RE or education in general, which have been presented in the debate about RE in Europe.

Not only in spite of, but because of, the variety of the various ways of dealing with religious plurality and RE in the individual European countries, a common framework for integrative RE, which ensures that all pupils in Europe learn about religious plurality in an educational approach, is necessary. Even though Peter Schreiner raises an important issue when he argues against the idea of developing "*the* European RE approach, which would ignore the richness of cultures and religions in Europe",[134] as well as the variety of European models for RE, this does not mean that Europe does not need a common general framework for an appropriate teaching about different religions.[135] On the contrary, despite all national, regional or local differences some common international standards for integrative RE are a prerequisite for the provision of an adequate environment for teaching and learning about different religions in schools. This is a point also made implicitly by Robert Jackson in his argument for a pluralistic RE[136] and explicitly by Tim Jensen in his account of the situation of RE in Europe.[137]

Unlike the prescription of certain topics and expected levels of attainment for children of certain ages, as have been presented e.g. in the national model syllabuses in England, this framework for integrative RE outlines a general educationally consistent model which may be modified – though not altered in its basic approach – to fit the situation in the individual countries. This general model dispenses with political and habitual concessions to interest groups beyond the immediate academic and educational partners for RE. In particular, a clear distinction is made between educational and religious interests in RE. Notwithstanding the fact that cooperation between educationists and religious communities with respect to the representation of individual religions

---

134 Schreiner 2002: RE in the European context, 90.
135 This is a point that Schreiner himself tentatively seems to make when he continues with his observation that speaking of different "biographies" of RE "should not hinder any discussion of some common or specific challenges to RE" (ibid).
136 Jackson 2004: Rethinking RE and Plurality.
137 Jensen, e.g. 2005: European and Danish RE.

in integrative RE is desirable, religious communities are not regarded as immediate partners for the design of the general framework of the subject, but the latter task is regarded as the responsibility of secular education authorities, based on expertise in the study of religions and education.

This framework for integrative RE is designed with regard to the secular character of the subject in the context of the educational task of schools in plural democracies in general. Therefore, this framework does not attempt to find a "middle way" between a secular and a religious character of RE, which is, for example, as the experiential approach in English RE has shown, in effect a religious approach. Neither does this framework intend to provide children with faith or spirituality, but takes an outsider perspective which, however, acknowledges insider perspectives. Furthermore, it tries to do away with privileging certain traditions over others – which still happens in confessional, but also even in some integrative approaches, e.g. when the subject-structure "Christianity and others" is chosen – but includes reflection about appropriate methodologies for an impartial approach to different religions as an integral element. Even though this framework has been designed particularly for the European situation, a global perspective has also been considered. Again, with some modifications, it can also be transferred to contexts beyond Europe, as has become evident in the exchange with scholars from other countries, for example, Canada, Indonesia, Japan and South Africa.

The criteria for this framework for integrative RE are based on cornerstones of the debates about theory and methodology in the academic disciplines which are held responsible for this kind of RE, the study of religions and education, as outlined in chapter I. However, in order not to design a concept on an academic drawing-board without any relation to existing concepts and practice, these theoretical presuppositions are considered in the light of the existing approaches to integrative RE in Europe discussed above. The following pages outline my proposal for a truly *educational*[138] integrative RE in the European context (3.1). After that, conclusions will be drawn about individual features of this kind of integrative RE (3.2), before the chapter concludes with an outlook on academic and political desiderata for integrative RE in Europe (3.3).

---

138 "Educational" is used in this context to emphasise that a consistent approach to integrative RE needs to be grounded in a framework which is based on non-religious educational principles, as outlined in chapter I.2.

3.1 The general character of integrative RE

The following is not a comprehensive concept for integrative RE but a clear statement of its general profile. As the experience with different models of teaching religions in schools in Europe has shown, in order to ensure that children learn not only superficially about the plurality of religions, it is necessary to introduce integrative RE as an individual school subject (i.e. not merely as a "learning dimension", even though cooperation beyond subject borders is also necessary)[139] from the first school year onwards (i.e. not only in secondary schools). The subject needs a clear non-religious profile which relates to the general task of education and an account of the situation of children and young people as an integral part of it. Integrative RE ought to be a normal part of any curriculum like other school subjects, for example, history, geography etc., without any kind of an exceptional status, be it with regard to its compulsion, its examination status, or its educational task of communicating values to the children. A clear statement of the subject profile, which is comprehensible for teachers, pupils and parents, making explicit the impartial approach to the plurality of religions, is necessary for its acceptance as an integrative obligatory school subject for all children of various religious or non-religious backgrounds. This general profile of integrative RE will be outlined in the next section (3.1.1). After that, the underlying concept of education will be discussed in delineation from other concepts of education (3.1.2), and the role of integrative RE in the context of wider cultural, social and political debates will be considered (3.1.3).

3.1.1 The profile of integrative RE

An important issue in the debates in different European countries about the character of integrative RE is the question as to what extent objectivity towards the variety of religions is possible.[140] Without any doubt, this issue is one of the key challenges of integrative RE. However, this problem is in fact not at all new, but has been a major concern in the academic study of religions for more than a hundred years. Many of the arguments put forward against integrative RE mirror arguments that were put forward against the discipline of the academic

---

139 See sections 2.2.3 and 2.3 of this chapter.
140 Cf. e.g. Giffionen and Bakker 2002: Interkulturelles und interreligiöses Lernen in der niederländischen Bildungspolitik, 28, with respect to the Netherlands. Cf. also the debate about LER in Germany (section 2.2.2 in this chapter).

study of religions in the early 20th century. Even though it took some time for the academic study of religions to develop a non-religious and impartial approach to the variety of religions and religious phenomena, it has presented a number of valuable approaches in the past decades. The debate in the study of religions (cf. chapter I.1) has shown that even though complete impartiality may be impossible, the very attempt to develop an impartial approach, and the complex methodological reflection related to this enterprise, makes this approach decisively distinct from religious approaches to the plurality of religions. Therefore, theory and methodology in the academic study of religions are relevant for the development of concepts for integrative RE.

Many of the questions raised with respect to integrative RE can be answered with reference to corresponding arguments in the academic study of religions. The study of religions has shown that there is a difference between a secular (i.e. non-religious) and a secularist (i.e. antireligious) approach to religions. Obviously, a secular, not a secularist, approach is appropriate for integrative RE. Furthermore, the study of religions has shown that there is a difference between absolute and methodological relativism[141] and, analogously, between absolute and methodological agnosticism. Denise Cush, for example, has transferred these ideas from the academic study of religions to integrative RE contexts, when she suggests envisaging a "positive pluralism" in education, as opposed to a negative pluralism that avoids encounters with or between religions, e.g. by leaving religious pluralism out of school education or by teaching RE in separative environments:

> "Positive pluralism does not teach that all faiths are equally valid like the relativist, or all paths to the same goal like the universalist. It takes the differences and incommensurability of world views seriously, but approaches them from a viewpoint of 'epistemological humility' or 'methodological agnosticism'."[142]

Similar ideas are put forward by Robert Jackson and the "conversational" approach to a "pluralistic RE" he advocates.[143] When due attention to the teachers' or pupils' own positions in relation to the study of different religions is called for in the debates about RE, it is important to take a close look at the motives and presuppositions behind such statements. Calls like this often seek to elicit a commitment to Christi-

---

141 Cf. e.g. Jensen 2002: RE in public schools - a must for a secular state, 86.
142 Denise Cush 1999: "Models of RE in a plural society: looking to the future", in Borowik (ed.): *Church-State Relations in Central and Eastern Europe*, Krakow: Nomos, 384, quoted in Jackson 2004: 166.
143 See Jackson 1997: RE. An Interpretive Approach, and 2004: Rethinking RE and Plurality. Issues in Diversity and Pedagogy.

anity, if not explicitly as one's actively practiced religion, then at least implicitly with respect to its influence on European culture, the latter often conceived of narrowly and very falsely as an exclusively Christian Europe.[144] Such conceptions of one's own presuppositions neglect the various kinds of religious, ideological, cultural and, no less importantly, social and political affiliations of different individuals as well as groups. The point that one's own presuppositions and contexts have to be taken into account and ought to be questioned is, without any doubt, a basic aspect of education, deserving permanent reconsideration. However, these contexts and presuppositions are manifold. Frequently, important influences like gender, social status or regional particularities (as e.g. eurocentrism) are disregarded. Furthermore, when "one's own tradition" is equated with a construct of a particular "world religion", beliefs and affiliations beyond institutionalised religion, which may be extremely dominant (for example, the capitalist worldview) as well as the internal diversity of what have been called "traditions" are neglected.

The impartial approach, however, meets with difficulties when the educational environment in which it is to be implemented is not impartial. This is, for example, the case in some federal states of Germany whose constitutions state that education in general is to be a Christian education (cf. chapter IV.2.2.1). Perhaps a subject like integrative RE has the potential to challenge these structures, which discriminate against all non-Christians. In many countries, official documents about value education or RE somehow prioritise particular religions, which are selected for representing the "cultural heritage" of education. In contrast to this, it is necessary to find formulations which pay attention to the plurality of religious and non-religious traditions and to the continuing debates which have shaped recent secular notions of education. Mentioning particular traditions always means excluding others. Therefore, in order to truly take account of plurality as a basis for integrative RE, any attempts to make particular religious traditions the general framework of integrative RE, have to be avoided. This also applies to formulations like "an integral concept of education, as found in the Judeo-Christian and Humanist traditions,"[145] which seem to imply that such an integral concept is less likely to be found in other traditions and, furthermore, disregards those aspects of Judeo-Christian and Humanist traditions that can be regarded as counterproductive to recent notions of education. A good way of finding appropriate formula-

---

144 For the debate about religion and culture in Europe see also below, section 3.1.3.
145 Schreiner 2005: RE in Europe, 2.

tions with respect to particular traditions may be to imagine similar situations in other parts of the world. For example, if a very devout Christian lived as an immigrant in a Muslim country and was asked to send his child to integrative RE there, what kind of concept for integrative RE would they be likely to accept?

The Norwegian example has shown that remains of catechesis or religious activity also cause problems for integrative models.[146] Any integrative RE has to pay attention to the difference between religious practice and learning about religions. However, a "grey area" of activities which may or may not be regarded as participation or practice will continue to exist. Therefore, it is important that reflection about this narrow ridge is included at all levels of planning integrative RE and that the children themselves are encouraged to make up their minds about it. A related question is to what extent religion may be simulated in RE in order to enable the pupils' understanding of individual phenomena.[147]

As the European comparison has shown, a consistent relationship between aims, contents and methods is crucial for the credibility of integrative RE. Contents and methods have to fit the aims of the subject. However, conversely, the formulation of aims must not result in distorted ways of representing individual religions in RE. Agreement can be achieved relatively easily over the descriptive dimension of the subject, concerning knowledge and understanding of different religions and an appropriate methodology,[148] which the pupils are meant to acquire. The crucial question is, however, to what extent integrative RE can or should be more than that. Some scholars emphasise that knowledge and understanding of a variety of religions, religious phenomena, secular worldviews and ethics, as well as a reflection upon appropriate methodologies for studying these, is already an important educational end in itself.[149] In fact, it would be an immense improvement for education in Europe if the latter were actually made an integral element of school education, analogous to the study of religions at universities. However, most RE scholars dealing with integrative RE also emphasise the fostering aspect of education, which is less explicit in university

---

146 Cf. Thomassen 2005: RE in a pluralistic society: experiences from Norway, 239.
147 This question is discussed by Antes 1999: Simulierung von Religion im Unterricht.
148 Even though agreement upon what is actually meant by "knowledge and understanding of different religions and an appropriate methodology" is far more difficult to attain. This will be taken up in the section on the representation of religions (3.2.3).
149 See e.g. Jensen 2005: European and Danish RE: human rights, the secular state, and 'Rethinking RE and Plurality'.

disciplines. The idea is that integrative RE also has, in addition to the aforementioned "descriptive"[150] dimension (often referred to as "learning about religions"), an "existential" dimension (often referred to as "learning from religions") which in some way or another pertains to the children's own conclusions from what they have learned about different religions.

The distinction between these two dimensions is perhaps the main difference between the academic study of religions, in which the existential dimension is regarded as a private matter, and concepts for integrative RE, which are often explicitly concerned with also supporting children at an existential level. However, as the experience with some English approaches has shown, this is a critical point at which some approaches to integrative RE fall back into confessional or religious models.[151] If integrative RE is to include some kind of an existential dimension, the crucial point is that this existential dimension cannot be religious but also has to remain within the general secular educational framework. This is mastered quite well in Sweden, where the idea is that one's own *livsfrågor* and *livsåskådning* may be clarified and put into contexts with the help of the study of other positions. Furthermore, a study of different religions is regarded as a prerequisite for taking responsible decisions as a citizen in a religiously plural country. Robert Jackson's concept of "edification", a new perspective on one's own ideas in the light of the study of other positions, which may result from the processes of acquiring knowledge and an understanding of different religions, also represents a non-religious approach to the existential dimension of integrative RE. However, Jackson emphasises that the results of these processes cannot be predicted. Neither can the pupils be provided with advice on how to make sense of the plurality of positions. This would necessarily result in a kind of universal theology as a general framework, which, however, fundamentally contradicts the conversational or methodologically agnostic approach to religions put forward in *educational* integrative RE.

If the plurality of beliefs and values is the starting point for integrative RE, on which values can the subject itself be based? Clearly, these values cannot be the values of any particular religion. Rather, a consideration of the ideological framework of education in general is necessary. If basic values like human rights, the equality of all human beings

---

150 The word "descriptive" is, of course, too narrow for the concept that it refers to. As we have seen in the existent approaches to integrative RE, this dimension involves much more than mere "decription" of religions, but aims at enabling the pupils to be able to analyse, compare and contrast different phenomena.

151 This was the case in the experiential approach as well as in the Stapleford project.

or democracy are chosen as a general basis for all school life, what this means for RE is that all religious traditions will have to be exposed to questions with respect to how their teachings and practice supports or contradicts these values. Furthermore, if criteria and values like democracy or human rights are really taken seriously in integrative RE, this subject will challenge at a grass-roots level the national and global structures which are often anti-democratic[152] and pay little attention to human rights.[153]

Having argued for a secular approach to RE, I have to admit that the distinction between religious and secular, as much as it is often useful, particularly in RE contexts, is ultimately misleading, but nevertheless necessary for the time being, particularly in order to clearly distinguish between theological and study-of-religions approaches to RE. This section has shown that secular RE is also necessarily based on values, beliefs, worldviews, views of life and concepts of the human being. Is, for example, the protection of human rights a religious or a secular value? Unlike the beliefs of individual religions, these are values agreed upon in international conventions. Even though having originated from particular contexts, they have been formally accepted by a majority of states. However, this does of course not mean that there is anything like agreement about what the consequences of such statements and conventions should be. If this very issue is taken up and discussed with reference to historical and contemporary problems, the critical and emancipatory impetus of the notion of education on which integrative RE is based, can be addressed.

3.1.2 The notion of education

It is important that the notion of education on which frameworks for individual school subjects build is made explicit. My conclusions about an appropriate notion of education for integrative RE refer to the debates about theory and methodology in the academic study of education, as outlined in chapter I.2 as well as to notions of education at work in the concepts for RE in Europe, as discussed above. The European comparison has shown that education systems in Europe are generally in transition, not only, but also with respect to RE. In this period of transition, conflicting notions of education, put forward by different

---

152 E.g. in undemocratic international organisations such as, for example, the so called "G8", the IMF, or NATO, as opposed to fairly democratic international organisations such as the UNO.
153 Cf. for example the immigration policy of the EU.

interest groups, compete with each other. The difference between these virtually incompatible understandings of the character of education can be exemplified in the distinction between the *transmission approach* and the *transformation approach* to education.[154] What is at stake in the debates about education is whether education ought to be an acquisition of standardised knowledge defined by economic, political and religious interest groups in order to reproduce existing economical, political and religious structures of society or if education ought to be directed towards the emancipation, autonomy, critical capacity and responsibility of the individual. These diametrically opposed notions of education are mirrored in the landscape of educational research. Here, a distinction has to be made between professional academic research and research that has been initiated by particular economic, political or religious interest groups.[155] However, to make this distinction at all is not an easy task, as these particular non-academic interests are frequently not made explicit.

Approaches to education in *professional academic research* have been outlined in chapter I.2 and were in one way or another also at work in almost all academic concepts for integrative RE which have been analysed in the subsequent chapters.[156] Concepts of education which ground in a critical educational theory, which integrates the aspects of *Erziehung* and *Bildung*, normally start with an analysis of the contexts of education and a critical evaluation of its social and historical character, including existing power structures and mechanisms that produce inequality or are generally directed against educational aims or principles. Wolfgang Klafki has presented a concept of general education (*Allgemeinbildung*) on which his critical and constructive didactics is based. This didactic model aims at promoting (1) *individual self-determination* of life and meaning with respect to e.g. social, vocational and religious matters, (2) *participation* in decision-making about cultural, economic, social and political issues as well as (3) *solidarity* in order to also grant self-determination and participation to others in the face of key challenges that characterise our epoch (*epochaltypische Schlüsselprobleme*). Education is understood as giving children opportunities to acquire key skills (*Schlüsselqualifikationen*) needed in order be responsible members of society, which are themselves to be based on individual self-determination, participation and solidarity. This notion of education

---

[154] See Freire 1997: Erziehung und Hoffnung. Cf. Schreiner 2002: RE in the European context, 97, Härenstam 2000: Kan du höra vindhästen, 136.
[155] For this issue see e.g. Jackson 2004: Current issues in research in RE.
[156] Especially in the works of Grimmitt, Jackson and Härenstam.

involves a radical reassessment of dominant concepts of achievement.[157]

With respect to didactics it is necessary to develop a holistic model which integrates different aspects of academic educational research: a reflection of the general character of education,[158] concepts of teaching,[159] learning and interaction.[160] For integrative RE, what has proved particularly relevant are the insights from research about intercultural education, which systematically considers the different processes involved in attempts to take seriously and understand other systems of perceiving reality, thinking, evaluating and acting. The aims of intercultural education, including (1) knowledge and understanding of different cultural traditions in their social and political contexts, (2) recognition of the subtle and pervasive mechanisms which are at work in the construction of cultures and "otherness" and (3) intercultural competence on different levels, including the cognitive, affective, emotional and behavioural levels,[161] are closely related to the aims of integrative RE as outlined in the variety of existing approaches. The different areas of intercultural learning, for example, social learning, global learning, continuous identity formation in relation to others, and practicing multiperspectivity, have also been important issues in recent international debates about integrative RE.[162]

These professional academic concepts of education lie in stark contrast to a number of concepts of education which have been put forward by particular interest groups or lobbies. Finding one's way through this maze of concepts for education is difficult, particularly for people who do not have professional experience in distinguishing between different types of research. Therefore, interest-group initiated research is frequently very present in political and public debates while the lobby for sound academic research is weak, if not non-existent. A general trend that can be observed in European education systems is an attempt to establish national and international standards for education in order to create more transparency and to make qualifications comparable.

---

157 For Klafki's approach see sections 2.1.4 and 2.2.1 of chapter I. For his general approach cf. Klafki 2001: Grundlinien eines gegenwarts- und zukunftsorientierten Bildungsbegriffs und didaktische Konsequenzen.
158 Cf. e.g. Klafki, see above.
159 Cf. e.g. the *Berlin* and *Hamburg Models*, see section 2.2.2 of chapter I.
160 Cf. e.g. concepts of critical communicative didactics, see section 2.2.3 of chapter I.
161 Cf. section 2.3.1 of chapter I.
162 See, for example, the contributions in Jackson (ed.) 2003: International Perspectives on Citizenship, Education and Religious Diversity.

However, this move towards standardisation and structural comparability is motivated by political and economic, rather than by educational, interests. In fact, it often involves a disregard for fundamental pedagogical principles. Education is alienated from its emancipatory and critical impetus when it is reduced to schooling, qualification and training in the name of a false sense of equality and comparability that relates to standardised tests at certain ages. The harsh discrepancy between lofty but empty political and economy-driven rhetoric and educational reality has been addressed most clearly by Michael Grimmitt. He criticises the fact that politicians frequently decide on short-sighted ideological and economic grounds, without taking any notice of relevant academic research. Education seems to be reduced to the production of human capital for economic growth, which is, in fact, a colonisation of the educational sector by economic interests.[163] In this context, integrative RE has a great potential, as it involves a critical analysis of worldviews and views of life, including the worldview and concepts of the human being behind these models of education, as well as a discussion of other options.

Considering the differences between these conflicting notions of education, from which further differences, for example, with respect to the concept of knowledge or the role of the teacher originate, a clear statement of the philosophy of education on which integrative RE can build is necessary. The framework for integrative RE which is suggested here, builds on a critical and emancipatory concept of education, as has been suggested by professional educationists (cf. chapter I.2). Therefore, my attempt to provide a common framework for integrative RE in Europe is not to be misunderstood as another voice in the rhetoric about standardisation, administration and management of education that currently dominates the political debate about education in Europe. It is meant rather as a call for a reconsideration of the basic principles of education and for leaving the responsibilities for education to those who are, in fact, qualified, i.e. professional educationists rather than political, economic or religious lobbies. My framework for integrative RE relates to the general character of the subject and not to the identification of some "standard knowledge" that can be tested in multiple choice tests. In view of the European social and political context, educators need to fight for a climate in which such a concept of education may regain its place.

---

163 See Grimmitt 2000: Introduction: The captivity and liberation of RE and the meaning and significance of pedagogy.

With respect to RE, conflicts between different interests in particular concepts of education have been particularly visible in the debates about confessional vs. non-confessional RE. Educators frequently identify a conflict between the interests of the pupils in receiving broad and balanced information about different religions (non-confessional RE) and the interests of the parents in having their children educated into a particular worldview (confessional RE). In Finland, for example, the right of the parents to having their children instructed in the way they wish is considered more important than the right of the pupils to unbiased information about religions.[164] In Germany, the current form of confessional RE almost exclusively serves the interests of the Protestant and Catholic churches in securing their influence on the young generation. Priorities are different in England, where the actual situation of the children is taken as a starting point and in Sweden, where preference is clearly given to the interests of the pupils in an emancipatory, educational approach.[165]

We have seen that integrative RE cannot be reduced to the transmission of testable standard knowledge about "world religions", as e.g. knowledge about the stories around the life of the Buddha or about the five pillars of Islam. The processes that take place in integrative RE are far more complex than that. Integrative RE encourages pupils to engage with their own beliefs and values in relation to understanding others. This is something different from the requirements of some "national or local syllabuses that specify the systematic coverage of large amounts of information, leaving little or no space for interaction, reflection and criticism".[166] Rather than trying systematically to cover too much information, confrontation with and participation in debates about religions, beliefs and values can help the pupils to clarify, challenge or illuminate their positions and thereby enable them to examine their own and others' ideas. A clear educational philosophy also involves an ideological framework for dealing with plurality and a clear statement about processes of "othering" and dichotomising vs. an appreciation of plurality, as well as an acknowledgement of and commitment to equality.[167] The latter is regarded as appropriate for integrative RE.

These educational presuppositions make it necessary that, in integrative RE, the pupils are presented with broad and balanced informa-

---

164 Olin 2000: RE in Finland – framework and practice.
165 For this issue cf. e.g. Almén 2000: RE in Sweden, Borevi 1997: Religion i skolan, Felderhof 2000: RE and human rights.
166 Jackson 2003: Citizenship, religious and cultural diversity and education, 22.
167 See Breidlid and Nicolaisen 2004: Multi-faith RE in a religiously-mixed context: some Norwegian perspectives, 78.

tion – as far as this is possible[168] – as well as being introduced to a methodological inventory, which together enable them to make up their own minds about these issues and take responsible decisions. This also involves thinking twice about preliminary decisions that educators have to take with respect to the general ideological framework, relating e.g. to the general perspective on religious diversity or the selection of teaching material and other sources. In a generally critical framework, these processes have to be made explicit so that pupils can learn to understand that these preliminary decisions and selections have been taken by somebody for particular reasons. Kjell Härenstam's remark that knowledge is always somebody's knowledge (*någons kunskap*) is a very relevant contribution to the debate.[169] With respect to the communication of knowledge about different religions, Tim Jensen recommends revitalising the Enlightenment tradition rather than searching for religious alternatives.[170] I fully agree with him that a truly secular perspective is needed, however the Enlightenment tradition and its effects also have to be considered critically. The dialectic of Enlightenment and its belief in progress as well as the subsequent instrumentalisation of reason for technical interests, as described by Horkheimer and Adorno, have to be kept in mind.[171] Critically taking up the Enlightenment tradition, however, can contribute to a truly educational account of religions and views of life, including an evaluation of the rhetoric about Enlightenment, democracy, freedom, human rights etc. in the face of actual political practice.

The debates about education have shown that views of education are normative and refer to different worldviews and concepts of individuals in relation to society. Professional concepts of education, which build on academic analyses of the social and political environments of pupils, have been found in conflict with concepts of education that are produced by certain lobbies, which provide their own analyses of the pupils' environments. This conflict remains an unresolved problem in the European educational landscape to this date. The concept of education which I suggest as a basis for a European framework for integrative RE is indebted to the academic tradition which focuses on emanci-

---

[168] That this is a difficult task does not mean that it is impossible, but that continuous attention to and critical reflection of one's own presuppositions is required. Jackson's idea of methodological self criticism (see 1997: RE. An Interpretive Approach, 57) may help to understand this general task.
[169] Härenstam 2000: Kan du höra vindhästen?, 145.
[170] Jensen 1997: Familiar and unfamiliar challenges to the study and teaching of religions, 218.
[171] Cf. my brief discussion of the contribution of critical theory to education, chapter I, section 2.1.

pation, liberation and integration as opposed to other concepts of education which are implicitly or explicitly indebted to the ideas of assimilation, exploitation and separation. The position of this concept of education with respect to integrative RE in relation to wider cultural, social and political debates will be discussed in the next section.

3.1.3 Integrative RE in the context of wider cultural, social and political debates

The last section has revealed the political character of education: education is neither planned in a neutral environment, nor does it take place on a neutral terrain. The debates about the aims of education as well as about integrative RE take place in the eye of the storm of wider debates about culture, religion, values and politics in different societies. We have seen that the political frameworks for RE are frequently not the educationally best solutions. Politicians who decide about these issues often have only vague, if any, ideas about the actual educational implications of their decisions. As political debates in various European countries have shown, the research to which politicians refer is frequently dated or cannot even really be called research, but rather information that lobbies have produced to support their claims. It has become the normal situation that politicians take decisions first and then expect researchers and educationists to follow after, rather than providing a basis for political decision making.[172] This situation is highly unsatisfactory and detrimental to the pupils as well as to society as a whole. A new relationship between academic research and politics is required, in which the task and character of education is derived from national and international conventions which have been adopted in democratic processes. These can be used as a basis for the design of general frameworks for individual schools subjects, for example integrative RE. These frameworks have to be drawn up by qualified professionals with academic educational expertise and not by other interest groups. For integrative RE, this means that educationists who have been educated in the study of religions and not representatives of religious communities are responsible for these frameworks. If the latter are consulted, it is important to be fully aware of their roles and strategies in these processes. It is high time that (religious, economic and

---

[172] This point, which was made by Geir Skeie (2004: An overview over RE research in Norway, 324) about the Norwegian situation is equally applicable to many other European countries.

other) lobbies are actually recognised as lobbies. As Jackson points out, this also means that RE researchers need to make their work more accessible to politicians and policy makers, who in turn need to recognise the value and relevance of RE research and make efforts to consult it.[173]

The general social and political climate with respect to religion and RE is also determined by the discrepancy between so-called secular states and the intimate church-state relations in most European as well as other countries. Jensen points out that the lack of integrative RE in many European countries indicates that the notion of religion, on which concepts for RE are based, is not really secular.[174] This creates confusion about the responsibility for religion in secular states and education systems, in particular the responsibility for RE, e.g. when cooperation with insiders, which is sensible in integrative RE, is mistaken for control by insiders.[175] Another important influence on the public opinion are the debates about the existence and the character of multicultural societies in Europe. In some countries, for example Great Britain, the multiethnic and multicultural composition of the society seems to be evident, while conservative politicians in other countries seem to try to conjure up their ideals of a supposedly lost cultural homogeneity by simply ignoring the actual composition of their country's inhabitants. In view of the Danish situation, Mette Buchard puts the latter strategy down to a fear of losing something when one's own position and frame of reference cannot claim unquestioned authority any longer.[176]

In the attempt to find common values for the religiously and culturally plural European states, reference is often made to the so-called "cultural heritage" of individual countries or Europe as a whole. This "cultural heritage" is frequently narrowly conceived of as the Christian tradition and Western Humanism, for example in Norway, whose national heritage programme, which prioritises Christianity, may be regarded as a threat to religious minorities, but also in Sweden, where the general school ethos (*värdegrund*) is related to the *kristen etik och västerlandsk humanism*. This construction of a uniform cultural heritage, which is often regarded as a legitimate guideline in the search for

---

173 Jackson 2004: Current issues in research in RE, 29.
174 Cf. Jensen 2002: RE in public schools – a must for a secular state, 85.
175 This was e.g. the case when suggestions for the revision of the curriculum of KRL in Norway were dismissed due to the criticism of church circles who wanted to keep the privileged position of Christianity in the curriculum, cf. Thomassen 2005: RE in a pluralistic society: experiences from Norway, 239ff.
176 Cf. Buchard 2004: RE in the school: approaches in school practice and research in Denmark, 117ff.

common values for the future, prioritises particular traditions while minoritising others. Jensen quite rightly asks why this kind of preaching cannot be left to the churches, and emphasises that, contrary to much contemporary Christian propaganda, today's Europe has not been shaped solely by so-called Christian ideas and values.[177] Furthermore, educational approaches have to critically evaluate all kinds of heritage, including – as we have seen above – the Enlightenment as well as Christian traditions whose heritage also includes e.g. the Inquisition, witch hunts, the crusades and the discrimination of women.

The diversity of religious and secular worldviews influences various wider social, political and historical issues in a number of ways. Therefore, rather than trying to construct a uniform cultural heritage, the relevance of the different traditions past and present, with all their positive and negative aspects ought to be taken into account. Not only contemporary Europe is religiously plural, but also the religious history of Europe is a plural one with periods of harmony as well as conflict between different religions, denominations and worldviews, including a wide tradition of philosophical criticism of "religion", which was normally directly addressed to the teachings and practice of Christianity. If we, for example, consider the history of religions in Europe in the 20th century, it is evident that topics relating to, for example, Judaism,[178] Islam,[179] Buddhism,[180] but also indigenous or so-called "pagan" religions[181] and philosophical traditions like Existentialism, to name but a selection, are part and parcel of the "European cultural heritage", if one is to use this notion at all. However, references to this notion in recent debates raise doubts about the actual motives behind them. The notion of cultural heritage seems to be used less as an analytical category for describing the history of religions and cultures in Europe and more as a prescriptive category which is used in order to justify the dominance of certain traditions over others with reference to similarly unequal structures that have existed in the past.

---

177 Jensen 2002: RE in public schools – a must for a secular state, 84, 88.
178 E.g. the holocaust, anti-Semitism, the situation of Jews in Germany after WWII, the policies of European states towards Israel etc.
179 E.g. Islam in different European countries past and present, migration and changing religious landscapes, issues concerning individual topics such as the debate about women wearing headscarves.
180 E.g. Western and Eastern understandings of Buddhism, the processes that occur when traditions are transferred to different contexts, the popular interpretation of Buddhism as meeting the needs of modern Western people, the recent popularity of people like the Dalai Lama or Thich Nhat Hanh.
181 E.g. the Sami tradition, Shamanism, the revival of "pagan" rituals and symbols.

Furthermore, in our global world a sole emphasis on Europe seems rather narrow. It is an urgent desideratum that the perspective is also widened beyond the borders of Europe, not only in integrative RE, but also, and very importantly, in other school subjects such as history. As Kjell Härenstam has argued, for example, with reference to the work of Edward Said and others who have criticised the limited perspective of much European discourse, the heritage of our contemporary world ought to be perceived as "humankind's cultural heritage".[182] Today's children and young people are inevitably confronted with local, regional and global challenges. Therefore, all these dimensions have to be in focus in school, in RE as well as in other subjects. Apart from local or regional relevance, religion is an evident factor in international relations and processes of globalisation. This is another reason why "no country can afford to see its educational provision in isolation."[183]

Considerations about integrative RE in the context of wider social, cultural and political issues and the tension between the quest for common values and expectations of religious freedom and tolerance towards diversity and otherness, have recently raised the question about the contribution of the study of religions and integrative RE to citizenship education. Important aspects of the international debate about RE and citizenship education, which is an explicit individual subject in some countries and an implicit general learning dimension relating to democratic values, virtues and political literacy in other countries, are collected in the book *International Perspectives on Citizenship, Education and Religious Diversity*, edited by Robert Jackson (2004). The notion of citizenship and its traditional focus on the participation of individuals in nation states has been challenged by the processes of globalisation, related e.g. to massive advances in information and communication technology, which have enhanced world trade but at the same time reinforced inequalities, particularly between the countries of the North and the South. In view of these developments, as Jackson puts it,

> "[t]hose committed to universal human rights, to the reduction of inequality or to the conservation of the environment ... find themselves at odds with government policies perceived as promoting narrow national interest at the expense of the poor or with policies of multinational companies seeming to show scant regard to the long-term future of the planet."[184]

The global context makes necessary a reconsideration of the notion of citizenship that takes account of the different affiliations of individuals.

---

182 See Härenstam 2000: Kan du höra vindhästen? 155f.
183 Jackson 2004: Current issues in research in RE, 29.
184 Jackson 2003: Citizenship, religious and cultural diversity and education, 3f.

Jackson suggests the concept of "differentiated citizenship", built on participatory structures for people of diverse backgrounds, in order to take account of different forms of plurality at various levels of society. For example with respect to Islam in Europe, he shows that the debates about religion need to be set in the context of complementary debates about the nation state, ethnicity and culture, and question common assumptions about members of Muslim diasporas in Western societies.[185] Data from field studies of religions can be used to illuminate issues relating to the debates about citizenship. For example, based on empirical research among Muslim young people in Norway, Sissel Østberg argues for a "transcultural" approach to citizenship, which combines local belonging, cultural diversity and global visions. A combination of cosmopolitanism and localism can be found among young Muslims in Europe today. Her argument is that findings like this have to be taken up in citizenship education, which ought to include the concept of transcultural citizenship. This kind of citizenship education together with other aspects of intercultural education and integrative RE may contribute to a positive stance towards plurality.[186] Considerations about RE and citizenship education relate directly to the political dimension of integrative RE and education in general, as they infer the tasks for education from plain analyses of social and political contexts. Jackson, for example, quotes from the Runnymede Trust's report *The Future of Multi-ethnic Britain* (2000), which suggests – with respect to the British situation – that the development of a sense of belonging and citizenship requires attention to underlying economic factors affecting cross-sections of the population:

> "Rather than concentrate on minorities based on ethnicity or religion, should we not urge Government increasingly to counter the emergence of an underclass, whose deepening exclusion – known to every youth magistrate – is a matter of shame to the whole nation? Of course this underclass has black, Asian (mainly Muslim) and white minorities within it – but it is the pains, injustices and problems of the underclass as a whole which require fundamental action. It is here that the question of racism, equalities etc. take on their sharpest edge."[187]

This rearrangement of social structures on different levels of society from local to global is also addressed by Heid Leganger-Krogstad. She

---

185 See Jackson 2003: Citizenship, religious and cultural diversity and education, 12ff.
186 See Østberg 2003: Cultural diversity and common citizenship.
187 Runnymede 2000: *The Report of the Commission on the Future of Multi-ethnic Britain*, London: Runnymede Trust, quoted in Jackson 2003: Citizenship, religious and cultural diversity and education, 13f.

refers to a quotation from the Nobel Lecture by Kofi Annan, general secretary of the United Nations:

> "Today's real borders are not between nations, but between powerful and powerless, free and fettered, privileged and humiliated. Today, no walls can separate humanitarian or human rights crisis in one part of the world from national security crises in another."[188]

Leganger-Krogstad uses such analyses of the global situation, which is mirrored in the children's lives, as a basis for her contextual approach to integrative RE which relates to local as well as global responsibility.[189]

I hope to have demonstrated that the interrelationships between integrative RE and citizenship education are many and manifold, yet only an illustration of these issues can be presented here. However, I would like to address one final point concerning common challenges for citizenship education and RE, which was raised by Judy Tobler, who identified "a glaring gender-blindness in modern citizenship theory that serves only to reinforce patriarchy and to privilege male citizens as the norm."[190] Tobler argues, that theory for RE and citizenship education can fruitfully contribute to each other in developing strategies to account for gender differences, based on a critical analysis of discourses on citizenship and religion with respect to the production of gendered subjectivity and intersubjectivity.[191] Common challenges and problems, as well as the interrelations between different aspects of social, cultural, political and religious life, demonstrate the close link between RE and citizenship education. Research findings in the study of religions have an important part to play in citizenship education. At the same time, integrative RE is itself an indispensable element of responsible citizenship education, if the challenges of globalisation are taken seriously and the differentiated character of citizenship with its local, regional, and global aspects is acknowledged.

---

188 Annan 2001: Nobel Lecture.
189 Leganger-Krogstad 2003: Dialogue among young citizens in a pluralistic RE classroom.
190 Tobler 2003: Learning the difference. RE, citizenship education and gendered subjectivity, 125.
191 Tobler 2003: Learning the difference. RE, citizenship education and gendered subjectivity.

3.2 Individual features of integrative RE

The following conclusions about individual features of integrative RE cover the name of the school subject (3.2.1), the concept of religion and the delineation of the subject matter (3.2.2), the representation of religions (3.2.3) and the organisation and transformation of the subject (3.3.4).

3.2.1 The name of the school subject

In order to be explicit about the general character of the subject, the actual name for integrative RE as an individual school subject ought to be consistent with the philosophy and contents of the approach. The European comparison has shown that debates about the name of integrative RE are often indicative of unresolved contradictions in the general concept. For example, Mette Buchard has shown for the Danish situation that the debate about the name of the subject *kristendomskundskab* in the Danish *folksskolen*, which has been meant to be non-confessional since 1975, is only the tip of the iceberg of a debate about fundamental questions concerning the relationship between religions, culture and society. Alternative suggestions for names, such as *religionskundskab* have given rise to debates about the responsibility for the subject (the study of religions vs. theology) as well as about the meaning of nationality and the idea of Danish culture being based on Lutheran values.[192] If one religion in particular is part of the name of the subject, doubts with respect to the true impartiality of the general approach are justified, as the debate about KRL (*Kristendoms- religions- og livssynskunnskap*) in Norway has shown. The name of the Bremen integrative model, called BGU (*Biblischer Geschichtsunterricht auf allgemein christlicher Grundlage*) may give rise to similar doubts about the approach and contents of the subject.

Names for the subject which also refer to ethics and worldviews or views of life have also been suggested for integrative RE. Between 1980 and 1994, integrative RE in Sweden was somewhat long-windedly called *människans frågor inför livet och tillvaron; religionskunskap* in order to emphasise the focus of the subject on implicit religion. However, the name was changed back to just *religionskunskap* in 1994, which incorporates explicit as well as implicit dimensions. Unlike in Sweden, scholars of religions in Germany have only felt responsible for those parts of the

---

192 Cf. Buchard 2004: RE in school: approaches in school practice and research in Denmark.

Brandenburg school subject *Lebensgestaltung-Ethik-Religionskunde* (LER), which deal explicitly with representing religions. This is a result of the way the German academic study of religions conceived of itself until very recently in general, and in particular a result of the lack of comprehensive reflection about a didactics of the study of religions in school. However, this disregards the potential of the methodology, and further resources existent in the study of religions for the other aspects of this subject, i.e. ethics and ways of life. If integrative RE is based on a sound educational approach, it is – in my view – not necessary to refer to the individual aspects of the subject in its name. This was probably also one insight which led to changing the name back to *religionskunskap* in Sweden. In fact, the Swedish *religionskunskap* or the German *Religionskunde* are very good names for the subject, as they refer to the generally impartial framework and avoid misunderstandings that the ambivalent English term *religious* education[193] may bring about with respect to the secular and simply not religious character of the subject.

3.2.2 The concept of religion and the delineation of the subject matter

As well as the academic study of religions, integrative RE needs an explicit outline of the concept of religion on which it is based, despite the difficulty of this task. This may serve as a delineation of the subject matter, but must not be misunderstood as an attempt to say what "religion" essentially is. We have seen that a variety of different and sometimes conflicting concepts of religion have been suggested in the academic study of religions itself.[194] However, even though no unquestioned definition has been found, convincing delineations of the subject matter have been presented, despite the contested nature of some of its borders. Taking seriously the basic epistemological presuppositions of the study of religions has led, if not really to anything like agreement about the concept of religion, then at least to a dynamic polycentrism of aspects that in different variations make up what scholars of religions regard as religion or religions.[195] A framework for integrative RE does not have to solve the problems that the academic study of religions has continued to struggle with up to this day. However, integrative RE has to build on basic insights from the academic study of religions with respect to a concept of religion which is accept-

---

193 The same problem arises, of course, in the term *religious studies*.
194 See section 1.2.1 of chapter I: The variety of concepts of religion.
195 See section 1.2.2 of chapter I: The "subject matter" or "field" of the study of religions.

able in an impartial framework. Therefore, a working concept of religion (which can and should remain a matter of debate) for integrative RE (1) must not be religious in itself, and therefore (2) also has to dispense with essentialising notions of "religion as such". Furthermore, (3) it has to refrain from universalising the features of any individual religion as well as from (4) over-emphasising any one aspect of religions. (5) It has to be broad enough to include a variety of traditions and phenomena, even and particularly beyond what has frequently been called "world religions", and has to be attentive to the actual diversity of religious phenomena as well as to local contexts and particularities. Finally (6), it cannot consider itself immune to criticism.

The European comparison of concepts of religion which underlie models for integrative RE mirror these criteria in the light of problems which have occurred in actual RE contexts. First of all, the survey has shown that there is no compromise between religious and non-religious concepts of religion as a basis for RE. Any attempt to find a middle way between the two results in a religious approach which is unacceptable in integrative RE, as e.g. problems arising from the experiential approach in England have revealed. However, this has already been demonstrated in the academic study of religions with respect to a criticism of the classical phenomenology of religion.[196] Therefore, such problems could have been avoided if the study of religions had been regarded as the responsible academic discipline for the development of method and theory for integrative RE from the very beginning. Secondly, if the notion of religion is to be secular, integrative RE necessarily has to include the study of a variety of "non-religious" worldviews and views of life along with what is traditionally conceived of as religion, as this very distinction between religious and non-religious has proved arguable at close inspection. The Swedish approach is consistent in this respect. In order to fully acknowledge the explicit as well as implicit dimensions of religion, which are relevant to the life of the pupils, the actual diversity of *livsåskådningar* have to be discussed rather than reducing the subject matter by working with problematical delineations such as a certain number of so-called "major world religions".[197] Thirdly, the phenomenon of religion has to be appreciated in its full ambivalent diversity. Any attempt to isolate positive aspects of individual religions or of "religion as such" represent normative constructs of religion that ignore its actual ambivalence. It is this very ambivalence that children have to learn to deal with. A presentation of

---

[196] Cf. section 1.1.2 of chapter I: Implications from the history of the study of religions.
[197] Cf. section 1.2.2 of this chapter about the concept of religion in English and Swedish RE.

domesticated versions of religion violates the children's right to broad and balanced information. The discrepancy between lofty moral ideals and actual practice is a recurrent phenomenon that children need to reflect upon. This also includes the ambivalence of concepts such as "democracy" or other philosophies and worldviews. All religious and secular worldviews or views of life need to be exposed to the same kind of critical study with respect to this very discrepancy. Fourthly, the study of concepts of religion underlying approaches to integrative RE has shown once again that using the terminology of one religious tradition for comparative descriptions of different religions without methodically reflecting this process frequently leads to misrepresentations of religions. This has, for example, been the case in the English national model syllabus for RE produced by the School Curriculum and Assessment Authority, in which almost exclusively Christian concepts were suggested for a comparative study of religions.[198] In contrast to this, the terminology for integrative RE has to start from the diversity of religions, not from one single religion which is used as a model for the study of others.

The delineation of the subject matter of integrative RE needs to combine the expertise of the academic study of religions with the selection of phenomena that are particularly relevant for the world of the pupils. Needless to say, it is impossible to study in RE the whole range of religions and religious phenomena that exist in the world. However, this makes it very important for the concept of religion, as well as for the general methodology, to be broad enough to be potentially applicable to this factual variety. Only then is exemplary learning with respect to further issues and questions possible. Care must be taken to ensure that an appropriate concept of religion is used from the very beginning when integrative RE takes place, i.e. already for very young children. Furthermore, once the children have the mental capability of understanding more complex issues, they need to be introduced to the debates about appropriate concepts of religion in an integrative environment, inclusive of the debate about the distinction between religious and non-religious. Furthermore, if an educational approach takes a truly critical perspective towards religions and worldviews, the *grand narratives* of religious traditions about themselves have to be contrasted with *small narratives* of individuals, and in particular with the *small narratives* of the pupils.[199] This also involves a study of the processes by which authority and truth claims are produced.

---

198 Cf. SCAA 1995: RE 16-19.
199 Cf. the work by Clive and Jane Erricker, e.g. 2000: The Children and Worldviews Project: A Narrative Pedagogy of RE.

Such a concept of religion for integrative RE makes possible a study of a wide range of phenomena, including, for example, (1) what is commonly understood by "religion", i.e. big and small, contemporary and ancient, indigenous and "world-" institutionalised religions in all their internal diversity, so-called new religious movements, as well as looser forms of individual or shared spirituality; (2) other worldviews and views of life, including capitalism (or: "the market economy"), with their respective grand and small narratives; (3) religion in the public sphere and religion as a social factor, including civil religion. Without any doubt, the traditions represented in the immediate surroundings of the pupils are of special relevance. This, however, must not diminish the generally broad perspective or deflect attention from national and global issues.

3.2.3 The representation of religions

The notion of religion underlying any approach to RE involves decisions about the framework in which religions are represented in RE. A reflected representation of religions includes a consideration of a number of prior decisions. These are not always uncontroversial, as, for example, the debates about a thematic vs. a systematic approach in England or the revision of the Norwegian curriculum with respect to the representation of religions in KRL have shown.

Frequent misrepresentations of religions are based on inadequate concepts of religion which refer e.g. to religion "as such" or religion as a thing or agent. Furthermore, representations of religion in RE often repeat and renew the well-known Christian and orientalist discourse on other religions with its dichotomies of "us" vs. "them". In confessional Christian RE misrepresentations have often resulted from approaching Christianity and other religions with different methodologies. While life themes or ultimate questions as starting points for approaching Christianity were actually related to the lives of the children with topics like love, relationships, death, turning points in life, illness, justice etc., the study of "other" religions often included not much more than a stereotypical representation of some information that was regarded as standard knowledge about these religions, which, however, did not in any way relate to the lives of the pupils. This meant that frequently the impression was created that "other" religions are something strange, irrational, pre-modern, ritualistic and definitely not an option for oneself. I myself experienced these processes when I sat in on classes on Hinduism with a teacher at a German grammar school as part of a teacher training course. Her teaching of Hinduism to pupils of about fifteen years of age, which concentrated on the study of ancient Vedic texts without any relation to the life of the pupils at all, resulted in the pupils' complete rejection of any possible relevance of Hindu teachings. Here, sound methods developed for teaching different religions, such as the teaching material developed in the Warwick RE-Project, would have helped to avoid this undesired outcome of this series of lessons on Hinduism.

However, integrative RE has not been immune to a misrepresentation of religions either. As we have seen, the use of concepts of one religion as a framework for the study of others has resulted in undue distortions. Furthermore, a religious, not secular, notion of religion as the framework for representing various religions has been one of the major causes of misrepresentations, as e.g. in the experiential approach in England. An impartial approach must not be confused with a universal theology of religions, which often builds on a preconceived universal essence or meaning of "religion" or religious phenomena. In order to avoid such confusions, a clear outline of the general framework for the representation of religions in an impartial approach is required and preliminary decisions about the approach to religious diversity have to be made explicit. The plurality of religions with sometimes similar, sometimes conflicting, ideas has to be acknowledged. The perspective of methodological (not absolute) agnosticism helps to avoid introducing the pupils to unquestioned paradigms.

An impartial approach to religions and the representation of religions, which builds on insights of the academic study of religions, involves attention to the background of those who study different religions, as well as attention to the voices of insiders as an integral part of such study. In order to do justice to the variety of positions, no decisions about truth can be taken from this perspective. The frequent claim that a study-of-religions approach to RE lacks "cooperation with faith communities, associations and organisations which give authentic testimony about beliefs and religious views"[200] is simply not true, as the survey of European approaches to integrative RE has shown. Various strategies for such a cooperation have been established for the representation of religions in integrative RE in the English, Swedish and Norwegian models. In integrative RE, the inclusion of insider voices may take different forms, including cooperation between educators and religious communities or individuals. However, as also in the academic

---

200 Schreiner 2002: RE in the European context, 90, just to give one example.

study of religions, such a cooperation is a complex task which requires a clear distribution of roles and responsibilities.[201]

In an educational approach, this cooperation should take place under the general responsibility of secular educational institutions and not of religious communities. Even though this cooperation has frequently worked well, some experiences have shown that educators ought to be alerted to the possibility that cooperation with believers might turn into domination by believers. This kind of cooperation seems to be particularly difficult with traditions that formerly enjoyed the privilege of having their own confessional RE in schools. For example, the right to veto of the Church of England in English agreed syllabus committees or the dominant position of the Norwegian Church in curriculum development for Norwegian integrative RE contradict the claim to impartiality. Further reforms towards a truly impartial approach are necessary. In Brandenburg in Germany, the Protestant Church terminated its cooperation in the test phase which preceded the introduction of integrative RE (*Lebensgestaltung-Ethik-Religionskunde*, LER) when it realised that the final decisions about the subject and the representation of religions were actually taken by educators and not representatives of religious communities. The organisers of LER managed to maintain the truly educational character of the subject against the massive pressure put on them by the two major churches in Germany.

In most European countries, powerful established religions are used to being granted a number of privileges that smaller and minority religions do not have.[202] In particular with respect to RE, being one religion among others in a generally impartial framework is a new situation and often poses a serious challenge to well-established religions. However, it is indispensable for the credibility of an educational approach that it is truly open towards the variety of religions and does not select only particular religions for cooperation. It is an important aspect of the English organisation of RE that members of all religious communities are invited to participate in the considerations about syllabuses, despite the inconsistency that the Church of England has a privileged position among the religions.[203]

---

201 For the relationship between scholars of religions and insiders cf. Pye 2004: Religionswissenschaft und Religionen: Eine riskante Nähe und ihre Notwendigkeit.
202 This is particularly evident in the educational sector, for example with respect to establishing private schools (e.g. in Norway) or presenting religious symbols (e.g. in Germany) as well as with respect to the representation of religions at universities and schools in general.
203 Cf. chapter II, section 1.2.

In integrative RE, cooperation with insiders about the representation of their particular religion is both welcome and helpful. However, this cooperation has to be organised and supervised by RE professionals trained in the study of religions. As in the study of religions, religious communities cannot have the last word about the representation of their religion, even though their view on this matter ought to be included. Most importantly, educators have to be aware of the diversity of insider voices and must not mistake the voices of "representatives" or people with high positions in religious communities for the actual diversity of views. Therefore, different forms of integrating insider voices are necessary. This is to be reflected in the selection of sources to be studied, the teaching material in general, and also in the planning of excursions or visits. The Warwick RE-Project has presented innovative material which draws on a well-reflected cooperation with believers, relating individual voices, which are taken as starting points, to local membership groups as well as wider religious traditions.

The selection of religions and religious phenomena from the broad "field" needs to be considered. A focus on contemporary religion, which is advisable with respect to the real-life environment of the pupils, should not completely dispense with an additional historical perspective and also a study of ancient religions, as these may help to better understand current phenomena. Furthermore, the notion "world religion" ought to be examined critically. Religions studied should also involve small and new religions as well as phenomena beyond institutionalised religion. For the representation of religions, a careful selection of sources is also important. The variety of sources (e.g. oral, written, visual, material) needs to be acknowledged, so that the focus is not narrowed down to just one of these, for example, religious texts. Furthermore, the selection of sources should also reflect different voices within traditions. Thus, it should not only refer to specialists' accounts of their religions, but also to the voices of "ordinary" members of the community. Children need to learn to distinguish between different kinds of sources, including insider and outsider sources, and consider the grey area between those.

In order to present a balanced account of the actual diversity of religious phenomena, the different aspects of religions need to be taken into account, so that no single aspect, for example texts or concepts, is over-emphasised. A good example of attention to the internal diversity of traditions is the focus on individuals, membership groups and the wider religious tradition in the Warwick RE project, which particularly focuses on the voices of individual children of different religions in Britain today. The complex relationships between majority and minority traditions to be considered and a critical account of traditional constructions of centres and peripheries is required, for example with respect to age, social status, gender or region. Representations of religions need to include religious dynamics and change, innovation and the fuzzy borders of traditions, which are never monolithic entities. Furthermore, power relations, including the power of description and the different ways of dealing with religious plurality, need to be reflected. Other representations of religions that the pupils may encounter beyond immediate school contexts, for example in the media, need to be discussed and contrasted with an impartial approach to religions in order to communicate knowledge about the various processes and contexts for different constructions of individual religions or "religion".

Integrative RE is a comparative subject and deals with individual religions as well as with similarities and differences between religions. It is incorrect to regard thematic (dealing with different themes, for example, death, in different religions) and systematic (studying the individual religions one by one) representations of religions as alternatives for the representation of religions in integrative RE, between which an approach for RE has to decide.[204] To use the concepts of the English debate, thematic and systematic representations of religions are not general either-or options, but both approaches have their place in different phases of representing religions in integrative RE. However, care has to be taken to avoid superficial comparisons which rather hinder than promote an understanding of the phenomena.[205]

The various processes and issues involved in representing religions in integrative RE cannot be dealt with comprehensively here. In addition to what I have said above I would like to draw attention to a few more points for consideration, which have emerged from the different European experiences with integrative RE:

(1) *Conflicting narratives*: Breidlid and Nicolaisen have presented strategies to avoid patronising the pupils and rather help them to deal with the factual diversity of sometimes conflicting narratives in a generally conversational approach.[206] Furthermore, postmodern criticism of representations of religions has addressed the distortion of the actual diversity of views by the construction of *meta-narratives* which silence the *small narratives* of minorities or indi-

---

[204] Cf. section 1.2.3 of chapter IV for more detailed conclusions about this debate in England.
[205] Cf. section 1.3.3. of chapter I for insights from the academic study of religions and section 1.2.3 of chapter IV for comparisons in integrative RE.
[206] Breidlid and Nicolaisen 2004: Multi-faith RE in a religiously-mixed context: some Norwegian perspectives, 74f.

viduals. Integrative RE needs to take up this kind of criticism in its continual reconsideration of the representation of religions.

(2) *Discriminatory elements*: Another important concern is discriminatory elements, which can be found in most religions, frequently, for example, with respect to the discrimination of women. For a study of such aspects of religions, it is important to approach all religions equally critically and not reproduce the stereotypes about religions that are frequently produced in public debates or in the media. For example, discriminatory elements in Buddhism have often been overlooked, as Buddhism is generally perceived of as an open and tolerant religion by people in Europe. However, like other major religions such as Christianity or Islam, many Buddhist traditions also include teachings and practice that discriminate against women.[207] Discriminating elements of religion may also relate to ethnicity or other factors. Breidlid and Nicolaisen's advice to contextualise those elements, e.g. with respect to their origins and interests, and to show the differences to the educational philosophy of the school, points at the critical impetus of integrative RE, which aims at understanding insider positions, but at the same time critically contrasts religious teachings and practice with the foundations of secular education, of which it is itself a part. Therefore, a clear outline of the ideological basis of the educational position is necessary, including an explicit statement about its dedication to social responsibility, non-discrimination, democracy, equality, solidarity etc. Perceiving the difference between the grand narratives which religious as well as secular traditions produce about themselves (including also the grand narrative about education in secular democracies) and actual practice is an important element of citizenship education.

(3) *Terminology*: Similarly to what is needed in the academic study of religions, it is necessary to develop an adequate terminology for the representation of religions in integrative RE. A meta-language which goes beyond insider concepts is necessary, even if this will be somewhat different at school and university levels. Furthermore, the pupils have to understand the problems concerned with finding an adequate terminology and work together towards using appropriate concepts. This is a means of introducing methodological self-criticism as an integral element of integrative RE.

---

207 A recent survey of the way Buddhist communities today deal with discriminatory elements of their traditions has been presented by Simone Heidegger (2006: Buddhismus, Geschlechterverhältnis und Diskriminierung. Die gegenwärtige Diskussion im Shin-Buddhismus Japans).

(4) *Teaching Christianity in a changed educational environment*: The comparison of models for integrative RE in Europe has shown that the changed learning environment in integrative approaches requires a reconsideration of the way the religion which RE formerly used to be almost exclusively about (in European countries i.e. Christianity), is taught now as one among others. Two English approaches, for example, were concerned with this question in particular.[208] The challenge is also to apply the same methodology to a religion that used to be taught with a quite different methodology and to place teaching Christianity in a truly integrative framework. These last steps still have to be taken in some integrative models, as can be seen with the example of Norway.

(5) *General issues concerning the representation of religions and cultures*: Various academic and non-academic debates about the representation of religions and cultures are also relevant to integrative RE. Integrative RE has to find its own responses to the challenges of postcolonial criticism, the debates about orientalism and occidentalism with their inherent processes of "othering" and the production of stereotypes of religions and cultures. Recent debates in the academic study of religions and intercultural education may be first guidelines for this task.[209]

3.2.4 Organisation and transformation

If integrative RE is to be designed as a compulsory subject for all pupils in Europe, it requires an organisation that is consistent with its general approach. As we have seen, in order to guarantee adequate provision, integrative RE has to be introduced as a subject in its own right, not just as a "learning dimension". The relevance and breadth of the subject matter require the subject to be taught to pupils of all ages from the very beginning of school life. Fears about the matter being too complex for young children have proved unfounded, if adequate methodologies are used. Experiences in England and Sweden have shown that integrative RE is very successful even at primary and preschool levels. It has been argued in this thesis that children are already confronted with different religions in nursery school (if not before, if their families are religiously mixed), which means that reflection about living in a religiously plural environment should not be postponed to later ages. Fur-

---

208 See sections 2.8 and 2.9 of chapter II.
209 Cf. chapter I.

thermore, if knowledge about religions is regarded as an element of education in general, all types of schools, including private religious schools, ought to offer integrative RE in order not to withhold this aspect of education from the children. For the same reasons, exemption from integrative RE should not be an option. There is no reason why this kind of education should not be provided for all children, without exception. If this idea is asserted, it may provide a particularly European approach to education as opposed to common practice e.g. in the United States of America where children may be withdrawn from several aspects of education (for example, biology lessons that contradict their parents' ideas of the creation of the world or of sex education) for religious reasons. A European approach to education may critically take up the Enlightenment tradition and grant the children the right to form their own opinion on the basis of broad and balanced information, unfiltered by religious ideologies. The right to exemption is an inconsistency e.g. of the English model or of LER in Brandenburg. In both models, integrative RE is intended for all children, but nevertheless exemption is possible. The Norwegian approach is more consistent in this respect. It allows exemption only from activities that may themselves be considered religious. However, the subject KRL itself is not yet truly ready for being made compulsory, as it still has a Christian bias. The Swedish model, where the right to exemption was abolished once the subject had found an adequate approach, which really is appropriate for all children, is most consistent in this respect.

Integrative RE has to be taught by professional teachers with a sound education in the academic study of religions and education. One's own religiosity or membership in a religious community are not qualifications for becoming an integrative RE teacher. As long as teachers are willing to apply an impartial approach in RE, their own religious affiliation is independent of the qualification for teaching integrative RE. Rather, knowledge about the different religions, about study-of-religions methodology as well as educational theory and practice are criteria which qualify prospective candidates for becoming teachers of integrative RE. Teaching material needs to correspond to the general profile of the subject. Therefore, textbooks have to reflect the particular methodology and the general approach of integrative RE. If other sources which have been produced, for example, by religious communities are used, the character of these sources has to be made explicit to the children. Syllabuses have to be drawn up by integrative-RE specialists, not religious specialists of individual religions. Curriculum development has to take the general character of the subject (cf. IV.3.1) as its starting point. As has already been stated with respect to the representation of religions, cooperation with believers is welcome as long as it does not turn into domination. It has to be clear that the general responsibility for integrative RE is with educationists, and not with the religious communities, despite possible cooperation, which often works without problems. This last step towards a truly *educational* approach still needs to be taken in some of the models.

Without any doubt, those religions which are majority religions in the local or national context have to be dealt with in depth in integrative RE. However, prescribed allocations for percentages of classroom time to be spent on teaching and learning about particular religions, as has been the case in some European models,[210] are educationally undesirable, as they disregard the dynamics of complex teaching and learning processes. Furthermore, the contexts in which such demands for prescribed time allocations occur, give rise to doubts about their truly educational intentions. Rather than being grounded in educational arguments, they seem to be regarded as useful means of prescribing Christian dominance.[211] A sound educational concept for integrative RE has to do without such prescriptions. However, it goes without saying that this does not question the fact that traditions with a particular local, national or regional influence ought to be studied in depth.

The European comparison has shown that introducing integrative RE as a compulsory subject is the only way to make sure that truly all children have the chance to learn about the diversity of religions from an educational perspective, which is not religious in itself. Separative and confessional models are simply not adequate for this task.[212] If the right to this aspect of education is to be granted to all children in Europe, integrative RE has to be introduced as an obligatory subject in all European countries. The current situation of RE in Europe seems to offer separative and integrative RE as alternatives to be decided between by the individual countries concerned. However, these two options are no real alternatives for teaching and learning about different religions. The relevance of integrative RE as a school subject is independent of the way opportunities are made available for introducing children to particular religious worldviews. The question is not if children learn about religions in a separative or in an integrative approach,

---

210 Cf. the regulations for KRL in Norway, which state that 55% of classroom time should be spent on teaching Christianity (Thomassen 2005: RE in a pluralistic society: experiences from Norway, 239), or complaints to the Secretary of State for Education in England about syllabuses which were not "mainly Christian" (cf. Jackson 2000: Law, Politics and RE in England and Wales, 90f.).

211 Christianity is the only religion for which such time allocations have explicitly been made.

212 Cf. section 2.2.3 of chapter IV.

but rather if children are taught about different religions by qualified teachers at all. Therefore, the introduction of integrative RE does not have to mean that additional confessional instruction cannot be retained for those who wish to attend this kind of religious activity in school, if it is offered by religious communities. However, confessional RE cannot be a *substitute* for integrative RE, but only an additional subject, as it has a completely different educational task and subject matter. Therefore, it is up to the individual countries which do not yet have integrative RE to decide if they wish to develop a completely new subject with its own teacher training programme, or if they prefer to transform existing separative RE programmes into integrative ones. Most existing integrative RE programmes have been developed out of confessional models. This involves a comprehensive reform of curricula, teaching material and teacher education. However, if countries regard confessional religious instruction as an indispensable part of education, introducing integrative RE as a new additional subject while retaining the tradition of also offering confessional RE, may be the only option. At any rate, no kind of confessional RE can fill the gap that the absence of integrative RE leaves. Furthermore, countries which already have integrative RE may have to revise its organisation in order to make the approach really consistent and truly educational.

3.3 Academic and political desiderata

Despite some approaches to integrative RE in Europe which take up the theory and methodology of the academic study of religions, in many countries the reflection about the didactics of the study of religions is still in its infancy. Contributing to the development of integrative RE at national and international levels has been on the agendas of only a tiny minority of scholars in the study of religions. Therefore, apart from a few exceptions, there has been only very little research about RE in schools, both on the conceptional as well as on the empirical level, within the academic discipline of the study of religions. In most countries this has changed only very recently, if at all, as RE is still regarded as a field for theologians and not scholars of religions. Since the study of religions as an academic discipline is not very well known among most politicians and even scholars of other disciplines, who continually confuse it with theology, it cannot wait until it is invited to participate in the debates about RE, but has to show – even if not called upon – the contribution its discipline can make to teaching about different religions at school. Otherwise, its place will continue to be taken by theologians who claim to be specialists for religion in general, particularly with respect to education.

The range of research desiderata with respect to integrative RE is wide. For example, research about the cognitive development of children with respect to their capacity to understand concepts is often dated and has been carried out only among very small groups of children. Further research is necessary to adapt teaching methods to the mental, social and emotional development of children. This kind of research can be a basis for decisions about what exactly can be taught at which levels and how teaching and learning may take place. Two other very urgent concerns are the development of adequate teaching material as well as teacher training programmes. Both have to actually take the basic profile of the subject as described in chapter IV.3.1.1 as their starting points and therefore be firmly grounded in the responsible academic disciplines, i.e. the study of religions and education, not in particular theologies. Some very good teaching material has been developed, for example, in England and Sweden. However, there is still a general lack of adequate teaching material, particularly in those countries which have only recently introduced integrative RE.

Teacher education for integrative RE is sometimes not yet entirely consistent. In particular, there is often no clear distinction between theology, with its bias in favour of one tradition, and the study of religions, with its attempt to apply an impartial approach. This distinction is, however, decisive if the subject is really designed for pupils of all religious backgrounds. If individual theologies are made part of teacher training programmes for integrative RE, this needs to be accompanied by clear reflection and an acknowledgement of the differences between the impartial approach needed for integrative RE and theological or religious approaches. Therefore, modules in which these theoretical and methodological issues are reflected are indispensable for sound teacher training programmes for integrative RE. Teachers have to understand the difference between a theological insider account of a religion and a study-of-religions perspective, for example with respect to recognition of the plurality of the sometimes conflicting voices of different insiders. A final example of academic desiderata is research about the effects of integrative RE on the children who take part in it. There is hardly any research at all about how the views of children on religious diversity develop in integrative RE. A recent study, published in Danish by Tim Jensen and others, indicates that pupils actually become more tolerant towards others' religions by way of integrative RE in Danish upper secondary schools.[213] Similar research is needed also for integrative RE in other countries.

Political desiderata relate to the promotion of RE policies which are consistent with academic concepts of education rather than giving in to diverse lobbies with vested interests in education. Politicians need to distinguish clearly between religious, ideological, economic and educational interests and make educational interests the prior concern in decisions about education. This also means distinguishing between the interests behind different types of research. Academic educational research, which is oriented towards the interests and basic rights of the pupils to individual self-determination, responsibility and solidarity, has to be distinguished from interest-group initiated research, which is produced to support the claims of certain lobbies. This task is difficult, particularly as there are no clear borders between these different types of research. Therefore, it is even more relevant that politicians are made aware of these issues and try to find their way through this maze in order to make truly educational interests the basis for their decisions. Furthermore, politicians need to support the development of truly secular and democratic approaches, which build on equal rights for all religious communities, but do not consider the interests of religious communities more important than the children's rights to broad and balanced information about the diversity of religions. This is an important aspect of finding responsible solutions for learning about different religions at national, international and global levels. Politicians have a responsibility for providing a suitable ambience, e.g. a political and social climate that encourages learning for living in a global world. This means that an initial attempt should be made to bridge the gap between rhetoric and practice in the educational sector[214] as well as in other fields.

---

213 See Andersen, Frederiksen et al. 2006: Hvor får de det dog fra? - Religiøs holdningsdannelse i gymnasieskolen.
214 E.g. with respect to the rhetoric about the right to education and equal opportunities vs. the commercialisation and ideologisation of education.

Epilogue
The potential of integrative RE

It is impossible to overlook the discrepancy between, on the one hand, statements about the philosophy of school education in general, as well as integrative RE in particular, and, on the other hand, the actual educational, political, social and economic situations in European countries. The idea of equal access to education and the concept of education as a means of enabling individual self-determination of life and meaning, participation and solidarity,[1] lies in stark contrast to the dominant trend towards regarding education as a commodity to be sold to those who can afford it[2] or as a means of reproducing existing power structures or currently influential ideologies, instead of fostering the development of a critical capacity.

If we regard these trends in education in the context of other political and social developments and recall the words of Kofi Annan, who, in his Nobel Lecture, said that

> "[t]oday's real borders are not between nations, but between powerful and powerless, free and fettered, privileged and humiliated. Today, no walls can separate humanitarian or human rights crisis in one part of the world from national security crises in another,"[3]

it becomes patently obvious that those who understand these global, regional and local interdependencies and have the means (intellectual, linguistic, institutional and economic) to articulate these problems have a special responsibility to make their knowledge accessible to others. One way of doing this is to promote a critical concept of education, which also includes a critical study of religions and worldviews. In the study of religions, as well as in integrative RE, it is important not to separate "religion" from its global and local social and political contexts, but to discern its function in social and political processes as a field in which much of the negotiation of power and privilege takes

---

1 Cf. Wolfang Klafki's concept of education, see e.g. Klafki 2001: Grundlinien eines gegenwarts- und zukunftsorientierten Bildungsbegriffs und didaktische Konsequenzen.
2 This concept of education is, for example, dominant in the current reform of higher education in many European countries.
3 Annan 2001: Nobel Lecture.

place. In principle, integrative RE involves an uncompromising analysis of all religions and worldviews, including also the dominant capitalist or "market economy" ideology, whose close analysis and criticism as a worldview still seems to be a taboo topic. The impartial methodology requires all religions and worldviews to be compared and contrasted with, for example, ideas of human rights or democracy. This is one of the important contributions that integrative RE has to make to citizenship education which builds on concepts of global, yet differentiated, citizenship. A comparison and contrast of different accounts of human rights and democracy and a close look at actual practice as well as local, regional and global consequences of any position may help to find some way through the maze of conflicting narratives and views of reality. Therefore, the kind of education that integrative RE implies may have its function in the development of more truly democratic structures as opposed to the current international order which is largely dependent on economic, financial and military power.

Another potential of integrative RE lies in its methodology, which takes heterogeneity as its starting point in a critical educational framework, in which methodological self-criticism is applied also to one's own presuppositions. This methodology may be a model for an impartial approach towards difference and diversity at a grass-roots level, with all its difficulties, which are, however, deliberately addressed rather than neglected or rendered insurmountable. The challenges of a plural situation are made the starting point for reflection in order to promote conversation, mutual understanding and respect. Learning to deal with diversity is a prerequisite for working out peaceful solutions for various kinds of conflicts. However, as was pointed out in chapter I.2.3, the relevance of multiperspectivity as well as other principles of intercultural education cannot be restricted to individual school subjects, such as history or integrative RE, but ought to be dimensions of any kind of education. This may help to put younger generations in a position to develop solutions to the problems and conflicts that older generations have produced and successfully maintained, for example the exploitation of natural resources, the degradation of human beings to human capital and a political order in which the gap between the privileged and the deprived is widening, despite the rhetoric of human dignity, human rights and democracy. Furthermore, dealing with the topic of diversity can provide a model for mediation and conflict resolution in a number of contexts. Acknowledging this as an indispensable element of education may help to promote globalisation also on intellectual, social and political levels.

Bibliography

Adorno, Theodor W. 1970: *Erziehung zur Mündigkeit. Vorträge und Gespräche mit Hellmut Becker*, Frankfurt: Suhrkamp.

—— 1972: *Soziologische Schriften I*, Frankfurt: Suhrkamp.

—— 1972: 'Theorie der Halbbildung [1959]', in: Adorno, Theodor W.: *Soziologische Schriften I*, Frankfurt: Suhrkamp, 93-121.

Ahlbäck, Tore (ed.) 1999: *Approaching Religion*, Åbo, Finland: Donner Institute for Research in Religious and Cultural History.

Alberts, Wanda 2005: 'European models of integrative religious education', in: Wasim, Alef Theria, Abdurrahman Mas'ud, et al. (ed.): *Religious Harmony: Problems, Practice and Education. Proceedings of the Regional Conference of the International Association for the History of Religions. Yogyakarta and Semarang, Indonesia, September 27th - October 3rd, 2004.*, Yogyakarta: Oasis, 247-258.

Albespy, Annie 2000: 'The French situation', in: Holm, Nils G. (ed.): *Islam and Christianity in School Religious Education. Issues, Approaches, and Contexts*, Åbo: Åbo Akademis trykeri, 249-254.

Alm, Lars-Göran 1997: *Religionskunskap för gymnasiet. A-kursen*, Stockholm: Natur och Kultur.

—— 1998: *Religionskunskap för gymnasiet. B-kursen*, Stockholm: Natur och Kultur.

Almén, Edgar 2000: 'Frestelser och vägmärken för undervisningen om kristendomen', in: Almén, Edgar, Ragnar Furenhed, et al. (ed.): *Livstolkning och värdegrund: att undervisa om religion, livsfrågor och etik*, Linköping: Linköpings Universitet, 176-191.

—— 2000: 'Religious Education in Sweden', in: Almén, Edgar and Hans Christian Øster (ed.): *Religious Education in Great Britain, Sweden and Russia. Presentations, Problem Inventories and Commentaries*, Linköping: Linköping University Electronic Press, 60-91.

—— 2000: 'Vad studerar vi som 'religion' - hur och varför studerar vi just det?' in: Almén, Edgar, Ragnar Furenhed, et al. (ed.): *Livstolkning och värdegrund: att undervisa om religion, livsfrågor och etik*, Linköping: Linköpings Universitet, 192-211.

Almén, Edgar, Ragnar Furenhed, et al. (ed.) 2000: *Livstolkning och värdegrund: att undervisa om religion, livsfrågor och etik*, Linköping: Linköpings universitet.

Almén, Edgar and Hans Christian Øster (ed.) 2000: *Religious Education in Great Britain, Sweden and Russia*. Presentations, Problem Inventories and Commentaries, Linköping: Linköping University Electronic Press.

Almén, Edgar and Carl Axel Aurelius 2000: Some Second Thoughts on Religious Education in Great Britain, Russia, and Sweden, in Edgar Almén and Hans Christian Øster (ed.): *Religious Education in Great Britain, Sweden and Russia*, Linköping: Linköping University Electronic Press, 125-138.

Andersen, Peter B. et al. (ed.) 2006: *Religion, skole og kulturel integration i Danmark og Sverige*, København: Museum Tusculanums Forlag.

Andersen, Peter B., Signe Frederiksen, et al. 2006: 'Hvor får de det dog fra? - Religiøs holdningsdannelse i gymnasieskolen', in: Andersen, Peter B. et al. (ed.): *Religion, skole og kulturel integration i Danmark og Sverige*, København: Museum Tusculanums Forlag, 359-371.

Andersson, Daniel and Åke Sander (ed.) 2005: *Det mångreligiösa Sverige - ett landskap i förändring*, Lund: Studentlitteratur.

Andree, Trees, Cok Bakker, et al. (ed.) 1997: *Crossing Boundaries. Contributions to Interreligious and Intercultural Education* (Documentation of the Research Symposium at the Utrecht University, Faculty of Theology, Center for Interreligious Learning, September 1996, with participants from Germany, Great Britain, Namibia, The Netherlands, Norway and South Africa), Münster: Comenius Institut.

Annan, Kofi 2001: *Nobel Lecture, Oslo* (http://nobelprize.org/nobel_prizes/peace/laureates/2001/annan-lecture.html, 4.7.2006).

Antes, Peter 1995: 'Religionspädagogik und Religionswissenschaft', in: Ziebertz, Hans-Georg und Werner Simon (ed.): *Bilanz der Religionspädagogik*, Düsseldorf: Patmos, 137-146.

—— 1999: 'Lebt der Mensch nur einmal? Einmaligkeit des Lebens und Wiedergeburt im Vergleich', in: Grözinger, Karl E., Burkhard Gladigow, et al. (ed.): *Religion in der schulischen Bildung und Erziehung: LER - Ethik - Werte und Normen in einer pluralistischen Gesellschaft*, Berlin: Berlin-Verlag Spitz, 107-118.

—— 1999: 'Simulierung von Religion im Unterricht?' in: Grözinger, Karl E., Burkhard Gladigow, et al. (ed.): *Religion in der schulischen Bildung und Erziehung: LER - Ethik - Werte und Normen in einer pluralistischen Gesellschaft*, Berlin: Berlin-Verlag Spitz, 187-195.

Antes, Peter, Armin W. Geertz, et al. (ed.) 2004: *New Approaches to the Study of Religion. Volume 1: Regional, Critical, and Historical Approaches*, Berlin/New York: deGruyter.

—— 2004: *New Approaches to the Study of Religion. Volume 2: Textual, Comparative, Sociological and Cognitive Approaches*, Berlin/New York: deGruyter.

Arlebrand, Håkan, Bengt Arvidsson, et al. 1998: *Relief A+B. Religionskunskap*, Malmö: Gleerups.

Aronson, Harry 1974: *Gymnasieeleven och livsfrågorna: studiematerial för lärare i soämnen, i första hand religionskunskap, på gymnaseiskolan*, Stockholm: Utbildningsförlag.

Asbrand, Barbara 2000: *Zusammen Leben und Lernen im Religionsunterricht. Eine empirische Studie zur grundschulpädagogischen Konzeption eines interreligiösen Religionsunterrichts im Klassenverband der Grundschule*, Frankfurt/M.: IKO - Verlag für interkulturelle Kommunikation.

Astley, Jeff and Leslie Francis (ed.) 1996: *Christian Theology and Religious Education: Connections and Contradictions*, London: SPCK (Society for Promoting Christian Knowledge).

Auernheimer, Georg 1997: 'Interkulturelle Pädagogik', in: Bernhard, Armin and Lutz Rothermel (ed.): *Handbuch Kritische Pädagogik. Eine Einführung in die Erziehungs- und Bildungswissenschaft*, Weinheim: Deutscher StudienVerlag, 344-356.

—— 1995[2]: *Einführung in die interkulturelle Erziehung*, Darmstadt: Wissenschaftliche Buchgesellschaft.

—— 2000: 'Ziele und Bedingungen interkultureller Bildung', in: Gerecht, Gonhild (ed.): *Grenzen überwinden - interkulturelle Bildung als Zunkunftschance*, Frankfurt: GEW Landesverband Hessen, 11-16.

—— 2003[3]: *Einführung in die interkulturelle Pädagogik*, Darmstadt: Wissenschaftliche Buchgesellschaft.

Auffarth, Christoph 1999: 'Dialog der Religionen: Vom Dialog vor dem Dialog', in: Grözinger, Karl E., Burkhard Gladigow, et al. (ed.): *Religion in der schulischen Bildung und Erziehung: LER - Ethik - Werte und Normen in einer pluralistischen Gesellschaft*, Berlin: Berlin-Verlag Spitz, 89-106.

Baden Württemberg 2005 [1983]: *Schulgesetz für Baden-Württemberg* (SchG) (http://www.leu.bw.schule.de/bild/SchG.pdf, 18.6.2006).

Bailey, Edward 1997: *Implicit Religion in Contemporary Society*, Kampen/Weinheim: Kok Pharos/Deutscher Studien Verlag.

Bakker, Cok 1997: 'Interreligiöser Religionsunterricht in den Niederlanden', in: Schreiner, Peter and Hans Spinder (ed.): *Identitätsbildung im pluralen Europa. Perspektiven für Schule und Religionsunterricht*, Münster et al.: Waxmann, 143-149.

—— 2001: 'School as a place of diversity', in: Heimbrock, Hans-Günter, Christoph Th. Scheilke, et al. (ed.): *Towards Religious Competence: Diversity as a Challenge for Education in Europe*, Münster: Lit, 203-221.

Bakker, Cok, Olaf Beuchling, et al. (ed.) 2002: *Kulturelle Vielfalt und Religionsunterricht. Entwicklungen und Praxis in vier europäischen Ländern*, Münster et al.: Lit.

Banton, Michael (ed.) 1966: *Anthropological Approaches to the Study of Religion*, London et al.: Routledge.

Barnes, Philip L. 1994: 'Rudolf Otto and the limits of religious description', *Religious Studies*, 30, 219-30.

—— 2000: 'Ninian Smart and the phenomenological approach to religious education', *Religion*, 30 (4), 315-332.

—— 2001: 'The contribution of professor Ninian Smart to religious education', *Religion*, 31 (4), 317-319.

Barnes, Philip L. and William K. Kay 1999: 'Developments in religious education in England and Wales (part 1): church and state, the 1988 Education Reform Act, and spirituality in schools', *Themelios. An International Journal for Theological and Religious Studies Students*, 25 (1), 23-38.

—— 2000: 'Developments in religious education in England and Wales (part 2): methodology, politics, citizenship and school performance', *Themelios. An International Journal for Theological and Religious Studies Students*, 25 (3), 5-19.

Barnikol, Horst-Martin and Rune Larsson 1993: *Religion och livsfrågor bland svenska och tyska ungdomar*, Bochum: Brockmeyer.

Bauer, Jochen 1996: 'Zwischen Religionenkunde und erfahrungsorientiertem Unterricht. Neuere religionsdidaktische Konzeptionen und England', in: Weiße, Wolfram (ed.): *Vom Monolog zum Dialog. Ansätze einer interkulturellen dialogischen Religionspädagogik*, Münster: Waxmann, 141-161.

Baumann, Martin 1995: "Merkwürdige Bundesgenossen' und 'naive Sympathisanten'. Die Ausgrenzung der Religionswissenschaft aus der bundesdeutschen Kontroverse um neue Religionen', *Zeitschrift für Religionswissenschaft*, 3, 111-136.

—— 1998: *Qualitative Methoden in der Religionswissenschaft. Hinweise zur religionswissenschaftlichen Feldforschung*, Marburg: Remid.

Baumfield, Vivienne, Catherine Bowness, et al. 1994: 'Model syllabuses: a contribution', *Journal of Beliefs and Values*, 15 (1), 3-5.

—— 1994: *A Third Perspective*, Plymouth: University College of St Mark and John.

—— 1995: 'Model syllabuses: the debate continues', *Resource*, 18 (1), 3-6.

Bellah, Robert N. 1970: *Essays on Religion in a Post-Traditional World*, New York et al.: Harper&Row.

Bellah, Robert N. and Phillip E. Hammond 1980: *Varieties of Civil Religion*, New York et al.: Harper&Row.

Benner, Dietrich, Michele Borrelli, et al. (ed.) 2003: *Kritik in der Pädagogik. Versuche über das Kritische in Erziehung und Erziehungswissenschaft*, Weinheim: Beltz.

Berg, Anna 2000: 'Synen på Islam i några läroböcker', *Religion & Livsfrågor*, 33 (1), 18-20.

Berger, Peter 1973: *The Social Reality of Religion*, Harmondsworth: Penguin.

Berner, Ulrich 1983: 'Gegenstand und Aufgabe der Religionswissenschaft', *Zeitschrift für Religions- und Geistesgeschichte*, 35 (2), 97-116.

Bernhard, Armin 1997: 'Bildung', in: Bernhard, Armin and Lutz Rothermel (ed.): *Handbuch Kritische Pädagogik. Eine Einführung in die Erziehungs- und Bildungswissenschaft*, Weinheim: Deutscher Studien Verlag, 62-74.

Bernhard, Armin and Lutz Rothermel (ed.) 1997: *Handbuch Kritische Pädagogik. Eine Einführung in die Erziehungs- und Bildungswissenschaft*, Weinheim: Deutscher Studien Verlag.

Bertram, Norbert (ed.) 1993: *Interkulturelles Verstehen und Handeln*, Pfaffenweiler: Centaurus.

Bianchi, Ugo, Claas J. Bleeker, et al. (ed.) 1972: *Problems and Methods of the History of Religions*, Leiden: Brill.

Binder, Susanne and Aryane Daryabegi 2003: 'Interkulturelles Lernen - Beispiele aus der schulischen Praxis', in: Fillitz, Thomas (ed.): *Interkulturelles Lernen. Zwischen institutionellem Rahmen, schulischer Praxis ung gesellschaftlichesm Kommunikationsprinzip*, Innsbruck: StudienVerlag, 33-84.

Birmingham (England) Education Department 1995: *The Birmingham Agreed Syllabus for Religious Education*, Birmingham: Birmingham City Council.

Bizeul, Yves et al. (ed.) 1997: *Vom Umgang mit dem Fremden: Hintergrund - Definitionen - Vorschläge*, Weinheim: Beltz.

Björlin, Ola 1996: *Livets Kurs*, Stockholm: Bonniers.

Borevi, Karin 1997: 'Religion i skolan', in: Karlsson, Pia and Ingvar Svanberg (ed.): *Religionsfrihet i Sverige*, Lund: Studentlitteratur, 37-69.

Borowik, Irena (ed.) 1999: *Church-State Relations in Central and Eastern Europe*, Krakow: Nomos.

Børresen, Beate 2002: 'Interkulturelle und interreligiöse Bildung in Norwegen', in: Bakker, Cok, Olaf Beuchling, et al. (ed.): *Kulturelle Vielfalt und Religionsunterricht. Entwicklungen und Praxis in vier europäischen Ländern*, Münster et al.: Lit, 101-105.

—— 2002: 'Kulturelle und religiöse Vielfalt in Norwegen', in: Bakker, Cok, Olaf Beuchling, et al. (ed.): *Kulturelle Vielfalt und Religionsunterricht. Entwicklungen und Praxis in vier europäischen Ländern*, Münster et al.: Lit, 97-100.

Bowker, John 1987: *Licensed Insanities: Religions and Belief in God in the Contemporary World*, London: Darton, Longman&Todd.

—— 2002: 'World religions. The boundaries of belief and unbelief', in: Broadbent, Lynne and Alan Brown (ed.): *Issues in Religious Education*, London/New York: RoutledgeFalmer, 210-217.

Braun, Willi and Russell T. McCutcheon (ed.) 2000: *Guide to the Study of Religion*, London/New York: Cassell.

Breidlid, Halldis and Tove Nicolaisen 2004: 'Multi-faith religious education in a religiously-mixed context: some Norwegian perspectives', in: Larsson, Rune and Caroline Gustavsson (ed.): *Towards a European Perspective on Religious Education. The RE Research Conference, March 11-14, 2004, University of Lund*, Skellefteå: Artos&Norma, 69-79.

Brezinka, Wolfgang 1972²: *Von der Pädagogik zur Erziehungswissenschaft: eine Einführung in die Metatheorie der Erziehung*, Weinheim et al.: Beltz.

Broadbent, Lynne and Alan Brown (ed.) 2002: *Issues in Religious Education*, London/New York: RoutledgeFalmer.

Brown, Adrian et al. (ed.) 1997: *God Talk: Science talk - A Teacher's Guide to Science and Belief*, Oxford: Lion.

Brown, Alan (ed.) 1987: *The Shap Handbook on World Religions in Education*, London: Commission for Racial Equality/Shap.

—— 1995: 'Christianity and other religions', in: Erricker, Clive (ed.): *Teaching Christianity: A World Religions Approach*, Cambridge: The Lutterworth Press, 10-14.

—— 2000: 'The Chichester Project: teaching Christianity: a world religions approach', in: Grimmitt, Michael (ed.): *Pedagogies of Religious Education. Case Studies in the Research and Development of Good Pedagogic Practice in RE*, Great Wakering: McCrimmons, 53-69.

—— 2002: 'The statutory requirements for Religious Education 1988-2001. Religious, political and social influences', in: Broadbent, Lynne and Alan Brown (ed.): *Issues in Religious Education*, London/New York: RoutledgeFalmer, 3-15.

Brown, Lyn M. and Carol Gilligan 1994: *Die verlorene Stimme. Wendepunkte in der Entwicklung von Mädchen und Frauen*, Frankfurt a.M. et al.: Campus.

Bruner, Jerome 1966: *Towards a Theory of Instruction*, Harvard University Press.

—— 1977: *The Process of Education*, Harvard University Press.

Buchardt, Mette 2004: 'Religious education in the school: approaches in school practice and research in Denmark', in: Larsson, Rune and Caroline Gustavsson (ed.): *Towards a European Perspective on Religious Education. The RE Research Conference, March 11-14, 2004, University of Lund*, Skellefteå: Artos&Norma, 117-126.

Bundesregierung der Bundesrepublik Deutschland 2000 [1949]: *Grundgesetz für die Bundesrepublik Deutschland* (http://www.bundesregierung.de/static/pdf/gg.pdf, 24.6.2006).

Bystrom Janarv, Görel and Ann Lagerström 1997: *Religiösa profiler*, Stockholm: Natur och Kultur.

Chambliss, Joseph J. (ed.) 1996: *Philosophy of Education. An Encyclopedia*, New York & London: Garland.

Chidester, David, Janet Stonier, et al. (ed.) 1999: *Diversity as Ethos: Challenges for Interreligious and Intercultural Education*, Cape Town: Institute for Comparative Religion in Southern Africa.

Clark, Elizabeth A. 2004: 'Engendering the Study of Religion', in: Jakeliæ, Slavica and Lori Pearson (ed.): *The Future of the Study of Religion. Proceedings of Congress 2000*, Leiden/Boston: Brill, 217-242.

Clifford, James 1986: 'Introduction: partial truths', in: Clifford, James and George E. Marcus (ed.): *Writing Culture: The Poetics and Politics of Ethnography*, Berkely: University of California Press, 1-26.

—— 1988: *The Predicament of Culture: Twentieth-Century Ethnography*, Literature and Art, Cambridge Mass.: Harvard University Press.

Clifford, James and George E. Marcus 1985: 'The making of ethnographic texts. A preliminary report', *Current Anthropology*, 26, 267-271.

—— (ed.) 1986: *Writing Culture: The Poetics and Politics of Ethnography*, Berkely: Universtiy of California Press.

Cooling, Trevor 1987: 'Christian doctrine in religious education', *British Journal of Religious Education*, 9 (3), 152-159.

—— 1994: *Concept Cracking: Exploring Christian Beliefs in School*, Nottingham: Stapleford.

—— 1996: 'Education is the point of RE - not religion? Theological reflections on the SCAA model syllabuses', in: Astley, J. and L. Francis (ed.): *Christian Theology and Religious Education: Connections and Contradictions*, London: SPCK (Society for Promoting Christian Knowledge), 165-183.

—— 1997: 'Theology goes to school: the story of the Stapleford Project', *Journal of Christian Education*, 40 (1), 47-60.

—— 2000: 'The Stapleford Project: theology as the basis for religious education', in: Grimmitt, Michael (ed.): *Pedagogies of Religious Education. Case Studies in the Research and Development of Good Pedagogic Practice in RE*, Great Wakering: McCrimmons, 153-169.

Copley, Terence 1997: *Teaching Religion. Fifty Years of Religious Education in England and Wales*, Exeter: University of Exeter Press.

—— 2000: *Spiritual Development in the State School. A Perspective on Worship and Spirituality in the Education System of England and Wales*, Exeter: University of Exeter Press.

—— 2004: 'Is UK religious education failing to address its own cultural context?' in: Larsson, Rune and Caroline Gustavsson (ed.): *Towards a European Perspective on Religious Education. The RE Research Conference, March 11-14, 2004, University of Lund*, Skellefteå: Artos&Norma, 80-89.

Crapanzano, Vincent 1986: 'Hermes' dilemma: the masking of subversion in ethnographic descriptions', in: Clifford, James and George E. Marcus (ed.): *Writing Culture: The Poetics and Politics of Ethnography*, Berkely: University of California Press, 51-76.

Cush, Denise 1999: 'Models of religious education in a plural society: looking to the future', in: Borowik, Irena (ed.): *Church-State Relations in Central and Eastern Europe*, Krakow: Nomos, 377-387.

CWVP 2006: *The Children and Worldviews Project* (http://www.cwvp.com, 4.7.2006).

Dahlin, Bo 2001: 'Religionsämnet i det postmoderna tillståndet', *Religion & Livsfrågor*, 34 (2), 14-17.

—— 2003: 'Genforskningen och människosynen - ett angeläget tema för religionsundervisningen', *Religion & Livsfrågor*, 36 (3), 18-21.

—— 2004 (second revised edition, 1998[1]): *Om undran inför livet: barn och livsfrågor i ett mångkulturellt samhälle*, Lund: Student-litteratur.

Dale, E.L. 1992: 'Kunnskap, reasjonalitet og didaktikk' in E.L. Dale: *Pedagogisk filosofi*, Oslo.

Debray, Régis 2002: *L'Enseignement du fait religieux dans l'école laïque*, Paris: Odile Jacob.

DfE (Department for Education) 1994: *Religious Education and Collective Worship, Circular 1794*, London: Department for Education.

Department of Education and Science 1985: *Education for All (The Swann Report)*, London: DES.

Döbert, Hans, Wolfgang Hörner, et al. (ed.) 2002: *Die Schulsysteme Europas*, Hohengehren: Schneider.

Doble, Peter 1995: 'Commitment and an open approach to teaching Christianity', in: Erricker, Clive (ed.): *Teaching Christianity: A World Religions Approach*, Cambridge: The Lutterworth Press, 15-22.

Doedens, Folkert and Peter Schreiner (ed.) 1996: *Interkulturelles und interreligiöses Lernen. Beiträge zu einer notwendigen Diskussion*, Münster: Comenius-Institut.

Doedens, Folkert and Wolfram Weiße (ed.) 1997: *Religionsunterricht für alle: Hamburger Perspektiven zur Religionsdidaktik*, Münster: Waxmann.

Dommel, Christa 2002: *Religious education in Bremen – a cousin of KRL? Considerations and perspectives of international educational research* (http://www.religion.uni-bremen.de/fileadmin/mediapool/religion/dateien /dommel/VortragNorwegen.pdf, 3.7.2006).

—— 2007: *Religions-Bildung im Kindergarten in Deutschland und England. Vergleichende Bildungsforschung für frühkindliche Pädagogik aus religionswissenschaftlicher Perspektive*, Frankfurt/Main: IKO.

Drobin, Ulf 1979: *Afrikanska religioner i västerländska belysningar: en idéhistorisk bakgrund*, Stockholm: Gotab.

DVRG (Deutsche Vereinigung für Religionsgeschichte), 2003: *Thematisches Raster* (http://www.uni-erfurt.de/religion_im_konflikt/beitraege.htm, 4.7.2006).

EAWRE 2006: *Kalender der Feste der Religionen* (http://www.eawre.org/cal_germ_05.htm, 28.6.2006).

EFTRE 2005: *Estonia* (http://re-xs.ucsm.ac.uk/eftre/reeurope/estonia_2005.html, 11.6.2006).

—— 2005: *Religious Education in Europe 2005* (http://re-xs.ucsm.ac.uk/eftre/reeurope.html, 25.05.2006).

Eggehorn, Ylva, Carl-Eric Weber, et al. 1996: *Religion*, Stockholm: Almqvist&Wiksell.

Eggert, Heike 1996: 'Interkultureller Religionsunterricht in den Niederlanden. Darstellung und kritische Analyse der Juliana van Stollberg Schule in Ede', in: Weiße, Wolfram (ed.): *Vom Monolog zum Dialog. Ansätze einer interkulturellen dialogischen Religionspädagogik*, Münster: Waxmann, 181-179.

Ehmann, Reinhard u.a. (ed.) 1998: *Religionsunterricht der Zukunft. Aspekte eines notwendigen Wandels*, Freiburg: Herder.

Eliade, Mircea 1954: *Die Religionen und das Heilige*, Salzburg: Müller.

—— 1957: *Das Heilige und das Profane*, Hamburg: Rowohlt.

Eliade, Mircea and Joseph M. Kitagawa (ed.) 1959: *The History of Religions: Essays in Methodology*, Chicago: Chicago University Press.

Eriksson, Keijo 1999: *På spaning efter livets mening. Om livsfrågor och livsåskådning hos äldre grundskolelever i en undervisningsmiljö som befrämjar kunskapande*, Malmö: Institutionen för pedagogik, lärarhögskolan.

Erling, Bernhard 1995: 'The fourth R: religious education in Sweden and the USA', *The Swedish-American Historical Quarterly*, 46 (3), 285-306.

Erricker, Clive 1982: *Christian Experience*, Guildord: Lutterworth Educational.

—— 1984: *Christian Ethics*, Guilford: Lutterworth.

—— 1995: 'Christianity in its cultural contexts', in: Erricker, Clive (ed.): *Teaching Christianity: A World Religions Approach*, Cambridge: Lutterworth, 30-36.

—— (ed.) 1995² [1987¹]: *Teaching Christianity: A World Religions Approach* (Foreword by Ninian Smart), Cambridge: Lutterworth.

—— 1998: 'Journeys through the heart: the effect of death, loss and conflict on children's worldviews', *Journal of Beliefs and Values*, 19 (1), 107-118.

—— 1998: 'Spiritual confusion: a critique of current educational policy in England and Wales', *International Journal for Children's Spirituality*, 3 (1), 51-63.

—— 2000: 'A critical review of religious education', in: Erricker, Clive and Jane Erricker (ed.): *Reconstructing Religious, Spiritual and Moral Education*, London/New York: RoutledgeFalmer, 15-35.

—— 2000: 'True stories and other dreams', in: Erricker, Clive and Jane Erricker (ed.): *Reconstructing Religious, Spiritual and Moral Education*, London/New York: RoutledgeFalmer, 1-11.

—— 2001: 'From silence to narration: a report on the research method(s) of the Children and Worldviews Project', *British Journal of Religious Education*, 23 (3), 156-164.

Erricker, Clive, Alan Brown, et al. (ed.) 1993: *Teaching World Religions. A Teacher's Handbook produced by the Shap Working Party on World Religions in Education*, Oxford: Heinemann.

Erricker, Clive, Jane Erricker, et al. 1997: *The Education of the Whole Child*, London: Cassell.

Erricker, Clive and Jane Erricker 2000: 'The Children and Worldviews Project: a narrative pedagogy of religious education', in: Grimmitt, Michael (ed.): *Pedagogies of Religious Education. Case Studies in the Research and Development of Good Pedagogic Practice in RE*, Great Wakering: McCrimmons, 188-206.

—— 2000: *Children's Spirituality and the Transformation of Religious Education*, London: Routledge.

—— 2000: 'Narrative constructions towards community', in: Erricker, Clive and Jane Erricker (ed.): *Reconstructing Religious, Spiritual and Moral Education*, London/New York: RoutledgeFalmer, 107-131.

—— 2000: *Reconstructing Religious, Spiritual and Moral Education*, London /New York: RoutledgeFalmer.

—— 2001: *Contemporary Spiritualities: Social and Religious Contexts*, London: Continuum.

Evangelische Kirche in Deutschland 1994: *Identität und Verständigung. Standort und Perspektiven des Religionsunterrichts*. Eine Denkschrift, im Auftrag des Rates der Ev. Kirche in Deutschland, Gütersloh: Kirchenamt der EKD.

Evans-Lowndes, Judith (ed.) 1991: *Planning RE in Schools*, Derby: Christian Education Movement.

Everington, Judith 1996: 'A question of authenticity: the relationship between educators and practitioners in the representation of religious traditions', *British Journal of Religious Education*, 18 (2), 69-77.

—— 1998: 'Evolution not revolution: an examination of the contribution of a curriculum project to the implementation of new agreed syllabuses', *British Journal of Religious Education*, 20 (3), 144-154.

—— 2000: 'Mission impossible? Religious education in the 1990s', in: Leicester, Mal, Celia Modgil, et al. (ed.): *Spiritual and Religious Education*, London/ New York: Falmer, 183-196.

Faber, Elisabeth 2005: *The Association of Danish Teachers of RE - Annual Report 2005* (http://re-xs.ucsm.ac.uk/eftre/reeurope/denmark_2005.html, 21.3.2006).

Falaturi, Abdoldjavad and Udo Tworuschka 1992: *A Guide to the Presentation of Islam in School Textbooks*, Birmingham: Centre for the Study of Islam & Christian-Muslim Relations.

—— 1996[3] (third revised edition): *Der Islam im Unterricht: Beiträge zur interkulturellen Erziehung in Europa*, Braunschweig: Georg-Eckert-Institut für Internationale Schulbuchforschung.

Fauth, Dieter 1998: 'Zur Didaktik der Religionswissenschaft', *Spirita*, 2, 4-8.

Felderhof, Marius C. 2000: 'Religious education and human rights', in: Holm, Nils G. (ed.): *Islam and Christianity in School Religious Education. Issues, Approaches, and Contexts*, Åbo: Åbo Akademis trykeri, 21-39.

Figl, Johann (ed.) 2003: *Handbuch Religionswissenschaft*, Göttingen: Vandenhoeck & Ruprecht.

Fillitz, Thomas (ed.) 2003: *Interkulturelles Lernen. Zwischen institutionellem Rahmen, schulischer Praxis und gesellschaftlichem Kommunikationsprinzip*, Innsbruck: StudienVerlag.

—— 2003: 'Methodische Reflexion', in: Fillitz, Thomas (ed.): *Interkulturelles Lernen. Zwischen institutionellem Rahmen, schulischer Praxis und gesellschaftlichem Kommunikationsprinzip*, Innsbruck: StudienVerlag, 341-347.

Flaake, Karin and Vera King (ed.) 1992: *Weibliche Adoleszenz. Zur Sozialisation junger Frauen*, Frankfurt a.M./New York: Campus-Verlag.

Flasche, Rainer 2000: 'Von der Selbstbeschränkung und Selbstbegründung der Religionenwissenschaft', in: Flasche, Rainer, Fritz Heinrich, et al. (ed.): *Religionswissenschaft in Konsequenz. Beiträge im Anschluß an Kurt Rudolph*, Münster et al.: Lit, 163-174.

Flasche, Rainer, Fritz Heinrich, et al. (ed.) 2000: *Religionswissenschaft in Konsequenz: Beiträge im Anschluß an Impulse von Kurt Rudolph*, Münster: Lit.

Florheden, Jörgen 1994: *Hinder och vägar* [lärares erfarenheter av att i religionsundervisningen utveckla förståelse och respekt för människor med olika religion och kultur], Göteborg: Dept. of Methodology, University of Goethenburg.

Francis, Leslie R., Jeff Astley, et al. (ed.) 2001: *The Fourth R for the Third Millenium. Education in Religion and Values for the Global Future*, Dublin: Lindisfarne.

Francis, Leslie R., William K. Kay, et al. (ed.) 1996: *Research in Religious Education*, Leominster/Macon: Gracewing/Smyth & Helwys.

Franck, Olof (ed.) 2002: *Mellan vidskepelse och vetenskap: att tro, att tvivla - och att veta*, Lomma: FLR.

—— (ed.) 2003: *Liksom värden, typ: moral och mening med fokus på skolan*, Lomma: FLR.

—— 2004: 'Tolkning som utmaning', *Religion & Livsfrågor*, 37 (3), 3-7.

Franke, Edith 1997: 'Feministische Kritik and Wissenschaft und Religionen', in: Klinkhammer, Gritt Maria, Tobias Frick, et al. (ed.): *Kritik an Religionen. Religionswissenschaft und der kritische Umgang mit Religionen*, Marburg: Diagonal, 107-119.

Franke, Edith and Michael Pye 2004: 'The Study of Religions and its contribution to problem-solving in a plural world', *Marburg Journal of Religion*, 9 (2), 1-15.

—— (ed.) 2006: *Religionen nebeneinander. Modelle religiöser Vielfalt in Ost- und Südostasien*, Münster et al.: Lit.

Freie Hansestadt Bremen 1947: *Verfassung der Freien Hansestadt Bremen* (http://www.verfassungen.de/de/hb/bremen47-index.htm, 16.9.2007).

Freire, Paulo 1997: 'Vorwort: Erziehung und Hoffnung', in: Bernhard, Armin and Lutz Rothermel (ed.): *Handbuch kritische Pädagogik*, Weinheim: Deutscher Studien Verlag, 7-10.

Freistaat Sachsen 2007 [2004]: *Schulgesetz* (http://www.sachsen-macht-schule.de/schule/1748.htm, 17.9.2007).

Fritzsche, Klaus Peter 1997: 'Multiperspektivität: eine Schlüsselkompetenz beim Umgang mit dem Fremden', in: Bizeul, Yves et al. (ed.): *Vom Umgang mit dem Fremden. Hintergrund, Definitionen, Vorschläge*, Weinheim: Beltz, 190-201.

Furenhed, Ragnar 2000: 'Den buddhistiska vägen', in: Almén, Edgar, Ragnar Furenhed, et al. (ed.): *Livstolkning och värdegrund: att undervisa om religion, livsfrågor och etik*, Linköping: Linköpings Universitet, 161-175.

—— 2000: 'Naturfolkens religion', in: Almén, Edgar, Ragnar Furenhed, et al. (ed.): *Livstolkning och värdegrund: att undervisa om religion, livsfrågor och etik*, Linköping: Linköpings Universitet, 143-160.

—— 2000: 'Undervisning och förståelse - exemplet religionskunskap', in: Almén, Edgar, Ragnar Furenhed, et al. (ed.): *Livstolkning och värdegrund: att undervisa om religion, livsfrågor och etik*, Linköping: Linköpings Universitet, 117-142.

Gadamer, Hans-Georg 1975: *Truth and Method*. [translated from the German original 1965²; translation edited by Garrett Barden and John Cumming]. London: Sheed and Ward.

Gardtman, Ulf Oom 2003: 'Konst och film i religionskunskaps-undervisningen', *Religion & Livsfrågor*, 36 (4), 4-6.

Gasparro, Giulia Sfameni (ed.) 2002: *Themes and Problems of the History of Religions in Contemporary Europe*. Proceedings of the International Seminar Messina, March 30-31 2001, Cosenza: Lionello Giordano.

Gates, Brian (ed.) 1996: *Freedom and Authority in Religions and Religious Education*, London/New York: Cassell.

Geels, Anton 1988: 'Buddhism som 'folkreligion'', in: Rosenquist, Ingrid (ed.): *Kulturmöten*, Oxie: FLR, 67-95.

Geertz, Armin W. 2000: 'Global perspectives on methodology in the study of religion', in: Geertz, Armin W. and Russell T. McCutcheon (ed.): *Perspectives on Method and Theory in the Study of Religion. Adjunct Proceedings of the XVIIth Congress of the International Association for the History of Religions Mexico City, 1995*, Leiden/Boston/Köln: Brill, 49-73.

—— 2004: 'Definition, categorization and indecision: or, how to get on with the Study of Religion', in: Kleine, Christoph, Monika Schrimpf, et al. (ed.): *Unterwegs. Neue Pfade in der Religionswissenschaft. Festschrift für Michael Pye zum 65. Geburtstag*, München: Biblion, 109-118.

Geertz, Armin W. and Russell T. McCutcheon (ed.) 2000: *Perspectives on Method and Theory in the Study of Religion*. Adjunct Proceedings of the XVIIth Congress of the International Association for the History of Religions Mexico City, 1995, Leiden/Bosten/Köln: Brill.

—— 2000: 'The role of method and theory in the IAHR', in: Geertz, Armin W. and Russell T. McCutcheon (ed.): *Perspectives on Method and Theory in the Study of Religion. Adjunct Proceedings of the XVIIth Congress of the International Association for the History of Religions Mexico City, 1995*, Leiden/Boston/Köln: Brill, 3-37.

Geertz, Clifford 1966: 'Religion as a cultural system', in: Banton, Michael (ed.): *Anthropological Approaches to the Study of Religion*, London et al.: Routledge, 1-46.

—— 1973: *The Interpretation of Cultures*, New York: Basic Books.

—— 1983: *Local Knowledge: Further Essays in Interpretive Anthropology*, New York: Basic Books.

—— 1987 [1983[1]]: *Dichte Beschreibung. Beiträge zum Verstehen kultureller Systeme*, Frankfurt a.M.: Suhrkamp.

—— 1988: *Works and Lives: The Anthropologist as Author*, Cambridge: Polity Press.

Gerecht, Gonhild (ed.) 2000: *Grenzen überwinden - Interkulturelle Bildung als Zukunftschance: Fachtagung der Gewerkschaft Erziehung und Wissenschaft. Donnerstag, 10. Febr. 2000, Frankfurt am Main*: GEW Landesverband Hessen.

Giles, Arthur 2002: 'The birth of a new Religious Studies at post-16', in: Broadbent, Lynne and Alan Brown (ed.): *Issues in Religious Education*, London/New York: RoutledgeFalmer, 150-162.

Gilligan, Carol 1982: *In a Different Voice: Psychological Theory and Women's Development*, Cambridge, Mass.: Harvard University Press.

—— 1999[5]: *Die andere Stimme. Lebenskonflikte und Moral der Frau*, München: Piper.

Gladigow, Burkhard 1988: 'Religionsgeschichte des Gegenstandes - Gegenstände der Religionsgeschichte', in: Zinser, Hartmut (ed.): *Religionswissenschaft. Eine Einführung*, Berlin: Reimer, 6-37.

Gladigow, Burkhard and Hans G. Kippenberg (ed.) 1983: *Neue Ansätze in der Religionswissenschaft*, München: Kösel.

Glaser, Barney G. and Anselm L. Strauss 1979: *The Discovery of Grounded Theory: Strategies for Qualitative Research*, New York: Aldine.

Gloy, Horst 1997: 'Dem interreligiösen Religionsunterricht gehört die Zukunft', *Neue Sammlung*, 37 (2), 231-254.

—— 1997: 'Was für eine Schule schulden wir unseren Kindern und Jugendlichen in einer sich verändernden Welt?' in: Doedens, Folkert and Wolfram Weiße (ed.): *Religionsunterricht für alle: Hamburger Perspektiven zur Religionsdidaktik*, Münster et al.: Waxmann, 11-22.

Goldman, Ronald J. 1964: *Religious Thinking from Childhood to Adolescence*, London: Routledge and Kegan Paul.

—— 1965: *Readiness for Religion*, London: Routledge and Kegan Paul.

Gottwald, Eckhart and Folkert Rickers (ed.) 1999: *Ehrfurcht vor Gott und Toleranz - Leitbilder interreligiösen Lernens. Grundsätze der Erziehung im Spannungsfeld multikultureller Beziehungen*, Neukirchen-Vluyn: Neukirchener.

Greschat, Hans-Jürgen 1988: *Was ist Religionswissenschaft?*, Stuttgart et al.: Kohlhammer.

Greschat, Hans-Jürgen 1994: *Mündliche Religionsforschung. Erfahrungen und Einsichten*, Berlin: Reimer.

Griffionen, Karin and Cok Bakker 2002: 'Interkulturelles und interreligiöses Lernen in der niederländischen Bildungspolitik', in: Bakker, Cok, Olaf Beuchling, et al. (ed.): *Kulturelle Vielfalt und Religionsunterricht. Entwicklungen und Praxis in vier europäischen Ländern*, Münster et al.: Lit, 23-28.

Grimmitt, Michael H. 1973: *What Can I Do in RE?*, Great Wakering, Essex: Mayhew-McCrimmon.

—— 1987: *Religious Education and Human Development*, Great Wakering, Essex: McCrimmons.

—— 1991: 'The use of religious phenomena in schools', *British Journal of Religious Education*, 13 (2), 77-88.

—— 2000: 'Constructivist Pedagogies of Religious Education Project: rethinking knowledge, teaching and learning in religious education', in: Grimmitt, Michael (ed.): *Pedagogies of Religious Education. Case Studies in the Research and Development of Good Pedagogic Practice in RE*, Great Wakering: McCrimmons, 207-226.

—— 2000: 'Contemporary pedagogies of religious education: what are they?' in: Grimmitt, Michael (ed.): *Pedagogies of Religious Education. Case Studies in the Research and Development of Good Pedagogic Practice in RE*, Great Wakering: McCrimmons, 24-52.

—— 2000: 'Introduction: the captivity and liberation of religious education and the meaning and significance of pedagogy', in: Grimmitt, Michael (ed.): *Pedagogies of Religious Education. Case Studies in the Research and Development of Good Pedagogic Practice in RE*, Great Wakering: McCrimmons, 7-23.

—— (ed.) 2000: *Pedagogies of Religious Education. Case Studies in the Research and Development of Good Pedagogic Practice in RE*, Great Wakering: McCrimmon.

Grimmitt, Michael H., Julie Grove, et al. 1991: *A Gift to the Child: Religious Education in the Primary School* (Teachers' Source Book), London: Simon&Schuster.

Grove, Julie 1991: 'Religion in the service of the child: a new strategy for primary religious education', in: Evans-Lowndes, Judith (ed.): *Planning RE in Schools*, Derby: Christian Education Movement, 32-34.

Grözinger, Karl E. 1999: 'Ethik - Religion und Philosophie. Deutungen des Gesetzes im Judentum', in: Grözinger, Karl E., Burkhard Gladigow, et al. (ed.): *Religion in der schulischen Bildung und Erziehung: LER - Ethik - Werte und Normen in einer pluralistischen Gesellschaft*, Berlin: Berlin-Verlag Spitz, 119-136.

Grözinger, Karl E., Burkhard Gladigow, et al. (ed.) 1999: *Religion in der schulischen Bildung und Erziehung: LER - Ethik - Werte und Normen in einer pluralistischen Gesellschaft*, Berlin: Berlin-Verlag Spitz.

—— 1999: 'Zur Einführung', in: Grözinger, Karl E., Burkhard Gladigow, et al. (ed.): *Religion in der schulischen Bildung und Erziehung: LER - Ethik - Werte und Normen in einer pluralistischen Gesellschaft*, Berlin: Berlin-Verlag Spitz, 9-15.

Gudjons, Herbert and Rainer Winkel (ed.) 1995[8]: *Didaktische Theorien*, Hamburg: Bergmann&Helbig.

Gustavsson, Caroline and Rune Larsson 2004: 'Religious education research for the future', in: Larsson, Rune and Caroline Gustavsson (ed.): *Towards a European Perspective on Religious Education. The RE Research Conference, March 11-14, 2004, University of Lund*, Skellefteå: Artos&Norma, 353-356.

Habermas, Jürgen 1974[3] [1963[1]]: *Theorie und Praxis. Sozialphilosophische Studien*, Frankfurt: Suhrkamp.

Hahn, Matthias, Michael Linke, et al. 1992: 'Welchen Religionsunterricht braucht die öffentliche Schule? Braunschweiger Ratschlag vom 8.Februar 1991 aus Anlaß des 60. Geburtstags von Prof. Dr. Reinhard Dross', in: Lott, Jürgen (ed.): *Religion - warum und wozu in der Schule?*, Weinheim: Deutscher Studien Verlag, 341-355.

Hallberg, Per-Gunnar 2000: 'Reflektioner kring kursplan 2000', *Religion & Livsfrågor*, 33 (3), 14-17.

Hammond, John 1991: 'Experiential learning in RE', *Norfolk Journal of Religious Education*, 1-5.

—— 1992: 'Turning to tradition', *Journal of Beliefs and Values*, 13 (2), 4-6.

—— 2002: 'Embodying the spirit. Realising RE's potential in the spiritual dimension of the curriculum', in: Broadbent, Lynne and Alan Brown (ed.): *Issues in Religious Education*, London/New York: RoutledgeFalmer, 189-200.

Hammond, John, David Hay, et al. 1990: *New Methods in RE Teaching: An Experiential Approach*, Harlow, Essex: Oliver&Boyd.

Hanlon, Dinah 2002: 'Not 'either-or', more a case of 'both-and'. Towards an inclusive gender strategy for religious education', in: Broadbent, Lynne and Alan Brown (ed.): *Issues in Religious Education*, London/New York: RoutledgeFalmer, 123-135.

Harbsmeier, Eberhard, Friedrich Schweitzer, et al. (ed.) 2001: *Elementarisering*, Løgumkloster: Folkekirkens Pædagogiske Institut.

Härenstam, Kjell 1993: *Skolboks-islam: analys av bilden av islam i läroböcker i religionskunskap*, Göteborg: Acta Universitatis Gothoburgensis.

—— 2000: *Kan du höra vindhästen?: religionsdidaktik - om konsten att välja kunskap*, Lund: Studentlitteratur.

—— 2000: 'How to choose knowledge for Swedish schools and text-books in RE, example: Tibetan Buddhism', *Panorama: International Journal of Comparative Religious Education and Values*, 12 (1), 27-42.

Hartmann, Sven G. 1992: *Barns livsfrågor som pedagogisk arena*, Linköping: Institutionen für pedagogik och psychologi.

—— 1994: 'Children's philosophy of life as the basis for religious education', *Panorama: International Journal of Comparative Religious Education and Values*, 6 (2), 104-128.

—— 1996: 'Uniformity and Pluralism in Swedish School Curriculum Development', *Panorama: International Journal of Comparative Religious Education and Values*, 8 (1), 123-134.

—— 2000: 'Hur religionsämnet formades', in: Almén, Edgar, Ragnar Furenhed, et al. (ed.): *Livstolkning och värdegrund : att undervisa om religion, livsfrågor och etik*, Linköping: Linköpings Universitet, 212-251.

Hase, Thomas 2000: *Quantitative Methoden in der Religionswissenschaft. Eine Erörterung ausgewählter Erhebungs- und Analyseverfahren*, Marbug: Remid.

Hasselrot, Titti and Lars Olov Lernberg 1980: *Tonåringen och livet: undersökning och diskussion kring tonåringen och livsfrågorna*, Stockholm: Liber Utbildningsförlag.

Hay, David 1985: 'Suspicion of the spiritual: teaching religion in a world of secular experience', *British Journal of Religious Education*, 7 (3), 140-147.

—— 1986: *Experiential Education in Religion as De-indoctrination*, Nottingham: Religious Experience Research Project.

—— 1990: *Religious Experience Today. Studying the Facts*, London: Mowbray.

—— 1992: 'How, in our time, can we learn about spirituality?' *Journal of Beliefs and Values*, 13 (2), 6-8.

—— 1998: 'The naturalness of relational consciousness', in: Hay, David and Rebecca Nye (ed.): *The Spirit of the Child*, London: HarperCollins, 141-158.

—— 2000: 'The Religious Experience and Education Project: experiential learning in religious education', in: Grimmitt, Michael (ed.): *Pedagogies of Religious Education. Case Studies in the Research and Development of Good Pedagogic Practice in RE*, Great Wakering: McCrimmons, 70-87.

Hay, David and John Hammond 1992: "When you pray, go to your private room'. A reply to Adrian Thatcher', *British Journal of Religious Education*, 14 (3), 145-150.

Hay, David and Rebecca Nye 1996: 'Investigating children's spirituality: the need for a fruitful hypothesis', *International Journal for Children's Spirituality*, 1 (1), 6-16.

—— 1998: *The Spirit of the Child*, London: HarperCollins.

Heidegger, Simone 2006: *Buddhismus, Geschlechterverhältnis und Diskriminierung. Die gegenwärtige Diskussion im Shin-Buddhismus Japans*, Münster: Lit.

Heiler, Friedrich 1920[2] [1918[1]]: *Das Gebet. Eine religionsgeschichtliche und religionspsychologische Untersuchung*, München: Reinhardt.

—— 1959: *Die Religionen der Menschheit in Vergangenheit und Gegenwart*, Stuttgart: Reclam.

—— 1961: *Erscheinungsformen und Wesen der Religion*, Stuttgart: Kohlhammer.

Heimann, Paul 1962: 'Didaktik als Theorie und Lehre', *Die Deutsche Schule. Zeitschrift für Erziehungswissenschaft und Gestaltung der Schulwirklichkeit*, 54 (9), 407-427.

Heimann, Paul, Gunther Otto, et al. (ed.) 1965: *Unterricht. Analyse und Planung*, Hannover: Schroedel.

Heimbrock, Hans-Günter, Christoph Th. Scheilke, et al. (ed.) 2001: *Towards Religious Competence: Diversity as a Challenge for Education in Europe*, Münster: Lit.

Heinrichs, Gesa 1996: 'Weltethos und Religionsunterricht. Eine kritische Untersuchung des Weltethosprogramms und der darauf bezogenen religionspädagogischen Überlegungen', in: Weiße, Wolfram (ed.): *Vom Monolog zum Dialog. Ansätze einer interkulturellen dialogischen Religionspädagogik*, Münster: Waxmann, 97-121.

Hellmann, Christian 2001: *Religiöse Bildung, Interreligiöses Lernen und Interkulturelle Pädagogik. Eine religionsgeschichtliche Untersuchung zur religiösen und interkulturellen Erziehung in der Moderne*, Frankfurt/M.: IKO - Verlag für interkulturelle Kommunikation.

Helve, Helena 1993: *The World View of Young People: A Longitudinal Study of Finnish Youth Living in a Suburb of Metropolitan Helsinki*, Helsinki: Suomalainen Tiedeakatemia.

—— 2000: 'The formation of gendered world views and gender ideology', in: Geertz, Armin W. and Russell T. McCutcheon (ed.): *Perspectives on Method and Theory in the Study of Religion. Adjunct Proceedings of the XVIIth Congress of the International Association for the History of Religions Mexico City, 1995*, Leiden/Boston/Köln: Brill, 245-259.

Helve, Helena and Michael Pye 2001-2002: 'Theoretical correlations between world-view, civil religion, institutional religion and informal spiritualities', *Temenos*, 37-38, 87-106.

Hertfordshire (England) County Council, Education Department 1995: *The Hertfordshire Agreed Syllabus of Religious Education*, Hertford: Hertfordshire Education Services.

Heydorn, Heinz-Joachim 1995: *Werke Band 2: Bildungstheoretische und pädagogische Schriften 1967-1970*, Vaduz: Topos.

—— 1995: *Werke Band 3. Bildungstheoretische und pädagogische Schriften. Über den Widerspruch von Bildung und Herrschaft*, Vaduz: Topos.

Hjärpe, Jan 2003: 'Att studera religioner och normsystem: från teologisk till antropologisk religionsvetenskap', in: Franck, Olof (ed.): *Liksom värden, typ: moral och mening med fokus på skolan*, Lomma: FLR, 41-53.

Högberg, Ole and Mats Sunqvist 1999: *Religionsboken*, Stockholm: Bonnier.

Holm, Nils G. (ed.) 1997: *The Familiar and the Unfamiliar in the World Religions: Challenges for Religious Education Today*, Åbo: Åbo Akademis trykeri.

—— 1997: 'Preface', in: Holm, Nils G. (ed.): *The Familiar and the Unfamiliar in the World Religions: Challenges for Religious Education Today*, Åbo: Åbo Akademis trykeri, 7-9.

—— 2000: 'Introduction', in: Holm, Nils G. (ed.): *Islam and Christianity in School Religious Education. Issues, Approaches, and Contexts*, Åbo: Åbo Akademis trykeri, 11-18.

—— (ed.) 2000: *Islam and Christianity in School Religious Education. Issues, Approaches, and Contexts*, Åbo: Åbo Akademis trykeri.

Holt, Mikael 2000: 'Denmark', in: Schreiner, Peter (ed.): *Religious education in Europe. A collection of basic information about RE in European countries*, Münster: Comenius-Institut, 27-30.

Horkheimer, Max 1970: 'Traditionelle und kritische Theorie [1937]', in: Horkheimer, Max: *Traditionelle und kritische Theorie. Vier Aufsätze*, Frankfurt: S. Fischer, 12-56.

—— 1970: *Traditionelle und kritische Theorie. Vier Aufsätze*, Frankfurt: S. Fischer.

Horkheimer, Max and Theodor W. Adorno 1998: *Dialektik der Aufklärung [1947]*, Frankfurt: S. Fischer.

—— 1998: 'Kulturindustrie, Aufklärung als Massenbetrug [1947]', in: Horkheimer, Max and Theodor W. Adorno: *Dialektik der Aufklärung*, Frankfurt: S. Fischer, 128-176.

Hormel, Ulrike and Albert Scherr 2004: *Bildung für die Einwanderungsgesellschaft. Perspektiven der Auseinandersetzung mit struktureller, institutioneller und interaktioneller Diskriminierung*, Wiesbaden: VS Verlag für Sozialwissenschaften.

Hull, John M. 1989: *The Act Unpacked. The Meaning of the 1988 Education Reform Act for Religious Education*, Birmingham/Isleworth: University of Birmingham/CEM.

—— 1991: *Mishmash. Religious Education in Multi-Cultural Britain. A Study in Metaphor*, Derbiy: CEM.

—— 1994: 'Editorial: 'model syllabuses'', *British Journal of Religious Education*, 17 (1), 2-4.

—— 1994: 'Geschichte und Entwicklung des Lehrplans für den Religionsunterricht in Birmingham - Kommunale und nationale Aspekte', in: Lohmann, Ingrid and Wolfram Weiße (ed.): *Dialog zwischen den Kulturen: erziehungswissenschaftliche und religionspädagogische Gesichtspunkte interkultureller Bildung*, Münster/New York: Waxmann, 275-280.

—— 1996: 'Freedom and authority in religious education', in: Gates, Brian (ed.): *Freedom and Authority in Religions and Religious Education*, London/New York: Cassell, 97-111.

—— 1996: 'A Gift to the Child: a new pedagogy for teaching religion to young children', *Religious Education*, 91 (2), 172-188.

—— 1998: 'Review of Robert Jackson (1997): Religious Education: An Interpretive Approach', *British Journal of Religious Education*, 20 (2), 125-8.

—— 2000: 'Religion in the Service of the Child Project: the gift approach to religious education', in: Grimmitt, Michael (ed.): *Pedagogies of Religious Education. Case Studies in the Research and Development of Good Pedagogic Practice in RE*, Great Wakering: McCrimmons, 112-129.

—— 2000: 'Religionism and religious education', in: Leicester, Mal, Celia Modgil, et al. (ed.): *Spiritual and Religious Education*, London/New York: Falmer, 75-85.

—— 2002: 'Der Segen der Säkularität: Religionspädagogik in England und Wales', in: Weiße, Wolfram (ed.): *Wahrheit und Dialog: Theologische Grundlagen und Impulse gegenwärtiger Religionspädagogik*, Münster et al.: Waxmann, 167-179.

—— 2002: 'Spititual development: interpretations and applications', *British Journal of Religious Education*, 24 (3), 171-182.

Introvigne, Massimo (ed.) 1998: *Schluß mit den Sekten*, Marburg: Diagonal.

Ipgrave, Julia 1999: 'Issues in the delivery of religious education to Muslim pupils: perspectives from the classroom', *British Journal of Religious Education*, 21 (3), 147-58.

Jackson, Robert 1994: 'Ethnography and religious education: a research report', *Panorama. International Journal of Comparative Religious Education and Values*, 6 (1), 115-130.

—— 1996: 'Re-examining 'religions' and 'culture' in religious education', in: Weiße, Wolfram (ed.): *Interreligious and intercultural education. Methodologies, conceptions, and pilot projects in South Africa, Namibia, Great Britain, The Netherlands and Germany*, Münster: 11-26.

—— 1997: 'Ethnographic studies of children and interpretive methods for religious education', in: Andree, Trees et al. (ed.): *Crossing Boundaries. Contributions to Interreligious and Intercultural Education*, Münster: Comenius-Institut, 65-73.

—— 1997: 'The law and politics of multifaith religious education in Britain', in: Andree, Trees et al. (ed.): *Crossing Boundaries. Contributions to Interreligious and Intercultural Education*, Münster: Comenius-Institut, 75-87.

—— 1997: *Religious Education. An Interpretive Approach*, London: Hodder & Stoughton.

—— 1999: 'The training of RE teachers in England and Wales. Some observations about power relations', *Panorama. International Journal of Comparative Religious Education and Values*, 11 (1/2), 80-86.

—— 2000: 'Law, politics and religious education in England and Wales: some history, some stories and some observations', in: Leicester, Mal, Celia Modgil, et al. (ed.): *Spiritual and Religious Education*, London/New York: Falmer, 86-99.

—— 2000: 'The Warwick Religious Education Project: the interpretive approach to religious education', in: Grimmitt, Michael (ed.): *Pedagogies of Religious Education. Case Studies in the Research and Development of Good Pedagogic Practice in RE*, Great Wakering: McCrimmons, 153-189.

—— 2001: 'Creative pedagogy in religious education: case studies in interpretation', in: Heimbrock, Hans-Günter, Christoph Th. Scheilke, et al. (ed.): *Towards Religious Competence: Diversity as a Challenge for Education in Europe*, Münster: Lit, 34-52.

—— 2003: 'Citizenship, religious and cultural diversity and education', in: Jackson, Robert (ed.): *International Perspectives on Citizenship, Education and Religious Diversity*, London/New York: RoutledgeFalmer, 1-28.

—— (ed.) 2003: *International Perspectives on Citizenship, Education and Religious Diversity*, London/New York: RoutledgeFalmer.

—— 2004: 'Current issues in research in religious education', in: Larsson, Rune and Caroline Gustavsson (ed.): *Towards a European Perspective on Religious Education. The RE Research Conference, March 11-14, 2004, University of Lund*, Skellefteå: Artos&Norma, 19-35.

—— 2004: 'Intercultural education and recent European pedagogies of religious education', *Intercultural Education*, 15 (1), 3-14.

—— 2004: *Rethinking Religious Education and Plurality. Issues in Diversity and Pedagogy*, London/New York: RoutledgeFalmer.

Jackson, Robert and Eleanor Nesbitt 1992: 'The diversity of experience in the religious upbringing of children from Christian families in Britain', *British Journal of Religious Education*, 15 (1), 19-28.

—— 1993: *Hindu Children in Britain*, Stoke on Trent: Trentham Books.

—— 1997: 'From fieldwork to school text: studying and representing British Hindu children', in: Andree, Trees et al. (ed.): *Crossing Boundaries. Contributions to Interreligious and Intercultural Education*, Münster: Comenius-Institut, 89-99.

Jäggle, Martin 1995: 'Religionspädagogik im Kontext interkulturellen Lernens', in: Ziebertz, Hans-Georg und Werner Simon (ed.): *Bilanz der Religionspädagogik*, Düsseldorf: Patmos, 243-258.

—— 2003: 'Religionen-Didaktik', in: Figl, Johann (ed.): *Handbuch Religionswissenschaft*, Göttingen: Vandenhoeck&Ruprecht, 817-833.

Jakeliæ, Slavica and Lori Pearson (ed.) 2004: *The Future of the Study of Religion. Proceedings of Congress 2000*, Leiden/Boston: Brill.

Jensen, Tim 1997: 'Familiar and unfamiliar challenges to the study and teaching of religions in an increasingly religious and multireligious context', in: Holm, Nils G. (ed.): *The Familiar and the Unfamiliar in the World Religions: Challenges for Religious Education Today*, Åbo: Åbo Akademis trykeri, 199-223.

—— 1999: 'Religion and religious education in a Europe of conflicting trends', in: Tidman, Nils-Åke (ed.): *Into the Third Millenium. EFTRE conference August 1998 in Copenhagen*, Lomma: FLR, 142-159.

—— 2002: 'From the History of Religions to the Study of Religions. Trends and tendencies in Denmark', in: Gasparro, Giulia Sfameni (ed.): *Themes and Problems of the History of Religions in Contemporary Europe. Proceedings of the International Seminar Messina, March 30-31 2001*, Cosenza: Lionello Giordano, 183-208.

—— 2002: 'Religious education in public schools - a must for a secular state: a Danish perspective', *Bulletin of the Council of Societies for the Study of Religion*, 31 (4), 83-89.

—— 2005: 'European and Danish religious education: human rights, the secular state, and 'Rethinking Religious Education and Plurality'', *Religion and Education*, 32 (1), 60-78.

Jensen, Tim and Mikael Rothstein (ed.) 2000: *Secular Theories of Religion. Current Perspectives*, Copenhagen: Museum Tusculanum Press.

Johannesson, Rudolf 1988: 'Skev bild av hinduismen i skolans läroböcker?' *Religion & Livsfrågor*, (3), 28-29.

Johansson, Peter 2003: 'Orientalism och panarabism i moderna populärmedier', *Religion & Livsfrågor*, 36 (4), 8-10.

Joy, Morny 2000: 'Beyond God's eyeview: alternative perspectives in the study of religion', in: Geertz, Armin W. and Russell T. McCutcheon (ed.): *Perspectives on Method and Theory in the Study of Religion*. Adjunct Proceedings of the XVIIth Congress of the International Association for the History of Religions Mexico City, 1995, Leiden/Boston/Köln: Brill, 110-140.

—— 2001: 'Postcolonial reflections: challenges for Religious Studies', *Method and Theory in the Study of Religion*, 13 (2), 177-195.

Jungclaussen, Emmanuel (ed.) 1992: *Ökumene - Ende oder Anfang? Zur Aktualität Friedrich Heilers*, Marburg: Pressestelle der Philipps-Universität.

Kallioniemi, Arto 1999: 'The challenges for religious education in the postmodern society: a Finnish approach', in: Tidman, Nils-Åke (ed.): *Into the Third Millenium. EFTRE conference August 1998 in Copenhagen*, Lomma: FLR, 28-37.

—— 2002: 'Adult senior secondary school students' concepts concerning religious education', *British Journal of Religious Education*, 24 (3), 208-222.

Karlsson, Pia and Ingvar Svanberg (ed.) 1997: *Religionsfrihet i Sverige*, Lund: Studentlitteratur.

Kaul-Seidman, Lisa, Jørgen S. Nielsen, et al. 2003: *Europäische Identität und kultureller Pluralismus: Judentum, Christentum und Islam in europäischen Lehrplänen; ein Projekt der Herbert-Quandt-Stiftung*, Bad Homburg v.d. Höhe: Herbert-Quandt-Stiftung.

—— 2003: *European Identity and Cultural Pluralism: Judaism, Christianity and Islam in European Curricula; a Project of the Herbert-Quandt-Stiftung*, Bad Homburg v.d. Höhe: Herbert-Quandt-Stiftung.

Kay, William K. 1996: 'Historical context: Loukes, Goldman, Hyde, Cox and Alves', in: Francis, Leslie J., William K Kay, et al. (ed.): *Research in Religious Education*, Leominster/Macon: Gracewing/Smyth & Helwys, 31-45.

—— 1997: 'Phenomenology, religious education and Piaget', *Religion*, 27 (3), 275-283.

—— 2000: British comment on the Swedish PPI, in Edgar Almén and Hans Christian Øster (ed.): *Religious Education in Great Britain, Sweden and Russia*, Linköping: Linköping University Electronic Press, 116-120.

King, Richard 1999: 'Orientalism and the modern myth of 'Hinduism'', *Numen*, 46 (2), 146-185.

King, Ursula 1989: 'Women and world religions', in: Wood, Angela (ed.): *Religions and Education. Shap Working Party 1969-89*, Isleworth: BFSS National RE Centre, 98-101.

—— 1990: 'Religion and gender', in: King, Ursula (ed.): *Turning Points in Religious Studies. Essays in Honour of Geoffrey Parrinder*, Edinburgh: Clark, 275-286.

—— (ed.) 1990: Turning *Points in Religious Studies. Essays in Honour of Geoffrey Parrinder*, Edinburgh: Clark.

—— (ed.) 1995: *Religion and Gender*, Oxford: Blackwell.

—— 2001: 'Introduction: spirituality, society, and the millennium - wasteland, wilderness, or new vision?' in: King, Ursula (ed.): *Spirituality and Society in the New Millennium*, Brighton/Portoand: Sussex Academic Press, 1-13.

—— (ed.) 2001: *Spirituality and Society in the New Millenium*, Brighton/Portland: Sussex Academic Press.

Kippenberg, Hans G. 1983: 'Diskursive Religionswissenschaft', in: Gladigow, Burkhard and Hans G. Kippenberg (ed.): *Neue Ansätze in der Religionswissenschaft*, München: Kösel, 9-28.

—— (ed.) 1991: *Religionswissenschaft und Kulturkritik: Beiträge zur Konferenz The History of Religions and Critique of Culture in the Days of Gerardus van der Leeuw (1890-1950)*; [Groningen 1-3 May, 1989], Marburg: Diagonal.

Kirklees Metropolitan Council, Education Service 1995: *Kirklees Agreed Syllabus for Religious Education 1995-2000*, Kirklees: Kirklees Metropolitan Council.

Klafki, Wolfgang 1958: 'Didaktische Analyse als Kern der Unterrichtsvorbereitung', *Die Deutsche Schule. Zeitschrift für Erziehungswissenschaft und Gestaltung der Schulwirklichkeit*, 50 (10), 450-471.

—— 1963: 'Das Problem der Didaktik', in: *Das Problem der Didaktik, 3. Beiheft zur Zeitschrift für Pädagogik*, 19-64.

—— 1985: *Neue Studien zur Bildungstheorie und Didaktik. Beiträge zur kritisch-konstruktiven Didaktik*, Weinheim/Basel: Beltz.

—— 1999: 'Braucht eine 'gute Schule' einen neuen Unterrichtsbereich LER?' in: Grözinger, Karl E., Burkhard Gladigow, et al. (ed.): *Religion in der schulischen Bildung und Erziehung: LER - Ethik - Werte und Normen in einer pluralistischen Gesellschaft*, Berlin: Berlin-Verlag Spitz, 197-209.

—— 2001: 'Grundlinien eines gegenwarts- und zukunftsorientierten Bildungsbegriffs', in: Harbsmeier, Eberhard, Friedrich Schweitzer, et al. (ed.): *Elementarisering*, Løgumkloster: Folkekirkens Pædagogiske Institut, 29-44.

—— 2001: 'Zur Frage eines zeitgemäßen Bildungsbegriffs', in: Harbsmeier, Eberhard, Friedrich Schweitzer, et al. (ed.): *Elementarisering*, Løgumkloster: Folkekirkens Pædagogiske Institut, 24-27.

—— 1969[10]: 'Didaktische Analyse als Kern der Unterrichtsvorbereitung [1959]', in: Roth, H., Wolfgang Klafki, et al. (ed.): *Didaktische Analyse. Grundlegende Aufsätze aus der Zeitschrift Deutsche Schule*, Hannover: Schroedel, 5-43.

Kleine, Christoph, Monika Schrimpf, et al. (ed.) 2004: *Unterwegs. Neue Pfade in der Religionswissenschaft. Festschrift für Michael Pye zum 65. Geburtstag*, München: Biblion.

Klinkhammer, Gritt Maria, Tobias Frick, et al. (ed.) 1997: *Kritik an Religionen. Religionswissenschaft und der kritische Umgang mit Religionen*, Marburg: Diagonal.

Knauth, Thorsten 1996: *Religionsunterricht und Dialog. Empirische Untersuchungen, systematische Überlegungen und didaktische Perspektiven eines Religionsunterrichts im Horizont religiöser und kultureller Pluralisierung*, Münster et al.: Waxmann.

Knauth, Thorsten and Wolfram Weiße 1996: 'Lernbereich Religion/Ethik und integrativer Religionsunterricht aus SchülerInnensicht. Empirische Erhebungen und konzeptionelle Überlegungen', in: Weiße, Wolfram (ed.): *Vom Monolog zum Dialog. Ansätze einer interkulturellen dialogischen Religionspädagogik*, Münster: Waxmann, 41-57.

Knoblauch, Hubert 2003: *Qualitative Religionsforschung. Religionsethnographie in der eigenen Gesellschaft*, Paderborn/München: Schöningh.

Kohli, Wendy 1996: 'Critical Theory', in: Chamberliss, J. J. (ed.): *Philosophy of Education. An Encyclopedia*, New York & London: Garland, 115-119.

Koppen, Jan Karel, Ingrid Lunt, et al. (ed.) 2002: *Education in Europe. Cultures, Values, Institutions in Transition*, Münster et al.: Waxmann.

Körber, Sigurd 1988: 'Didaktik der Religionswissenschaft', in: Cancik, Hubert, Burkhard Gladigow et al. (ed.): *Handbuch religionswissenschaftlicher Grundbegriffe*, vol. 1, Stuttgart: Kohlhammer, 195-215.

Krausen, Halima 1996: 'Aus muslimischer Sicht: Anmerkungen zum neuen Hamburger Lehrplan Religion Primarstufe', in: Weiße, Wolfram (ed.): *Vom Monolog zum Dialog. Ansätze einer interkulturellen dialogischen Religionspädagogik*, Münster: Waxmann, 179-180.

Kremer, Armin 1997: 'Didaktik', in: Bernhard, Armin and Lutz Rothermel (ed.): *Handbuch Kritische Pädagogik. Eine Einführung in die Erziehungs- und Bildungswissenschaft*, Weinheim: Deutscher Studien Verlag, 74-84.

Kriesel, Peter 1998: 'Wenn die Magd zur Herrin wird. Erfahrungen mit einem untauglichen Kooperationsmodell', in: Ehmann, Reinhard u.a. (ed.): *Religionsunterricht der Zukunft. Aspekte eines notwendigen Wandels*, Freiburg: Herder, 97-103.

—— 1999: 'Anmerkungen zum Beitrag der Religionswissenschaft für die Allgemeinbildung der Schüler und Lehrkräften in der Schule', in: Grözinger, Karl E., Burkhard Gladigow, et al. (ed.): *Religion in der schulischen Bildung und Erziehung: LER - Ethik - Werte und Normen in einer pluralistischen Gesellschaft*, Berlin: Berlin-Verlag Spitz, 59-69.

Kristensen, W. Brede 1954: *Religionshistorisk Studium*, Oslo: Olaf Noris Forlag.

—— 1960: *The Meaning of Religion: Lectures in the Phenomenology of Religion*, The Hague: Nijhoff.

Kron, Friedrich W. 1993: *Grundwissen Didaktik*, München/Basel: E.Reinhardt.

Krüger-Potratz, Marianne 2002: 'Kulturelle Differenz - Skizze zu einem Reizwort', in: Wulf, Christoph and Christine Merkel (ed.): *Globalisierung als Herausforderung der Erziehung. Theorien, Grundlagen, Fallstudien*, Münster et al.: Waxmann, 59-63.

Kunert, Hubertus 1997: 'Erziehung', in: Bernhard, Armin and Lutz Rothermel (ed.): *Handbuch Kritische Pädagogik. Eine Einführung in die Erziehungs- und Bildungswissenschaft*, Weinheim: Deutscher Studien Verlag, 57-62.

Laermans, Rudi, Bryan Wilson, et al. (ed.) 1998: *Secularization and Social Integration*, Louvain: Louvain University Press.

Lähnemann, Johannes 1998: *Evangelische Religionspädagogik in interreligiöser Perspektive*, Göttingen: Vandenhoeck&Ruprecht.

Lärarförbundet 1998: *Lpfö - Läroplaner för förskolan*, Stockholm: Lärarförb.

Land Baden-Württemberg 1953: *Verfassung des Landes Baden-Württemberg* (http://www.verfassungen.de/de/bw/bw53-index.htm, 16.9.2007).

Land Baden-Württemberg, Ministeriums für Kultus, Jugend und Sport 2005 [1983]: *Schulgesetz für das Land Baden-Württemberg* (http://www.kultus-und-unterricht.de/schulgesetz_20.pdf, 16.9.2007).

Land Berlin, Senatsverwaltung für Bildung, Wissenschaft und Forschung 2006 [2004]: *Schulgesetz für das Land Berlin* (http://www.belin.de/imperia/md/content/senbildung/rechtsvorschriften/schulgesetz.pdf, 16.9.2007).

Land Brandenburg, Ministerium für Bildung, Jugend und Sport 2007 [1996]: *Gesetz über die Schulen im Land Brandenburg* (http://www.mbjs.brandenburg.de/sixcms/media.php/1238/schulgesetz2006_lesefassung.pdf, 16.9.2007).

Land Mecklenburg Vorpommern 1993: *Verfassung des Landes Mecklenburg Vorpommern* (http://www.verfassungen.de/de/mv/mv93-index.htm, 16.9.2007).

Land Mecklenburg-Vorpommern, Ministerium für Bildung, Wissenschaft und Kultur 2006: *Schulgesetz für das Land Mecklenburg-Vorpommern* (www.kultus-mv.de/_sites/bibo/gesetze/schulgesetz_neu.pdf, 16.9.2007).

Lankshear, David 2000: 'Religious education in England and Wales', in: Schreiner, Peter (ed.): *Religious Education in Europe. A Collection of Basic Information About RE in European Countries*, Münster: ICSS/Comenius-Institut, 56-59.

Larochelle, Marie, Nadine Bednarz, et al. (ed.) 1998: *Constructivism and Education*, Cambridge, UK: Cambridge University Press.

Läroplanskommittén 1992: *Skola för bildning: huvudbetänkande*, Stockholm: Allmänna förlag.

Larsson, Ove 1991: *Religionen i skolan och skolans religionsunder-visning: elevers uppfattningar av fenomenet religion och skolämnet religions-kunskap i årskurs 9*, Göteborg: Göteborgs Universitet, Institutionen för metodik i lärarutbildningen.

Larsson, Rune 1992[3] (third revised edition, 1985[1]): *Introduktion till religionspedagogiken*, Lund: Teologiska insitutionen.

—— (ed.) 1996: *Nordisk religionspedagogik 1993-1995*: material framlagt vid Nordisk religionspedagogisk forskar-konferens på stiftsgården Åkersberg, Höör, den 12-16 augusti 1995, Lomma: Religionspedagogiska Institutet.

—— 1996: 'A reformed school and religious education in Sweden', *Panorama: International Journal of Comparative Religious Education and Values*, 8 (1), 72-82.

—— 1997: 'Pluralität als Herausforderung', in: Schreiner, Peter and Hans Spinder (ed.): *Identitätsbildung im pluralen Europa. Perspektiven für Schule und Religionsunterricht*, Münster et al.: Waxmann, 17-26.

—— 1997: 'Religionsunterricht in einer Schule für alle - Schweden', in: Schreiner, Peter and Hans Spinder (ed.): *Identitätsbildung im pluralen Europa. Perspektiven für Schule und Religionsunterricht*, Münster et al.: Waxmann, 177-190.

—— 2000: 'Sweden', in: Schreiner, Peter (ed.): *Religious Education in Europe. A Collection of Basic Information About RE in European Countries*, Münster: ICSS/Comenius-Institut, 159-164.

Larsson, Rune and Caroline Gustavsson 2004: 'Introduction', in: Larsson, Rune and Caroline Gustavsson (ed.): *Towards a European Perspective on Religious Education. The RE Research Conference, March 11-14, 2004, University of Lund*, Skellefteå: Artos&Norma, 9-17.

—— (ed.) 2004: *Towards a European Perspective on Religious Education. The RE Research Conference, March 11-14, 2004, University of Lund*, Skellefteå: Artos&Norma.

Leganger-Krogstad 2001: 'Religious education in a global perspective: a contextual approach', in: Heimbrock, Hans-Günter, Christoph Th. Scheilke, et al. (ed.): *Towards Religious Competence: Diversity as a Challenge for Education in Europe*, Münster: Lit, 53-73.

—— 2003: 'Dialogue among young citizens in a pluralistic religious education', in: Jackson, Robert (ed.): *International Perspectives on Citizenship, Education and Religious Diversity*, London/New York: RoutledgeFalmer, 169-190.

Lehmann, Karl (ed.) 1998: *Religionsunterricht in der offenen Gesellschaft. Ein Symposion im Bonner Wasserwerk*, Köln: Kohlhammer.

Leicester, Mal, Celia Modgil, et al. (ed.) 2000: *Spiritual and Religious Education*, London: Falmer.

Leimgruber, Stephan 1995: *Interreligiöses Lernen*, München: Kösel.

Leont'ev, Aleksej Nikolaevic 1981: *Problems of the Development of Mind*, Moscow: Progressive Publishers.

Lersch, Rainer 2005: 'Modellierungen der Didaktischen Fragestellung - Entwicklungen und Perspektiven für ein Modell der 'ganzen' Didaktik', in: Stadtfeld, Peter and Bernhard Dieckmann (ed.): *Allgemeine Didaktik im Wandel*, Bad Heilbrunn: Verlag Julius Klinkhardt, 68-95.

Liljefors Persson, Bodil 2004: 'Religious studies and learning - and beyond! Grasping the global field of religious education research from a local perspective', in: Larsson, Rune and Caroline Gustavsson (ed.): *Towards a European Perspective on Religious Education. The RE Research Conference, March 11-14, 2004, University of Lund*, Skellefteå: Artos&Norma, 212-221.

Lohmann, Georg 1999: 'Zehn Thesen zum Verhältnis von Ethik und Religion im Ethikunterricht', in: Grözinger, Karl E., Burkhard Gladigow, et al. (ed.): *Religion in der schulischen Bildung und Erziehung: LER - Ethik - Werte und Normen in einer pluralistischen Gesellschaft*, Berlin: Berlin-Verlag Spitz, 155-167.

Lohmann, Ingrid and Wolfram Weiße (ed.) 1994: *Dialog zwischen den Kulturen: erziehungshistorische und religionspädagogische Gesichtspunkte interkultureller Bildung*, Münster/New York: Waxmann.

Lombaerts, Herman and Didier Pollefeyt (ed.) 2004: *Hermeneutics and Religious Education*, Leuven: Peeter.

Lott, Jürgen (ed.) 1992: *Religion - warum und wozu in der Schule?*, Weinheim: Deutscher Studien Verlag.

—— 1998: *'Wie hast Du's mit der Religion?': das neue Schulfach 'Lebensgestaltung - Ethik - Religionskunde' (LER) und die Werteerziehung in der Schule*, Gütersloh: Gütersloher Verlagshaus.

—— 2001: *Lebensgestaltung-Ethik-Religionskunde* (http://www.religion.uni-bremen. de/lott, 28.4.2006).

Loukes, Harold 1961: *Teenage Religion*, London: SCM.

Luckmann, Thomas 1991: *Die unsichtbare Religion*, Frankfurt: Suhrkamp.

Lyotard, Jean-François 1979: *La condition postmoderne: rapport sur le savoir*, Paris: Les Éditions de Minuit.

Marcuse, Herbert 1967: *Der eindimensionale Mensch: Studien zur Ideologie der fortgeschrittenen Industriegesellschaft*, Neuwied: Luchterhand.

—— (ed.) 1979: *Schriften Band 3. Aufsätze aus der Zeitschrift für Sozialforschung*, Frankfurt: Suhrkamp.

—— 1979 [1937]: 'Philosophie und kritische Theorie', in: Marcuse, Herbert (ed.): *Schriften Band 3. Aufsätze aus der Zeitschrift für Sozialforschung*, Frankfurt: Suhrkamp, 227-249.

Martin, Luther H. 2000: 'Comparison', in: Braun, Willi and Russell T. McCutcheon (ed.): *Guide to the Study of Religion*, London/New York: Cassell, 45-56.

Maybury, Jill 2000: 'Religious education in England and Wales: contemporary approaches', in: Holm, Nils G. (ed.): *Islam and Christianity in School Religious Education. Issues, Approaches, and Contexts*, Åbo: Åbo Akademis trykeri, 69-84.

Mbiti, John S. 1969: *African Religions and Philosphy*, London: Heinemann.

McCutcheon, Russell T. 2000: 'Critics not caretakers: the scholar of religion as public intellectual', in: Jensen, Tim and Mikael Rothstein (ed.): *Secular Theories of Religion. Current Perspectives*, Copenhagen: Museum Tusculanum Press, 167-181.

Meijer, Wilna A. 2004: 'Tradition and reflexivity in religious education', in: Lombaerts, Herman and Didier Pollefeyt (ed.): *Hermeneutics and Religious Education*, Leuven: Peeters,

Mercier, Carrie 1996: *Muslims*, Oxford: Heinemann.

Mertens, Gerhard 1999: 'Identität/Identitätsfindung', in: Reinhold, Gerd, Guido Pollak, et al. (ed.): *Pädagogik Lexikon*, München: Oldenbourg, 268-270.

Mette, Norbert 1994: 'Religion(en) im Bildungsauftrag öffentlicher Schulen', in: van der Ven, Johannes A. and Hans-Georg Ziebertz (ed.): *Religiöser Pluralismus und Interreligiöses Lernen*, Kampen/Weinheim: 277-289.

Meyer, Karlo 1998: *Zeugnisse fremder Religionen im Unterricht. 'Weltreligionen' im deutschen und englischen Religionsunterricht*, Neukirchen-Vluyn: Neukirchener.

Michaels, Axel 1997: 'Einleitung', in: Michaels, Axel (ed.): *Klassiker der Religionswissenschaft*, München: Beck, 7-16.

—— (ed.) 1997: *Klassiker der Religionswissenschaft. Von Friedrich Schleiermacher bis Mircea Eliade*, München: C. H. Beck.

Mikaelsson, Lisbeth 2004: 'Gendering the history of religion', in: Antes, Peter, Armin W. Geertz, et al. (ed.): *New Approaches to the Study of Religion. Volume 1: Regional, Critical, and Historical Approaches*, Berlin/New York: deGruyter, 295-315.

Miller, Anne-Marie 2000: *Directory of Agreed Syllabuses for Religious Education 1998-2000 (London Boroughs, English Counties, Channel Islands and Wales)*, Norwich: Keswick Hall Centre for Research & Development in Religious Education.

Ministery of Education Consolidation 1999: 'Act on the Folkskole. The Danish Primary and Lower Secondary School (Act No. 55 of 17 January 1995)', in: Tidman, Nils-Åke (ed.): *Into the Third Millenium. EFTRE conference August 1998 in Copenhagen*, Lomma: FLR, 15-19.

Minton, David 1995: 'The political dimension of Christianity', in: Erricker, Clive (ed.): *Teaching Christianity: A World Religions Approach*, Cambridge: The Lutterworth Press, 23-29.

Morgan, Peggy 2001: 'Ninian Smart', *Religion*, 31 (4), 345-347.

Mott-Thornton, Kevin et al. 1996: 'Language, dualism and experiential religious education: a critical appraisal of the debate between Adrian Thatcher and the Authors of *New Methods in R.E. Teaching*', *British Journal of Religious Education*, 18 (3), 155-165.

Müller, Friedrich Max 1979: *Essays. 1. Beiträge zur vergleichenden Religionswissenschaft*, Leipzig: Engelmann.

—— 1976²: *Einleitung in die vergleichende Religionswissenschaft*, Straßburg: Trübner.

Münzner, Eva-Maria 1998: 'Religionsunterricht im Spiegel von LER', in: Ehmann, Reinhard u.a. (ed.): *Religionsunterricht der Zukunft. Aspekte eines notwendigen Wandels*, Freiburg: Herder, 90-96.

Myrgård, Stefan 2000: 'Ny kurs för religionskunskap i grundskolan?' *Religion & Livsfrågor*, 33 (3), 6-9.

—— 2000: 'Ny kurs... för religionskunskapen!' *Religion & Livsfrågor*, 33 (1), 11.

Nesbitt, Eleanor 1993: 'Drawing on the ethnic diversity of Christian tradition in Britain', *Multicultural Teaching*, 11 (2), 9-12.

—— 1998: 'Bridging the gap between young people's experience of their religious traditions at home and school: the contribution of ethnographic research', *British Journal of Religious Education*, 20 (2), 102-114.

—— 1999: 'Diversity as ethos in society: negotiating power relations', in: Chidester, David, Janet Stonier, et al. (ed.): *Diversity as Ethos: Challenges for Interreligious and Intercultural Education*, Cape Town: Institute for Comparative Religion in Southern Africa, 116-132.

—— 2001: 'Ethnographic research at Warwick: some methodological issues', *British Journal of Religious Education*, 23 (3), 144-155.

—— 2001: 'What young Hindus believe: some issues for the researcher and the RE teacher', in: Heimbrock, Hans-Günter, Christoph Th. Scheilke, et al. (ed.): *Towards Religious Competence: Diversity as a Challenge for Education in Europe*, Münster: Lit, 150-162.

—— 2002: 'Ethnography and religious education', in: Broadbent, Lynne and Alan Brown (ed.): *Issues in Religious Education*, London/New York: RoutledgeFalmer, 111-122.

Nestvogel, Renate 2002: 'Zum Verhältnis von 'interkulturellem Lernen', 'globalem Lernen' und 'Bildung für eine nachhaltige Entwicklung", in: Wulf, Christoph and Christine Merkel (ed.): *Globalisierung als Herausforderung der Erziehung. Theorien, Grundlagen, Fallstudien*, Münster et al.: Waxmann, 31-44.

Netto, Brian 1989: 'On removing theology from religious education', *British Journal of Religious Education*, 11 (3), 163-168.

—— 1990: 'Multi-faith RE and experiential learning', in: Hammond, John and David Hay (ed.): *New Methods in Teaching RE: An Experiential Approach*, Harlow, Essex: Oliver&Boyd, 197-198.

Newman, Fred and Lois Holzman 1997: *The End of Knowing: A New Developmental Way of Learning*, London: Routledge.

Noormann, Harry (ed.) 2000: *Ökumenisches Arbeitsbuch Religionspädagogik*, Stuttgart et al.: Kohlhammer.

Nordén, Åsa 2002: 'Har nytida fysik religiös betydelse?' in: Frank, Olof (ed.): *Mellan vidskepelse och vetenskap*, Lomma: FLR, 178-193.

Nye, Malory 2000: 'Religion, post-religionism, and religioning: religious studies and contemporary cultural debates', *Method and Theory in the Study of Religion*, 12 (4), 447-476.

Nye, Rebecca and David Hay 1996: 'Identifying children's spirituality: how do you start without a starting point?' *British Journal of Religious Education*, 18 (3), 144-154.

OFSTED (Office for Standards in Education) 1997: *The Impact of New Agreed Syllabuses on the Teaching and Learning of Religious Education. A Report from the Office of Her Majesty's Chief Inspector of Schools*, London: The Stationary Office.

Ohlemacher, Jörg (ed.) 1991: *Religion und Bildung in Europa: Herausforderungen, Chancen, Erfahrungen*, Göttingen: Vandenhoeck&Ruprecht.

Ohlsson, Sven-Göran 2002: 'Att förnya och vidga religionskunskaps-ämnet', *Religion & Livsfrågor*, 35 (4), 3.

Öhrvall, Inger 2004: 'Religionskunskap och demokrati', *Religion & Livsfrågor*, 37 (1), 7-8.

Olin, Camilla 2000: 'Religious education in Finland - framework and practice', in: Holm, Nils G. (ed.): *Islam and Christianity in School Religious Education. Issues, Approaches, and Contexts*, Åbo: Åbo Akademis trykeri, 109-123.

O'Loughlin, Michael 1992: 'Engaging teachers in emancipatory knowledge construction', *Journal of Teacher Education*, 45 (5), 336-346.

Østberg, Sissel 2003: 'Cultural diversity and common citizenship: reflections on ethnicity, religion, nationhood and citizenship among Pakistani young people in Europe', in: Jackson, Robert (ed.): *International Perspectives on Citizenship, Education and Religious Diversity*, London/New York: RoutledgeFalmer, 93-108.

Østnor, Arna 1997: 'Ny læreplan i Religion og etikk: Prosess og produkt', *Religion og Livssyn*, 9 (1), 4-8.

Otto, Gert 1992: 'Allgemeiner Religionsunterricht - Religionsunterricht für alle', in: Lott, Jürgen (ed.): *Religion - warum und wozu in der Schule?*, Weinheim: Deutscher Studien Verlag, 359-374.

—— 1997: 'Das Ende des konfessionellen Religionsunterrichts. Auswege aus einer Sackgasse', *Pädagogik*, 49 (10), 48-53.

Otto, Rudolf 1969: *The Idea of the Holy [1917[1], Germ.]*, Oxford et al.: Oxford University Press.

—— 1979 [1917[1]]: *Das Heilige. Über das Irrationale in der Idee des Göttlichen und sein Verhältnis zum Rationalen*, München: Beck.

Oxfordshire County Council, Education Service 1999: *Religious Education in Oxfordshire: The Agreed Syllabus*, Oxford: Oxfordshire County Council.

Pahnke, Donate (ed.) 1993: Blickwechsel. *Frauen in Religion und Wissenschaft*, Marburg: Diagonal.

—— 1993: 'Feministische Aspekte einer religionswissenschaftlichen Anthropologie', in: Pahnke, Donate (ed.): *Blickwechsel. Frauen in Religion und Wissenschaft*, Marburg: Diagonal, 13-41.

Palmer, Martin 1995: *'Studying Religions in Social Sciences at school'. Report on the 65th European Teachers Seminar Donaueschingen, Germany, 24-29 October 1994*, Strasbourg: Council for Cultural Co-operation.

Piaget, Jean 1950: *The Psychology of Intelligence*, London: Routledge and Kegan Paul.

Plöger, Wilfried 1999: *Allgemeine Didaktik und Fachdidaktik*, München: Fink.

Pollack, Detlef 1995: 'Was ist Religion? Probleme der Definition', *Zeitschrift für Religionswissenschaft*, 3 (2), 163-190.

Pollitt, Helmar-Ekkehart 1997: 'World religions in education in spite of confessional education in Austria', in: Holm, Nils G. (ed.): *The Familiar and the Unfamiliar in the World Religions: Challenges for Religious Education Today*, Åbo: Åbo Akademis trykeri, 156-161.

Pörschke-Hansen, Beate 1996: 'Wahrheitsanspruch der Religionen, Dialogbereitschaft und Religionspädagogik. Anstöße durch die pluralistische Theologie der Religionen', in: Weiße, Wolfram (ed.): *Vom Monolog zum Dialog. Ansätze einer interkulturellen dialogischen Religionspädagogik*, Münster: Waxmann, 123-140.

Potter, Maureen 1990: 'The Durham pilot project', in: Hammond, John and David Hay (ed.): *New Methods in Teaching RE: An Experiential Approach*, Harlow, Essex: Oliver&Boyd, 184-185.

Projektet Barn och Livsfrågor 1975: *Små barn och stora frågor: en probleminventering bland lärare om livsfrågor i förskolan, på lågstadiet och på fritidshem: en rapport från BaLi-projektet*, Stockholm: Lärarhögskolan.

Pye, Michael 1969: 'The transplantation of religions', *Numen*, 16 (3), 234-239.

—— 1972: *Comparative Religion: An Introduction through Source Materials*, Newton Abbot: David&Charles.

—— 1982: 'The Study of Religion as an autonomous discipline', *Religion*, 12 (1), 67-76.

—— (ed.) 1989: *Marburg Revisited. Institutions and Strategies in the Study of Religion*, Marburg: Diagonal.

—— 1991: 'Reflections on the treatment of tradition in comparative perspective, with special reference to Ernst Troeltsch and Gerardus van der Leeuw', in: Kippenberg, Hans G. and Brigitte Luchesi (ed.): *Religionswissenschaft und Kulturkritik*, Marburg: Diagonal, 101-111.

—— 1994: 'Religion: shape and shadow', *Numen*, 41 (1), 51-75.

—— 1999: 'Methodological integration in the study of religions', in: Ahlbäck, Tore (ed.): *Approaching Religion*, Åbo: Donner Institute for Research in Religious and Cultural History, 189-205.

—— 2000: 'Westernism unmasked', in: Jensen, Tim and Mikael Rothstein (ed.): *Secular Theories of Religion. Current Perspectives*, Copenhagen: Museum Tusculanum Press, 211-230.

—— 2002: 'Memes and models in the Study of Religions', in: Gasparro, Giulia Sfameni (ed.): *Themes and Problems of the History of Religions in Contemporary Europe. Proceedings of the International Seminar Messina, March 30-31 2001*, Cosenza: Lionello Giordano, 245-259.

—— 2004: 'Religionswissenschaft und Religionen: Eine riskante Nähe und ihre Notwendigkeit (ABSCHIEDSVORLESUNG)', *Marburg Journal of Religion*, 9 (1), 1-17.

Pye, Michael, Edith Franke et al. (ed.) 2006: *Religious Harmony. Problems, Practice, and Education. Proceedings of the Regional Conference of the International Association for the History of Religions. Yogyakarta and Semarang, Indonesia. September 27th – October 3rd, 2004*. Berlin/New York: Walter de Gruyter.

Pyysiäinen, Markku 1999: 'The challenge of the students for religious education: a Finnish view', in: Tidman, Nils-Åke (ed.): *Into the Third Millenium. EFTRE conference August 1998 in Copenhagen*, Lomma: FLR, 38-53.

QCA (Qualifications and Curriculum Authority) 2004: *Religious Education. The Non-Statutory National Framework*, London: QCA.

Rajan, Rajeswari Sunder 1993: *Real and Imagined Women: Gender, Culture and Postcolonialization*, New York: Routledge.

Rankin, John 1995: 'Christianity as a world religion: the educational implications', in: Erricker, Clive (ed.): *Teaching Christianity: A World Religions Approach*, Cambridge: The Lutterworth Press, 2-9.

—— 1999: '30 years on...', in: *Shap Journal World Religions in Education 1999/2000: Can I Teach Your Religion?*, 13-16.

Read, Garth, John Rudge, et al. 1992: *How Do I Teach RE? The Westhill Project RE 5-16*, Cheltenham: Stanley Thornes.

Reich, Hans H., Alfred Holzbrecher, et al. (ed.) 2000: *Fachdidaktik interkulturell. Ein Handbuch*, Opladen: Leske+Budrich.

Reinhold, Gerd, Guido Pollak, et al. (ed.) 1999: *Pädagogik-Lexikon*, München: Oldenbourg.

Rickers, Folkert 1999: 'Eine religionspädagogische Stellungnahme zur Einführung des Faches 'Praktische Philosophie' in Nordrhein-Westfalen', in: Gottwald, Eckart and Folkert Rickers (ed.): *Ehrfurcht vor Gott und Toleranz - Leitbilder interreligiösen Lernens*, Neukirchen-Vluyn: 127-142.

Rickers, Folkert and Eckhart Gottwald (ed.) 1999: *Vom religiösen zum interreligiösen Lernen: Wie Angehörige verschiedener Religionen und Konfessionen lernen*, Neukirchen-Vluyn: Neukirchener.

Ricoeur, Paul 1988: *Time and Narrative*, Chicago: University of Chicago Press.

Roald, Anne Sofie 2002: 'Den muslimska traditionen. Några historiska och moderne aspekter av debatten om förhållandet mellan uppenbarelse och förnunft', in: Frank, Olof (ed.): *Mellan vidskepelse och vetenskap: att tro, att tvivla - och att veta*, Lomma: FLR, 160-177.

Robson, Geoff 1995: *Christians*, Oxford: Heinemann.

Rockstroh, Elke 1998: 'Erfahrungsbericht aus Brandenburg zum neuen Schulfach 'Lebensgestaltung - Ethik - Religionskunde'', in: Ehmann, Reinhard u.a. (ed.): *Religionsunterricht der Zukunft. Aspekte eines notwendigen Wandels*, Freiburg: Herder, 104-107.

Rodhe, Birgit and Sten Rodhe 1996: 'Tradititon, identity, authority in Swedish religious education', *Panorama: International Journal of Comparative Religious Education and Values*, 8 (1), 39-49.

Rodhe, Sten and Bo Nylund 1995[2] [1993[1]]: *Nya Studietexter i religionskunskap*, Uppsala: Almqvist&Wiksell.

—— 1998: *Religionskunskap*, Stockholm: Almqvist&Wiksell.

Rohr, Elisabeth 2003: 'Interkulturelle Kompetenz. Ein gemeinsamer und gegenseitiger Lernprozess in einer sich globalisierenden Welt', *Wege zum Menschen*, 55 (8), 507-520.

Ronnås, John et al. 1969: *Tonåringen och livsfrågorna: elevattityder och undervisningen i livsåskådning och etik på grundskolans hög-stadium:* elevundersökningar och metodiska förslag av en arbetsgrupp inom Skolöverstyrelsen, Stockholm: SÖ-förlaget.

Rosenquist, Ingrid (ed.) 1988: *Kulturmöten*, Oxie: FLR.

Roth, Hans Joachim 2000: 'Allgemeine Didaktik', in: Reich, Hans H., Alfred Holzbrecher, et al. (ed.): *Fachdidaktik interkulturell. Ein Handbuch*, Opladen: Leske+Budrich, 11-53.

Roth, Heinrich, Wolfgang Klafki, et al. (ed.) 1969[10]: *Didaktische Analyse. Grundlegende Aufsätze aus der Zeitschrift Deutsche Schule*, Hannover et al.: Schroedel.

Rudge, John 1993: *RE and Spiritual Development*, Birmingham: Westhill College.

—— 2000: 'The Westhill Project: religious education as maturing pupils' patterns of belief and behaviour', in: Grimmitt, Michael (ed.): *Pedagogies of Religious Education. Case Studies in the Research and Development of Good Pedagogic Practice in RE*, Great Wakering: McCrimmons, 88-111.

Rudge, Linda 2002: 'Review of Clive and Jane Erricker (2000): Reconstructing Religious, Spiritual and Moral Education', *British Journal of Religious Education*, 24 (3), 229-231.

Rudolph, Kurt 1978: 'Die 'ideologiekritische' Funktion der Religionswissenschaft', *Numen*, 25 (1), 17-39.

—— 2000: 'Some reflections on approaches and methodologies in the study of religions', in: Jensen, Tim and Mikael Rothstein (ed.): *Secular Theories of Religion. Current Perspectives*, Copenhagen: Museum Tusculanum Press, 231-247.

Rudvall, Göte and Hans-Martin Stimpel 1998: *Bildungspolitik. Schulen und Hochschulen in Schweden*, Göttingen: Cuvillier.

Rydahl, John 2005: *The Association of Danish Teachers of RE in Primary and Lower Secondary School: Annual Report 2005* (http://re-xs.ucsm.ac.uk/eftre/reeurope/denmark_2005.html, 21.3.2006).

Said, Edward 1978: *Orientalism*, London: Routledge and Kegan Paul.

—— 1989: 'Representing the colonized: anthropology's interlocutors', *Critical Inquiry*, 15 (2), 205-25.

—— 1993: *Culture and Imperialism*, London: Chatto and Windus.

SCAA (School Curriculum and Assessment Authority) 1994: *Model Syllabuses for Religious Education - Faith Communities' Working Group Reports*, London: SCAA.

—— 1994: *Model Syllabuses for Religious Education - Model 1: Living Faiths Today*, London: SCAA.

—— 1994: *Model Syllabuses for Religious Education - Model 2: Questions and Teachings*, London: SCAA.

—— 1995: *Religious Education 16-19*, London: SCAA.

—— 1995: *Spiritual and Moral Development*, London: SCAA.

—— 1996: *Education for Adult Life: The Spiritual and Moral Development of Young People*, London: SCAA.

Schäfer Karl-Hermann and Klaus Schaller (ed.) 1971: *Kritische Erziehungswissenschaft und kommunikative Didaktik*, Heidelberg: Quelle & Meyer.

Schalk, Peter (ed.) 2003: *Religion im Spiegelkabinett. Asiatische Religionsgeschichte im Spannungsfeld zwischen Orientalismus und Okzidentalismus*, Uppsala: Uppsala University Library.

Schmitt, Rudolf 1979: *Kinder und Ausländer. Einstellungsänderung durch Rollenspiel. Eine empirische Untersuchung*, Braunschweig: Westermann.

Schneider, Hans J. 1999: 'Propädeutik statt Therapie. Eine Anmerkung zur Studienordnung 'Lebensgestaltung - Ethik - Religionskunde' der Universität Potsdam', in: Grözinger, Karl E., Burkhard Gladigow, et al. (ed.): *Religion in der schulischen Bildung und Erziehung: LER - Ethik - Werte und Normen in einer pluralistischen Gesellschaft*, Berlin: Berlin-Verlag Spitz, 169-185.

Schools Council 1971: *Religious Education in Secondary Schools*, London: Evans/Methuen.

Schreiner, Peter 1999: 'Different approaches to RE/RS in European schools - the Scandinavian Approach in a European Context', in: Tidman, Nils-Åke (ed.): *Into the Third Millenium. EFTRE conference August 1998 in Copenhagen*, Lomma: FLR, 111-129.

—— 2000: *Religious Education in Europe. A Collection of Basic Information about RE in European Countries*, Münster: Comenius-Inst.

—— 2001: 'Towards a European oriented religious education', in: Heimbrock, Hans-Günter, Christoph Th. Scheilke, et al. (ed.): *Towards Religious Competence: Diversity as a Challenge for Education in Europe*, Münster: Lit, 253-267.

—— (ed.) 2002: *Committed to Europe's Future. Contributions from Education and Religious Education; A Reader*; a Publication of the Coordinating Group for Religious Education in Europe and the Comenius-Institut, Protestant Centre for Studies in Education, Münster: CoGREE.

—— 2002: 'Different approaches - common aims? Current development of religious education in Europe', in: Schreiner, Peter (ed.): *Committed to Europe's Future. Contributions from Education and Religious Education. A Reader.*, Münster: Comenius-Institut, 95-100.

—— 2002: 'Religious education in the European context', in: Broadbent, Lynne and Alan Brown (ed.): *Issues in Religious Education*, London/New York: RoutledgeFalmer, 86-98.

—— 2005: *Religious Education in Europe*
(http://www.cimuenster.de/pdfs/themen/europa2.pdf, 16.4.2006).

Schreiner, Peter and Hans Spinder (ed.) 1997: *Identitätsbildung im pluralen Europa. Perspektiven für Schule und Religionsunterricht*, Münster et al.: Waxmann.

Schultze, Herbert, Hans-Mikael Holt, et al. 1996: 'The teaching of world religions in continental Europe', in: Gates, Brian (ed.): *Freedom and authority in religions and religious education*, London/New York: Cassell, 176-187.

Schulz, Wolfgang 1981[3]: *Unterrichtsplanung. Mit Materialien aus Unterrichtsfächern*, München et al.: Urban&Schwarzenberg.

Schulz, Wolfgang 1995[8]: 'Die lehrtheoretische Didaktik', in: Gudjons, Herbert and Rainer Winkel (ed.): *Didaktische Theorien*, Hamburg: Bergmann & Helbig, 29-45.

Secco, Luigi 1993: 'Interkulturelle Pädagogik: Probleme und Konzeptionen. Ein Weg zwischen Studien und Positionen', in: Bertram, Norbert (ed.): *Interkulturelles Verstehen und Handeln*, Pfaffenweiler: Centaurus,

Segal, Robert A. 2001: 'In defense of the comparative method', *Numen*, 48 (3), 339-373.

Selander, Gunilla 1997: *Gymnasisten och det heliga. Två elevundersökningar och några religionsdidaktiska/metodiska uppsatser*, Malmö: Utvecklingsavdelningen, Lärarhögskolan.

—— 2000: 'Att välja lärobok på gymnasiet', *Religion & Livsfrågor*, 33 (1), 12-16, 21.

Selander, Sven-Åke 1993: *Undervisa i religionskunskap*, Lund: Student-litteratur.

—— 1994: *Livstolkning. Om religion, livsåskådning och etik i skolan i ett didaktiskt perspektiv. En förutsättningsanalys*, Malmö: Utvecklingsavdelningen, Lärarhögskolan.

—— 1999: 'State, church and school in the Scandinavian countries - in a European perspective', in: Tidman, Nils-Åke (ed.): *Into the Third Millenium. EFTRE conference August 1998 in Copenhagen*, Lomma: FLR, 142-159.

—— 2000: 'Religionskunskapen på gymnasiet i kursplanen 2000', *Religion & Livsfrågor*, 33 (3), 10-12.

Shap: The Shap Working Party on World Religions in Education
(http://www.shap. org/, 3.7.2006).

Sharpe, Eric J. 1975: *Comparative Religion. A History*, London: Duckworth.

Sieg, Ursula 1998: "Religionsunterricht für alle'. Interreligiöses Lernen von Anfang an!' in: Ehmann, Reinhard u.a. (ed.): *Religionsunterricht der Zukunft. Aspekte eines notwendigen Wandels*, Freiburg: Herder, 132-141.

Sjödin, Ulf 1995: *En skola - flera världar. Värderingar hos elever och lärare i religionskunskap i gymnasieskolan*, Lund: Plus Ultra.

Skeie, Geir 2002: 'The concept of plurality and its meaning for religious education', *British Journal of Religious Education*, 25 (2), 47-59.

—— 2003: 'Nationalism, religiosity and citizenship in Norwegian majority and minority discourses', in: Jackson, Robert (ed.): *International Perspectives on Citizenship, Education and Religious Diversity*, London/New York: RoutledgeFalmer, 51-66.

—— 2004: 'An overview of religious education research in Norway', in: Larsson, Rune and Caroline Gustavsson (ed.): *Towards a European Perspective on Religious Education. The RE Research Conference, March 11-14, 2004, University of Lund*, Skellefteå: Artos&Norma, 317-331.

Skogar, Björn 2000: 'I stormens öga - några inledande teoretiska vägval i religionsdidaktiken', in: Almén, Edgar, Ragnar Furenhed, et al. (ed.): *Livstolkning och värdegrund. Att undervisa om religion, livsfrågor och etik*, Linköping: Linköpings Universitet, 102-116.

Skolverket 2000: *Kursplan religionskunskap grundskola*
(http://www3.skolverket.se/ki03/front.aspx?sprak=SV&ar=0506& infotyp=24&skolform=11&id=3886&extraId=2087, 13.3.2006).

—— 2000: *Kursplan religionskunskap gymnasieskola*
(http://www3.skolverket.se/ki03/front.aspx?sprak=SV&ar=0506& infotyp=8&skolform=21&id=RE&extraId=, 13.3.2006).

—— 2000: *Upper Secondary School*
(http://www3.skolverket.se/ki03/front.aspx?sprak=EN&ar=0506& infotyp=8&skolform=21&id=RE&extraId=, 28.6.2006).

—— 2001: *Compulsory School. Syllabuses*
(http://www3.skolverket.se/ki/eng/comp.pdf, 13.3.2006).

—— 2001: *Programme Manual. Programme goal and structures*, core subjects, subject index for upper secondary school
(http://www3.skolverket.se/ki/eng/pgm_eng.pdf, 13.3.2006).

—— 2001: *Social Science Programme. Programme goal, structure and syllabuses*
(http://www3.skolverket.se/ki/eng/sp_eng.pdf, 13.3.2006).

—— 2004: *Det svenska skolsystemet*
(http://www.skolverket.se/content/1/c4/08/36/V007_1%20Det%20svenska% 20skolsyst.pdf, 13.3.2006).

—— 2005: *Democracy and Fundamental Values*
(http://www.skolverket.se/content/1/c4/12/57/en_demokrati.pdf, 30.5.2006).

—— 2005: *Demokrati och värdegrund*
(http://www.skolverket.se/content/1/c4/08/48/demokrati.pdf, 13.3.2006).

—— 2005: *Gymnasieskolan*
(http://www.skolverket.se/sb/d/740, 28.6.2006).

—— 2005: *The Swedish School System* (http://www.skolverket.se/sb/d/354, 13.3.2006).

Slee, Nicola 1989: 'Conflict and reconciliation between competing models of religious education: some reflections on the British scene', *British Journal of Religious Education*, 11 (3), 126-135.

Smart, Ninian 1968: *Secular Education and the Logic of Religion*, London: Faber&Faber.

—— 1975: 'What is religion?' in: Smart, Ninian and Donald Horder (ed.): *New Movements in Religious Education*, London: Temple Smith, 13-22.

—— 1989: 'Worldview analysis: a way of looking at our field', in: Wood, Angela (ed.): *Religions and Education. Shap Working Party 1969-89*, Isleworth: BFSS National RE Centre, 97-98.

—— 1996: *Dimensions of the Sacred: An Anatomy of the World's Beliefs*, London: HarperCollins.

—— 1995: 'Foreword', in: Erricker, Clive (ed.): *Teaching Christianity: A World Religions Approach*, Cambridge: The Lutterworth Press, vii-viii.

—— 2000: Reflections on Religious Education in Russia, Sweden and England, in in Edgar Almén and Hans Christian Øster (ed.): *Religious Education in Great Britain, Sweden and Russia*, Linköping: Linköping University Electronic Press, 102-106.

Smart, Ninian and Donald Horder (ed.) 1975: *New Movements in Religious Education*, London: Temple Smith.

Smith, David 1999: *Making Sense of Spiritual Development*, Nottingham: Stapleford Centre.

Smith, Jonathan Z. 1998: 'Religion, religions, religious', in: Taylor, Mark C. (ed.): *Critical Terms for Religious Studies*, Chicago/London: The University of Chicago Press, 269-284.

Smith, Wilfred Cantwell 1959: 'Comparative religion: wither and why?' in: Eliade, Mircea and Joseph M. Kitagawa (ed.): *The History of Religions*, Chicago: Chicago University Press, 31-58.

—— 1978: *The Meaning and End of Religion*, London: SPCK.

Söderblom, Nathan 1913: 'Holiness (general and primitive)', in: Hastings, James (ed.): *Encyclopaedia of Religion and Ethics Vol. 6*, Edinburgh/New York: T.&T.Clark, 731-741.

Spinder, Hans 1991: 'Religionsunterricht in Europa. Eine Dokumentation der Intereuropean Commission on Church and School (ICSS)', in: Ohlemacher, Jörg (ed.): *Religion und Bildung in Europa. Herausforderungen, Chancen, Erfahrungen*, Göttingen: Vandenhoeck&Rup-recht, 183-227.

—— 2000: 'Netherlands', in: Schreiner, Peter (ed.): *Religious Education in Europe. A Collection of Basic Information About RE in European Countries*, Münster: ICSS/Comenius-Institut, 117-122.

Spiro, Milford E. 1966: 'Religion: problems of definition and explanation', in: Banton, Michael (ed.): *Anthropological Approaches to the Study of Religion*, London et al.: Routledge, 85-126.

Stadtfeld, Peter and Bernhard Dieckmann (ed.) 2005: *Allgemeine Didaktik im Wandel*, Bad Heilbrunn: Verlag Julius Klinkhardt.

—— 2005: 'Einleitung', in: Stadtfeld, Peter and Bernhard Dieckmann (ed.): *Allgemeine Didaktik im Wandel*, Bad Heilbrunn: Verlag Julius Klinkhardt, 7-11.

Statistisk Centralbyrå 2003: *Statistics Norway: Population* (http://www.ssb.no/norge_en/bef_en/, 18.6.2006).

Steinert, Wilfried Wolfgang 1998: 'LER - Ein Erfahrungsbericht aus Brandenburg', in: Ehmann, Reinhard u.a. (ed.): *Religionsunterricht der Zukunft. Aspekte eines notwendigen Wandels*, Freiburg: Herder, 77-89.

Stolz, Fritz 1997[2] [1988[1]]: *Grundzüge der Religionswissenschaft*, Göttingen: Vandenhoek&Ruprecht.

Svare, Marit 2003: *Rapport fra Norge/ Report from Norway* (http://re-xs.ucsm.ac.uk/eftre/reeurope/norway_2003.html#eng, 21.3.2006).

Svensson, Jonas 2004: 'Mänskliga rättigheter och islam', *Religion & Livsfrågor*, 37 (1), 14-18.

Svingby, Gunilla 1987: *Sätt kunskapen i centrum!*, Stockholm: Liber Utbildningsförlag.

Taylor, Mark C. (ed.) 1998: *Critical Terms for Religious Studies*, Chicago/London: The University of Chicago Press.

Teece, Geoff 1997: 'Why John Hick's theory of religions is important for RE', *Resource, The Journal of The Professional Council for RE*, 20 (1), 3-6.

ten Broek, Bart and Cok Bakker 2002: 'Wie ein interreligiöses Curriculum aussehen könnte', in: Bakker, Cok, Olaf Beuchling, et al. (ed.): *Kulturelle Vielfalt und Religionsunterricht. Entwicklungen und Praxis in vier europäischen Ländern*, Münster et al.: Lit, 44-52.

Thatcher, Adrian 1991: 'A critique of inwardness in religious education', *British Journal of Religious Education*, 14 (1), 22-27.

The London Borough of Redbridge, 1995: *Exploration and Response: the Redbridge Agreed Syllabus for Religious Education*.

The Stapleford Centre 2006 (http://www.stapleford-centre.org, 25.6.2006).

The Swedish Institute 2006: *SWEDEN.SE - The Official Gataway to Sweden* (http://www.sweden.se, 28.6.2006).

Thomas, Alexander (ed.) 1988: *Interkulturelles Lernen im Schüleraustausch*, Saarbrücken/Fort Lauderale: Breitenbach.

—— 1988: 'Psychologisch-pädagogische Aspekte interkulturellen Lernens im Schüleraustausch', in: Thomas, Alexander (ed.): *Interkulturelles Lernen im Schüleraustausch*, Saarbrücken/Fort Lauderale: Breitenbach, 77-99.

Thomassen, Einar 2005: 'Religious education in a pluralistic society: experiences from Norway', in: Wasim, Alef Theria, Abdurrahman Mas'ud, et al. (ed.): *Religious Harmony: Problems, Practice and Education. Proceedings of the Regional Conference of the International Association for the History of Religions. Yogyakarta and Semarang, Indonesia, September 27th - October 3rd, 2004*, Yogyakarta: Oasis, 237-246.

Thulin, Birgitta and Sten Elm 1995: *Religion*, Malmö: Interskol.

Tidman, Nils-Åke (ed.) 1999: *Into the Third Millenium- / EFTRE conference, August 1998 in Copenhagen*, Lomma: FLR.

—— 2004: 'Kunskap för hela människan', *Religion & Livsfrågor*, 37 (4), 22-23.

Tiele, Cornelius Petrus 1899 [1898[1], Dutch]: *Einleitung in die Religionswissenschaft. 1. Morphologie*, Gotha: Perthes.

Tobler, Judith 2003: 'Learning the difference: religious education, citizenship and gendered subjectivity', in: Jackson, Robert (ed.): *International Perspectives on Citizenship, Education and Religious Diversity*, London/New York: RoutledgeFalmer, 125-143.

Trond, Enger 1998: 'Religious education for all pupils - the Norwegian way', *Panorama*, 10 (2), 122-134.

Tworuschka, Udo 1982: *Methodische Zugänge zu den Weltreligionen. Einführung für Unterricht und Studium*, Frankfurt am Main: Diesterweg.

—— 1994: 'Weltreligionen im Unterricht oder Interreligiöses Lernen?' in: van der Ven, Johannes A. and Hans-Georg Ziebertz (ed.): *Religiöser Pluralismus und Interreligiöses Lernen*, Kampen/Weinheim: 171-196.

—— 1997: 'Challenges of Religionswissenschaft today. Theoretical and methodological considerations', in: Holm, Nils G. (ed.): *The Familiar and the Unfamiliar in the World Religions: Challenges for Religious Education Today*, Åbo: Åbo Akademis trykeri, 114-126.

—— 2004: *Religiopolis - Weltreligionen erleben* (CD), Leipzig: Klett.

Tyloch, Witold (ed.) 1990: *Studies on Religions in the Context of Social Sciences. Methodological and Theoretical Relations*, Warsaw: Polish Society for the Science of Religions.

Tylor, Edward B. 1873: *Primitive Culture: Researches into the Development of Mythology, Philosophy, Religion, Language, Art, and Custom, vol. 1* [1871], London: Murray.

Utbildningsdepartement 1994: *Curriculum for the Non-Compulsory School System Lpf 94* (http://www.skolverket.se/publikationer?id=1072, 28.6.2006).

—— 1994: *Lpf-94. 1994 års läroplan för de frivilliga skolformerna. Gymnasieskolan, gymnasiesärskolan, den kommu-nala vuxenutbildningen, statens skolor för vuxna och vuxen-utbildningen för utvecklingsstörda*, Stockholm: Utbildningsdepartement.

—— 1994: *Lpo-94. Läroplan för det obligatoriska skolväsendet, föreskoleklassen och fritidshemmet*, Stockholm: Utbildningsdepartment.

UK Parliament 1988: *Education Reform Act*, London: Her Majesty's Stationery Office.

—— 1993: *Education Act*, London: Her Majesty's Stationary Office.

van der Leeuw, Gerardus 1938: *Religion in Essence and Manifestation: A Study in Phenomenology*, London: Allen&Unwin.

van der Leeuw, Gerardus 1956[2]: *Phänomenologie der Religion*, Tübingen: Mohr.

van der Ven, Johannes A. and Hans-Georg Ziebertz (ed.) 1994: *Religiöser Pluralismus und interreligiöses Lernen*, Kampen/Weinheim: Kok/Deutscher Studien Verlag.

—— 1995: 'Religionspädagogische Perspektiven zur interreligiösen Bildung', in: Ziebertz, Hans-Georg und Werner Simon (ed.): *Bilanz der Religionspädagogik*, Düsseldorf: Patmos, 259-273.

van Draat, Hans Fijn 2005: *Religious Education in Nederlands* (http://rexs.ucsm.ac.uk/eftre/reeurope/netherlands_2005.html, 21.3.2006).

von Glaserfeld, Ernst 1995: *Constructivism: A Way of Knowing and Learning*, London: Falmer Press.

Vygotsky, Lev Semenovich 1962: *Thought and Language*, Cambridge, USA: Massachusats Institute of Technology.

—— 1978: *Mind in Society: The Development of Higher Psychological Processes*, Cambridge, USA: Harvard University Press.

Waardenburg, Jacques 1978: *Reflections on the Study of Religion*, The Hague: Mouton.

—— 1986: *Religionen und Religion. Systematische Einführung in die Religionswissenschaft*, Berlin/New York: deGruyter.

—— 1992: 'Friedrich Heiler und die Religionsphänomenologie - eine kritische Würdigung', in: Jungclaussen, Emmanuel (ed.): *Ökumene - Ende oder Anfang?: zur Aktualität Friedrich Heilers*, Marburg: Pressestelle der Philipps-Universität, 22-51.

Wach, Joachim 1924: *Religionswissenschaft. Prolegomena zu ihrer wissenschaftstheoretischen Grundlegung*, Leipzig: J.C. Hinrichs.

Warne, Randi R. 2000: 'Making the gender-critical turn', in: Jensen, Tim and Mikael Rothstein (ed.): *Secular Theories of Religion. Current Perspectives*, Copenhagen: Museum Tusculanum Press, 249-260.

Warwickshire (England) County Council 1996: *Warwickshire Agreed Syllabus for Religious Education*, Leamington Spa: Warwickshire County Council.

Wasim, Alef Theria, Abdurrahman Mas'ud, et al. (ed.) 2005: *Religious Harmony: Problems, Practice and Education. Proceedings of the Regional Conference of the International Association for the History of Religions. Yogyakarta and Semarang, Indonesia, September 27th - October 3rd, 2004*, Yogyakarta: Oasis.

Watzlawick, Paul (ed.) 1984: *The Invented Reality: How do we know what we believe we know?*, New York: Norton.

Wayne, Elizabeth, Judith Everington, et al. 1996: *Hindus*, Oxford: Heinemann.

Weber, Carl-Eric 1997: 'Religionsundervisning som kulturell och existentiell utmaning', *Didactica Minima*, 11 (4), 15-27.

Weiße, Wolfram 1996: ''Dialogischer Religionsunterricht'. Eine Einführung', in: Weiße, Wolfram (ed.): *Vom Monolog zum Dialog. Ansätze einer interkulturellen dialogischen Religionspädagogik*, Münster: Waxmann, 3-17.

—— (ed.) 1996: *Interreligious and Intercultural Education. Methodologies, concepts and pilot projects in South Africa, Namibia, Great Britain, the Netherlands, and Germany*, Münster: Comenius Institut.

—— 1996: 'Ökumenisch-interkulturelles Lernen und interreligiöse Dialogerfahrungen', in: Weiße, Wolfram (ed.): *Vom Monolog zum Dialog. Ansätze einer interkulturellen dialogischen Religionspädagogik*, Münster: Waxmann, 77-96.

—— 1996: 'Religionsunterricht für alle. Reform- und Lehrplanarbeit für einen interkulturell geöffneten, dialogischen Religionsunterricht in Hamburg (Anhang: Lehrplanentwurf Religion Primarstufe vom Sept.1995)', in: Weiße, Wolfram (ed.): *Vom Monolog zum Dialog. Ansätze einer interkulturellen dialogischen Religionspädagogik*, Münster: Waxmann, 163-177.

—— (ed.) 1996: *Vom Monolog zum Dialog. Ansätze zu einer interkulturellen dialogischen Religionspädagogik*, Münster/New York: Waxmann.

—— (ed.) 2002: *Wahrheit und Dialog: Theologische Grundlagen und Impulse gegenwärtiger Religionspädagogik*, Münster et al.: Waxmann.

—— 2003: 'Difference without discrimination. Religious education as a field of learning for social understanding?' in: Jackson, Robert (ed.): *International Perspectives on Citizenship, Education and Religious Diversity*, London/New York: RoutledgeFalmer, 191-208.

Weiße, Wolfram and Folkert Doedens (ed.) 2000: *Religiöses Lernen in einer pluralen Welt: religionspädagogische Ansätze in Hamburg*, Münster et al.: Waxmann.

Werler, Tobias 2002: 'Schweden', in: Döbert, Hans, Wolfgang Hörner, et al. (ed.): *Die Schulsysteme Europas*, Hohengehren: Schneider, 452-469.

Westerberg, Boel 2002: 'Undervisningens innehåll är alltid ett val', *Religion & Livsfrågor*, 35 (4), 6-7.

Westerberg, Boel and Linnér Bengt 1997: *Tio frågor till livet. Teman för A-kursen i religionskunskap på gymnasiet*, Stockholm: Natur och Kultur.

Westerman, Wim 1996: "Geestelijke Stromingen': a distinctive feature of religious education in the Netherlands', in: Gates, Brian (ed.): *Freedom and authority in religions and religious education*, London/New York: Cassell, 179-182.

Wiberg, Anna 2000: 'Religious education in a Swedish upper secondary school perspective', in: Holm, Nils G. (ed.): *Islam and Christianity in School Religious Education. Issues, Approaches, and Contexts*, Åbo: Åbo Akademis trykeri, 125-134.

Wiebe, Donald 2000: 'Problems with the family resemblance approach to conceptualizing religion', in: Geertz, Armin W. and Russell T. McCutcheon (ed.): *Perspectives on Method and Theory in the Study of Religion. Adjunct Proceedings of the XVIIth Congress of the International Association for the History of Religions Mexico City, 1995*, Leiden/Boston/Köln: Brill, 314-322.

Wilson, Bryan 1998: 'The secularization thesis. Criticisms and rebuttals', in: Laermans, Rudi, Bryan Wilson, et al. (ed.): *Secularization and Social Integration*, Louvain: Louvain University Press, 45-65.

Winkel, R. 1995[8]: 'Die kritisch-kommunikative Didadaktik', in: Gudjons, H., R. Teske, et al. (ed.): *Didaktische Theorien*, Hamburg: 79-93.

Wood, Angela 1989: *Religions and Education. Shap Working Party 1969-89*, Isleworth: BFSS National RE Centre.

Woodward, Peter, Riadh El-Droubie, et al. (ed.) 1998[2] [1986[1]]: *Festivals in World Religions*, Norwich: RMEP.

WRERU (Warwick Religions and Education Research Unit), 2006: *Current WRERU Research Projects* (http://www2.warwick.ac.uk/fac/soc/wie/wreru/aboutus/research_projects/current/, 4.7.2006).

Wright, Andrew 1993: *Religious Education in the Secondary School: Prospects for Religious Literacy*, London: David Fulton.

—— 1996: 'Language and experience in the hermeneutics of religious understanding', *British Journal of Religious Education*, 18 (3), 166-180.

—— 1997: 'Hermeneutics and religious understanding. Part one: the hermeneutics of modern religious education', *Journal of Beliefs and Values*, 18 (2), 203-216.

―― 1997: 'Mishmash, religionism and theological literacy. An appreciation and critique of Trevor Cooling's hermeneutical programme', *British Journal of Religious Education*, 19 (3), 143-156.

―― 1998: 'Hermeneutics and religious understanding. Part two: Towards a critical theory of religious education', *Journal of Beliefs and Values*, 19 (1), 59-70.

―― 1998: *Spiritual Pedagogy. A Survey, Critique and Reconstruction of Contemporary Spiritual Education Pedagogy in England and Wales*, Abingdon: Culham College Institute.

―― 1999: *Discerning the Spirit. Teaching Spirituality in the Religious Education Classroom*, Abingdon: Culham College Institute.

Wright, Andrew 2000: 'The Spiritual Education Project: cultivating spiritual and religious literacy through a critical pedagogy of religious education', in: Grimmitt, Michael (ed.): *Pedagogies of Religious Education. Case Studies in the Research and Development of Good Pedagogic Practice in RE*, Great Wakering: McCrimmons, 170-187.

―― 2000: *Spirituality and Education*, London: Falmer.

―― 2001: 'Religious literacy and democratic citizenship', in: Francis, Leslie R, Jeff Astley, et al. (ed.): *The Fourth R for the Third Millennium. Education in Religion and Values for the Global Future*, Dublin: Lindisfarne, 201-219.

―― 2003: 'Context, competence and cultural diversity: religious education in a European setting', *Journal of Beliefs & Values*, 24 (1), 111-118.

Wright, Andrew and Anne-Marie Brandom 2000: *Learning to Teach Religious Education in the Secondary School: a Companion*, London: Routledge/Falmer.

Wulf, Christoph (ed.) 1995: *Education in Europe: An Intercultural Task*, Münster/New York: Waxmann.

Wulf, Christoph 1995: 'Paradigms of educational theory. The development of educational science in Germany', in: Wulf, Christoph (ed.): *Education in Europe: An Intercultural Task*, Münster/New York: Waxmann, 35-42.

―― 2003: *Educational Science. Hermeneutics, Empirical Research, Critical Theory*, Münster et al.: Waxmann.

Wulf, Christoph and Christine Merkel (ed.) 2002: *Globalisierung als Herausforderung der Erziehung. Theorien, Grundlagen, Fallstudien*, Münster et al.: Waxmann.

Ziebertz, Hans-Georg und Werner Simon (ed.) 1995: *Bilanz der Religionspädagogik*, Düsseldorf: Patmos.

Ziebertz, Hans-Georg and Johannes A. van der Ven 1996: 'Religion in religious education. An empirical study in the Netherlands and Germany', *Panorama*, 8 (1), 135-145.

Zinser, Hartmut (ed.) 1988: *Religionswissenschaft. Eine Einführung*, Berlin: Reimer.

—— (ed.) 1991: *'Herausforderung Ethikunterricht'. Ethik/ Werte und Normen als Ersatzfach in der Schule*, Marburg: Diagonal.

—— 1992: 'Warum brauchen wir einen Ersatzunterricht? - Zum 'Ersatzunterricht' für das Fach Religion aus der Sicht der Religionswissenschaft', in: Lott, Jürgen (ed.): *Religion - warum und wozu in der Schule?*, Weinheim: Deutscher Studien Verlag, 437-449.

Index

"A Gift to the Child" (Religion in the Service of the Child Project) 3, 100, 120-129, 179, 294, 296, 301, 305, 306
achievement 65, 85, 329, 362
Adorno, Theodor W. 58f, 70, 365
agreed syllabus 87, 93-100, 103-107, 142, 291f, 316, 322, 378
Almén, Edgar 61, 219f, 224, 227-230, 236, 239-241, 249, 251, 263, 272, 288, 298f, 302f, 307, 364
alternative or substitute subjects 2, 315, 318, 324, 330-332, 337, 341, 347, 349
Annan, Kofi 371, 388
Antes, Peter 3, 341, 358
anthropology 13, 22, 32, 34, 49, 52, 74, 77, 109, 143f, 147, 149-152, 161, 167, 285, 297, 302
Auernheimer, Georg 75-85
Auffarth, Christoph 76
Bailey, Edward 20
Barnes, Philip L. 87, 91
Baumann, Martin 25, 43
Bellah, Robert N. 20
Berlin 67, 69, 72f, 332, 362
Berner, Ulrich 20f, 29f, 38f, 41-44
BGU (Unterricht in Biblischer Geschichte auf allgemein christlicher Grundlage) 335, 372
Bildung 55f, 58f, 63-66, 68, 75, 324f, 341, 361
Brandenburg 1, 65, 329, 332, 336-340, 373, 378, 383
Breidlid, Halldis 325, 327, 349f, 364, 380f
Bremen 5, 332, 335-338, 340, 372
Bremer Klausel (Bremen Clause) 335, 337f
bridging 154, 161, 207, 302, 307
Bruner, Jerome 112, 197f

Buddhism 368, 381
  in the Study of Religions 45
  in English RE 101f, 114, 152, 292
  in Swedish RE 230, 234, 242, 247, 251-263, 269f, 273-276, 286, 299
Canada 83, 354
Chichester Project 93, 187-196, 302
Christianity 293, 302-304, 313, 318, 325f, 328-331, 334f, 337, 342-344, 348f, 353, 357, 367, 375f, 383f
  in the Study of Religions 16f, 48, 54,
  in English RE 84, 87f, 94f, 103, 105, 107, 123, 128, 134, 139, 141, 144f, 150, 152, 154, 163f, 172, 187f, 190-194, 196, 198-203, 205, 207-210,
  in Swedish RE 214, 218-220, 222, 224f, 227, 232f, 241f, 266, 268, 272, 277f,
Church of England 87, 94, 105, 292, 378
Church of Sweden 16, 213f, 219, 241, 269
citizenship 108, 163, 309, 314, 318, 321, 323, 327, 334, 369, 370f, 381, 389
civil religion 20, 188, 191, 269, 376
Clifford, James 32, 52, 148f
comparability 363
confessional RE 1-3, 61, 65, 88, 144, 195, 219, 273, 302, 315-320, 322-326, 329-333, 335-339, 341f, 344, 346-352, 354, 359, 364, 372, 376, 378, 384
constructivism 173-179, 305, 307f
constructivist approach 173-179, 305, 307
content-centred/subject-centred 172, 180, 204, 206, 221, 223,
Cooling, Trevor 196-210
cooperation with religious communities 103, 152, 292f, 339, 353, 367, 377-379, 384
Copley, Terence 94, 96f, 110, 310

Crapanzano, Vincent 32, 52, 148f
critical approach 139, 162-173, 295f, 306, 309
critical educational theory 55, 57f, 60-63, 77, 172, 196, 361
critical impetus 172, 308, 360, 363, 381
critical theory 55, 58-62, 71, 365
cultural heritage 80, 151, 270, 272f, 304, 357, 367-369
curriculum development 111f, 121, 142, 144, 161, 219, 222f , 292, 316, 336, 342, 378
Cush, Denise 356
Denmark 6, 21, 32, 230f, 318, 324, 347, 367, 372
descriptive dimension of RE 119, 227f, 248, 270, 307, 358
Deutsche Vereinigung für Religionswissenschaft (DVRW/DVRG) 10, 27, 341
Dialectic of Enlightenment 58f, 365
didactics of the study of religions 2f, 5, 373, 385
Dommel, Christa 335, 337
Durkheim, Émile 18, 32f
EAWRE (European Association for World Religions in Education) 93, 313
edification 143, 149, 154, 159, 207, 306, 359
education about religions 316, 322f, 342
education from religion 316, 322
education into religion 316, 322
EFTRE (European Forum for Teachers of RE) 6, 298, 313, 314-316
Eliade, Mircea 17, 23, 30, 33f, 41, 133, 135, 145, 172, 244, 296
emancipation 30, 56, 57, 60-63, 67, 70f, 73, 170-172, 174, 177f, 270, 294, 308-310, 323, 340, 360f, 363f
Enlightenment 25, 58, 62, 180, 318, 365, 368, 383
environment, the 64, 102, 234, 275, 288, 369
epoché 18, 44, 145-147

equality 62, 71, 77, 79, 215, 218, 232, 278, 304, 308, 310, 349, 359, 363f, 381, 387, 388
Erricker, Clive 92, 179-186, 188f, 191f, 194f, 304, 306, 309, 320, 375
Erziehung 55-57, 59, 66, 75, 329, 341, 361
Estonia 6
ethnocentrism 81, 254, 261, 265, 283, 300
ethnography 52, 142, 148f, 152f, 155, 160-162, 177f, 185, 302, 327
Everington, Judith 100, 104, 142, 151, 153, 154, 157-160, 293f
existential dimension of RE 202, 224-226, 247f, 270, 307, 309, 359
Existentialism 227, 274f, 297, 368
experiential approach 130-141, 294, 301, 354, 359, 374, 377
Faith Communities' Working Group Reports 99, 104, 201
Finland 61, 220, 230f, 318, 322, 347, 349, 364
Flasche, Rainer 9, 35, 37, 41, 45, 48, 53
framework for integrative RE in Europe 6, 290, 340, 343, 352-354, 363, 365
Franke, Edith 2, 5, 9, 24, 26-28, 42f, 50, 54
Frankfurt School 55, 57, 58, 60, 63, 70
Freire, Paolo 171, 361
Furenhed, Ragnar 227, 238f, 248, 250-254, 256, 262-264, 282f
Gadamer, Hans-Georg 160, 166, 285
Geertz, Armin W. 14, 19f, 22, 31-33, 42, 46, 52, 144, 147f, 239, 285
Geertz, Clifford 14, 19f, 22, 31-33, 42, 46, 52, 144, 147f, 239, 285
geestelijke stromingen (GS) 344-346
gender 23f, 26, 50, 52, 64, 79, 82, 149, 161f, 174, 201, 215, 218, 232f, 246, 252, 278, 327f, 357, 371, 380
Germany 1-3, 6, 8, 10, 25f, 57, 72, 75, 84, 231, 290, 315f, 318f, 321f, 324, 328-343, 347-349, 355, 357, 364, 368, 372, 378

globalisation 74, 76, 80, 309, 369, 371, 389
Goldman, Ronald 87f, 112, 197, 222, 306
Gombrich, Richard 256-259
Habermas, Jürgen 58, 60, 70, 166
Hamburg 1, 67, 69-73, 321, 332-335, 337, 340, 362
Hammond, John 20, 130-138, 141, 262
Hardy, Alister 130
Härenstam, Kjell 219, 254-263, 265f, 269-273, 277-281, 283-287, 299f, 308f, 361, 365, 369
Hartmann, Sven G. 218-225
Hay, David 130-138, 141, 170, 262
headscarf 330
Heiler, Friedrich 16f, 133f, 145, 277, 296
Heimann, Paul 66f, 69
Helve, Helena 20f
Heydorn, Heinz-Joachim 56, 61-63
Hick, John 112f, 115, 119, 139
Hinduism 292, 297, 299, 343, 345, 376
  in the Study of Religions 21f, 53
  in English RE 114, 123f, 142, 150, 152, 155, 156-158, 172, 176,
  in Swedish RE 230, 234, 251, 258, 273- 277
Holm, Niels G. 4, 312, 314
Horkheimer 57-59, 70, 365
Hormel, Ulrike 75, 80, 82, 84f
Hull, John 94f, 105f, 110, 119-121, 125-127, 203, 209
human capital 363, 389
human rights 25f, 30, 62, 76f, 80, 190, 218, 231f, 269, 276, 308, 310, 326, 352, 358- 360, 364f, 369, 371, 388f
IAHR (International Association for the History of Religions) 4f, 10, 19, 23, 27, 42, 46, 51
identity 59, 64f, 82f, 113, 116, 124, 132, 180, 208, 228, 253, 331, 336, 343, 362
ideology-criticism 21, 25f, 30, 36, 61f, 185f, 306, 336
implicit religion 20, 37, 301, 307, 372
inequality 61-64, 79, 84, 177, 303, 361, 368f
informal spiritualities 20

institutionalised religion 20, 295, 304, 357, 376, 379
intercultural education 55, 74-85, 271, 314, 321, 362, 370, 382, 389
interest groups 37, 292f, 350, 353, 361f, 366, 387
internal diversity of religions 152, 188-190, 195, 200f, 297, 300, 304f, 357, 376, 379
interpretive approach, the 142-162, 184f, 207, 262, 285, 293, 297, 306, 320f
Ipgrave, Julia 142, 155, 321
Islam 4, 83, 292, 297, 299, 306, 312, 314, 325, 328, 330f, 341, 364, 368, 370, 381
  in English RE 139, 150, 152, 163-165, 207f, 210
  in Swedish RE 230- 232, 234, 239f, 246, 266- 268, 273-281
Islam in Europe 248, 266f, 276, 306, 370
Jackson, Robert 4f, 91, 107, 126, 142-154, 159-162, 185, 270, 277, 285, 293, 296, 302, 306, 309, 314f, 320f, 323, 328, 350, 353, 356, 359, 361, 364f, 367, 369, 370
Jäggle, Martin 3
Jensen, Tim 4-6, 21, 34, 43, 312f, 315, 317-321, 323, 348, 351-353, 356, 358, 365, 367f, 386
Joy, Morny 22, 49-51, 186
Kay, William 87, 307
Keown, Damien 256f, 259
King, Richard 22
King, Ursula 23, 50, 93
Kippenberg, Hans G. 11, 32, 265, 341
Klafki, Wolfgang 55, 61, 63-69, 72, 74, 340, 348, 361f, 388
Knauth, Thorsten 2, 333
Körber, Sigurd 3
Kristensen, W. Brede 46f, 145f
KRL (Kristdendoms- religions- og livssynskunnskap) 324-326, 328, 348, 351, 367, 372, 376, 383f
Krüger-Potratz, Marianne 78f
Lähnemann, Johannes 3
Larsson, Rune 219, 222, 249, 314
LEA (Local Education Authority) 87, 94

learning about religions 96, 98, 100, 103, 108, 227, 306, 312, 322, 347, 358f
learning dimension 324, 343, 345f, 351, 355, 369, 382
learning from religion 96, 98, 100, 103, 108f, 143, 204, 208, 270, 322, 359
Leganger-Krogstad, Heid 327, 370f
LER (Lebensgestaltung-Ethik-Religionskunde) 65, 336-341, 348, 355, 373, 378, 383
literacy (religious, spiritual, theological) 162, 167-172, 320f
livsfråga 117, 212, 222-224, 226, 229f, 234-237, 238, 248-250, 273, 275, 283, 287f, 298f, 359
livstolkning 224f, 229f, 233, 237f, 247
livsåskådning 219, 221, 223, 230, 233f, 236, 241, 244, 248-251, 270f, 273, 287, 297, 299, 359
Lott, Jürgen 335f, 338-340, 348
Loukes, Harold 87f, 112, 222
Luckmann, Thomas 20
Lyotard, Jean-François 180f
Marcuse, Herbert 58-60
Marxism 32, 89, 227
McCutcheon, Russell T. 13, 19, 25-27, 36, 42-46
media 27, 59, 65, 69, 73, 114, 156, 272, 278, 281, 306, 342, 380f
mediation 27, 71, 85, 389
methodological agnosticism 9, 18, 30, 43, 51, 356, 359
Meyer, Karlo 3
Michaels, Axel 34
Mikaelsson, Lisbeth 23
model syllabuses 94, 96f, 99-104, 108, 153, 160, 178, 201, 207, 209, 245, 292-297, 303, 353, 375
moral education 90, 124f
Müller, F. Max 14f
multicultural education 75, 80, 151, 321
multiperspectivity 40, 74, 83f, 362, 389
narrative approach 179-186, 297, 306

narratives 36, 83, 150, 153, 167, 179f, 183, 186, 198, 203, 208, 237, 320, 326f, 380, 389
  grand or small narratives 179-185, 297f, 304f, 375f, 380f
  meta-narratives 182, 185, 198, 380
national curriculum 105f, 108f, 215f, 291
naturreligion 263f
Nesbitt, Eleanor 142, 152, 155f, 160f
Nestvogel, Renate 75-77, 80f
Netherlands 6, 15, 83, 290, 324, 343-346, 350f, 355
new religious movements / new religions 26, 31, 93, 215, 227, 233f, 239, 246, 275f, 312, 336, 376, 379
new-style phenomenology 146-148, 152
Nicolaisen, Tove 325, 327, 349f, 364, 380f
Norway 2-6, 230, 290, 318, 321, 324-328, 347-351, 358, 366f, 370, 372, 376-378, 382f, 384
Nye, Malory 22
Nye, Rebecca 135, 137
occidentalism 21f, 382
orientalism 20-22, 43, 49, 52, 150, 382
Østberg, Sissel 327, 370
othering 18, 303, 364, 382
Otto, Gert 1, 336, 338, 340
Otto, Gunther 67, 69
Otto, Rudolf 16, 125f, 129, 133f, 145, 146, 243f, 296
Pahnke, Donate 23f, 30, 48, 50
philosophy of education 58, 84, 299, 363, 364, 381
Piaget, Jean 88, 112, 117, 173f, 197
postcolonial criticism/postcolonial theory 21f, 49f, 186
private schools 291, 320, 325, 343f, 346, 378
pupil-centred 172, 180, 204, 206, 222-224
Pye, Michael 2, 5, 9, 11-13, 19f, 27-29, 31, 37f, 42-45, 47-49, 51, 54, 172, 240, 378

representatives of religions 25, 87, 94f, 104-106, 153, 201, 292, 333f, 342, 348, 366, 378f
research
  about RE in the European context 3, 302, 306, 312- 315, 326- 328, 333, 339, 361-363, 366f, 369f, 372, 385- 387
  in education 69f, 72, 77
  in the Study of Religions 12, 19, 21, 28, 31f, 34, 42-45, 48, 50f
  related to RE in England 121, 142, 146, 152f, 155f, 159-162, 179, 185
  related to RE in Sweden 223, 235, 278, 280, 287
Ricoeur, Paul 160
Rohr, Elisabeth 79f
Rudge, John 112-119
Rudolph, Kurt 25f, 32, 36, 39, 48
SACRE (Standing Advisory Council for Religious Education) 94f, 321
Said, Edward 21, 52, 150, 273, 369
SCAA (School Curriculum and Assessment Authority) 96, 99-104, 153, 160, 178, 201, 207, 245, 293, 295, 297, 303, 375
Schalk, Peter 22
Scherr, Albert 75, 80, 82, 84f
Schreiner, Peter 6, 298, 314-317, 320- 323, 351, 353, 357, 361, 377
Schulz, Wolfgang 67, 69f, 73
secularisation 20, 152, 213, 220, 238f, 279, 292, 312
Selander, Sven-Åke 219, 250f
self-criticism 147, 150, 152, 162, 308, 365, 381, 389
self-determination 62, 64, 67, 73, 361, 387f
separative RE 1-3, 6, 322-326, 328-330, 332f, 336-338, 340, 342, 347-352, 356, 384f
Sharpe, Eric J. 14
Skeie, Geir 325, 327, 366
Skolverket 211, 215-218, 226-230, 236f, 239, 245-247, 282
Smart, Ninian 4f, 35, 37, 41, 86, 88-91, 93, 112, 120, 144f, 188, 222, 237, 250, 270f, 291, 295f, 308

Smith, Jonathan Z. 33-35
Smith, Wilfred Cantwell 46f, 112, 139, 144, 150-152, 165
social responsibility 21, 25, 27, 36, 381
Socialism 273, 297
Söderblom, Nathan 16, 145, 243f
spiritual development 100, 105, 112, 115f, 119, 182f, 204, 233, 260, 270, 273, 294, 309
spiritual education 162, 166, 171, 309
spirituality 92, 115, 117, 119, 129-132, 135, 141, 162, 164-166, 171, 189, 239, 294, 299, 309, 317, 354, 376
Spiro, Milford E. 11, 35
standardisation 94, 106, 109, 216, 291, 310, 353, 361f, 363
Stapleford Project 187, 196-210, 298, 302f, 306f, 359
Stolz, Fritz 9, 45f, 48f, 54
subject matter 72
  of confessional RE 385
  of integrative RE 1, 89, 91, 117, 145, 161, 180f, 186, 222, 297, 306, 339, 344, 350f, 372-375, 382
  of the study of religions 8, 11, 15, 17, 28, 31f, 36f, 40-42, 47, 53
teacher training 6, 70, 84-86, 94, 109- 111, 177, 217, 226, 254f, 283, 285, 296, 316, 319, 326f, 331f, 335f, 341f, 346f, 349, 377, 385f
terminology 54, 145, 241, 261, 265f, 296, 303, 317, 375, 381
textbooks for RE 4, 6, 297, 327, 345f, 383
  in England 142, 153f, 185, 193, 306
  in Sweden 212, 218, 228, 234-236, 241, 243f, 254-256, 259f, 269, 271, 273- 281, 287, 300
thematic or systematic representation of religions 10, 90, 96f, 99, 115, 145, 193, 206f, 209, 300, 326, 376, 380
Thomassen, Einar 2, 4, 325f, 328, 348, 358, 367, 384
Tiele, Cornelius Petrus 15
truth claims 9, 12, 143, 163, 167, 171- 173, 182, 185f, 375
Tworuschka, Udo 3, 4, 341

Index

..., 12, 16, 19, 51,
..., 359, 377
...ardus 16, 18, 145,
..., 217f, 224f, 233f, 262f,
..., 82, 293, 299, 310, 367
...ev Semenovich 174
...ourg, Jacques 9, 34f, 37, 39,
..., 126, 146-148, 277
..., Joachim 10

Warne, Randy 24, 50
Warwick RE Project 142f, 149, 153-157, 160, 162, 379
Weiße, Wolfram 2, 321, 333f, 348
Westhill Project 112-121, 126, 173, 207, 295, 298, 301, 306f
Wiebe, Donald 11, 27
Wilson, Bryan 312
Wright, Andrew 96, 100, 139f, 162- 173, 209, 296, 301, 309, 320